The
Bible Knowledge
Commentary

HISTORY

The

Bible Knowledge
Commentary

HISTORY

John F. Walvoord and Roy B. Zuck
GENERAL EDITORS

DAVID C COOK
transforming lives together

THE BIBLE KNOWLEDGE COMMENTARY: HISTORY
Published by David C Cook
4050 Lee Vance Drive
Colorado Springs, CO 80918 U.S.A.

David C Cook U.K., Kingsway Communications
Eastbourne, East Sussex BN23 6NT, England

The graphic circle C logo is a registered trademark of David C Cook.

The website addresses recommended throughout this book are offered as a resource
to you. These websites are not intended in any way to be or imply an endorsement
on the part of David C Cook, nor do we vouch for their content.

LCCN 2017955601
ISBN 978-0-8307-7263-6
eISBN 978-0-8307-7290-2

© 1984, 2018 John F. Walvoord and Roy B. Zuck
Previously published as part of *The Bible Knowledge Commentary:
Old Testament*, ISBN 978-0-9714100-1-5.

Cover Design: Nick Lee
Cover Photo: Getty Images

Printed in the United States of America
First Edition 2018

1 2 3 4 5 6 7 8 9 10

010818

CONTENTS

PREFACE

The Bible Knowledge Commentary series is an exposition of the Scriptures written and edited solely by Dallas Seminary faculty members. It is designed for pastors, laypersons, Bible teachers, serious Bible students, and others who want a comprehensive but brief and reliable commentary on the entire Bible.

Why another Bible commentary when so many commentaries are already available? Several features make this series a distinctive Bible study tool.

The Bible Knowledge Commentary series is written by faculty members of one school: Dallas Theological Seminary. This commentary interprets the Scriptures consistently from the grammatical-historical approach and from the pretribulational, premillennial perspective, for which Dallas Seminary is well known. At the same time, the authors often present various views of passages where differences of opinion exist within evangelical scholarship.

Additionally, this commentary has features that not all commentaries include. (a) In their comments on the biblical text, the writers discuss how the purpose of the book unfolds, how each part fits with the whole and with what precedes and follows it. This helps readers see why the biblical authors chose the material they did as their words were guided by the Holy Spirit's inspiration. (b) Problem passages, puzzling Bible-time customs, and alleged contradictions are carefully considered and discussed. (c) Insights from modern conservative biblical scholarship are incorporated in this series. (d) Many Hebrew, Aramaic, and Greek words, important to the understanding of certain passages, are discussed. These words are transliterated for the benefit of readers not proficient in the biblical languages. Yet those who do know these languages will also appreciate these comments. (e) Throughout the series, dozens of maps, charts, and diagrams are included; they are placed conveniently with the Bible passages being discussed, not at the end of each book. (f) Numerous cross references to related or parallel passages are included with the discussions on many passages.

The material on each Bible book includes an *Introduction* (discussion of items such as authorship, date, purpose, unity, style, unique features), *Outline, Commentary,* and *Bibliography.* In the *Commentary* section, summaries of entire sections of the text are given, followed by detailed comments on the passage verse by verse and often phrase by phrase. All words quoted from the New International Version of the Bible appear in boldface type, as do the verse numbers at the beginning of paragraphs. The *Bibliography* entries, suggested for further study, are not all endorsed in their entirety by the authors and editors. The writers and editors have listed both works they have consulted and others which would be useful to readers.

Personal pronouns referring to Deity are capitalized, which often helps make it clear that the commentator is writing about a Member of the Trinity. The word LORD is the English translation of the Hebrew YHWH, often rendered *Yahweh* in English. *Lord* translates *'Ǎdōnāy.* When the two names stand together as a compound name of God, they are rendered "Sovereign LORD," as in the NIV.

The consulting editors—Dr. Kenneth L. Barker and Dr. Eugene H. Merrill on the Old Testament, and Dr. Stanley D. Toussaint on the New Testament—have added to the quality of this commentary by reading the manuscripts and offering helpful suggestions. Their work is greatly appreciated. We also express thanks to Lloyd Cory, Victor Books Reference Editor, to Barbara Williams, whose careful editing enhanced the material appreciably, to Production Coordinator Myrna Jean Hasse, to Jan Arroyo, and other people in the text editing department at Scripture

Press, who spent many long hours keyboarding and preparing pages for typesetting, and to the several manuscript typists at Dallas Theological Seminary for their diligence.

This commentary series is an exposition of the Bible, an explanation of the text of Scripture, based on careful exegesis. It is not primarily a devotional commentary, or an exegetical work giving details of lexicology, grammar, and syntax with extensive discussion of critical matters pertaining to textual and background data. May this commentary deepen your insight into the Scriptures, as you seek to have "the eyes of your heart ... enlightened" (Eph. 1:18) by the teaching ministry of the Holy Spirit.

This book is designed to enrich your understanding and appreciation of the Scriptures, God's inspired, inerrant Word, and to motivate you "not merely [to] listen to the Word" but also to "do what it says" (James 1:22) and "also ... to teach others" (2 Tim. 2:2).

John F. Walvoord
Roy B. Zuck

Editors

John F. Walvoord, B.A., M.A., TH.M., Th.D., D.D., Litt.D.
Chancellor Emeritus
Professor Emeritus of Systematic Theology

Roy B. Zuck, A.B., Th.M., Th.D.
Senior Professor Emeritus of Bible Exposition
Editor, *Bibliotheca Sacra*

Consulting Editors

Old Testament
Kenneth L. Barker, B.A., Th.M., Ph.D.
Writer, Lewisville, Texas

Eugene H. Merrill, B.A., M.A., M.Phil., Ph.D.
Distinguished Professor of Old Testament Studies

New Testament
Stanley D. Toussaint, B.A., Th.M., Th.D.
Senior Professor Emeritus of Bible Exposition

Series Contributing Authors

Walter L. Baker, B.A., Th.M., D.D.
Associate Professor Emeritus of World
Missions and Intercultural Studies
Obadiah

Craig Blaising, B.S. Th.M., Th.D., Ph.D.
Professor of Christian Theology Southern
Baptist Theological Seminary Louisville,
Kentucky
Malachi

J. Ronald Blue, B.A., Th.M.
President Emeritus CAM International
Dallas, Texas
Habakkuk

Sid S. Buzzell, B.S., Th.M., Ph.D.
Professor of Bible Exposition Colorado
Christian University Lakewood,
Colorado
Proverbs

Donald K. Campbell, B.A., Th.M., Th.D.
President Emeritus
Professor Emeritus of Bible Exposition
Joshua

**Robert B. Chisholm, Jr., B.A., M. Div.,
Th.M., Th.D.**
Professor of Old Testament Studies
Hosea, Joel

Thomas L. Constable, B.A., Th.M., Th.D.
Chairman and Senior Professor of Bible
Exposition
1 and 2 Kings

Jack S. Deere, B.A., Th.M., Th.D.
Associate Senior Pastor Trinity
Fellowship Church Amarillo, Texas
Deuteronomy, Song of Songs

Charles H. Dyer, B.A., Th.M., Th.D.
Provost and Senior Vice-President of
Education
Moody Bible Institute Chicago, Illinois
Jeremiah, Lamentations, Ezekiel

Gene A. Getz, B.A., M.A., Ph.D.
Senior Pastor
Fellowship Bible Church, North Plano,
Texas
Nehemiah

Donald R. Glenn, B.S., M.A., Th.M.
Chairman and Senior Professor of Old
Testament Studies
Ecclesiastes

John D. Hannah, B.S., Th.M., Th.D.
Chairman and Distinguished Professor
of Historical Theology
Exodus, Jonah, Zephaniah

Elliott E. Johnson, B.S., Th.M., Th.D.
Senior Professor of Bible Exposition
Nahum

F. Duane Lindsey, B.A., B.D., Th.M., Th.D.
Former Registrar, Research Librarian,
and Assistant Professor of Systematic
Theology
Leviticus, Judges, Haggai, Zechariah

John A. Martin, B.A., Th.M., Th.D.
Provost
Robert Wesleyan College
Rochester, New York
Ezra, Esther, Isaiah, Micah

Eugene H. Merrill, B.A., M.A., M.Phil., Ph.D.
Distinguished Professor of Old
Testament Studies
*Numbers, 1 and 2 Samuel, 1 and 2
Chronicles*

J. Dwight Pentecost, B.A., Th.M., Th.D.
Distinguished Professor Emeritus of
Bible Exposition
Daniel

John W. Reed, B.A., M.A., M.Div., Ph.D.
Director of D.Min. Studies
Senior Professor Emeritus of Pastoral
Ministries
Ruth

Allen P. Ross, B.A., M.A., M.Div., Ph.D.
Professor of Old Testament Studies
Trinity Evangelical Episcopal Seminary
Ambridge, Pennsylvania
Genesis, Psalms

Donald R. Sunukjian, B.A., Th.M., Th.D., Ph.D.
Professor of Christian Ministry and
Leadership
Talbot School of Theology La Mirada,
California
Amos

Roy B. Zuck, B.A., Th.M., Th.D.
Editor, Bibliotheca Sacra
Senior Professor of Bible Exposition
Job

*Authorial information based on original edition of the Bible Knowledge Commentary set. At the time of the commentary's first printing, each author was a faculty member of Dallas Theological Seminary.

Abbreviations

A. General

act.	active	n., nn.	note(s)
Akk.	Akkadian	n.d.	no date
Apoc.	Apocrypha	neut.	neuter
Aram.	Aramaic	n.p.	no publisher, no place of
ca.	*circa*, about		publication
cf.	*confer*, compare	no.	number
chap., chaps.	chapter(s)	NT	New Testament
comp.	compiled, compilation,	OT	Old Testament
	compiler	p., pp.	page(s)
ed.	edited, edition, editor	par., pars.	paragraph(s)
eds.	editors	part.	participle
e.g.	*exempli gratia*, for example	pass.	passive
Eng.	English	perf.	perfect
et al.	*et alii*, and others	pl.	plural
fem.	feminine	pres.	present
Gr.	Greek	q.v.	*quod vide*, which see
Heb.	Hebrew	Sem.	Semitic
ibid.	*ibidem*, in the same place	sing.	singular
i.e.	*id est*, that is	s.v.	*sub verbo*, under the word
imper.	imperative	trans.	translation, translator,
imperf.	imperfect		translated
lit.	literal, literally	viz.	*videlicet*, namely
LXX	Septuagint	vol., vols.	volume(s)
marg.	margin, marginal reading	v., vv.	verse(s)
masc.	masculine	vs.	versus
ms., mss.	manuscript(s)	Vul.	Vulgate
MT	Masoretic text		

B. Abbreviations of Books of the Bible

Gen.	Ruth	Job	Lam.	Jonah
Ex.	1, 2 Sam.	Ps., Pss. (pl.)	Ezek.	Micah
Lev.	1, 2 Kings	Prov.	Dan.	Nahum
Num.	1, 2 Chron.	Ecc.	Hosea	Hab.
Deut.	Ezra	Song	Joel	Zeph.
Josh.	Neh.	Isa.	Amos	Hag.
Jud.	Es.	Jer.	Obad.	Zech.
				Mal.

Matt.	Acts	Eph.	1, 2 Tim.	James
Mark	Rom.	Phil.	Titus	1, 2 Peter
Luke	1, 2 Cor.	Col.	Phile.	1, 2, 3 John
John	Gal.	1, 2 Thes.	Heb.	Jude
				Rev.

C. Abbreviations of Bible Versions, Translations, and Paraphrases

ASV	American Standard Version
JB	Jerusalem Bible
KJV	King James Version
NASB	New American Standard Bible
NEB	New English Bible
NIV	New International Version
RSV	Revised Standard Version

Transliterations

Hebrew

Consonants

א – '	ד – ḏ	י – y	ס – s	ר – r
ב – b	ה – h	כ – k	ע – '	שׂ – ś
ב – ḇ	ו – w	כ – ḵ	פ – p	שׁ – š
ג – g	ז – z	ל – l	פ – p̄	ת – t
ג – ḡ	ח – ḥ	מ – m	צ – ṣ	ת – ṯ
ד – d	ט – ṭ	נ – n	ק – q	

Daghesh forte is represented by doubling the letter.

Vocalization

בָה – bâh	בָ – bā	בֹ – bo[1]	בְ – bĕ
בוֹ – bô	בֹ – bō	בֻ – bu[1]	בְ – b
בוּ – bû	בֻ – bū	בֶ – be	בָה – bāh
בֵ – bê	בֵ – bē	בִ – bi[1]	בָא – bā'
בֶ – bè	בִ – bī	בֲ – bă	בֵה – bēh
בִ – bî	בַ – ba	בֳ – bŏ	בֶה – beh

[1] In closed syllables

Greek

α, ᾳ	– a	ξ	– x	γγ	– ng
β	– b	ο	– o	γκ	– nk
γ	– g	π	– p	γξ	– nx
δ	– d	ρ	– r	γχ	– nch
ε	– e	σ, ς	– s	αἰ	– ai
ζ	– z	τ	– t	αὐ	– au
η, ῃ	– ē	υ	– y	εἰ	– ei
θ	– th	φ	– ph	εὐ	– eu
ι	– i	χ	– ch	ηὐ	– ēu
κ	– k	ψ	– ps	οἰ	– oi
λ	– l	ω, ῳ	– ō	οὐ	– ou
μ	– m	ῥ	– rh	υἰ	– hui
ν	– n	ʽ	– h		

An Overview of Old Testament History

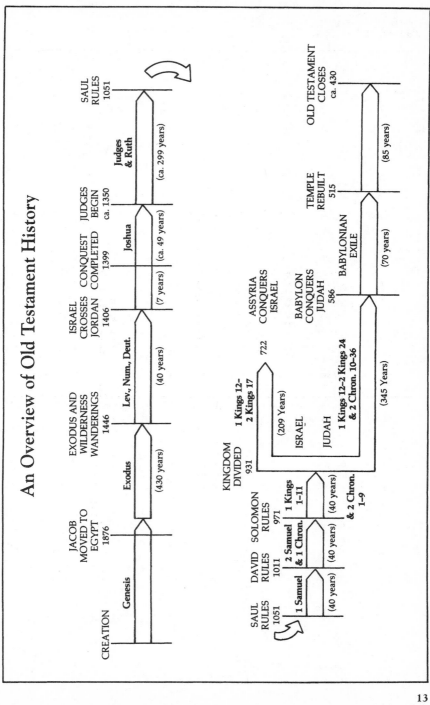

Biblical Weights and Measures

BIBLICAL UNIT		AMERICAN EQUIVALENT	METRIC EQUIVALENT
WEIGHT			
talent	*(60 minas)*	75 pounds	34 kilograms
mina	*(50 shekels)*	1 1/4 pounds	0.6 kilogram
shekel	*(2 bekas)*	2/5 ounce	11.5 grams
pim	*(2/3 shekel)*	1/3 ounce	7.6 grams
beka	*(10 gerahs)*	1/5 ounce	6 grams
gerah		1/50 ounce	0.6 gram
LENGTH			
cubit		18 inches	0.5 meter
span		9 inches	23 centimeters
handbreadth		3 inches	7 centimeters
CAPACITY			
Dry Measure			
cor [homer]	*(10 ephahs)*	6 bushels	220 liters
lethech	*(5 ephahs)*	3 bushels	110 liters
ephah	*(10 omers)*	1/2 bushel	22 liters
seah	*(1/3 ephah)*	7 quarts	7.3 liters
omer	*(1/10 ephah)*	2 quarts	2 liters
cab	*(1/18 ephah)*	1/2 pint	0.3 liter
Liquid Measure			
bath	*(1 ephah)*	6 gallons	22 liters
hin	*(1/6 bath)*	4 quarts	4 liters
log	*(1/72 bath)*	1/3 quart	0.3 liter

The information in this chart, while not being mathematically precise, gives approximate amounts and distances. The figures are calculated on the basis of a shekel equaling 11.5 grams, a cubit equaling 18 inches, and an ephah equaling 22 liters.

JOSHUA

Donald K. Campbell

INTRODUCTION

Title of the Book. In the Hebrew text the book bears the superscription Yᵉhôšūaʹ, the name of its leading figure, Joshua. His name and the title of the book mean "Yahweh saves" or "Yahweh is salvation." The title therefore suitably describes what God used Joshua to do, as recorded in this book, namely, to save His people by conquering Canaan and apportioning it to Israel as their promised homeland.

Place in the Canon. In the English Old Testament Joshua appears as the first of the 12 historical books (Josh.–Es.). This follows the Septuagint (the Gr. trans. of the OT) in which the books are grouped into the Pentateuch (Gen.–Deut.), History (Josh.–Es.), Poetry (Job–Song), and Prophecy (Isa.–Mal.). In the Hebrew canon the books are identical, but the groupings are different. They are divided into the Law, the Prophets, and the Writings. The Book of Joshua therefore in this case heads the second division of the Old Testament, the Prophets. The "Prophets" in turn are divided into the "Former Prophets" (Josh.–2 Kings, not including Ruth) and the "Latter Prophets" (Isa.–Mal. without Lam. and Dan.). The "Writings" include (in this order) Psalms, Job, Proverbs, Song of Solomon, Ruth, Ecclesiastes, Lamentations, Esther, Daniel, Ezra, Nehemiah, 1 and 2 Chronicles. Scholars have debated the reason for placing the Book of Joshua among the "Prophets." Some have suggested it was because he held the office of prophet. Others say the historical books, the "Former Prophets," illustrate the principles preached by the prophets.

Authorship. The Bible does not identify the author of this book. Many liberal scholars consider it a composite of the documents which supposedly underline the Pentateuch, but a strong case can be made for unity of composition by a single author (e.g., Gleason L. Archer, *A Survey of Old Testament Introduction*. Chicago: Moody Press, 1964, pp. 252-3). Any discussion of authorship should keep the following matters in mind: (1) An eyewitness wrote many parts of the book (cf. the "we" and "us" references in 5:1, 6; and the vivid descriptions of the sending of the spies, the crossing of the Jordan, the capture of Jericho, the battle of Ai, etc.). (2) An early authorship is required by internal evidence (Rahab was alive at the time of writing [6:25]; the Jebusites still inhabited Jerusalem [15:63]; Canaanite cities are mentioned by archaic names, such as Baalah for Kiriath Jearim and Kiriath Arba for Hebron [15:9, 13]; Tyre had not yet conquered Sidon which it did in the 12th century [13:4-6]; the Philistines were not a national menace to Israel as they became after their invasion about 1200 B.C.). (3) Joshua had written parts of the book (cf. 8:32; 24:26). (4) Other parts of the book were clearly written after Joshua's death (cf. 24:29-30—the record of his death; 15:13-14—Caleb's conquest of Hebron [also recorded in Jud. 1:1, 10, 20]; Josh. 15:15-19—Othniel's conquest of Debir [also recorded in Jud. 1:11-15]; Josh. 19:47—the Danites' conquest of Leshem [also recorded in Jud. 17–18]). In light of these factors many evangelical scholars ascribe the book to Joshua himself as the main author with minor additions made by Eleazar the high priest and his son Phinehas.

Date. Since an eyewitness wrote much of the book (see the previous section "Authorship"), the date of writing is closely related to the date of the events. Again there is considerable disagreement among scholars on the date of the Conquest of Canaan under Joshua. Some place the Conquest in the 15th century B.C., whereas others date the Conquest in the 13th century B.C. (For more on this subject see the *Introduction* to Ex.) Key verses in deciding the issue are 1 Kings 6:1 and Judges 11:26. According to 1 Kings 6:1 the Israelites left Egypt 480 years before the fourth year of Solomon, that is, before 966 B.C. Adding these figures gives an Exodus date of 1446 B.C. The beginning of the Conquest was 40 years later (after the wilderness wanderings) or 1406 B.C. The evidence from Judges 11:26 confirms this. Jephthah said the period from the Conquest to his time was 300 years (Jud. 11:26). Adding 140 years to cover the period from Jephthah to the fourth year of Solomon gives a total of 480, which agrees with 1 Kings 6:1 (40 years for the wilderness wanderings, plus 300 for the period from the Conquest to Jephthah, plus 140 from Jephthah to the fourth year of Solomon equals 480 years). Since the actual Conquest lasted seven years (cf. comments on Josh. 14:10), the land was probably occupied about 1399 B.C. The book, apart from minor additions, could have been completed soon after that.

Purpose. The purpose of the Book of Joshua is to give an official account of the historical fulfillment of the Lord's promise to the patriarchs to give Israel the land of Canaan by holy war. A "holy war" was a conflict with religious overtones rather than one with a political motivation of defense or expansion. This can be seen in both the opening charge (1:2-6) and the concluding summary (21:43).

Specifically, the conquest of Canaan under Joshua's leadership was based on the Abrahamic Covenant. God, having dealt with all nations, made Abraham the center of His purposes and determined to reach the lost world through Abraham's seed. The Lord made a contract or covenant with Abraham, promising unconditionally to give a land, a posterity, and spiritual blessing to the patriarch and his descendants (Gen. 12:2-3). Soon thereafter God said He was giving the land to Israel forever (cf. Gen. 13:15). The boundaries of the land were then given to Abraham (Gen. 15:18-21). Later God affirmed that the rightful heirs to the Promised Land were Isaac and his descendants (Gen. 17:19-21). Thus the Book of Joshua records the fulfillment of the patriarchal promise as Israel appropriat-

ed the land pledged to her by her faithful God centuries before. That the nation was later dispossessed reflects not on the character of God but on the fickleness of a people who took divine blessings for granted, fell into the worship of their neighbors' gods, and therefore came under the chastisement God had warned them about (cf. Deut. 28:15-68). But Israel must possess the land forever according to the promise, something that awaits the return of Messiah and the redemption of Israel. According to the Prophet Isaiah, the Messiah will be a "second Joshua," who will "restore the land and . . . reassign its desolate inheritances" (Isa. 49:8).

Paul taught that the events of the Exodus and Conquest are meaningful for Christians in that those events possess significance as types (cf. 1 Cor. 10:1-11). The Greek form of the name "Joshua" ("Yahweh saves" or "Yahweh is salvation") is "Jesus." As Joshua led Israel to victory over her enemies and into possession of the Promised Land, and as he interceded for the nation after it had sinned and been defeated, so does Jesus. He brings the people of God into a promised rest (Heb. 4:8-9); intercedes for His own continually (Rom. 8:34; Heb. 7:25); and enables them to defeat their enemies (Rom. 8:37; Heb. 2:14-15).

OUTLINE

COMMENTARY

I. The Invasion of Canaan (1:1–5:12)

A. The commissioning of Joshua (chap. 1)

1. JOSHUA'S LISTENING TO THE LORD (1:1-9)

1:1 The words, **After the death of Moses**, link this book with Deuteronomy (cf. Deut. 34:1-9). Before Moses' death **Joshua** was designated his successor (cf. Num. 27:15-23; Deut. 3:21-22; 31:1-8). Joshua had been **Moses'** young **aide** for a number of years (Ex. 24:13; 33:11; Num. 11:28). Joshua was from the tribe of Ephraim (Num. 13:8), and lived 110 years (Josh. 24:29).

Joshua may have felt a sense of loneliness, and waited expectantly near the Jordan River to hear the voice of God. He was not disappointed. When God's servants take time to listen, He always communicates. In the present Age He usually speaks through His written Word. But in the Old Testament He spoke in dreams by night, in visions by day, through the high priest, and occasionally in an audible voice.

1:2. In whatever way God communicated with Joshua, the message came through clearly. **Moses** God's **servant was dead.** (Interestingly Moses is called "the servant of the LORD" 3 times in Josh. 1 [vv. 1, 13, 15; cf. Ex. 14:31], and 13 times elsewhere in the Book of Josh. And at the end of Joshua's life he too was called "the servant of the LORD" [Josh. 24:29].) But though Moses was dead, God's purpose was quite alive, and Joshua was now the key figure to fulfill God's program. His instructions were explicit. Joshua was to assume immediate command of **all** the **people** and lead them across **the Jordan River into the land** God was **about to give to them.** No one can question God's right to give Canaan **to the Israelites** for He owns all the earth. As a psalmist later affirmed, "The earth is the LORD's, and everything in it, the world, and all who live in it" (Ps. 24:1).

1:3-4. Though the land was God's gift to Israel, it could be won only by hard fighting. The Lord gave them title to the **territory** but they had to possess it by marching on **every** part. The boundaries established by God and **promised** to Abraham (Gen. 15:18-21) and **Moses** (Deut. 1:6-8) were to extend from the wilderness on the south to the **Lebanon** mountain range on the north, and from **the Euphrates** River on the east **to the Great Sea,** the Mediterranean, **on the west.** The added expression, **all the Hittite country,** probably refers not to the extensive empire of that name north of Canaan but to the fact that in ancient times the whole population of Canaan or any part of it was sometimes called "Hittite" (cf. Gen. 15:20). "Pockets" of Hittite peoples existed here and there in Canaan.

Thirty-eight years earlier Joshua had explored this good and fruitful land as 1 of the 12 spies (Num. 13:1-16; there [Num. 13:8] he is called "Hoshea," a variant spelling of his name). The memory of its beauty and fertility had not dimmed. Now he was to lead the armies of Israel to conquer that territory.

What is the extent of these boundaries? The territory actually conquered and possessed in the time of Joshua was much less than what was promised in Genesis 15:18-21. Even in the time of David and Solomon, when the land reached its greatest extent, the outlying districts were only within Israel's sphere of influence.

When will the nation of Israel fully possess the land? The prophets have declared that at the time of Christ's return to earth He will regather the Jews and reign in the land over a converted and redeemed Israel. Full and complete possession of the land awaits that day (cf. Jer. 16:14-16; Amos 9:11-15; Zech. 8:4-8).

1:5. As Joshua faced the tremendous task of conquering Canaan, he needed a fresh word of encouragement. From personal observation Joshua knew that the Canaanites and others were vigorous people who lived in strongly fortified cities (cf. Num. 13:28-29). Frequent battles kept their warriors in trim fighting condition. And for the most part the land was mountainous, a fact that would make war maneuvers most difficult. But when God gives a command He often accompanies it with a promise, so He assured Joshua a lifetime of continuous victory over his enemies, based on His unfailing presence and help. The words **I will never leave you** (cf. Josh. 1:9) may be rendered, "I will not drop or abandon you." God never walks out on His promises.

1:6. Flowing from this strong affirmation that God would never let Joshua down was God's threefold call to courage. First, Joshua was commanded to **be strong and courageous** (cf. vv. 7, 9, 18) **because** of *God's promise* of the land. Strength and fortitude would be required for the strenuous military campaign just ahead, but Joshua was to keep uppermost in his mind the fact that he would succeed in causing Israel **to inherit the land** because it had been promised **to their forefathers,** that is, to Abraham (Gen. 13:14-17; 15:18-21; 17:7-8; 22:16-18), Isaac (Gen. 26:3-5), Jacob (Gen. 28:13; 35:12), and the entire nation, the seed of Abraham (Ex. 6:8), as an eternal possession. And Joshua now at last was to **lead** the children of Israel into possession of this Promised Land. What a strategic role he was to play at this crucial time in his nation's history!

While in any given generation the fulfillment of this great and significant promise depends on Israel's obedience to God, there can be no question that the Bible affirms her right to the land. By divine contract the title is hers even though she will not possess it totally and enjoy it fully until she is right with God.

1:7-8. Second, Joshua was again commanded to **be strong and very courageous,** being **careful to obey all the Law of Moses.** This command is based on *God's power* through His Word. This is a stronger exhortation, indicating that greater strength of character would be required to obey God's Word faithfully and fully than to win military battles! The emphasis in these verses is clearly on a written body of truth. Many critics argue that the Scriptures did not appear in written form until several centuries later but here is a clear reference to an authoritative **Book of the Law.**

To enjoy prosperity and **be . . . successful** in the Conquest of Canaan Joshua was to do three things with regard to the Scriptures: (a) The Law was not to **depart from** his **mouth;** he was to talk about it (cf. Deut. 6:7); (b) He was to **meditate on it day and night,** to think about it (cf. Ps. 1:2; 119:97); (c) He was to **do everything written in it,** to obey its commands fully and to act by it (cf. Ezra 7:10; James 1:22-25).

Joshua's life demonstrates that in a practical way he lived according to the teachings of the Law of Moses, the only portion of the Word of God then in written form. This alone explains the victories he achieved in battle and the success that marked his entire career. In one of his farewell addresses to the nation just before he died he urged the people to live in submission to the Scriptures (Josh. 23:6). Tragically they heeded this charge for only a short time. In succeeding generations the people of Israel refused to be guided by God's authoritative revelation, and they all did what they chose (Jud. 21:25). Rejecting an objective standard of righteousness, they chose a subjective one characterized by moral and spiritual relativism. This in turn plunged the nation into centuries of religious apostasy and moral anarchy.

1:9. The third call to courage addressed to Joshua was based on the promise of *God's presence.* This did not minimize the task Joshua faced. He would encounter giants and fortified cities, but God's presence would make all the difference.

Joshua probably had times when he felt weak, inadequate, and frightened. Perhaps he considered resigning before the Conquest even began. But God knew all about his feelings of personal weakness and fear and told Joshua three times, **Be strong and courageous** (vv. 6-7, 9; cf. v. 18). God also urged him **not** to **be** afraid or **discouraged** (cf. Deut. 1:21; 31:8; Josh. 8:1). These charges with their accompanying assurances (God's promise, God's power, and God's presence) were sufficient to last a lifetime. Believers in all ages can be uplifted by the same three assurances.

2. JOSHUA'S COMMANDING THE OFFICERS (1:10-15)

The Lord had spoken to Joshua. Now Joshua was to speak to the people, which he did without delay. Joshua's commands had a ring of certainty. The new leader had taken charge with confidence. The situation Joshua and the people faced was not easy. In fact his situation closely paralleled the dilemma Moses and the Israelites encountered at the Red Sea (Ex. 14). In both cases the obstacle occurred at the beginning of the leaders' ministries. Both were impossible to overcome by natural means. Both demanded implicit trust in and absolute dependence on God's miracle-working power.

1:10-11. Two matters demanded attention. First, provisions had to be gathered, for even though the daily manna had not yet ceased **the people** were to gather some of the fruit and grain from the plains of Moab for themselves and their cattle. The order to "prepare" was given by **Joshua** to **the officers** (lit., "scribes"), who like present-day adjutants or staff officers relayed their commanding officer's orders to the people. In **three days** (cf. 2:22) the Conquest would begin.

1:12-15. Joshua's second item of business was to remind the tribes of Reuben, Gad, and **the half-tribe of Manasseh** that though they had received their inheritance **east of the Jordan,** they were committed to fight with their **brothers**

and assist in conquering **the land** west of Jordan (Num. 32:16-32; Deut. 3:12-20). The key word here is **remember,** and their response (Josh. 1:16-18) shows they had not forgotten their promise and were ready to stand by it. In fact they were to serve as shock troops in leading the attack on Canaan (v. 14, **cross over ahead of your brothers**).

3. JOSHUA'S RECEIVING SUPPORT FROM THE PEOPLE (1:16-18)

1:16-18. The response of the two and one-half Transjordanian tribes was enthusiastic and wholehearted. It must certainly have reflected the attitude of all the tribes at this crucial time of preparation for the invasion. What an encouragement this was to the new leader to be sure that the people were united in supporting him. Their pledge of loyalty and obedience (**we will go. . . . we will obey you**) included the solemn declaration that anyone guilty of disobedience would be executed. The tribes even encouraged Joshua to **be strong and courageous!** (cf. vv. 6-7, 9)

But there was one condition: they were willing to follow **Joshua** if he showed clear evidence that he was being led by **God** (v. 17). This was a wise precaution and one to be carefully followed lest Israel's leaders turn out to be false prophets or "blind leaders of the blind."

B. The spying out of Jericho (chap. 2)

Joshua had been 1 of the 12 spies who had explored the land (Num. 13–14). Now as he faced westward and viewed the land God promised across the turbulent Jordan, it was natural for him to secure information necessary for a successful battle. That battle was the first in a long, difficult war.

1. THE SPIES' COMMISSION TO JERICHO (2:1)

2:1. Looming in the middle of the path the invaders must take was the walled city of **Jericho,** the key citadel of the Jordan Valley which commanded the passes into the central highlands. But before attacking it Joshua needed complete information about this fortress—its gates, fortified towers, military force, and the morale of its people. So two secret agents were chosen and sent on a carefully concealed mission. Not even the Israelites were to know of it lest an unfavorable

report dishearten them as it had their fathers at Kadesh Barnea (Num. 13:1–14:4).

Taking their lives in their hands the **two spies** left **Shittim,** seven miles east of the Jordan, and probably traveled north, swimming across the flooded river (cf. 3:15) at some fords. Turning south they approached Jericho from the west side and soon were moving along its streets, mingling with the people.

How the spies chose **the house of a prostitute named Rahab** is not revealed. While some suggest they saw her walking the streets and followed her, it seems better to believe that in the providence of God the men were led **there.** God's purpose for the visit of the spies to Jericho included more than securing military information. A sinful woman was there whom God in His grace purposed to spare from the judgment soon to fall on the city. So the Lord, moving in a mysterious way, brought together two secret agents of the army of Israel and a harlot of Canaan who would become a proselyte to the God of Israel.

Some, from the time of Josephus to the present, have attempted to soften the situation by arguing that Rahab was only an innkeeper, but the New Testament references to her (Heb. 11:31; James 2:25) indicate that she was an immoral woman. This in no way impugns the righteousness of God who used such a person in the fulfillment of His purposes. Instead this incident serves to bring His mercy and grace into bold relief (cf. Matt. 21:32; Luke 15:1; 19:10).

2. THE SPIES' SHIELDING BY RAHAB (2:2-7)

2:2-3. The disguise of the spies was not adequate. The entire city was on alert, knowing about the camp of Israel opposite them across the Jordan. Someone detected the agents, followed them to Rahab's **house,** and quickly returned to report to **the king. The king,** responding with alacrity, sent messengers who demanded of **Rahab** that the spies be surrendered. In keeping with oriental custom the privacy of even a woman such as Rahab was respected and the king's men refrained from bursting into her house and searching it.

2:4-6. But apparently Rahab also had suspicions about the identity of the **two** visitors. When she saw the soldiers approaching her house she took the spies and hid then beneath **the stalks of flax** which had been placed on her flat **roof** for drying. After flax stalks were pulled up at harvesttime, they were soaked in water for three or four weeks to separate the fibers. Then, after drying in the sun, the flax was made into linen cloth.

Hastening down to open her front door to the king's messengers, she freely admitted that two strangers had come to her house, but how could she know their identity and mission? "They **left** here **at dusk,** just about the time **the city gate** is closed," she lied. "But if you hurry **you** can probably **catch . . . them.**"

2:7. The soldiers took Rahab at her word, made no search of her property, but quickly **set out** on a wild-goose chase due east **to the fords of the Jordan,** the most likely escape route.

Was Rahab wrong to lie since her falsehood protected **the spies**? Are there some situations in which a lie is acceptable?

After all, some say, this was a cultural matter, for Rahab was born and raised among the depraved Canaanites among whom lying was universally practiced. She probably saw no evil in her act. Further, if she had told the truth the spies would have been killed by the king of Jericho.

But such arguments are not convincing. To argue that the spies would certainly have perished if Rahab had been truthful is to ignore the option that God could have protected the spies in some other way. To excuse Rahab for indulging in a common practice is to condone what God condemns. Paul quoted a prophet of Crete who said that Cretans' were inveterate liars, and then added, "This testimony is true. Therefore, rebuke them sharply, so that they will be sound in the faith" (Titus 1:13). The lie of Rahab was recorded but not approved. The Bible approved her faith demonstrated by good works (Heb. 11:31), but not her falsehood. (However, some explain Rahab's lying by saying that deception is allowable in war.)

3. THE SPIES' INTELLIGENCE INFORMATION FROM RAHAB (2:8-11)

2:8-11. A most remarkable conversation then took place. The king's messengers were gone and Rahab climbed to the

roof of her home where she talked with the two **spies** in the darkness. One is hardly prepared for her declaration of faith which follows. First, she disclosed that she believed that **the LORD,** the God of Israel, had **given** them the **land** of Canaan. Though the army of Israel had not yet crossed the Jordan River, Rahab stated in effect, "the Conquest is as good as over." Second, she revealed to the spies the priceless information that the inhabitants of Jericho as well as the rest of Canaan were utterly demoralized: **All who live in this country are melting in fear because of you.** (Cf. v. 24, and v. 11, **our hearts sank and everyone's courage failed.**) This is as God had said it would be (Ex. 23:27; Deut. 2:25). Since a major objective of the spy mission was to assess the morale of the enemy, this word was indeed "music to their ears." But why the terror? Because of the power of Israel's God which parted **the Red Sea** for the Hebrew slaves 40 years before, and more recently gave them victories over **Sihon and Og,** the mighty **kings of the Amorites east of the Jordan** (Num. 21:21-35). Now that same God was closing in on them and they knew they could not win.

Then Rahab declared her faith in Israel's God: **For the LORD your God is God in heaven above and on the earth below.** Responding to the word she had received about the mighty working of God, Rahab believed, trusting in His power and mercy. And that faith saved her. But how could Rahab have such a remarkable faith and still be a harlot, and so glibly tell lies? The answer would seem to be that as she responded in belief to the message she heard about God's works, she later responded to further messages concerning God's standards of life and obeyed. After all, spiritual maturity is gradual, not instantaneous. Even John Newton, who wrote the gospel song "Amazing Grace," continued for some time after his conversion in the slave trade before he was convicted about this base and degrading practice and gave it up.

4. THE SPIES' PROMISE TO RAHAB (2:12-21)

2:12-13. Rahab demonstrated her faith not only by protecting the spies (Heb. 11:31; James 2:25) but also by showing concern for her family's safety.

Admittedly she sought her family's physical deliverance, but she must have desired also that they too become a part of God's people, serving the one true God of Israel instead of being enslaved to the Canaanites' vile and degrading idolatry.

She pursued this urgent matter delicately but persistently, pressing the spies to make a pact with her because of her cooperation with them.

When Rahab asked for **kindness** (hesed) to be shown to her **family** she used a significant and meaningful word. Found about 250 times in the Old Testament, hesed means loyal, steadfast, or faithful love based on a promise, agreement, or covenant. Sometimes the word is used of God's covenant-love for His people and sometimes, as here, of relationships on the human level. Rahab's request was that the spies make a hesed agreement with her and her father's family, just as she had made a hesed agreement with them by sparing their **lives**.

2:14. The response of the spies was immediate and decisive. "**When the Lord gives us the land,** that is, Jericho, we will keep the hesed agreement. **If you don't** report our mission we will protect you and your family or forfeit **our** own **lives**" (author's paraphrase).

2:15-20. As the spies prepared to go they again confirmed the pact by repeating and enlarging the conditions Rahab must abide by. First, her **house** must be marked by a **scarlet cord** hung from **the window.** Because of the position of the house on **the city wall** (see comments on v. 21 about the house on the wall) the cord would be clearly seen by the Israelite soldiers again and again as they would march around the walls (6:12-15). Her home would be clearly marked out and no soldier, however fierce and eager he might be in the work of destruction, would dare violate the oath and kill anyone in that **house.**

Second, Rahab and her **family** were to remain **in the house** during the attack on Jericho. If anybody would wander out and was killed the guilt for his death would be **his own,** not the invaders'. Finally, the spies again emphasized that they would be free of this **oath** of protection if Rahab exposed their mission.

2:21. To these conditions Rahab **agreed,** and after the spies left she **tied the scarlet cord in the window.** She probably also hurried and told her family to gather in her house. The door of her house was a door to safety from the judgment soon to fall on Jericho (cf. Gen. 7:16; Ex. 12:23; John 10:9).

Their mission completed, the spies and Rahab exchanged parting instructions concerning their escape (cf. Josh. 2:15-16). Jericho at this time was surrounded by two walls about 15 feet apart. Planks of wood spanned the gap and then houses were built on this foundation. Probably due to the pressure of space in the small city, Rahab's house was one of those built "on the wall." In this way it was "part of the city wall" (v. 15).

5. THE SPIES' RETURN TO JOSHUA (2:22-24)

2:22-24. The spies were carefully lowered by a rope through a window of Rahab's house (v. 15). Their escape would have been more difficult, if not impossible, had it been necessary for them to go out the city gate. Scarcely a half-mile west of Jericho are limestone cliffs about 1,500 feet high, honeycombed with caves. Here the spies hid (in **the hills**) for **three days** (cf. 1:11) **until the** soldiers of Jericho gave up the hunt. Then under cover of darkness the spies swam back across the Jordan, made their way quickly to the camp at Shittim (cf. 2:1), and reported **to Joshua** about their strange and stirring adventure and the alarm and utter despondency of the Canaanites. Their conclusion was, **The Lord has surely given the whole land into our hands** for **all the people are melting in fear** (cf. v. 9; Ex. 23:27; Deut. 2:25). How different from the report of the majority of the spies at Kadesh Barnea who said, "We can't attack those people; they are stronger than we are" (Num. 13:31).

C. The crossing of the Jordan (chap. 3)

1. PREPARATION FOR THE CROSSING (3:1-4)

3:1. Joshua was a man of action. The spies having reported in, Israel's leader began immediate preparations to cross the Jordan and invade Canaan. As yet Joshua had no knowledge of how this massive group of people was to cross the swollen river (cf. v. 15). But believing that God would somehow make it possible, he moved them all, bag and baggage, the seven miles **from Shittim . . .**

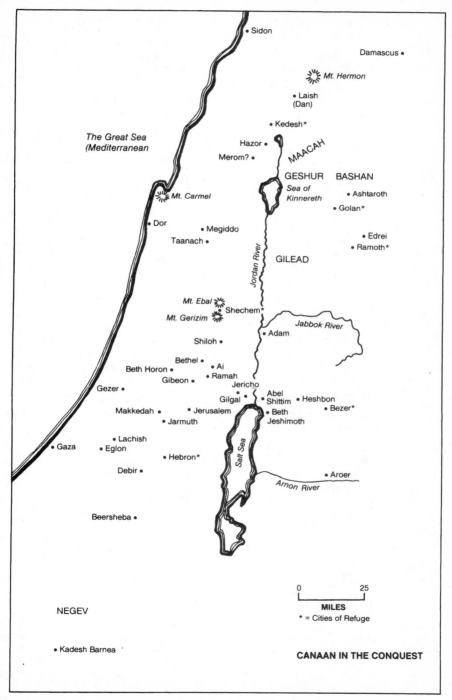

CANAAN IN THE CONQUEST

to the Jordan. (Shittim is probably the same as Abel Shittim, mentioned in Num. 33:49.)

3:2-3. Having arrived at the river they stopped for **three days.** Time was no doubt needed for the leaders to organize the crossing and pass instructions on to the people. The delay also gave everyone an opportunity to get close and see the river, now a strong and rapid current due to the melting of the winter snows of Mount Hermon in the north. They must have faltered at the seeming impossibility of the crossing.

At the end of the third day of waiting **the people** were given instructions. The pillar of cloud would no longer lead them but they were instead to follow the **ark of the covenant.** No army scouts would advance first into the land but rather **priests** bearing the ark (cf. v. 11). And since the ark symbolized **the LORD** Himself, it was Yahweh who led His people into Canaan.

3:4. With the ark going ahead the people were to fall in behind, or possibly to spread around it on three sides. But they were to **keep** their **distance** by some 3,000 feet. Why? Probably to remind them of the sacredness of **the ark** and the holiness of the God it represented. They were to have no casual or careless intimacy with God but a profound spirit of respect and reverence. God was to be considered not "the Man upstairs" but the sovereign and holy God of all the earth.

The distance was also essential so that the largest possible number of this great population could see the ark. God was about to lead them over unfamiliar ground, over a **way** they had not taken **before.** It was new territory so without the Lord's guidance and leadership the people would not know which direction to take.

2. CONSECRATION FOR THE CROSSING (3:5-13)

3:5. As the day for the crossing approached **Joshua** commanded **the people** to sanctify or **consecrate** themselves. It would be easier to understand if he had said, "Sharpen your swords and check your shields!" But spiritual not military preparation was needed at this time because God was about to reveal Himself by performing a great miracle in Israel's midst. As a person would prepare scrupulously to meet someone of earthly

fame so it was appropriate for the Israelites to prepare for a manifestation of the God of all the earth. The same command was heard at Sinai when the previous generation prepared itself for the majestic revelation of the Lord in the giving of the Law (Ex. 19:10-13).

But that was not all. The people of Israel were to *expect* God to work a miracle. They were to be eager, gripped by a sense of wonder. Israel was not to lose sight of their God who can do the incredible and the humanly impossible.

3:6-8. The LORD then told **Joshua** how they would make the crossing, and explained to Joshua that this miracle would magnify or **exalt** him as the leader **of the people.** It was time to establish Joshua's credentials as God's representative to guide **Israel.** What better way to accomplish this than for Joshua to direct their passage through a miraculously parted **river?** After the crossing the people did in fact revere Joshua (4:14), knowing that God was **with** him (3:7; cf. 1:5, 9).

3:9-13. But when **Joshua** passed on **the words** of **God** to the people he did not disclose the special promise that he would be exalted by this miraculous event. Rather he told them that this miracle would certify that the living God, in contrast with the dead idols worshiped by the heathen, was in their midst. Further, besides opening a way across the flooded **Jordan,** the living God would also **drive out** the seven groups of people inhabiting the land. The promise, **the living God is among you,** became the watchword of the Conquest, the key to victory over the enemies in the land. It is a promise that appears on almost every page of this book: "I will be with you!" It is a promise that still sustains the Lord's people—the assurance of His presence. Since God is **the Lord** ('*ăḏôn*, "master") **of all the earth** (cf. Ps. 97:5), He was certainly capable of getting His people across a river.

3. COMPLETION OF THE CROSSING (3:14-17)

3:14-15a. The day of the crossing of **the Jordan,** the day when Israel was to enter Canaan, finally arrived. The people folded their tents and followed the ark-bearing **priests** to the brink of **the Jordan.** It was the time of the barley **harvest,** the month of Nisan (March-April), the first month of their year (4:19). The river was **at flood stage**—a foreboding sight to the priests and people and a severe test of their faith. Would they hesitate in fear or would they advance in faith, believing that what God had promised (about the water stopping, 3:13) would actually happen?

3:15b-17. Dramatic things happened the moment **the priests** carrying **the ark** of the covenant stepped into the muddy, swirling waters. **The water from upstream stopped flowing** (cf. v. 13). Piling up **at a town called Adam,** waters from other streams were **completely cut off** so as not to enter the Jordan. **So the people crossed over opposite Jericho.** This is reminiscent of the Red (Reed) Sea crossing (cf. Ex. 15:8; Ps. 78:13).

Though the place named "Adam" is found only here it is usually identified with Tell ed-Damiyeh, about 16 miles north of the ford opposite Jericho. A wide stretch of riverbed therefore was dried up, allowing the people with their animals and baggage to hurry across (cf. Josh. 4:10).

How could this sensational event occur? Many insist that this was no miracle since the event can be explained as a natural phenomenon. They point out that on December 8, 1267 an earthquake caused the high banks of the Jordan to collapse near Tell ed-Damiyeh, damming the river for about 10 hours. On July 11, 1927 another earthquake near the same location blocked the river for 21 hours. Of course these stoppages did not occur during flood season. Admittedly God could have employed natural causes such as an earthquake and a landslide and the timing would have still made it a miraculous intervention. But does the biblical text allow for such an interpretation of this event?

Considering all the factors involved it seems best to view this occurrence as a special act of God brought about in a way unknown to man. Many supernatural elements were brought together: (1) The event came to pass as predicted (3:13, 15). (2) The timing was exact (v. 15). (3) The event took place when the river was at flood stage (v. 15). (4) The wall of water was held in place for many hours, possibly an entire day (v. 16). (5) The soft, wet river bottom became **dry** at once (v. 17). (6) The water returned immedi-

ately as soon as the people had crossed over and **the priests** came up out of the river (4:18). Centuries later the Prophets Elijah and Elisha crossed the same river on dry ground to the east (2 Kings 2:8). Soon thereafter Elisha crossed back over the river on dry ground. If a natural phenomenon is necessary to explain the Israelites' crossing under Joshua, then one would have to conclude that two earthquakes occurred in quick sequence for Elijah and Elisha, which seems a bit presumptuous.

By this great miracle, the crossing of **the Jordan** River at flood stage by a nation of about 2 million people, God was glorified, Joshua was exalted, **Israel** was encouraged, and the Canaanites were terrorized.

For Israel the crossing of the Jordan meant they were irrevocably committed to a struggle against armies, chariots, and fortified cities. They were also committed to walk by faith in the living God and to turn from walking according to the flesh as they had often done in the wilderness.

For believers today, crossing the Jordan represents passing from one level of the Christian life to another. (It is not a picture of a believer dying and entering heaven. For the Israelites Canaan was hardly heaven!) It is a picture of entering into spiritual warfare to claim what God has promised. This should mean the end of a life lived by human effort and the beginning of a life of faith and obedience.

D. The erecting of memorials (chap. 4)

4:1-3. It was important that Israel never forget this great miracle. So that the Israelites would remember how God acted on their behalf on this historic day God had them erect a 12-stone memorial. This memorial celebrated the crossing of the Israelite multitudes over the dry riverbed of **the Jordan.**

The LORD told **Joshua** to direct **12 men,** previously chosen (cf. 3:12), to carry **12 stones from the** bed of the river to the place of the first night's encampment.

4:4-8. Calling **the 12** tribal representatives **together** Joshua instructed them. They were to return to **the middle of the** riverbed and **each** one was to bring back one **stone.** These stones would be a vivid reminder (**a memorial**) of God's work of deliverance (cf. v. 24) and an effective means for the Israelites to teach their young (vv. 6-7; cf. vv. 21-24).

The response of the 12 **men** was immediate and unquestioning. They could well have feared reentering the Jordan. After all, how long would it stay dry? Whatever fears they may have had were put aside and they unhesitatingly obeyed God's instructions.

4:9. **Joshua** joined these men on their strange mission, and while they were wrenching up great stones from the bed of the river, he **set** another pile of **12 stones** (NIV marg.) in the riverbed itself to mark the precise **spot where the priests** stood with **the ark of the covenant.** This was apparently done on Joshua's own initiative and expressed his desire to have a personal reminder of God's faithfulness at the very beginning of the Conquest of Canaan.

4:10-18. All was now accomplished that **the LORD . . . commanded.** In anticipation of **the Jordan** flowing again the details of the crossing were reviewed. (1) **The priests** and **the ark remained** in the riverbed while **the people hurried** across (v. 10; cf. 3:17). (2) The **armed** men of the Transjordanian tribes, not hampered with families and goods, led the crossing (4:12-13). (3) As soon as all the people had crossed and the special mission for the memorials was completed, **the priests** left the riverbed—they were the first ones in and the last ones out—and resumed their position at the head of the people (vv. 11, 15-17). (4) Immediately **the Jordan** resumed its flow (v. 18).

Thus all the tribes participated in the crossing, though **Reuben, Gad, and the half-tribe of Manasseh** sent only representative armies. The rest of those two and one-half tribes remained on the east side to protect their homes and cities (cf. v. 13). The population of males in those tribes 20 years of age or older totaled 136,930 (Num. 26:7, 18, 34). The **40,000** soldiers (Josh. 4:13) were 29 percent of that adult male population—less than one of every three adult males.

Alexander Maclaren wrote, "The one point made prominent is the instantaneous rush back to the impatient torrent as soon as the curb was taken off. Like some horse rejoicing to be free, the tawny flood pours down, and soon everything looks 'as aforetime' except for the new rock, piled by human hands, round which the water chafed" (*Exposi-*

tions of Holy Scripture. London: Hodder & Stoughton, 1908, 3:119).

One can imagine what it must have been like for the Israelites to stand on the riverbank, watching the hurrying torrent covering up their path, and then lifting their eyes to look at the opposite side where they had stood that morning. There was no returning now. A new and exciting chapter in their history had begun.

4:19-20. But this was no time for reflection. **Joshua** led **the people** to **Gilgal,** their first encampment in Canaan, about two miles from **Jericho.** There **the 12 stones . . . taken out of the Jordan** were **set up,** perhaps in a small circle. The name Gilgal means "circle," and may have been taken from an ancient circle of stones of pagan significance. If so, the more recent circle commemorating Yahweh's great work would serve to counteract the idolatrous association of the site.

4:21-23. The purpose of the stones was clearly pedagogical: to remind Israel for generations to come that it was **God** who brought them through **the Jordan** (cf. vv. 6-7) just as He had taken their fathers through **the Red Sea.**

But how were the **future** generations to know what the stones meant? The answer is clear. Parents were to teach God's ways and works to their children (cf. Deut. 6:4-7). A Jewish father was not to send his inquisitive child to a Levite for answers to his questions. The father was to answer them himself.

4:24. However, besides serving as a visual aid for parental instruction of children, the memorial stones had a broader purpose: **that all the peoples of the earth might know that the hand of the LORD is powerful.** As the families of Israel spent their first night in the land, their hearts may well have been filled with uncertainty and fear. The mountains rising steeply to the west looked foreboding. But then the people looked at the 12 stones taken out of the Jordan and were reminded that God had done something great for them that day. Surely they could trust Him for the days ahead.

E. The consecration of the Israelites (5:1-12)

Under Joshua's leadership and by miraculous intervention some 2 million soldiers and civilians crossed the Jordan.

A beachhead was quickly established at Gilgal, and from every human point of view it was time to strike immediately at the strongholds of Canaan. After all, the morale of the people of Canaan had utterly collapsed in the face of one old and two recent news items that had spread through the land: (a) that the God of Israel had dried up the Red (Reed) Sea (2:10); (b) that the Israelites had defeated the powerful kings of the Amorites in Transjordan (2:10); (c) that Yahweh had also dried up the waters of the Jordan River so that the Israelites could cross over into Canaan (5:1; cf. 4:24).

As this news spread, so did fear. What better time to strike a paralyzing blow? Certainly the military leaders of Israel must have favored an immediate all-out offensive.

But this was not God's plan. He is never in a hurry though His children often are. From God's point of view Israel was not yet ready to fight on Canaan's soil. There was some unfinished business—and it was spiritual in character. It was time for renewal. Consecration must precede conquest. Before God would lead Israel to victory, He would lead them through three experiences: (a) the renewal of circumcision (5:1-9), (b) the celebration of the Passover (v. 10), and (c) the appropriation of the land's produce (vv. 11-12).

1. THE RENEWAL OF CIRCUMCISION (5:1-9)

5:1-3. When the nations of the land were filled with terror (cf. 4:24) **the Lord** commanded **Joshua** to **circumcise** the sons of Israel. He obeyed, even though it must have been difficult for him as a military commander to incapacitate his entire army in that hostile environment.

5:4-7. An explanation is given. Though **all the men** of Israel **had been circumcised** before they left **Egypt,** they **died** in the wilderness because of their disobedience at Kadesh Barnea (Num. 20:1-13; cf. Num. 27:14; Deut. 32:51). **Their sons** born during the wilderness wanderings were not **circumcised,** which was further evidence of their parents' spiritual indifference. This sacred rite therefore needed to be performed on this new generation.

5:8-9. After all the males were circumcised . . . the Lord acknowledged the completed task by declaring, **Today I have rolled away the reproach of Egypt from you.** Since the Israelites were slaves in Egypt, they did not practice circumcision until they were about to leave. No doubt the Egyptians prohibited the practice since it was reserved for their own priests and upper-class citizens. "The reproach of Egypt" may refer to the Egyptians' mocking the Israelites for not having possessed the land of Canaan.

Another indication of this event's importance is the fact that a new significance was attached to the name **Gilgal** (NIV marg.). Not only was the meaning "circle" to remind Israel of the memorial stones (see comments on 4:19-20), but now the related idea of "rolling" would commemorate Israel's act of obedience at the same site.

But why was circumcision so important? The Bible's answer is clear. Stephen, in his dynamic speech before the Sanhedrin, declared that God "gave Abraham the covenant of circumcision" (Acts 7:8). Circumcision, then, was no ordinary religious rite; it was rooted in the Abrahamic Covenant, a contract guaranteeing the everlasting continuation of Abraham's seed and their everlasting possession of the land (Gen. 17:7-8). In this connection God adopted circumcision as the "sign" or symbol of that contract (Gen. 17:11). God instructed Abraham that every male in his household as well as every male descendant of his was to be circumcised. And Abraham immediately obeyed (Gen. 17:23-27).

But why did God choose circumcision as the symbol of His covenant with Abraham and his seed? Why not some other sign or work? The act of circumcision itself symbolized a complete separation from the widely prevalent sins of the flesh: adultery, fornication, and sodomy. Further, the rite had spiritual overtones not only in relation to sexual conduct but in every phase of life. "Circumcise your hearts, therefore, and do not be stiffnecked any longer" (Deut. 10:16; cf. Deut. 30:6; Jer. 4:4; Rom. 2:28-29).

So Israel was to understand that circumcision was not simply a cutting of flesh; also their lives were to be holy. This is why at Gilgal God said, in effect, "Before I fight your battles in Canaan you must have this mark of the covenant in your flesh." **Joshua** understood the cruciality of this divine requirement and led all males in unhesitating obedience.

Paul affirmed that a Christian has been "circumcised" in Christ (Col. 2:11). This circumcision is spiritual not physical, relating not to an external organ but to one's inward being, the heart. This circumcision takes place at the time of salvation when the Holy Spirit joins a believer to Christ. At that time one's sinful nature is judged (Col. 2:13). A Christian is to recognize that fact (Rom. 6:1-2) even though his carnal nature remains a part of him during this life. He is to treat his carnal nature as a judged and condemned (though not yet executed) enemy.

2. THE CELEBRATION OF THE PASSOVER (5:10)

5:10. Israel, **camped at Gilgal,** now kept **the Passover.** Without circumcision they would have been unqualified to participate in this important event (Ex. 12:43-44, 48). Interestingly the nation arrived across the Jordan just in time to celebrate the Passover on **the 14th day of the month** (Ex. 12:2, 6). God's timing is always precise!

This was only the third Passover the nation had observed. The first was observed in Egypt the night before their deliverance from bondage and oppression (Ex. 12:1-28). The second was observed at Mount Sinai just before the people broke camp and moved toward Canaan (Num. 9:1-5).

Apparently the Passover was not observed during the wilderness wanderings, but now at Gilgal in Canaan the feast was again observed. The recent Jordan crossing was so similar to the crossing of the Red (Reed) Sea that vivid memories were brought back to those who had been in Egypt (persons under 20 at the time of the Exodus were not excluded from Canaan). No doubt many an Israelite remembered how his father killed a lamb and sprinkled its blood on the doorpost and lintel. Those now in Canaan could still hear the awful death cries of the Egyptians' firstborn. Then there was the excitement of the midnight departure, the terror of the Egyptian pursuit, and the thrill of walking between walls of water to escape Egypt.

Now they were reliving it again. As the lambs were slain they were assured that as the Red Sea crossing was followed by the destruction of the Egyptians, so

the crossing of the Jordan would be followed by the defeat of the Canaanites. So remembering the past was an excellent preparation for the tests of the future.

3. THE APPROPRIATION OF THE LAND'S PRODUCE (5:11-12)

5:11. The morning **after** Israel had eaten **the Passover** and were prepared for battle **they ate some of the produce of the land.** Since they gave evidence of wanting to be fully obedient to the Law of God it is probable that they first brought the wave-offering of a sheaf of grain, prescribed in Leviticus 23:10-14. Then the people ate freely of the harvest, including **unleavened** cakes and parched corn. **Roasted** ears of **grain** are still considered a delicacy in the Middle East and are eaten as a substitute for bread.

God had promised to bring Israel into a land of abundance, "a land with wheat and barley, vines and fig trees, pomegranates, olive oil, and honey" (Deut. 8:8). Now at last they had tasted the fruit of the land and realized it was a foretaste of blessings to come.

5:12. The next day **the manna stopped.** For 40 long years it had continued (cf. Ex. 16:4-5), but now it ceased as suddenly as it had begun, demonstrating that its provision was not a matter of chance but of special providence.

It is noteworthy that God did not discontinue the **manna** when Israel despised it (Num. 11:6), or even when the unbelieving generation turned away from Kadesh Barnea and wandered in the trackless wilderness. At least for the sake of their children He continued to give it, till they grew and entered the land of promise. Then God stopped performing this miracle since natural **food** was available.

II. The Conquest of Canaan (5:13–12:24)

A. Introduction: The divine Commander (5:13-15)

God had just brought the Israelites through three events: the rite of circumcision, the celebration of the Passover, and eating the produce of Canaan. All of these were for Israel's edification. Next came an experience for Joshua alone. It too was extremely meaningful and would shortly be shared with the people.

5:13. It seemed obvious that the next

step would be the capture of **Jericho.** But since no divine message of instruction had yet come to **Joshua** (as before the crossing of the Jordan), he went out to reconnoiter the seemingly impregnable city. Was Joshua perplexed as he viewed the secure walls of Jericho? The spies reported at Kadesh Barnea that the cities of Canaan were "large, with walls up to the sky" (Deut. 1:28). Despite Joshua's long military experience he had never led an attack on a fortified city that was prepared for a long siege. In fact, of all the walled cities in Palestine, Jericho was probably the most invincible. There was also the question of armaments. Israel's army had no siege engines, no battering rams, no catapults, and no moving towers. Their only weapons were slings, arrows, and spears—which were like straws against the walls of Jericho. Joshua knew the battle of Jericho must be won because, now that they had crossed the Jordan, Israel's troops had no place to which they could retreat. Further, they could not bypass the city because that would leave their women, children, goods, and cattle at Gilgal exposed to certain destruction.

Pondering these heavy thoughts, Joshua was startled when something came across his sphere of vision. **He** lifted **up** his eyes to see a Soldier brandishing His **sword.** Instinctively he challenged the Stranger, saying in effect, "Who goes there—friend or foe?" If He were a friend, an Israelite, He was off limits and had some explaining to do. Especially was this true since Joshua had given no command for anyone to draw a sword! If the Stranger were an enemy, **Joshua** was ready to fight!

5:14. The response was startling and revealing. Something occurred that convinced Joshua this was no mortal soldier. As with Abraham under the oak at Mamre, Jacob at Peniel, Moses at the burning bush, and the two disciples at Emmaus, there was a flash of revelation and Joshua knew he was in the presence of God. It seems clear that Joshua was indeed talking to the Angel of the Lord, another appearance in Old Testament times of the Lord Jesus Christ Himself (cf. 6:2).

The **Commander of the army of the LORD** stood **with a drawn** sword, indicating that He would fight with and for Israel. But the sword also shows that

God's long-suffering delay of judgment was over and the iniquity of the Amorites was now full (cf. Gen. 15:16). The Israelites were to be the instruments by whom judicial punishment would fall.

What kind of a military force did this divine Commander lead? The "army of the LORD" was surely not limited to the army of Israel though it may have been included. More specifically, it referred to the angelic host, the same "army" of heaven that later surrounded Dothan when Elisha and his servant appeared to be greatly outnumbered by the Aramean army (2 Kings 6:8-17). In the Garden of Gethsemane at the time of His arrest, Jesus referred to this heavenly army when He said that 12 legions of angels were ready to defend Him (Matt. 26:53). In Hebrews 1:14 they are described as "ministering spirits sent to serve those who will inherit salvation." Though invisible, they serve and care for God's children in times of great need.

Joshua, recognizing his heavenly visitor with the drawn sword, **fell** on his face and worshiped, saying, in effect, "Speak, Lord, for Your servant is listening."

5:15. The reply of the Lord to Joshua was brief but urgent. Remove **your sandals, for the place where you are standing is holy.** The presence of the holy God sanctified this spot in a strange and defiled land (cf. a similar command to Moses, Ex. 3:5).

This was a deeply significant experience for Joshua. He had anticipated a battle between two opposing armies, Israelite and Canaanite. He had thought this was to be his war and that he was to be the general-in-charge. But then he confronted the divine Commander and learned that the battle was the Lord's. The top general **of the LORD's army** had not come to be an idle Spectator of the conflict, or even an ally. He was in complete charge and would shortly reveal His plans for capturing the citadel of Jericho.

How comforting all this was for **Joshua.** He did not need to bear the heavy burden and responsibility of leadership alone. By removing his sandals he gladly acknowledged that this battle and the entire conquest of Canaan was God's conflict and that he was merely God's servant.

B. The central campaign (chaps. 6–8)

The pattern of divine strategy for the conquest of Canaan was based on geographic factors. From their camp at Gilgal near the Jordan River the Israelites could see steep hills to the west. Jericho controlled the way of ascent into these mountains, and Ai, another fortress, stood at the head of the ascent. If the Israelites were to capture the hill country they must certainly take Jericho and Ai. This would put them on top of the hill country and in control of the central ridge, having driven a wedge between the northern and southern sections of Canaan. Israel could then engage the armies of the south in battle followed by the more remote enemy in the north. But first, Jericho must fall—and it would if Joshua and the people followed the Lord's plan of action.

1. THE CONQUEST OF JERICHO (CHAP. 6)

a. The strategy of the conquest of Jericho (6:1-7)

6:1. Jericho was a beleaguered city. Orders had been given to close all the gates, and no traffic was permitted **in** or **out**. As Rahab had disclosed to the spies (2:11) the residents of Jericho were filled with terror because of **the** advancing **Israelites** (cf. 5:1).

6:2. But there this impressive fortress stood, in full view of Joshua whose conversation with the Commander of the Lord's army continued. This Commander, **the LORD** Himself, promised victory to **Joshua** and announced that He had given **Jericho into** his **hands**. The city, **its king,** and its army would all fall to Israel. The tense of the Hebrew verb is prophetic perfect (**I have delivered**), describing a future action as if it were already accomplished. Since God had declared it, the victory was assured.

6:3-5. The battle plan Joshua was to use was most unusual. Ordinary weapons of war such as battering rams and scaling ladders were not to be employed. Rather Joshua and his **armed men** were to **march around the city once** a day **for six** successive **days** with **seven priests** blowing **trumpets** preceding **the ark** of the covenant. **On the seventh day** they were to circle Jericho **seven times** and then **the wall of** Jericho would **collapse** and the city would be taken.

In the Bible the number seven often symbolizes completeness or perfection. There were seven priests, seven trumpets, seven days, seven circuits of the wall on the seventh day. Though God's plan of action may have seemed foolish to men it was the perfect scheme for this battle.

What was the significance of the blaring **trumpets**? These instruments were "jubilee trumpets" (lit. Heb.) used in connection with Israel's solemn feasts to proclaim the presence of God (Num. 10:10). The conquest of Jericho was not therefore exclusively a military undertaking but also a religious one, and the trumpets declared that the Lord of heaven and earth was weaving His invisible way around this doomed city. God Himself, in effect, was saying in the long blasts of these priestly trumpets, "Lift up your heads, O you gates; be lifted up, you ancient doors, that the King of glory may come in" (Ps. 24:7). When Christ returns, He, the King of glory, will enter cities in triumph. The conquest of Jericho was a similar kind of triumphant victory.

6:6-7. No battle strategy appeared more unreasonable than this one. What was to prevent the army of Jericho from raining arrows and spears down on the defenseless Israelites pursuing their silent march? Or who could stop the enemy from rushing out of the city gates to break up Israel's line, separating and then slaughtering them? **Joshua** was an experienced military leader. Certainly these and similar objections to the divine strategy flashed into his mind. But unlike Moses at the burning bush who argued with lengthy eloquence against the Lord's plan (cf. Ex. 3:11–4:17) Joshua responded with an unquestioning obedience. He lost no time in calling together **the priests** and soldiers, passing on to them the directions he had received from his Commander-in-chief.

b. The sequence of the conquest of Jericho (6:8-21)

6:8-9. It was perhaps a little after dawn when a long procession began to unwind out of the camp of Israel. First came **the armed guard** marching under tribal banners, then **seven priests** with **trumpets**; next **the ark** of God; and last **the rear guard**. The army thus had prominent places in the procession but Jericho would fall not through their prowess but because of the power of God.

6:10-11. Preserving absolute silence (except for the seven priests blowing their trumpets) this strange parade made its way toward Jericho and then **around the city** like a serpent. Jericho then covered about eight or nine acres and required less than 30 minutes to march around. When the circuit was completed, to the amazement of the Canaanites who probably anticipated an immediate attack, the Israelites **returned** quietly **to camp.**

6:12-14. The same procedure was followed **for six days.** No fortress had ever been conquered in this fashion. This strange strategy was probably given to test the faith of **Joshua.** He did not question; he trusted and obeyed. This procedure was also designed to test Israel's obedience to God's will. And that was not easy in this case. Every day they were exposing themselves to ridicule and danger. A Jericho soldier may have looked down from the wall on the army of Israel and asked, "Do they think they can frighten us into surrender by the sound of their rams' horns?" And the rest may have joined in a loud chorus of raucous laughter.

Probably the Israelites received their orders on a daily basis so that their obedience was not a once-for-all matter but a new challenge every morning. That is the way God often deals with His children. They are required to do their "daily march" with little or no knowledge of tomorrow (Prov. 27:1; James 4:14; cf. Matt. 6:34).

The faith of the Israelites triumphed over their fear that the enemy would attack. They also triumphed over any expectation of ridicule and scorn. Never before and seldom after this historic event did the thermometer of faith rise this high in Israel.

6:15-20a. On that fateful **seventh day** the procession made the circuit of the walls **seven times.** This parade—consisting of the armed guard, the seven **trumpet**-blowing **priests,** the priests carrying the ark of the covenant, and the rear guard—may have taken about three hours. (On the word **devoted** in vv. 17-18 see comments on v. 21.) (As Joshua recorded, Israel experienced disastrous consequences because of an immediate violation of God's instruction in vv. 18-

19.) At the end of the seventh circuit the clear voice of **Joshua** rang out, **Shout! For the Lord has given you the city!** Also he told them to spare **Rahab** and her family (cf. 2:8-13). So when the priests blasted on **the trumpets . . . the people gave a loud shout.** That shout reverberated through the hills around, startling wild animals and terrorizing the dwellers of Jericho in their homes. At that moment **the wall** of Jericho, obeying the summons of God, **collapsed** (lit., "fell in its place").

6:20b-21. The men of Israel clambered over the debris. Finding the inhabitants paralyzed with terror and unable to resist, the soldiers utterly destroyed all human and animal life in Jericho, except for Rahab and her household (cf. v. 17). Though critics have charged that this destruction is a blemish on the Old Testament, it is clear that Israel was acting on divine command. The responsibility for this destruction rests therefore with God and not the Israelites.

The city of Jericho and everything in it was "to be devoted (*hērem*) to the Lord" (v. 17). The NASB renders those words "shall be under the ban," a more literal translation. Verse 21 includes a verb form of that noun *hērem*: **They devoted** (*wayyaharîmû,* from *hāram*) **the city to the Lord.** The idea is that the city's contents were to be given over to the Lord by totally destroying them. To convey this, the NIV adds **and destroyed.** (The verb *hāram* is trans. "totally destroyed" in 10:28, 35, 37, 39-40; 11:11-12, 21 and "destroy them totally" in 11:20; cf. 1 Sam. 15:3, 8-9, 15, 18, 20. The noun *hērem* is trans. "devoted" or "devoted things" in Josh. 6:17-18; 7:1, 11-12, 15; 1 Sam. 15:21; "devoted to destruction" in Lev. 27:29; "set apart for destruction" in Deut. 7:26. Sometimes, however, the idea of destruction is not in the word; cf., e.g., Lev. 27:21, 28.)

The contents of Jericho were to be given "to the Lord" as the firstfruits of the land. Just as the firstfruits of a crop, given to the Lord, pointed to more crops to come, so the conquest of Jericho signified that Israel would receive all of Canaan from Him. No loot from Jericho was to be taken by the people. In carrying out the *hērem,* people and animals were to be killed (Josh. 6:17, 21), and other things were either to be destroyed or set apart, as in this case, for the purposes of the sanctuary. These items included "silver and gold and the articles of bronze and iron" (v. 19). All was "devoted" either to destruction or to the Lord's "treasury"; all was to be forfeited by the people.

Furthermore, God has the right to visit judgment on individuals and nations in sin. Is there evidence that the iniquity of the Canaanites was full? Few would question that the idolatrous worship and licentious lifestyle attested by archeological discoveries (e.g., the Ras Shamra tablets) justified the divine judgment on Jericho.

Finally, God's purpose was to bless the nation of Israel in the land and to use her as a channel of blessing to the world. But this would be greatly hindered if they were infected by the degenerate religion of the Canaanites. Gleason Archer declares, "In view of the corrupting influence of the Canaanite religion, especially with its religious prostitution . . . and infant sacrifice, it was impossible for pure faith and worship to be maintained in Israel except by the complete elimination of the Canaanites themselves" (*A Survey of Old Testament Introduction*. Chicago: Moody Press, 1964, p. 261).

Sin is desperately contagious. To compromise with evil is dangerous and invites spiritual disaster.

Various suggestions have been made as to why the walls of Jericho fell at the precise moment when the people shouted: (1) An earthquake caused the destruction. (2) Israelite soldiers undermined the walls while the others marched. (3) Vibrations set up by the trumpet blasts and soldiers' shouts caused the collapse. (4) Shock waves caused by the marching feet of the Israelites were responsible. However, it was a supernatural event. This is clear from the fact that all the wall was destroyed except the portion by the house of Rahab. Actually it is unnecessary to determine the exact means God employed in this or any other miracle. A New Testament writer, reviewing this event centuries later, was content to write, "By faith the walls of Jericho fell, after the people had marched around them for seven days" (Heb. 11:30).

Archeological evidence for the collapse of Jericho's walls in Joshua's day is not as clear as was once supposed. This can be explained by the fact that further excavations have determined that in its long history Jericho has had some 34 walls. (Jericho is one of the oldest cities in the world. Many archeologists hold that it was inhabited as early as 7000 B.C.) The many earthquakes in the area, the thoroughness of Joshua's destruction of the city, and the process of erosion over five centuries until it was refortified in Ahab's time (1 Kings 16:34) also contributed to the meager remains and the extreme difficulty of relating these remains to the time of Joshua's attack. The most significant evidence seems to be extensive pottery remains found on the mound and in the tombs of the area. These findings point to an occupancy of Jericho until about 1400 B.C. Under the pottery is a thick burned layer of ash representing a major destruction. This no doubt points to Joshua's destruction and burning (Josh. 6:24) of the city. (For a thorough discussion of the archeology of Old Testament Jericho, see Leon Wood, *A Survey of Israel's History*. Grand Rapids: Zondervan Publishing House, 1970, pp. 94-9.)

c. The sequel to the conquest of Jericho (6:22-27)

As the story of this great Old Testament event moves quickly to its end, two matters are briefly mentioned: the rescue of Rahab and the burning, sacking, and curse on the city.

6:22-25. Like an oasis in this doleful account of Canaanite extermination is the story of Rahab's deliverance. Before the **city** was **burned** (v. 24), **Rahab** was **spared.** Joshua kept the promise made to Rahab by the two spies (cf. 2:12-21) and sent those same **young men** to the **house** where the scarlet cord hung from the window. She and **her entire family** followed them without hesitation to the appointed **place outside** the doomed city. Rahab and her family, being Gentiles, had to be ceremonially cleansed; the men were no doubt circumcised before they could be identified with the people of Israel. Rahab's history is an example of the grace of God operating in the lives of an individual and **her family.** Regardless of her past life she was saved by faith in the living God and even became a part of the messianic line (Matt. 1:5). In keeping with the biblical pattern, Rahab and her family were spared from divine judgment (cf. Gen. 7:1; 1 Thes. 5:9) because of their faith.

6:26. Devoting **Jericho** to destruction (cf. comments on v. 21) included the pronouncing of a curse on anyone who would dare to refortify the **city** by rebuilding **its foundations** or **its gates.** Though the site was later occupied for brief periods (18:21; Jud. 3:13; 2 Sam. 10:5) the prohibition against the rebuilding was not violated until the days of King Ahab, 500 years later. Then, as an indication of the apostasy of that period, Hiel the Bethelite attempted to rebuild Jericho's walls, but it cost him the lives of his two sons Abiram and Segub (1 Kings 16:34).

6:27. But the chapter recording the spectacular victory in Israel's first battle in Canaan does not end on a minor note. The final words take the reader back to the triumph and its effects: **So the LORD was with Joshua** (cf. 1:5, 9; 3:7), **and his fame spread throughout the land.** The secret to success at Jericho was not Joshua's military genius or his army's skill in warfare. Victory came because he and the people fully trusted God and obeyed His commands (1:6-9).

2. THE DEFEAT AT AI (CHAP. 7)

Unexpectedly Israel next tasted defeat. Up to this point in the Conquest the army Joshua led had experienced only victory. The possibility of a military defeat was the remotest thing from the Israelites' minds, particularly after the triumph over Jericho. Yet God's people are never more vulnerable, never in greater danger, than right after they have won a great victory.

Ai was the next objective on Israel's path of conquest. It was smaller than Jericho but was at a strategic junction of two natural routes ascending from Jericho to the hill country around Bethel. Defeating Ai would also lead to the ultimate control of the main "ridge route" running from north to south along the central highlands.

Many archeologists have identified Ai with the site et-Tell ("the ruin"). Excavations at et-Tell, however, have not yet produced evidence of a settlement there in the time of Joshua. The geography of the area fits perfectly with the details found in Joshua 8. So perhaps the king of Ai was the leader of forces mobilizing for

the battle which occurred at a place that was *already* a ruin rather than a city. Some archeologists, however, are looking for alternative locations of Ai and excavations are underway at the nearby site of Khirbet Nisya.

Though there may still be some question regarding the location of Ai, the importance of the happenings there can be seen from the amount of biblical material given over to a discussion of Israel's defeat (chap. 7) and her victory at that site (chap. 8).

a. Disobedience (7:1)

7:1. The chapter opens with the ominous word **But.** The gladness of victory was soon replaced by the gloom of defeat. And all this was because of the disobedience of one man. Jericho was placed under God's ḥērem ("ban for destruction"; 6:18-19), meaning that everything living was to be put to death and valuable objects were to be dedicated to the Lord's treasury. No Israelite soldier was to help himself to the booty—but that temptation was too strong for one man.

Though one might wish to give credit to the discipline of Joshua's forces because only one of his soldiers gave in to temptation, even this one did not escape God's notice. God saw Achan's sin in taking **some** of **the devoted things,** and because of it God's wrath **burned against** the entire nation. He considered them collectively responsible and withheld His blessing until the matter was made right. In fact it is apparent that Israel's history would have ended here if God's anger had not been turned away.

b. Defeat (7:2-5)

7:2. Unaware of Achan's disobedience and eager to take advantage of the first victory, **Joshua** made preparations for the next battle by sending spies 10 miles northwest of **Jericho to Ai,** which was **east of Bethel.** This seems to have been his regular practice (cf. 2:1). (**Beth Aven** ["house of evil"] later was a nickname [Hosea 10:5] for Bethel ["house of God"]. But here it seems to be another place about three miles north of **Ai.**)

7:3. When the spies **returned** they spoke with great confidence. They said that **Ai** could easily be conquered with only **two or three thousand men.** The city had **only a few men**, they said. But the spies were wrong. Actually Ai had 12,000 men and women, or about 6,000 men (8:25). Later, when God gave the orders to **Joshua,** He told him, "Take the whole army" (8:1). Though smaller than Jericho, Ai was well fortified and her soldiers well entrenched. Israel was guilty of underestimating the strength of her enemy and of overestimating her own strength. On this occasion there is no mention of prayer and no evidence of dependence on God.

It is a deadly error to underrate the enemy's power. Christians often fail to realize that their enemies are powerful (Eph. 6:12; 1 Peter 5:8). So believers suffer the consequences in ignominious spiritual defeat.

The calamity that befell Israel was due, at least in part, to minimizing the enemy and to assuming that one victory guaranteed another. But life simply does not work that way. Yesterday's victory does not make a believer immune from defeat today. He must continually depend on the Lord for strength. Speaking of a Christian's conflict with evil Paul wrote, "Be strong in the Lord and in His mighty power" (Eph. 6:10).

7:4-5. But Joshua sent only **3,000 men** to **Ai,** where sadly they did not conquer but **were routed.** They rushed in terror down the steep pass which they had so confidently climbed in the morning, till the pursuers caught them at some **stone quarries,** where **36** Israelite soldiers were slain. The rest escaped and returned to camp.

As the report of the defeat spread rapidly through the camp the people were utterly demoralized. **The hearts of the people melted, and became like water.** Even though this was Israel's only defeat in the seven-year Conquest of Canaan, the significant matter was not the loss itself or even the deaths of the 36 soldiers. Israel was suddenly filled with terrible misgivings that the Lord's help had been withdrawn. They knew of no reason why it should have been. Had God changed His mind?

c. Dismay (7:6-9)

7:6-9. Joshua also was stunned by the defeat. In keeping with ancient rites of mourning the leader and the elders **tore** their **clothes** and **the elders** put **dust**

on their heads (cf. Job 1:20; 2:12). They **fell** on their faces **before the ark of the LORD . . . till evening.** Then Joshua's perplexity was verbalized as he asked the Lord three questions: (1) **Why did You . . . bring** us here—**to destroy us?** (2) **What can I say, now that Israel has been** defeated? (3) **What then will You do** to protect **Your** reputation?

Joshua seemed to blame God for the defeat and did not even consider that the cause might have been elsewhere. In his first question he even adopted the thinking of the spies against whom he had so vehemently protested at Kadesh (cf. Num. 14:2-3). Joshua's greatest concern was that the news of this defeat might somehow reduce the respect of the heathen for God's **own great name.** Consequently their **name** would be wiped out, that is, they would be destroyed and never remembered.

d. Directions (7:10-15)

7:10-11. The Lord's reply **to Joshua** was brusque. **Stand up! What are you doing down on your face?** God then explained the cause of the defeat and the need for action. The cause of the disaster was with Israel, not God—**Israel** had **sinned.** In His indictment God angrily used an accumulation of verbs. Advancing from the general to the particular He charged Israel with sinning, violating the **covenant,** appropriating **some of the devoted things** (haḥērem, "things devoted for or designated for destruction"; cf. 6:18-19 and comments on 6:21), stealing, lying, and concealing the **stolen** goods. (The goods are named in 7:21.) Till these transgressions were repudiated and expiation made for them, the sin of one person was considered the sin of the nation.

7:12. After the fall of Jericho it was recorded, "So the LORD was with Joshua" (6:27). But now the grim announcement came from God, **I will not be with you anymore unless** this sin is judged and the **devoted** things are destroyed.

7:13-15. The LORD then revealed the steps to be followed in the purging process. First, **the people** were to **consecrate** themselves. No victory over **their enemies** was possible till this problem was dealt with. Second, they were to gather on the next day to identify the offender, presumably by casting lots (cf. comments on vv. 16-18), exposing first the guilty **tribe,** then **the clan,** then **the family,** and finally the individual. Third, the culprit and all his possessions (not merely the stolen goods) were then to be burned. This sin was considered by God **a disgraceful thing.** Achan's sin was in deliberate disobedience to God's instruction (6:18), and it made the entire nation liable to destruction. If the Israelites did not destroy the Canaanites' goods, God might destroy the Israelites!

e. Discovery (7:16-21)

7:16-18. **Joshua** rose **early** on the fateful day. All **Israel** was assembled for the ritual of determining the offender. This was probably done by drawing lots, perhaps by taking inscribed potsherds out of a jar. But since God knew who was guilty, why did He not simply reveal his identity to Joshua? The answer is that this dramatic method would impress on the nation of Israel the seriousness of disobeying God's commands. Since the method took time it would also give the guilty person an opportunity to repent and confess his sin. If Achan had responded in this way and thrown himself on the mercy of God no doubt he would have been pardoned as was the guilty David centuries later (Pss. 32:1-5; 51:1-12).

There was a grim silence as the process narrowed from the selection of the tribe of **Judah** to **the clan of the Zerahites,** to the family of **Zimri,** and finally to the trespasser himself, **Achan.** This was no quirk of fate; it was the direction of God's providence. Solomon described the process well: "The lot is cast into the lap, but its every decision is from the LORD" (Prov. 16:33).

7:19-21. Strangely, **Achan** had remained silent throughout the entire procedure, though surely fear gripped him and his heart may have pounded furiously as each step brought his discovery nearer. At length **Joshua** addressed **Achan** tenderly but firmly, for though Joshua hated the sin he did not despise the sinner. A public confession confirming the supernatural exposure of the guilty person was necessary.

Achan's response was straightforward and complete. He confessed his sin and gave no excuses. But neither did he express sorrow for disobeying God's order, betraying his nation for booty, and causing the defeat of Israel's troops and the death of 36 men. Any remorse he may have felt was probably only because he got caught.

The three crucial steps in Achan's sin are familiar: he **saw;** he **coveted;** he **took.** Eve took the same tragic steps in the Garden of Eden (Gen. 3:6), as did David with Bathsheba (2 Sam. 11:2-4).

The objects Achan took from Jericho and hid **in the ground inside** his **tent** included (a) **a beautiful robe from Babylonia,** perhaps acquired by someone in Jericho who traded with a Babylonian, (b) **200 shekels of silver,** weighing about 5 pounds, and (c) a **50-shekel** (1¼-pound) **wedge of gold.** Achan may well have reasoned, "After all, I have been deprived of the good things of life these many years in the wilderness. Here is a beautiful new and stylish garment and some silver and gold. How could God want to withhold these things from me? They will never be missed, and I am entitled to some pleasure and prosperity." But there was a specific command against taking any of Jericho's booty. (Joshua had told the people that *all* the silver and gold were to be put in the Lord's treasury, Josh. 6:19.) God's Word can never be rationalized away without penalty.

f. Death (7:22-26)

7:22-25. Achan's confession was quickly verified; the stolen objects were found where he said they were. They were then **spread . . . out before the LORD** to whom they belonged. Then the wretched man was led out **to the Valley of Achor** with the spoil, all his family, his animals, and all his other belongings. The fatal stones felled Achan and his children, and fire consumed their bodies and belongings. Having stolen "devoted" objects Achan himself became contaminated and under the doom of destruction. Since children were not to be executed for their father's sins (Deut. 24:16) it is assumed that Achan's family (except for his wife, who was not mentioned) were accomplices in the crime (cf. comments on Num. 16:28-35).

7:26. The final stroke was accomplished by the raising of a historical marker, **a large pile of rocks,** over the body of **Achan.** This seems to have been a common method of burial for infamous individuals (cf. 8:29). It served in this case that good purpose of warning Israel against the sin of disobeying God's express commands.

The Hebrew words for Achan and Achor are probably related. Thus Achan, which possibly means "troubler," was buried in **the Valley of Achor,** the Valley of "Trouble." But because Israel was willing to deal with the sin problem in her midst, God's burning **anger** (7:1) was **turned** away and He was ready to lead them again to victory.

3. THE VICTORY AT AI (CHAP. 8)

a. The setting of the battle (8:1-2)

8:1. The momentum Israel had achieved by the miraculous crossing of the Jordan and the supernatural victory over Jericho was stopped by the defeat at Ai. Gloom and despair permeated not only all those in the camp but also the heart of Joshua.

But with Achan's crime judged, God's favor toward Israel was restored and He reassured **Joshua** that He had not forsaken him or the people. When Joshua heard God's words of encouragement his heart quickened, for these were the same words Moses spoke in Kadesh Barnea when he sent out the 12 spies (Deut. 1:21). They were also the words Moses said to Joshua 40 years later when he was turning the reins of leadership over to the younger man (Deut. 31:8). And Joshua heard them again when God spoke to him just after the death of Moses (Josh. 1:9). Now at this crucial time in Joshua's life it was good to be reminded and reassured that God was ready to lead if Joshua were ready to listen to *His* plan, which he was.

God's plan involved using all the fighting men of Israel. Though the primary cause of the defeat at Ai was Achan's sin, a secondary cause was underrating the enemy (cf. 7:3-4). That error would now be rectified. God said for Joshua to **go up and attack Ai** and He promised to turn the place of defeat into a place of victory.

8:2. Before the actual plan of battle was revealed to Joshua he was told that the spoil of **Ai** and also its **livestock** could be taken by Israel. Jericho had been placed under the ban but Ai was not.

What an irony! If only Achan had suppressed his greedy and selfish desires and obeyed God's word at Jericho he would later have had all his heart desired and God's blessing too. The path of obedience and faith is always best.

b. The sequence of the battle (8:3-29)

The order of events at Ai differed entirely from that at Jericho. The Israelites did not march around the walls of Ai seven times. The city's walls did not fall miraculously. Israel had to conquer the city through a normal combat operation. God is not limited to any one method of working. He is not and will not be stereotyped in His operations.

8:3-9. The strategy for the capture of Ai was ingenious. It involved placing **an ambush behind** (west of) **the city.** God Himself had told **Joshua** to do this (vv. 2, 8). The outworking of this plan involved three contingents of soldiers. The first was a group of valiant warriors who were sent by **night** to hide just **west** of the city of **Ai.** Their assignment was to rush into the city and burn it after its defenders had deserted it to **pursue** Joshua and his army. This unit numbered **30,000,** and while this seems like an excessively large number of soldiers to hide near the city, the presence of large rocks in the region made it possible for all these men to remain hidden.

8:10-11. The second contingent was the main army which walked the 15 miles from Gilgal **early the next morning** and camped in plain view on the **north** side **of Ai.** No doubt this **entire force** included many thousands of soldiers. Led by **Joshua,** this army was a diversionary force to decoy the defenders of **Ai** out of **the city.**

8:12-13. The third contingent was another **ambush** numbering **5,000 men** who were positioned **between Bethel and Ai** to cut off the possibility of reinforcements from Bethel aiding the men of Ai. **Joshua** was in **the valley** north of Ai, a deep ravine in the hills.

8:14-22. The plan worked to perfection. **When the king of Ai saw** Israel's army he took the bait. Pursuing the Israelites who pretended defeat, **the city of Ai** was left unguarded. At Joshua's signal the other troops **quickly** entered and **set the city on fire.** The consternation of **the men of Ai** was complete as they witnessed the billows of flame and **smoke**

rising into the sky. Before they could gather their wits they were caught in a pincer movement of Israelite soldiers and were destroyed.

8:23-29. After killing all Ai's soldiers, Israel's army reentered the city and killed all its inhabitants. The dead soldiers and citizens totaled **12,000.** Plunder was taken from the city by Israel's soldiers as God had said they could do (v. 2). The city was made a heap of ruins. Ai's king, previously spared, was hanged on a tree till evening and then was buried beneath a pile of stones (cf. Achan's similar burial, 7:26). The king's body was taken off the tree at sunset because of God's command (Deut. 21:22-23; cf. Josh. 10:27).

Thus Israel, restored to God's favor, won a great victory. After failure came a second chance. One defeat or failure does not signal the end of a believer's usefulness for God.

c. The sequel to the battle (8:30-35)

8:30-31. After the victory of Ai Joshua did a strange and militarily foolish thing. Instead of securing the central sector of the land with further victories he led the Israelites on a spiritual pilgrimage. Why? Simply because Moses . . . had commanded it (Deut. 27:1-8).

Without delay Joshua led the men, women, children, and cattle from their camp at Gilgal northward up the Jordan Valley to the place specified, the mountains of Ebal (Josh. 8:30) and Gerizim (v. 33) which are at Shechem. The march of about 30 miles was not difficult or dangerous since they passed through a sparsely populated area. But how did the Israelites avoid a confrontation with the men of the city of Shechem, a fortress which guarded the entrance to the valley between the mountains?

The Bible does not record every battle of the Conquest and the record of the capture of Shechem may have been omitted. Or the city at that time may have been in friendly hands or it may simply have surrendered without resistance. But why was this location chosen? These mountains are located in the geographic center of the land and from either peak much of the Promised Land can be seen. Here then, in a place that represented all the land, both at the time of entrance into Canaan and also when his leadership was ending (cf. 24:1), Joshua challenged the people to renew their covenant vows to the Lord.

The solemn and significant religious ceremonies at this location involved three things. First, an altar of uncut stones was erected on Mount Ebal and sacrifices (consisting of burnt offerings and fellowship offerings; cf. Lev. 1; 3) were offered to the LORD. Jericho and Ai, in which false gods of the Canaanites were worshiped, had fallen. Israel now publicly worshiped and proclaimed her faith in the one true God.

8:32. Second, Joshua set up some large stones. On their surfaces he wrote a copy of the Law of Moses. How much of the Law was inscribed is not stated. Some suggest only the Ten Commandments were written, while others think the stone inscription included the contents of at least Deuteronomy 5-26. Archeologists have discovered similar inscribed pillars or stelae six to eight feet long in the Middle East. And the Behistun Inscription in Iran is three times the length of Deuteronomy.

8:33-35. Third, Joshua read . . . the Law to the people. Half of the people were positioned on the slopes of Mount Gerizim to the south, the other half were on the slopes of Mount Ebal to the north, and the ark of the covenant surrounded by priests was in the valley between. As the curses of the Law were read one by one, the tribes on Mount Ebal responded, "Amen!" As the blessings were likewise read the tribes on Mount Gerizim responded "Amen!" (Deut. 11:29; 27:12-26) The huge natural amphitheater which still exists there made it possible for the people to hear every word and with all sincerity Israel affirmed that the Law of the Lord was indeed to be the Law of the land.

From this point on the history of the Jews depended on their attitude toward the Law which had been read in their hearing that day. When they were obedient there was blessing; when they were disobedient there was judgment (cf. Deut. 28). It is tragic that the affirmations of this momentous hour faded so quickly.

C. The southern campaign (chaps. 9-10)

Israel's failure to consult the Lord was a major factor in her defeat at Ai and the prayerlessness of her leaders was about to precipitate another crisis.

It all came about when it was least expected. The people had just returned to camp at Gilgal after hearing the Law of God read to them at Mounts Ebal and Gerizim. Much of the Law was inscribed on stones as Israel affirmed her willingness to obey God's Word. It was a time of spiritual victory; it was also a time for a subtle attack from Satan. When God's people think they "have it made" they are most vulnerable to the enemy's assault.

This story unfolds in the next two chapters of the Book of Joshua—the alliance with the Gibeonites (chap. 9) and the defense of the Gibeonites (chap. 10).

1. THE ALLIANCE WITH THE GIBEONITES (CHAP. 9)

a. The deception of the Gibeonites (9:1-15)

9:1-2. Israel's victories over Jericho and Ai aroused the whole country to concerted action. These verses prepare the reader for the southern and northern campaigns of the Conquest, described in chapters 10 and 11.

The frightened **kings** are grouped according to three geographical areas: those from **the hill country** of central Palestine, **the western foothills** (valleys or lowlands), and the coastal plain stretching north to **Lebanon.** That they were not able to unite as planned into one fighting force is a tribute to the success of Joshua's strategy in driving a wedge through the backbone of Canaan.

But powerful confederations did form in both the north and the south. Truces were declared in tribal wars and deadly enemies were ready to make common cause against the invasion force of God's people.

9:3. Not all Israel's enemies wanted to fight. The Gibeonites were convinced they could never defeat Israel in war so they pursued peace. Located in the hill country only six miles northwest of Jerusalem and about the same distance southwest of Ai, **Gibeon** was known as "an important city" (10:2) and was head of a small confederation including three neighboring towns (cf. 9:17).

9:4-6. After consultation they adopted an ingenious plan to send emissaries to **Joshua** disguised as weary and worn travelers who had been on a long journey. One morning **in the** Israelite **camp at Gilgal** this strange deputation arrived, their **wineskins** old and patched, their **sandals** worn thin, their **clothes** dirty and torn, and their bread **dry and moldy.** As the visitors passed through the bystanders to seek out Joshua, the Israelites no doubt wondered who the strangers were, where they came from, and why they were there.

Untruthful answers were given as soon as the Gibeonites found Joshua. They told him, **We have come from a distant country; make a treaty with us.** But why the emphasis on being from a far country and the deceptive performance to "prove" it? Apparently the Gibeonites had become aware of the provisions in the Mosaic Law permitting Israel to make peace with cities that were at a considerable distance, but requiring them to wipe out completely the cities of the seven nearby Canaanite nations (Deut. 20:10-18; 7:1-2).

9:7. At first Joshua and his staff were hesitant and not altogether convinced. They said **But perhaps you live near us.** It was well for them to be on their guard for things are not always what they seem to be. Evil men often try to take advantage of the righteous.

The travelers from Gibeon were called **Hivites** (cf. 11:19); they were descendants of Canaan, a son of Ham (Gen. 10:17). Possibly the Hivites were also the Horites (in Gen. 36:2 Zibeon was called a Hivite, but in Gen. 36:20 he was called a Horite).

9:8-13. **Joshua** probed with questions and the wily Gibeonites told their tale. They insisted that they came from a great distance to show respect to the powerful **God** of the Israelites, to be allowed to live at peace as Israel's **servants.** Word had reached them of what God had done for the Israelites **in Egypt** (probably the plagues and the crossing of the Red [Reed] Sea) and of God's victories over **Sihon** and **Og** (Num. 21:21-25; Deut. 2:26–3:11). Interestingly, however, they made no mention of Israel's recent victories over Jericho and Ai because if they had come from a far country they would not have heard of these recent battles. Pursuing this clever ruse they presented their credentials—moldy **bread,** patched **wineskins,** ragged **clothes,** and worn-out **sandals**—and the suspicion of Joshua and the leaders dissipated.

9:14-15. Caught off guard by the cunning strategy of the Gibeonites, **the leaders of** the Israelites concluded a formal **treaty** with **them.** But **Joshua** and the Israelites made at least two mistakes. First, in sampling **their provisions** they accepted as evidence things that were highly questionable. If the visitors were true ambassadors with power to conclude a treaty with another nation they should have had more substantial credentials. It was foolish of Joshua not to demand them.

The second and primary reason for Israel's failure is stated in verse 14: the leaders **did not** seek direction from God. Did Joshua think the evidence to be so beyond question that they needed no advice from Yahweh? Did he think the matter too routine or unimportant to "bother" God with it? Whatever the cause it was a mistake to trust their own judgment and make their own plans. This holds true for believers in all ages (James 4:13-15).

b. The discovery of the ruse (9:16-17)

9:16-17. In **three days** Israel learned that they had been "taken" because the **Gibeonites** lived only about 25 miles from Gilgal, in Canaan proper and not in some far country. An exploratory force confirmed the fraud by discovering the nearby location of **Gibeon** and its three dependent **cities.** "A lying tongue lasts only a moment" (Prov. 12:19). Sooner or later trickery and deceit are exposed. Truth will win out.

c. The decision of the leaders (9:18-27)

9:18-19. How provoked **the Israelites** were when they discovered they had been duped! The people in fact wanted to disregard the treaty and destroy the Gibeonites, but Joshua and his staff said that the enemies' deception did not nullify the treaty. The agreement was sacred because it had been ratified **by** an **oath** in the name of **the LORD, the God of Israel** (cf. v. 15). To break it would bring down the wrath of God on Israel, a tragedy that later came to pass during David's reign because Saul disregarded this oath (cf. 2 Sam. 21:1-6).

9:20-27. Joshua and the princes were men of integrity, men who stood by their word. Though humiliated by what had transpired they did not want to bring disgrace on God and His people by breaking a sacred treaty. Yet, though Israel would not go back on their pledge the deceivers must be punished. **Joshua** therefore addressed **the Gibeonites,** rebuking them for their dishonesty, and announced that they were cursed to perpetual slavery. This slavery would take the form of their being **woodcutters and water carriers for** the Israelites. In order to keep the Gibeonites' idolatry from defiling the religion of Israel their work would be carried out in connection with the tabernacle where they would be exposed to the worship of the one true God.

So the very thing the Gibeonites hoped to attain they lost. They desperately wanted to remain free men; in the end they became slaves. But the curse became a blessing. It was on behalf of the Gibeonites that God worked a great miracle (cf. 10:10-14). Later the tabernacle was pitched at Gibeon (2 Chron. 1:3); still later some Gibeonites helped Nehemiah rebuild Jerusalem's wall (Neh. 3:7). Such is the grace of God. He is still able to turn a curse into a blessing. Though it is usually true that the natural consequences of sin must run their course, the grace of God can not only forgive but also overrule mistakes and often bring blessings out of sins and failures.

2. THE DEFENSE OF THE GIBEONITES (CHAP. 10)

a. The cause of the conflict (10:1-5)

10:1-2. Attention shifted suddenly from Gibeon to **Jerusalem,** five miles south. Near panic had seized **Adoni-Zedek** its **king** and for good reason. The treacherous surrender of the Gibeonite cities completed an arc beginning at Gilgal and extending through **Jericho** and **Ai** to a point just a few miles northwest of Jerusalem. The handwriting was on the wall. Jerusalem's security was being severely threatened. If the advances of Israel's armies continued without challenge Jerusalem would soon be surrounded and captured.

10:3-4. So the **king of Jerusalem** sent an urgent message to four other kings of southern Canaan stressing the fact that **Gibeon** had **made peace** with Israel, a traitorous and punishable act.

This might pave the way for other cities to surrender in like manner. It was a signal for war. Immediate action had to be taken against Gibeon.

10:5. There was a quick response. Little time elapsed before the united force of a **five**-king southern confederacy was laying siege **against Gibeon.** The **kings** were **of the Amorites,** that is, of Canaan's hill country (cf. comments on Gen. 14:13-16).

b. The course of the conflict (10:6-15)

10:6. Faced with certain slaughter, **the Gibeonites** sent a runner to **Joshua in . . . Gilgal** with an insistent appeal for **help** against the overwhelming force that pressed on them.

But why should Joshua respond to this cry for help from the very people who had deceived him? Why not just sit back and let the Canaanites fight among themselves? The Israelites would then be rid of evidence of an embarrassing failure.

10:7-8. That this was not an option for Joshua is made clear by his immediate reaction. Some suggest that this is evidence that the covenant between Israel and the Gibeonites' league was a mutual defense pact. But the scriptural record does not state that. And it seems preposterous that Israel would obligate herself in a treaty to go to the rescue of a "distant" nation which Israel assumed about the Gibeonites when the treaty was adopted.

The reason for Joshua's response lies in the area of military strategy. Up to this time Israel's army attacked one fortified city at a time, at best a long and drawn-out offensive procedure for conquering the entire land of Canaan. But now Joshua sensed he had the strategic break he needed. The combined Amorite armies of southern Canaan were camped together in an open field outside Gibeon. An Israelite victory would break the backs of the enemy forces of the entire region. Furthermore God assured **Joshua** that he need **not be afraid of them** (cf. 1:9; 8:1) for God would give him victory.

Gathering his forces, **Joshua** and his men **marched** the 25 miles **from Gilgal** to Gibeon under cover of darkness. It was a tiresome journey with an ascent of 4,000 feet up steep and difficult terrain. There was no opportunity to rest. The army was fatigued and faced a powerful foe. Clearly God must intervene or all would be lost.

10:9-10. Motivated by God's promise of victory, **Joshua** led a **surprise** attack on the Amorite armies of the south, possibly while it was still dark. Panic seized the enemy and after a short stand in which many were killed they broke and fled in wild **confusion** toward the west. Their escape route was through a narrow pass and down the Valley of Aijalon with the Israelites in hot pursuit. This was not the only time that the highroad which led down from the central hill country has been the scene of a rout; in A.D. 66 the Roman general Cestius Gallus fled down this descent before the Jews.

10:11. The Amorites however were not able to escape. Using the forces of nature to fight for Israel **the LORD** caused **large hailstones** to fall on the enemy with deadly precision so that **more** were killed in this way than by **swords.**

This entire passage provides a striking illustration of the interplay between the human and divine factors in achieving victory. Verses 7-11 alternate between Joshua (and Israel) and the Lord. They all played important parts in the conflict. The soldiers had to fight but God gave the victory.

10:12. But **the day** of the battle of Beth Horon was wearing on and **Joshua** knew that the pursuit of the enemy would be long and arduous. At the most the military leader had 12 hours of daylight ahead of him. He clearly needed more time if he were to realize the fulfillment of God's promise (v. 8) and see the total annihilation of his foes. Joshua therefore took to **the LORD** an unusual request: **O sun, stand still over Gibeon, O moon, over the Valley of Aijalon.**

10:13-15. It was noon and the hot **sun** was directly overhead when Joshua uttered this prayer. **The moon** was on the horizon to the west. The petition was quickly answered by the Lord. Joshua prayed in faith, and a great miracle resulted. But the record of this miracle has been called the most striking example of conflict between Scripture and science because, as is well known, the sun does not move around the earth causing day and night. Instead, light and darkness come because the earth rotates on its axis around the sun. Why then did Joshua address the sun rather than the earth? Simply because he was using the language of observation; he was speaking from the perspective and appearance of things on earth. People still do the same thing, even in the scientific community. Almanacs and journals record the hours of sunrise and sunset, yet no one accuses them of scientific error.

The "long day" of Joshua 10, however, must be explained. What *did* actually happen on that strange day? The answers are numerous (an eclipse, clouds over the sun, refraction of the sun's rays, etc.). But the best explanation seems to be the view that in answer to Joshua's prayer God caused the rotation of the earth to slow down so that it made one full rotation in 48 hours rather than in 24. It seems apparent that this view is supported both by the poem in verses 12b-13a and the prose in verse 13b. (**The Book of Jashar** is a Heb. literary collection of songs written in poetic style to honor the accomplishments of Israel's leaders; cf. David's "lament of the bow" in 2 Sam. 1:17-27.)

God stopped the cataclysmic effects that would have naturally occurred, such as monstrous tidal waves and objects flying around. Evidence that the earth's rotation simply slowed down is found in the closing words of Joshua 10:13: **The sun . . . delayed going down about a full day.** The sun was thus abnormally slow or tardy in getting to sunset, that is, its progression from noon to dusk was markedly lethargic, giving Joshua and his soldiers sufficient time to complete their victorious battle.

An important fact that should not be overlooked is that the sun and moon were principal deities among the Canaanites. At the prayer of Israel's leader Canaan's gods were compelled to obey. This disturbance to their gods must have been terribly upsetting and frightening to the Canaanites. The secret of Israel's triumph over the coalition of Canaanites is found in the words, **Surely the LORD was fighting for Israel!** In answer to prayer Israel experienced the dramatic intervention of God on their behalf and victory was assured.

c. The culmination of the conflict (10:16-43)

10:16-24. Taking every advantage of the extended day **Joshua** continued in

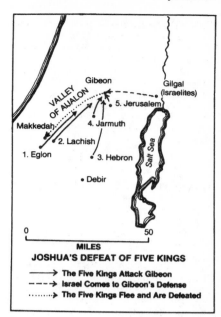

JOSHUA'S DEFEAT OF FIVE KINGS
→ The Five Kings Attack Gibeon
---→ Israel Comes to Gibeon's Defense
······→ The Five Kings Flee and Are Defeated

hot pursuit of the enemy. **The five** strong **kings** and their armies had left their fortified cities to fight Israel in the open. Now Joshua was determined to prevent their retreating back to **their** walled **cities.** When word came that **the five kings** had **hidden in** a **cave** Joshua himself did not stop to deal with them but vigorously pursued the Amorite soldiers, killing all but a **few** who escaped to **their fortified cities.** Then returning to the guarded **cave** he brought out the captured **kings** and executed them. But first, following an eastern custom of conquerors, often pictured on Egyptian and Assyrian monuments, **Joshua** instructed his field **commanders to put** their **feet** on the kings' **necks.** This was a symbol of the complete subjugation of the defeated enemy.

10:25-27. Then, using words identical to those God had given him, **Joshua** urged his soldiers **not** to **be afraid** or **discouraged** (cf. 1:9; 8:1) but to **be strong and courageous** (cf. 1:6-7, 9). The victory over the Amorite kings was a sample of Israel's future victories in Canaan, for Joshua said, **This is what the LORD will do to all the enemies you are going to fight. Joshua . . . killed the kings** and their bodies were exposed by **hanging** till sundown (cf. 8:29). Then they were thrown **into the cave** which was blocked

by great **rocks,** as had been done earlier
(10:18). These rocks became another memorial of Israel's victorious march
through Canaan.

10:28-39. The defeat of the five kings
and their armies sealed the doom of
southern Canaan. In a series of quick
raids **Joshua** attacked the key military
centers themselves to destroy any further
military capability. First he **took Makkedah** (v. 28), **Libnah** (v. 29), **Lachish** (v.
31), and **Eglon** (v. 34). These cities, ranging roughly from north to south, guarded
the approaches to the southern highlands. Centuries later both Sennacherib
and Nebuchadnezzar followed the same
strategy in their attacks on Judah.

Joshua next drove into the heart of
the southern region and defeated its two
chief walled cities, **Hebron** (v. 36) and
Debir (v. 38).

But Jerusalem and Jarmuth, two of
the five confederates (v. 5), were bypassed. No explanation is given as to
why the defeat of the city of Jarmuth is
not mentioned. As for Jerusalem, no
doubt Israel's troops were too weary to
undertake this difficult task as they returned to camp at Gilgal. At any rate this
pagan "island" in the land was to be
troublesome to the tribes of Judah and
Benjamin until it was conquered by David (2 Sam. 5:7).

10:40-43. The extent of Israel's campaign in the south is summarized in
verses 40-41 (cf. 11:16). The **region of
Goshen,** *not* the Goshen in Egypt (Gen.
45:10; 46:34; 47:1, 4, 6), was probably the
area around Debir in southern Canaan. A
town named Goshen was 1 of 11 towns
"in the hill country" which included
Debir (Josh. 15:48-51). Perhaps the area
was named for the town. The impressive
sweep of victories recorded in Joshua 10
is given credibility by the concluding
statement, **All these kings and their
lands Joshua conquered in one campaign because the Lord, the God of Israel, fought for Israel.**

With such confidence, **Joshua** and
his tired army **returned** to **Gilgal** to make
preparations for completing their task.

D. *The northern campaign (11:1-15)*

After the exhausting military campaign in the south, Joshua was not to
enjoy any prolonged period of recuperation before facing an even greater

challenge, a massive coalition of forces
in the north. But he was equal to the
task.

Israel's leader was both a military
genius and a spiritual giant. Militarily,
his tactics were skillful: (1) His battles
were all offensive. When he learned that
an attack was impending, he preceded it
by an attack of his own. (2) He used the
element of surprise (e.g., against the five
Amorite kings besieging Gibeon, 10:9;
against the many kings at the Waters of
Merom, 11:7; and against Ai when he
staged a decoy-rout, 8:14-19). (3) He sent
his soldiers to harry the retreating enemy, to prevent them from reaching their
cities (10:19-20).

Spiritually, Joshua served as an example to the people: he stood by the
promise his spies made to Rahab; he kept
faith with the deceptive Gibeonites; he
could have used his position for personal
gain but he did not.

With such a leader at the helm of
affairs in Israel, the Conquest entered its
final phase.

1. THE CONFEDERATION (11:1-5)

11:1-3. The alarm of **the northern**
Canaanite **kings** was aroused by Joshua's
crushing victories in the south. **Jabin,
king of Hazor,** organized a desperate attempt to stop the conquest of the land by
the army of Israel. No doubt his attempt
would have had a better chance of success if he had joined the coalition of
Adoni-Zedek (10:1-3), marching in force
from the north to merge with the southern armies to crush Israel at Gibeon. But
God restrained Jabin from that move and
now he reacted to the crisis with dispatch
and near panic.

Messengers fanned out rapidly to
the north, south, east, and west, with an
urgent call to arms. This may have been
quite similar to the summons Saul issued
later to Israel to follow him to Jabesh
Gilead, killing a yoke of oxen and sending pieces of the animals by couriers who
cried, "This is what will be done to the
oxen of anyone who does not follow Saul
and Samuel" (1 Sam. 11:7). **Kinnereth**
(Josh. 11:2; cf. 13:27; 19:35; Num. 34:11;
Deut. 3:17; 1 Kings 15:20) is an early
name for the Sea of Galilee and also the
name of a town on the coast of the lake.
"Kinnereth," meaning harp, may refer to
the lake's harp-like shape. The New Tes-

tament sometimes refers to the Sea of Galilee as the Lake of Gennesaret, a Greek spelling for the Hebrew Kinnereth (e.g., Luke 5:1).

11:4-5. Though there was no love lost among those **kings** of the north, the threat of annihilation forced them into an alliance and they rendezvoused a few miles northwest of the Sea of Galilee in a plain near the **Waters of Merom.**

The combined army was impressive. Not only did it include soldiers **as numerous as the sand on the seashore,** but in addition they had **horses and chariots** in great numbers. Josephus, a Jewish historian of the first century A.D., speculated that this northern confederacy included 300,000 infantry soldiers, 10,000 cavalry troops, and 20,000 chariots.

The odds against the Israelites seemed overwhelming. How could Joshua hope to win this battle?

2. THE CONFLICT (11:6-15)

The vast host of Canaanites were pitched at the Waters of Merom (v. 5). It was probably their plan, after organizing their detachments and adopting a strategy, to sweep down the Jordan Valley and attack Joshua at Gilgal. But Joshua did not wait for the battle to come to him; he was in fact already marching toward Merom, a five-day trek from his home base. And as he marched he had a lot of time to think about the immense array awaiting him. No doubt he trembled at the prospect of the battle that loomed before him.

11:6. Then God spoke. The promise He gave **Joshua** was unmistakably clear: **Do not be afraid of them** (cf. 1:9; 8:1) **because by this time tomorrow I will hand all of them over to Israel, slain.** This was just what Joshua needed and Israel's leader took God's promise at face value, believing that He would give them the victory over their formidable foe. God even told Joshua specifically **to hamstring** (cripple by cutting the leg tendons) **their horses and** to **burn their chariots** (cf. comments on 11:9).

11:7-9. The battle took place in two phases. The next day **Joshua** surprised the enemy, attacking them **at the Waters of Merom** and chasing **them** westward to the coast (**to Greater Sidon** and **to Misrephoth Maim**), **and** eastward **to the Valley of Mizpah.** Following God's di-

rection (v. 6) to the letter Joshua killed all of the enemy, **burned their chariots,** and lamed **their horses.**

But why did God command such drastic action, burning the chariots and hamstringing the horses? Because the Canaanites used horses in their pagan worship (and so later did Judah; cf. 2 Kings 23:11). Also there was danger that Israel might trust in these new weapons of war rather than in the Lord. The Psalmist David declared, "Some trust in chariots and some in horses, but we trust in the name of the LORD our God" (Ps. 20:7).

11:10-14. In the second phase of the conflict in northern Canaan **Joshua** returned after routing the enemy army and **captured** all the cities of the defeated kings. **Hazor,** however, was singled out for special treatment, probably because it was by far the largest city of ancient Palestine (200 acres in size, compared with Megiddo at 14 and Jericho at 8). Occupying a position of immense strategic importance **Hazor** dominated several branches of an ancient highway which led from Egypt to Syria and on to Assyria and Babylon. This location on the trade routes contributed to the city's wealth. **Hazor** alone among the northern cities was both seized and **burned.** Though **Joshua** may have decided to save the other captured **cities** for later Israelite use, he determined to make an example of **Hazor,** capital **of all these kingdoms** (city states) and the convener of their armies. If great Hazor could not escape, the Canaanites would be forced to acknowledge that any city could be burned if Joshua so decreed.

11:15. Thus a decisive victory was won in the north. And the key was obedience to God. **Joshua . . . left nothing undone of all that the LORD commanded Moses.**

E. The review of the victories (11:16–12:24)

Victory in the north brought the formal end of the Conquest. But before giving the record of how the land was apportioned among the tribes, the author paused to review and summarize the scope of Israel's triumphs in Canaan. He included a description of the conquered geographic areas (11:16-23) and a list of the defeated kings (chap. 12).

1. THE CONQUERED AREAS (11:16-23)

11:16-17. The battles fought by **Joshua** and his troops ranged over lands that stretched from border to border, from south to north, and from east to west. **The hill country,** the **Negev,** the **Goshen** area, **the western foothills, the Arabah, and the mountains** refer to the central and southern portions of the land (cf. 10:40). "The Negev" is the desert area southwest of the Dead Sea and "the Arabah" is the depression of the Jordan Valley north and south of the Dead Sea. **Mount Halak** is in the southern desert region; **Baal Gad** (exact location unknown) was in the far north, **in the Valley of Lebanon** perhaps 30-40 miles north of the Sea of Galilee.

11:18:20. The period of the Conquest lasted **a long time.** Victory did not come easily or quickly; it rarely does. Yet in all the military confrontations only one city, **Gibeon,** sought **peace.** The rest were taken **in battle,** God having **hardened their hearts** (cf. comments on Ex. 4:21; 8:15) to fight **Israel** so that they might be destroyed. The Canaanites' day of grace was gone. They had sinned against the light of God's revelation in nature (Ps. 19:1; Rom. 1:18-20), in conscience (Rom. 2:14-16), and in His recent miraculous works at the Red (Reed) Sea, the Jordan River, and Jericho. Now the sovereign God confirmed the hearts of these unrepentant people in their stubborn unbelief before judging them.

11:21-22. Special mention is made of **the Anakites,** the giants who had terrified the spies 45 years before (Num. 13:33; cf. comments on Josh. 14:10), of whom it was asked, "Who can stand up against the Anakites?" (Deut. 9:2) But under **Joshua** those supposedly invincible foes were utterly **destroyed. Only** a few remained, in the remote cities of **Gaza, Gath, and Ashdod**—which later proved to be an unfortunate oversight on Joshua's part because in David's time Goliath came from Gath to defy Israel and her God (1 Sam. 17).

11:23. The section concludes with a declaration that summarizes the Book of Joshua as a whole. **So Joshua took the entire land** (cf. v. 16). This looks back and condenses the history of the Conquest in chapters 1–11. **And he gave it as an inheritance to Israel according to their tribal divisions.** These words look forward and summarize the distribution of the land in chapters 13–22.

But how is the statement, "Joshua took the entire land," to be understood when later it was written that "there are still very large areas of land to be taken over"? (13:1) To the Hebrew mind the part stands for the whole. It thus only needs to be demonstrated that Joshua took key centers in all parts of the land to validate the statement that he had conquered the whole land.

A.J. Mattill, Jr. has meticulously analyzed the conquest of Canaan by surveying the geographical divisions of the land and the representative parts of it subdued by Joshua ("Representative Universalism and the Conquest of Canaan," *Concordia Theological Monthly* 35. January 1964:8-17). Included are conquered sites on the coastal plain, the Shephelah (foothills), the central plateau, the Jordan Valley, and the Transjordan plateau. No area was totally bypassed. Joshua did indeed take the entire land, just as God promised he would if he followed the divine Word rather than human wisdom (cf. 1:8). Also see comments on 21:43-45. On the concluding statement **Then the land had rest from war** (11:23), see comments on these words in 14:15.

2. THE CONQUERED KINGS (CHAP. 12)

Chapter 12, in concluding the story begun in chapter 1, gives a detailed catalog of the kings defeated by Israel. The preceding chapters obviously then list only the major battles. Only here is the complete list of conquered kings found. It is not claimed that Israel occupied all these cities. Certainly Joshua did not have sufficient manpower to leave a controlling garrison in each place. Joshua no doubt expected the respective tribes to occupy those towns.

12:1-6. First were recorded the victories under **Moses** on the **east** side **of the Jordan.** These were important victories over **Sihon** and **Og.** Sihon had ruled over a stretch of land about 90 miles south to north from **the Arnon Gorge** at about the midpoint of **the Sea of the Arabah** (also called **the Salt Sea** and the Dead Sea) up to **the Sea of Kinnereth** (cf. comments on 11:2). Og ruled over a stretch of land extending north from Sihon's northern boundary for about 60 miles (cf. Num. 21:21-35; Deut. 2:24–

3:17). This territory was assigned to the tribes of Reuben and Gad and the half tribe of Manasseh (Num. 32; cf. Josh. 13:8-13). (On **Geshur** and **Maacah** see comments on 13:13.)

12:7-24. In this section 16 **kings** of southern Canaan are enumerated first (vv. 9-16) and then 15 kings of northern Canaan (vv. 17-24).

It is surprising to find recorded **31 kings** in a land approximately 150 miles from north to south and 50 miles from east to west. But it must be remembered that these kings reigned over city-states and had only local authority. Apart from the confederations formed by the kings **of Jerusalem** (10:1-5) and **Hazor** (11:1-5), the lack of a central government in Canaan made the Israelites' task easier than it would have been otherwise.

As to the meaning of Joshua's victories one writer stated, "There has never been a greater war for a greater cause. The battle of Waterloo decided the fate of Europe, but this series of contests in far-off Canaan decided the fate of the world" (Henry T. Sell, *Bible Study by Periods*. Chicago: Fleming H. Revell Co., 1899, p. 83).

III. The Division of Canaan (chaps. 13–21)

A. The portions for the two and one-half tribes (chap. 13)

Having successfully removed the major military threats to Israel's survival in Canaan, Joshua the aged soldier now became an administrator. The land conquered by bloody warfare had to be assigned to the various tribes and Joshua would oversee this important transaction. It would be a service less exhausting and more suited to his advancing years.

To many people this section of the Book of Joshua, with its detailed lists of boundaries and cities, seems tedious. Someone has said, "Most of this long section reads like a real estate deed." And that is precisely what is found in these lengthy narrations—legal descriptions (after the manner of that ancient day) of the areas allocated to the 12 tribes. Title deeds are important documents so these should not be regarded as insignificant or superfluous.

This was a climactic moment in the life of the young nation. After centuries in Egyptian bondage, decades in the barren wilderness, years of hard fighting in Canaan, the hour had arrived when the Israelites could at last settle down to build homes, cultivate the soil, raise families, and live in peace in their own land. The days of land allotment were a happy time for Israel.

1. THE DIVINE COMMAND TO DIVIDE THE LAND (13:1-7)

13:1a. God directed **Joshua** to divide the land west of the Jordan at this time because he was **very old.** Since Joshua died at the age of 110 (24:29), he probably was at least 100 at this time. God's commission to Joshua had included not only conquering the land but also distributing it among the tribes (cf. 1:6). He must therefore move on quickly to this new assignment.

13:1b-7. The land that remained **to be taken over** is described from south to north and included Philistia (vv. 2-3; see comments on the Philistines at Gen. 21:32); Phoenicia (Josh. 13:4), called here **the land of the Canaanites** but designating the inhabitants of the Syro-Palestinian coastland; and **Lebanon** (vv. 5-6). All this land was now to be allotted to the **nine** and one-half **tribes** since God promised to **drive . . . out** all the enemy (v. 6).

2. THE SPECIAL GRANT TO THE EASTERN TRIBES (13:8-33)

13:8-13. Joshua was next called on to recognize and confirm what had already been done by **Moses** on the **east** side **of the Jordan.** The tribes of Reuben, Gad, and the half-tribe of Manasseh, possessing large herds of cattle, were anxious to settle in the rich grazing lands of the Transjordan. But only after their men agreed to fight alongside their brothers to win Canaan proper did Moses agree to give them their land (Num. 32). A survey of the area of Transjordan is given in these verses (Josh. 13:9-12; cf. 12:1-5). **Geshur and Maacah** (already mentioned in 12:5) were not defeated by **the Israelites,** and the reason for this is not given. These countries were located east and northeast of the Sea of Kinnereth (Sea of Galilee).

13:14. The tribe of Levi received no specific territory of land as did the other tribes (cf. v. 33; 14:3-4; 18:7). Instead the Levites received 48 towns with pastureland for their flocks and herds (14:4;

21:41) as Moses had specified (Num. 35:1-5).

13:15-32. Reuben (vv. 15-23) received **the territory** previously occupied by Moab, east of the Dead Sea. **The tribe of Gad** inherited the portion in the center of the region, in the original land **of Gilead** (vv. 24-28).

The allotment to **the half-tribe of Manasseh** (vv. 29-31) was the rich tableland **of Bashan** east of the Sea of Kinnereth.

Centuries before the land was divided Jacob, when dying, had uttered prophecies regarding his sons. His prophecy about his firstborn Reuben was foreboding (cf. Gen. 49:3-4; 35:22). Though Reuben was the firstborn and entitled to a double portion (Deut. 21:17), neither he nor his tribe received it. Now after more than four centuries the punishment for Reuben's sinful deed was passed on to his descendants; the right of the firstborn passed over to his brother Joseph who received two portions, one for Ephraim and the other for Manasseh (Gen. 48:12-20).

Was the request of the two and one-half tribes to settle in Transjordan a wise one? History would seem to answer no. Their territories had no natural boundaries to the east and were therefore constantly exposed to invasion by the Moabites, Canaanites, Arameans, Midianites, Amalekites, and others. And when the king of Assyria looked covetously toward Canaan, Reuben, Gad and the half-tribe of Manasseh were the first to be carried into captivity by the Assyrian armies (1 Chron. 5:26).

13:33. By contrast with the rich though dangerous inheritance of these tribes, it is twice emphasized in this chapter (vv. 14, 33) and twice later (14:3-4; 18:7) that **the tribe of Levi** received **no inheritance** from **Moses.** At first this may seem puzzling, but closer examination reveals that in lieu of territorial possessions the tribe of Levi was allotted the sacrifices or offerings (13:14), the priesthood (18:7), and **the LORD** Himself (13:33). Who could have dreamed of a greater inheritance?

The two and one-half tribes chose, as Lot did, on the basis of appearance (cf. Gen. 13:10-11), and their inheritance was ultimately lost to them. On the other hand the Levites, requesting no portion, were given an **inheritance** of abiding spiritual significance.

B. The portion for Caleb (chap. 14)

1. INTRODUCTION (14:1-5)

14:1-5. With the recording of the allotments by **Moses** in Transjordan completed, the account turns to the distribution of the land in **Canaan** proper to the remaining **nine-and-a-half tribes.** The explanation is repeated regarding the dealings with the Reubenites, the Gadites, and the half-tribe of Manasseh; and the arrangements for the tribe of Levi (cf. 13:14, 33; 18:7). Also the method by which the allocations in Canaan were to be made was specified: the land was to be **assigned by lot** (14:2; 18:8; 19:51). **The LORD had** instructed **Moses** that each tribe was to receive territory proportionate to its population with the casting of lots to determine its location (Num. 26:54-56). According to Jewish tradition the name of a tribe was drawn from one urn and simultaneously the boundary lines of a territory from another. This method designated each tribal inheritance. But blind chance did not decide the tribal location, for God was superintending the whole procedure (cf. Prov. 16:33). The inequities of assignments that existed and that caused some tensions and jealousies among the tribes should have been accepted as a part of God's purpose, not as something that was arbitrary and unfair.

2. CALEB AT KADESH BARNEA (14:6-9)

14:6-9. The time for casting lots arrived and the tribe **of Judah,** receiving the first portion, assembled **at Gilgal.** Before the lots were cast **Caleb,** a "grand old man of Israel," stepped forward to remind **Joshua** of a promise the Lord had made to him 45 years earlier: "I will give him and his descendants the land he set his feet on, because he followed the LORD wholeheartedly" (Deut. 1:36). Caleb's life was ebbing away and he must make a choice. What did he still want most of all? In a remarkable address to Joshua he reviewed the highlights of his life and made his request. His brief autobiography highlighted events **at Kadesh Barnea,** during the wilderness wanderings, and the Conquest.

Caleb is introduced in this passage as the **son of Jephunneh the Kenizzite.**

According to Genesis 15:19 the Kenizzites were a tribe of Canaan in Abraham's day. Caleb's family then was originally outside the covenant and commonwealth of Israel as were Heber the Kenite (Jud. 4:17), Ruth the Moabitess (Ruth 1:1-5), Uriah the Hittite (2 Sam. 11:3, 6, 24), and others. It is apparent that the Kenizzites in part at least joined the tribe of Judah before the Exodus. So their faith was not hereditary but was the fruit of conviction. And Caleb displayed that faith throughout his long lifetime.

Standing before General Joshua, his old friend and fellow spy (Num. 14:6), 85-year-old Caleb (Josh. 14:10) told the story of that never-to-be forgotten day, 45 years before (v. 10), when the 2 of them stood alone against the other 10 spies and the cowardly mob. For Moses had sent 12 spies into Canaan (Num. 13:2); 2 of them were Caleb and Joshua (Num. 13:6, 8). When the spies returned 10 of them praised the land itself but fearfully concluded Israel could not conquer it (Num. 13:27-29, 31-33). Caleb, **however,** dared to disagree (Num. 13:30), and when the fears of the people threatened to bring national rebellion Joshua joined his colleague in urging the people to trust God for victory (Num. 14:6-9). For Caleb's leadership against the unbelieving spies and people, **God** singled him out for blessing and promised him a special reward (Num. 14:24; Deut. 1:36).

Caleb's testimony (Josh. 14:6-12) was simple. He had spoken on that memorable day **according to** his **convictions.** He did not minimize the problems—the giants and the fortified cities—but he magnified God. To him, God was greater than the biggest problem. Caleb had faith in *the power of God.* Not so the other spies. They magnified the problems and thereby minimized God. But Caleb would not follow the crowd. He did not once consider sacrificing his own convictions in order to make the majority report unanimous. Instead he **followed the Lord** his **God wholeheartedly** (cf. v. 14).

3. CALEB DURING THE WILDERNESS WANDERINGS AND THE CONQUEST (14:10-11)

14:10. The autobiographical story continued as Caleb reminisced about God's faithfulness to him over many years. First he affirmed that God had

kept him **alive** the past **45 years** as He had promised. Actually Caleb was the recipient of two divine promises: one, that his life would be prolonged, and the other, that he would someday inherit the territory he had bravely explored near Hebron. But 45 years is a long time to wait for the fulfillment of a pledge, a long time for faith to live on a promise. Yet Caleb did wait through the weary years of the wilderness wanderings and the demanding years of the Conquest. Caleb had strong faith in *the promises of God.* They sustained him in his difficult times.

Caleb's remarks provide information for determining the length of the conquest of Canaan by the Israelites. Caleb stated (v. 7) that he was 40 years old when he went to spy out the land. The wilderness wanderings lasted 38 years, thus bringing Caleb's age to 78 at the beginning of the Conquest. Caleb then said he was **85** at the end of the Conquest. So the Conquest lasted 7 years. This is confirmed by Caleb's reference (v. 10) to God's sustaining grace for 45 years since Kadesh Barnea (38 years of the wanderings plus 7 years of the Conquest).

14:11. Interestingly as an octogenarian, Caleb said he felt **as strong** and **vigorous** at 85 as he had at 40!

4. CALEB AT HEBRON (14:12-15)

14:12-14. Caleb concluded his speech to **Joshua** with an astounding request. At age 85, when he might have asked for a quiet place to spend his last days raising some vegetables or flowers, he instead requested that he be given the same section of land that had struck fear into the hearts of the 10 spies. This was the **inheritance** he desired in fulfillment of God's earlier promise. Though most older people are more apt to talk about old conflicts than to take on new ones, **Caleb** was ready for one more good battle. He was eager to fight **the Anakites** at **Hebron** and take that city for his possession. Caleb chose a large and foreboding task. Not that he was filled with pride in his own ability. Rather he believed God would be with him. Caleb had faith in *the presence of God.*

With flashing eyes and a strong voice he concluded, **The Lord helping me, I will drive them out just as He said.** And drive them out he did, as Joshua

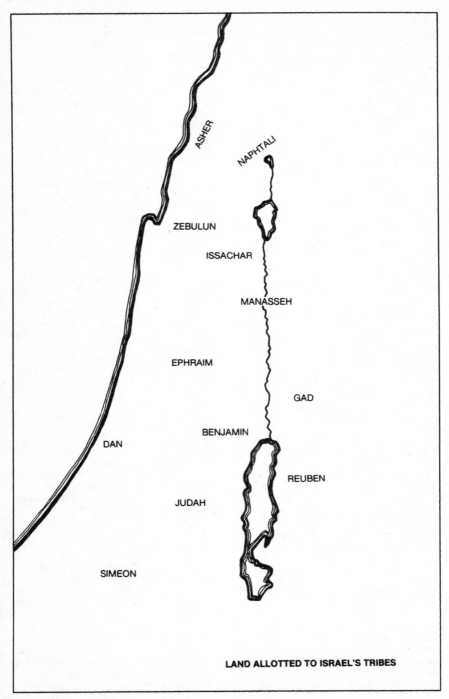

LAND ALLOTTED TO ISRAEL'S TRIBES

(15:13-19) recorded. Joshua's response to Caleb's request was twofold: (a) he **blessed Caleb,** that is, he set him apart for God's enablement so he would be enriched and successful in his task, and (b) Joshua **gave him Hebron,** a statement which emphasizes that this land grant was a legal transaction.

14:15. A historical note explaining the previous name of **Hebron** as **Kiriath Arba** ends the story. **Arba** was a giant **among the Anakites,** a nation of giants, a fact that causes the heroic faith of Caleb to stand out even more vividly. The concluding words, **Then the land had rest from war** (cf. 11:23 for the same expression at the end of the Conquest proper), show what faith in the Lord can accomplish with respect to land yet to ·be possessed.

C. *The portions for the nine and one-half tribes (15:1–19:48)*

1. THE ALLOTMENT FOR THE TRIBE OF JUDAH (CHAP. 15)

15:1-12. Caleb's request having been granted, Joshua returned to the business of dividing the land west of the Jordan among the nine and one-half tribes (see the map). **Judah** was the first to receive an inheritance and as the largest tribe her portion exceeded that of any of the others. Jacob's prophecy regarding Judah and his seed was remarkably fulfilled in her land allotment after the Conquest. First, Judah was surrounded by enemies (Gen. 49:8-9). The Moabites were on the east, Edomites on the south, Amalekites to the southwest, and Philistines to the west. Thus hemmed in by fierce foes, Judah would need strong rulers such as David to survive. Second, the land allotted to Judah was ideally suited to the planting of vineyards (Gen. 49:11-12). It was from a Judean valley (the Valley of Eshcol) that the spies cut down the gigantic cluster of grapes (Num. 13:24). Third, Judah was the tribe from which the Messiah would come (Gen. 49:10; Matt. 1:1, 3; Luke 3:23, 33).

Judah's **southern boundary** (Josh. 15:2-4) extended from the south end of the Dead **Sea** westward to the river **of Egypt (Wadi** el-Arish). The **northern** border extended from the northern tip of the Dead Sea westward to **the Great Sea,** the Mediterranean (vv. 5-12). These two bodies of water were the eastern and western

limits. Composed mainly of the territory conquered by Joshua in his southern campaign (chap. 10), the area included some fertile tracts, but large parts were mountainous and barren.

15:13-19. Included in Judah's portion was **Hebron (Kiriath Arba;** cf. 14:15) which had been granted **to Caleb.** The record describes how that courageous warrior claimed and enlarged this inheritance (after Joshua's death), aided by a brave nephew **Othniel** who became his son-in-law (cf. Jud. 1:1, 10-15, 20) and later a judge (Jud. 3:9-11).

15:20-63. The **towns** of **Judah** are next listed according to their locations in the four main geographic regions of the tribe: **29 towns** plus **their villages** in the south or **Negev** (vv. 21-32); 42 **towns** plus **villages** in **the western foothills** or Shephelah (vv. 33-47); 38 **towns** plus **villages** in the central **hill country** (vv. 48-60); **6 towns** plus **villages** in the sparsely populated wilderness of Judah which slopes down toward the Dead Sea (vv. 61-62). The number of towns in the Negev is said to be 29 (v. 32), but 36 are listed (vv. 21-32). This is explained by the fact that seven of these were later given to Simeon's tribe: Moladah, Hazar Shual, Beersheba, Ezem, Eltolad, Hormah, and Ziklag (19:1-7). **Judah** inherited well over 100 cities and seems to have occupied them with little or no difficulty with the significant exception of Jerusalem. **Judah could not** dislodge **the Jebusites, who were living in Jerusalem** (15:63). Was it that the men of Judah "could not" or that they "would not"? Was the failure because of lack of strength or a lack of faith? The account of Judah's inheritance ends on an ominous and foreboding note.

2. THE ALLOTMENTS FOR THE JOSEPH TRIBES (CHAPS. 16–17)

a. The territory of Ephraim (chap. 16)

16:1-3. The powerful house of **Joseph** made up of the tribes of Ephraim and Manasseh, inherited the rich territory of central Canaan. Because Joseph kept the whole family alive during the famine in Egypt, the patriarch Jacob ordained that Joseph's two sons, Ephraim and Manasseh, should be made founders and heads of tribes with their uncles (cf. Gen. 48:5). Their territory in Canaan was in many respects the most beautiful and fertile.

16:4-10. Located immediately north of the **territory** to be assigned to Dan and Benjamin, the allotment of **Ephraim** stretched from **the Jordan** to the Mediterranean and included the sites of some of Joshua's battles as well as **Shiloh** where the tabernacle would remain for about 300 years. To encourage unity some of Ephraim's **towns** were located in the territory of Manasseh (v. 9).

But the men of Ephraim, like those of Judah, **did not** completely drive out **the Canaanites** from their region. Motivated by a materialistic attitude, they chose to put the Canaanites in **Gezer** under tribute to gain additional wealth. That proved to be a fatal mistake for in later centuries, in the time of the Judges, the arrangement was reversed as the Canaanites rose up and enslaved the Israelites. In addition to the historical lesson there is a spiritual principle here. It is all too easy for a believer to tolerate and excuse some pet sin only to wake up some day to the grim realization that it has risen up to possess and drive him to spiritual defeat. It pays to deal with sin decisively and harshly.

b. The territory of Manasseh (17:1-13)

17:1-2, 7-10. The descendants of **Makir, Manasseh's firstborn,** settled in Transjordan (vv. 1-2). The remaining heirs settled in Canaan proper and were given the territory north of Ephraim extending also from the Jordan River to the Mediterranean Sea (vv. 7-10).

17:3-6. Special note is taken of the five **daughters** of **Zelophehad,** a great-great grandson of Manasseh. Because their father died without **sons** they, as **the Lord** had declared in this and other such cases, should receive the **inheritance** (cf. Num. 27:1-11). They now went to the high priest **Eleazar** (Aaron's son, Josh. 24:33) who with **Joshua** and the tribal **leaders** oversaw the allotments to the tribes (cf. 19:51). These five women claimed and received their portion within the territory of **Manasseh.** This incident is significant, for it shows a concern for the rights of women at a time when most societies regarded them as mere chattel.

17:11-13. Several cities located in the tribes of **Issachar and Asher** were given to **Manasseh.** These were the Canaanite fortresses of **Beth Shan, Ibleam . . . Dor, Endor, Taanach, and Megiddo.** (Dor, **the**

third in the list, was also known as **Naphoth.**) Apparently it was considered necessary for military purposes that these cities be held by a strong tribe. The decision, however, was in vain for the sons of Manasseh, like the Ephraimites, chose tribute over triumph.

c. The complaint of Ephraim and Manasseh (17:14-18)

17:14-15. The descendants of **Joseph** registered a belligerent complaint with **Joshua,** claiming that their **allotment** was too small in light of their large population. With tact and firmness **Joshua** challenged them first to **clear** the trees and settle in the forested **hill country** (v. 15). He suggested that they combine their energies to drive out the Canaanites (v. 18).

17:16-18. But this was not what they wanted to hear. They insisted that **the hill country** was **not** sufficient **for** them **and** that **the Canaanites** in the region possessed **iron chariots,** probably chariots of wood covered with iron. Again **Joshua** reminded his fellow tribesmen that they were **numerous and very powerful** and fully capable of expanding their territory by clearing the **hill country** and driving out the enemy **Canaanites.** While there is some similarity between this section and the one recording Caleb's request (14:6-15), their outlooks were opposite. Caleb's request was motivated by faith, whereas that of the Josephites stemmed from fear. The purpose, however, of this episode may well be to alert the Israelites to the fact that the tribes had to act in courageous faith if they were to possess the Promised Land fully.

3. THE ALLOTMENTS FOR THE REMAINING
   TRIBES (18:1–19:48)

a. Introduction (18:1-10)

18:1-3. Before the final divisions of the land were made the Israelites moved en masse from Gilgal to **Shiloh,** about 20 miles northwest, from the Jordan Valley to the hill country. Why? Probably because Shiloh, located in the center of the land, was a convenient location where the tabernacle (**the Tent of Meeting**) could remind the people that the key to prosperity and blessing in the land was worshiping and serving Yahweh. The dissatisfaction of the sons of Joseph with their allotment (17:14-18) was an ominous foreshadowing of the future disintegration of the nation because of self-interest. To counteract this tendency the tabernacle was **set up** in Shiloh to promote a sense of national unity.

Further, when the Israelites were thus assembled for erecting the tabernacle and celebrating the new worship center Joshua sensed that a feeling of war-weariness had overtaken them. They were exhausted in the struggle for the conquest of Canaan, so they stopped in the middle of the task of allocating the **tribes. Seven** were still without homes, apparently content to continue a nomadic and purposeless existence such as they had experienced in the wilderness. Their listlessness provoked **Joshua** who took steps to prod them into action. He reproached them sharply: **How long will you wait before you begin to take possession of the land that the** LORD**, the God of your fathers, has given you?** Apparently the tribes were to initiate matters relating to territorial allocations. Joshua probably viewed every passing day as a day lost in the program of completely occupying the land, a day in which the enemy could return or become more firmly entrenched.

18:4-7. Joshua was for action but not before careful preparations were made. Directing the appointment of a commission of 21 men, **3** from **each** of the seven unassigned tribes, he sent them to **make a** topographical **survey of the** remaining **land.** How long this complex task took is not stated, but it was obviously a job that required time and skill. Josephus wrote that these men were experts in geometry. Probably their parents had mastered the science of land surveying in Egypt. Who among them dreamed that their children would ever put that knowledge to use so strategically in their land of promise?

18:8-10. Writing their expert observations **on a scroll,** the surveyors then **returned** to **Shiloh** where **Joshua** proceeded to **cast lots** (see comments on 14:1-5; cf. 19:51) to determine the portions of territory to be allotted to the remaining **seven** tribes.

b. The territory of Benjamin (18:11-28)

18:11-28. Benjamin was assigned the land that lay between **Judah and Joseph,** a reference to Ephraim, thus minimizing the incipient rivalry between these leading tribes. Though their area was covered by mountains and ravines, extending only 25 miles from east to west and 15 miles at its widest point from north to south, it included many cities that were important in biblical history—**Jericho . . . Bethel . . . Gibeon, Ramah . . . Mizpah,** and **the Jebusite city . . . Jerusalem** (vv. 21-28). So the site of the future temple in Jerusalem was in the tribe of Benjamin, a fulfillment of Moses' prophecy (Deut. 33:12).

c. The territory of Simeon (19:1-9)

19:1-9. Because **Judah** had **more** territory than it **needed** (v. 9), and in fulfillment of Jacob's prophecy (cf. Gen. 49:5-7), **Simeon** was given land in the southern section of Judah's **territory** with 17 **towns and their villages.** But it was not long before Simeon was to lose her individuality as a tribe, for her territory was incorporated eventually into that of Judah and many of her citizens migrated north to Ephraim and Manasseh (cf. 2 Chron. 15:9; 34:6). This explains why after the division of the kingdom following Solomon there were 10 tribes in the north and only 2 in the south (Judah and Benjamin).

d. The territory of Zebulun (19:10-16)

19:10-16. According to Jacob's prophecy **Zebulun** would "live by the seashore and become a haven for ships" (Gen. 49:13). She was assigned a portion in lower Galilee which many consider to have been landlocked. However, it is possible to understand that a strip of land extended to the Mediterranean Sea forming an enclave in Issachar's territory. Strangely omitted is the city of Nazareth which was within the borders of Zebulun's allotment. (The **Bethlehem** mentioned in Josh. 19:15 is not the Bethlehem village in Judah [Micah 5:2] where Jesus was born.)

e. The territory of Issachar (19:17-23)

19:17-23. Lying east of Zebulun and south of the Sea of Galilee **Issachar** was to occupy the fertile and beautiful valley of **Jezreel,** also a noted battlefield. Until the time of David, however, its people remained in the mountainous district at the eastern end of the valley.

f. The territory of Asher (19:24-31)

19:24-31. Asher was assigned the Mediterranean coastal lands from Mount **Carmel** north to **Sidon** and **Tyre.** By virtue of her vital position she was to protect Israel from northern coastal enemies such as the Phoenicians. By David's time Asher had faded into insignificance though her tribal identity was not lost. Anna the prophetess, who along with Simeon gave thanks for the birth of Jesus, was from the tribe of Asher (cf. Luke 2:36-38).

g. The territory of Naphtali (19:32-39)

19:32-39. Adjacent to Asher on the east, **Naphtali** had **the Jordan** River and the Sea of Galilee as its eastern boundary. While not highly significant as a region in the Old Testament period, Naphtali occupied lands that were important in New Testament history because the Galilean ministry of Jesus Christ was centered there. Isaiah the prophet contrasted Naphtali's early gloom (due to Assyrian invasion) with its glory when Christ would be there (cf. Isa. 9:1-2; Matt. 4:13-17).

h. The territory of Dan (19:40-48)

19:40-48. The least desirable portion fell to **Dan.** Surrounded by Ephraim and Benjamin on the north and east and by Judah on the south, her boundaries coincided with theirs so Dan's borders are not described. Only towns are included, which numbered 17. Not only was their original location too small but after part of the territory of Dan was lost to the Amorites (Jud. 1:34) most of the tribe migrated to the far north, and **attacked** and **settled in** the city of **Leshem** (Laish) opposite the northern sector of Naphtali **and named it Dan** (cf. Jud. 18; Gen. 49:17).

So God provided for the needs of each tribe, though in some cases parts of their inheritances were still in the hands of the enemy. The Israelites were to possess the land by faith, trusting God to enable them to defeat their foes. Centuries later Jeremiah purchased a field held by the invading Babylonian army (Jer. 32). And centuries after that a Roman citizen arranged to buy some ground on which the attackers of Rome were camped. Similarly Israel was to claim her tribal inheritances by faith. Failure to do

so would be to live in poverty and weakness, conditions which God did not desire for His people.

D. The portions for Joshua, manslayers, and Levites (19:49–21:45)

1. THE SPECIAL PROVISION FOR JOSHUA (19:49-51)

19:49. Whereas Caleb's **inheritance** was determined first (14:6-15), Joshua's was last. Only after all the tribes had received their allotments did **Joshua** ask for his. What a selfless spirit he possessed, and how his behavior contrasts with many political leaders who use their positions and influence to enrich themselves and their families.

19:50-51. Joshua's choice of land further reveals his humility. He asked for **Timnath Serah,** a city in the rugged, infertile, mountainous district of his own tribe (**Ephraim**), when he could have appropriated land in the fairest and most productive area of Canaan. With deep appreciation for his godly leadership the sons of Israel granted Joshua his modest request, **and he built up the town and settled there.** In one of the final pictures of this stalwart leader, Joshua is seen as a builder (in addition to his being a general and an administrator). The combination is rare among God's servants.

All the tribes received their **territories . . . by lot** (see comments on 14:1-5).

2. THE ASSIGNMENT OF CITIES OF REFUGE (CHAP. 20)

One of the first ordinances after the announcement of the Ten Commandments provided for the future establishment of cities of refuge (Ex. 21:12-13). These cities, providing havens for unintentional manslayers, are discussed in detail in Numbers 35:6-34 and Deuteronomy 19:1-14. The present chapter discusses their appointment after the Conquest (see their locations on the map "Canaan in the Conquest" near Josh. 3).

The fact that these cities are discussed in four books of the Old Testament marks them as being of great importance. It is apparent that God wished to impress on Israel the sanctity of human life. To put an end to a person's life, even if done unintentionally, is a serious thing, and the cities of refuge underscored this emphatically.

In the ancient world blood revenge was widely practiced. The moment a person was killed, his nearest relative took responsibility for vengeance. This ancient rite of vendetta was often handed down from one generation to another so that increasingly larger numbers of innocent people died violently. The need in ancient Israel for the refuge that these special cities provided is evident.

20:1-3. A clear distinction is made in the Old Testament between premeditated murder and accidental manslaughter (cf. Num. 35:9-15 with Num. 35:16-21). In the case of murder the nearest kinsman became **the avenger of blood,** killing the guilty party. But if a **person** killed another **accidentally** he was provided a place of asylum in one of six **cities of refuge.** However, he had to hurry to the nearest shelter without delay. According to Jewish tradition the roads leading to these cities were kept in excellent condition and the crossroads were well marked with signposts reading, "Refuge! Refuge!" Runners were also stationed along the way to guide the fugitives.

20:4-6. Having arrived at the **gate** of a refuge city, the manslayer was to present **his case** (breathlessly!) to **the elders of that city** who formed an ancient court of law (cf. Job 29:7; Deut. 21:19; 22:15). A provisional decision would then be made to grant him asylum till a **trial** could be held in the presence of **the assembly.** If acquitted of premeditated murder he was returned to the city of refuge where he lived till **the high priest** died, after which the manslayer was free to return to his **home.** That could be many years later. Involuntary manslaughter was therefore something to be carefully avoided. Many have puzzled over the meaning of the high priest's **death** in relation to the change in the status of the manslayer. The best explanation may be that the change in priestly administration served as a statute of limitations ending the fugitive's exile in the **city** of refuge.

20:7-9. The six designated cities were located on both sides of the Jordan River. On the west side were **Kedesh in Galilee . . . of Naphtali, Shechem in . . . Ephraim,** and **Hebron in . . . Judah.** The cities **on the east side** were **Bezer** in the south in **Reuben, Ramoth** in the region of **Gilead in the tribe of Gad,** and

Golan in the northern territory of **Bashan** in Manasseh's **tribe.**

But why is there no record in the Old Testament of a single instance in which this merciful provision of deliverance was utilized? Some critics suggest that these cities were not part of the Mosaic legislation but that this provision was instituted after the Exile. Yet the postexilic books likewise do not refer to their use, so other critics have suggested that the cities were not occupied till the time of Christ. In the face of such shifting arguments it is better to recognize the historicity of these accounts and to explain the silence of the record by the obvious fact that the scriptural authors were selective about what they recorded. Once the provision was made, it was apparently not important to document specific cases of its use.

Israel's benefit of sanctuary reminds believers of Psalm 46:1, "God is our refuge and strength, an ever present help in trouble," and of Romans 8:1, "Therefore, there is now no condemnation for those who are in Christ Jesus." The writer of the Epistle to the Hebrews may have had the Old Testament cities of refuge in mind when he wrote that believers may have great encouragement because they "have fled to take hold of the hope offered to" them (Heb. 6:18). The cities of refuge, then, seem to typify Christ to whom sinners, pursued by the avenging Law which decrees judgment and death, may flee for refuge. Paul's frequent expression "in Christ" speaks of the safety and security possessed by every believer.

3. THE APPOINTMENT OF LEVITICAL CITIES (21:1-42)

21:1-3. The last and crowning act of distribution was now described. The leaders of the tribe of Levi stepped forward and laid claim to the **towns** which had been promised to them by **Moses** (cf. Num. 35:1-8). These 48 towns **with pasturelands,** including the 6 towns of refuge, were now assigned to **the Levites.**

21:4-7. The distribution is described according to the three main branches of the tribe of Levi corresponding to Levi's three sons—**Kohath . . . Gershon,** and **Merari** (see the chart "Moses' Ancestry from Abraham," near Ex. 6:18).

21:8-19. **Thirteen** towns for the Kohathites were listed first. **Nine** were in the tribes of **Judah and Simeon,** including **Hebron (a city of refuge)** and **four** in the tribe of **Benjamin.** These 13 were **for the priests,** Aaron's **descendants.**

21:20-26. Ten more cities, including **Shechem (a city of refuge),** were assigned the other branches of the Kohathites in **Ephraim . . . Dan,** and western **Manasseh.** Thus the priestly cities fell ultimately within the Southern Kingdom of Judah where the temple would be built in its capital city, Jerusalem.

21:27-33. The 13 **Levite** cities **of the Gershonites** were located in eastern **Manasseh . . . Issachar . . . Asher,** and **Naphtali.** Two cities of refuge were included here, **Golan in Bashan** and **Kedesh in Galilee.**

21:34-40. The **Merarite** descendants of Levi received **12** cities in **Zebulun** and in the Transjordanian tribes of **Reuben** and **Gad,** including **Ramoth,** a city of refuge **in Gilead.** So 10 of the 48 Levite cities were east of the Jordan—2 in the half-tribe of Manasseh (v. 27), and 4 each in Reuben (vv. 36-37) and Gad (vv. 38-39).

This scattering of the tribe of Levi among the other tribes fulfilled Jacob's curse on Levi as well as Simeon (Gen. 49:5, 7) for their senseless murder of the Shechemites (Gen. 34). In the case of Levi's descendants God overruled to preserve their tribal identity and make them a blessing to all Israel. He did this because the Levites stood with Moses at a time of acute crisis (Ex. 32:26) and because Phinehas (a Levite and Eleazar's son) vindicated God's righteous name in the plains of Moab (Num. 25).

21:41-42. But at the time of the assignment many of the Levites' **towns** were under Canaanite control and had to be conquered. Apparently the **Levites** did not always succeed and the other tribes did not offer to help. This would appear to be the simplest explanation for the lack of complete correlation between the list of Levitical cities here and the list in 1 Chronicles 6:54-81. (See the chart on Levite towns on p. 599.)

The potential for good in the dispersion of Levites among the other tribes was almost unlimited. Moses, in his final blessing of the tribes, said of Levi, "He teaches Your precepts to Jacob and Your Law to Israel" (Deut. 33:10). The solemn responsibility and high privilege of the Levites was to instruct Israel in the Law of the Lord, to maintain the knowledge of His Word among the people. Especially in the north and east the Levites ought to have been barriers against the idolatry of Tyre and Sidon, as well as against the heathen practices of the desert tribes.

Someone has estimated that no one in Israel lived more than 10 miles from 1 of the 48 Levite towns. Thus every Israelite had nearby a man well-versed in the Law of Moses who could give advice and counsel on the many problems of religious, family, and political life. And it was essential that Israel obey the Word of God in all areas of life because without this their prosperity would cease and their privileges would be forfeited. But the final word is a sad one. The Levites did not live up to their potential; they did not fulfill their mission. If they had, idolatry and its corrupting influence might never have spread over the land of Israel.

4. SUMMARY OF THE CONQUEST AND DISTRIBUTION (21:43-45)

21:43-45. Here the long section describing the allocation of territories and towns ends. The historian looked back to the beginning and summarized the Conquest and division of the land with emphasis on the faithfulness of God. God had kept His promise to give Israel **the land. . . . rest on every side,** and victory over **their enemies.** In fact the Lord faithfully performed every part of His obligation; **not one of** His **promises . . . failed.** This did not mean that every corner of the land was in Israel's possession, for God Himself had told Israel they would conquer the land gradually (Deut. 7:22). Neither do these concluding statements ignore the tragedies that would develop during the period of the Judges, but those would be Israel's fault, not God's. Yet the unfaithfulness of Israel in no way impugned the faithfulness of God. Paul affirmed this fact in his words to Timothy, "If we are faithless, He will remain faithful, for He cannot disown Himself" (2 Tim. 2:13).

Some theologians have insisted that the statement in Joshua 21:43 means that the land promise of the Abrahamic Covenant was fulfilled then. But this cannot be true because later the Bible gives additional predictions about Israel possessing the land after the time of Joshua (e.g.,

Amos 9:14-15). Joshua 21:43, therefore, refers to the extent of the land as outlined in Numbers 34 and not to the ultimate extent as it will be in the messianic kingdom (Gen. 15:18-21). Also though Israel possessed the land at this time it was later dispossessed, whereas the Abrahamic Covenant promised Israel that she would possess the land forever (Gen. 17:8).

IV. Conclusion (chaps. 22–24)

A. A border dispute (chap. 22)

A rash and impetuous judgment when the Eastern tribes returned to their own inheritances threatened to bring the newly settled communities into a disastrous civil war. It was a dangerous and potentially explosive situation. The enemy lurked nearby, no doubt eagerly hoping that just such a divisive conflict would take place so they could regain their lost territories. But in God's providence the tragedy was averted and Israel learned some valuable and important lessons.

1. THE ADMONITION OF JOSHUA (22:1-8)

22:1-4. The Eastern tribes of Reuben, Gad, and **the half-tribe of Manasseh** had performed well. Called before their general, they were commended for keeping their word to God, **Moses,** and Joshua, by fighting alongside their **brothers** in all the struggles of the conquest of Canaan (cf. Num. 32; Josh. 1:16-18; 4:12-14). For seven long years these men were separated from their wives and families but now the battles were over, the land was divided, and it was time to go home. So Joshua dismissed those soldiers with honor.

22:5-8. As the weary but happy soldiers left, they took with them a substantial portion of spoils from the enemy, with instructions from Joshua to share **the plunder** with their **brothers** who had remained at home (v. 8). Extensive **wealth** was acquired by the soldiers, including **herds,** metals, and **clothing.** But why should those who had not endured any of the pain and peril of the conflict enjoy any of the spoils? Possibly many of the men who remained behind would have preferred to go to war, but who then would have raised the crops and protected the women and children? The principle was firmly established that honors and rewards do not go only to those who carry arms but also to those who stay home to perform the commonplace duties (1 Sam. 30:24).

The returning soldiers also left with six solemn exhortations by Joshua ringing in their ears: (a) **be very careful to keep the commandment and the Law,** (b) **love the LORD your God,** (c) **walk in all His ways,** (d) **obey His commands,** (e) **hold fast to Him, and** (f) **serve Him with all your heart and all your soul.** This charge, short but passionate, called for obedience, love, fellowship, and service. Their military obligations were fulfilled, but Joshua reminded them of their abiding spiritual commitments which were conditions for God's continued blessing. Like an anxious parent who sees a son or daughter leave home for a place where the young person would be separated from spiritual influences, Joshua delivered his earnest charge to the departing warriors. He was perhaps fearful that their separation from the rest of the tribes might cause them to drift away from worshiping the Lord and to embrace idolatry.

2. THE SYMBOLIC ACTION OF THE EASTERN TRIBES (22:9-11)

22:9-11. Leaving **Shiloh,** the armies of the Eastern tribes headed excitedly for home. As they approached the **Jordan** River their minds were probably flooded with memories of the miraculous crossing seven years before, of the remarkable victory over nearby Jericho, and of the other triumphs shared with their brothers from whom they had so recently separated. A sense of isolation from the other tribes began to sweep over them. But this was not simply because an ordinary river would separate the Eastern from the Western tribes, for the Jordan is not an ordinary river. Mountains on each side rise to heights above 2,000 feet and the Jordan Valley nestled in between is in effect a great trench 5 to 13 miles wide. During a part of the year the intense heat greatly discourages travelers. This then was a very pronounced river boundary and may have contributed to the fear of these tribesmen that they and their brethren would permanently drift apart. After all, "out of sight" is often "out of mind." What then could be done to keep alive the ties of comradeship forged by those long years of united struggles? What could be done to symbolize the unity between the people on both sides of the river, to remind everyone that they were all the children of the promise?

The answer suggesting itself to the minds of those soldiers was that they should build a huge **altar,** one that could be seen from a great distance, **an imposing altar** that would witness their right to the original altar at the tabernacle. So they erected such an altar **on the Israelite** (western) **side** of the Jordan River. Why did they not build some other kind of monument? Because they knew that the true basis of their unity was their common worship centered in the sacrifices at the altar.

3. THE THREAT OF WAR (22:12-20)

22:12. But the symbol of unity was misconstrued as a symbol of apostasy. When word reached the other tribes they **gathered at Shiloh,** the site of the one true altar (1 Sam. 4:3), prepared **to go to war against** the armies of the Eastern tribes. On the basis of what they had heard (Josh. 22:11) the Israelites concluded that this was rebellion against God, that the others had set up a second altar of sacrifice contrary to the Mosaic Law (Lev. 17:8-9).

"They thought the holiness of God was being threatened. So these men, who were sick of war said, 'The holiness of God demands no compromise.' I would to God that the church of the 20th century would learn this lesson. The holiness of the God who exists demands that there be no compromise in the area of truth" (Francis A. Schaeffer, *Joshua and the Flow of Biblical History,* p. 175).

22:13-14. Faced with apparent compromise and disobedience of God's commands the Israelites called for a war of judgment against their brothers. And though one must admire their zeal for truth and their jealousy for purity of worship, it is good that wisdom prevailed over rashness. A decision was made to begin by vigorously remonstrating the two and one-half tribes in the hope that they would abandon their project. War could thereby be avoided. Eleazar's son **Phinehas,** noted for his righteous zeal for the Lord (Num. 25:6-18), headed a deputation of **10** tribal rulers whose responsibility was to confront the others.

22:15-20. Arriving at the scene of the new altar the appointed group charged the Eastern tribesmen with turning **away from the Lord** (vv. 16, 18) and being **in rebellion against Him** (v. 16; cf. vv. 18-19). They reminded the easterners that **the sin of Peor** brought God's judgment on the whole nation (Num. 25), as did the sin of **Achan** (Josh. 22:20; cf. chap. 7). Now the entire congregation was in jeopardy again because of their daring act of rebellion. Such a sin would bring God's anger on the entire nation (22:18; cf. v. 20). Finally it was magnanimously suggested that if those in the two and one-half tribes felt the **land** east of Jordan was **defiled,** that is, not hallowed by God's presence, the Western tribes would make room for them on their side of Jordan. This was a generous, loving offer potentially involving great cost.

4. THE DEFENSE OF THE EASTERN TRIBES (22:21-29)

The Israelite delegation was about to learn how false her rash judgments and stern denunciations had been. The facts behind erecting the great altar by Jordan now came to light.

22:21-23. Instead of responding to the fierce reproof in anger, the Eastern tribes in candor and sincerity solemnly repudiated the charge that the altar they erected was in rebellion against God. Invoking **God** as a witness they swore twice by His three names—El, Elohim, Yahweh (**the Mighty One, God, the Lord**), affirming that **if** their act was **in rebellion** against God and His commands concerning worship they deserved His judgment.

22:24-25. Why then was the second altar built? They earnestly explained that it was occasioned by the geographic separation of their people and the effect this might have on future generations.

22:26-29. The Eastern tribesmen made it clear that they were fully aware of God's laws governing Israel's **worship;** their recently erected **altar** was **not** intended as a place **for burnt offerings and sacrifices** (cf. v. 23) **but as a witness** to all **generations** that the Transjordanian tribes had a right to cross the Jordan and worship at Shiloh. This **altar** was only a copy of the true worship center and an evidence of their right to frequent that one. While their concern for the spiritual welfare of future generations was admirable, it would appear that the action of the two and one-half tribes was unnecessary. God had ordained in the Law that all Israelite males were to appear at the sanctuary three times a year (Ex. 23:17). This, if heeded, would preserve the unity of all the tribes both spiritually and politically. Furthermore, the building of another altar was also a dangerous precedent. John J. Davis comments, "The unifying factor in ancient Israel was not her culture, architecture, economy, or even military objectives. The long-range unifying factor was her worship of Jehovah. When the central sanctuary was abandoned as the true place of worship, the tribes then developed independent sanctuaries, thus alienating themselves from other tribes and weakening their military potential. The effects of this trend are fully seen in the period of the Judges" (*Conquest and Crisis*, p. 87).

5. THE RECONCILIATION OF THE TRIBES (22:30-34)

22:30-34. There was a happy ending to this grave crisis. The explanation of the representatives of the Eastern tribes was fully accepted by **Phinehas** and his delegation as well as by the other tribes when report was made to them. In fact the nine and one-half tribes on the west of the Jordan **were glad . . . and praised God.** In concluding the whole matter **Phinehas** expressed deep gratitude that no sin had been committed and that the wrath of God was not incurred.

In a book describing the occupation and distribution of the Promised Land why should this single incident be treated in such detail? Simply because it illustrates certain principles that were vital to Israel living together in the land harmoniously and under God's full blessing. The same principles apply to those in God's family today:

1. It is commendable for believers to be zealous for the purity of the faith. Compromise of truth is always costly.

2. It is wrong to judge people's motives on the basis of circumstantial evidence. It is important to get all the facts, remembering that there are always two sides to every dispute.

3. Frank and open discussion will often clear the air and lead to reconciliation. But such a confrontation should be

approached in a spirit of gentleness, not arrogance (Gal. 6:1).

4. A person who is wrongly accused does well to remember the wise counsel of Solomon, "A gentle answer turns away wrath, but a harsh word stirs up anger" (Prov. 15:11).

B. The last days of Joshua (23:1–24:28)

The Book of Joshua ends with the old soldier saying farewell. His parting addresses were tinged with sadness, as are nearly everyone's last words. They expressed the deep concern of Joshua who observed a growing complacency on the part of Israel toward the remnants of the Canaanites, an easy acceptance of joint occupancy of the land which was to have been exclusively theirs. With Israel's enemies practically vanquished, Joshua knew well the danger of the people's "letting down." Before his departure from active leadership he felt compelled to warn them that continued obedience to God's commands was essential to continued enjoyment of His blessing. Though some have suggested that these final chapters contain two reports of the same event, it seems better to view chapter 23 as Joshua's challenge to Israel's leaders, and chapter 24 as his charge to the people.

1. JOSHUA'S FINAL CHALLENGE TO THE LEADERS (CHAP. 23)

a. The first round (23:1-8)

23:1-2. Some 10 or 20 years after the end of the Conquest and distribution of the land **Joshua . . . summoned** Israel's **leaders,** probably to Shiloh where the tabernacle was located, to warn them earnestly of the dangers of departing from Yahweh. It was a solemn meeting. No doubt Caleb was there, along with Eleazer the priest, and the soldiers of the Conquest who had exchanged their swords for plowshares and were now heads of families, **elders,** and **judges.**

They had come without hesitation in response to Joshua's call to hear the last words of their great chief. And the **old** veteran spoke on one theme—God's unfailing faithfulness to **Israel** and their corresponding responsibility to be faithful to Him. Three times he repeated his central message (vv. 3-8, 9-13, 14-16). Three times, fearful they would not hear and heed, he emphasized the faithfulness of

God and the responsibility of **Israel**.

23:3-5. Avoiding any temptation to elevate himself Joshua reminded the leaders of Israel that their enemies had been defeated solely because **the LORD their God** had **fought for** them. The battles were the Lord's, not his. A psalmist reiterated this affirmation (Ps. 44:3). As for the Canaanites, who still lingered about the country, **the LORD . . . God** would **push them out** also so that Israel could **take possession of** the **land** they partially occupied.

23:6-8. Turning to impress the Israelites with their responsibility, Joshua passed on the very words Yahweh had armed him with when He instructed him to cross the Jordan: **Be . . . strong; be careful to obey** (cf. 1:6-9). Courage and obedience were the graces that led to the successful Conquest of Canaan and they were no less essential now (cf. 22:5). Specifically Joshua dreaded Israel's conformity to the heathen **nations** around them so he forbade all contact and fraternization, knowing that his people would backslide step by step till in the course of their decline they would prostrate themselves before the shrines of the pagan deities (cf. 23:16). Instead he exhorted them **to hold fast to the LORD** (cf. 22:5).

b. The second round (23:9-13)

23:9-13. Returning to his theme Joshua again affirmed God's past faithfulness to Israel. Yahweh fought their battles for them (cf. v. 3), and though some of the Canaanites still remained in the land, wherever an enemy had been encountered he had been overcome.

Israel was then solemnly exhorted, on the basis of divine interventions on their behalf, **to love . . . God** (cf. 22:5). This would require diligence and watchfulness because of the near presence of their corrupt neighbors. The temptation would be strong to forsake Yahweh and cleave to the people of Canaan, even intermarrying **with them**, a fateful decision and one fraught with peril to Israel. This danger was graphically described by Joshua in terms of the dire results that would follow. First, **God** would **no longer drive out these nations** but they would remain to mar Israel's inheritance. Second, the Canaanites among them would be like **snares and traps** to entangle

them, **whips** to lash them, and **thorns** that fly back into their faces stabbing their **eyes**. Third, miseries and troubles would increase for Israel until they would be dispossessed of their **good land** (cf. 23:15-16.).

Joshua did not contemplate any possibility of neutrality as he posed the choice to be made. They would either go with Israel's God or the people of Canaan. So it is today. There is no middle course. "No one can serve two masters" (Matt. 6:24; cf. Matt. 12:30).

c. The third round (23:14-16)

23:14-16. Like a masterful preacher, Joshua restated his discourse, this time emphasizing that he was a dying man, hoping that this would make his words sink more deeply into their hearts. Once more he spoke of God's punctilious faithfulness to every promise (cf. **good promises** in 21:45); once more he warned of the doom caused by disobedience. Joshua's deep anxiety was about the nations that were left in the land. As the old soldier looked into the future he foresaw Israel's sinful compromise with them and the tragic fate that would inevitably overtake the people of God. God's **anger** would **burn against** them, and they would **perish from the** land (cf. **good land** in 23:13, 15-16).

The terrible climax of this message to the nation's leaders emphasized the fact that Israel's greatest danger was not military—it was moral and spiritual. If Joshua were alive today the strong likelihood is that he would say the same thing to this nation.

2. JOSHUA'S FINAL CHARGE TO THE PEOPLE (24:1-28)

Joshua's last meeting with the people took place at Shechem. Whether this second gathering occurred soon after the previous one, whether it was held on an anniversary of the earlier, or whether it was after a long interval cannot be determined.

The geographical setting is of interest. Shechem, a few miles northwest of Shiloh, was where Abraham first received the promise that God would give his seed the land of Canaan. Abraham responded by building an altar to demonstrate his faith in the one true God (Gen. 12:6-7). Jacob too stopped at Shechem on his return from Paddan Aram and buried there the idols his family had brought with them (Gen. 35:4). After the Israelites completed the first phase of the conquest of Canaan they journeyed to Shechem where Joshua built an altar to Yahweh, inscribed the Law of God on stone pillars, and reviewed these laws for all the people (Josh. 8:30-35). Joshua had good reason, therefore, to convene the Israelites at this location. Certainly the stones on which the Law had been written were still standing, vivid reminders of that significant event. From this moment on, that beautiful valley between Mount Ebal and Mount Gerizim would be associated with this poignant farewell scene as their honored leader spoke to them for the last time.

The literary form of this discourse has occasioned much interest and comment. It is now rather well known that the rulers of the Hittite Empire in this period (ca. 1450–1200 B.C.) established international agreements with their vassal states obligating them to serve the Hittite kings in faithfulness and obedience. These suzerainty (overlordship) treaties followed a regular pattern and required periodic renewal. Joshua 24 contains, in the standard suzerainty treaty form of that time, a covenant-renewal document in which the people of Israel were called on to confirm their covenant relationship with God (cf. "Structure" in *Introduction* to Deut.). The parts of the covenant renewal, like a suzerainty treaty, included a preamble (vv. 1-2a), a historical prologue (vv. 2b-13), the stipulations for the vassals with the consequences of disobedience (vv. 14-24), and the writing of the agreement (vv. 25-28). The Mosaic Covenant established at Sinai was not an everlasting covenant; hence it needed to be renewed in every generation. That renewal was now transacted in a formal and impressive ceremony.

a. Reviewing their blessings (24:1-13)

24:1-13. **God** was identified as the Author of the covenant and **Israel** as **the people** (vv. 1-2a). Following this preamble is the historical prologue (vv. 2b-13) in which Yahweh reviewed His past blessings on His subjects. He brought them out of Ur of the Chaldees (vv. 2b-4), **out of Egypt** (vv. 5-7), and into Canaan (vv. 8-13). Some have said **the hornet** (v.

12; Ex. 23:28; Deut. 7:20) refers to Egyptian armies that may have attacked Canaan before the Conquest. Others say the hornet refers figuratively to the panic experienced by the people of Canaan on hearing of what God had done for Israel (cf. Deut. 2:25; Josh. 2:10, 24; 5:1). Still others suggest that this referred to literal hornets.

It was God who spoke in this recapitulation of Israel's history; 18 times the personal pronoun "I" is used: **I took . . . I gave . . . I assigned . . . I sent . . . I afflicted . . . I brought . . . I delivered,** etc. Like a Hittite king reviewing the benevolent acts he had performed for his vassal subjects, God reviewed the marvelous deeds He had performed for Israel's benefit. Any greatness Israel achieved was not by her effort but through God's grace and enablement. From first to last Israel's conquests, deliverances, and prosperity were because of God's good mercies and were not of their own making.

b. Rehearsing their responsibilities (24:14-24)

24:14-15. The stipulations of the covenant renewal were then stated: Israel must **fear the Lord and serve Him.** In the Hittite treaties all other foreign alliances were to be rejected; so in this covenant Israel was to reject alliances with all foreign gods. Joshua boldly challenged them to **choose** between **the gods** of Ur their ancestors **worshiped** (cf. v. 2) **beyond the River** (i.e., the Euphrates), **the gods of the Amorites** in Canaan, and Yahweh. Then, adding example to exhortation, Israel's venerated leader assured them that whatever their choice his mind was made up, his course clear: **as for me and my household, we will serve the Lord.**

24:16-18. **The people** responded with alacrity, moved by the force of Joshua's arguments and the magnetism of his example. They despised the very thought of forsaking the **God** who had delivered them **out of Egypt . . . that land of slavery . . . protected** them in the wilderness, and brought them into the land of promise. "Perish the thought that we should ever be guilty of such ingratitude," was their instant reply. They promised that they too would **serve the Lord.**

24:19-21. Joshua spoke again. He

was not at all satisfied with their burst of enthusiasm. Did he detect some traces of insincerity? Had he hoped that the people would bring forth their idols for destruction as Jacob's family had done here some centuries before? (Gen. 35:4; Josh. 24:14, 23) There was no such response so Joshua bluntly declared, **You are not able to serve the LORD. He is a holy God; He is a jealous God. He will not forgive your rebellion and your sins.** Of course Joshua did not mean that God was not a God of forgiveness. He meant that God was not to be worshiped or served lightly, and that to **forsake** Him deliberately to **serve** idols would be a presumptuous, willful, high-handed sin for which there was no forgiveness under the Law (Num. 15:30). Such sin would result in **disaster.** Once more **the people** responded to Joshua's probing words, earnestly reaffirming their purpose to **serve** Yahweh.

24:22-24. Joshua spoke a third time, pointedly challenging them to serve as **witnesses against** themselves if they did turn aside from God. And the people immediately replied **Yes, we are witnesses.**

Joshua then spoke a fourth and final time, coming again to the point he had mentioned at the beginning. **Now then . . . throw away the foreign gods that are among you** (cf. v. 14). He had heard the pledge on their lips; now he challenged them to prove their sincerity by their works. Knowing that many of them were secretly practicing idolatry Joshua forthrightly demanded that they remove their foreign gods. Without the slightest hesitation the people shouted, **We will serve the LORD our God and obey Him.** They said they would be obedient servants of God, not slaves of Egypt or of other gods. (The words "serve," "served," and "serving" occur 13 times in vv. 14-24.)

There could be no mixing of allegiance to God with idol-worship. A firm choice had to be made then as in every generation. People must choose between expediency and principle, between this world and eternity, between God and idols (cf. 1 Thes. 1:9).

c. The reminders of their pledge (24:25-28)

24:25-26a. Realizing that further words would be fruitless, and semi-satisfied with the genuineness and sincerity of the people's consecration, **Joshua** sol-

emnly renewed the **covenant.** He wrote down their agreement **in the Book of the Law of God,** which was probably placed beside the ark of the covenant (cf. Deut. 31:24-27). Among the Hittites likewise the suzerainty treaty was placed in the sanctuary of the vassal state.

24:26b-27. As a final reminder Joshua also apparently inscribed the statutes of the covenant on **a large stone** slab which was **set up** beneath **the oak** at this sacred location. Archeologists excavating the site of Shechem have uncovered a great limestone pillar which may be identified with the memorial referred to here. Joshua **said** this **stone** was **a witness,** as if it had **heard all the** transactions of the covenant.

24:28. Thus leading **the people** of Israel in a sacred ritual of covenant renewal by which they pledged to fear and follow the Lord God, **Joshua** completed his last public act. With the memories of this solemn occasion indelibly impressed on their minds the Israelites returned to their homes in possession of their **inheritance.**

C. The appendix (24:29-33)

24:29-31. Three burials—each of them in Ephraim—mark the close of the Book of Joshua. First it is recorded that **Joshua . . . died at the** advanced **age of 110** years **and** was **buried in his** own town (cf. 19:50). No greater tribute could be paid to him than the fact that he was called simply **the servant of the LORD.** He aspired to no greater rank than this.

24:32. The burial of **Joseph's bones** is also recorded. His dying request was that he be buried in the Promised Land (Gen. 50:25). Moses, knowing of this request, took Joseph's bones with him in the Exodus (Ex. 13:19). Now after the long years of the wanderings and the Conquest, Joseph's remains, which had been embalmed in Egypt (Gen. 50:26) more than 400 years earlier, were now laid to rest in **Shechem** (cf. Gen. 33:18-20).

24:33. The third burial mentioned is that of the high priest **Eleazar, son** and successor **of Aaron.** It was his privilege to be associated with Joshua in the distribution of the land (Num. 34:17; Josh. 14:1; 19:51) and to direct the ministry of tabernacle worship in the crucial years of the Conquest and settlement of Canaan.

Recording three burials is a strange way to end a book like Joshua! But these three peaceful graves testify to the faithfulness of God, for Joshua, Joseph, and Eleazar once lived in a foreign nation where they received God's promise to take His people back to Canaan. Now all three were at rest within the Promised Land. God kept His word to Joshua, Joseph, and Eleazar—and to all Israel. And this encourages God's children today to count on God's unfailing faithfulness.

BIBLIOGRAPHY

Blaikie, William G. *The Book of Joshua.* The Expositor's Bible. New York: Hodder & Stoughton, n.d. Reprint. Minneapolis: Klock & Klock Christian Publishers, 1978.

Bush, George. *Notes on Joshua.* New York: Newman & Ivison, 1852. Reprint. Minneapolis: James & Klock Publishing Co., 1976.

Campbell, Donald K. *No Time for Neutrality.* Wheaton, Ill.: Scripture Press Publications, Victor Books, 1981.

Cohen, A. *Joshua and Judges.* London: Soncino Press, 1950.

Davis, John J. *Conquest and Crisis.* Grand Rapids: Baker Book House, 1969.

Garstang, John. *Joshua–Judges.* London: Constable & Co., 1931. Reprint. Grand Rapids: Kregel Publications, 1978.

Jensen, Irving L. *Joshua: Rest-Land Won.* Everyman's Bible Commentary. Chicago: Moody Press, 1966.

Kaufmann, Yehezkel. *The Biblical Account of the Conquest of Palestine.* Jerusalem: Magnes Press, 1953.

Miller, J. Maxwell, and Tucker, Gene M. *The Book of Joshua.* The Cambridge Bible Commentary. Cambridge: Cambridge University Press, 1974.

Pink, Arthur W. *Gleanings in Joshua.* Chicago: Moody Press, 1964.

Redpath, Alan. *Victorious Christian Living.* Westwood, N.J.: Fleming H. Revell Co., 1955.

Schaeffer, Francis A. *Joshua and the Flow of Biblical History.* Downers Grove, Ill.: Inter-Varsity Press, 1975.

Woudstra, Martin H. *The Book of Joshua.* The New International Commentary on the Old Testament. Grand Rapids: Wm. B. Eerdmans Publishing Co., 1981.

JUDGES

F. Duane Lindsey

INTRODUCTION

Title and Place in the Canon. The English title "The Book of Judges" can be traced back through the Latin (*Liber Judicum*) and the Greek Septuagint (*Kritai*, "Judges") to the Hebrew *šōp̄ᵉṭîm* ("judges"). The title is appropriate as long as the English concept of legal arbitration is expanded to general administrative authority including military deliverance from Israel's enemies.

In the English Bible the Book of Judges is found in those books popularly classified as "the historical books." In the Hebrew Bible it is placed in the division of "the Prophets" (preceded by "the Law" and followed by "the Writings"), specifically "the former Prophets" containing Joshua, Judges, Samuel, and Kings.

Authorship and Date of Writing. Internal evidence in the Book of Judges suggests that it was written during the early days of the monarchy—after the coronation of Saul (1051 B.C.) but before the conquest of Jerusalem by David (1004 B.C.). The following three facts support this suggestion: (1) The stylistic motto—"in those days Israel had no king"—repeated toward the end of the book (17:6; 18:1; 19:1; 21:25) looks backward from a period when Israel did have a king. (2) The statement about Jerusalem that "to this day the Jebusites live there" (1:21) is most clearly explained as written before David's conquest of the city (cf. 2 Sam. 5:6-7). (3) The reference to Canaanites in Gezer suggests a date before the time the Egyptians gave that city to Solomon's Egyptian wife as a wedding present (cf. 1 Kings 9:16).

Though there is no internal evidence identifying the author of Judges, the Talmud (Tractate *Baba Bathra* 14b) ascribes to Samuel the Books of Judges, Ruth, and Samuel. Though difficult to substantiate,

identifying Samuel as the author of Judges harmonizes with the internal evidence mentioned above and the known fact that Samuel was a writer (1 Sam. 10:25). Judges thus appears to have been written between about 1040 and 1020 B.C. Earlier sources, both written and oral, were no doubt used by the inspired author who chronicled this theologically selective history of Israel from the death of Joshua to the rise of the monarchy.

Chronology of the Period of the Judges. Scholars agree that the period of the Judges began with the death of Joshua and ended with the coronation of Saul and the beginning of the monarchy. But scholars differ on how much time elapsed between these two events. Since most scholars agree that the monarchy began under Saul in 1051 B.C., the debate centers on the date of Joshua's death. The problem concerns particularly the date of the Exodus under Moses which many conservative scholars place at 1446 B.C. while most liberal scholars maintain a later date (ca. 1280/60 B.C.). The conservative argument rests on the literal use of the numbers recorded in 1 Kings 6:1 and Judges 11:26. (See the *Introduction* to the Book of Ex. for a discussion of the date of the Exodus.) Scholars who follow the later date of the Exodus consequently date the period of the Judges from about 1220 to 1050 B.C., whereas many who accept the early date of the Exodus say the period of the Judges began about 1390–1350 B.C. and ended about 1050 B.C.

The evidence for beginning the period of the Judges about 1350 B.C. is strong (cf. Eugene H. Merrill, "Paul's Use of 'About 450 Years' in Acts 13:20," *Bibliotheca Sacra* 138. July-September 1981:249-50). The elders who outlived Joshua (Josh. 24:31; Jud. 2:7) would have been no more than 20 years of age in 1444 B.C. when the spies entered the land (Num. 13:2; 14:29), two years after the

Exodus. If they lived to about the age of 110 (Joshua's age at his death; Josh. 24:29), the oldest of them would have died about 1354 B.C. (Having been born in 1464 B.C. or later, and living no more than 110 years of age would date their deaths at 1354 B.C.) The idolatry leading to the first oppression (that by Cushan-Rishathaim, Jud. 3:8) seems to have begun *after* these elders died (2:7).

The next datable event recorded in Judges was the occupation of Gilead by the Ammonites. Jephthah said this took place 300 years (11:26) after the Israelite occupation of Transjordan (ca. 1406 B.C.). Thus 1106 B.C. marked either the beginning of Jephthah's judgeship (probably) or the beginning of the Ammonite invasion 18 years earlier (possibly). The dates of the judgeship of Samson (ca. 1105–1085 B.C.) and the leadership of Eli (ca. 1144–1104 B.C.), and Samuel (ca. 1104–1020 B.C.), can be reconstructed fairly accurately (with Samson's and Samuel's years overlapping) from the rather certain dates of Saul's reign (Merrill, pp. 250-2).

Insufficient evidence is available to support clearly any of the conflicting proposals regarding the *exact* dates for most of the other judges. Contrast, for example, the dates set forth by J. Barton Payne, "Chronology of the Old Testament," *Zondervan Pictorial Encyclopedia of the Bible*. Grand Rapids: Wm. B. Eerdmans Publishing Co., 1975, 1:829-45; Merrill F. Unger, *Archaelogy and the Old Testament*. Grand Rapids: Zondervan Publishing House, 1954, pp. 158-87; John C. Whitcomb, Jr., "Chart of Old Testament Patriarchs and Judges," Study-Graph, 3rd rev. ed. Chicago: Moody Press, 1968; and Leon J. Wood, *Distressing Days of the Judges*, pp. 10-21, 303-4, 341-2, 409-11.

Adding the length of the rule of each judge with its preceding oppression comes to 410 years (if the Philistine oppression and the judging by Samson are reckoned independently), a period too extended to fit the time between Joshua and Saul. Therefore scholars agree that the periods of some oppressions and judgeships overlapped. Such an overlapping of judges is to be expected since many (if not all) of the judges probably ruled in geographically limited portions of Israel.

Historical and Theological Setting. *Historically* the Book of Judges is the sequel to the Book of Joshua. The two books are linked together by the repeated record of Joshua's death (Jud. 2:6-9; cf. Josh. 24:29-31). Joshua's military achievements "broke the back" of the Canaanite military coalition throughout the land (Josh. 11:16-23) but left large areas yet to be possessed by the individual tribes (Josh. 13:1; Jud. 1:2-36). Canaanite enclaves raised their heads time and again during the period of the Judges (4:2). The book not only looks back to Joshua's victories but also looks forward to the establishment of the monarchy in Israel (cf. 17:6; 18:1; 19:1; 21:25; also cf. 8:23 with 1 Sam. 8:7; 12:12).

Theologically the period of the Judges formed a transition between Yahweh's mediatorial activity through Moses and Joshua and His mediatorial rule through the anointed kings of the monarchy. During the period of the Judges, Yahweh raised up His chosen deliverers whom He anointed with His Spirit to rescue His people Israel from their enemies. It seems ironic that Yahweh had previously given His people into the hands of these enemies as punishment for their sins (cf. comments on Jud. 3:1-6).

The Function of the Judges. The Hebrew word šōpēṭ ("judge, deliverer") has a wider connotation than the English word "judge." It was a general term for leadership combining the executive (including military) and judicial aspects of governing. Thus the judges of Israel were primarily military and civil leaders, with strictly judicial functions included as appropriate (cf. 4:5).

Purpose and Theme. The purpose of the Book of Judges was to demonstrate divine judgment on Israel's apostasy. More particularly the book recorded Israel's disobedience to Yahweh's kingship as mediated through her sovereignly appointed and Spirit-empowered leaders, and the subsequent need for a centralized hereditary kingship as the means through which Yahweh would continue to exercise His kingship over the nation Israel. Israel's disobedience to Yahweh and her worship of Canaanite gods resulted in her failure to experience divine blessing and the full conquest of her ene-

The Judges of Israel

Oppressors	Years of Oppression	Judges	Years of Judging	References
Arameans	8	1. Othniel	40	Judges 3:7-11
Moabites	18	2. Ehud	80	Judges 3:12-30
Philistines	?	3. Shamgar	?	Judges 3:31
Canaanites	20	4. Deborah	40	Judges 4–5
Midianites	7	5. Gideon*	40	Judges 6–8
?	?	6. Tola	23	Judges 10:1-2
?	?	7. Jair	22	Judges 10:3-5
Ammonites	18	8. Jephthah	6	Judges 10:6–12:7
?	?	9. Ibzan	7	Judges 12:8-10
?	?	10. Elon	10	Judges 12:11-12
?	?	11. Abdon	8	Judges 12:13-15
Philistines	40	12. Samson	20	Judges 13–16

*Abimelech, Gideon's son (Jud. 9), though often considered a judge, is not included here because he usurped authority over Shechem and God did not appoint him as judge.

mies (cf. 3:1-6). The Canaanite influence in moral and social areas led to Israelite apostasy and anarchy, demonstrating the need for a centralized hereditary monarchy in Israel.

OUTLINE

I. Prologue: Causes Introducing the Days of the Judges (1:1–2:5)
 A. The political-military background—the partial conquest of Canaan by Israel (chap. 1)
  1. The success of Judah and Simeon in conquering southern Canaan (1:1-20)
  2. The failure of Benjamin to displace the Jebusites (1:21)
  3. The partial success of the house of Joseph in occupying central Canaan (1:22-29)
  4. The failure of Israelite tribes in northern Canaan (1:30-33)
  5. The confinement of Dan to the hill country by the Amorites (1:34-36)
 B. The religious-spiritual background—the covenant of the Lord broken by Israel (2:1-5)
  1. The pronouncement by the

Angel of the Lord (2:1-3)
  2. The response by the people of Israel (2:4-5)
II. Documentary: Cases Exhibiting the Deeds of the Judges (2:6–16:31)
 A. The introduction to the history of the judges (2:6–3:6)
  1. A summary of the passing of Joshua (2:6-10)
  2. The pattern of the period of the Judges (2:11-19)
  3. The results of the broken covenant (2:20-23)
  4. The identification of the remaining nations (3:1-6)
 B. The description of the oppressions and deliverances (3:7–16:31)
  1. The deliverance by Othniel from the oppression of Cushan-Rishathaim (3:7-11)
  2. The deliverance by Ehud from the oppression of Eglon (3:12-30)
  3. The deliverance by Shamgar from the oppression of the Philistines (3:31)
  4. The deliverance by Deborah and Barak from the oppression of the Canaanites (chaps. 4–5)

5. The deliverance by Gideon from the oppression of the Midianites (6:1–8:32)
6. The judgeships of Tola and Jair following the usurpation of Abimelech (8:33–10:5)
7. The deliverance by Jephthah from the oppression of the Ammonites (10:6–12:7)
8. The judgeships of Ibzan, Elon, and Abdon (12:8-15)
9. The deliverance by Samson from the oppression of the Philistines (chaps. 13–16)
III. Epilogue: Conditions Illustrating the Days of the Judges (chaps. 17–21)
  A. Religious apostasy: The idolatry of Micah and the migration of the Danites (chaps. 17–18)
    1. The idolatry of Micah the Ephraimite (chap. 17)
    2. The migration of the Danites to the north (chap. 18)
  B. Moral degradation: The atrocity of Gibeah and the war with the Benjamites (chaps. 19–21)
    1. The atrocity against the concubine of the Levite (chap. 19)
    2. The war against the tribe of Benjamin (chap. 20)
    3. The preservation of the tribe of Benjamin (21:1-24)
    4. The characteristics of the period of the Judges (21:25)

COMMENTARY

I. Prologue: Causes Introducing the Days of the Judges (1:1–2:5)

The actual account of the heroic deeds of the judges is preceded by what amounts to two introductory sections (1:1–2:5 and 2:6–3:6). The second of these two sections, forming a theological analysis of the era of the Judges, is more properly the literary introduction to the rest of the book. However, it is preceded by a background introduction which treats both political-military features (the partial conquest of Canaan by Israel) and religious-spiritual factors (the broken covenant with Yahweh by Israel).

A major problem of interpretation which arises in this background section (1:1–2:5) is that of its chronological relationship to the death of Joshua. This

great leader's death (previously recorded in Josh. 24:29-31) is again narrated in summary fashion in Judges 2:6-10, especially verses 8-9. Judges 2:10 and following obviously refer to events experienced by the new generation which came to maturity after the death of Joshua. But how do the events of Judges 1:1–2:5 relate to Joshua's death? The book opens with the apparently unambiguous statement, "After the death of Joshua" (1:1), followed by a seeming sequence of events concerning the tribal occupation of Canaan. But if these events followed Joshua's death, why is Joshua's death narrated in 2:8?

Three answers are given to these questions. Some scholars regard all the events of 1:1–2:5 as taking place after Joshua's death, with the second introduction which begins in 2:6 providing a further recapitulation of his death. According to this view apparent parallels between Judges 1 and the Book of Joshua actually refer to two different series of events—the initial military achievements by the army of Israel under the leadership of Joshua, and the subsequent tribal possession of individual areas allotted by Joshua for actual occupation. This view faces many problems including the fact that when all the tribes of Israel were assembled by Joshua (Josh. 24:1), the tribes gathered from their allocated inheritances (Josh. 24:28), thus indicating that at least a significant degree of tribal occupation had already occurred (Josh. 15:13-19).

A second view regards at least Judges 1:11-15 (events associated with the conquest of Debir by Othniel) as parallel with Joshua 15:16-19. According to this view, the narrative in Judges 1 begins after the death of Joshua but changes (perhaps at v. 10) to the pluperfect tense (the tense distinction is a contextual decision in Heb.), and should read, for example, "they had advanced" (v. 10). Though this view is possible, it seems to disrupt the apparent sequence noted throughout the chapter.

A third view recognizes the opening phrase of the book ("After the death of Joshua") as a heading for the Book of Judges as a whole, with the actual events following Joshua's death not being narrated till after the record of that death in 2:8. This view poses fewer chronological

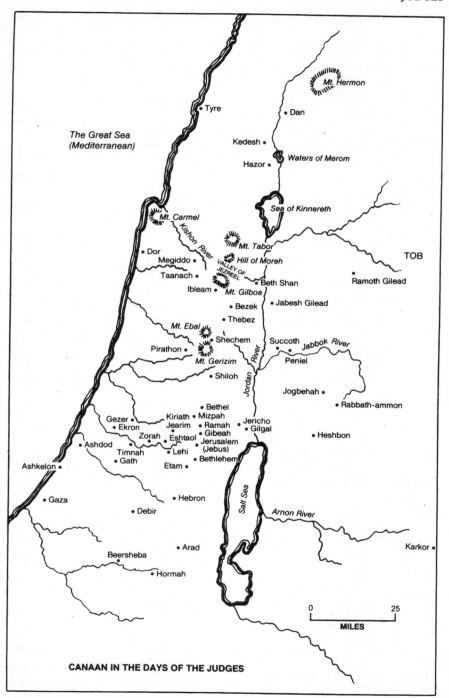

The Great Sea
(Mediterranean)

Mt. Hermon

Tyre

Dan

Kedesh

Waters of Merom

Hazor

Sea of Kinnereth

Mt. Carmel

Kishon River

Mt. Tabor

Dor

Hill of Moreh

TOB

Megiddo

VALLEY OF JEZREEL

Taanach

Beth Shan

Ramoth Gilead

Ibleam

Mt. Gilboa

Bezek

Jabesh Gilead

Thebez

Mt. Ebal

Shechem

Succoth

Jabbok River

Pirathon

Peniel

Mt. Gerizim

Shiloh

Jordan River

Jogbehah

Bethel

Mizpah

Rabbath-ammon

Gezer

Kiriath

Ramah

Jericho

Ekron

Jearim

Gibeah

Gilgal

Heshbon

Zorah

Eshtaol

Jerusalem
(Jebus)

Ashdod

Timnah

Lehi

Bethlehem

Ashkelon

Gath

Etam

Salt Sea

Gaza

Hebron

Debir

Arnon River

Arad

Karkor

Beersheba

Hormah

0   25
MILES

CANAAN IN THE DAYS OF THE JUDGES

problems, and it does justice to the flow of thought in chapter 1.

Whichever view is taken, it is clear that the tribal wars of occupation (chap. 1) occurred after the national wars of conquest under Joshua and his allotment of the tribal territories. Tribal possession of these territories surely began before Joshua's death, whether the record of Judges 1 refers to this phase of occupation or to a later phase of occupation after his death.

A. The political-military background—the partial conquest of Canaan by Israel (chap. 1)

1. THE SUCCESS OF JUDAH AND SIMEON IN CONQUERING SOUTHERN CANAAN (1:1-20)

a. The divine affirmation of Judah's primacy (1:1-2)

1:1-2. The Israelites' desire to **fight . . . the Canaanites** was in harmony with Joshua's command for them to occupy their allotted tribal territories (Josh. 18:3; 23:5). Though **the land** was given by God, and conquered under and divided by **Joshua,** it was still necessary for each tribe to fight to displace the Canaanites yet remaining. The method whereby they **asked** and **the LORD answered** is not specified, but probably involved the ministry of the high priest at the tabernacle, whether by use of the Urim and Thummim (cf. Ex. 28:30; Num. 27:21; 1 Sam. 14:37-43) or by a verbal form of divine guidance. God's selection of **Judah** (the names of the sons of Jacob throughout this chapter refer to tribal entities) for military preeminence corresponds with Judah's divine elevation in Jacob's patriarchal blessing (Gen. 49:8). On the location of the 12 tribes see the map "Land Allotted to Israel's Tribes" near Joshua 14.

b. The Judean agreement with Simeon (1:3)

1:3. The tribal military alliance of **Judah** and Simeon was a logical one since the **allotted** inheritance of **the Simeonites** was within the southern boundaries of the tribe of Judah (Josh. 19:1-9). Also Judah and Simeon had a natural bond as offspring of Jacob and Leah (Gen. 29:33-35). Their common enemy was **the Canaanites,** probably used here as a generic term for all the inhabitants of Canaan in the area west of the Jordan River. In a more restricted sense, the term "Canaanites" sometimes refers to the inhabitants of the coastal plain and the valleys, whereas the inhabitants of the hill country are sometimes designated as Amorites (Num. 13:29; cf. Jud. 1:34-36; 3:5).

c. The God-given victory at Bezek (1:4-7)

1:4-7. The LORD gave victory to **Judah** as they fought **the Canaanites and Perizzites.** The latter group may have been an indigenous people distinct from the Canaanites. Or the term may be social rather than ethnic, referring to "villagers." Judah defeated **10,000 men at Bezek,** probably the same Bezek (modern Khirbet Ibziq) in Manasseh south of Mount Gilboa where Saul mustered his army to attack the Ammonites at Jabesh Gilead (1 Sam. 11:8-11). **Adoni-Bezek** is probably a title meaning "prince of Bezek." However, some scholars identify the name with Adoni-Zedek, a king of Jerusalem (Josh. 10:1, 3). The barbarous act by which the Israelites **cut off his thumbs and big toes** was neither commanded nor commended by God; yet it was recognized by **Adoni-Bezek** as an act of divine retribution since he had done the same thing to **70 kings** (apparently over a long period of time). Though barbarous by modern standards, this act was pragmatic since the loss of the thumbs made it difficult to hold a weapon, and the loss of the big toes hindered one's footing in combat. Since the major function of a king was to lead in battle (cf. 2 Sam. 11:1), this mutilation apparently disqualified him from further royal office. His own people took him to the important Canaanite city-state of **Jerusalem** to live out his days.

d. The successful attack on Jerusalem (1:8)

1:8. Judah's initial success in destroying **Jerusalem** may refer only to the unfortified southwest hill (modern Mount Zion). In any case, **Judah** failed to displace the Jebusites permanently (cf. Josh. 15:63), and the Benjamites were not any more successful (Jud. 1:21).

e. The Judean conquest in the South and the West (1:9-20)

(1) A summary of the conquest. **1:9.** The region of Canaan south of Jerusalem, corresponding with the tribal allotment of **Judah** (including Simeon), is divided geographically into **the hill country** (the

central mountain range straddling the ridge route from Jerusalem to Hebron), **the Negev** (the semiarid transitional region running east and west from Beersheba), **and the western foothills** (lit., "the Shephelah"), lying between the hill country and the coastal plain (which is not mentioned till vv. 18-19).

(2) The conquest of Hebron. **1:10.** The former name of **Hebron** (meaning "confederacy") was **Kiriath Arba** (meaning "city of four," possibly suggesting an early confederacy of four cities), though some have identified it with Arba, the father of Anak, who may have founded the city (cf. Josh. 14:15; 15:13; 21:11; Jud. 1:20). Hebron is located about 19 miles south by southwest of Jerusalem in a valley lying about 2,800 feet above sea level. Hebron was well known to Abraham (Gen. 13:18) and would later become the Judean capital for the first seven and one-half years of David's reign (2 Sam. 5:5). The populous clans of **Sheshai, Ahiman, and Talmai,** who were descended from Anak (cf. Jud. 1:20; Josh. 15:14) and were indigenous to the south hill country (Num. 13:22, 28; Josh. 11:21-22), were **defeated** by the men of Judah in or near Hebron. Either on this or a previous occasion, Caleb was the leader in defeating Hebron (Jud. 1:20; cf. Josh. 15:14).

(3) The conquest of Debir. **1:11-15.** The strategic royal Canaanite city of **Debir** (cf. Josh. 10:38; 12:13) was at one time identified by scholars with Tell Beit Mirsim, about 11 miles west by southwest of Hebron, but has been more recently identified as Khirbet Rabud, eight miles southwest of Hebron. It is not known why its former name was **Kiriath Sepher** (meaning "city of writing"). **Caleb** had been promised Hebron by Moses because he was one of the two faithful spies who came back from Canaan (Num. 14:24; Josh. 14:6-15; Jud. 1:20). Debir seems also to have been allotted to Caleb, but after conquering Hebron, he enlisted other leaders for the attack on Debir. He did this by offering his **daughter Acsah in marriage to the man who** would undertake the capture of Debir. **Othniel,** Caleb's **younger brother** (or "nephew" if "younger brother" refers to **Kenaz**), captured the city and hopefully the heart of Acsah.

If Kenaz was the personal name of Othniel's father, he may have had the same mother as Caleb, whose father was "Jephunneh the Kenizzite" (Num. 32:12). Or "son of Kenaz" may mean "Kenizzite" (an Edomite clan associated with the tribe of Judah; cf. Gen. 36:11). Caleb and Othniel would still have been natural Judahites if their mother was of the tribe of Judah. Othniel's reward was the waiver of the customary gift to the bride's family. **Acsah** urged **Othniel** to seek **a field** from **Caleb, and** she herself requested **springs of water** as a bridal blessing (**special favor**) from her father. His abundant response was the gift of **the upper and lower springs.** It is noteworthy that the water supply system at Khirbet Rabud depended solely in the dry season on the upper and lower wells of 'Alaqa about two miles north of the site.

(4) The dwelling place of the Kenites. **1:16.** The Kenites were a nomadic people associated with the Amalekites (cf. 1 Sam. 15:6) and Midianites (cf. Ex. 18:1 with Jud. 1:16). **Moses' father-in-law,** Jethro, was a priest of Midian (Ex. 18:1). **The City of Palms** was the Jericho oasis (Deut. 34:3; Jud. 3:13). **The people of the Desert of Judah** may have been Amalekites. **Arad** (cf. Num. 21:1-3) is Tell Arad, 16 miles south of Hebron though some scholars identify the ancient Canaanite Arad with Tel el-Milḥ, another eight miles to the southwest.

(5) The conquest of Hormah. **1:17.** The Judahites joined **the Simeonites** (cf. v. 3) in attacking one of their allotted cities, **Zephath** (cf. Josh. 19:4), believed to be Tel Masos/Khirbet el-Meshash, about seven miles east of Beersheba. It had been taken earlier (Num. 21:2-3) but now **they totally destroyed the city.** "Totally destroyed" translates the Hebrew ḥāram, indicating a holy war in which a city and its occupants were totally "devoted" to destruction (cf. comments on Josh. 6:21). This was reflected in the name given the city—**Hormah** (meaning "devotion or "destruction").

(6) The victory over coastal cities. **1:18.** The cities of **Gaza, Ashkelon, and Ekron** (later associated with Ashdod and Gath in the Philistine pentapolis) were located on the coastal plain. That **Judah . . . took** these cities is contradicted by the Septuagint's "did not take," a translation perhaps influenced by the state-

ment in verse 19 that "they were unable to drive the people from the plains." But this does not negate Judah's initial victory over the cities; it only means that the **men of** Judah were unable to displace the inhabitants and occupy the cities.

(7) The restricted occupation of conquered cities. **1:19.** As **Judah . . . took possession of the hill country,** the LORD **was with** them (cf. v. 22). The stated reason for their inability **to drive the people from the plains** was not the Lord's absence but the enemies' **iron chariots,** introduced by the Philistines about 1200 B.C. But the author later records God's rebuke (2:2-3) which linked nondisplacement of the land's peoples to Israel's disobeying the Mosaic Covenant.

(8) The allotment of Hebron to Caleb. **1:20.** This summary statement relates the defeat of **Hebron** (v. 10) to the occupation of that city by **Caleb,** as **promised** by **Moses** (cf. Num. 14:24; Deut. 1:36; Josh. 14:9; 15:13). Caleb was apparently the leader of the men of Judah in the defeat of the three families **of Anak** (Jud. 1:10, 20).

2. THE FAILURE OF BENJAMIN TO DISPLACE THE JEBUSITES (1:21)

1:21. Jerusalem was located on the boundary between Judah and Benjamin. Following Judah's partial and/or temporary victory at Jerusalem (v. 8), **the Jebusites,** who could not be dislodged by **the Benjamites,** continued to dwell on the fortified southeast hill until the time of David (2 Sam. 5:6-9). **The Jebusites** were the Canaanite inhabitants of the city also known as Jebus (Jud. 19:10-11).

3. THE PARTIAL SUCCESS OF THE HOUSE OF JOSEPH IN OCCUPYING CENTRAL CANAAN (1:22-29)

a. *The success of the whole house of Joseph in conquering Bethel (1:22-26)*

1:22-26. The key to the victory of **the house of Joseph** (i.e., Ephraim and Manasseh; cf. Gen. 48) over the city of **Bethel** was that **the LORD was with them** (cf. Jud. 1:19). Their faith in Yahweh and obedience to His covenant stipulations for occupying Canaan brought victory from Him. Yet their failure to displace the Canaanites from other cities mentioned in verses 27-29 demonstrated a growing condition of disobedience and a lack of faith (cf. 2:1-5). **Bethel** ("house of

God"), a city rich in Israelite history (e.g., Gen. 12:8; 28:10-22; 35:1-15), was situated on the border between Ephraim and Benjamin in the central highlands 10 or 12 miles north of Jerusalem. It was strategically located on the north-south trade route, and was a junction for traffic from the Mediterranean seacoast on the west and from the Jordan Valley via Jericho on the east. Bethel has commonly been identified with modern Beitin about 12 miles north of Jerusalem, though some evidence favors el-Bireh 2 miles farther south (cf. David Livingston, "Location of Biblical Bethel and Ai Reconsidered," *Westminster Theological Journal* 33. November 1970:20-44; and "Traditional Site of Bethel Questioned," *Westminster Theological Journal* 34. November 1971:39-50).

When **the spies** who were sent to reconnoiter Bethel were unable to discover any hidden entrance to **the city,** they promised safety to an occupant who revealed the needed access. After the defeat of the city, this man took his family to northern Syria (i.e., **the land of the Hittites;** cf. Josh. 1:4), perhaps his ancestral home, where he established **a city** called **Luz,** named after the ancient name of Bethel (Jud. 1:23).

b. *The failure of Manasseh in occupying southern Jezreel (1:27-28)*

1:27-28. The determination of **the Canaanites** to remain in key cities guarding the Jezreel Valley was stronger than the faith of the tribe of **Manasseh** to displace them. Israel's eventual compromise to put the Canaanites to **forced labor** (cf. vv. 30, 33, 35) demonstrated the incomplete obedience that was characteristic of several tribes, as stated in the remainder of chapter 1. The cities are not listed in exact geographical sequence, which would be (from east to west) **Beth Shan,** strategically located east of the Harod Valley; **Ibleam . . . Taanach,** and **Megiddo,** guarding key entrances into the Jezreel Valley; and **Dor,** located on the coast south of Mount Carmel.

c. *The failure of Ephraim in displacing the Canaanites from Gezer (1:29)*

1:29. Gezer was strategically located on Ephraim's southwest border at the entrance to the Aijalon Valley. It guarded the crossroads of the eastern branch of the coastal highway and the major west-to-east route through the Aijalon Valley to Jerusalem or Bethel. Like Manasseh farther north, **Ephraim** allowed **the Canaanites . . . to live there among them** (cf. vv. 27-28).

4. THE FAILURE OF ISRAELITE TRIBES IN NORTHERN CANAAN (1:30-33)

a. Zebulun's failure to displace the Canaanites (1:30)

1:30. The incomplete obedience of **Zebulun** resembled that of Manasseh and Ephraim for they merely subjected **the Canaanites** of **Kitron** and **Nahalol** to **forced labor.** These unidentified cities may have been located on the northwestern edge of the Valley of Jezreel.

b. Asher's failure to displace the Canaanites (1:31-32)

1:31-32. The greater disobedience of **Asher** is evident in that **the people of Asher lived among the Canaanite inhabitants of the land** rather than merely putting to forced labor those whom they allowed to live among them, as Manasseh and Zebulun had done (cf. vv. 28, 30). The Canaanite cities listed in verse 31 were located in the area later known as Phoenicia.

c. Naphtali's failure to displace the Canaanites (1:33)

1:33. The tribe of **Naphtali** likewise **lived among the Canaanite inhabitants of the land,** though they did make **forced laborers** (cf. vv. 29-30, 35) of **those living in Beth Shemesh** and **Beth Anath.** Sites in both Upper and Lower Galilee have been suggested for these cities.

5. THE CONFINEMENT OF DAN TO THE HILL COUNTRY BY THE AMORITES (1:34-36)

1:34-36. The Amorites (cf. comments on v. 3) did not allow **the Danites . . . to come down into the plain** even though the Danites eventually put them to **forced labor** in the cities of the Shephelah. That the Amorites basically confined the Danites **to the hill country** eventually led to the migration of the Danites to Laish north of the Sea of Galilee (cf. chap. 18), for the reduced territory of Dan extended little more than four miles from **Aijalon** on the west, at the entrance to the hill country, to Dan's border with Benjamin on the east.

B. *The religious-spiritual background— the covenant of the Lord broken by Israel (2:1-5)*

1. THE PRONOUNCEMENT BY THE ANGEL OF THE LORD (2:1-3)

2:1a. The Angel of the LORD (Heb., *Yahweh*) **went up from Gilgal to Bokim.** The Angel of the Lord was not merely "an angel"; He was a theophany—an appearance of the second Person of the Trinity in visible and bodily form before the Incarnation. Prominent during the time of Moses (Ex. 3:2-15; Num. 22:22-35) and Joshua (Josh. 5:13-15), this divine manifestation also appeared during the period of the Judges to Gideon (Jud. 6:11-24) and to the parents of Samson (13:3-21). The Angel of the Lord was Deity for He was called Yahweh (e.g., Josh. 5:13-15; Jud. 6:11-24; Zech. 3) and God (e.g., Gen. 32:24-32; Ex. 3:4), and had divine attributes and prerogatives (cf. Gen. 16:13; 18:25; 48:16). Yet this Messenger of the Lord was also distinct from Yahweh, thus indicating a plurality of Persons within the Godhead (cf. Num. 20:16; Zech. 1:12-13). New Testament allusions suggest that the Angel of the Lord in the Old Testament was Jesus Christ (cf. John 12:41; 1 Cor. 10:4; John 8:56; Heb. 11:26).

"Gilgal" was where the Israelites first camped after they crossed the Jordan. There they were circumcised and dedicated to covenant faith and obedience (Josh. 5:2-12). Gilgal was near Jericho, and perhaps should be identified with Khirbet al-Mafjar about one and one-half miles northeast of Old Testament Jericho. The "oak of weeping" near Bethel (Gen. 35:8, NIV marg.) has been suggested as a possible site for "Bokim" ("weepers"), but that location remains uncertain.

2:1b-2. The Angel of the Lord obviously spoke as Yahweh Himself, for He used the covenantal formula to refer to His redemptive mercies in the Exodus and the gracious establishment of the Mosaic **Covenant** (cf. Ex. 19:4; 20:2; Josh. 24:2-13). He rehearsed the divine prohibition to the Israelites regarding Canaanite alliances (**you shall not make a covenant with the people of this land**) and idolatry (**you shall break down their altars**; cf. Ex. 23:32-33; 34:12-16; Num. 33:55; Deut. 7:2, 5, 16; 12:3). Then the Angel, speaking as Yahweh, affirmed the fact of Israel's disobedience (cf. the covenant with the Gibeonites, Josh. 9; and the continuance of the Canaanites in forced labor, Jud. 1:28, 30, 33, 35). God emphasized Israel's disobedience with a question designed to stir their consciences: **Why have you done this?** (cf. NEB, "Look what you have done!")

2:3. As a result of Israel's disobedience, the divine aid by which Israel would have driven out the Canaanites was withheld (cf. 2:20–3:6). Intermarriage with the Canaanites led to tolerance of and even participation in their idolatry. The form of their disobedience which incurred divine wrath became in turn the form of the punishment placed on them. The **snare** of Canaanite idolatry anticipated the cycles in the days of the Judges.

2. THE RESPONSE BY THE PEOPLE OF ISRAEL (2:4-5)

2:4-5. The weeping of **the Israelites** left little more than the place name (**Bokim,** "weeping") for it apparently did not express true repentance since the people did not turn permanently from their disobedience. The **sacrifices** offered **to the Lord** at Bokim seem to have been only an external ritual rather than an expression of true faith.

II. Documentary: Cases Exhibiting the Deeds of the Judges (2:6–16:31)

A. The introduction to the history of the judges (2:6–3:6)

This section further answers the question, Why were some Gentile nations left in the land? Whereas 1:1–2:5 forms a historical introduction to the book, this section is a literary introduction to the judges' deeds, telling the repeating cycles of history that formed the pattern during the rules of the Judges.

1. A SUMMARY OF THE PASSING OF JOSHUA (2:6-10)

Judges 2:6-9 corresponds with Joshua 24:29-31, thus linking together the close of the book of Conquest under Joshua and the book which records the deeds of the judges.

a. Israel's obedient years before and after Joshua's death (2:6-7)

2:6-7. Joshua's dismissing of Israel (cf. Josh. 24:28) apparently followed the covenant renewal ceremony at Shechem, described in Joshua 24:1-27. From Shechem each tribe was to return to its **own inheritance** to complete the occupation of the land, to eliminate the local inhabitants, and to destroy the pagan altars. In general this was accomplished as **the people served the Lord** for the period of time embracing the **lifetime of Joshua and of the elders who outlived him** (cf. Josh. 24:31). This service was a faithful response to **all the great things the Lord had done for Israel** in the Exodus from Egypt, the wilderness wanderings, and the initial Conquest of the land.

b. Joshua's obituary (2:8-9)

2:8-9. In contrast with Moses (cf. Josh. 1:1-9; Num. 27:12-23), **Joshua** died without appointing a successor, thus setting the stage for the period of the Judges. Joshua's epitaph, identifying him as **the servant of the Lord,** linked him with other theocratic servant-rulers (Moses, Josh. 1:1; the kings, 2 Sam. 3:18; 2 Chron. 32:16; and the promised Messiah, Isa. 52:13; 53:11). **At the age of 110,** Joshua **died** and was **buried** at **Timnath Heres** (also known as Timnath Serah, Josh. 19:50; 24:30), traditionally identified with Tibneh about 18 miles north by northwest of Jerusalem.

c. The rise of a new faithless generation (2:10)

2:10. The new **generation** of Israelites that **grew up** after their faithful fathers died was distinguished by its faithlessness toward the Lord. That they **knew neither the Lord nor what He had done for Israel** could imply a failure of the older generation to communicate God's acts to them (cf. Deut. 6:7). But the word "knew" probably has the sense of "acknowledge" (cf. Prov. 3:6, where "know" is trans. "acknowledge"), thus indicating unbelief rather than ignorance. They rejected both the Lord's grace toward them and their responsibilities toward Him. This led to the idolatrous practices cited in the verses that follow.

2. THE PATTERN OF THE PERIOD OF THE JUDGES (2:11-19)

A history of over three centuries is synthesized in these verses. The author directs attention to a recurring sequence of events in the period of the Judges (illustrated most clearly in the narrative about Othniel in 3:7-11): (a) the *sin* or rebellion of Israel through idolatry or apostasy (2:11-13, 17; 3:7, 12; 4:1; 6:1; 10:6; 13:1), (b) the *servitude* of Israel to foreign peoples due to retribution from the Lord (2:14-15; 3:8), (c) the *supplication* or repentance of Israel (3:9a; cf. 2:18), (d) the *salvation* (military deliverance) and restoration to favor by the Lord through a Spirit-empowered deliverer (judge, vv. 16-18; 3:9b-10), and (e) a period of *silence* when the people and the land had rest, that is, cessation of war (3:11). Before long, however, the pattern was repeated. Yet this was more than just a cycle; it was also a descending spiral (cf. 2:19).

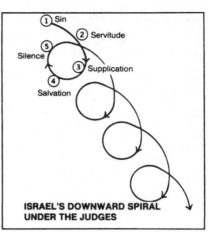

ISRAEL'S DOWNWARD SPIRAL UNDER THE JUDGES

a. The sin or defection of the Israelites (2:11-13)

2:11-13. Israel's sin is highlighted in terms of her forsaking **the Lord . . . who had brought them out of Egypt** and serving or worshiping the **various gods of the peoples around them** (v. 12), identified as **the Baals** (v. 11) or **Baal and the Ashtoreths** (v. 13). The word "baal," which can mean "lord" or "husband," corresponds with the analogy of idolatry as spiritual adultery (cf. v. 17). "Baal" was the Canaanite name for the Syrian god Hadad, god of storms and wars. The plural "Baals" (*beʿālîm*) suggests the many local varieties of the worship of Baal (cf. Baal Peor, Num. 25:3; Baal Gad, Josh. 11:17; Baal-Berith, Jud. 9:4; Baal-Zebub, 2 Kings 1:2). In Canaan the goddess Ashtoreth was the consort of Baal, known in Syria as 'Athtart and in Babylonia as Ishtar. (Cf. comments on a different goddess, Asherah, mentioned in Jud. 3:7.) Ashtoreth was the goddess of fertility. Baal worship involved the most debasing immorality imaginable.

b. The defeat and distress of the Israelites (2:14-15)

2:14-15. The Lord's (cf. v. 12) **anger** was His righteous response to Israel's sin and spiritual adultery. The vivid imagery of a slave dealer (**He sold them to their enemies**) indicates the severity of the divine displeasure the Lord manifested in chastening His people. These enemies were located **all around** Israel, as illustrated by the various **raiders who plun-**

dered **them** during the days of the Judges. Israel's defeat at the hands of her enemies (v. 15; cf. Lev. 26:17; Deut. 28:25, 48) was the result of **the hand of the Lord** and in response to the previous warning which **He had sworn to them.** Psalm 106:34-42 is a poetic paraphrase of Judges 2:11-15. Because of her defeats in battle, Israel was **in great distress.**

c. The deliverance by the judges (2:16-19)

This introductory summary of Israel's "pattern" in the days of the Judges does not specifically mention the supplication of Israel by which "they cried out to the Lord" but this is a recurring part of the pattern in 3:9, 15; 4:3; 6:6-7; 10:10. The supplication may be implied in 2:18 in that "they groaned under those who oppressed and afflicted them."

2:16. This summary statement of deliverance attributes it to **judges** whom **the Lord raised up** to save Israel **out of the hands of these raiders.**

2:17. It is not clear whether verse 17 refers to continued idolatry even during the period of rest in each judge's lifetime, or whether it views the period of the Judges as a whole, referring to the renewed spiral of disobedience after each judge's demise. In either case, Israel's sin is evident—they **prostituted themselves to other gods** and **turned from the way . . . of obedience to the Lord's commands.** Since the practices of those who worshiped the Canaanite fertility gods involved sexual prostitution, the phrase "prostituted themselves" was literal as well as figurative.

2:18-19. Once God had **raised up a judge,** the deliverance from the enemy was effective during the rest of that judge's lifetime because **the LORD had compassion on** His people. **But when the judge died,** Israel reactivated her downward spiral of progressive deterioration by following **ways even more corrupt than** the immediately preceding corrupt generation. (The "fathers" of v. 17 seems to refer to the obedient generation of Joshua's day, while the **fathers** of v. 19 refers to the preceding generation.)

3. THE RESULTS OF THE BROKEN COVENANT (2:20-23)

2:20-23. This paragraph, along with the next one (which identifies the remaining enemy nations still in the land, 3:1-6), concludes the theological analysis of the period of the Judges. Whereas the pattern identified in 2:11-19 related to surrounding nations that came in and plundered various tribes of Israel, 2:20–3:6 refers to Canaanite peoples already in the land which Israel failed to displace because of lack of faith and obedience.

The LORD allowed the Canaanite nations **to remain** in the land for four reasons: (1) He chose to punish Israel for her apostasy in turning to idolatry (2:2, 20-21; cf. Josh. 23:1-13). In identifying themselves with the peoples of the land through marriage and subsequent idolatry (cf. Jud. 3:6), the Israelites **violated the covenant** that the Lord gave **their forefathers** (cf. Josh. 23:16). Therefore, as God had promised (Josh. 23:4, 13), He would **no longer drive out before them any of the nations Joshua left when he died.** (2) The Lord left the Canaanites in the land **to test** Israel's faithfulness to Himself (Jud. 2:22; 3:4). This provided each generation with an opportunity to **keep the way of the LORD** (cf. "the way of obedience," 2:17) or to continue in the rebellion of their immediate ancestors. (3) The Lord left the Canaanites in the land to give Israel experience in warfare (see comments on 3:2). (4) Another reason is stated in Deuteronomy 7:20-24—to prevent the land from becoming a wilderness before Israel's population increased sufficiently to occupy the whole land.

4. THE IDENTIFICATION OF THE REMAINING NATIONS (3:1-6)

3:1-2. The list of remaining **nations** is prefaced with two of the reasons the Lord allowed them to remain in the land—**to test** the **Israelites** (previously indicated in 2:22; cf. 3:4), and **to teach warfare to the descendants of the Israelites who had not had previous battle experience,** that is, experience in the kind of "holy warfare" conducted during Joshua's conquest of the land. Thus "warfare" is probably not just "how to fight" but how to fight successfully, depending on the Lord to give the victory.

3:3. This list and the list in verse 5 both mention the Canaanites and the Hivites. **The Canaanites** are those peoples mentioned in 1:27-33. **The Hivites** are thought to be the Horites who were previously associated with the Upper Mesopotamian kingdom of Mittanni. The Horites who were best known in Joshua's time were the Gibeonites, the occupants of a confederacy of city-states including Gibeon (Josh. 9:7, 17). The Hivite people listed here lived **in the Lebanon mountains from Mount Baal Hermon to Lebo Hamath** (probably modern Lebweh in the Beqaa Valley 14 miles northeast of Baalbek). **The Philistines,** organized as a pentapolis (a confederacy of five cities), inhabited the southern coastal cities of Ashdod, Ashkelon, Ekron, Gath, and Gaza. Because of the prominence of the city of Sidon at this time, the Canaanite people known as the Phoenicians were also called **the Sidonians.**

3:4. This is the third time the Lord's purpose, **to test the Israelites,** is mentioned (cf. 2:22; 3:1).

3:5-6. **The Israelites** descended three steps in their cultural accommodation to paganism: (a) they **lived among the Canaanites,** (b) they intermarried with them, and (c) they **served their gods.** Each step is a natural one leading on to the next. The resulting departure from the Lord has already been described several times in connection with their oppression by foreign raiders (2:11-19). (On the Canaanites and **Hivites,** see comments on 3:3; on the **Hittites,** see comments on 1:26; on the **Amorites,** see comments on 1:3; on the **Perizzites,** see comments on 1:4; and on the **Jebusites,** see comments on 1:21.)

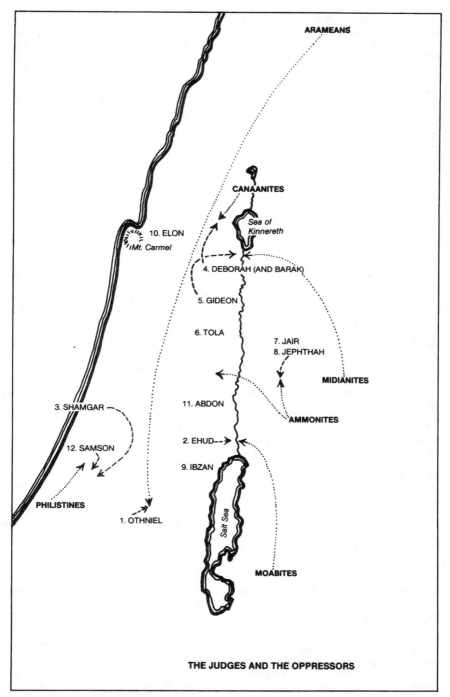

THE JUDGES AND THE OPPRESSORS

B. The description of the oppressions and deliverances (3:7–16:31)

1. THE DELIVERANCE BY OTHNIEL FROM THE OPPRESSION OF CUSHAN-RISHATHAIM (3:7-11)

This cameo description of Othniel's judgeship maximizes the literary structure and historical pattern of the heroic deeds of the judges while it minimizes the historical detail of this particular deliverance.

a. The defection of Israel (3:7)

3:7. The episode begins with mention of Israel's idolatry. This was a deliberate act of putting Yahweh out of mind and choosing to serve **the Baals** (cf. 2:11) **and the Asherahs** (wooden pillars or images used as objects of idolatrous worship; cf. Ex. 34:13; Deut. 16:21; Jud. 6:25). Asherah was the goddess of the sea in Ugaritic literature in Syria; she was the consort of El. Asherah should not be confused with Ashtoreth, the consort of Baal, in 2:13.

b. The distress under the Arameans (3:8)

3:8. Cushan-Rishathaim is a name meaning "Cushan of Double Wickedness." **Aram Naharaim** is literally "Syria of the Two Rivers," referring to Upper Mesopotamia. Since it seems strange for such a distant nation to plunder Israel, especially in the area of Judah where Othniel lived, some scholars have regarded "Aram" as an alteration of "Edom" (a slight difference in one Hebrew letter), which was located appropriately close to Judah in the south. However, it would not have been unusual for an ambitious **king** in Mesopotamia to invade Canaanite territory, especially at a time when Egypt to the southwest (which had nominal control over Canaan) was weak. In this case, Cushan subjected **the Israelites . . . for eight years.**

c. The deliverance by Othniel (3:9-10)

3:9-10. In response to Israel's supplication (**they cried out to the Lord**), Yahweh **raised up . . . Othniel** as **a deliverer** who, when **the Spirit of the Lord came upon him** (cf. 6:34; 11:29; 13:25; 14:6, 19; 15:14), **became Israel's judge and went to war.** Othniel had already been introduced (1:11-15) as **Caleb's younger brother** (cf. Josh. 15:13-19). As the Lord

sold the Israelites "into the hands of" the oppressing Arameans (Jud. 3:8), so also He gave the enemy **king . . . into the hands of Othniel.**

d. The duration of peace (3:11)

3:11. Thus **peace** was secured **for 40 years,** the remainder of the life of **Othniel.**

2. THE DELIVERANCE BY EHUD FROM THE OPPRESSION OF EGLON (3:12-30)

a. The defection of Israel (3:12a)

3:12a. The downward spiral began as **once again the Israelites did evil in the eyes of the Lord** (cf. v. 7). This evil was obviously their disobedience to the Mosaic Covenant, forsaking Yahweh to worship other gods (cf. 2:17, 19).

b. The distress under the Moabites (3:12b-14)

3:12b-14. Once again the sovereign control of God over human affairs is noted in that He **gave Eglon king of Moab power over Israel.** The Moabites were descendants of Lot by his older daughter's incestuous relationship with him (Gen. 19:30-38). They lived in the land east of the Dead Sea between the Arnon and Zered Rivers. They occupied the territory of Reuben to about 25 miles north of the Arnon, and then followed Joshua's route of entrance into the land and captured the Jericho oasis (**the City of Palms**). Israelites had apparently reoccupied Jericho but without refortifying it with city walls because of the curse on whoever did this (cf. Josh. 6:26).

The Moabites were aided in this conflict by **the Ammonites and Amalekites.** The Ammonites were the northeastern neighbors of the Moabites and were related to them as the descendants of Lot by his younger daughter (Gen. 19:38). The Amalekites were bitter enemies of Israel (cf. Ex. 17:8-13; Deut. 25:17-19) who lived a nomadic life in the land south of Beersheba. **The Israelites** (i.e., the Benjamites and perhaps some Ephraimites) **were subject to Eglon for 18 years.**

c. The deliverance by Ehud (3:15-29)

3:15a. Following the Israelites' supplication, **the Lord . . . gave them a deliverer—Ehud, a left-handed man.** The term "left-handed" is literally "one bound in the right hand." Left-handedness does not seem to have handicapped the Benjamites. In fact, they had 700 lefties who were excellent at slinging stones (cf. 20:16). In Ehud's case, being left-handed would provide an opportunity for a daring deed.

3:15b-19a. Since **the Israelites sent** Ehud **with** the **tribute** (probably consisting of domestic animals as well as gold or silver and other precious commodities), he was probably a recognized leader in Benjamin. He had personally **made a double-edged sword** (probably a dagger without a hilt) which was short enough (about 18 inches long) to be **strapped to his right thigh under** his long outer garment. After presenting the **tribute to Eglon . . . who was a very fat man** (cf. v. 22), **Ehud** dismissed his attendants who **carried** the heavy tribute, but immediately **turned back** at Gilgal to seek further audience with **King** Eglon. **The idols near Gilgal** were a well-known landmark, whether "idols" means "sculptured stones" (RSV) or "graven images" (ASV marg.). Possibly the reference is to the memorial of 12 stones which Joshua's men had taken from the Jordan River (Josh. 4:1-7).

3:19b-22. **Ehud** intrigued **the king** with the offer of **a secret message,** and so gained private access to Eglon in **the upper room of his summer palace.** Stating **I have a message from God for you,** Ehud plunged his hitherto concealed dagger **into the king's belly** so deeply that **the fat closed in over it.** The concealment of the dagger was accomplished by its unexpected location on Ehud's **right thigh,** from which he deftly grabbed it **with his left hand.**

3:23-26. Ehud's escape was well planned. To gain time he **locked** the **doors** of the king's **upper room,** and left undetected, or at least unhindered. His necessary time for escape was gained because the king's **servants** delayed outside his locked door, figuring that the king was **relieving himself** (lit., "covering his feet," a euphemism for body elimination; cf. 1 Sam. 24:3). When they realized they must be mistaken, they finally **unlocked** the **doors** and discovered their slain king. Meanwhile **Ehud** again **passed** the landmark (**idols;** cf. Jud. 3:19) at Gilgal **and escaped to Seirah** (an unidentified place in Ephraim).

3:27-29. By means of **a trumpet** blast, Ehud summoned Israelite men whom he led into battle against the disarrayed Moabites. He made no claims for himself but affirmed to the Israelites, **The LORD has given Moab, your enemy, into your hands.** His battle strategy was to seize **the fords of the Jordan** where the fleeing Moabites had to cross to return to their country. The Israelites **struck down about 10,000 Moabites** without allowing any to escape across the Jordan River.

d. The duration of peace (3:30)

3:30. The defeat of the Moabites was so decisive that they became **subject to Israel.** As a result of the deliverance through Ehud, **the land had peace** for an unprecedented **80 years,** the longest period of rest during the time of the Judges.

3. THE DELIVERANCE BY SHAMGAR FROM THE OPPRESSION OF THE PHILISTINES (3:31)

3:31. Shamgar's judgeship appears to have transpired after Ehud's deliverance but before his death (the historical notice in 4:1 continues after Ehud's death rather than after Shamgar's). The name **Shamgar** is Hurrian, but this may infer no more than Hurrian influence on his parents, not that he was a non-Israelite. That he **saved Israel** marks him out as a judge though the only item recorded is that he **struck down 600 Philistines with an oxgoad.** Whether this tally was a lifetime total or the number in a single episode is not indicated. His weapon was a sharp metal-tipped stick about 8 or 10 feet long used to direct animals. The other end usually had a chisel-like blade for cleaning a plow.

4. THE DELIVERANCE BY DEBORAH AND BARAK FROM THE OPPRESSION OF THE CANAANITES (CHAPS. 4–5)

The focus of attention switches to the Northern tribes (cf. 4:6; 5:14-15, 18) who were oppressed by a coalition of Canaanites united under Jabin of Hazor (4:2), apparently a descendant of King Hazor who was conquered by Joshua (Josh. 11:1-13). Unlike the preceding oppressions by foreign invaders, this one was instigated at the hands of the Canaanite population of the land, some of the same people that the Israelites had failed to drive out of northern Canaan (cf. Jud. 1:30-33).

a. The defection of Israel
(4:1)

4:1. That **the Israelites once again did evil** indicated their continuing tailspin into the idolatrous practices of the Canaanites (cf. 2:19; 3:7, 12). This defection seems to have reappeared only **after Ehud died,** indicating his positive influence in leading the people as judge. The dating of this chapter with the judgeship of Ehud suggests that Shamgar's deliverance of Israel (3:31) occurred during rather than after Ehud's period of leadership.

b. The distress under the Canaanites
(4:2-3)

4:2-3. About 200 years earlier **the Lord** had freed Israel from slavery in Egypt. Now, in contrast, He **sold them into the hands of** the Canaanites as punishment for their sins (cf. 2:14; 3:8; 1 Sam. 12:9). **Jabin** was probably a hereditary title (cf. a different Jabin in Josh. 11:1-13). **Hazor** (Tell el-Qedaḥ) was the most important northern Canaanite stronghold in northern Galilee about 8½ miles north of the Sea of Kinnereth (Galilee). Neither Hazor nor its king Jabin play an active role in the narrative in Judges 4–5, for attention is centered on **Sisera,** the Canaanite **commander** from **Harosheth Haggoyim** (cf. 4:13, 16) sometimes identified with Tell el-'Amar (located by a narrow gorge where the Kishon River enters the Plain of Acre about 10 miles northwest of Megiddo). The Canaanite oppression was severe because of their superior military force, spearheaded by **900 iron chariots** (cf. v. 13). The oppression lasted **for 20 years,** so that **the Israelites** again **cried to the Lord for help.**

c. The deliverance by Deborah and Barak
(4:4–5:31a)

(1) The leadership of Deborah. **4:4-5. Deborah** (whose name means "honeybee") was both **a prophetess** and a judge (she **was leading Israel**). She first functioned as a judge in deciding **disputes** at her **court,** located about 8 or 10 miles north of Jerusalem **between Ramah and Bethel in the hill country of Ephraim.** She was apparently an Ephraimite though some have linked her with the tribe of Issachar (cf. 5:15). Nothing else is known about her husband **Lappidoth** (meaning "torch," not to be identified

with Barak, meaning "lightning").

(2) The commissioning of Barak (4:6-9). **4:6-7.** Deborah summoned **Barak** who was from the town of **Kedesh in Naphtali,** a city of refuge (Josh. 20:7), usually identified as Tel Qedesh, five miles west by northwest of Lake Huleh, close to the Canaanite oppressors in Galilee. An alternate site, Khirbet el-Kidish on the eastern edge of the Jabneel Valley, about a mile from the southwest shore of the Sea of Galilee, is more closely located to Mount Tabor where the army of Israel was mustered by Barak. Deborah, speaking as the Lord's prophetess, commanded Barak to muster **10,000 men** from the tribes **of Naphtali and Zebulun and lead** them **to Mount Tabor.** Conical Mount Tabor rises to 1,300 feet and was strategically located at the juncture of the tribes of Naphtali, Zebulun, and Issachar in the northeast part of the Jezreel Valley. (Issachar, not mentioned in this chapter, is mentioned in Jud. 5:15.) Mount Tabor was a place of relative safety from the Canaanite **chariots** and a launching ground from which to attack the enemy below. The message from God informed Barak that He would be in sovereign control of the battle (**I will lure Sisera . . . and give him into your hands**).

4:8-9. Regardless of his motivation, Barak's conditional reply to Deborah (**if you don't go with me, I won't go**) was an unfitting response to a command from God. Perhaps **Barak** simply wanted to be assured of the divine presence in battle, represented by His prophetess-judge **Deborah.** It is noteworthy that Barak is listed among the heroes of faith (Heb. 11:32). **Deborah** agreed to go but said that Barak's conditional response to the divine command (**the way you are going about this**) was the basis for withholding the honor of victory over Sisera from **Barak** (**the Lord will hand Sisera over to a woman**). Barak no doubt thought she meant herself, but the statement was prophetic, anticipating the role of Jael (Jud. 4:21).

(3) The gathering of the troops. **4:10-13.** Accompanied by **Deborah,** Barak led **10,000 men** from the tribes of **Zebulun and Naphtali . . . to Mount Tabor.** Parenthetically (in anticipation of vv. 17-22), an explanation is given that the nomad, **Heber the Kenite, had left** his clan in

southern Judah (cf. 1:16) **and pitched his tent . . . near Kedesh.** On **Hobab** as **Moses' brother-in-law** (or father-in-law, NIV marg.), see comments on Numbers 10:29. When **Sisera** heard of Barak's action, he positioned his army with its **900 iron chariots** (cf. Jud. 4:3) near **the Kishon River,** probably in the vicinity of Megiddo or Taanach (cf. 5:19) in the Jezreel Valley.

(4) The defeat of the Canaanites. **4:14-16.** At Deborah's command **(Go!)** and encouragement (**the LORD has given Sisera into your hands**), **Barak** led his men **down Mount Tabor** against the much stronger forces of Sisera. As promised by **Deborah . . . the LORD routed Sisera and all his chariots and army.** The means used by God were both human (**by the sword**) and divine (bringing an unseasonable and violent storm that mired the chariots in the floodwaters of the Kishon; cf. 5:20-22). **Sisera abandoned his chariot and fled on foot,** apparently in a northeastern direction past Mount Tabor, while Barak's forces **pursued** the grounded Canaanites till **not a man was left.**

(5) The flight and death of Sisera. **4:17-22. Sisera . . . fled on foot** in the direction of Kedesh (a city of refuge) or perhaps Hazor, and ran toward the tents of **Heber the Kenite** who had **friendly relations** (*šālôm,* "peace") with **Jabin king of Hazor. Jael, the wife of Heber,** offered Sisera all the expected Near-Eastern hospitality, for she **covered him** either with a fly-net or with a rug for concealment, **gave him a drink** of milk, probably yogurt (cf. 5:25), and stood at **the tent** door to divert intruders as he slept. However, **Jael** apparently did not share her husband's allegiance to King Jabin, for as soon as Sisera was **fast asleep,** she took **a tent peg** and with a **hammer . . . drove** it **through his temple into the ground** (cf. 5:26), an unusual breach of Near-Eastern hospitality! Since Bedouin women had the task of pitching the tents, she was an expert with the implements she used. **Jael** then attracted the attention of **Barak** who was going **by in pursuit of Sisera,** and showed him the corpse. Thus Deborah's prophecy (cf. 4:9) was fulfilled, for two women received honor for the defeat of Sisera—Deborah who started it and Jael who finished it.

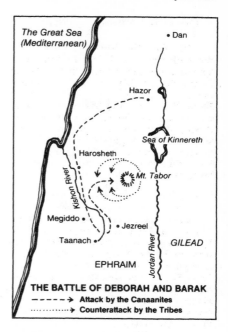

THE BATTLE OF DEBORAH AND BARAK
- - - - → Attack by the Canaanites
· · · · · · · · · · → Counterattack by the Tribes

(6) The destruction of Jabin. **4:23-24.** The defeat of Jabin's army initiated a period of constant decline in Galilee until **Canaanite** forces were no longer a threat to Israel.

(7) The hymn of victory (5:1-31a). **5:1.** This ancient poem, which may have been initially preserved in a collection such as "the Book of the Wars of the LORD" (Num. 21:14) or "the Book of Jashar" (Josh. 10:13), is literally a victory hymn (well known in examples from the 15th to 12th centuries B.C. in Egypt and Assyria). This hymn was no doubt written by **Deborah** herself (cf. Jud. 5:7-9) though **Barak** joined with her in voicing its theme (v. 1). With profound simplicity the hymn ascribes to Yahweh, the covenant God of Israel, victory over Sisera and the Canaanites. It also fills in a few incidental gaps in the narrative not given in chapter 4. It is noteworthy that the theme of blessing and cursing is prominent throughout. The victory hymn has five parts: (a) the heading of the hymn (5:1), (b) the praise by Deborah (vv. 2-11), (c) the muster of the tribes (vv. 12-18), (d) the defeat of the Canaanites (vv. 19-30), and (e) the concluding prayer of cursing and blessing (v. 31a).

5:2-5. The opening call to **praise the** LORD is related to the rise of the volunteer spirit in Israel among both **princes** and **people** (v. 2). A typical proclamation of praise (v. 3) is followed by a historical recital of the Lord's previous saving deeds (vv. 4-5). Yahweh is identified as **the One of Sinai** (cf. Ps. 68:8) and associated with events prior to the crossing of the Jordan under Joshua. The mention of **Seir** (cf. Deut. 33:2) and **Edom** (cf. Hab. 3:3, which mentions Teman, an Edomite town) has led some scholars to locate Mount Sinai just east of the Arabah Valley (south of the Dead Sea), but this is unlikely.

5:6-8. **Deborah** next described the contemporary situation of distress that gripped the Northern tribes of **Israel** (cf. 3:31; 4:2-3) till she **arose a mother in Israel.** Outside the fortified (walled) cities, Israelite **life** in the villages and on the roadways came to a standstill because of the oppression by the Canaanites, which came right up **to the city gates.** This distress was rooted in Israel's idolatry—**they chose new gods.**

5:9-11. Deborah praised God because of faithful leaders and **volunteers among the people** who responded in the time of crisis. She called on rich (**who ride on white donkeys**) and poor (**who walk along the road**) alike to hear the song of victory. The **righteous acts of the** LORD were those by which He had intervened to bring salvation and victory to His **people.**

5:12-18. The **song** of victory itself begins with a call for **Deborah** and **Barak** to initiate the action. Blessing is pronounced on those tribes that responded freely to the muster for battle—**Ephraim . . . Benjamin. . . . Makir** (a division of the tribe of Manasseh, usually the portion east of the Jordan but here perhaps the combined tribe or just the division west of the Jordan; cf. Num. 26:29; 27:1), **Zebulun,** and **Issachar** (Jud. 5:14-15). The explanation about Ephraim's **roots** being **in Amalek** (v. 14) apparently indicates that the Ephraimites lived in the central hill country previously occupied by the Amalekites. A series of taunts implying curses (cf. the curse on the Israelite city of Meroz in v. 23 for failing to render aid during the battle) is directed against the tribes of **Reuben. . . . Gilead** (apparently Gad and perhaps part of Manasseh),

Dan, and **Asher** (vv. 15-17). The tribes of **Zebulun** (cf. v. 14) and **Naphtali,** however, are praised for their parts in the battle (v. 18; cf. 4:6, 10).

5:19-22. The **kings of Canaan** were from the confederacy of Canaanite city-states under Jabin of Hazor whose army was commanded by Sisera. The battle zone included **Taanach** (located five miles southeast **of Megiddo**). The highly poetic language—**from the heavens the stars fought . . . against Sisera**—does not imply a belief that the stars caused rain, but simply affirms divine intervention in the battle. As implied in verse 21, God's intervention took the form of an unseasonable rain (the Canaanites would never have risked taking their chariots into marshy territory in the rainy season) which turned the dry riverbed of the **Kishon** into a raging torrent (cf. 1 Kings 18:40).

5:23-27. A **curse** was pronounced on **Meroz** (perhaps located on the route of Sisera's flight) for failure to aid in the battle, but a blessing was pronounced on **Jael** for her act of slaying Sisera (cf. 4:21-22), an act apparently regarded as expressing faithfulness to the covenant people of Israel with whom her clan had been identified through Moses. The vivid picture of Sisera's death (5:26-27) was not intended to narrate the steps of the physical action, but to describe metaphorically and in slow motion, so to speak, the fall of a leader.

5:28-30. The pathos of the fallen general is amplified by an ironic description of **Sisera's mother** awaiting the unrealizable return of her son from battle. Her anxiety—**Why is his chariot so long in coming?**—and the hopeful excuses of his delay made by one of her maidens and herself contrast vividly with the real situation.

5:31a. It is appropriate for a hymn describing Yahweh's victory over idolatrous enemies to conclude with a curse on evil **enemies** and a blessing on those who are faithful to Yahweh. To be **like the sun when it rises** means to have a life full of blessing.

d. The duration of peace (5:31b)

5:31b. The deliverance of Israel from Canaanite power under the judgeship of Deborah brought **peace** to **the land** for **40 years.**

5. THE DELIVERANCE BY GIDEON FROM THE
OPPRESSION OF THE MIDIANITES (6:1–8:32)

a. The defection of Israel (6:1a)

6:1a. The downward cycles (see the sketch near 2:11-15) of apostasy (**again the Israelites did evil in the eyes of the Lord;** cf. 3:7, 12; 4:1) and deliverance continued in the case of Gideon whose judgeship receives the most extensive narration in the Book of Judges (100 verses comprising three chapters). The story of Samson is comparable, consisting of 96 verses in four chapters.

b. The distress under the Midianites (6:1b-6)

6:1b-6. The **seven years** of oppression under **the hands of Midianites** was divine chastening for Israel's idolatry and evil practices. This relatively brief period of oppression was sandwiched in between two 40-year periods of peace (5:31; 8:28). The Midianites were descendants of Abraham and Keturah (Gen. 25:1-2) and were defeated by Israel during the wilderness wanderings (Num. 22:4; 25:16-18). They were a nomadic people who came from near the Gulf of Aqabah and ranged throughout the Arabah and Transjordania, apparently at this time subduing the Edomites, Moabites, and Ammonites as they crossed the Jordan into Canaan as far north as the Jezreel Valley (Jud. 6:33), and as far south and east as **Gaza** (v. 4), perhaps moving westward across the Jezreel Valley and southward along the coastal plain.

The strength of Midianite oppression forced **the Israelites** to hide **themselves** and their produce **in mountain clefts, caves, and strongholds.** However, this was not a continual occupation (like the preceding one of the Canaanites) but a seasonal invasion at harvesttime, **whenever the Israelites planted their crops.** The Midianites' major goal was the appropriation of **the crops** for themselves and their animals. But the cumulative effect of these invasions on Israelite agriculture and food cycles was devastating. Midianite allies included the **Amalekites** (from south of Judah; cf. 3:13) **and other eastern peoples,** a general term for the nomads of the Syrian desert, possibly including some Ammonites and Edomites. On these annual predatory invasions, in typical nomadic style, the oppressors **camped on the land** in such numbers and with such devastation that

they were compared to **swarms of locusts** (cf. 7:12). The Midianites and their allies traveled on innumerable **camels** (cf. 7:12) whose range of distance and speed (as high as 100 miles per day) made them a formidable long-range military threat. This is the first reference to an organized raid using camels (cf. Gen. 24:10-11). The impoverishment that came to Israel drove her to cry **out to the Lord for help.** This cry does not seem to have been an indication of repentance for sin because they apparently were not aware of the moral cause behind the enemy's oppression until the Lord sent a prophet to point this out (cf. Jud. 6:7-10).

c. The deliverance by Gideon (6:7–8:27)

(1) The censure of Israel by a prophet. **6:7-10. The Lord . . . sent** an unnamed **prophet** (the only prophet mentioned in the book besides the Prophetess Deborah) to remind Israel of her covenant obligations to **the Lord,** who had delivered them from **Egypt** (cf. Ex. 34:10-16; Deut. 7; Jud. 3:5-6), **not to worship the gods of the Amorites.** The prophet rebuked them for their continued disobedience (**But you have not listened to Me** [God]). This message is similar to that from the Angel of the Lord at Bokim (cf. 2:1-3).

(2) The call of Gideon by the Angel of the Lord (6:11-24). **6:11-12a.** The story of Gideon is introduced not by an affirmation that "God raised up a deliverer named Gideon," but rather by a narration of *how* God raised him up. Gideon's call or commission resulted from a confrontation with **the Angel of the Lord** (who is "the Lord," v. 14; cf. comments on 2:1), who appeared to him as a sojourning stranger and **sat down under the oak in Ophrah.** Since Gideon's father **Joash** was an **Abiezrite** (a clan of Manasseh, Josh. 17:2), this Ophrah was not the place located in Benjamin but rather a northern site possibly near the border of Manasseh in the Jezreel Valley. Possible site identifications are el-Affula (six miles east of Megiddo) or et-Taiyiba (Hapharaim, eight miles northwest of Beth Shan). Gideon's act of **threshing wheat in a winepress** reflected both his fear of discovery by **the Midianites** and the smallness of his harvest. Normally wheat was threshed (the grain separated from the wheat stalks) in an open area on

a threshing floor (cf. 1 Chron. 21:20-23) by oxen pulling threshing sledges over the stalks.

6:12b-13. The Angel's introductory remark affirmed the Lord's presence with **Gideon (you** is sing.) and described Gideon as a **mighty warrior** ("mighty man of valor," KJV; the words *gibbôr ḥāyil* are also applied to Jephthah, 11:1; and to Boaz, Ruth 2:1). Though this description may have been spoken in satire (at this point Gideon was anything but a mighty warrior!), it probably reflected Gideon's potentiality through divine enablement, as well as expressing his notable rank in the community.

Gideon's initial response ignored the singular pronoun "you" (Jud. 6:12), for he replied, **If the LORD is with us** (pl. pronoun). Gideon questioned the divine promise in view of his people's present circumstances. He correctly concluded, however, that **the LORD** had **put** them **into the hand of Midian.**

6:14. "The Angel of the LORD" (vv. 11-12) now spoke as **the LORD** and commissioned Gideon to **Go . . . and save Israel out of Midian's hand.** The words **the strength you have** perhaps assumed the divine presence previously mentioned (v. 12).

6:15. But, Gideon objected, **My clan is the weakest . . . and I am the least.** This objection might have stemmed from typical Near-Eastern humility, but perhaps it also reflected a good amount of reality.

6:16. God's reassurance reaffirmed His presence with Gideon (**I will be with you**) and the ease with which he would accomplish victory over **the Midianites** (**as if they were but one man**).

6:17-21. Gideon requested **a sign** to confirm the Lord's promise. This request was granted (cf. v. 21). Meanwhile Gideon's uncertainty regarding the exact identity of his supernatural Visitor prompted him to offer typical Near-Eastern hospitality. The word for **offering** or gift (*minḥâh*), which he proposed to **set . . . before** the Visitor, could refer to a freewill offering in Israel's sacrificial system, or it could refer to tribute offered as a present to a king or other superior (cf. 3:15). The large amount of food prepared by Gideon—goat's **meat** and **broth,** and **bread** made **from an ephah** (one-half bushel) **of flour**—reflected both

his wealth in a destitute time and the typical excessiveness of Near-Eastern hospitality. He no doubt planned to take the leftovers home for his family! But **the Angel of the LORD touched** the food offering **with the tip of** His **staff** and consumed it by **fire,** thus providing the sign Gideon had requested (6:17; cf. Lev. 9:24; 1 Kings 18:38). Then **the Angel . . . disappeared.**

6:22-24. Gideon's consternation probably reflected his fear of impending death because of seeing the divine presence (cf. Ex. 33:20). When **the LORD** assured **Gideon** he was **not going to die . . . Gideon built an altar** and named it **the LORD is Peace.**

(3) The destruction of Baal's altar by Gideon (6:25-32). **6:25-26. The LORD** gave Gideon a test of obedience. If Gideon was to deliver Israel from the Midianites, he must not only achieve military victory over the enemy but also must remove the cause of idolatry which initially led the Lord to give His people over to the Midianites (cf. v. 1). Therefore God commanded Gideon to destroy his **father's altar to Baal** with its accompanying **Asherah pole** (a cult object probably representing Asherah, Ugaritic goddess of the sea; cf. comments on 3:7). Gideon was then to construct **a proper kind of altar to the LORD,** kindle a fire with **the wood of the Asherah pole,** and offer one of his father's bulls (probably intended originally as a sacrificial animal for Baal) **as a burnt offering** to the Lord.

6:27. Gideon's obedience to God's command should not be minimized by his use of **10 . . . servants** (dismantling a Canaanite altar was a massive task), or by the fact that **he did it at night** (the Baal-worshipers would obviously have prevented it if he had tried to do this during the day).

6:28-32. The resultant hostility of the community against Gideon was defused by his father's sage advice. Their investigation of the overnight vandalism quickly implicated **Gideon,** whose execution they demanded. **But Joash,** perhaps repentant and inspired by his son's remarkable actions, wisely proclaimed, **If Baal really is a god, he can defend himself.** Perhaps this implied that the people should not overstep Baal's prerogative of self-defense (cf. Elijah's irony about **Baal,** 1 Kings 18:27). This wise advice appealed to the people who then **called Gideon** by the name of **Jerub-Baal,** meaning **Let Baal contend.** Though they apparently applied the name derogatively, it might have later assumed an honorable signification as a witness against Baal's inability to defend himself (cf. Jud. 7:1; 8:29; and comments on Jerub-Baal in 9:1).

(4) The preparation of Gideon for battle. **6:33-35.** Gideon's commission by the Lord seems to have preceded the next (and final) annual invasion of **the Midianites** and their allies. They **crossed . . . the Jordan** River not far south of the Sea of Kinnereth **and camped** in typical Bedouin fashion in the rich agricultural area of the Jezreel Valley. The Lord's deliverance of His people through Gideon began as **the Spirit of the LORD came upon Gideon** (cf. 3:10; 11:29; 13:25; 14:6, 19; 15:14), providing divine enablement through the Holy Spirit's personal presence. Gideon immediately began to muster men, summoning his Abiezrite clan (cf. 6:11, 24) with **a trumpet** and the rest of the tribe of **Manasseh** along with the tribes of **Asher, Zebulun, and Naphtali** by means of **messengers.**

(5) The signs concerning the fleece of Gideon. **6:36-40.** Gideon's apparent lack of faith in seeking a miraculous sign from **God** (cf. Matt. 12:38; 1 Cor. 1:22-23) seems strange for a man who is listed among the heroes of faith (Heb. 11:32). In fact **Gideon** already had a sign from God at the time of his commission (Jud. 6:17, 21). It is noteworthy, however, that Gideon was not using the **fleece** to discover God's will, for he already knew from divine revelation what God wanted him to do (v. 14). The sign related to a confirmation or assurance of God's presence or empowerment for the task at hand. **God** condescended to Gideon's weak faith and saturated the **wool fleece** with **dew,** so much so that Gideon **wrung out . . . a bowlful of water.** Perhaps **Gideon** had second thoughts about the uniqueness of this event since the surrounding **threshing floor** might naturally dry before the fleece. So he requested the opposite— **This time make the fleece dry and the ground covered with dew.** God patiently **did so,** and Gideon was reassured to continue his assignment.

(6) The reduction of the army of Gideon (7:1-8a). **7:1-2. Gideon . . . camped at the spring of Harod** (probably En

Harod at the foot of Mount Gilboa, a spring that winds eastward to the Jordan River through the Harod Valley) with all his men, who numbered 32,000 (v. 3). The Midianite force of 135,000 (cf. 8:10) was camped three or four miles **north of them** at the foot of **the hill of Moreh,** the prominent hill rising like a sentinel to guard the eastern entrance to the Jezreel Valley. God, whose **strength** does not depend on numbers (cf. Ps. 33:16), purposed to **deliver Midian** to Israel through a few men so Israel would **not boast** that they had won the battle themselves. **Gideon** was no doubt perplexed by God's words, **You have too many men.**

7:3-6. The means by which the size of Gideon's force was reduced was twofold: (a) **22,000** fearful recruits were summarily dismissed (in harmony with Deut. 20:8) and allowed to return to their homes; and (b) 9,700 apparently lesswatchful men who failed a simple test were also discharged (Jud. 7:4-8; or at least were granted a leave of absence; cf. v. 23).

The permission to **leave Mount Gilead** is puzzling since Gilead was across the Jordan River to the east. Some scholars view "Gilead" as an early copyist's error for "Gilboa," the mount near Gideon's army. Or another Mount Gilead may have been nearby, since some of Gilead's descendants lived on the western side of Jordan. Though the test given to the 9,700 seems simple enough, the words describing it are somewhat ambiguous. As **the men** drank from the spring, **Gideon** was to **separate those who lap the water with their tongues like a dog from those who kneel down to drink.** But how does one "lap . . . like a dog" without "kneel[ing] down" to place his face near the water? Some writers have suggested that a "non-kneeler" scooped the water up in one hand (holding his weapon in the other) from which he **lapped** the water with his tongue. Others have suggested that each used his hand to bring the water to his mouth much as a dog uses his tongue to bring water to his mouth. Whatever the explanation, the test probably identified those who were watchful, though some think it was strictly an arbitrary test for reducing the number of men. Historian Josephus even believed the **300 men** who passed the test were less watchful, which resulted in a greater recognition of God's power.

7:7-8a. *Now with just a few fighters,* Gideon was again reassured by a divine promise: *With the 300 men . . . I will save you and give the Midianites into your hands* (cf. 6:14). Gideon's 300 men acquired *the provisions and trumpets of* those who returned *to their tents.*

(7) The encouragement of Gideon concerning victory (7:8b-15). **7:8b-11a.** In spite of all the encouragement and assurance previously given Gideon, the Lord knew that he was *afraid to attack,* so God provided two further means of encouragement: (a) a direct divine word (*go down against the camp, because I am going to give it into your hands;* cf. vv. 7, 14-15), and (b) a providentially planned dream narrated by a Midianite and overheard by Gideon (vv. 13-14).

7:11b-15. Gideon *and Purah his servant* stalked the outskirts of the Midianite *camp* with its innumerable tents spread out *in the valley* like *locusts* (cf. 6:5), tents which were outnumbered only by the myriads of *camels* (cf. 6:5). A beautiful demonstration of God's providence was exhibited: Gideon arrived just *as a man was telling a friend his dream* about *a round loaf of barley bread* which *came tumbling into the Midianite camp* and *overturned* a tent which it struck. The other Midianite *responded,* perhaps in jest, that *this* must refer to *the sword of Gideon . . . the Israelite* into whose hands *God has given* us *Midianites.* However, the divinely intended symbolism is clear (barley bread aptly described the poverty-stricken Israelites, and the tent referred to the nomadic Midianites). Gideon correctly understood it as an encouragement from the Lord that *Israel* would be victorious over Midian. Spontaneously worshiping *God* after this message, Gideon *returned to the* Israelite *camp* and proceeded immediately to marshal his forces, passing on to them the same assurance God had given him— *The Lord has given the Midianite camp into your hands* (cf. 7:7, 9, 14).

(8) The victory over the Midianites by Gideon. **7:16-22.** Gideon divided his small band *into three companies* of men, whose strategic but strange weapons were *trumpets and empty jars . . . with torches inside.* They arrived at the edge of the Midianite *camp* at the providential time of *the beginning of the middle*

watch (10:00 P.M.), **just after they had changed the guard** (when the retiring guards would still be milling about their tents). In Gideon's day the first watch was from 6 P.M. to 10 P.M.; the middle watch was from 10 P.M. to 2 A.M.; and the morning watch started at 2 A.M. and went to 6 A.M.

At this critical moment the Israelites **blew their trumpets and broke the jars** (both making a terrible noise and revealing the glowing torches), and **shouted** loudly, **A sword for the Lord and for Gideon!** This battle cry indicated their confidence in the Lord to give them victory and also identified them to the Midianites and aroused fear in them. The word for **trumpets** is šôp̄ārôṯ, "made from animal horns"; they gave a sharp, shrill sound. The jars were pitchers probably made of clay. The confusion in the Midianite camp was unbelievable as they imagined a much larger Israelite force attacking them and as they perhaps mistook their own retiring guards for Israelites. This divinely planned confusion caused the Midianites **to turn on each other with their swords** while the Israelites apparently watched in safety **around the camp.** The Midianite **army fled to** the southeast to **Beth Shittah** (an immediate field site) and **Abel Meholah** toward the Jordan River. Abel Meholah was perhaps Tell Abu Sus, about 24 miles south of the Sea of Kinnereth (Galilee). (Abel Meholah was where Elisha was living when Elijah called him to be his protégé, 1 Kings 19:16.) The army apparently fled in that direction in order to cross the Jordan to reach **Zererah** (possibly Zarethan or Tell es-Saidiya) and **Tabbath** (Ras Abu Ṭalbat).

(9) The summons of Gideon for reinforcements. **7:23-24a.** Gideon summoned reinforcements **from Naphtali, Asher, and all Manasseh** to pursue the fleeing **Midianites.** Those who responded probably included the earlier contingents of Gideon's men who had been dismissed. Gideon also requested aid of the Ephraimites, who were well situated, to cut off **the Midianites** at strategic locations, preventing them from fording **the Jordan** River.

(10) The capture of Oreb and Zeeb by the Ephraimites. **7:24b-25.** The men of Ephraim quickly secured the fords **of the Jordan** (the site of **Beth Barah** is cur-

rently unknown) and **also captured two of the Midianite leaders, Oreb** (meaning "raven") **and Zeeb** (meaning "wolf"), whose **heads** they brought **to** Gideon according to typical Near-Eastern military practice.

(11) The diplomacy of Gideon toward the Ephraimites. **8:1-3.** However, **the Ephraimites . . . criticized** Gideon **sharply** for not inviting them to participate in the initial conflict near the Hill of Moreh (7:1). The "gentle answer" of **Gideon** (cf. Prov. 15:1) demonstrated his tactful diplomacy in the face of Ephraimite jealousy and averted intertribal warfare (cf. Jud. 12:1-6 where Jephthah reacted adversely to Ephraimite jealousy). In Gideon's parable **the full grape harvest of Abiezer** seems to refer to the initial victory in the camp of Midian (Gideon was an Abiezrite, 6:11) and **the gleanings of Ephraim's grapes** (affirmed as a greater victory) then refers to the "mopping up" operations which included slaying the two **Midianite** leaders.

(12) The pursuit of the Midianites into Transjordan (8:4-21). **8:4-9.** Though the Israelite reinforcements destroyed many of the fleeing Midianites, a sizable group, including two Midianite kings, **Zebah and Zalmunna,** escaped beyond **the Jordan** in a southeasterly direction. They were rapidly pursued by **Gideon and his 300 men** who sought food from **the men of Succoth** (v. 5) and **the men of Peniel** (vv. 8-9), two Israelite cities in the Transjordan territory of Gad (cf. Gen. 32:22, 30; Josh. 13:27). Both communities refused aid to **Gideon,** perhaps through fear of reprisal by the Midianites. However, this was tantamount to allying themselves with the Midianites against the Lord and His chosen deliverer. Therefore similar to the earlier curse on the city of Meroz in Deborah's time (cf. Jud. 5:23), Gideon threatened to punish them in retribution for their virtual hostility. To the people of **Succoth** he said, **I will tear** (lit., "thresh") **your flesh with desert thorns and briers** (cf. 8:16). This may mean he would drag them over thorns like a threshing sledge over grain, or "thresh" them by drawing threshing sledges over them. Whatever the exact meaning, death seemed the inevitable result. To the people of **Peniel** he gave the threat, **I will tear down this tower** (cf. v. 17). The tower was possibly a fortress

where people went for safety, like the tower of Shechem (9:46-49) or the tower of Thebez (9:50-51).

8:10-12. The two Midianite kings **(Zebah and Zalmunna)** arrived with a surviving force of only **15,000 men** at **Karkor,** an unidentified site thought to be near the Wadi Sirhan well east of the Dead Sea. The 15,000 was a mere 11 percent of the total Midianite force of 135,000. **Gideon** followed a caravan **route . . . east of Nobah** (perhaps Quanawat in eastern Bashan) **and Jogbehah** (modern el-Jubeihat 15 miles southeast of Peniel) and launched a surprise attack on the Midianites, **captured** the two kings, and routed their **army.**

8:13-17. Returning northwest to **the Pass** ("ascent") **of Heres** (an unidentified site) **Gideon** forced **a young man of Succoth** to write down **the names of the** city's **77 officials. Gideon** then carried out his previous threat to punish **the elders** of the city (cf. v. 7). **He also** fulfilled his threat to punish the city **of Peniel** (cf. v. 9).

8:18-21. With the two Midianite kings in hand, Gideon interrogated them regarding an otherwise unrecorded incident—the slaying of several **brothers** of his **at Tabor,** the conical small mountain just north of the Hill of Moreh. It is not stated whether this took place in the current invasion or on a previous Midianite invasion of the Jezreel Valley. Since Gideon felt obligated by the duty of blood revenge (cf. Deut. 19:6, 12), probably his brothers were murdered in their homes or fields, not in battle. Gideon asked **Jether his oldest son** to **kill them.** This was an honor that the **boy** was not prepared to undertake, though it would have been a fitting insult to the kings to be slain by an untried opponent. They bravely invited Gideon to fulfill the revenge himself, considering it an honor to be slain by the courageous Gideon. **Gideon** obliged them and **took the ornaments** (probably moon-shaped) **off their camels' necks** (cf. Jud. 8:26) as the spoils of war.

(13) The refusal of kingship by Gideon. **8:22-23.** Following this significant victory, **the Israelites** turned **to Gideon** with the request that he **rule** as king over them, that is, establish a ruling dynasty **(you, your son, and your grandson). Gideon** declined both the **rule** and the dynasty (but one of his sons, Abimelech,

would later speak for himself; cf. 9:1-6). Probably Gideon spoke words more significant than he realized when he affirmed the theocratic kingship of Yahweh—**The LORD will rule over you.**

(14) The snare of the ephod of Gideon (8:24-27). **8:24-26.** Though he rejected kingship, Gideon did take occasion to indulge in a form of virtual taxation by requesting a **share of the plunder** in the form of **gold earrings,** the total weight coming to about 43 pounds. The term **Ishmaelites** originally referred to another nomadic tribe descended from Hagar (Gen. 16:15) but the term apparently took on a broader usage so that it is here applied to the Midianites.

8:27. Gideon took the **gold** he received and made **an ephod, which he placed in Ophrah, his town.** Whatever Gideon's intentions were in this act, the people worshiped this ephod, and **it became a snare to Gideon and his family.** The nature of this ephod is not clear. It may have been patterned after the short outer garment worn by the high priest (Ex. 28:6-30; 39:1-21; Lev. 8:7-8). But rather than being worn as a garment, Gideon's golden ephod was apparently erected and became an idol. In some sense he may have usurped the function of the priest and/or established a rival worship center to the tabernacle. In the end Gideon seems to have returned to the syncretistic society out of which God had called him to deliver Israel.

d. The duration of peace (8:28)

8:28. As a result of **Gideon's** rout of the Midianites **the land enjoyed peace 40 years.** This is the last period of peace recorded in the Book of Judges. The subsequent activities of Jephthah and Samson did not seem to produce an interim of peace or delay the nation's decline.

e. The death of Gideon (8:29-32)

8:29-32. Though **Jerub-Baal** (i.e., Gideon; cf. 6:32; 7:1) declined the kingship, he generally lived like a king (**he had many wives** who bore him **70 sons**). He also had a **concubine . . . in Shechem** (who characteristically lived with her parents' family) who **bore him a son . . . named Abimelech.** This set the stage for the next downward spiral in Israel's history of apostasy, a spiral which began in earnest after the death of **Gideon.**

6. THE JUDGESHIPS OF TOLA AND JAIR FOLLOWING THE USURPATION OF ABIMELECH (8:33–10:5)

It may be significant that none of the judgeships recorded in the rest of the Book of Judges resulted in a designated period of peace (contrast 3:11, 30; 5:31; 8:28). This seems to fit the general pattern of progressive political and social decline and moral degeneration in the book. The event that launched the declining phase of the period of the Judges was the abortive kingship of Abimelech. Abimelech, a son of Gideon by a concubine, was not called a judge. In fact his rule included some elements of oppression which were eliminated only by his death and by the subsequent positive judgeship of Tola (who lived in the same general area of the central highlands).

a. The defection of Israel (8:33-35)

8:33-35. As though they had been waiting for it with expectancy, Gideon's death triggered Israel's immediate return to idolatry (cf. 2:19). Instead of worshiping Yahweh with thanksgiving for all His deliverances, **they set up Baal-Berith as their god,** who had a central shrine at Shechem (9:3-4) where he was also worshiped as El-Berith (9:46). Their accompanying failure **to show gratitude to the family of Jerub-Baal (that is, Gideon;** cf. 6:32; 7:1; 8:29) may have accounted for the apparent ease with which his sons were soon slain by Abimelech (9:5).

b. The distress under Abimelech (chap. 9)

(1) The conspiracy of Abimelech at Shechem (9:1-6). **9:1.** (Interestingly in chap. 9 Gideon is always called **Jerub-Baal,** and never Gideon. Cf. comments on "Jerub-Baal" in 6:32.) **Abimelech** was a **son** of Gideon by a concubine (8:31), a secondary wife who might live with her own family and be visited occasionally by her husband. In this social environment, Abimelech was no doubt shunned by his half-brothers (cf. his retaliation, 9:5) but he was accepted by **his mother's** family who lived **in Shechem.**

The city of Shechem had been a significant religious center since the time of Abraham (Gen. 12:6-7). It was located in the narrow valley between the prominent hills of Gerizim and Ebal, the site of the recitation under Joshua of the blessings and cursings of the Law (Josh. 8:30-35) and of the further covenant renewal ceremony before Joshua's death (Josh. 24:1-28). Shechem was situated on a strategic crossroads of the latitudinal route ascending from the coastal highway in the west and descending to Adam, on the Jordan River, and the longitudinal route along the central ridge from Jerusalem in the south to the northern accesses to the Jezreel Valley.

9:2-5. Abimelech appealed to his Shechemite heritage in offering himself to **the citizens of Shechem** in place of a corporate rule by **Jerub-Baal's sons,** who may have had neither the desire nor the following to be kings anyway. Some **silver** from the public **temple of Baal-Berith** was donated to **Abimelech . . . to hire reckless adventurers** as his personal cadre. Their first assignment was to murder Abimelech's **70 brothers** on **one stone,** implying a mass public execution. Significantly **Jotham,** Gideon's **youngest son . . . escaped.**

9:6. Following the successful removal of potential contenders for power (or was Abimelech's real motive personal vengeance?), **Abimelech** was crowned **king** by the ordinary **citizens of Shechem** and by the upper class who lived in the section of the city called **Beth Millo** ("house of the fortress"). The coronation took place beside **the great tree** (perhaps a well-known sacred tree; cf. Gen. 12:6; 35:4) **at the pillar** (cf. Josh. 24:26). It is doubtful that Abimelech's authority extended much beyond several cities in the vicinity of Shechem.

(2) The response of Jotham to the Shechemites (9:7-21). **9:7.** Gideon's youngest son **Jotham,** who had escaped the massacre by Abimelech (v. 5), courageously **climbed up on the top of Mount Gerizim** southwest of the city, **and shouted** out to the **citizens of Shechem.** He probably spoke from a triangular rock ledge on the side of Gerizim which forms a natural pulpit from which one can be heard as far away as Mount Ebal across the valley. Jotham's speech is noteworthy for its form and content as the first of one of the Bible's few fables (a short story in which animals or inanimate objects, like trees, are personified). Its purpose was to call the Shechemites to account before God (**Listen to me . . . so that God may listen to you**) for accepting as a leader the worthless· murderer Abimelech.

9:8-15. The major point of Jotham's parable was that only worthless people seek to lord it over others, for worthy individuals are too busy in useful tasks to seek such places of authority. The features of the parable are clear. **The trees** were seeking a **king,** but were turned down, in turn, by (a) **the olive tree** (v. 8), the most ancient of trees which is busy producing **oil** to be used to honor **both gods and men** (v. 9); (b) **the fig tree** (v. 10), the most common of trees in Israel whose **fruit** is a staple food (v. 11); and (c) **the vine** (v. 12), whose vintage produces **wine which cheers both gods** (i.e., in libations) **and men** (v. 13). In desperation the trees invited **the thornbush** (the buckthorn or bramblebush was used to kindle cooking fires in the wilderness areas of Palestine) to **be** their **king** (v. 14). The qualified acceptance by the thornbush was conditioned on the trees taking **refuge in** its **shade** (v. 15). Jotham employed extreme irony in this statement, for the puny **thornbush** at the foot of other trees scarcely casts a shadow. The threat of **fire** coming **out of the thornbush,** however, was real for farmers feared the wildfires that could spread quickly through the dried tinder of thornbushes.

9:16-20. Jotham then applied the parable, which stressed the worthless "bramble king" Abimelech, to rebuke the Shechemites for accepting such a worthless leader. This rebuke actually took the form of a curse (v. 20; cf. v. 57). Jotham began the rebuke with three conditional clauses (v. 16). After a parenthesis (vv. 17-18) describing the good deeds of Gideon and the bad deeds of **Abimelech,** Jotham restated the rebuke: **If then you have acted honorably and in good faith toward Jerub-Baal** (i.e., Gideon), "then may you and **Abimelech** enjoy your relationship!" (v. 19) **But if** the opposite was true (which was Jotham's obvious assumption), **let fire . . . consume** both Shechemites and **Abimelech.** This appropriate statement is specifically designated as a "curse" in verse 57.

9:21. It is evident that the Shechemites responded negatively to Jotham's rebuke for he **fled . . . to Beer** ("well"), which is such a common place name in Israel that to try to identify it is only guesswork.

(3) The revolt of the Shechemites un-

der Gaal (9:22-29). **9:22-25. Three years** of life under the leadership of **Abimelech** set the stage for a Shechemite revolt. **An evil** (demonic) **spirit** was **sent** by **God** to fulfill Jotham's curse by arousing distrust or jealousy in the Shechemites, who **set men on the hilltops to ambush and rob** the caravans and other travelers on the strategic trade routes through **Shechem.** Such action would reduce travel and deprive **Abimelech** of tributes and tolls from travelers. That God would send an evil spirit, a demon, shows that He sovereignly rules over all the universe. Even Satan could not attack Job without God's permission (Job. 1:12; 2:6).

9:26-29. The undisciplined populace of **Shechem** found a new leader in **Gaal son of Ebed,** who **moved** into Shechem **with his brothers** (perhaps his personal army of brigands). At the time of grape harvest (June-July) the Shechemites held a pagan religious **festival** comparable to but earlier than the Israelite Feast of Ingathering or Tabernacles, which was in September-October (cf. Deut. 16:13-15). At this time of festivity, **they cursed Abimelech** and **put their confidence in** Gaal, who ridiculed both **Abimelech** and **Zebul** his deputy, who was Shechem's governor (Jud. 9:30). Gaal exhorted them to **serve the men of Hamor,** the ancestor of their clan (Gen. 34:26) rather than the half-breed Abimelech. This suggests that a large portion of the Shechemite populace were native Canaanites. Gaal boldly challenged the absent Abimelech, **Call out your whole army!**

(4) The retaliation of Abimelech against Gaal (9:30-49). **9:30-33.** Zebul (cf. v. 28), **the governor of the city,** was angered by the rebel **Gaal.** So Zebul warned **Abimelech,** who lived in nearby Arumah (v. 41), perhaps Khirbet el-Urma between Shechem and Shiloh, to bring his troops **during the night** and **advance against the city** at **sunrise** to kill **Gaal.**

9:34-41. Abimelech went to **Shechem,** concealed **his** troops in **four companies,** and began to move on the city at sunrise. **When Gaal** mentioned their early morning movement, **Zebul** claimed they were only **shadows of the mountains.** But **Gaal** persisted in recognizing them as **people . . . coming down from the center of the land** (lit., "the navel of the land," apparently a reference to Gerizim located centrally in the central high-

lands). **The soothsayers' tree** may have been the oak of Moreh (Gen. 12:6). When he could deceive **Gaal** no longer, **Zebul** goaded him into leading his forces outside the protective walls of the city to **fight** against Abimelech's troops. After all his bragging, **Gaal** had no other choice but to engage in the encounter, and his Shechemite followers were soundly defeated by **Abimelech.** Then Abimelech returned to **Arumah** while those Shechemites faithful to **Zebul drove Gaal and his brothers out of Shechem.**

9:42-45. However, Abimelech's anger had not receded and his fear of further Shechemite revolt led him to **ambush the people** while they worked in **the fields. Two companies** carried out the slaughter while Abimelech secured **the city gate** with a third company. By evening he had **captured** the **city** and **destroyed** it, having **killed** its inhabitants. He then **scattered salt over it,** symbolic of a sentence of infertility so it might remain barren forever (cf. Deut. 29:23; Jer. 17:6). Archeology has confirmed this 12th-century destruction of Shechem, which remained a ruin till rebuilt by Jeroboam I as his capital (1 Kings 12:25).

9:46-49. These verses probably explain an incident within the city, included in the destruction previously recorded in verse 45, rather than a subsequent event outside the destroyed city. **On hearing** of either the slaughter in the fields (vv. 43-44) or the capture of the city gate (v. 44), the Shechemites who had retreated into **the tower of Shechem** (probably the same as the Beth Millo of v. 6), secured themselves in **the stronghold of the temple of El-Berith** (an alternate title for Baal-Berith, v. 4), probably a part of the tower of Shechem. **Abimelech** and his troops **cut . . . branches** from **Mount Zalmon** (perhaps either Mount Gerizim or Mount Ebal) and **set** them **on fire over** the stronghold, so that **about 1,000 men and women . . . died.**

(5) The ignoble death of Abimelech at Thebez. **9:50-55. Abimelech** next **besieged . . . and captured** Thebez, probably to be identified with modern Tubas about 10 miles northeast of Shechem on the road to Beth Shan. This city apparently was a dependency of Shechem which, under Abimelech's control, had

joined in the revolt. Attempting a repeat performance of Shechem, **Abimelech** sought to set . . . **fire** to **the tower** (within **the city**) where **the people** had **fled.** However, **a woman dropped an upper millstone on his head and cracked his skull.** The "upper millstone" was either a cylinder-shaped stone from a handmill (about 8 or 10 inches in length and several inches thick) or the large upper stone of a regular mill (about 12 to 18 inches in diameter with a hole in the middle and several inches thick). As he was dying Abimelech (like Saul, 1 Sam. 31:4) commanded **his armor-bearer** to **kill him.** Abimelech did not want it said that **a woman** had killed him. The followers of **Abimelech** (here identified as **Israelites**) **went home** when they **saw** that he **was dead.**

(6) The fulfillment of the curse of Jotham. **9:56-57.** The sacred historian recorded the divine providence behind the destruction of Shechem and the death of Abimelech: **God repaid the wickedness that Abimelech had done** to Gideon and his family; **God also made the men of Shechem pay for all their wickedness.** Thus **the curse of Jotham,** Gideon's **son,** was fulfilled (cf. v. 20).

c. The deliverances under Tola and Jair (10:1-5)

Tola and Jair were among the so-called "minor judges" but they were no less significant in delivering Israel during the period before the monarchy. The judgeship of Tola in particular was a temporary counteraction to the decay under Abimelech. The judgeship of Jair in Gilead anticipated the judgeship of the next major judge, Jephthah, in the same geographical area.

10:1-2. Since **Tola** was a deliverer in **the hill country of Ephraim,** but was **a man of Issachar,** his judgeship may have affected the adjacent tribe of Manasseh where Abimelech's petty kingdom had been established. Since no foreign oppressors are mentioned, his acts of deliverance (he **rose to save Israel**) may have related to internal strife and the sad state of affairs (including Abimelech's rule) which followed the positive influence of Gideon. Tola judged **Israel 23 years** before his death. The site of **Shamir,** his place of residence and burial, has not been identified.

10:3-5. After Tola's judgeship, **Jair . . . led Israel 22 years** in **Gilead,** in the Transjordanian area of Manasseh. His noble status is evidenced by his large progeny of **30 sons,** who each had a donkey as his status symbol (cf. 12:14). The "tent villages of Jair" (**Havvoth Jair**) were a group of towns in Bashan named by an earlier Jair (Num. 32:39-42; Deut. 3:14) which were relatively permanent since they were still there in the days of the author of the Book of Judges. Jair's burial place, **Kamon,** may be modern Qamm in Gilead.

7. THE DELIVERANCE BY JEPHTHAH FROM THE OPPRESSION OF THE AMMONITES (10:6–12:7)

Judges 10:6-16 seems to be an expanded theological introduction to the judgeships of both Jephthah (10:17–12:7) and Samson (chaps. 13–16) since the oppressors introduced in 10:7 are simultaneously the Ammonites (in the east) and the Philistines (in the west).

a. The defection of Israel (10:6)

10:6. Noteworthy is the numerical correspondence between the seven groups of pagan gods (v. 6) and the seven nations which oppressed Israel (v. 11). **The Baals and the Ashtoreths,** as noted earlier, were the gods of the Canaanites (cf. 2:13). **The gods of Aram** included Hadad or Rimmon (2 Kings 5:18), while **the gods of Sidon** were the Phoenician Baal and Asherah (cf. 1 Kings 16:31-33; 18:19). Moab's chief god was Chemosh (cf. 1 Kings 11:5, 33; 2 Kings 23:13), Ammon's was Milcom or Molech (1 Kings 11:33; Zeph. 1:5), and the Philistines' was Dagon (Jud. 16:23). Amazingly **the Israelites** worshiped these gods of surrounding nations and at the same time **forsook the Lord and no longer served Him.**

b. The distress under the Ammonites (10:7-9)

10:7-9. The Lord again chastened His straying people by foreign oppressors—**the Philistines** in the west (anticipating the narrative of Samson, chaps. 13–16) and **the Ammonites** in the **east,** who oppressed Israel **for 18 years.** Ammon was a Transjordanian kingdom northeast of Moab which was allied with Eglon of Moab in the time of Ehud (3:13). The Ammonites oppressed **Gilead,** the

Some of the Pagan Gods and Goddesses Worshiped in Nations Surrounding Israel

Names	Nations
1. Baal	Aram, Phoenicia, Canaan
2. Asherah	Aram, Phoenicia, Canaan
3. Ashtoreth	Aram, Phoenicia, Canaan
Other name: 'Athtart (sometimes called Astarte; also known in Babylonia as Ishtar)	Aram
4. Hadad = Rimmon (the Arameans' name for Baal)	Aram
5. Adad = Hadad	Mesopotamia
6. Chemosh	Moab
7. Milcom = Molech	Ammon
8. Dagon	Philistia
9. Resheph	Aram

Transjordanian area occupied in the south by the tribe of Gad and in the north by the half-tribe of Manasseh. **The Ammonites also crossed the Jordan,** probably on periodic raids **against Judah, Benjamin, and the house of Ephraim** (the area of the central highlands).

c. The repentance of Israel (10:10-16)

10:10-16. In previous times of distress Israel's calling on **the LORD** was not an evidence of repentance for her sin (cf. 3:9, 15; 4:3). At the time of the Midianite invasions, the Lord sent a prophet to point out her need for repentance (6:7-10). However, on this occasion **the Israelites** demonstrated genuine repentance, first confessing their sins (**We have sinned against You**) and then, after **the LORD** rebuked them (let **the gods you have chosen. . . . save you**), they remained steadfast in their confession of sin and took action to get **rid of the foreign gods** and serve **the LORD.** His mercy toward **Israel's misery** led Him to raise up Jephthah as a deliverer. **The Maonites** (10:12) may refer to the Midianites (cf. v. 12, LXX) or to a clan descended from someone with the Canaanite name of Maon.

d. The deliverance by Jephthah (10:17–12:6)

(1) The selection of Jephthah by the elders of Gilead (10:17–11:11). **10:17–11:6.** In response to the Ammonite invasion of **Gilead, the Israelites assembled and camped at Mizpah** (probably Ramath Mizpeh [Khirbet Jalad, about 14 miles northeast of Rabbath-ammon, i.e., modern Amman] or Ramoth Gilead [Tel Ramith, about 40 miles north of Rabbath Ammon]). The first task of Israel was to search for a military **commander.** Their search led them to seek **Jephthah** (11:4-6), a notorious leader of men whose earlier family history is summarized in 11:1-3. Like Abimelech (cf. chap. 9), Jephthah was probably a half-Canaanite (**his mother was a prostitute**). He was driven from home by his half brothers (11:2). **In the land of Tob** (probably north of Ammon and east of Manasseh) he **gathered around** himself **a group of adventurers** (v. 3, probably meaning "a band of brigands").

11:7-11. The elders of Gilead persisted in the face of Jephthah's rebuke (v. 8). They cemented their promise that Jephthah would be their civil leader **over . . . Gilead** after he won a military victory by making a formal and solemn oath with **the LORD** as **witness** (v. 10).

This was followed by a formal swearing-in ceremony at **Mizpah**. In contrast with the judgeship of Gideon, who was initially called by the Lord, Jephthah was initially called by other men. However, **the LORD** was called to witness their selection (vv. 10-11) and He placed His Spirit on Jephthah to achieve victory (v. 29).

(2) The diplomacy of Jephthah with the Ammonite king (11:12-28). **11:12-13.** Surprisingly Jephthah's first step as commander of Gilead was to seek a non-military settlement to the conflict. Through **messengers** he asked **the Ammonite king** why he had **attacked** Gilead. The king's reply came in the form of an accusation—**When Israel came up out of Egypt, they took away my land**—which Jephthah proceeded to demonstrate was untrue (vv. 14-27). Yet the Ammonite **king** offered peace to Jephthah for the return of the land. **The Arnon** and **the Jabbok** are rivers that formed the southern and northern boundaries of Ammon. South of the Arnon was Moab. The Arnon flows into the Dead Sea and the Jabbok into the Jordan River.

11:14-22. Jephthah applied his knowledge of Israel's history (learned either from written or oral sources) to refute **the Ammonite** king's claim. In passing, **Jephthah** indicated that **Israel** had acquiesced to the refusal of **Edom** (cf. Num. 20:14-21) and **Moab** to permit passage through their lands (Jud. 11:17-18). However, when Israel circled the borders of Edom and Moab, **and camped on the other side of the Arnon** (the more usual northern **border of Moab**), **Sihon king of the Amorites** also refused **Israel** passage northwest to the Jordan River, and **fought** against **Israel. The LORD** gave Israel the victory and **Israel took over all the land of the Amorites . . . from the Arnon to the Jabbok**—the land now under dispute between the Ammonites and the Gileadites (cf. v. 13). This area was really southern Gilead (the rest of Gilead was north of the Jabbok River), and its southern portion (from the Arnon to a line extending eastward from the north end of the Dead Sea) was periodically in Moabite hands.

11:23-24. Jephthah thus argued that **the LORD** had given this land to **Israel.** He concluded this point of his argument by indicating that Ammon should be sat-

isfied with the land that their **god Chemosh** had given them and should not contest the land **the LORD** had **given** Israel. Historically Chemosh was the god of the Moabites, and Milcam (or Molech) was god of the Ammonites. However, Jephthah seemed to be referring to the god of that portion of the land which had previously belonged to the Moabites before Sihon had pushed Moab south of the Arnon. Another explanation is that the Moabites were in alliance with the Ammonites in this attack on Gilead, so that Jephthah was really addressing the Moabites at this point in his argument. A third possibility is that the Ammonites had adopted the worship of Chemosh by this time.

11:25-27. Jephthah also argued that **Balak . . . king of Moab,** to whom part of the area in question used to belong, had consented to Israel's right to this area. In fact, Jephthah claimed, the land at the time of the Ammonite invasion had been Israel's **for 300 years** without any surrounding nations contesting it. Thus Jephthah denied any wrongdoing on Israel's part against Ammon. Ammon was in the **wrong** by warring **against** Israel.

11:28. Jephthah's attempt at diplomacy failed since **the king of Ammon . . . paid no attention to** his **message.**

(3) The empowerment of Jephthah by the Lord. **11:29.** The purpose of **the Spirit of the LORD** coming on **Jephthah** was to provide divine enablement in his military leadership against the pagan oppressors whom the Lord had been using to chasten His people (cf. 3:10; 6:34; 13:25; 15:14). The presence of the Holy Spirit with Old Testament leaders was primarily for the purpose of accomplishing services for God, not specifically for holy living. Thus the presence of the Spirit with Jephthah was not necessarily related to his vow or its fulfillment, recorded in the following verses. Jephthah's trip through **Gilead and Manasseh** was apparently to recruit his army.

(4) The vow of Jephthah to the Lord. **11:30-31.** That **Jephthah made a vow to the LORD** was not unusual in the Mosaic dispensation. Jephthah may have made the vow in anticipation of thanksgiving for divinely provided victory over the **Ammonites.** While the vow showed

JUDGES

Jephthah's zeal and earnestness, many have thought it was also characterized by rashness. Some scholars have sought to protect Jephthah from this charge by translating verse 31, "it will be the LORD's *or* I will offer it up as a burnt offering." However, the NIV more likely reflects Jephthah's intention—**I will sacrifice it as a burnt offering.**

(5) The victory of Jephthah over Ammon. **11:32-33.** God fulfilled Jephthah's request and **gave** the Ammonites **into his hands.** Jephthah **devastated 20** Ammonite-occupied **towns** in Gilead, and so **subdued Ammon.** Aroer (Khirbet Arair) was located about 14 miles east of the Dead Sea near the intersection of the Arnon River or the southern boundary of Reuben and the "King's Highway," on the main north-south trade route.

Abel Keramim may be identified with Naur about eight miles southwest of Rabbath Ammon (modern Amman). The site of **Minnith** is not known but was probably near Abel Keramim.

(6) The action of Jephthah concerning his daughter. **11:34-40.** Victorious **Jephthah** was met at the door of his house by **his** rejoicing **daughter,** who was jubilantly celebrating her father's victory over Ammon. Emphasis is placed on the fact that **she was an only child.** Anticipating the fulfillment of his vow, Jephthah expressed his great chagrin and sorrow in typical Near-Eastern fashion by tearing **his clothes** (cf., e.g., Gen. 37:29, 34; 44:13; Josh. 7:6; Es. 4:1; Job 1:20; 2:12). His statement, **I have made a vow to the LORD that I cannot break,** may reflect his ignorance of the legal option to redeem (with silver) persons who were thus dedicated (cf. Lev. 27:1-8). Also the Mosaic Law expressly prohibited human sacrifices (cf. Lev. 18:21; 20:2-5; Deut. 12:31; 18:10). Therefore many scholars conclude that when Jephthah **did to her as he had vowed** (Jud. 11:39), he commuted his daughter's fate from being a burnt sacrifice to being a lifelong **virgin** in service at Israel's central sanctuary. Other scholars believe Jephthah's semi-pagan culture led him to sacrifice her as a burnt offering. Strong arguments have been advanced for both views (cf. Wood, *Distressing Days of the Judges,* pp. 288-95; Merrill F. Unger, *Unger's Commentary on the Old Testament,* 2 vols. Chicago: Moody Press, 1981, 1:331).

Most of the arguments for or against Jephthah's offering his daughter as a human sacrifice can be used to defend either position and therefore are not conclusive. For example, the grief of both Jephthah and his daughter readily fits either her death or her perpetual virginity. In either case she would die childless (whether sooner or later) and Jephthah would lack descendants. Her asking for **two months to roam . . . and weep . . . because** she would **never marry** may be one of the stronger arguments for the virginity view. But this could also mean she was wailing in anticipation of her death which of course would render her childless. Though Jephthah made his rash vow, he probably knew something about the prohibitions of the Mosaic Law against human sacrifice. Yet his half-pagan background, combined with the general lawless spirit dominating the period of the Judges (cf. 17:6; 21:25), could readily account for his fulfilling this vow. The record of the local annual custom that arose to remember Jephthah's daughter (11:39-40) lacks sufficient detail to support either viewpoint strongly.

Even the existence of a group of young women serving at the tabernacle is not demonstrably evident from the passages used to support this (Ex. 38:8; 1 Sam. 2:22). Nor does the appeal to the law of options for vows (Lev. 27) apply directly to this situation. Nothing is said there about substitutionary service to God for the sacrifice—only the substitution of monetary payment. Therefore in the absence of any clear evidence indicating the girl's dedication to tabernacle service as a perpetual virgin, the more natural interpretation of the euphemism that Jephthah "did to her as he had vowed" seems to be that he offered his daughter as a human sacrifice.

Whichever position is taken, the attitude of Jephthah's daughter is worth noting. Whether by death or by perpetual sanctuary service, she was to bear no children. This was a cause of great sorrow in ancient Israel. Yet she submitted herself to her father's vow: **You have given your word to the LORD. Do to me just as you promised.** An **Israelite custom,** though probably somewhat localized, developed from the incident. **Each year the young women of Israel** went **out for four days to commemorate the daughter of**

92

Jephthah the Gileadite.

(7) The conflict of Jephthah with Ephraim. **12:1-6.** The Ephraimites had been attacked by **the Ammonites** (cf. 10:9) but the former's land had apparently not been occupied by the Ammonites as was true of Jephthah's Gileadites. Nevertheless the Ephraimites reacted against **Jephthah** because he had not invited their aid in defeating Ammon. In contrast with Gideon's tactful handling of a similar situation (cf. 8:1-3), **Jephthah** asserted that they had not responded to his call (though the record is silent concerning such an invitation), so he gained **victory over** Ammon without their help. Insults by **the Ephraimites** then led to their destruction by **the Gileadites. The Gileadites** even killed straggling survivors who tried to ford **the Jordan** River to return to **Ephraim.** The Ephraimites were easily identified by their colloquial pronunciation of the Hebrew sound *sh* which they pronounced as an *s*. This civil conflict in Israel cost the Ephraimites **42,000** lives, a high price for jealousy!

e. The death of Jephthah (12:7)

12:7. Following the victory over the Ammonites, **Jephthah led** (i.e., judged) **Israel six years** until his death.

8. THE JUDGESHIPS OF IBZAN, ELON, AND ABDON (12:8-15)

Three minor judges followed Jephthah, in various areas of Israel.

12:8-10. Ibzan . . . led Israel as judge, apparently from his hometown **of Bethlehem.** It is not indicated whether this was Bethlehem in Judah or Bethlehem in Zebulun (cf. Josh. 19:10, 15). Ibzan's community status is evidenced by his large family of **30 sons and 30 daughters,** and his political alliances are suggested by his seeking marriages both for **his sons** and **daughters . . . outside his clan.** He judged **Israel seven years** before he **died.**

12:11-12. Elon the Zebulunite led Israel 10 years. Nothing is recorded about him except his place of burial— **Aijalon** (an unidentified city) **in the land of Zebulun.**

12:13-15. Abdon, who was from **Pirathon in Ephraim** (located seven miles west by southwest of Shechem), **had 40 sons and 30 grandsons,** each with his own donkey, the status symbol of nobil-

ity (cf. the judge Jair, whose 30 sons each rode a donkey; 10:4). Abdon's **eight**-year judgeship may have involved some conflict with **the Amalekites.**

9. THE DELIVERANCE BY SAMSON FROM THE OPPRESSION OF THE PHILISTINES (CHAPS. 13–16)

a. The defection of Israel (13:1a)

13:1a. Israel's monotonous downward spiral climaxed with the seventh recorded apostasy in the Book of Judges (cf. 3:5-7, 12-14; 4:1-3; 6:1-2; 8:33-35; 10:6-9). This apostasy appears to have been a phase of the idolatrous worship previously described in 10:6 (which included "the gods of the Philistines"), because a resulting oppression by the Philistines (in the west) is mentioned in 10:7 to complement that by the Ammonites (in the east).

b. The distress under the Philistines (13:1b)

13:1b. The depths of Israelite apostasy and the greatness of Philistine strength were causes for the unprecedented length of oppression—**40 years**—though **the Philistines** continued as a threat until the early years of David's reign (cf. 2 Sam. 5:17-25). Though earlier Philistine settlements had been present in Palestine (cf. Gen. 21:32-34; 26:1-18; Jud. 1:18-19), the Philistines arrived in large numbers during the invasion of the Sea Peoples about 1200 B.C. They organized a pentapolis or confederation of five cities—Gaza, Ashkelon, and Ashdod on the strategic coastal highway, and Gath and Ekron on the edge of the Shephelah or Judean foothills (cf. Josh. 13:3).

When the Philistine aggression moved eastward into the land of Benjamin and Judah, the Israelites accepted that domination without resistance (cf. 14:4; 15:11) till the time of Samuel (cf. 1 Sam. 7:10-14).

How was it that Samson's parents, who were Danites, were still living in the Sorek Valley when much earlier the tribe of Dan had migrated north? (Jud. 18) Apparently a few of the Danite clans stayed behind and did not move northward.

c. The deliverance by Samson (13:2–16:31)

Unless the repentance mentioned in 10:10-16 includes the western Israelites who were being oppressed by the Philistines (cf. 10:7)—which is unlikely in view of their apparent acceptance of the Philistine domination (cf. 15:11)—there is no mention of Israel's cry to God before He raised up Samson as a deliverer (contrast 3:9, 15; 4:3; 6:7; 10:10). Since Samson judged Israel 20 years (15:20; 16:31), beginning apparently at about age 20, his entire life span must have approximated the 40-year Philistine oppression which began before his birth (cf. 13:5). He was thus a contemporary of Samuel who with God's help subdued the Philistines after Samson's death (cf. 1 Sam. 7:10-14).

(1) The birth of Samson (13:2-24). **13:2-5.** Samson's parents were **from the clan of the Danites,** perhaps implying that the bulk of the tribe of Dan had already made the move northward to the Huleh Valley (cf. chap. 18), so that only a clan or two remained in their original tribal inheritance. The childless **wife** of **Manoah** of **Zorah** was visited by **the Angel of the Lord.** Zorah, the highest point in the Shephelah, was on a high ridge north of the Sorek Valley and about 14 miles west of Jerusalem. Originally Zorah was a city of Judah (Josh. 15:20, 33), but later it was allotted to the tribe of Dan (Josh. 19:40-41). In this theophany (cf. comments on Jud. 2:1-2) the Lord foretold the **birth** of her **son,** Samson, and said that he was to **be a Nazirite.** A Nazirite (meaning "devoted" or "consecrated") was a person whose vow of separation **to God** included abstaining from **fermented drink,** refraining from cutting his hair, and avoiding contact with dead bodies (Num. 6:2-6). Nazirite vows were normally for a limited period of time but Samson was to be a Nazirite of God all his life (Jud. 13:7). His mother was to share for a time in part of the Nazirite vow (vv. 4, 7, 14). Besides being set apart as a Nazirite, Samson was chosen by God to **begin the deliverance of Israel from the hands of the Philistines.** The completion of this task would be left to Samuel (1 Sam. 7:10-14) and David (2 Sam. 5:17-25).

13:6-8. When Manoah's wife reported to him her encounter with this One whom she described as **a Man of God,** who **looked like an Angel . . . Manoah prayed** for His reappearance to **teach** them **how to bring up the boy.**

13:9-18. In response to Manoah's prayer **the Angel of God** (another title for the Angel of the Lord) reappeared, first to his wife and then to **Manoah,** but He merely repeated His previous instructions (vv. 13-14). Not fully realizing the divine character of his Guest (v. 16b), **Manoah** invited the Messenger to stay for a meal. **The Angel** indicated that any provisions should be offered **to the Lord** as **a burnt offering.** On asking the Angel's **name,** Manoah was informed, **It is beyond understanding.**

13:19-23. Then **Manoah** sacrificed a **young goat** (cf. v. 15) with a **grain offering** (cf. Lev. 2) **on a rock to the Lord.** He and his wife were amazed as **the Angel of the Lord ascended in the flame** that blazed up from **the altar.** Realizing the identity of the divine Messenger, **Manoah** expressed fear of impending death because of their having **seen God** (cf. Gideon's similar response, Jud. 6:22-23). Manoah's **wife** more practically pointed out that God's acceptance of the sacrifice and the promise of a son indicated that immediate death was not God's plan for them.

13:24. In fulfillment of the words of the divine Messenger, Manoah's wife **gave birth to . . . Samson** (a name related to the word for "sun"), who **grew** up under the blessing of **the Lord.**

(2) The moving of Samson by the Holy Spirit. **13:25.** One day **the Spirit of the Lord began to stir** Samson, that is, to empower him to begin to deliver Israel. This happened at **Mahaneh Dan** ("Camp of Dan"; cf. 18:11-12 for the origin of the name) **between Zorah** (Samson's home; cf. 13:2) **and Eshtaol** (a town about one and one-half miles east by northeast of Zorah). Samson was later buried between these two towns (16:31; also cf. 18:2, 8, 11). Samson's leadership as judge or deliverer did not take the form of leading an army against the Philistines. Rather it consisted of his being a lone champion for the cause of his people. His exploits, the record of which begins in chapter 14, distracted the Philistines from more serious invasions into the tribal areas of Benjamin and Judah.

(3) The marriage of Samson to a Philistine woman (chap. 14). **14:1-4.** Samson's exploits with the Philistines began with his desire for **a young Philistine woman** who lived in **Timnah** (probably modern Tell el-Batashi, four miles north-

west down the Sorek Valley from Beth Shemesh). Since marriages were contracted by the parents (cf. Gen. 21:21), **Samson** insisted that his parents **get her for** him **as his wife.** Since marriage with a non-Israelite was expressly forbidden by the Mosaic Law (Ex. 34:16; Deut. 7:3), his parents objected to his marrying a Philistine (cf. Jud. 14:3). Other peoples around Israel, whether Egyptians or Semites, practiced circumcision, but the Philistines did not. By citing this fact Samson's parents were deriding the Philistines.

Though Samson's parents objected to his marrying a Philistine, they allowed Samson's wishes to prevail. They **did not know that this was from the LORD, who was seeking an occasion to confront the Philistines.** This does not mean that breaking the Law was desired by God but that Samson's decision was overruled by God for His own purpose and glory.

14:5-7. Samson took his parents **down to Timnah** to arrange the wedding. He apparently turned aside into **the vineyards of Timnah,** perhaps to obtain grapes, where he was attacked by **a young lion.** Under the empowerment of **the Spirit of the LORD** (cf. 14:19; 15:14) **he tore the lion apart with his bare hands,** probably in the manner Near-Easterners rend a young goat, pulling it in half by the hind legs. That he did not tell **his father** or **mother** about this implies that they had proceeded on to Timnah to complete the betrothal arrangement. When Samson arrived in Timnah, he could then actually talk to **the woman,** perhaps for the first time (before he had only "seen" her, 14:2), and **he liked her.**

14:8-9. Some time later, when the betrothal period was completed, he was on his way to the wedding. Again **he turned aside** into the vineyards, this time **to look at the lion's carcass** in which he discovered **a swarm of bees and some honey.** He **scooped out** the honey to eat it, and shared it with **his parents** without informing them of its source. While the Nazirite law strictly prohibited contact with a dead person, the purpose of this was to avoid ceremonial uncleanness (Num. 6:7). Since touching the carcass of even a clean animal made a person (with the obvious exception of an officiating priest) ceremonially unclean (Lev. 11:39-40), probably Samson's scooping the honey from the lion's carcass was a viola-

tion of his Nazirite vow. His participation in the wedding feast (Jud. 14:10) may also have violated his vow to abstain from fermented drink. However, only one Nazirite qualification was specifically indicated before his birth—"No razor may be used on his head" (13:5). Later a violation of this specific practice would lead to the removal of the power of God's Spirit from him (16:17-20).

14:10-14. At the **seven**-day wedding ceremony, **Samson** conducted the customary **feast** (lit., "drinking party") and was accompanied by **30 companions** (typical "friends of the bridegroom," apparently provided by the Philistine family). **Samson** told his companions **a riddle,** the meaning of which he made more challenging with a wager of **30 linen garments** (large rectangular sheets often used as undergarments) **and 30 sets of clothes** (festal garments, often embroidered). Solving Samson's poetically phrased riddle—**Out of the eater, something to eat; out of the strong, something sweet**—would require a knowledge of his having taken honey from the lion's carcass.

14:15-18. Unable to solve the riddle after three days, the companions threatened **Samson's** bride and her family with **death** if she would not obtain the answer for them. They implied that she might have been involved in a scheme with Samson to **rob** them by means of the wager. Samson withstood bridal tears till **the seventh day** of **the feast** when the time to solve the riddle would expire (cf. v. 12). Then Samson's weakness to give in to the tears or pleadings of a woman (cf. 16:16) was expressed. **He finally told her** and **she in turn explained the riddle** to the 30 Philistines. When they informed Samson of the solution which, like the riddle, they phrased in poetic parallelism, Samson retorted concerning his bride with a scornful but picturesque figure of speech: **If you had not plowed with my heifer, you would not have solved my riddle.** In calling her a "heifer" he was ridiculing her for her untamed and stubborn spirit (cf. Jer. 50:11; Hosea 4:16).

14:19-20. To fulfill his obligation in the wager (cf. v. 12) Samson attacked **30** Philistines in **Ashkelon** (23 miles southwestward on the Mediterranean coast—far enough away not to be associated with Samson in Timnah) and took **their clothes** to the Philistines **who had explained the riddle.** God overruled Samson's foolishness by the enabling power of **the Spirit of the LORD** (cf. v. 6; 15:14) to accomplish His purpose of disrupting the Philistine status quo of easy dominance over Israel (cf. 14:4). Still angry, Samson **went up to his father's house** in Zorah without returning to his wife on the seventh night of the wedding to consummate the marriage. The bride's father, to avoid the disgrace of what he perceived as an annulment (cf. 15:2), gave her to the best man.

(4) The conflicts of Samson with the Philistines (15:1–16:3). **15:1-5. Samson** later (in **the wheat harvest,** i.e., May) returned to Timnah with a present of **a young goat** (cf. 13:15, 19) for **his wife.** Samson's marriage was apparently the ṣadîqa type in which the bride remained with her parents and was visited periodically by her husband (cf. 8:31). Thus Samson's present was probably not a reconciliation gift for his previous behavior, but merely the expected gift on a husband's periodic visit. However, **Samson** soon discovered that his bride had been given to another by **her father** who thought Samson **hated her** (the word is used in a divorce context in Deut. 24:3).

Unimpressed with the offer of marriage to **her younger sister,** Samson again vented his anger on **the Philistines,** this time by burning their **grain** (wheat, Jud. 15:1) fields. He did this by fastening **torches** to the **tied . . . tails** of pairs of **300 foxes** (the Heb. word can also mean jackals which run in packs and are more easily caught). The fiery destruction included the dry **shocks** of grain already harvested along with the dry **standing grain** yet to be harvested and spread also to **the vineyards and olive groves** (thus destroying the land's three main crops; cf. Deut. 7:13; Hag. 1:11).

15:6-8. When the Philistines learned that **Samson** caused the destruction, they retaliated by burning **his wife . . . and her father to death** (apparently destroying the entire Timnite household). Motivated again by personal **revenge,** Samson **viciously . . . slaughtered many of** the **Philistines** and then walked to **a cave in the rock of Etam.** The term "viciously" is literally "leg on thigh," a wrestling metaphor for a ferocious attack. Though there

is a town named Etam about 2 miles southwest of Bethlehem in Judah (about 17 miles from Timnah), another possibility is to identify the site with a cleft above the Wadi Isma'in about 2½ miles southeast of Zorah.

15:9-14. Pursuing Samson, **the Philistines . . . camped in Judah . . . near Lehi** (lit., "jawbone"; perhaps modern Khirbet es-Siyyaj). When the Judeans learned the reason for the Philistine show of force, they sought **Samson** with **3,000 men** to turn him **over to the Philistines.** Apparently satisfied with the status quo, they asked **Samson, Don't you realize that the Philistines are rulers over us?** When the Judeans **agreed** not to kill him themselves, **Samson** (not wanting to shed Israelite blood) let them surrender him to **the Philistines. They bound him with two new ropes,** but these **became like charred flax and . . . dropped from his hands** when he came near the jubilant Philistines. Again special strength was given him by **the Spirit of the LORD** (cf. 14:6, 19).

15:15-17. Grabbing **a fresh jawbone of a donkey** (an old one would have been too brittle), **Samson** slaughtered **1,000** Philistines. His words of triumph included a play on the Hebrew ḥāmôr which can mean either "donkey" or "heap." Thus the phrase translated **I have made donkeys of them** is often translated "heaps upon heaps" (NASB) and interpreted to mean something like, "I have piled them in heaps." **The place** where this happened was **Ramath Lehi,** which probably means "the hill (height) of the jawbone."

15:18-19. The next incident in Samson's life was God's provision of water for him. Samson was extremely **thirsty** after his difficult effort in the hot, dry climate. His cry **to the LORD** was miraculously answered as **God opened up the hollow place** (maktēš, lit., "mortar," i.e., basin) **and water came out.** This place where Samson's strength was restored **was** still **called En Hakkore** ("spring of the caller") when the Book of Judges was completed (**it is still there**).

15:20. Samson's leadership over **Israel,** summarized at this point, is also noted in 16:31. The **20 years** (about 1069–1049 B.C.) would cover Samson's adult life until his death in Gaza (cf. 16:30-31).

16:1-3. The incident of Samson's removing the doors of Gaza showed that his physical strength was unmatched except by his moral weakness. No reason is given why **Samson went to Gaza,** perhaps the most important Philistine city, which was near the coast about 35 miles southwest of his home in Zorah. Whatever the reason, his sensual inclinations overcame him and he spent **the night** with **a prostitute.** Aware of Samson's presence in the city, the Philistines **of Gaza . . . lay in wait for him all night at the city gate,** planning to **kill him** when he left **at dawn.** However, **Samson** arose in **the middle of the night,** apparently catching them by such surprise that he escaped even though he pulled away **the doors of the city gate, together with the two posts . . . bar and all.** In fact, he **carried** the doors **to the top of the hill that faces Hebron.** Whether this is a hill outside of Gaza that has a view eastward toward Hebron, or whether Samson carried the doors uphill 37 miles to a hill outside of Hebron, is not clear from the text. Local tradition identifies the hill as El Montar just east of Gaza. There seems to be no reason why Samson would carry the doors farther, since he had already insulted the people of the city by removing its gate of security.

(5) The downfall of Samson at the hands of Delilah (16:4-22). **16:4-14.** Samson **fell in love with a woman** named **Delilah** (though she was probably a Philistine, she had a Semitic name meaning "devotee", so she may have been a temple prostitute). She was at least the third woman with whom Samson had been involved (cf. 14:1-2; 16:1). The town where Delilah lived **in the Valley of Sorek** (where Samson spent most of his life) is not named, whether Har-heres (Beth Shemesh), or Timnah, or some other town.

The Philistine **rulers** devised a plot to capture Samson. The Bible does not say how many rulers were involved, but probably the number was five, one for each of the major Philistine cities. They hired Delilah to learn **the secret of his great strength and how** to **overpower . . . and subdue him.** The rulers each promised to give her the exorbitant amount of **1,100 shekels of silver,** equal to many thousands of dollars. **Delilah** made three fruitless attempts to gain Samson's confidence and **secret.** Each time he teased her by inventing a means

whereby he would **become as weak** as **any other man** and could be captured: (a) if he were **tied** up with **seven fresh thongs** (i.e., bowstrings prepared from animal viscera); (b) if he were **tied** up with **new ropes that have never been used** (but the effectiveness of this had already been disproven; 15:13); and (c) if his hair (getting closer to the truth) was woven **into the fabric on the loom. Delilah** futilely tried each method, apparently while **Samson** slept (as in 16:13), and seemed to tease him by crying out, **Samson, the Philistines are upon you!** (vv. 9, 12, 14) when in reality she was testing the success or failure of each method before the Philistines, **hidden in the room** (vv. 9, 12), dared show themselves.

16:15-17. Samson finally revealed the source of his strength, which was not a magical secret, as the Philistines had supposed, but a supernatural enablement from the Spirit of **God** (cf. 13:25; 14:6, 19; 15:14). This enablement was associated with Samson's special separation to the Lord through his **Nazirite** status, which was especially symbolized by his uncut hair (13:5). Samson explained his Nazirite status to Delilah when he could no longer bear her nagging him for his secret. He said that if his **head were shaved,** he **would become as weak as any other man.** This was not because his strength was in his hair but because cutting it would manifest his disobedience to the Lord, a disobedience that had already begun by his revealing the truth to Delilah whom he had no reason to trust.

16:18-22. Samson's indiscretion led to his imprisonment by **the Philistines.** This time **Delilah** sensed that **Samson had told her everything,** so she set the trap again and had **his hair** shaved while he slept **on her lap.** As a fruit of his foolish disobedience to the Lord, Samson's **strength left him.** Apparently Samson was also bound since, when Delilah cried out **The Philistines are upon you!** he attempted to **shake** himself **free.** The tragic fact was that **he did not know that the LORD had left him.** The departure of the Spirit of the Lord was tantamount to discharging him from his role as judge.

The powerless Samson was then **seized** by the Philistines who blinded him **and took him down to Gaza,** a just retribution they no doubt thought for his stealing its city gate (vv. 1-3). They bound **him with bronze shackles** and **set him to grinding** meal between millstones **in the prison,** a woman's work. This may have been a handmill with a saddle-quern (cf. comments on 9:53), since it is not certain that large animal-turned mills were used that early. As time passed while Samson was in prison, his **hair** (the symbol of his Nazirite dedication, 13:5) **began to grow again.** Since the physical growth of his hair would be expected, the point of this observation must have been the anticipation of Samson's renewed strength for one last act of revenge against the Philistines (cf. 16:28-30).

(6) The revenge of Samson on the Philistines. **16:23-30.** The time came for the Philistine **rulers . . . to offer a great sacrifice to Dagon their god.** Dagon was a West Semitic grain deity (cf. 1 Sam. 5:2-7; 1 Chron.10:10) adopted by the Philistines from the Amorites. Since they believed that their **god** had **delivered Samson . . . into** their **hands. . . . they called Samson out of the prison** to **entertain** them (apparently expecting to see some acts of strength, or perhaps just to mock their now-powerless opponent). A Philistine temple was typically a long inner chamber with two major **pillars** supporting the roof. A large group of Philistines (including some **3,000** people **on the roof**) watched **Samson perform,** apparently in an outer court. What his "performing" included is not known. Afterward blind **Samson** had **the servant who** was guiding him take him to **the pillars that support the temple,** on the pretext of resting **against them.** However, he then **prayed to the LORD** for one final feat of strength to obtain **revenge on the Philistines. Samson . . . bracing himself against** the pillars (whether between them pushing outward, or adjacent to them leaning forward), **said, Let me die with the Philistines!** and **pushed with all his might.** God granted his final prayer and **the temple** was demolished, killing **more** people in Samson's death than he had slain **while he lived.** Previously he had killed at least 1,030 Philistines (30 in Ashkelon, 14:19; and 1,000 at Ramath Lehi, 15:14-17).

(7) The burial of Samson by his relatives. **16:31.** Samson's **whole family** (his **brothers**) who had not been mentioned till this incident (**went down** to Gaza and brought Samson's body back for burial **between Zorah** (his birthplace, 13:2) **and Eshtaol** (cf. 13:25; 18:2, 8, 11) in Manoah's **tomb.** Thus ended Samson's **20 years** of judgeship over **Israel** (cf. 15:20). Though Samson had great ability and was endowed with physical power by the Holy Spirit, he gave in to temptation several times and suffered the consequences. His life is a stern warning to others who are prone to follow the path of sensuality.

III. Epilogue: Conditions Illustrating the Days of the Judges (chaps. 17–21)

Theologically chapters 17–21 constitute an epilogue giving illustrations of the religious apostasy and social degradation that characterized the period of the Judges. Those conditions were viewed by the author (probably early in the monarchy) as indicative of the anarchy which prevailed when "Israel had no king" (17:6; 18:1; 19:1; 21:25). Historically the events recorded in these chapters form an appendix to the book, having transpired fairly early in the preceding history. An early date is indicated by the presence of the grandsons of both Moses (18:30) and Aaron (20:28) and by reference to the ark at Bethel (20:27-28). Possibly the events in chapters 17–18 took place in the days of Othniel, the first judge.

The epilogue consists of two major sections: (1) Chapters 17–18 interweave stories of the household idolatry of Micah the Ephraimite who hired the Levite Jonathan, Moses' grandson (18:30), as his personal priest, and the migration and tribal idolatry of the Danites. (2) Chapters 19–21 narrate an atrocity perpetrated on another Levite's concubine at Gibeah, and the ensuing civil war against the recalcitrant tribe of Benjamin, leading to its near annihilation.

A. Religious apostasy: The idolatry of Micah and the migration of the Danites (chaps. 17–18)

1. THE IDOLATRY OF MICAH THE EPHRAIMITE (CHAP. 17)

a. The acquisition of an image by Micah (17:1-5)

17:1-5. It is ironic that **a man named Micah** (meaning "Who is like Yahweh?")

should establish an apostate shrine with an unlawful priesthood. Such a situation came about, in part, when he heard his mother . . . utter a curse against the thief who had stolen her 1,100 shekels of silver, and then confessed, I took it. (These 1,100 silver shekels are not to be confused with the 1,100 silver shekels that each of the Philistine rulers gave Delilah, 16:5, 18.) As a reward for such "honesty," his mother sought to neutralize her curse with a blessing (The Lord bless you, my son!). Her subsequent consecration of the silver to the Lord . . . to make a carved image was in disobedience to the command in Exodus 20:4, and reflects the idolatrous Canaanite influence on the Israelites during this period.

The phrase a carved image and a cast idol suggests two objects of false worship, an image carved out of stone or wood, and a cast idol made out of melted metal poured into a mold. But some scholars think the phrase is a hendiadys (referring to only one molded image), perhaps a wooden idol overlaid with silver which Micah's mother had made and placed in the house. However, in Judges 18:18 the objects are clearly distinct. Micah's mother paid a silversmith 200 silver shekels—equal to several thousand dollars—to make those objects of worship. These were not the only idols in Micah's aberrant shrine (lit., "house of god[s]"), for he had an ephod (possibly as an object of worship; cf. 8:24-27; or for a priest to wear) and some idols ($t^e r \bar{a} p\hat{i}m$; cf. Gen. 31:17-50). He then installed one of his sons as his priest to conduct worship in this shrine (later Micah installed another priest, Jud. 17:12).

b. *The characteristics of the period of the Judges (17:6)*

17:6. The author, writing from the viewpoint of the early monarchy, explained Micah's religious lawlessness as a characteristic of a period without the centralized authority of a king (cf. 18:1; 19:1; 21:25).

c. *The acquisition of a Levitical priest by Micah (17:7-13)*

17:7-13. A young Bethlehem Levite (Moses' grandson, Jonathan son of Gershom; cf. 18:30) moved to the hill country of Ephraim where he was employed by Micah to be his father (a term of honor; cf. Gen. 45:8; 2 Kings 6:21; 13:14) and priest. Micah took care of him like one of his sons. So Micah installed the Levite (cf. Jud. 18:4) as his priest (in addition to Micah's own son, who was made a priest, 17:5). Micah rejoiced because of his superstitious notion that having a Levite (a young man; cf. 18:3) for his priest would bring blessings from the Lord, when in fact it was forbidden in the Law (cf. Num. 3:10). The Levite, of course, was as much (or more) to blame for having accepted the position. These acts of disobedience to God's Law were typical of the Israelites in the time of the Judges.

2. THE MIGRATION OF THE DANITES TO THE NORTH (CHAP. 18)

a. *The problem of the Danites (18:1)*

18:1. This chapter repeats the refrain of the epilogue that Israel had no king (17:6; 19:1; 21:25). This lack of a central authority to muster an Israelite army no doubt aggravated the problem faced by the tribe of Dan, namely, Dan's inability (or lack of faith) to come into an inheritance. The Danites were being pushed by the Amorites (1:34-35; cf. Josh. 19:47) and later the Philistines (with the rest of Israel; cf. Jud. 13:1; 14:4; 15:11). Dan was forced more and more eastward into the territory of Benjamin and Ephraim. Because of Dan's cramped living conditions its people decided to seek a new territory.

b. *The mission of the spies (18:2-10)*

18:2-6. The clans of the Danites sent five warriors from Zorah and Eshtaol (cf. 13:25; 16:31) to explore the land. Early in their journey they lodged for the night in the house of Micah in the hill country of Ephraim (cf. 17:1). There they recognized the voice (probably the Judean accent) of Micah's priest (the young Levite Jonathan; cf. 17:12) and inquired concerning his presence and activities in Ephraim. When they learned that he was functioning as a priest, they superstitiously sought some word of God's blessing on their mission. One wonders about the source of the priest's confident answer: Your journey has the Lord's approval. The outward success of their mission did not correspond with the Lord's revealed plan for the tribe of Dan, and eventuated in the establishing of a major center of idolatry (cf. 18:30-31; 1 Kings 12:28-30).

18:7. As **the five** spies continued to explore the land they eventually **came to Laish** (Leshem in Josh. 19:47; modern Tell el-Qadi) about 25 miles north of the Sea of Kinnereth and 27 miles east of Tyre. Located on the north edge of the fertile Huleh Basin, the **land lacked nothing** and **the people . . . were prosperous.** Their town was also isolated from **the Sidonians** by the Lebanon range of mountains, and from Syria by Mount Hermon and the Anti-Lebanon range, so that they were without close military allies. Possibly Hazor had already been destroyed (Jud. 4:2, 23-24), though this may raise some chronological problems concerning the Levite as Moses' grandson (cf. 18:30).

18:8-10. Returning home, the five spies reported **an unsuspecting people and a spacious land . . . that lacks nothing whatever.** They encouraged the Danites to **attack** Laish without hesitation. They felt that **God** had given it to them. Though their theological affirmation is debatable, their anticipated victory seemed inevitable.

c. The expedition against Laish (18:11-28a)

18:11-13. The Danites armed **600 men . . . for battle** who first camped **near Kiriath Jearim** (about six miles east of the Zorah-Eshtaol area). Their campsite, **Mahaneh Dan** ("Camp of Dan"), was where Samson later first sensed the work of God's Spirit in his life (13:25). The Danites then **went on** to **Ephraim** where Micah (cf. 17:1; 18:2) lived.

18:14-21. The five spies then informed their fellow warriors about the house and shrine of Micah (cf. 17:5). While the fighters waited outside, the five men **greeted** Micah's **priest,** and then proceeded to steal Micah's **image, ephod,** and idols. When **the priest** challenged them, they told him, **Be quiet!** and invited him to become their tribal **priest** rather than just a **household** priest. He gladly accepted the offer and **went with** them carrying Micah's **ephod, the other household gods, and the carved image** (cf. 17:4-5). Anticipating

that Micah might pursue them, the Danites sent their families and **possessions** on ahead of them and formed a rear guard.

18:22-26. Micah soon discovered his loss, and accompanied by his friends and neighbors he pursued **the Danites. Micah** accused them of appropriating his **gods** and **priests.** But when they intimidated him with threats of violence he reluctantly but wisely **turned around and went back home.** His pathetic question concerning his idols—**What else do I have?**—reflects the emptiness of idolatry.

18:27-28a. The **peaceful and unsuspecting people** of **Laish** (cf. v. 7) were no match for the determined Danites who defeated them **and burned down their city.** The people of Laish were 27 miles **from Sidon** (cf. v. 7) **and had no** allies to come to their rescue.

d. The establishment of idolatry at Dan (18:28b-31)

18:28b-31. The Danites rebuilt the city and **named it Dan after their** tribal **forefather.** More significantly (and sadly), they established a tribal center of idolatrous worship under the priesthood of **Jonathan son of Gershom** (cf. Ex. 2:22) which extended through his descendants **until the time of the captivity of the land.** Many scholars refer this to either the Assyrian captivity of Israel in 722 B.C. (2 Kings 17:6) or the captivity of the Galilean population under Tiglath-Pileser III in 733-732 B.C. (2 Kings 15:29). However, an early monarchial date of the authorship of Judges suggests that the statement refers to an earlier unknown captivity (some have suggested the Philistine capture of the ark; cf. 1 Sam. 4:11). For **Moses** the Hebrew text has inserted a superlinear *n* into the name of Moses (*mōšeh*) to make it read "Manasseh" (*mᵉnaššeh*). This was apparently a pious scribe's attempt to relieve Moses' grandson, Jonathan, of involvement with idolatry. The reference to **the house of God . . . in Shiloh** (modern Seilun 19 miles north of Jerusalem) implies that the worship at the Danite shrine opposed the true worship of the Lord at Shiloh (cf. Josh. 18:1). This false worship in Dan was a forerunner of that of Jeroboam I who later established a Northern Kingdom shrine at **Dan** (cf. 1 Kings 12:28-31).

B. Moral degradation: The atrocity of Gibeah and the war with the Benjamites (chaps. 19–21)

1. THE ATROCITY AGAINST THE CONCUBINE OF THE LEVITE (CHAP. 19)

a. The reconciliation of the Levite with his concubine (19:1-9)

19:1a. This chapter opens with the slogan, **In those days Israel had no king** (cf. 17:6; 18:1; 21:25). This indicates that chapters 19–21 illustrate the *anarchy and injustice* that prevailed when the Israelites did not have the centralized authority of a king. Chapters 17–18 illustrate the *idolatry* that characterized the nation.

19:1b-9. The **Levite** mentioned in this chapter is not Micah's Levite (chaps. 17–18) though both had connections with **Bethlehem in Judah** and both lived **in the hill country of Ephraim.** The **remote area** (lit., "backside of") was off the main north-south ridge route. This Levite's **concubine** (a second-status wife, a practice that was never divinely approved; cf. 8:31) **was unfaithful to him** (lit., "played the harlot"), after which she returned to **her father's house in Bethlehem. Four months** later the Levite traveled to Bethlehem where he initiated a reconciliation with his concubine. He was **gladly welcomed** by his **father-in-law** who, with typical Near-Eastern hospitality, entertained him for four days and part of a fifth before the Levite decided he could **stay** no longer.

b. The arrival of the Levite's entourage at Gibeah (19:10-15)

19:10-15. The Levite took his servant, **his two . . . donkeys** (cf. v. 3), **and his concubine,** and traveled northward six miles to pass by **Jebus** (a name for Jerusalem used only here in vv. 10-11 and 1 Chron. 11:4-5, so named for the Amorite group of Jebusites who lived there). He declined his servant's suggestion to **spend the night** in Jebus because it was **an alien city, whose people** were **not Israelites.** The Levite determined to move on to more friendly territory (an ironic and unfortunate decision in view of the following events). So they pressed four miles farther north **to Gibeah** (modern Tell el-Ful) where **they stopped to spend the night.** However, though they **sat in the city square,** the hospitality of

the Benjamites was not forthcoming.

c. The hospitality of the old man from Ephraim (19:16-21)

19:16-21. At the last minute they were saved from a night of danger **in the city square** by **an old man from the hill country of Ephraim** who invited them to **spend the night** at **his house** in Gibeah.

d. The assault by the wicked men of Gibeah (19:22-26)

19:22-26. Reminiscent of the wicked Sodomites in the time of Lot (cf. Gen. 19:1-11), **the wicked men** (or "worthless men"; lit., "sons of Belial"; cf. 1 Sam. 1:16; 2:12) **of** Gibeah **surrounded the house** and demanded that the old man send out the Levite to satisfy their homosexual desires. Considering the laws of hospitality more important than chivalry toward the opposite sex, **the old man** offered them instead his **virgin daughter** and the Levite's **concubine.** The men either did not hear or refused his offer, but when the Levite thrust **his concubine . . . outside to them,** they took her and sexually **abused her throughout the night. At daybreak** she was released to return; she fell **at the door** of the house where she died.

e. The call of the Levite for tribal vengeance (19:27-30)

19:27-30. When the Levite **stepped out** of the door **to continue on his way** (not to look for his concubine!), he discovered her corpse **in the doorway,** and **put her on his donkey and set out for home.** The Levite next performed an almost unbelievable cruelty, cutting **up his concubine limb by limb** (lit., "according to her bones," like a priest preparing a sacrifice) **into 12 parts** (apparently one for each tribe) to be **sent . . . into all the areas of Israel** (cf. 1 Sam. 11:7; 1 Kings 11:30). While this is difficult for modern readers to understand (as well as for the Levite's contemporaries; Jud. 19:30; cf. Hosea 9:9), he meant to arouse the nation to action by calling for a national judicial hearing. Perhaps he was charging them with the responsibility of removing the bloodguiltiness that rested on the entire nation for his concubine's death. The people who **saw** a part of her were appalled and bewildered as to what to do.

2. THE WAR AGAINST THE TRIBE OF BENJAMIN (CHAP. 20)

The Benjamite war narrated in this chapter resulted from the inquiry into the death of the Levite's concubine (cf. chap. 19). It describes an unusually dark hour in Israel's history.

a. The assembly of Israel at Mizpah (20:1-11)

20:1-7. In response to the Levite's call for an inquest, **all the Israelites from Dan to Beersheba** (i.e., from the northern to southern boundaries of Israel; this is a stereotyped expression written from the perspective of the early monarchial author) **and from the land of Gilead** (here referring to all the Transjordanian tribes) **assembled.** They gathered **before the LORD in Mizpah** (Tell en-Nasba, eight miles north of Jerusalem and only four miles north of Gibeah; not the Mizpah in Gilead; cf. 10:17; 11:29). The reference to **400,000 soldiers** need not be understood as 400 contingents or 400 family units, as some scholars have suggested.

The Benjamites were not officially represented at **Mizpah** since the men who raped the concubine were from Gibeah in Benjamin. Apparently, however, the tribe of Benjamin received 1 of the 12 parts of the concubine (cf. 19:29; 20:6). On request, **the Levite** explained the circumstances of his concubine's rape and death, and called for Israel's **verdict.**

20:8-11. The verdict was unanimous: **All the people rose as one man** against the town of **Gibeah** to **give them what they deserve** by launching an attack. One-tenth of the Israelites' troops collected supplies for those who did the fighting.

b. The rejection of the verdict by the Benjamites (20:12-13)

20:12-13. The Benjamites rejected the request of the other tribes **to surrender those wicked men of Gibeah** for execution in order to **purge the evil** (of bloodguiltiness) **from Israel.** Therefore **Israel** took the final step and attacked Gibeah.

c. The mustering of the troops for battle (20:14-18)

20:14-16. Having rejected the request of their fellow **Israelites** (cf. v. 13), **the Benjamites** mobilized **26,000 swordsmen** plus **700 . . . left-handed** men from Gibeah who were all experts with slings.

20:17-18. As noted previously (v. 2), the 11 tribes had the advantage of a much larger army—**400,000** men. They **went up to Bethel** (meaning "house of God") to inquire of the Lord (probably through the high priest's Urim and Thummim; cf. Lev. 8:8; Num. 27:21; Deut. 33:8) concerning which tribe should lead the attack **against the Benjamites.** The Lord's answer was, **Judah shall go first.** Since the tabernacle (or similar central sanctuary where the high priest could be consulted) was located in Shiloh both before (cf. Josh. 18:1) and after (cf. 1 Sam. 1:9) this incident, some scholars refer "Bethel" here not to the city but to "the house of God" which was at Shiloh (cf. Jud. 18:31, "the house of God was in Shiloh"). However, in 18:31 and elsewhere when the sanctuary is called "the house of God" the Hebrew phrase is *bêt-hā'ĕlōhîm*, not just *bêt-'ēl* (as in 20:18, 26). Possibly the central sanctuary was moved back and forth between Shiloh and Bethel, perhaps more than once. So it is preferable to regard Bethel in verses 18 and 26 as the city on the central ridge route 10 or 12 miles north of Jerusalem.

d. The victories of Benjamin over Israel (20:19-28)

20:19-23. The location and topography of **Gibeah** made it easy to defend. **The Benjamites came out of Gibeah,** attacked the Israelite **battle positions,** and slayed **22,000 Israelites.** The Israelites **encouraged one another** and regrouped at the same battle **positions** for another day's fighting. In view of their defeat they also **went up** to Bethel **and wept before the LORD,** inquiring this time whether they should continue **to battle against the Benjamites.** The Lord's answer was affirmative: **Go up against them.**

20:24-28. The strategy and events of the previous day were repeated on **the second day,** but **this time** Israel lost "only" **18,000** men. This second defeat motivated **the Israelites** to return to Bethel where they wept **before the LORD** and **fasted . . . and presented burnt offerings and fellowship offerings to the LORD** (cf. 21:4). Perhaps one reason the Lord permitted their initial defeats was to bring them back in a spirit of repentance to the neglected sacrificial worship. This time their inquiry about whether they should continue the battle not only received a positive reply (**Go**) but also included a promise of victory (**tomorrow I will give them into your hands**). The mention of **Phinehas son of Eleazar** (i.e., Aaron's grandson) implies that he was instrumental in procuring the oracle from the Lord. It also indicates that this event occurred not much later than the death of Joshua (cf. 18:30).

e. The defeat of the Benjamites by Israel (20:29-46)

A general account of the battle (vv. 29-36a) is followed by a detailed and supplementary account (vv. 36b-46).

20:29-36a. God's promise of victory (v. 28) did not lead to presumption on Israel's part, for they reviewed and improved their battle strategy by setting **an ambush around Gibeah.** This was accomplished as follows: The Israelites **took up** the same battle **positions as before** and then deliberately fled as **the Benjamites** launched their attack, so that **the Benjamites** were **drawn away from the city.** Joshua had used a similar ambush strategy against Ai (Josh. 8:1-29). **Then 10,000 of Israel's finest men** attacked **Gibeah** frontally, and **the LORD** gave them victory in battle. The **Benjamites** lost **25,100** soldiers—almost their entire force of 26,700 (Jud. 20:15).

20:36b-46. These verses supplement the previous account by detailing the ambush and the aftermath of the major battle. As the Benjamites were drawn away from the city (cf. vv. 31-32), the Israelites who were waiting **in ambush** dashed **into Gibeah,** slaying the population and setting the city on fire. **The smoke of the whole city going up into the sky** was a prearranged signal for the retreating **Israelites** to turn on the **terrified** Benjamites who **fled** toward **the desert** (eastward; cf. v. 43). Before 600 Benjamites finally escaped to **the rock of Rimmon** (v. 45; cf. v. 47), they suffered a total loss of approximately **25,000 Benjamite swordsmen** (the more exact figure of 25,100 is given in v. 35). The narrative groups their deaths in stages of the battle—**18,000** (v. 44), **5,000 . . . along the roads,** and **2,000** (v. 45).

f. The aftermath of the defeat of Benjamin (20:47-48)

20:47-48. Six hundred Benjamite warriors were able to reach the defensible

stronghold of **the rock of Rimmon** (modern Rammun, four miles east of Bethel), **where they stayed four months** (until they received terms of peace from the Israelites; cf. 21:13-14). They were the only survivors from the entire tribe of Benjamin since the Israelite soldiers destroyed and burned **all the towns** of the Benjamites. Since the destruction included **the animals and everything else they found,** apparently they had placed the Benjamite towns "under the ban" as in holy war (cf. comments on 1:17).

3. THE PRESERVATION OF THE TRIBE OF BENJAMIN (21:1-24)

a. The national concern for the completeness of Israel (21:1-7)

21:1-7. The atrocity of Gibeah (19:25-26) had been punished and blood-guiltiness had been removed from Israel by the deaths of the Benjamites (20:35). However, with the war and destruction behind them, the Israelites became aware of another painful problem—1 of the 12 tribes of Israel had been nearly exterminated and since only 600 males remained alive, Benjamin was in danger of extinction. The problem was complicated by the fact that the Israelites **had taken an oath at Mizpah** not to **give** their **daughters in marriage** to a Benjamite (cf. 21:7, 18). Of course it was contrary to the Mosaic Law for the remaining 600 Benjamites to marry non-Israelites (cf. Ex. 34:16; Deut. 7:3). A secondary matter faced by the Israelites was the fulfillment of another **solemn oath** to **put to death** any **Israelites** who had **failed to assemble** at Mizpah. The primary matter of Benjamite extinction resulted in another period at Bethel when the Israelites **sat before God until evening, raising their voices and weeping bitterly.** The content of their lament was, **Why should one tribe be missing from Israel today?** They also participated in sacrificial worship, giving **burnt offerings and fellowship offerings** (cf. Jud. 20:26).

b. The expedition of Israel against Jabesh Gilead (21:8-12)

21:8-12. In researching their secondary problem (cf. v. 5), the Israelites **discovered that no one from** the town of **Jabesh Gilead** (located about nine miles southeast of Beth Shan and two miles east of the Jordan River) had responded to the call to Mizpah. So they fulfilled their vow by having **12,000** soldiers exterminate the people of **Jabesh Gilead**, except that they spared the **400** virgins of the city as a step toward solving the primary problem of Benjamite extinction.

c. The reconciliation of Israel with Benjamin (21:13-18)

21:13-18. The assembly of Israelites next **sent** to the 600 surviving **Benjamites** a formal **offer of peace** (šālôm, implying restoration to covenantal participation). They accepted the peace offer and were granted the 400 virgins **of Jabesh Gilead.** Israelite grief continued, however, because 200 Benjamites were still without **wives.**

d. The provision of the maidens from Shiloh (21:19-24)

21:19. The Israelites conceived a plan, based on a loophole in their oath, which they suggested to the Benjamites. The oath said the Israelites could not "give" (vv. 1, 7, 18) their daughters to the Benjamites, but it said nothing about their daughters being "taken." Conveniently the girls of nearby **Shiloh** (about 13 miles north by northeast of Mizpah) would soon be participating in a local harvest feast where they would dance in the fields near the vineyards. **Lebonah** (modern el-Lubbān) was about 3 miles north of Shiloh.

21:20-24. The 200 **Benjamites** were to **hide in the vineyards** until the festivities were in progress, and then each was to **rush from the vineyards and . . . seize a wife . . . and go to the land of Benjamin.** The Israelites would then explain the situation to the men of Shiloh, that they were **innocent** (of breaking the oath of Mizpah; v. 1) since they **did not give** their **daughters** to the Benjamites. So the extinction of the tribe of Benjamin was averted, **the Benjamites. . . . rebuilt the towns and settled in them,** and **the Israelites . . . went home.** Though the people were guilty of scheming to get around their oath, the tribe of Benjamin was saved from extinction.

4. THE CHARACTERISTICS OF THE PERIOD OF THE JUDGES (21:25)

21:25. The Book of Judges concludes with a final restatement of human failure concerning the moral and social anarchy

of this period which preceded the monarchy. As stated three times before, **Israel had no king** (cf. 17:6; 18:1; 19:1). The fact that **everyone did as he** wished is a sad commentary on the deplorable spiritual condition of the nation in those days. Though Israel suffered under the oppression of many enemies, God's grace was repeatedly evident when the people turned to Him in repentance. The Book of Judges illustrates both God's justice and His grace—justice in punishing sin and grace in forgiving sin.

BIBLIOGRAPHY

Armerding, Carl Edwin. "Judges." In The New Layman's Bible Commentary. Grand Rapids: Zondervan Publishing House, 1979.

Boling, Robert G. Judges: Introduction, Translation, and Commentary. The Anchor Bible. Garden City, N.Y.: Doubleday & Co., 1975.

Bruce, F.F. "Judges." In The New Bible Commentary. 3rd ed. Grand Rapids: Zondervan Publishing House, 1970.

Cundall, Arthur E., and Morris, Leon. Judges; Ruth. The Tyndale Old Testament Commentaries. Chicago: InterVarsity Press, 1968.

Davis, John J., and Whitcomb, John C. A History of Israel: From Conquest to Exile. Grand Rapids: Baker Book House, 1980.

Enns, Paul P. Judges. Bible Study Commentary. Grand Rapids: Zondervan Publishing House, 1982.

Garstang, John. Joshua–Judges. Grand Rapids: Kregel Publications, 1978.

Gray, John. Joshua, Judges, and Ruth. Greenwood, S.C.: Attic Press, 1967.

Inrig, Gary. Hearts of Iron, Feet of Clay. Chicago: Moody Press, 1979.

Keil, C.F., and Delitzsch, F. In Commentary on the Old Testament in Ten Volumes. Vol. 2. Reprint (25 vols. in 10). Grand Rapids: Wm. B. Eerdmans Publishing Co., 1982.

Soggin, J. Alberto. Judges: A Commentary. Old Testament Library. Philadelphia: Westminster Press, 1981.

Wood, Leon. Distressing Days of the Judges. Grand Rapids: Zondervan Publishing House, 1975.

RUTH

John W. Reed

INTRODUCTION

Title and Authorship. The Book of Ruth is named for a Moabitess who had married a Hebrew man living in Moab. After the death of her husband, Ruth migrated with Naomi, her widowed Hebrew mother-in-law, to Bethlehem in Israel. There God providentially provided for her and led her to marry Boaz, a prosperous Hebrew farmer. Ruth became the great-grandmother of King David. She is listed in the genealogy of Christ in Matthew 1:5.

Ruth and Esther are the only two books in the Bible named for women. Esther was a Hebrew woman who married a Gentile king. God used Esther in a strategic time in the history of Israel to help preserve the nation from destruction. Ruth, on the other hand, was a Gentile woman who married a Hebrew man. God used Ruth to perpetuate the line of the Messiah, the Lord Jesus Christ.

The Book of Ruth is read annually by orthodox Jews on the Feast of Pentecost. This feast commemorates the giving of the Law on Mount Sinai and occurs at the time of the beginning of the offering called the Firstfruits of the Harvest (Ex. 23:16). Ruth's betrothal took place during this festive harvest season, when barley was being winnowed (Ruth 3:2; cf. 1:22).

No one knows for sure who wrote the Book of Ruth. Jewish tradition has attributed the book to Samuel. If he was the author, the book would have been written near the time when David was anointed king of Israel. One of the reasons, then, for Samuel's writing the Book of Ruth could have been to justify David's claim to the throne (through Ruth and Boaz, his great-grandparents).

Most conservative scholars place the date of the writing of Ruth in the Monarchy, either in the time of David or Solomon. Since Solomon is not mentioned in the genealogy at the end of the book (4:18-21), one might deduce that the book was written in David's time. On the other hand an old custom that had ceased to be practiced—the exchanging of the sandal—was explained (4:7). This has caused some to think that the Solomonic period was more likely since additional time would have passed for the custom to have fallen into disuse. Hals has discussed the matter of authorship in further detail (*The Theology of the Book of Ruth*, pp. 65-75).

Historical and Literary Features. The Book of Ruth gleams like a beautiful pearl against a jet-black background. The action recorded in the narrative took place during the period of the Book of Judges (Ruth 1:1). Those days were the dark ages of Israel's history. The victories of Joshua had been followed by periods of spiritual declension with but brief periods of revival. As the time of the Judges wore on, the apostasy deepened till the book ended in corruption and bloody civil strife.

The period of the Judges was marked by weak faith and irresponsible conduct. Even Gideon, who exhibited great faith against overwhelming odds during the destruction of the invading Midianites, Amalekites, and eastern desert tribes (Jud. 7:12, 17-21), later failed to seek God's advice in the everyday affairs of his judgeship (Jud. 8:16-17, 21, 27). Gideon had many wives and concubines, who bore him 70 sons (Jud. 8:29-32).

After Gideon's death Abimelech, a son by his concubine in Shechem, killed all the other sons except one and established himself as a godless and bloody king (Jud. 9).

Since Ruth was the great-grandmother of David (Ruth 4:17), who began his rule at Hebron in 1010 B.C., the experiences in the Book of Ruth occurred in the last half of the 12th century. This means that Ruth may have been a contemporary of Gideon (see the chart "The Judges of Israel" in the *Introduction* to Jud.).

The sensual activities of the judge Samson became an archetype of a hero who is mighty in physical strength but weak in spiritual and moral character.

Against this background of national irresponsibility and weak character Ruth, a Moabitess, and Boaz, a Hebrew landowner, shone as bright examples of purity, faith, and responsible living. The Ruth narrative provided a gratifying reminder that even in the darkest times God was at work in the hearts of His faithful remnant.

The degree of permissiveness in Israel was a theme repeated often in the Book of Judges and restated in the book's last verse: "In those days Israel had no king; everyone did as he saw fit" (Jud. 21:25). By contrast the Book of Ruth provides a view of people who acted responsibly, rather than permissively, and with faith in God's sovereign, superintending control.

Ruth also stood in stark relief against the dark background of her own Moabite ancestry. Moses detailed the somber story of the nation of Moab's origin (Gen. 19:30-38). Lot's two daughters despaired of any future after the destruction of Sodom and Gomorrah. In faithless irresponsibility they got their father drunk enough that he would have sex with them in the cave where they lived. The fruits of their incest were Moab and Ben-Ammi. These sons became the founders of the Moabites and the Ammonites, respectively, nations that often warred against Israel.

Ruth the Moabitess broke the tradition of her idolatrous people and her irresponsible ancestor, Lot's older daughter. Ruth became a believer in the God of the Hebrews. She sought her fulfillment as a mother through the righteous requirements of the Mosaic Law. She proved herself to be worthy of being named with the finest women of Israel.

The practice of levirate marriage (the requirement that a man marry the widow of his deceased brother, Deut. 25:5-6) and the activity of the kinsman-redeemer provided an additional backdrop for the narrative. Ruth 4:9-17 discloses the specific

aspects of this practice as Boaz took the kinsman-redeemer responsibility and married the widowed Ruth. In this account is a strong overtone of grace since Boaz was not within the immediate circle of levirate responsibility. In other words he was not a brother of the deceased Mahlon. His willing acceptance of this responsibility showed the genuine quality of his character, as well as his love for Ruth.

This willing action of Boaz placed him in contrast with his ancestor, Judah, 1 of Jacob's 12 sons. Judah had not acted responsibly in the case of his daughter-in-law, Tamar. Judah had three sons by his Canaanite wife. Judah's eldest son married Tamar, also a Canaanite. This son, Er, was wicked and God took his life (Gen. 38:7). Judah gave his second son, Onan, to Tamar to perform the levirate responsibility of raising up a son for his dead brother.

Onan "knew that the offspring would not be his" (Gen. 38:9), for children born to him and Tamar would perpetuate not his name but the name of his brother Er. So Onan, though he enjoyed sexual relations with Tamar, spilled his sperm on the ground. Because his refusal to fulfill the levirate responsibility displeased God, Onan also died (Gen. 38:10).

After Onan's death Judah did not give his third son, Shelah, to Tamar. It appeared that the family line would cease. But after Judah became a widower, Tamar posed as a harlot and seduced Judah. She conceived and bore twins, Perez and Zerah. Judah, in spite of Tamar's actions, declared that she was more righteous than he because he had refused to fulfill his responsibility and give his third son to her (Gen. 38:11-30).

When the elders at the gate of Bethlehem witnessed the levirate transaction between Boaz and Ruth, they blessed their union with mention of Perez, whom Tamar bore to Judah (Ruth 4:9-12). Ruth stood in contrast with Tamar in that she gained her levirate fulfillment honorably according to the Mosaic Law, whereas Tamar used a disguise and seduction. Without the births of Perez (to Tamar) and Obed (to Ruth and Boaz) the line from Judah to David would have been broken.

The grace of God was evident in that

He included several non-Israelites in the line of David. Since this was the line through which Christ came, it foreshadowed God's inclusion of Gentiles in the work of David's greater Son, the Lord Jesus Christ. Four non-Israelite women are mentioned in Christ's genealogy in Matthew 1—Tamar (Matt. 1:3), Rahab (Matt. 1:5), Ruth (Matt. 1:5), and Uriah's wife, who was Bathsheba (Matt. 1:6). Tamar was a Canaanite, who became the mother of Judah's children, Perez and Zerah. Rahab was a Canaanite harlot in Jericho who became an ancestress of Boaz (cf. comments on Ruth 4:21). Ruth was a Moabitess who became the mother of Obed. Since Bathsheba, the mother of Solomon by David, had been the wife of Uriah, the Hittite, it was probable that she too was a Hittite.

The Book of Ruth is beautifully written with a symmetrical design. It is a "romantic quest" that began in tragic circumstances and ended in joyous fulfillment. It is a book of seeking. Ruth sought a home, provision, a husband, and ultimately a son. Though she was widowed and without offspring, God gave her a husband and a son.

Naomi lost her husband and her two sons in Moab. In her depression she failed to realize the value of her Moabitess daughter-in-law, Ruth. But the book ends with Naomi's depression turned to joy. Her neighbors reminded her that Ruth was more valuable to her than seven sons. Naomi held in her arms Obed, her grandson. But her neighbors called Obed Naomi's "son" (4:17) because the levirate obligation had been willingly undertaken by the godly Boaz.

Mother-in-law jokes are today part of the stock repartee of comedians. This may have been the case in Naomi's insensitive day as well. But Ruth's love and care for her aging mother-in-law stands as a model for all generations. The fact that Boaz was careful to provide for Naomi along with Ruth indicated that his spirit was in tune with Ruth's in this regard. This is the best of all mother-in-law stories and should be told repeatedly.

Theological Emphasis. The writer of Ruth stressed several theological truths. Several names of God were used profusely in the book. "LORD" (*Yahweh*) was

used 17 times, "God" (*'ĕlōhîm*) 3 times (1:16 [twice]; 2:12), and "Almighty" (*šadday*) twice (1:20-21). Yahweh was the name that spoke of God's essential nature as a present active force in the lives of His covenant people.

On two occasions the author spoke directly of God's sovereign, superintending grace on behalf of the main characters in the Book of Ruth: (1) Naomi learned "in Moab that the LORD had come to the aid of His people by providing food for them" (1:6). (2) Ruth had been barren for several years in Moab before her husband Mahlon died. Later, as the wife of Boaz, "the LORD enabled her to conceive, and she gave birth to a son" (4:13).

Eight times the characters in the book spoke of God's activity (1:13, 20-21 [four times]; 2:20; 4:12, 14). The Lord was regularly petitioned to answer prayers on their behalf (1:8-9; 2:12; 4:11-12). Five times blessing from the Lord was invoked on behalf of faithful people (2:4 [twice], 19-20; 3:10). Ruth and Boaz committed themselves to carry out their responsibilities in light of God's fidelity (1:17; 3:13). Boaz commended Ruth for seeking refuge under the wings of Israel's God (2:12).

Clearly God would always act responsibly and carry out His plan. The question was whether the people in the Book of Ruth would respond in a responsible manner. Elimelech seemed irresponsible in leaving Bethlehem and going to Moab (1:2). But Naomi acted responsibly in returning (1:7). Orpah returned to her home and her Moabite gods; in contrast Ruth chose to follow Naomi's God and to care for Naomi (1:14-17). Though the nearest kinsman refused to redeem, faithful Boaz acted responsibly in providing redemption (3:12; 4:1-10). Various forms of the Hebrew words "redeem," "redeemer," "redemption," and "kinsman-redeemer" are used 20 times in the book, thus making redemption one of the book's key words.

Another key word is *ḥesed*, which speaks of loyalty borne out of love and kindness toward those to whom a person is responsible. Naomi asked that the Lord would show His *ḥesed* to her daughters-in-law (1:8). Naomi also spoke of the Lord's *ḥesed* to her ("the living") because of what Boaz had done for Ruth (2:20). Boaz affirmed the *ḥesed* of Ruth when she asked him to marry her instead of seeking a younger man. This kindness, Boaz said, was even greater than her earlier kindness to Naomi (3:10). Boaz performed an act of ḥeseḏ when he went beyond the bounds of what was required of him in marrying Ruth.

Message. The book's message may have been an affirmation of King David's rights to the throne of Israel. The display of God's providence in bringing this to pass can challenge all Christians to believe that God is at work in their lives as well.

The truth of the book for all ages might be stated as follows: The Lord is faithful in His business of loving, superintending, and providentially caring for His people. God's people should also be about His business in the ordinary activities of daily living. Since God's people are recipients of His grace they, like Ruth and Boaz, should respond in faithful obedience to Him and in gracious acts toward other people.

During a period of great irresponsibility in Israel's history the Book of Ruth was a clear call to responsible living. Clearly this message is needed today as well.

Boaz is an illustration of the greater One who came from his family, the Lord Jesus Christ. Boaz acted in grace to redeem Ruth; Christ acted in grace by giving Himself as the Redeemer to provide redemption for all mankind.

OUTLINE

COMMENTARY

I. Introduction (1:1-5)

The narrative begins with the necessary mention of the time, names, places, and events. The mood was somber and foreboding. A famine forced a family in Bethlehem to move to a foreign land. This situation became an opportunity for God to demonstrate His grace. The unfolding of the story revealed how God providentially worked to meet needs.

A. A tragic sojourn (1:1-2)

1:1. The events recorded in the Book of Ruth occurred in the period of **the Judges,** probably during the administration of the judge Gideon (see "Historical and Literary Features" under *Introduction*). The **famine in the land** was probably God's acting in judgment on His sinning people. Many years later in Elijah's day God sent another famine as judgment on Israel for worshiping Baal (1 Kings 16:30–17:1; 18:21, 37; 19:10).

Divine control of the crops was a major factor in the development of events in the Book of Ruth. During the period of the Judges, worship of the Canaanite god Baal was common among the Israelites (Jud. 2:11; 3:7; 8:33; 10:6, 10). Baal was believed to be owner of the land and to control its fertility. Baal's female counterpart was Ashtoreth. Sexual intercourse between these two gods was believed to regulate fertility of the earth and its creatures.

God had commanded the Israelites under Joshua's leadership to purge the land of the Canaanites and their idols (Deut. 7:16; 12:2-3; 20:17). The failure of the Israelites to do so (Josh. 16:10; Jud. 1:27-33) left them open to the temptation to look to the idols rather than to God for agricultural blessing. Perhaps the cultic prostitution and sexual practices used in the worship of Baal also enticed the Hebrew people. Interestingly Gideon's father had built an altar to Baal, but Gideon had destroyed it (Jud. 6:25-34). The Ruth narrative shows the wisdom of trusting in God and His providence rather than in Canaanite gods.

Bethlehem was about five miles south of Jerusalem. Later Obed, son of Ruth and Boaz, was born in Bethlehem and Obed's grandson David was born in Bethlehem (Ruth 4:18-21; 1 Sam. 17:58). Bethlehem, of course, would also be the birthplace of David's greater Son, the Lord Jesus Christ (Luke 2:4-7).

A man from Bethlehem decided to take his family to **Moab,** about 50 miles east on the other side of the Dead Sea. He intended to live there for a short period. Nothing is said about why he chose Moab. Probably he had heard that there was no famine there. However, the unfolding events indicate that it was an unwise choice, and that Bethlehem, not Moab, was the place where God would bless him. The inhabitants of Moab were excluded from the congregation of the Lord (Deut. 23:3-6). (On the origin of the Moabites see "Historical and Literary Features" under *Introduction*; cf. Gen. 19:30-38.) They were worshipers of the god Chemosh, a deity whose worship was similar to that of Baal.

1:2. The man's name was Elimelech, his wife was **Naomi,** and their **two sons were Mahlon and Kilion.** Some Bible students make much of the fact that the name Elimelech means "My God is king," but he may or may not have lived up to his name. (See comments on vv. 20-21 for a wordplay on Naomi's name.) The term **Ephrathites** was a designation for the inhabitants of Ephrath (also spelled Ephratah and Ephratha), another name for Bethlehem (cf. 4:11; Gen. 35:19; 48:7; Micah 5:2).

B. A depressing emptiness (1:3-5)

1:3. Naomi faced the distressing problem of her husband's death. How long they had lived in Moab before Elimelech's death is not known. But Naomi, though widowed, sorrowing, and in a foreign land, had hope while **her two sons** were still alive. Naomi now became the central figure in the narrative.

1:4. Naomi's two sons **married Moabite women . . . Orpah and Ruth.** These marriages were not condemned.

Though the Mosaic Law prohibited Israelites from marrying the Canaanites (Deut. 7:3), the Law did not say Israelites could not marry Moabites. However, Solomon's experience later showed that the greatest problem in such a marriage is the temptation to serve the gods of one's foreign wife (1 Kings 11:1-6; cf. Mal. 2:11). No doubt orthodox Israelites would have thought that marrying Moabite women was unwise. The Book of Ruth does not record the length of these marriages but they were childless. Not till Ruth 4:10 does the reader learn which son (Mahlon) married Ruth. **They . . . lived** in Moab **about 10 years** which was probably longer than the family intended to stay (cf. "for a while," 1:1).

1:5. Then Naomi's two sons **died.** Jewish tradition has regarded the death of these three males (Elimelech, **Mahlon, and Kilion**) as God's punishment for their leaving Bethlehem. Though that is possible, the text does not indicate it. **Naomi** had now accumulated a great load of personal grief. **Her husband** and her only **sons** had died before their time. She was a stranger in a foreign land. If the family name were to carry on, there had to be an heir. But having no sons, Naomi **was left without** hope. Her Moabitess daughters-in-law offered her no apparent means to an heir.

II. Seeking a Home by Faith (1:6-22)

The main narrative portion now begins. Dialogue was the primary device used by the author. Fifty-nine of the 84 verses in the book contain dialogue, beginning in verse 8. Naomi resolved to return home, and in so doing she believed that she had to leave her daughters-in-law in Moab because she thought that would be best for them. She received a surprise when Ruth resolved to return with her.

A. A loving choice (1:6-18)

1:6-7. Naomi learned that rain had come to her homeland. The famine was ended and God provided **food** (crops from the field and fruit from the trees). It was **the LORD** who had stopped the famine and given rain; it was not Baal, who the Canaanites believed was the god who sent rain. **Return** is a key word in Ruth. Hebrew forms of this word are used several times in this first chapter. Here is an apt illustration of repentance. Naomi reversed the direction she and her husband had taken. She turned away from **Moab** and the errors of the past. She turned her back on the tragic graves of her loved ones and headed **back** to **Judah,** her homeland.

1:8 Naomi, sensing that the prospects of her daughters-in-law for remarriage in Israel would be slight, urged them to stay in Moab. Her telling each of them to return to her **mother's home** was unusual in a male-dominated society. Since Naomi was thinking of their remarriages, she may have referred to their mothers because her daughters-in-law would have discussed their wedding plans with their mothers.

The word **kindness** is the Hebrew word *ḥeseḏ*. It is an important word in the Book of Ruth (cf. 2:20; 3:10) and throughout the Old Testament. It speaks of God's covenant loyalty to His people. It involves grace in that it was extended even when it was not deserved. Here divine will and human action went hand in hand. Both God and humans were doers of *ḥeseḏ*. The basis of Naomi's blessing was the gracious actions of Ruth and Orpah to their husbands and to Naomi. Both young women were worthy in the eyes of their mother-in-law, so she wanted God to be good to them. Though they were foreigners, they had married Israelite men and thus were under God's covenant.

1:9-10. Naomi then asked that God would give **each of** them a place of **rest** with **another husband.** This became a key issue in the book. Marriage meant security for a woman. And yet ironically Ruth seemed to be giving up this possibility by leaving Moab. Naomi's kisses were intended as farewells, but both women stated their desire to return with Naomi. Possibly a custom in that day required this.

1:11. Three times **Naomi** insisted that they **return** to Moab (vv. 11-12, 15). They needed to be sure to remarry. In the ancient Near East a woman without a husband was in a serious situation because she lacked security. And widows were especially needy. Naomi referred to the *levirate custom* in Israel in which a brother was responsible to marry his deceased brother's wife in order to conceive a son and perpetuate his brother's name

and inheritance (Deut. 25:5-10). Naomi pointed out that this would not be possible in their case since she had no **more sons.**

1:12-13. Naomi said that she was past the age of childbearing. Even if she did acquire a new **husband** and have **sons** it was ridiculous to think that Orpah and Ruth would **wait** for them to grow **up.**

Naomi seemed a bit insensitive to the grief of her daughters-in-law. She thought that her case was **more bitter** than theirs because they still had potential for childbearing. She regarded her plight as a result of **her mother-in-law's** affliction (cf. vv. 20-21). Naomi was apparently in a stage of grief that caused her to speak in anger against God. And yet she was still a woman of faith. She had no doubt that God was actively involved in their lives (cf. vv. 8-9; 2:20). She saw God as sovereign and the ultimate cause of life's issues.

1:14. Orpah should not be unduly criticized for returning to Moab. She was obeying the wishes of **her mother-in-law.** Nothing more is said in the Book of Ruth about Orpah. Presumably she remarried in Moab.

Ruth, however, did the unexpected. Though Orpah chose to seek a husband, **Ruth clung to** Naomi, apparently choosing to follow and serve her widowed mother-in-law rather than seek a husband. In Ruth's mind the decision probably meant that she would never have a husband or children. James would have considered her concern for her widowed mother-in-law a profoundly religious act (James 1:27).

1:15. Naomi again urged Ruth to return to her home. She cited the example of Orpah's obedience to her request. Naomi was aware that the decision to return meant the continuing influence of the Moabite **gods** including Chemosh the chief god (Num. 21:29; 1 Kings 11:7), but the importance of Ruth's having a husband seemed to outweigh this concern. Naomi did not make it easy for Ruth to come to faith in the God of Israel.

1:16. Ruth had endured three entreaties of her mother-in-law to return home to Moab (vv. 11-12, 15). But she chose life with Naomi over her family, her national identity, and her religious idolatry. In one of the most beautiful expressions of commitment in all the world's literature to that of Naomi. She confessed allegiance to the **people** of Israel (**your people**) and to the **God** of Israel (**your God**). Here was a stirring example of a complete break with the past. Like Abraham Ruth decided to leave her ancestors' idolatrous land to go to the land of promise. And Ruth did it without the encouragement of a promise. In fact she made her decision despite Naomi's strenuous encouragement to do otherwise.

1:17. Ruth's decision was so strong that it included reference to death and burial. She would stay with Naomi to death and beyond. To seal the quality of her decision, Ruth invoked judgment from Israel's God if she were to break her commitment of loyalty to her mother-in-law. Ruth's conversion was complete. The events that followed show that her life matched her confession.

1:18. Naomi then **stopped urging** Ruth to go back to Moab. Since Ruth had invoked God's name in her commitment (v. 17), Naomi acquiesced. Nothing more could be said. The Book of Ruth says nothing about Naomi welcoming her daughter-in-law to the fold of those who trusted in Israel's God. **Ruth** had leaped by faith the barriers that had been thrown up before her.

B. A bittersweet return (1:19-22)

1:19. The **two women** made the arduous journey **to Bethlehem.** The exclusively female character of this portion of chapter 1 continued, for **the whole town** of Bethlehem spoke through its **women.** Their question, **Can this be Naomi?** suggests that they remembered Naomi and that she had experienced an observable change, obviously for the worse.

1:20. Naomi's grief and depression, that had expressed itself toward God (v. 13), continued. She stated that her name **Naomi,** which means "sweetness or pleasantness," was improper for her in her condition. She said she should be called **Mara,** which means "bitter." Her reason was that **the Almighty** (*šadday*) had **made** her **life very bitter.** By speaking of God as "the Almighty" she emphasized His great power (or "provisions"; cf. comments on Gen. 17:1). This great God could not be resisted. The disaster He sent could not be averted. Na-

omi had such faith in God and His personal involvement in her life that she knew the bitter things she experienced were from Him. Her grief was real; obviously she took God seriously.

1:21. Naomi's complaint became specific. Years before she **went away** to Moab **full,** with a husband and two sons, but now she came **back empty.** Her grief and depression did not enable her to recognize her Moabitess daughter-in-law as of any significant worth. Later, however, she experienced great benefit through Ruth (4:15). **Naomi** was sure her problem was all God's fault. Her return home had only intensified the depth of her grief. She saw nothing ahead but the loneliness, abandonment, and helplessness of widowhood. Her complaint began and ended with a reference to **the Almighty,** the name of the all-powerful God. But in the face of her deep tragedy God would soon proceed to act in gracious mercy.

1:22. This verse provides a transition toward hope for **Naomi,** as well as Ruth. God was not really her antagonist but would through His sovereign, superintending providence act with favor toward both widows.

Naomi had left Bethlehem because of a food famine. She **returned** with a famine in her soul. **The barley harvest** in **Bethlehem,** however, must have been a welcome sight. But Naomi in her depression might not have been impressed. (The barley harvest was in the month of Nisan [March-April]. See the chart "Calendar in Israel," near Ex. 12.)

Naomi thought she was returning empty-handed, but she had **Ruth the Moabitess** with her. And the harvest was ripe; there was hope.

III. Seeking Provisions Responsibly (chap. 2)

Ruth was now a believer (cf. v. 12). She was in the land of Israel. How would she act? Since Moabites were excluded from the congregation of Israel (Deut. 23:3), she was there by grace. The events in Ruth 2 show how she was received. In this chapter another person, Boaz, a wealthy farmer, is introduced. Would he be a responsible member of the godly congregation of Israel? Naomi was home. Would her grief assuage and her depression heal? By their words and their actions these three persons revealed their true characters.

A. A God-guided happening (2:1-3)

2:1. The female dominance in the story now was modified by reference to an important male. **Boaz** was a near **relative** of **Elimelech,** Naomi's deceased husband (1:2-3; cf. 2:3). Boaz was a man of outstanding qualities. The Hebrew words *'îš gibbôr ḥayil,* translated **man of standing,** are literally, "a mighty man of valor." These same words are used of Gideon and Jephthah, each of whom was called a "mighty warrior" (Jud. 6:12; 11:1). They were men of valor—capable, efficient, and worthy in battle. Boaz was a mighty man of valor, capable in his community, and lived an exemplary lifestyle (cf. *ḥayil,* used of Ruth, in Ruth 3:11).

2:2. The author again reminded the readers that **Ruth** was a **Moabitess** (cf. 1:22), perhaps to highlight the favorable treatment she was to receive from Boaz. Ruth understood the rights of the poor in Israel to gather grain in a field after the harvesters had passed through. The corners of the field were to be left for the poor to reap (Lev. 19:9-10; 23:22). Some generous landowners were known to have left as much as one-fourth of their crop for the needy and aliens. Ruth did not wait for **Naomi** to serve her; she took the initiative. **Naomi** encouraged Ruth to **go.**

2:3. Because **Boaz** was already introduced into the plot (v. 1), it is clear that Ruth was not in Boaz's **field** by mere chance. She had moved forward in obedience to her rights in the Law of God and was guided by grace into the place God provided. The same providence that later led the Magi to Bethlehem (Matt. 2:1-8) directed Ruth to the appropriate Bethlehem field. Again the author stated that Boaz **was from the clan of Elimelech** (cf. Ruth 2:1). This fact is important to the unfolding of events.

B. A well-deserved kindness (2:4-17)

2:4. The spiritual tone of **Boaz** and his workers was warm and vigorous. When he **greeted** them with the blessing, **The LORD be with you,** they responded similarly, **The LORD bless you.** Faith in the Lord was active in their lives. Boaz spoke the language of faith. Would his actions also fit his words?

2:5-6. When **Boaz** noted a new **young woman** in his field among the gleaners, his interest was stirred. When he asked who she was, **the foreman** identified the new gleaner as **the Moabitess who** had returned **from Moab with Naomi.** Some have felt that the foreman's reference to Moab was intended as a derogatory statement, but the text does not indicate this.

2:7. The foreman added that Ruth had asked permission to **glean . . . among the sheaves** (i.e., bundles of barley grain). He said she had **worked steadily from** the time she came in the **morning . . . except for a short rest in the shelter** that apparently was provided for the workers. He noticed that she was a diligent worker.

2:8-9. **Boaz** addressed **Ruth** as **my daughter** (cf. 3:10-11) in reference to the age difference between them. He was closer to the age of Naomi (cf. "younger men," 3:10). Boaz not only spoke of his faith in the Lord (2:4); his life corresponded with his words. When he told Ruth to continue gleaning in his field, he apparently meant that she should glean there throughout the several weeks of harvesting (cf. v. 23) barley (March-April) and wheat (June-July). Normally the gleaners would move in after the harvesters had left an area. But Ruth was invited to **follow along** with the **servant girls** as they worked in the reaping. Boaz assured Ruth that she would be protected from any remarks or other embarrassing incidents that might have come from the male workers (cf. v. 15). When she got **thirsty,** she need not be concerned about drawing water. She could **drink from** that provided for the workers. In these several ways Boaz was providing for Ruth beyond what was required by the Law (cf. v. 16).

2:10. Ruth responded with utter humility. **She bowed down with her face to the ground,** a gesture common in the ancient Near East, mentioned frequently in the Bible (cf., e.g., Gen. 19:1; 42:6; 43:26; 48:12; Josh. 5:14; 2 Sam. 1:2). She was surprised by the **favor** (cf. Ruth 2:2, 13) she received from this important man. The word "favor" (*ḥēn,* "grace, favor, acceptance") is used often in the Old Testament (e.g., Gen. 6:8; 18:3; 30:27; Ps. 84:11; Prov. 3:4, 34 ["grace"]). Ruth had expected the opposite of the treatment she received. She was a recipient of grace and was grateful. Yet she was eager to find out **why** she had been singled out for such unusual treatment since she was **a foreigner** and a stranger.

2:11. **Boaz** knew much **about** Ruth. News about her had traveled rapidly throughout the small town. Boaz, deeply moved by what Ruth had **done for** Naomi, spoke to Ruth in words of high affirmation. His words about her leaving her parents and her **homeland . . . to live with a people** she had not met are reminiscent of God's words when He called Abram (Gen. 12:1).

2:12. Boaz prayed that God would reward Ruth as repayment for the kindness she had displayed to her mother-in-law. He strengthened his request by asking that she be **richly rewarded by . . . the God** she had **come to** trust. He used a figure of speech known as a zoomorphism, comparing part of God to some aspect of an animal. He said she had taken **refuge** under God's **wings,** like a chick under the wings of its mother hen (cf. Pss. 17:8; 36:7; 57:1; 61:4; 63:7; 91:4; Matt. 23:37). She was trusting in God's protection. Soon Boaz would be used by God to answer his own prayer.

2:13. Though Boaz's words could have stirred her to pride, Ruth continued to respond in humility. Naomi had given no words of encouragement to Ruth, but this man spoke comforting words that warmed her soul. She mentioned her gratitude for his **favor** (cf. vv. 2, 10), **comfort,** and kind words, and hoped they would **continue.** She felt she was less important than Boaz's **servant girls.**

2:14. **Boaz** continued his kindness to Ruth. He invited her to eat the good food provided for himself and his **harvesters.** She was not left to fend for herself as gleaners usually were. He provided for her more than she could eat, either to show his genuine concern for and interest in her, or to allow her to have some to take home to her mother-in-law (cf. v. 18). The **wine vinegar** was apparently a delicacy that enhanced the meal. **Roasted grain** was a staple food in that day. It consisted of barley roasted on an iron plate over an open fire.

2:15-16. Ruth did not linger at the meal. After she returned to gleaning, **Boaz** ordered his workers to do more

than let her glean among them. In addition they were deliberately to drop handfuls of **stalks** of barley in her path so that she would have abundant provision. This too was beyond what Boaz was required by the Law to do (cf. v. 9). Nor were his men to **rebuke her** or hinder her in any way.

2:17. After working hard all day **Ruth . . . threshed the barley,** beat out the grain from the stalks, and had **an ephah.** This was about half a bushel, an unusually generous amount for one day of gleaning. It weighed about 30 pounds and was enough food for many days.

C. An expression of joy (2:18-23)

Ruth's return home to Naomi ended Naomi's emptiness and filled the older woman with anticipation, thankfulness, and hope.

2:18. When Ruth brought home the ephah of barley grain, the results of her toil, Naomi **saw** the large amount. Also **Ruth** gave Naomi the extra portion **she had** saved from her lunch (cf. v. 14). Here was a widow who was not overlooked in the daily supply of food (cf. Acts 6:1). Naomi would be cared for by Ruth.

2:19. Naomi requested the name of Ruth's benefactor and prayed a blessing on him before Ruth answered her question. **Ruth** disclosed that she had **worked** in the field of **Boaz.**

2:20. **Naomi** repeated her blessing, now knowing to whom it should be applied (cf. v. 19a). Her night of sorrow with its fog of depression had broken into the dawning of a new day of joy. As God was the source of her sorrow (1:20-21), He was now the source of her joy. God's **kindness** (*ḥeseḏ*; cf. 3:10 and comments on 1:8) again rested on **the living,** Ruth and herself.

Naomi's mind immediately perceived the significance of the situation. Even **the dead** might soon be blessed, in that the name of Elimelech, her dead husband, could live on through her faithful daughter-in-law, Ruth. Boaz was a **close relative,** but more than that, he was a **kinsman**-redeemer. He could act as a redeemer of property and persons. He could act as a *levir*, a Latin term for brother-in-law. Boaz could redeem by fulfilling the levirate law, which required a brother of a deceased man to marry his widow and raise up a son to his name (Deut. 25:5-10). Though Boaz was not a brother to Mahlon, Ruth's deceased husband (Ruth 4:10), he was a close relative to the family and could act as a *levir* if he so desired. Naomi sensed the willingness of Boaz. No explanation is given as to why Naomi did not mention the nearer kinsman-redeemer (cf. 3:12).

2:21-22. Ruth had more good news. Boaz had invited her to remain in his field throughout the harvest (cf. vv. 8, 23). Naturally Naomi encouraged Ruth to accept Boaz's generosity. Perhaps to emphasize her need to stay there, **Naomi** reminded **Ruth** of the danger that might lurk in another **field**. This was a reminder of the especially low morals in the days of the Judges and Ruth.

2:23. Ruth's loyalty was revealed in her obedience to Naomi's words. She gleaned with Boaz's **servant girls** (cf. v. 8) for the several weeks of **the barley and wheat harvests,** and **lived with** Naomi during that time. However, the tension in the plot continued, for the harvest would soon come to an end. What would happen to the widows after the harvest was over?

IV. Seeking Redeeming Love (chap. 3)

Naomi was no longer depressed. She became a matchmaker and prepared Ruth to seek the love of her willing kinsman-redeemer, Boaz. The turning point in the narrative is at hand.

A. A plan for redemption (3:1-5)

During the weeks of the barley and wheat harvests (cf. 2:23), Naomi had time to put her plan together. When the time was right she acted.

3:1. Naomi was a persistent person (cf. 1:8-15). She was now resolved to seek rest and security for her daughter-in-law through marriage. Ruth had given up the possibility of remarriage in order to care for the aging Naomi, but now marriage suddenly again became a possibility. It was customary for Hebrew parents to arrange marriages for their children (Jud. 14:1-10). **To find a home** is literally to "find rest" (cf. Ruth 1:9), to be settled and secure in a home with a husband.

3:2. Naomi pointed out that since **Boaz** was a relative of theirs, he could be a **kinsman**-redeemer for Ruth. He had an

open and willing heart. So Naomi suggested Ruth go to **the threshing floor** that evening. The people of Bethlehem took turns using the threshing floor. The floor was a flat hard area on a slightly raised platform or hill. In threshing, the grain was beaten out from the stalks with flails (cf. 2:17) or was trodden over by oxen. Then in **winnowing** the grain was thrown in the air and the wind carried the chaff away. The grain was then removed from the threshing floor and placed in heaps to be sold or stored in granaries.

Threshing and winnowing were a time of great festivity and rejoicing. Naomi knew that Boaz was threshing his grain on the day that she had chosen for her plan. She also knew that Boaz would be sleeping near his grain that night, to protect it.

3:3. Ruth was to prepare herself by washing and perfuming herself. The words **best clothes** may be rendered "a large outer garment." This was to keep her identity from being detected. She was to observe Boaz **eating and drinking** but was not to **let him know** of her presence.

3:4. After Boaz finished eating and drinking, Ruth was to observe **the place where** he retired for the night. Under cover of darkness Ruth was to **go** to Boaz, **uncover his feet, and lie down** there. (On the meaning of the uncovering of the feet, see the comments on v. 7.) Boaz, Naomi said, would then **tell** Ruth what she was **to do.** The implication was clear that Ruth should do whatever he requested.

3:5. Ruth stated that she would act in full and unquestioned obedience to the directions of her mother-in-law (cf. 2:22-23).

B. A claim for redemption (3:6-9)

The preparation for the redemption experience had been carefully made. Now the plan had to be carried out.

3:6. Ruth **went** to **the threshing floor** and carried out the plan in exact detail as matchmaker Naomi had laid it out.

3:7. Some commentators suggest that what **Ruth** did presented an opportunity for immorality. But nothing in the passage supports this. Her mother-in-law had complete confidence in the integrity of the kinsman-redeemer. **Boaz** could be trusted to act responsibly. And Ruth was recognized by everyone as "a woman of noble character" (v. 11). The uncovering of the **feet** was a ceremonial act that was completely proper. Probably the scene took place in the dark so that Boaz had the opportunity to reject the proposal without the whole town knowing about it.

3:8-9. Something startled Boaz **in the middle of the night. He turned** to discover that **a woman** was **lying at his feet.** Boaz asked for the identity of his unusual guest (cf. 2:5). Ruth responded in humility (cf. 2:10): **I am your servant Ruth.** She had put herself under the wings of Yahweh (2:12), and now she asked to be put under the wings of Boaz. In the phrase **the corner of your garment** the word "corner" is kānāp, which is translated "wing" in 2:12. She used a poetic image that had its source in the blessing that Boaz had given her. A Moabitess widow was calling the attention of a noted Hebrew to his responsibility. He could now follow through on his benediction (2:12) by becoming Ruth's **kinsman-redeemer** and providing her with the security of marriage.

C. A pledge of redemption (3:10-15)

Boaz joyfully received Ruth's proposal. The tension of the plot continued, however, because another kinsman had a prior claim on her.

3:10. Boaz gave no hint that Ruth had embarrassed him by her actions or that she had done something that was not within her rights or against the customs of the day. Rather than thinking suggestive thoughts as some might have done in such a setting, he immediately blessed Ruth: **The LORD bless you.** He again used the phrase **my daughter,** a reminder of their age difference (cf. 2:8; 3:11). He commended Ruth for her act of **kindness** ("loyalty," ḥeseḏ; cf. comments on 1:8) that was **greater than** her decision to serve her mother-in-law. Boaz also commended her for not going **after** a **younger** man. He seemed to believe Ruth could have readily found such a match. He praised her for being willing to marry an older man in order to fulfill her commitment to her first husband, Mahlon (cf. 4:10), and the family name of Elimelech.

3:11. Boaz then relieved any imme-

diate fears Ruth might have had by saying that he would **do** as she requested. He might have sensed that she was apprehensive over how he might interpret her bold proposal. Boaz told her that **all** his **fellow townsmen** (lit., the "people of the gate," probably referring to the elders of Bethlehem) considered her a person of the highest reputation. **Noble character** translates ḥayil ("valor, worth, ability"), the same word used of the worthiness of Boaz (2:1; cf. Prov. 12:4; 31:10, 29 ["noble"]). They were truly a good match!

3:12. The narrative, however, was not nearing the end. Still another complication had to be unraveled. Boaz had already looked into the legal aspects of the proposed marriage; perhaps he had anticipated her request. He knew that Ruth by her marriage into Elimelech's family had a relative who was more closely related to her than he was. But Boaz would do all he could to see that the outcome would be one that satisfied Ruth's request.

3:13. Boaz acted responsibly in two ways: (1) He did not send her home in the middle of **the night.** He would protect her and he would touch her only if she could be rightfully his. (2) Also he protected the rights of her nearer kinsman. If the other relative wanted **to redeem,** that was his right. But if the nearer kinsman was **not willing,** Boaz would **surely** do so. He covered his pledge with a **vow.** There was no doubt about how Boaz wanted the matter to eventuate.

3:14. Ruth **lay at his feet until** early **morning.** She arose before daylight. Boaz did not want her life complicated by village gossips, so he urged her not to **let it be known** she had been at **the threshing floor.** Nothing had happened that was improper but gossipers are not careful about facts.

3:15. Into Ruth's **shawl** Boaz put **six measures of barley** for her and Naomi. Naomi was entering more and more into the fullness of her wise decision to return to Bethlehem. The "measure" was probably the seah (one-third of an ephah or about 10 pounds). Thus six seahs would equal about 60 pounds. Ruth was a strong woman to be able to carry such a heavy load. Probably Boaz placed the burden **on her** head.

Some Hebrew manuscripts read,

Then he went back to town, but others have "she" in place of "he." Since Ruth returned to Bethlehem at that time and Boaz a bit later that morning (4:1), both renderings ("she" and "he") fit the facts.

D. An anticipation of redemption (3:16-18)

Naomi eagerly sought to know the outcome of Ruth's adventure and predicted that Boaz would quickly resolve the issues that day. Whatever the outcome as to who the redeemer would be, it would be Ruth's day of redemption.

3:16-17. Naomi sought to know how it had gone with **Ruth.** As before, she called Ruth **my daughter** (v. 1; 2:2; cf. 1:11-13; 3:18). Ruth gave her a full report and added that **Boaz had** given her the **barley** so that Naomi could share in Ruth's future fulfillment. Naomi had done her matchmaking well and had earned a reward. The aged widow could then rest assured that she would not be forgotten in the future.

3:18. Naomi and Ruth had done all they could. The initiative now rested with Boaz. Boaz would **not rest** till he had **settled the matter** that day.

V. Receiving Redemption's Loving Rewards (4:1-13)

With the action having turned in his direction, Boaz now took the initiative. Would the nearer kinsman take what had been offered to Boaz?

A. A refusal of redemption (4:1-8)

4:1. Boaz went up to the town gate of Bethlehem. The town gate was where personal business and civic affairs of the people were transacted. The threshing floor was below the level of the city itself, and for that reason Boaz went "up" to the gate. The area was quite hilly. **The kinsman-redeemer** closer to Elimelech (3:12) **came** by the gate and **Boaz** asked him to **sit down.** The fact that the man's name was not given may have been poetic justice since he refused to become the redeemer. The words **my friend** became a catch phrase in Israel. Rabbinic writings used the designation for an unknown "John Doe."

4:2. Boaz called together **10 of** Bethlehem's **elders,** and they also sat down. They would serve as witnesses of the legal transaction (vv. 4, 9-11). Why he

chose 10 is not stated. (Centuries later 10 became the number necessary for a Jewish marriage benediction or a quorum for a synagogue meeting.) This was now a man's world where a public decision was to be made on an important matter that profoundly affected the women who had brought it to this point.

4:3. Boaz had a carefully planned strategy. He unfolded the elements in the case step by step. First, he explained that **Naomi** (and Ruth; cf. v. 5) had a field for sale **that belonged to** Naomi's late husband. No information is given as to how she came to possess it. Her poverty apparently required that she sell it. But if possible the land should remain in the family (cf. Jer. 32:6-12).

4:4. The nearer kinsman had the first right to the property and Boaz was **next** after him. If Ruth's closer relative would not **redeem** (purchase) it, Boaz was prepared to do so. The man then agreed to **redeem** the piece of land.

4:5. But then **Boaz** explained that when the nearer kinsman redeemed the **land,** he must also acquire **Ruth the Moabitess.** Apparently at the death of Elimelech the property had passed to Mahlon so Mahlon's **widow** Ruth was included in the redemption responsibility. A son, to whom the property would belong, should be raised up to perpetuate the family **name.**

4:6. When the nearer **kinsman** heard this stipulation about marriage, he refused his right of purchase. He feared that his **own estate** might be endangered. So he gave the right of redemption to Boaz. Why did he change his mind? (Cf. "I will redeem it," v. 4b, with "I cannot redeem it," v. 6.) Perhaps he was too poor to sustain the land and a wife. Or, as some have suggested, perhaps he feared to marry a Moabitess lest the fate of Mahlon, Ruth's first husband (v. 10), befall him. Perhaps the best view is that when he learned from Boaz that Ruth owned the property along with Naomi (v. 5), he knew that if Ruth bore him a son, that son would eventually inherit not only the redeemed property but probably part of his own estate too. In that sense the nearer redeemer would "endanger" his estate. However, if only Naomi were the widow (not Naomi *and* Ruth), then no son from the levirate marriage would inherit part of the redeemer's estate because Naomi was past childbearing.

4:7-8. A legal transaction was finalized not by signing a paper but by a dramatic symbolic act that others would witness and remember. The passing of the **sandal** symbolized Boaz's right to walk on the land as his **property** (cf. Deut. 1:36; 11:24; Josh. 1:3; 14:9). After giving his **sandal** to **Boaz,** the unknown **kinsman** moved from the scene and into anonymity. But the name of Boaz has been remembered in all succeeding generations (cf. Ruth 4:14).

B. An accomplished redemption (4:9-12)

Boaz moved quickly to complete the transaction. He claimed and received the right of redemption, both for Elimelech's land and for Ruth, who was the only widow left capable of giving birth to a son who would perpetuate the family name.

4:9-10. Boaz called **the elders** to witness the transaction as he took possession of Naomi's **property** and **acquired Ruth the Moabitess** (cf. 1:22; 2:2, 21; 4:5). Boaz evidenced no reluctance to call Ruth a Moabitess. He respected her as a worthy person. He would raise a son to continue the name of Elimelech and of Elimelech's son, Mahlon. In verses 9-10 all the family members were mentioned again except Orpah. She had also faded into anonymity with the nameless nearer kinsman. Though not stated, it may be assumed that with Ruth, Boaz also took responsibility for **Naomi.** This logically followed from the commitment Ruth had made to her mother-in-law. This was later confirmed by the Bethlehem women (v. 15). Boaz is a beautiful illustration of the Lord Jesus Christ who became mankind's Kinsman-Redeemer and who makes things right before God the Father for those who trust in Him.

4:11. The elders gave willing witness to this redemption transaction. They blessed Boaz with the desire that the Lord make Ruth a fertile mother. Their mentioning **Rachel and Leah** has significance. Rachel, named first, had been barren for many years before she bore children. Similarly Ruth had been barren in Moab.

The elders prayed that Boaz would **have standing** (*ḥayil*) **in Ephrath.** This word *ḥayil* ("valor, worth, ability") is

used of Boaz (2:1) and of Ruth (3:11). Ephrath (also spelled Ephrath and Ephrathah) was another name for **Bethlehem** (cf. Gen. 35:19; 48:7; Micah 5:2). The elders prayed that Boaz would be **famous** in Bethlehem. God abundantly answered their prayers as many have witnessed.

4:12. The elders also prayed for numerous and distinguished progeny for Boaz. Their prayer acknowledged that children are a gift from God (**offspring the Lord gives you**; cf. Ps. 127:3). Little did they realize that from this union would issue Israel's greatest kings including David and the Eternal King, the Lord Jesus Christ. **Perez** may have been named here: (a) because of the levirate connection with **Tamar** (see the *Introduction*), (b) because Perez's descendants had settled in Bethlehem (1 Chron. 2:5, 18, 50-54; note "Ephrathah" and "Bethlehem" in 1 Chron. 2:50-51), and (c) because Perez was an ancestor of Boaz (Ruth 4:18-21).

C. A rewarded redemption (4:13)

4:13. This climax to the narrative is brief but full of meaning. Marriage, God-given conception, and the longed-for heir were all mentioned in a few words.

Ruth had been barren in Moab for the entire period of her marriage to Mahlon (1:4-5). Now her faithful obedience was rewarded as God gave her conception. In a sense this foreshadowed the miraculous birth of the Son of God that would take place in Bethlehem when the fullness of time had come (Luke 1:26-38; 2:1-7; Gal. 4:4). The sojourn in Moab lasted at least 10 years (Ruth 1:4). By contrast, within a few short weeks of their return to Bethlehem, Naomi and Ruth had experienced blessing that was rich and full.

VI. Conclusion (4:14-21)

This conclusion of the narrative contrasts beautifully with its introduction (1:1-5). Deep sorrow turned to radiant joy; emptiness gave way to fullness.

A. A joyful filling (4:14-17)

4:14. Naomi again moved to the center of the scene. **The women** of Bethlehem who had witnessed Naomi's emptiness when she returned (1:19) now praised God that she had received **a kinsman-redeemer.** Had Naomi not been past the time of childbearing (1:12; 4:15) she might have been the one at the feet of Boaz that night on the threshing floor (3:7). The women knew this and they spoke of Boaz as the kinsman-redeemer of Naomi as surely as if she had gone there. They blessed Boaz with a blessing similar to that of the elders (cf. 4:11). They asked that Boaz be **famous** in **Israel**, a request that God granted. The Book of Ruth is filled with benedictions and blessings of Israel's people (1:8-9; 2:4, 12, 20; 3:10; 4:11-12, 14-15).

4:15. The women predicted that Boaz would care for Naomi by renewing her **life** and giving her security for her **old age.** Ruth, whom Naomi had not thought worth mentioning when she came to Bethlehem, was declared by the women to be of more worth **than seven sons.** Seven sons symbolized the supreme blessing that could come to a Hebrew family (cf. 1 Sam. 2:5; Job 1:2). Ruth's worth was related to the occasion of the **birth** of her son.

4:16-17. Naomi became the nurse for **Obed.** This may have been a formal act of adoption. The women of Bethlehem named the boy Obed which means "worshiper." Naomi accepted the name. She, the empty one, was now full. The bitter one was now blessed. Naomi had **a son** (actually a grandson but "son" in Heb. often means "descendant"). In time God's providential purpose became clear. The child became the grandfather of King **David.**

B. A surprising genealogy (4:18-21)

Perez's family line provided documentation for God's providential care. The seemingly ordinary events in the Book of Ruth (e.g., travels, marriages, deaths, harvesting, eating, sleeping, purchasing land) revealed the guiding activity of the sovereign God.

4:18-20. Perez was the son of Judah through Tamar (Gen. 38:12-30; Ruth 4:12). **Hezron** was among the family of Jacob that went to Egypt (Gen. 46:12). **Ram** is mentioned in 1 Chronicles 2:9. **Amminadab** was the father-in-law of Aaron (Ex. 6:23). **Nahshon** was head of the house of Judah (Num. 1:7; 7:12; 10:14).

4:21. Salmon was **the father of Boaz.** According to Matthew 1:5, Boaz's mother was Rahab, the Canaanite harlot from Jericho. However, Rahab lived in Joshua's time, about 250-300 years earlier. Probably, then, Rahab was Boaz's "mother" in the sense that she was his ancestress (cf. "our father Abraham," Rom. 4:12, which means "our ancestor Abraham").

Obed, Boaz and Ruth's son, became **the father of Jesse,** who became **the father of David** (1 Sam. 17:12). (See the chart "David's Ancestry from Abraham," near 1 Sam. 16:1-13.) Jesus Christ's lineage, through Mary, is traced to David (Matt. 1:1-16; cf. Rom. 1:3; 2 Tim. 2:8; Rev. 22:16). Christ is therefore called "the Son of David" (Matt. 15:22; 20:30-31; 21:9, 15; 22:42). Christ will someday return to earth and will sit on the throne of David as the millennial King (2 Sam. 7:12-16; Rev. 20:4-6).

In spite of all appearances to the contrary, the faithful God had been about His business on Ruth's behalf. Believers should also be about His business. The rewards of responsible living are always the sweet fruit of God's grace.

BIBLIOGRAPHY

Atkinson, David. *The Message of Ruth: The Wings of Refuge.* Downers Grove, Ill.: InterVarsity Press, 1983.

Barber, Cyril J., *Ruth: An Expositional Commentary.* Chicago: Moody Press, 1983.

Campbell, Edward F., Jr. *Ruth.* The Anchor Bible. Garden City, N.Y.: Doubleday & Co., 1975.

Cundall, Arthur E., and Morris, Leon. *Judges and Ruth.* The Tyndale Old Testament Commentaries. Downers Grove, Ill.: InterVarsity Press, 1968.

Enns, Paul P. *Ruth.* Bible Study Commentary. Grand Rapids: Zondervan Publishing House, 1982.

Gray, John. *Joshua, Judges and Ruth.* Greensboro, S.C.: Attic Press, 1967.

Hals, Ronald M. *The Theology of the Book of Ruth.* Philadelphia: Fortress Press, 1969.

Leggett, Donald A. *The Levirate and Goel Institutions in the Old Testament with Special Attention to the Book of Ruth.* Cherry Hill, N.J.: Mack Publishing Co., 1974.

Lewis, Arthur. *Judges/Ruth*. Everyman's Bible Commentary. Chicago: Moody Press, 1979.

McGee, J. Vernon. *Ruth: The Romance of Redemption*. Pasadena, Calif.: Thru the Bible Books, n.d.

Trible, Phyllis. "A Human Comedy: The Book of Ruth." In *Literary Interpretations of Biblical Narratives*. Vol. 2. Nashville: Abingdon Press, 1982.

Wood, Leon. *Distressing Days of the Judges*. Grand Rapids: Zondervan Publishing House, 1975.

1 SAMUEL

Eugene H. Merrill

INTRODUCTION

Names. The Books of 1 and 2 Samuel take their names from the Prophet Samuel, who is the first important character in the first book. The earliest Hebrew manuscripts made no division between the two books. They simply entitled the whole collection "Samuel." The Septuagint was the first version to divide the material into two parts. That division has persisted to the present day in all translations and versions, including Hebrew-printed Bibles.

Author. The authorship of 1 and 2 Samuel is anonymous, though one can hardly doubt that Samuel himself may have written or supplied information for 1 Samuel 1:1–25:1, all of which describes his life and career up to and including his death. It is impossible, however, to say anything with certainty about the authorship of the remainder of 1 Samuel and of 2 Samuel.

Date. The date of the composition of the books cannot be determined with any degree of precision. There is no hint that the author(s) knew anything about the fall of Samaria in 722 B.C., and yet he (or one of the authors) clearly lived in the post-Solomonic era, after the division of the kingdom between Israel and Judah (931 B.C.). This is indicated by the reference to Ziklag, a Philistine city which, the narrator wrote, "has belonged to the kings of Judah to this day" (1 Sam. 27:6, NASB), and by references to Israel and Judah (11:8; 17:52; 18:16; 2 Sam. 5:5; 11:11; 12:8; 19:42-43; 24:1, 9).

Historical Setting. The events described in 1 and 2 Samuel center about the lives of three important figures—Samuel, Saul, and David. First Samuel opens with the narrative of Samuel's birth, an event which occurred toward the end of the 12th century, about 1120 B.C. Second Samuel concludes with a story of royal succession in which David on his deathbed made provision for his son Solomon to follow him on the throne. This must be dated at 971 B.C. The entire period, then, consists of about 150 years.

The 300 or so years of the history of Israel under the Judges were marked by political, moral, and spiritual anarchy and deterioration. The situation was so pervasive that even the sons of Eli, the high priest at the end of the 12th century, had completely apostatized and had used their priestly office for their own gain and licentious pursuits. Just when it seemed that the nation would cave in on its own rottenness, God intervened and in response to godly Hannah's prayers gave young Samuel to her and the nation. Samuel's strong leadership as judge, prophet, and priest provided respite to the people from both internal and external threat. Unfortunately, however, when he became old and a successor was needed, it was evident to all that his own sons were unfit to take his place. This factor, coupled with the encroachments of the Ammonites on the east side of the Jordan River, prompted Israel to demand of Samuel that he give them a king "like all the other nations" (1 Sam. 8:5, 20). Though disturbed by this request, which implied the rejection of Yahweh as their King, Samuel granted it and selected Saul to be king, a selection determined and sanctioned by Yahweh Himself. Thus the monarchy was established in Israel. The circumstances and timing of its creation were improper, to be sure, but the concept of human royalty was part of the plan of God as revealed as early as the time of the patriarchs (Gen. 17:6, 16; 35:11; Deut. 17:14-20). Finally, with the selection and anointing of David, Israel's second king, Samuel lived to see the inauguration of the dynastic kingship which God had promised as part of His messianic, redemptive plan (Gen. 49:10; Num. 24:17). The Books of Samuel, then, embrace that critical period of Israel's history from judgeship to monarchy, from loose tribal affiliation to strong central government.

Purpose. The Books of Samuel provide an account of the history of Israel from the end of the 12th through the beginning of the 10th centuries before Christ. But, as is always true of biblical history, these books should be viewed theologically and not as mere recountings of events divorced from the purposes and plan of God. Since it might be argued that the major theme of biblical theology concerns the establishment of the sovereignty of God over all things, the specific purpose of 1 and 2 Samuel is to show how that sovereignty was delegated to the nation Israel, especially through its line of divinely elected Davidic kings. David and his dynasty demonstrate what it means to rule under God. Also through David's royal house his greater Son, Jesus Christ, eventually became incarnate. Christ perfectly exercised kingship in His own life, and provided in His death and resurrection the basis on which all people who believe can reign with and through Him (2 Sam. 7:12-16; Ps. 89:36-37; Isa. 9:7).

OUTLINE

I. The Preparations for the Monarchy (chaps. 1–9)
  A. Samuel's birth and childhood (chap. 1)
    1. Samuel's family (1:1-3)
    2. Hannah's problem (1:4-8)
    3. Hannah's prayer (1:9-18)
    4. Samuel's birth (1:19-23)
    5. Samuel's presentation to God (1:24-28)
  B. Hannah's song (2:1-10)
    1. Hannah's exulting in the Lord (2:1)
    2. Hannah's extolling of the Lord (2:2-8)
    3. Hannah's expectation from the Lord (2:9-10)
  C. The situation at Shiloh (2:11-36)
    1. Samuel's progress (2:11, 26)
    2. The sins of the priesthood (2:12-17, 22-25)

3. The blessing of Samuel's family (2:18-21)
    4. The rejection of the priesthood (2:27-36)
  D. Samuel's call (chap. 3)
    1. The divine voice (3:1-10)
    2. The divine message (3:11-14)
    3. Samuel's vindication (3:15-21)
  E. The ark (chaps. 4–7)
    1. The capture of the ark (chap. 4)
    2. The power of the ark (chap. 5)
    3. The return of the ark (6:1–7:1)
    4. The restoration of the ark (7:2-17)
  F. Selection of a king (chaps. 8–9)
    1. The demand for a king (8:1-9)
    2. The nature of the king (8:10-18)
    3. The introduction of the king (8:19–9:14)
    4. The choice of the king (9:15-27)
II. The Period of Saul (1 Sam. 10–31)
  A. Saul's ascendancy (chaps. 10–14)
    1. Saul's choice by Israel (chap. 10)
    2. Saul's first victory (chap. 11)
    3. The address by Samuel (chap. 12)
    4. Saul's first rebuke (chap. 13)
    5. Jonathan's peril (chap. 14)
  B. Saul's rejection (chap. 15)
  C. Saul and David (chaps. 16–26)
    1. On friendly terms (chaps. 16–17)
    2. On unfriendly terms (chaps. 18–26)
  D. Saul's death (chaps. 27–31)
    1. David at Ziklag (chap. 27)
    2. Saul at Endor (chap. 28)
    3. David's return to Ziklag (chaps. 29–30)
    4. The battle of Gilboa (chap. 31)

COMMENTARY

I. The Preparations for the Monarchy (chaps. 1–9)

A. Samuel's birth and childhood (chap. 1)

1. SAMUEL'S FAMILY (1:1-3)

1:1-3. Samuel was the son of **Elkanah . . . an Ephraimite** from **Ramathaim** Zophim. This area, otherwise known simply as Ramah ("the height"), was in the hill country about 15 miles north of Jerusalem. Perhaps, according to Eusebius, it is to be identified with Arimathea, the home of Joseph of Arimathea of New Testament times. (Ramah was Samuel's birthplace [vv. 19-20], residence [7:17], and burial place [25:1].) Elkanah's description as an Ephraimite appears troublesome since Samuel served as a priest, an office reserved exclusively for Levites. However, Elkanah was a direct descendant of Levi (1 Chron. 6:33-38) and was therefore qualified to function in a priestly capacity. He was a Levite by lineage but an Ephraimite by residence. One indication of how lawless were the times in which Samuel was born is his father's bigamous marriages. Often in those days (though it was never sanctioned by God), a man whose wife was infertile would take a second wife by whom he could bear **children** (Gen. 16:1-3; 30:3-4, 9-10; etc.). This explains why Elkanah **had two wives** and why **Hannah,** the beloved but barren one, so fervently desired a son.

2. HANNAH'S PROBLEM (1:4-8)

1:4-8. Because a Hebrew man's posterity was bound up in his having a son to perpetuate his name, his wife's inability to conceive a son was regarded as a curse from God. (According to Deut. 7:13-14 having children was a sign of God's blessing. Conversely the Israelites considered the inability to bear children as a curse.) But Hannah's barrenness did not diminish Elkanah's love for **her.** In fact he gave her twice what he gave **Peninnah,** his second wife, when they took their offerings to the LORD at **Shiloh,** the place some 15 miles north of Ramah where Joshua had located the tabernacle (Josh. 18:1). This antagonized Peninnah, so she belittled **her rival** Hannah (1 Sam. 1:6-7). One thinks of the jealousy which Jacob's bigamy wrought in Rachel's heart (Gen. 30:1). None of Elkanah's assurances of devotion had any beneficial effect upon Hannah and her sorrow (1 Sam. 1:8). Her only resort was to cast herself entirely on the mercies of God.

3. HANNAH'S PRAYER (1:9-18)

1:9-18. The Law required all adult Hebrew males to appear at the tabernacle or temple of **the LORD** for the three major religious festivals of the year (Ex. 23:14-17). At this period of history the tabernacle was at **Shiloh** about 15 miles north of

Ramah. Elkanah regularly attended the festivals with his wives, and **Hannah** there poured out her soul to God in petition for **a son.** On one such occasion Hannah **made a vow** that if God would grant her request she would **give** her son **to the LORD for** as long as he lived. This dedication of her son was a commitment to the Nazirite vow, described in Numbers 6:1-8. It was the same vow undertaken by the parents of Samson when they dedicated to **the LORD** under nearly identical circumstances (Jud. 13:2-5). So intense was Hannah's silent prayer that **Eli,** the high **priest** who was seated nearby, noted the movement of **her lips** and assumed **she was** intoxicated. When the priest learned about her true plight, he assured her that **God** would answer her prayer.

4. SAMUEL'S BIRTH (1:19-23)

1:19-20. Shortly after Hannah's return to **Ramah,** she **conceived** and in due **course** bore **a son** whom she **named . . . Samuel.** Though the name technically means "his name is God" or something similar, **Hannah** may, by assonance, have understood the name to mean "asked of God." She had "asked" (*šā'al*) God for a son, and He had "heard" (*šāma'*) her. "Samuel," then, would be associated with *šāmûa' 'ēl*, "heard of God," because **she** had **asked the LORD for him.**

1:21-23. At the next **annual** festival **Elkanah** went to Shiloh to offer **sacrifice to the LORD** (cf. v. 3), but this time he also paid **his vow** to the Lord. This payment of the vow must have consisted of the offering of Samuel himself whom Elkanah (and Hannah) had promised to give if the Lord would answer their prayers for a son (cf. Lev. 27:1-8; Num. 30:1-8).

Hannah and Samuel **did not** accompany Elkanah, for Samuel was not yet **weaned** and was therefore totally dependent on his mother. **Elkanah** saw the wisdom in this and agreed that Hannah and Samuel might remain at home. However, he was perhaps fearful that the temporary withholding of Samuel from the service of the Lord might jeopardize the Lord's favor (in giving them a son who would survive and mature) and so Elkanah prayed that **the Lord** might **make good His word.**

5. SAMUEL'S PRESENTATION TO GOD (1:24-28)

1:24-28. After Hannah had **weaned** her son, she fulfilled her pledge and **took** him to **Shiloh** to offer **him to the LORD** as a lifelong Nazirite. Since it was customary for a child to be nursed until he was about three years of age (see the apocryphal 2 Maccabees 7:27), the lad Samuel would be no unusual burden for **Eli** and the priestly staff at Shiloh. Also Samuel would be old enough to learn the rudiments of tabernacle service.

B. Hannah's song (2:1-10)

This is one of the earliest and most stirring poems in the Old Testament. So messianic in character is it that Mary, the mother of Jesus, incorporated it into her own song of triumph, the Magnificat, in which she praised God for having selected her to be the human mother of Jesus, the Messiah (Luke 1:46-55).

1. HANNAH'S EXULTING IN THE LORD (2:1)

2:1. Hannah, with clear reference to her rival Peninnah, spoke of her joy **in the LORD** who had helped her achieve satisfaction at last. Horns, used by animals for defense and attack, symbolized strength. Thus Hannah spoke of her **horn** in describing the strength that had come to her because God had answered her prayer.

2. HANNAH'S EXTOLLING OF THE LORD (2:2-8)

2:2-8. Through His attributes such as holiness, strength (a **Rock**), knowledge, and discernment (vv. 2-3), and in view of His actions toward both the ungodly and the godly (vv. 4-8), the Lord demonstrates His awesome sovereignty in human affairs. Especially pointed is Hannah's reference (v. 5) to herself and Peninnah respectively: **She who was barren has borne seven children, but she who has had many sons pines away.** Hannah eventually had five other children (v. 21), but the expression "seven children" here symbolizes the full granting of her desire for a son. The breaking of **the bows** (v. 4), satisfying of the **hungry** (v. 5), raising of the dead (v. 6), and elevating of **the poor** (vv. 7-8) refer to the principle that the final disposition of all things is in the hand of **the LORD.** He who created the world (v. 8) was able to cause Hannah to triumph.

3. HANNAH'S EXPECTATION FROM THE LORD (2:9-10)

2:9-10. In addition to stating that **the LORD** blesses **His saints but** brings **the wicked** to destruction (v. 9), Hannah closed her poem with the prophetic announcement that the Lord **will give strength to His king and exalt the horn of His anointed.** The reference to a king here in this premonarchial passage has led many critics to maintain that the poem is a redaction from a later period which was placed in Hannah's mouth. This is unnecessary, of course, if one accepts the possibility of predictive prophecy. In addition, the notion of a coming human king was in no way foreign to Israel's expectation since **the LORD** had clearly intimated this as early as the time of Abraham (see *Introduction*). The word parallel to "king" (v. 10) is "anointed," a translation of *māšîaḥ* ("Messiah"). This is the first Old Testament reference to an individual's being "the Anointed One." Though it may be unwarranted to make a direct connection between Hannah's prophecy and Jesus the Messiah, it is evident that the juxtaposition of "king" and "anointed one" points to the royal nature of the anointed one(s) whom God would raise up (see Ps. 89:20-24).

C. The situation at Shiloh (2:11-36)

1. SAMUEL'S PROGRESS (2:11, 26)

2:11, 26. Immediately after the return of his parents to their **home** young **Samuel** began his training **under Eli** (v. 11), a training which was characterized by his development physically, but especially morally and spiritually (v. 26). He grew **in stature and in favor with the LORD and with men,** an appropriate description of a son who, like Mary's, had come as a blessing of God to the world (Luke 2:52).

2. THE SINS OF THE PRIESTHOOD (2:12-17, 22-25)

2:12-17, 22-25. The human reason for the birth of Samuel had been recounted. He came in response to a godly mother's prayer. Now it was important to see the divine reason. The Book of Judges asserts, "In those days Israel had no king; everyone did as he saw fit" (Jud. 21:25). This was also true of the priests. **Eli,** though apparently a moral man himself, had lost control of his priestly **sons** who went so far as to appropriate for themselves the choice **meat** of the sacrificial animals which rightfully belonged to **the LORD** as His **offering** (1 Sam. 2:12-17). Moreover, they engaged in ritual fornication in the very precincts of the tabernacle at Shiloh in accord with Canaanite cultic practice (vv. 22-25).

3. THE BLESSING OF SAMUEL'S FAMILY (2:18-21)

2:18-21. As though to show the contrast between the ungodly and the godly about which Hannah had sung, the narration now contrasts the family of **Samuel** with that of Eli. Though Samuel's **mother** had given **Samuel** to **the LORD**, she retained her maternal love and responsibility. She came yearly to Shiloh to attend to the needs of her son. Nor did **the LORD** forget **Hannah.** As is so often the case, He gave her not only what **she** had **prayed** for but much more—in her case **three sons and two daughters** (cf. the example of Rachel, Gen. 30:22-24; 35:16-18).

4. THE REJECTION OF THE PRIESTHOOD (2:27-36)

2:27-36. It is no wonder that God rejected the priesthood of Eli and his **sons.** After reviewing the circumstances of the selection of Eli's ancestors to be priests of **the LORD** over **Israel** (vv. 27-28), an unnamed **man of God** announced **to Eli** that his priesthood would end because it had violated the conditions for its ongoing existence (vv. 29-33). Yet **the LORD** would not terminate the office of priest altogether for He would **raise up . . . a faithful priest** (v. 35) whose line of succession (**house**) would be **firmly** established and who would **minister before** His **anointed one** (i.e., the king) forever. In human terms this was fulfilled when the priesthood was taken from Abiathar, descendant of Aaron's son Ithamar, and given to Zadok, descendant of Aaron's son Eleazar (1 Kings 2:27, 35). But in the ultimate sense the "faithful Priest" and "Anointed One" are One and the same, the Lord Jesus Christ. He is both Priest and King (Ps. 110; Heb. 5:6; Rev. 19:16).

D. Samuel's call (chap. 3)

For centuries God had rarely visited His people with revelation (v. 1). Now He had one to whom He could entrust His message. He called the young lad Samuel.

1. THE DIVINE VOICE (3:1-10)

3:1-10. Though Samuel had been dedicated to the Levitical ministry at Shiloh and had undergone training in the things of **the LORD,** he **had not yet been** addressed by the direct revelation of God (v. 7). At last the time came for **the LORD** to fulfill His promise to remove Eli's priesthood and establish another, so the divine silence was broken. While **Samuel** was reclining **in the** tabernacle (the meaning of the Heb. *hêkāl,* **temple,** v. 3) attending to the burning **lamp,** he heard the voice of **the LORD,** which he mistakenly took to be that of **Eli.** Finally Eli discerned that the lad was being addressed by **the LORD** so he advised him to submit himself to whatever **the LORD** would have him do.

2. THE DIVINE MESSAGE (3:11-14)

3:11-14. The message consisted of the announcement that the promised removal of Eli's family from the priesthood was about to occur. It was an announcement so shocking that it would cause **the ears** of the people to ring like hammer blows on a bell. The reason is explicitly stated—Eli's **sons** were wicked, and though **he knew** it **he failed to restrain them.** Though the message was given right then to Eli through Samuel, Eli himself lived for a short time thereafter, and indeed the priesthood continued in his family for three more generations. This is clear from 14:3—Ahijah served as priest to King Saul. He is identified as the great-grandson of Eli through Phinehas and Ahitub. The prophecy to Samuel came to pass fully when Abiathar, son of Ahijah (the same as Ahimelech of 22:9-12), was apparently replaced by King David with Zadok after Abiathar sided with Adonijah against Solomon (1 Kings 1:7-8; 2:27, 35). Thus the time between prophecy and fulfillment was more than 130 years. Yet it did come to pass and the priesthood switched to Zadok, a descendant of Aaron's son Eleazar, and it remained with his offspring throughout Israel's subsequent history.

3. SAMUEL'S VINDICATION (3:15-21)

3:15-21. This first act of **Samuel** as a prophet was recognized by **Eli** as having come from **God.** This was only the beginning of a public ministry as prophet, which would last through a lifetime and be recognized by all the people as a divine calling. The **word** of **the LORD** had been rare in those days (v. 1). Now, however, it would be common, for God had found a man to whom He could entrust it. The sign that **Samuel** was a spokesman for God was the fact that God **let none of his words fall to the ground** (v. 19), that is, everything he prophesied came to pass. **All Israel from Dan to Beersheba** (the northernmost and southernmost towns in Israel—a distance of about 150 miles) **recognized that Samuel was . . . a prophet of the LORD.** There was no clearer indication that a man was called to be a prophet than the fact that his predictive word invariably was fulfilled (Deut. 18:21-22). When it was understood that Samuel's credentials as a prophet were established, a new era was under way. Revelation through priest and ephod was passing away, and revelation through prophets was beginning.

E. The ark (chaps. 4–7)

1. THE CAPTURE OF THE ARK (CHAP. 4)

The Philistines, Israel's principal enemy during the period of the last of the Judges (Jud. 10:6-8; 13–16), were a non-Semitic people whose origins were most likely in Crete or in some other part of the Aegean Sea area (Gen. 10:14; see Jer. 47:4; Deut. 2:23; Amos 9:7). They came to Canaan in two different migrations, one as early as Abraham's time (2000 B.C.) and the other about 1200 B.C. They lived in five main towns on the southern Canaan coast—Gaza, Ashkelon, Ekron, Gath, and Ashdod. They were technologically advanced, pioneering in the use of iron and in other skills (1 Sam. 13:19-20). The primary god of their pantheon was Dagon, a deity worshiped also in upper Mesopotamia as a grain god. Some scholars suggest that the Philistine Dagon was represented as having a human torso and upper body and a fish's tail. It may well be that the originally seafaring Philistines brought their fish god with them to Canaan and then adapted him to the Semitic god Dagon (or Dagan, as it is known outside the Bible), because of their need to become a grain-producing people (Jud. 15:3-5).

4:1-11. When Samuel was yet a youth, Israel was attacked by **the Philistines at Aphek,** a site about 25 miles west of Shiloh. When it was clear that the Philistines would win, the Israelites **sent men to Shiloh** to bring the **ark of the covenant** to the battlefield, superstitiously supposing that its presence, like a good-luck charm, would turn the tide. The ark *did* represent the presence of **the LORD** in battle (Num. 10:35; Josh. 6:6) but only when the people carried it in faith and by divine leading. Even **the Philistines** were terrified when they knew **the ark** was in **the camp** of Israel, for they had heard about its association with Israel's **mighty gods** who had brought that people out of Egypt more than 300 years before (1 Sam. 4:6-8). Nonetheless, summoning their courage, they **fought** on and **defeated** Israel. In the process **the ark . . . was captured** and the **sons** of Eli, its keepers, were slain (v. 11).

4:12-22. When **Eli,** back at **Shiloh,** learned that **the ark** had been taken by **the** pagan **Philistines** and that his **sons** were **dead,** he **fell backward off his** seat, broke **his neck,** and **died.** Shortly thereafter **his daughter-in-law,** Phinehas' **wife,** died as she **gave birth . . . to a son** whom **she named,** appropriately enough, **Ichabod,** "there is no **glory**" (*'î kābôḏ*). Since the presence of **the ark** represented the presence **of God** in Israel, its capture suggested that not only was **the ark** gone but **God** Himself and all His **glory** were now in enemy hands. To the pagans it was conceivable that gods could be taken into exile (Isa. 46:1-2), but the Israelites should have known that their omnipresent God could not be taken away from them. How heathen Israel's perception of God had become!

2. THE POWER OF THE ARK (CHAP. 5)

5:1-5. That the Lord of Israel was not only omnipresent but also omnipotent was a fact that **the Philistines** were about to learn. Bearing **the ark** like a trophy of conquest, they took it first to the **temple** of **Dagon** at **Ashdod,** some 50 miles southwest of Shiloh. There they laid it at Dagon's feet (or tail) as though to say that **Dagon** was victor and the **LORD** his prisoner. But the **next** morning **Dagon** lay prostrate **before the ark.** Restored to his pedestal once again, **Dagon,** on **the following** day, again lay in submission before **the LORD,** this time shattered and broken. **Only his** torso **remained** intact. **Head and hands** were **broken off** and lay scattered across **the threshold** or podium. The word translated "threshold" (*miptān*) may also and perhaps ought to be understood as the pedestal on which the idol stood. So embarrassed were the Philistines over this misfortune of their god that they forever after refused to set foot on the scene of his calamity.

5:6-12. The Philistine **people** were affected as well, for the Lord sent a plague on the inhabitants **of Ashdod** which was evidently carried by mice ("rats," NIV; 6:4-5) and caused large **tumors** to erupt on their bodies (5:6). The nature of the plague is unclear but seemed to consist of growths particularly in the rectal area as the Hebrew *'ōpel* indicates. Perhaps it was a hemorrhoid-like condition, as suggested in many versions.

In complete despair over this turn of events, the Ashdodites decided to send **the ark** on **to Gath,** some 12 miles southeast and toward Israel. The same disaster befell the Gathites, however (v. 9); so finally **the ark** was moved **to Ekron** where its deadly reputation had already preceded it. The citizens of Ekron fared no better than the others and at once determined to send **the ark** (the chest which, in their view, contained **the God of Israel**) back to its own land. This seems naive to modern readers, but people in all times have attempted to box God in and manipulate Him to their own convenience.

3. THE RETURN OF THE ARK (6:1–7:1)

6:1-12. After suffering the humiliation of their god Dagon and the painful and fatal consequences of God's **plague,** the **Philistine** lords decided to **return** the **ark of the LORD** to Israel. In accordance with their superstitious techniques they consulted their **priests** and **diviners** who advised them to **send** the ark **back** accompanied with tokens of tribute in the form of **five gold tumors and five gold rats,** representing the five Philistine cities (vv. 17-18). These offerings to **Israel's God** would indicate their acknowledgment of His superiority (v. 5). Furthermore **the ark** should be sent on a **new** driverless **cart,** as a further test of the source of their troubles. If the animals (**two cows** still nursing their young and

not previously **yoked,** v. 7) pulled **the cart** directly back to Israel it would be clear that Israel's God had indeed caused their affliction. **But if** they wandered aimlessly about, the Philistines could attribute their misfortune to mere **chance.**

Though not much is known about divination from the Old Testament, since it was forbidden to Israel, divination texts abound from the ancient Near Eastern world. They indicate both the techniques employed to discover the intent of the gods and those used to avert portended evil. Frequently, as in the present story, it would take a binary form, that is a given test would be applied to which a yes or no response would be possible. Perhaps Gideon's use of the fleece reflects such a divinatory practice, though stripped of pagan overtones. The casting of lots would be similar. In any event, the deepest suspicions of the Philistines were confirmed when the animals made their way **straight** back to Israel. It was obvious that **the LORD** had been at the root of all their troubles.

6:13–7:1. The Israelites were so overjoyed to see **the ark** after seven months (6:1) that they offered a sacrifice of **the cows** to the LORD at **Beth Shemesh,** the border town where the ark had been directed, about 15 miles west of Jerusalem (see the map "The Wanderings of the Ark of the Covenant"). Unfortunately **the people of Beth Shemesh** not only **rejoiced** at the return of **the ark** (6:13) and **offered . . . sacrifices** in worship (6:14-15), but they desecrated it by opening it and looking inside (6:19) perhaps to see if the stone tablets of the Law were still there. This violated the Mosaic statute that only **Levites** could handle **the ark** and not even they could touch it directly, to say nothing of looking within it (Num. 4:5, 15, 20). Disobedience in this respect would bring death. The sin of the people of Beth Shemesh was a deliberate, "high-handed" violation of the clear will of God (1 Sam. 6:19; cf. 2 Sam. 6:6-7). (According to the NIV and a few Heb. mss., **70** people were put **to death.** Most Heb. mss., however, have 50,070. This seems an unusually large number, but it may be accounted for in some yet-unknown way.) The point, of course, is that not only unbelievers (the Philistines) suffer when the Law of **the LORD** is disre-

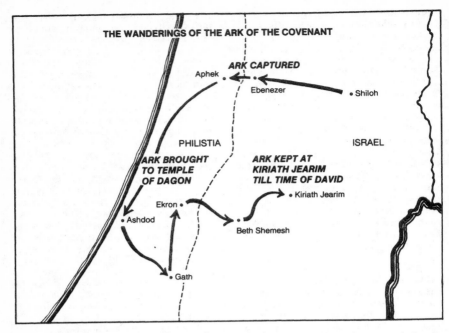

THE WANDERINGS OF THE ARK OF THE COVENANT

ARK CAPTURED

Aphek • • • Ebenezer • Shiloh

PHILISTIA   ISRAEL

ARK BROUGHT TO TEMPLE OF DAGON

ARK KEPT AT KIRIATH JEARIM TILL TIME OF DAVID

Ekron •   • Kiriath Jearim

• Ashdod   • Beth Shemesh

• Gath

garded; believers (the Israelites) also suffer when they do not conform to His strict requirements. After this disaster at Beth Shemesh **the ark** was moved again (1 Sam. 6:21), this time to **Kiriath Jearim** (modern Abu Ghosh, about 10 miles northwest of Jerusalem). No doubt **the ark** was taken there rather than to Shiloh, because the latter was destroyed by the Philistines, perhaps after the battle of Aphek (chap. 4; cf. Jer. 26:9). The ark remained in the custody of the family of Abinadab (1 Sam. 7:1) for about 100 years.

4. THE RESTORATION OF THE ARK (7:2-17)

The return of the ark to Kiriath Jearim seemed to be a tangible sign that God was once again among His people to bless them and deliver them from all their oppressors. The mere presence of the ark did not guarantee God's favor, however, as Israel had learned at the battle of Aphek. Rather, it was submission to the God of the ark that was essential (v. 4).

7:2. After **the ark** was at **Kiriath Jearim** for **20 years** Samuel addressed the Israelites (v. 3). In other words, the ark was in Kiriath Jearim for 20 years before

Samuel undertook his first recorded public ministry. In actual fact the ark remained at Kiriath Jearim for about 100 years. It was taken there just after the battle of Aphek (1104 B.C.) and remained until David brought it from there to Jerusalem in his first year as king over *all* Israel (1003 B.C.; see 2 Sam. 5:5; 6:1-11).

7:3-4. After these 20 long years with the ark at Kiriath Jearim, **Samuel** challenged the people **of Israel** to prove their loyalty to **the LORD** by abandoning their **foreign gods** and turning to **the LORD . . . only.** The plural **Baals** and **Ashtoreths** describe the many local shrines of those Canaanite nature deities. Baal, variously identified as son of El (chief of the Canaanite pantheon) or as son of Dagan (the Mesopotamian deity), was particularly recognized as the god of thunder and rain whose task was to make the earth fertile annually. Ashtoreth (or Astarte) was goddess of both love and war, as were her Babylonian and Greek counterparts Ishtar and Aphrodite respectively. She apparently functioned with Baal as a fertility deity and by their sexual union in some magical way the earth and all its life supposedly experienced annual rejuvenation and fruitfulness. (See the chart "Some of the Pagan Gods and Goddesses Worshiped in Nations Surrounding Israel," near Jud. 10:6.)

7:5-9. Samuel next summoned the people to **Mizpah,** some seven miles north of Jerusalem, and there prayed for them and **offered** sacrifice to **the Lord** on their **behalf** (v. 9). This was a common place of assembly for Israel. In the time of the Judges the elders of the tribes gathered there to decide Benjamin's fate following the murder of a Levite's concubine (Jud. 19:1–20:1, 3; 21:1, 5, 8). Later, Saul was presented to Israel as king at Mizpah (1 Sam. 10:17). It was even the capital of Judah after the destruction of Jerusalem by the Babylonians (2 Kings 25:23, 25). The town of Mizpah should probably be identified with modern Tell en-Nasbeh.

7:10-17. When **the Philistines** learned of the assembly, they attacked **Israel** at **Mizpah** but **the Lord,** in a mighty demonstration of power (by **thunder),** defeated them. In commemoration of this great triumph **Samuel** erected on the site **between Mizpah and Shen** (whose location is unknown), a monument which he called **Ebenezer,** literally, the "stone of [God's] help." This apparently ended Philistine occupation of **Israelite** soil though **the Philistines** came later time and time again to harass Israel (13:5; etc.). **Amorites** (7:14) refers to the hill-dwellers of southern Canaan (see Num. 13:29; Josh. 10:5). Thereafter **Samuel continued** to judge . . . **Israel** in a **circuit** (approx. 50 miles in circumference) including **Bethel . . . Gilgal . . . Mizpah,** and his hometown, **Ramah** (see the map "The Cities of Samuel").

F. Selection of a king (chaps. 8–9)

After the battle of Ebenezer (7:12), about 1084 B.C. (see comments on 7:2), the nation of Israel was content to follow Samuel's leadership for the next 30 years or so. Israel had made abortive attempts to establish a human monarchy during the days of the Judges (see Jud. 8:22-23; 9), actions contrary to the theocratic ideal of the kingship of the Lord Himself. But when Samuel had grown old and it appeared he would not live much longer, the people again expressed the desire for a king. God had such a king in mind, one who would be raised up and identified in His own good time (Deut. 17:14-15), but

that time had not yet come. Thus the stage was set for an encounter between Samuel and the people.

1. THE DEMAND FOR A KING (8:1-9)

8:1-6. Shortly before 1051 B.C., the year Saul became king (**when Samuel** was 65-70 years **old),** the people of **Israel,** aware of Samuel's advanced age and of the wickedness of **his sons** (vv. 3, 5) demanded of the prophet that he select **a king** to rule over them. Samuel's sons, who had been serving as judges **at Beersheba** in Judah, no doubt reminded Israel of the sons of Eli (2:12, 22). Probably the people were afraid that they might return to the wicked days the nation had known before Samuel had been raised up by the Lord. Samuel's sons, **Joel** and **Abijah** were **dishonest** judges, accepting **bribes** and perverting, rather than upholding, **justice. Samuel,** of course, was grieved that they should seek **a king,** for God, who had redeemed them from Egypt to be His people, was their King.

8:7-9. But **the Lord told** Samuel that **the people** were rejecting **not** him **but** God. Furthermore God would permit them to have a **king,** but they would live to regret their hasty impulse.

The request for a human king was not in itself improper, for God had promised such a leader (see *Introduction*). But the refusal to wait for God's timing was clearly displeasing to the Lord and to His prophet. In the face of impending conflict with the Ammonites (see 12:12-13) the people wanted a king "such as all the other nations have" (8:5). Even after witnessing the leadership of the Lord in stunning victory over the Philistines at Ebenezer, Israel demanded a fallible, human leader.

2. THE NATURE OF THE KING (8:10-18)

8:10-18. At last **Samuel** relented. He told **the people** God would give them what they wanted, but **the king** would be a despot, a demanding dictator who would enrich himself at the people's expense. He would press them into his military and domestic enterprises (vv. 11-13, 16, 17). He would appropriate their properties to his own use (vv. 14, 16) and would inflict heavy taxes on them (vv. 15, 17). And **when** all this happened it would be too late to complain, for the people would have reaped the conse-

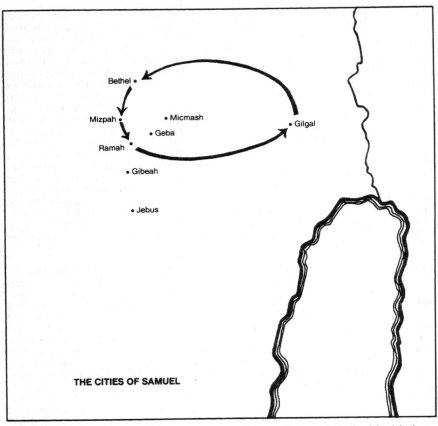

THE CITIES OF SAMUEL

quences of their own fleshly desires (v. 18). Shortly after Saul ascended the throne many of these predictions came to pass (14:52) and continued to mark the long history of the monarchy in both Israel and Judah (2 Sam. 15:1; 1 Kings 12:12-15; 21:7).

3. THE INTRODUCTION OF THE KING (8:19–9:14)

8:19–9:2. After **the LORD** had agreed to let **the people** have **a king . . . like all the other nations, Saul** was introduced in the story. He was a tall and striking **Benjamite** (9:1) who appeared quite naive and unkingly in many ways. He hailed from the town of Gibeah (10:26), where the concubine of a Levite who had sought hospitality was raped and killed (Jud. 19). Excavations at Tel el-Ful, just three miles north of Jerusalem, have established it as the site of ancient Gibeah. Though **a son** of **Kish,** a man of some

influence (1 Sam. 9:1), Saul had little to commend him to the high position of **king** except his physical impressiveness (9:2). God had to convince both Saul and **the people** that he was the proper candidate.

9:3-11. On a mission to find some lost **donkeys** belonging to his **father Kish,** Saul approached the region **of Zuph** (in **the hill country of Ephraim;** cf. 1:1, the home of Samuel). It occurred to Saul's **servant** that since Samuel was a **seer** he could help **find** the animals. In Saul's day a **prophet** was known primarily as **a seer** (*rō'eh*) undoubtedly because the major thrust of his ministry was associated with receiving divine revelation, even in matters as mundane as finding **lost** animals. Later prophets served more as proclaimers of revelation, spokesmen for God (*nābî'*), though of course all prophets were both seers and proclaimers. Samuel, for example, was expressly described by both terms (9:11; 3:20).

9:12-14. When Saul and his servant arrived in Samuel's **town,** they found that the prophet was on his way to a nearby **high place** (a place of worhip on a hill) to offer **a sacrifice.** Undaunted, they continued on until they located him.

4. THE CHOICE OF THE KING (9:15-27)

9:15-27. Meanwhile **the LORD had revealed . . . to Samuel** that Saul was on his way and that he was the divine choice for king (vv. 15-17). This does not mean that Saul satisfied God's ultimate requirements but only that He was graciously letting the **people** have their own way. When the two met (by God's providential control), **Samuel** not only put Saul's mind at ease concerning the **lost** beasts but also told him that he was God's choice for king (v. 20). Astounded, **Saul** could only reply that he was unworthy of this high honor (v. 21). The transparency and humility of Saul are evident at this stage of his career. **Samuel** then invited **Saul** to sit with him as guest of honor at the sacrificial feast (vv. 22-24) and then to spend the night in his home in **the town** below. Next morning **Samuel** detained him so that he might communicate with him alone (with Saul's **servant** going **on ahead**) the revelation of **God** about his selection as king (vv. 25-27).

II. The Period of Saul (chaps. 10–31)

A. Saul's ascendancy (chaps. 10–14)

1. SAUL'S CHOICE BY ISRAEL (CHAP. 10)

10:1-8. As **Samuel** prepared to reveal God's purposes to Saul, he first anointed him with **oil.** In the Old Testament anointing with oil symbolized the setting apart of a person or even an object for divine service (Ex. 30:23-33). It was also accompanied by the presence and power of the Holy Spirit (1 Sam. 10:6, 10; 16:13). When Samuel **poured** oil **on Saul's head,** that act represented God's approval of Saul as **leader** of His people. In confirmation to both Saul and the people of his divine call and commission, Saul would that he would experience three signs: (a) he would **meet two men near Rachel's tomb at Zelzah on the border of Benjamin** and Ephraim, who would tell him of the whereabouts of the lost **donkeys**; (b) he would meet **three**

men at the (oak) **tree of Tabor,** somewhere between Zelzah and Gibeah, who would give him **two loaves of bread;** and (c) he would **meet a procession of prophets** descending **from the high place** at **Gibeah.** Remarkably, he would join in with the prophets in their **prophesying** as **the Spirit** of God enabled him and he would **be changed into a different person.** This is frequently taken to mean that Saul was converted or spiritually regenerated. However, such language for spiritual renewal is foreign to the Old Testament, and Saul's subsequent attitudes and behavior do not bear out that this was his experience (16:14; 18:12; 28:15-16). Actually the Spirit made the inexperienced and unlettered Saul able to assume kingly responsibilities in much the same way as the judges before him were blessed (Jud. 6:34; 11:29; 13:25; 14:6, 19; 15:14).

10:9-13. After **Saul** left **Samuel,** the promised **signs** came to pass. So amazed were the witnesses to Saul's dramatic and powerful change of character that they created a proverb which thereafter was quoted to describe a totally unexpected and unexplainable phenomenon: **Is Saul also among the prophets?** This does not suggest, of course, that Saul became part of the prophetic ministry led by Samuel, but only that he was able to exercise a prophetic gift, at least on this occasion, though never having received prophetic training. This was a remarkable and convincing sign of God's presence and power in Saul's life.

Further evidence that Saul did not actually become a prophet lies in the stem of the Hebrew verb here. **He joined in their prophesying** means literally, "He acted like a prophet among them," that is, to all outward appearances he was a prophet because he was able to enter into their activities.

10:14-16. Saul told **his uncle** about finding **the donkeys** with Samuel's help, **but** Saul **said** nothing **about the kingship.**

10:17-27. Sometime later **Samuel** gathered the leaders **of Israel** together **at Mizpah,** a favorite place for assembly in Samuel's day (cf. 7:5-6). After reminding them of their foolish insistence on having **a king** apart from the directive will of **God,** he set about to demonstrate God's selection of Saul by a process of elimination (10:18-19). By lot or some similar means the choice was made of **tribe,** that **of Benjamin . . . clan,** that of Matri; and family, that **of Kish** (vv. 20-21). But when **Saul** was **chosen,** he was nowhere **to be found.** Indicative of his unassuming humility were his initial attempts to avoid the glare of publicity (v. 22) and his refusal to be vindictive against those who ridiculed his selection as king (v. 27). But the masses were convinced of his eminent suitability for the high office and in jubilation cried out, **Long live the king!**

However, in the eyes of the Lord, Saul was disqualified. The prophetic word of Jacob was that the scepter (of kingship) would not depart from Judah (Gen. 49:10). The promised dynasty of kings which would eventually produce the Messiah must originate in Judah. Saul as a Benjamite could not, then, meet the basic prerequisite of lineage. Nonetheless the people had made their demand, and **the Lord** had acquiesced. All that **Samuel** could do was invest Saul with his authority and responsibility as outlined in **a scroll** prepared for this occasion of coronation (1 Sam. 10:25). Undoubtedly the scroll included the Mosaic regulations for kingship found in Deuteronomy 17:14-17. Interestingly **valiant men** were immediately attracted to Saul **in Gibeah** (see comments on 1 Sam. 9:1).

2. SAUL'S FIRST VICTORY (CHAP. 11)

11:1-6. No sooner had Saul begun his rule than a distant but important part of his kingdom was attacked by the Ammonites. This was the city of **Jabesh Gilead,** about 25 miles south of the Sea of Galilee, east of the Jordan River. Saul's special concern for this community may well lie in possible ancestral ties which he had there. Judges 19–21 records the story of the civil war between Benjamin and the other tribes, which resulted in the annihilation of all but 600 men of Benjamin. With no wives and children it is apparent that the tribe would become extinct. To prevent this the leaders of Israel proposed that the virgin women of any town which had not sent troops to combat Benjamin should be seized and given to these survivors as wives. When it was discovered that Jabesh Gilead had failed in this respect, the 400 virgins of the city were captured and given to the

Benjamites. Since Saul was a Benjamite, it is entirely possible that his ancestry sprang in part from Jabesh Gilead.

When **Saul** learned of the plight of Jabesh Gilead, a city so hopelessly besieged by the Ammonites that defeat was inevitable, he became enraged (1 Sam. 11:6) and set about to raise an army capable of delivering the place. So confident was **Nahash,** king of Ammon, that he made **a treaty** with Jabesh Gilead to the effect that if they surrendered he would pluck out every **right eye.** If they resisted, Nahash would probably kill them. The **Jabesh** elders asked for **seven days** of grace in which to find help. Nahash agreed, to spare the expense of a long and costly siege, assuming that Saul, who did not even have an army, would be powerless to intervene.

11:7-15. Saul, hearing of the people's plight, **cut up two oxen** and **sent the pieces . . . throughout Israel,** saying that **anyone who** would **not follow Saul and Samuel** would have their **oxen** similarly dissected. This method of getting the attention of the tribes is remarkably similar to that of the Levite of Ephraim who dissected his concubine's corpse and sent the parts to the various tribes, a part of the story from Judges 19–21 (see comments on Jud. 19:27-30). After assembling 330,000 soldiers **at Bezek,** 12 miles west of **Jabesh Gilead,** Saul marched all night and early in the morning (**the last watch** was the last third of the night) engaged **the Ammonites** in battle, **and slaughtered them.** The distinction between **Israel** and **Judah** (cf. 1 Sam. 15:4; 17:52; 18:16) indicates that 1 Samuel was written after the nation was divided in 931 B.C. into the Northern and Southern Kingdoms. After this decisive victory **Saul** was hailed as a hero and became firmly entrenched in his monarchical role. And he gave **the Lord** all the glory. This achievement convinced even **Samuel** that God had His hand on Saul, so the prophet convened another assembly at **Gilgal** so that the people could **reaffirm the kingship.** Though the evidence is somewhat meager the occasion described is likely a covenant-renewal ceremony, perhaps on the occasion of Saul's first anniversary as king. The presence of **the Lord,** the **king,** and **the people** would suggest this, particularly in light of the sacrificial festival which highlighted the event (1 Sam. 11:15).

3. THE ADDRESS BY SAMUEL (CHAP. 12)

12:1-5. As **Samuel** had spoken to them earlier about his age and the imminence of his death, so now again he addressed the assembly of **Israel,** this time after Saul had become **king** and had distinguished himself. As though now to reestablish his credibility among them, Samuel asked whether or not the people had ever detected any moral or spiritual flaw in his life. (By contrast, flaws had certainly been evident in his **sons,** 8:3.) The answer, of course, was no. Samuel's intent was to show that just as he could be trusted in the past so his word for the present and the future could also be accepted with confidence.

12:6-25. A critical point had been reached in Israel's history. **The people** had demanded and had been given **a king,** contrary to the precise purposes and will of **God.** And that king had led them to a glorious victory in his very first campaign! Now the question was, Would Israel see this victory as evidence of God's blessing and give Him the glory, or would they interpret it as a human achievement devoid of divine enablement? Samuel anticipated that question and sought to direct the people to a fresh recognition of the sovereignty of God and to the need to worship and praise Him as the Source of all their blessing. He did this first by reminding them of how God had redeemed them from **Egypt** and brought them into Canaan (vv. 6-8). He then recounted their disobedience under the Judges (vv. 9-11). (**Jerub-Baal**, v. 11, was another name for "Gideon," Jud. 6:32. **Barak** in the NIV is lit., in the Heb., "Bedon" [see NIV marg.]. Bedon was either another name for Barak or another judge mentioned only here in the OT.) Next Samuel pointed out that the Ammonite menace had prompted them to request a human **king,** a request to which **the LORD** had graciously acceded (1 Sam. 12:12-15). Finally **Samuel** appealed to **the LORD** to **send** a sign from heaven both to authenticate his own warnings of judgment and to cause the people to revere the God who had called them and who desired to bless and use them (vv. 16-18). The Lord reminded them that their insistent demand **for a king,** though He would grant it, was still

an evil request because it was premature and wrongly motivated.

When **the people** witnessed the display of **thunder and rain,** a phenomenon unheard of in early summer, the time of **wheat harvest** (v. 17), they turned to **Samuel** in earnest penitence and asked the prophet to **pray** that **God** might forgive their hastiness in seeking a king (v. 19). In a marvelous manifestation of the grace of God, **Samuel** related to **the people** that God would bless them in spite of their wrong choice if they would only be steadfast in their obedience from this point on. The past could not be undone but their future was untainted and could be devoted to the Lord (vv. 20-22). And Samuel also, as a true mediator, pledged to keep praying for the people. (Centuries later Jeremiah spoke of Samuel as a great man of prayer, Jer. 15:1.) Failure to do so, Samuel said, would be **sin against** God! (1 Sam. 12:23) If the people would respond affirmatively, they could expect God's continued blessing on their nation. But if they did not, they could expect the judgment of God on them (vv. 24-25).

4. SAUL'S FIRST REBUKE (CHAP. 13)

13:1. If the setting of the reaffirmation of Saul's kingship and Samuel's address on that occasion is the first anniversary of his coronation, it may be that the events of this chapter occurred after his second anniversary. This is a possible interpretation of the textually difficult passage translated by the NIV as **Saul was 30 years old when he became king, and he reigned over Israel 42 years.** The Hebrew is literally, "Saul was years old when he began to reign and he reigned two years over Israel." Obviously a figure has dropped out of the first part of the statement, and the second part cannot mean that he reigned for a total of only two years. Old Testament chronology implies—and Paul in his address at Pisidian Antioch (Acts 13:21) distinctly teaches—that Saul reigned for 40 years, no doubt a round number but close to the actual figure. There is no reason to think that the number "two" is suspect, however, for all manuscripts and versions retain it. It is only the desire to see 1 Samuel 13:1 as a regular formula for kingship (as in 2 Sam. 2:10; 5:4; 1 Kings 14:21; 22:42; etc.) that leads many scholars to postulate that "40" or some other figure

1 SAMUEL

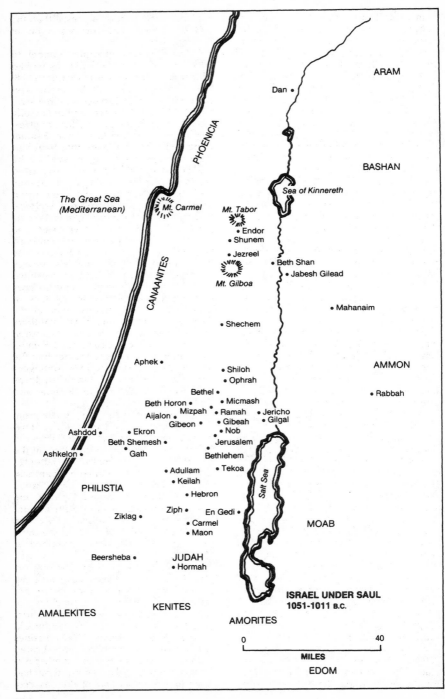

134

is missing. In the context, however, the historian is not introducing a kingship formula (why do so here, well into Saul's reign?), but is probably indicating that the Ammonite threat had come in Saul's first year and now, in his second, the Philistines must be encountered.

A problem remains with the first part of the Hebrew statement, "Saul was years old. . . ." Many scholars, following Origen (ca. A.D. 185–254), postulate "30" (so NIV). Since Jonathan, Saul's son, was already grown then and served as a military commander, Saul would have been older than 30. It is more likely that the figure to be supplied is "40" though this too is difficult to reconcile with the description (1 Sam. 9:2) that Saul was, at the time of his anointing, "an impressive young man." Of course "young" in this latter passage may not be a good translation for the Hebrew *bāḥûr*, a word that could be rendered "choice."

The best translation of 13:1 would seem to be, "Saul was [40] years old when he began to reign, and he reigned over Israel for two years." This is further supported by the next verse which begins with a verb in the preterite tense, a construction indicating a close connection with the previous clause. "Saul chose . . . " (v. 2) implies that after he had reigned for two years Saul began to select and train a regular army, not the larger militia he had used previously.

13:2-15. Having learned from his recent experience with the Ammonites, **Saul** set about to create a standing army of **3,000** trained troops—2,000 under his direct control and **1,000** under his son **Jonathan.** These he stationed at **Micmash** and **Gibeah** respectively, in order to avert Philistine attacks. After a preliminary encounter **at Geba,** halfway between Micmash and Gibeah, **the Philistines** (with **3,000 chariots, 6,000 charioteers** and innumerable foot **soldiers**) pushed the Israelite troops eastward all the way to **Gilgal** (vv. 3-7). This is the first of Israel's three major battles with the Philistines in Saul's reign (cf. 17:1-54; 31:1-6). (Though the Heb. reads "30,000 chariots," this is problematic because this would mean 5 chariots for every charioteer. The Heb. words for "30,000" and for "3,000" look almost alike. The one could easily be mistaken for the other when the text was being copied. Perhaps this suggests that the text of 1 Sam. has suffered a bit in transmission.)

There **Saul** waited for **Samuel** to come and offer sacrifice (13:8) as he had been told to do two years earlier (10:8; see comments on 13:1-2). But on the seventh day, the day **Samuel** was to arrive, **Saul** could wait no longer and unlawfully took on himself the priestly task of **offering** community sacrifice. Then **Samuel** came and when he knew that **Saul** had taken liberties by offering the sacrifice, he rebuked him with the words, **You acted foolishly.** Because of this deed, Samuel said, Saul's dynasty would come to an end (**Your kingdom will not endure**), and that of another man would take its place, **a man after** God's **own heart.** The severity of God's judgment on Saul must be seen in the light of God's holiness. As in the instance of the people's careless handling of the ark at Beth Shemesh, so Saul had now violated the holy standards of the Lord by disobeying the Law of Moses (Lev. 6:8-13) and the word of His Prophet Samuel (1 Sam. 10:8). That there was the possibility of the eternal duration of Saul's dynasty is clear from 1 Samuel 13:13, but this in no way teaches that the rise of David's dynasty is contingent on the fall of Saul's. All Samuel said was that Saul's kingship would end and someone else's would begin.

13:16-18. Having taken **Geba** from the Philistines (v. 3), **Saul and . . . Jonathan,** after the incident with Samuel at Gilgal, were once again attacked by **the Philistines** from **Micmash.** The latter divided themselves into **three** companies of **raiding parties,** one of which **turned** north of Micmash **toward Ophrah,** the second southwest **toward Beth Horon, and the third** east **toward . . . Zeboim** (the Jordan Valley). The rest of the overconfident Philistine army remained at Micmash.

13:19-23. This parenthetical note explains that the Israelites were at a big disadvantage because they were not skilled in the manufacture and use of iron; **the Philistines** had kept them from metallurgy for fear the Israelites would **make swords** and **spears. The Philistines** had apparently learned sophisticated metallurgy from the Hittites or other Anatolian peoples with whom they had come in contact as part of the Sea People's migration from the Aegean Sea area to Canaan around 1200 B.C. Israel had to depend on the Philistines for iron weapons and tools (v. 20). In wartime such services were not available, so **only Saul and . . . Jonathan had** iron weapons (v. 22).

5. JONATHAN'S PERIL (CHAP. 14)

14:1-14. With the resumption of the skirmish against the Philistines, **Saul** camped near the capital **Gibeah** (v. 2), with **about 600 men.** But **Jonathan** undertook a secret mission into the enemy camp itself near Micmash. On the way Jonathan and his **armor-bearer** passed between two cliffs named **Bozez** and **Seneh** (v. 4). As they came through the narrow crevice they were spotted by **the Philistines,** who challenged them to a contest (v. 12). Having undertaken his mission with confidence in **the LORD** (vv. 6, 10), **Jonathan** knew that he and his servant would prevail. Together they **killed some 20** of the enemy in a small field.

14:15-23. Jonathan's heroic encounter shocked and frightened the Philistines. **Saul's lookout** could see the enemy in flight. Knowing that this must have come about because of some Israelite involvement, the king checked to determine who among his troops had undertaken this independent action. **Jonathan and his armor-bearer** were missing.

Meanwhile **Ahijah** the priest (cf. v. 3) came bearing **the ark of** the Lord (vv. 18-19). **It was** still housed at Kiriath Jearim (7:1) but as a symbol of the presence of the Lord, it was summoned by Saul to the battle. When **Saul** saw that the Philistines were in total disarray, he ordered Ahijah to **withdraw** his **hand** (i.e., from the sacred lots, the Urim and Thummim, 14:19; cf. Ex. 28:29-30; 1 Sam. 14:40-42). The will of God was now clear so **Saul,** with Israelite defectors and refugees, achieved a great triumph (vv. 20-23).

14:24-48. Prior to this **Saul had** commanded all his men to fast until they had defeated the Philistines. As hungry as they were in the battle, they refused to eat anything, even some **honey** in the forest, for **they feared** the curse that attended their vow to fast. **Jonathan had not** known of the vow, **so when he** came

across the honey he ate it and was immediately refreshed (**his eyes brightened**; cf. v. 29). The rest of Saul's army was so famished that after the victory they took the Philistine animals, slaughtered them, and ate them without proper draining of **the blood** (vv. 32-33; cf. Lev. 17:10-14). This so alarmed **Saul** that he hastily built **an altar** on which to offer a propitiatory sacrifice to the Lord (1 Sam. 14:35).

Saul then determined to pursue and **plunder** the **Philistines** further but could not get an **answer** from the Lord (v. 37). This meant to **Saul** that someone had violated the fast, and by means of the **lot** (i.e., the Urim and Thummim, vv. 41-42; cf. v. 19) he discovered it was his own **son Jonathan.** Only the interposition of Saul's **men** prevented Jonathan's execution (v. 45).

The major campaigns of **Saul** are listed in verses 47-48 and include victories over **Moab,** Ammon, **Edom . . . Zobah** (the Arameans), **the Philistines,** and even **the Amalekites,** though his success over the latter was tempered by his lack of complete obedience to God (cf. 15:20-23).

14:49-52. The royal family consisted of Saul; his wife **Ahinoam;** his three **sons . . . Jonathan,** Ishvi (not the same as Ish-Bosheth or Esh-Baal; cf. 1 Chron. 10:2 where Ishvi is the same person as Abinadab); **and Malki-Shua;** his daughters **Merab** and **Michal** (David's first wife; cf. 1 Sam. 18:27); and **Abner,** who served as Saul's **commander** of the **army.**

Ishvi is probably not the same as Ish-bosheth because Ish-bosheth was apparently Saul's youngest son born after Saul began to reign. For that reason he is not listed in 1 Samuel 14:49 but is listed in the total list of Saul's sons in 1 Chronicles 8:33 (cf. comments on 2 Sam. 2:8).

According to 1 Chronicles 8:33 and 9:39 **Ner** was Saul's grandfather (Ner's son was **Kish** and Kish's **son** was **Saul**), but in 1 Samuel 14:50 Ner appears to be Saul's uncle and Abner his cousin. In 1 Chronicles Abner, though not mentioned, would be Saul's *uncle,* for Abner was Ner's son (1 Sam. 14:50). This seeming contradiction is eliminated by the Hebrew of 1 Samuel 14:50b, which says literally, "Abner son of Ner, uncle of Saul," with the understanding that the ambiguous "uncle of Saul" refers not to Ner but to Abner. Charted, this relationship was as follows:

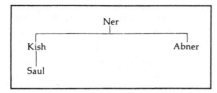

Ner
Kish   Abner
Saul

B. Saul's rejection (chap. 15)

15:1-8. Long before the time of Saul, in the days of the wilderness wandering, Israel had been savagely attacked from the rear by **the Amalekites,** a deed the Lord had promised to avenge someday (Ex. 17:8-16). The time had now come, so **Samuel** commanded Saul to **destroy** the Amalekites **totally,** that is, to "place them under the ban (ḥērem) of holy war" (1 Sam. 15:3; cf. vv. 8-9, 15, 18, 20-21; Deut. 20:16-18; see comments on Josh. 6:21). However, **Saul** was to spare **the Kenites** since they had **shown kindness** to Israel in the wilderness wandering (1 Sam. 15:6; cf. Ex. 18:9-10 [Jethro was a Kenite, Jud. 1:16]). **Saul** proceeded to do the bidding of Samuel (1 Sam. 15:7-8) but not entirely.

15:9-35. When **Saul** saw the fatness of the Amalekite **sheep and cattle** and when he considered the enhancement of his own glory and prestige in bringing back **Agag, king of** Amalek, as prisoner, he could not resist returning them as public exhibits of his leadership (v. 9). That this was Saul's intent is clear from verse 12, which speaks of Saul's erecting **a monument** to **his own honor** at **Carmel** (in Judah, not the Carmel on the upper Mediterranean coast). When accosted by **Samuel** (v. 14), **Saul** tried to justify his disobedience by claiming that the animals were brought as **sacrifice to the Lord** (vv. 13, 15), and were brought because of the insistence of **the soldiers** (vv. 20-21). But **Samuel** responded with a statement of principle that is timeless in its application: **To obey is better than sacrifice, and to heed is better than the fat of rams** (v. 22). In addition to disobeying, Saul was guilty of **rebellion . . . arrogance,** and rejecting God's **word** (v. 23).

The result for **Saul** was the Lord's rejection of him **as king** (v. 26), symbolized by Saul's tearing of Samuel's **robe** (vv. 27-28). This repudiation of Saul and selection of a replacement (David) did not mean that God had misled Samuel or even changed **His mind** (v. 29). Rather, God had from the beginning chosen another, one who would be "after His own heart" (cf. 13:14; 16:1). Though still recognized by the people as their king for about 15 more years, **Saul** was deposed by **the Lord** right then (cf. 16:14), and **Samuel** executed **Agag** (15:32-33). The finality of it all was not missed by **Samuel** for from that day Samuel never visited the **king** again (v. 35). The estrangement between **Samuel** and **Saul** represents that which now existed in permanent form between the Lord Himself and the disobedient king. Though God had permitted Saul to reign in response to the demand of the people, that very concession now **grieved** the heart of **the Lord** (v. 35).

C. Saul and David (chaps. 16–26)

1. ON FRIENDLY TERMS (CHAPS. 16–17)

a. The choice and anointing of David (16:1-13)

16:1-13. After Saul's further rebellion against the Lord and his subsequent rejection by **the Lord,** Samuel was commissioned to seek out the **one** who would succeed Saul on the throne of **Israel.** This one had already been identified as "a man after [God's] own heart" (13:14) and "one of [Saul's] neighbors" who was "better than" he (15:28). David had been chosen from eternity past to be ruler of Israel. The rejection of Saul did not force **the Lord** to a new course of action. Rather, God's action followed His omniscient plan in such a way as to use Saul's disobedience as the human occasion for implementing His higher plan. God had permitted the people to have the **king** of their choice. Now that that king and their mistake in choosing him had been clearly manifested, God proved the superiority of His own wisdom in raising up a king who would come in fulfillment of His perfect will.

After an undetermined length of time in which **Samuel** lamented the rejection of **Saul,** the Lord commanded the prophet to go to **Bethlehem** to select a son of **Jesse . . . to be king** (16:1-3). Jesse was the grandson of Ruth and Boaz (Ruth 4:18-21), and so was in the line of promise (see the chart "David's Ancestry from Abraham"). As the wives of Jacob gave birth to a royal house (Gen. 35:11; 49:10), so Ruth would produce the Davidic dynasty (Ruth 4:11). God did not tell Samuel to be deceptive, but rather to combine the anointing with the business of sacrificing (1 Sam 16:2). **The elders** in **Bethlehem** may have wondered if **Samuel** had come for judgment (v. 4).

After the **seven** older **sons of Jesse** were disqualified one by one (vv. 5-10), **David** was singled out by **the LORD** and **anointed** by **Samuel** (vv. 11-13). The anointing, as in the experience of Saul, was accompanied by the coming of **the Spirit** of God mightily on the young lad (v. 13). This was the supernatural authentication of God's will. Later David was anointed king over Judah (2 Sam. 2:4) and then over Israel (2 Sam. 5:3).

b. David as Saul's musician (16:14-23)

16:14-23. As David was invested by the Spirit, that same **Spirit** left **Saul.** This is evidence of the fact that the presence or absence of the Holy Spirit in the Old Testament says nothing about salvation but only that His power worked in those whom God selected for service (cf. Jud. 3:10; 6:34; 13:25; 14:6; 1 Sam. 10:10; 16:13).

With the departure of the Spirit of God, Saul became **tormented** by **an evil spirit** which **God** permitted to come (v. 14; cf. vv. 15-16; 18:10; 19:9). Whether this spirit had sinful or only harmful characteristics, it is quite certain that it was a demonic, satanic instrument (cf. Job 1:12; 2:6; 1 Kings 22:19-22). In his troubled state Saul could find relief only in music, so he commanded that a musician be found (1 Sam. 16:15-17). In His providence God arranged that **David** be the one, so the shepherd boy was introduced to the palace of the king (vv. 18-21). The Holy Spirit empowered **David** to drive away **the evil spirit** that overwhelmed **Saul** (v. 23). Harps had already been mentioned in connection with prophesying (10:5). Later Elisha, when seeking a revelation from the Lord, also requested that a harp be played (2 Kings 3:15). Also Asaph, Heman, and Jeduthun prophesied with harps, lyres, and cymbals (1 Chron. 25:1).

c. David's triumph over Goliath (chap. 17)

17:1-51. Sometime after David commenced his role of court musician, Israel was again in peril at the hands of **the Philistines.** The armies were drawn up on opposite sides of **the Valley of Elah,** a few miles southwest of Jerusalem (vv. 2-3). Apparently intimidated by each other, they decided that the outcome should be determined by a contest of champions who would engage each other in combat. **The Philistines** offered **Goliath,** a giant (about 9'9" tall!), but Israel could find no one worthy, not even **Saul** (vv. 4-11). Goliath **wore a bronze helmet** and **a coat of scale armor** weighing **5,000 shekels,** that is, about 125 pounds, and **bronze greaves.** He was armed with **a bronze javelin,** and a long **spear** with a 15-pound **iron** tip! (v. 7) At last **David** heard of the dilemma and, having been sent to the **camp** of **Israel** with provisions for his **brothers** (vv. 12-22), begged **Saul** to let him take on **the Philistine** (vv. 23-32). Reluctantly **Saul** agreed and **David,** armed only with his confidence in God, a **sling,** and **five smooth stones,** slew Goliath and brought back his severed **head** in triumph (vv. 33-51).

17:52-58. When the conflict was over, **Saul** inquired as to the identity of the young warrior and learned that he was David, **son** of Jesse (vv. 55, 58). Why could not Saul recognize David, who had already served him for some time as musician and armor-bearer? One answer is that Saul was not asking who David was but for the first time was curious about David's family connections: **Whose son is that young man?** (v. 55; cf. v. 25) When David himself was interrogated he did not say, "I am David," but only, **I am the son of your servant Jesse of Bethlehem** (v. 58). Another and perhaps better solution is that David's previous service had been brief and intermittent and now several years had passed since Saul had last seen him. If, for example, David had been only 12 years old when he came as Saul's musician and had stayed off and on for only a year or so, he might have been 17 or 18 by the time of the Philistine episode and no longer recognizable to Saul. This view is strengthened by the fact that after David joined himself to Saul this time, the king "did not let him return to his father's house" (v. 15; 18:2). This implies that David's previous tenure

DAVID'S ANCESTRY FROM ABRAHAM

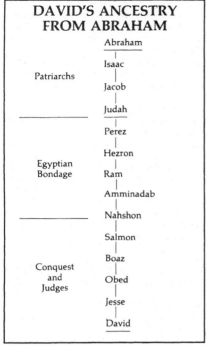

	Abraham
	Isaac
Patriarchs		
	Jacob
	Judah
	Perez
	Hezron
Egyptian Bondage		
	Ram
	Amminadab
	Nahshon
	Salmon
	Boaz
Conquest and Judges		
	Obed
	Jesse
	David

had not been permanent. In any event, one need not posit two sources for chapters 16 and 17 or view the accounts as irreconcilable.

2. ON UNFRIENDLY TERMS (CHAPS. 18–26)

a. David's flight from Saul (chaps. 18–20)

(1) David's popularity. **18:1-7. David,** as has been seen, was not only chosen from eternity to be the founder of the messianic dynasty of kings, but he was also providentially prepared by the Lord to undertake his royal responsibilities. David had served as a shepherd in the fields and had the loving, protective heart of a shepherd, a fitting attribute of a king. He had learned responsibility and courage by confronting and slaying wild beasts that threatened his flock (17:34-36). He had learned to play the harp, a skill that would make him sensitive to the aesthetic side of life and that would help him compose the stirring psalms which extol the Lord and celebrate His mighty exploits. David had been brought into the palace of the king as musician and warrior so that he might acquire the experience of statecraft. Though an un-

initiated novice at the time of his anointing, he was eminently equipped to be king of Israel at his coronation some 15 years later. But his education was not always pleasant. With his rising popularity among the people came a deterioration of his relationship with **Saul,** for the king became insanely jealous of Israel's new hero.

After David's dramatic victory over Goliath, Saul brought him into his palace once again, this time as a commander of his **army** (18:5). David's favored position in the court was further strengthened by the personal affection felt for him by **Jonathan,** Saul's oldest son (vv. 1, 3). So close did this friendship become that **Jonathan,** though heir apparent to the throne of Israel (cf. 20:31), stripped himself of his own royal regalia and placed it on **David** in recognition of David's divine election to be king (18:4; cf. 23:17). More than once the covenant of friendship between the two men would work to David's advantage. Meanwhile David became so effective militarily that his exploits were celebrated in song: **Saul has slain his thousands, and David his tens of thousands.**

(2) Saul's jealousy (18:8–20:42). **18:8-16.** So enraged was **Saul** at the diminishing of his glory that he, inspired by the demonic **spirit** (v. 10; cf. 16:14-16; 19:9), tried to **spear** David (18:10-11; 19:9-10). But God delivered **David** and gave him even greater popularity (18:12-16).

18:17-30. When **Saul** then saw that he could not destroy **David** personally, he determined to let **the Philistines** kill him. This he arranged by proposing that **David** marry his oldest **daughter, Merab.** Saul had already reneged on one marital promise to David (17:25). **David** protested, however, that he was a commoner and had no sufficient bridal **price** (18:25, *mōhar,* not "dowry" as in KJV and others). Before anything further could develop, **Merab . . . was given** to another man (v. 19). Again **Saul** offered his second daughter, **Michal,** who at that time loved **David** (v. 20; cf. 2 Sam. 6:16). But again **David** argued that he was unsuitable to be a **son-in-law** of the king because of his low status (1 Sam. 18:23). In an act of apparent generosity **Saul** waived the usual bridal payment and demanded only that David kill **100** Philistines and bring back their **foreskins** (v. 25), a requirement he more than met by slaying 200 (v. 27). Saul had been hoping, of course, that the exploit would cost David his life (v. 25). As a result, Saul was again afraid of David (v. 29; cf. vv. 12, 15). But David became Saul's son-in-law by marrying Michal (v. 27), and his military success and his popularity increased (v. 30).

Chapter 19. After an initial and successful attempt by Jonathan to soothe his father's feelings toward David (vv. 1-7), Saul set in motion further steps to destroy David. First he tried to slay him once more with his own hand (vv. 9-10); then he hired conspirators to murder him in his bed, a plot foiled by Michal (vv. 11-17). Next Saul sent men to Naioth at Ramah where David had taken refuge with Samuel (vv. 18-24). (Ramah was Samuel's hometown.) Their efforts were also unsuccessful for they, and later Saul, were overwhelmed by the Spirit of God who came on them and caused them to "act like prophets" (NIV, prophesied, vv. 20-21, 23-24). This means that they fell into a trance or an ecstatic state, a condition which immobilized them and made them incapable of accomplishing their evil intentions.

20:1-23. Having become persuaded of the irremedial nature of Saul's hostility toward him, David sought to learn its source and to determine if there might be a means of reconciliation. The test would be Saul's response to David's absence from the New Moon feast (v. 5), held on the first day of every month (Num. 28:11-15). If Saul became upset about David's absence, then David would know that there was no hope of patching up their differences. If, however, the king was amenable, then all was not lost (1 Sam. 20:6-8). Jonathan would approach his father on the matter and communicate the results to David by signaling with arrows (vv. 18-23).

20:24-42. At first Saul . . . thought David was absent because he was ceremonially unclean (v. 26). But then Saul's response was what David feared. After David's absence on the second day, Saul was filled with rage toward David and also toward Jonathan (vv. 30, 33). As long as David lived, Saul said, there was no hope that his own dynasty would continue (v. 31).

With heavy heart Jonathan signaled to David the next morning by his words

to a boy and with arrows (vv. 34-40). Jonathan and David met and wept together (v. 41). It was obvious that friendship with Saul was impossible. But Jonathan said that his own bond of loyalty with David would never be broken (v. 42). Jonathan was giving up a kingdom for the love of a friend.

b. David's life in exile (chaps. 21–26)

As far as can be determined, David was a young man of no more than 20 when he was forced to leave Saul's palace and his own home because of Saul's relentless determination to destroy him. Driven to the wilderness area of Judah, the logical place because of his familiarity with it from childhood, David lived out a "Robin Hood" existence for nearly 10 years. This period of time is reckoned from the fact that David was 30 when he began to rule over Judah at Hebron (2 Sam. 5:4), his accession occurring immediately after Saul's death (2 Sam. 2:10-11). David had spent a year and four months among the Philistines just before that (1 Sam. 27:7) and, as just suggested, was only about 20 when exiled from Saul. The events of chapters 21–26 must then represent only a fraction of David's activity during this period. But God was teaching David many things in those days, lessons David still shares with all who read his psalms which find their setting in this turbulent period of his life (see, e.g., Pss. 18; 34; 52; 54; 56–57). All these things were surely working together to prepare David to be the kind of leader who would glorify God and inspire His people.

(1) David at Nob and Gath (chap. 21). 21:1-6. It is difficult to trace the history of the tabernacle after the capture of the ark in 1104 B.C. The ark itself rested at Kiriath Jearim since then (7:2; 2 Sam. 6:3-4), but the tabernacle is not mentioned or even hinted at till 1 Samuel 21, when it was presumed to be at Nob, the "city of priests," where David fled after he made his final break with Saul. Just as David had earlier sought sanctuary with Samuel at Ramah (19:18), so now he went to find sanctuary with Ahimelech (also known as Ahijah), the priest at Nob (21:1), halfway between Jerusalem and Gibeah. Hungry from his flight, David asked the priest for bread (v. 3). There was no ordinary bread, the priest replied (v. 4), but

only the holy showbread (Ex. 25:30, KJV) which had been desacralized by being replaced with fresh bread (1 Sam. 21:6; cf. Lev. 24:5-9). This could be eaten, as Jesus suggested later on (Matt. 12:3-4), but ordinarily only by the priests and certainly only by those who were ceremonially pure (1 Sam. 21:4-5; Lev. 15:18). David's eating illustrated a concession that the Law permitted—life is more holy than bread (Matt. 12:7-8).

21:7-15. While **David** was at Nob, he was spotted by a spy of Saul, **Doeg the Edomite,** who informed Saul of David's whereabouts (v. 7; 22:9). Taking Goliath's **sword** which had been kept by the priests at Nob (21:8-9), **David** immediately **fled** for his life and, throwing all caution to the winds, fled to **Gath,** hometown of the dead Philistine hero Goliath (v. 10). Recognized by **Achish,** the lord **of Gath,** David pretended to be insane and so escaped Philistine reprisal (vv. 11-13). This is in line with the practice of the ancient world to regard the **insane** as being in some sense an evil portent and so exempt from harm lest the gods be provoked.

(2) David at Adullam. **Chapter 22.** David next moved to **Adullam,** about 20 miles southwest of Jerusalem and 10 miles northeast of **Gath** (v. 1). There he took residence in **the cave** along with **400** other **men** who, for various reasons, were refugees (v. 2). Meantime, sensing a threat to his own family, **David** took them to **Moab** (vv. 3-4), perhaps to live among the kinfolk of his own greatgrandmother Ruth. **David** then **went to the forest of Hereth,** east of Adullam, in **Judah** (v. 5), no doubt to be among his own people over whom God had anointed him to reign.

As soon as **Saul** found out about David's return to Judah, he began to blast his followers for their failure to communicate all they knew about David's activities, particularly his close relationship with Jonathan (vv. 6-8). To soothe Saul **Doeg,** who had seen David at Nob, told the king how the priest **at Nob** had assisted David in his need. In his paranoia **Saul** concluded that **Ahimelech** and the other **priests** were conspirators **against** him, and after calling for them and listening to their self-defense he ordered them slain (vv. 11-16). Only **Doeg** was willing to undertake the gruesome assignment. He **killed** the **85** priests of **Nob** together with their families and livestock (vv. 17-19).

David then was joined by **Abiathar** (vv. 20-23), **son of** the priest **Ahimelech,** who **fled to** David after Saul exterminated the whole priestly community. This marked the beginning of David's priestly staff which would later lead the tabernacle worship in Jerusalem.

(3) David in the wilderness (chaps. 23–24). **23:1-18.** While in flight from Saul, **David** did more than remain in hiding. He also fought on behalf of his beleaguered people against the ever-menacing **Philistines.** First, having consulted **the** LORD by means of the ephod's sacred lots (v. 2; cf. v. 6), he delivered the town **of Keilah,** near the Philistine border, 15 miles southwest of Bethlehem (vv. 1-5). But the people "repaid" his kindness by betraying him to **Saul** (vv. 7-12). So he withdrew with **600** men, who remained faithful to him (v. 13; cf. 27:2; 30:9; 2 Sam. 15:18), **to the Desert of Ziph** (1 Sam. 23:14), a desolate hilly and wooded area between Hebron and the Dead Sea. He was joined there (**at Horesh in the desert**) briefly by **Jonathan,** who again confirmed the legitimacy of David's kingship (vv. 16-18).

23:19-29. The Ziphites also betrayed **David** to Saul (vv. 19-23). **David** became aware of this (vv. 22-25), so he escaped to **the Desert of Maon,** 10 miles southeast of Hebron. **Saul** pursued him there, but was temporarily called back to defend Israel against another Philistine raid (vv. 27-28). That gave David opportunity to go to **En Gedi** (v. 29), an oasis 10 miles north of Masada on the Dead Sea.

Chapter 24. Saul caught up with **David** at En Gedi and nearly found him. The LORD had other plans, however, and Saul's life was in David's hands as the king went **to relieve himself** (lit., "cover his feet," a euphemism, v. 3) in the same **cave** where **David** was hiding. So close was **David** that he **cut off a** piece of the king's **robe** as evidence of his opportunity to kill him. But even this act convicted **David,** who would not think of harming Saul bodily (vv. 5-7). **David** would not hurt the king, for he regarded **Saul** as the LORD's **anointed** (vv. 6, 10; cf. 26:9, 11, 23). Yet, as **David** said, **the king** had no just cause for hunting him down (24:14-15). In repentance, **Saul** acknowledged

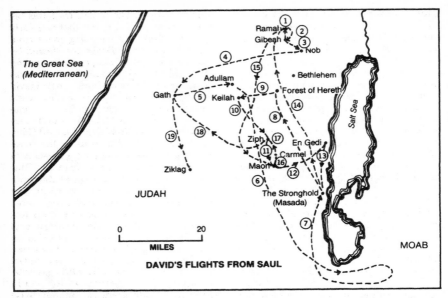

The Great Sea (Mediterranean)

Ramah
Gibeah
Nob
Bethlehem
Adullam
Forest of Hereth
Gath
Keilah
Salt Sea
Ziph
En Gedi
Carmel
Maon
Ziklag
JUDAH
The Stronghold (Masada)
MOAB

0   20
MILES

DAVID'S FLIGHTS FROM SAUL

David's righteousness (vv. 17-19) and the fact that David would indeed **be king** (v. 20).

(4) David and Nabal. **Chapter 25.** The chapter opens with the death and burial of **Samuel** at **Ramah.** Then **David moved** to **the Desert of Maon** (v. 1; cf. 23:24). There in dire circumstances David thought of **a certain man** named **Nabal,** who **had 1,000 goats and 3,000 sheep,** indicative of his great wealth (25:2-3). Appealing to his past protective attitude toward Nabal (v. 7; cf. vv. 15-16, 21), **David** asked him for provisions to sustain him and his men in the wilderness.

Nabal, however, with utter contempt, refused to comply (vv. 4-11). This so angered **David** that he took **about 400 men** with him to take forcibly from Nabal what he wanted. Were it not for the intervention of **Abigail** Nabal's wife, Nabal surely would have been slain. She learned about **Nabal's** foolish reply from **one of the servants.** To avert **disaster** she **took** with her food supplies in sufficient abundance to meet David's requirements (vv. 14-19). When **she met him,** she begged him not to punish her husband for, she said, **He is just like his name**—a **fool** (nābāl, "foolish"). Instead, she continued, God would bless David and would eventually make him king (v. 28). For him to kill the senseless **Nabal** would

only burden **his conscience** needlessly (v. 31). Impressed by her wisdom, **David** followed her advice and gratefully **accepted** the food **she had brought** (vv. 32-35).

Abigail's judgment was vindicated shortly thereafter when **Nabal,** after a drunken night, found out how narrow an escape he had had from **David.** The news so shocked him that he had a **heart attack** and died in **about 10 days** (vv. 36-38). **David** saw in this turn of events a sign from God. Obviously struck by the beauty and character of **Abigail,** he proposed marriage to her, a proposal she gladly accepted. Thus David added another wife to **Ahinoam** and **Michal,** whom he had previously **married,** though in his absence from Gibeah, **Saul had given** the latter **to Paltiel** (vv. 43-44; cf. 2 Sam. 3:15-16).

(5) Saul's final pursuit of David. **Chapter 26.** Once again **Saul** learned from **the Ziphites** about David's place of **hiding,** so the king and **3,000 chosen men** went to **the hill of Hakilah** (cf. 23:19) in **the Desert of Ziph** to **search** for **David.** Again the Lord miraculously delivered His chosen one who this time came—with **Abishai,** a skilled and faithful soldier and **Joab's brother** (26:6; cf. 2 Sam. 2:24; 10:14; 18:12; 21:17; 23:18)—so close to the sleeping king that **David**

stole both his **spear and water jug**
(1 Sam. 26:5-12). Again **David** dared not
harm **the LORD's anointed** (vv. 9, 11, 23;
cf. 24:6, 10).

After crossing the ravine opposite
Saul, **David** shouted **to Abner,** who supposedly guarded Saul, and tauntingly
chided him for his carelessness in allowing **the king's spear and water jug** to be
taken (26:13-16). **Saul** then awoke and
once more heard David's plea that he be
left alone. If God were leading Saul in the
pursuit, then David would repent (v. 19).
If, however, men were responsible, they
should **be cursed** by God because they
had intervened in God's purposes by
driving David **from** both his home (**inheritance,** v. 19) and his public worship
of God (**Go, serve other gods,** v. 19).

So evident to **Saul** was God's protection of his young rival that he could only
confess his own wickedness (v. 21) and
recognize fully and finally that **David**
was destined to be the shepherd of Israel
(v. 25). So far as can be determined **Saul**
became resigned to his fate and never
again tried to interfere with the will of
God for the kingdom and its next anointed leader (cf. 27:4).

D. Saul's death (chaps. 27–31)

1. DAVID AT ZIKLAG (CHAP. 27)

Chapter 27. Though **Saul** at long last
had decided that further pursuit of **David**
was fruitless because the Lord had ordained him for the throne, **David** did not
know this. **So** he reluctantly **left** Judah to
find refuge among **the Philistines** (v. 1).
This move accomplished two important
objectives: (a) it delivered him from any
possible danger from Saul, and (b) it ingratiated him with the Philistines so he
had no further need to fear them. No less
important, this 16-month (v. 7) respite
(from the time of his Philistine sojourn
until the death of **Saul**) gave him opportunity to develop even further his combat
and leadership skills. He needed this
time to stabilize himself in view of what
he knew must be the soon end of Saul's
dynasty and the beginning of his own.

So after many years of running from
Saul, **David** finally led his immediate
family (his two wives, v. 3, **Ahinoam of
Jezreel** [cf. 25:43] **and Abigail of Carmel**
[cf. 25:42]) and **600** followers (27:2; cf.
23:13; 30:9; 2 Sam. 15:18) to **Gath** and
threw himself on the mercy of **Achish,** a

Philistine ruler. **David** had tried this before (1 Sam. 21:10-15), but that was early
in the period of his estrangement from
Saul. At that time **David** was feared by
Achish and barely escaped with his life.
But now it was clear to all that **David** was
Saul's mortal enemy and that David
could even be useful to the Philistines in
their ongoing struggle with Israel. A relationship of lord and vassal was undertak-
en then between **Achish** and **David** (27:5-
6). According to the terms of the covenant they made, David pledged loyalty to
Achish in return for a fiefdom. This
Achish granted in the town of **Ziklag,** a
small settlement on the southern frontier
of Philistia between Gaza and Beersheba.

This remained David's headquarters
for over **a year,** until the death of Saul
and David's subsequent move to Hebron
(v. 7; 2 Sam. 1:1-2). From there he carried
out pillaging raids against various desert
peoples, including **the Geshurites** (a tribe
bordering the Philistines on the south,
Josh. 13:2), **the Girzites** (an otherwise
unknown people living between the Philistines and Egypt), **and the Amalekites**
(1 Sam. 27:8), killing the people and loot-
ing all their livestock and other goods (v.
9). These raids were in the region of the
modern Gaza strip, toward the Desert of
Shur, east of the present Suez Canal (v.
8). But **David** reported to **Achish** that his
attacks were against his own tribe **Judah,**
or **Jerahmeel,** or **the Kenites,** fabrications
which endeared him all the more to the
Philistines and persuaded them that he
was a true and loyal subject (v. 12).

2. SAUL AT ENDOR (CHAP. 28)

28:1-2. A day came when **the Philistines** resolved to make another massive
assault **against Israel.** Whether they were
encouraged to do so because of the obvious instability of the now-aged king Saul
and his nation, or because of David's apparent shift of allegiance, or for some
other reason, is not clear. But they felt
that the time was then propitious. The
result, of course, was that **David** found
himself in a most compromising position,
for he would now be called on to demonstrate his loyalty to his new lord by fighting against his own people!

28:3-6. Meanwhile **Saul** also found
himself in a desperate situation. **Samuel
was dead** (cf. 25:1), and **the Philistines**
were camped **at Shunem** (in the Valley of

Jezreel). **Saul, who was at Gilboa,** five miles northwest of Mount Gilboa, **was afraid.** He had purged out the **mediums** ('*ōbôt*, "necromancers," those who communicate with the dead) **and spiritists** (*yidd*e'ōnîm, "soothsayers," *those who contact the spirits, v. 3*). And **the LORD** refused to **answer** Saul's inquiry for help.

28:7-14. Saul at last resorted to a celebrated **medium** at nearby **Endor** who had somehow survived the purge. Disguising **himself** . . . **Saul** made his way **at night** to Endor, in the Valley of Jezreel just north of Mount Moreh. After putting her at ease, **Saul** asked the medium to contact **Samuel.** Drawing on the demonic powers of necromancy (Deut. 18:10-11), she called up the apparition of **Samuel.** So startled was she by Samuel's appearance that she immediately realized that the work was of God and not herself and that her disguised nocturnal visitor was King **Saul.** This implies that she did not really expect to raise up Samuel but only a satanic imitation. After she described the vision as **a spirit** ('*ĕlōhîm*, "mighty one") and as **an old man** clad in **a robe** . . . **Saul knew it was Samuel.** That Samuel's appearance, even in visionary form, was not the expected result clearly teaches that necromancers or mediums have no real power over the deceased, especially the righteous, but can only produce counterfeits. Samuel's appearance here is explained by the intervention of the Lord who graciously permitted Saul one last encounter with the prophet whom he had first sought so long ago in pursuit of his father's lost donkeys (1 Sam. 9:6-9).

28:15-25. But **Samuel** did not have good news this time. He rebuked **Saul** for his impiety and informed him that **the kingdom** was **torn** . . . **out** of his **hands and given** . . . **to David.** Also just as the **LORD** had rejected him as king because of his sin in the Amalekite affair (15:7-26), so He would deliver him **to the Philistines** and bring about his death and that of his **sons.** After reluctantly accepting refreshment (a butchered **calf** and freshly **baked bread without yeast**) from the medium, **Saul** arose and dejectedly walked off into the **night.**

3. DAVID'S RETURN TO ZIKLAG (CHAPS. 29–30)

a. *David's dilemma (chap. 29)*

Chapter 29. On the eve of the battle the **Philistines** had rendezvoused **at Aphek,** precisely where they had defeated Israel and captured the ark about 90 years earlier (4:10-11). **Israel** took up positions **by the spring in Jezreel,** on the flank of Mount Gilboa, some 40 miles northeast of Aphek. Among the troops of **Achish,** lord of Gath, were **David and his men.** Though **Achish** had implicit confidence in **David** (29:3) and argued with the other leaders that he should be allowed to fight against **Saul,** he was outvoted (vv. 6-7, 9). Understandably the other **commanders** feared that in the heat of **battle** David would defect to Israel (v. 4). **David,** offering a feeble protest (v. 8) but obviously greatly relieved, was discharged and returned to Ziklag.

b. *David's diplomacy (chap. 30)*

30:1-7. In David's absence from **Ziklag,** Amalekite raiding parties had **burned** the town and **carried . . . off** his family and everyone else as prisoners. After great lament (v. 4) and his men's threat to stone him, **David inquired of the LORD** through **Abiathar the priest** concerning His will in the matter. The inquiry was made by means of **the ephod,** the high priest's apronlike garment which contained the Urim and Thummim, the sacred stones used to discern the will of God (cf. Ex. 28:30).

30:8-31. Assured of victory (v. 8), **David** and his **men** pursued the Amalekites **to the Besor Ravine** (the Wadi el-Arish, some 20 miles south of Ziklag). When they finally **found** them (with the help of **an Egyptian . . . slave of an Amalekite** [vv. 11-15]), David's **400 men** who were rugged enough to stand the rigorous march (vv. 9-10) defeated **the Amalekites (except** for **400 young** Amalekites who escaped on camelback, v. 17) and retrieved all their families and property intact (vv. 17-20). **The 200** who had remained behind by **the Besor Ravine** (vv. 10, 21) wanted a share of the Amalekite booty. (On David's 600 men, see 23:13; 27:2; 2 Sam. 15:18.) So reasonable did their request sound to **David** that he established a principle **that day** that would thereafter prevail: **The share of the man who stayed with the supplies is to be the same as that of him who went down to the battle** (1 Sam. 30:24). But David's diplomatic masterstroke was his return of the properties stolen by the

Amalekites from the cities and towns **of Judah** (vv. 26-31). Never would they forget his concern for them, and when the time came for him to declare his kingship at **Hebron** he no doubt enjoyed their enthusiastic support.

4. THE BATTLE OF GILBOA (CHAP. 31)

31:1-6. Just as Samuel had prophesied (28:19), **the Philistines** quickly and easily defeated **Israel** in the broad plains of the Valley of Jezreel where they, with their chariots (2 Sam. 1:6), had an overwhelming tactical advantage (cf. Josh. 17:16; Jud. 4:3, 13, for the use of iron chariots by the Canaanites in this same area). **Saul,** with **three of his** four **sons**— all but Ish-Bosheth (see 2 Sam. 2:8)—**fled** from **Mount Gilboa. Saul** was overtaken, however, and mortally **wounded** after **his sons** had been slain. Fearing that he might be found by the Philistines and tortured to death (1 Sam. 31:4), he asked **his armor-bearer** to kill him, an order his attendant refused to obey. **Saul** then, in violation of an Israelite taboo, committed suicide (v. 5), an act rarely known among Israelites in the Old Testament (cf. Abimelech [Jud. 9:54], Samson [Jud. 16:30], Ahithophel [2 Sam. 17:23], and Zimri [1 Kings 16:18]). His death by his own hand climaxed a life which had been led in independence of God.

31:7-10. When the Israelites learned that their king was dead, **they abandoned their** cities and took to the wilderness. **The Philistines** eventually came on the bodies of **Saul and his three sons,** decapitated the king, displayed **his armor in the temple of** the goddess Ashtoreth (cf. comments on 7:3-4), and impaled **his body** on the city **wall of Beth Shan,** a prominent town on the eastern slopes of Mount Gilboa overlooking the Jordan Valley.

31:11-13. So horrified were **the people of Jabesh Gilead** when they became aware of this desecration that they removed **the bodies of Saul and his sons** under cover of **night** and brought **them** to their own city, just 10 miles across the Jordan. Probably to hide their mutilation **they burned** the corpses and **buried** the **bones.** This last act of respect was a tribute of a grateful people to the fact that Saul's first public deed was the rescue of this same city from the Ammonites 40 years before (11:1-11). And one cannot forget that Saul's own tribe, Benjamin, found much of its more recent historical origins in Jabesh Gilead (Jud. 21:8-12). For whatever reasons, the courageous actions of the people of Jabesh Gilead would not be forgotten by David when he at last came to power (2 Sam. 2:4-7). Later David had Saul's and Jonathan's bones exhumed and reburied in Benjamin (2 Sam. 21:11-14).

BIBLIOGRAPHY

Ackroyd, Peter R. *The First Book of Samuel.* Cambridge: Cambridge University Press, 1971.

Carlson, R.A. *David, the Chosen King.* Stockholm: Almquist and Wiksell, 1964.

Crockett, William Day. *A Harmony of the Books of Samuel, Kings, and Chronicles.* Grand Rapids: Baker Book House, 1951.

Davis, John J. *The Birth of a Kingdom: Studies in 1 and 2 Samuel and 1 Kings 1–11.* Winona Lake, Ind.: BMH Books, n.d.

Hertzberg, H.W. *1 and 2 Samuel: A Commentary.* Philadelphia: Westminster Press, 1964.

Jorden, Paul J., and Streeter, Carole S. *A Man's Man Called by God.* Wheaton, Ill.: Scripture Press Publications, Victor Books, 1980.

Keil, C.F., and Delitzsch, F. "The Books of Samuel." In *Commentary on the Old Testament in Ten Volumes.* Vol. 2. Reprint (25 vols. in 10). Grand Rapids: Wm. B. Eerdmans Publishing Co., 1982.

Kirkpatrick, A.F. *The First Book of Samuel.* Cambridge: Cambridge University Press, 1891.

Laney, J. Carl. *First and Second Samuel.* Everyman's Bible Commentary. Chicago: Moody Press, 1982.

McKane, William. *1 and 2 Samuel.* Torch Bible Commentaries. London: SCM Press, 1963.

Meyer, F.B. *Samuel.* Chicago: Fleming H. Revell Co., n.d. Reprint. Fort Washington, Penn.: Christian Literature Crusade, 1978.

Vos, Howard F. *1, 2 Samuel.* Grand Rapids: Zondervan Publishing House, 1983.

Whybray, R.N. *The Succession Narrative.* Naperville, Ill.: Alec R. Allenson, 1968.

Wood, Leon J. *Israel's United Monarchy.* Grand Rapids: Baker Book House, 1979.

2 SAMUEL

Eugene H. Merrill

INTRODUCTION

See the *Introduction* to 1 Samuel.

OUTLINE

COMMENTARY

I. David at Hebron (chaps. 1–4)

A. Lament for Saul and Jonathan (chap. 1)

1:1-10. Shortly after **David returned** to Ziklag (cf. 1 Sam. 27:6) from his successful punitive raid against the Amalekites (2 Sam. 1:1), he was met by a runner who had returned from Gilboa with the news of **the death of Saul** and his sons (vv. 2-4). When pressed for details, the messenger claimed that he had come on the wounded **Saul** (vv. 5-6), identified himself as **an Amalekite** (vv. 7-8), and when urged to do so by the king had mercifully put him to death (vv. 9-10). This man's report, differing from the account in 1 Samuel 31:3-6, was fabricated. Perhaps he called himself an Amalekite to protect Saul from the charge that he asked a fellow Israelite to do the unthinkable—to kill his own king, the Lord's anointed (cf. 2 Sam. 1:14, 16).

1:11-16. So enraged was **David,** after his grief was somewhat assuaged at the end of the day (vv. 11-12), that he commanded the alleged **Amalekite** to be executed (vv. 13-15). His false testimony, far from ingratiating him with David, had sealed his doom. It is ironic that Saul lost his kingdom because he failed to annihilate the Amalekites, and now one who said he was an Amalekite died because he claimed to have destroyed Saul.

1:17-27. David's public expression of grief over the deaths of Saul and Jonathan has been preserved in a poem, "The Song of **the Bow**" (vv. 19-27). This in turn is part of a now-lost longer composition referred to by the historian as the **Book of Jashar** (cf. Josh. 10:13). The same epic contained the short quatrain sung by Joshua on the occasion of the defeat of the Amorite league (Josh. 10:12-13).

In David's song, which opens and closes with the refrain, **How the mighty have fallen!** (2 Sam. 1:19, 27; cf. 1:25) **David** warned against telling of the tragedy in Philistia lest the Philistine maidens **rejoice** (v. 20) just as the Israelite maidens had sung of the triumphs of Saul and David years before (1 Sam. 18:7). David then cursed the **mountains of Gilboa** for having been the stage of **Saul** and Jonathan's heroic but fruitless defense against the enemy (2 Sam. 1:21-22). The undying loyalty of **Jonathan** comes in for special praise as David viewed father and son knit together **in life . . . and in death** (v. 23). Even though **Saul** had oppressed the people at times, he had also, David said, brought them luxury and bounty (v. 24). But it was **Jonathan** whom David celebrated with special pathos. All the years of their unbroken friendship are captured in his stirring tribute, **Your love for me was wonderful, more wonderful than that of women.**

B. Battle between David and Abner (chap. 2)

2:1-4a. David had looked back and lamented the past, but with the death of Saul came the future to which he had looked since the day of his anointing by Samuel more than 15 years before (1 Sam. 16:13). There was a power vacuum, particularly in **Judah,** now that Saul and three of his sons by his wife Ahinoam were gone. (Saul had two other sons by his concubine Rizpah, 2 Sam. 21:8, 11.) **David,** therefore, sought the mind of God and was told to go **to Hebron** where, at last, he was formally installed by oil-anointing as **king over . . . Judah.** (Later he was anointed a third time, as king of the entire nation, 5:3.) This was a decisive and important move for it immediately alienated him from the Philistines with whom he had taken refuge and made an alliance; it signified the quasi-independence of Judah from Israel, an attitude which would find complete expression at the division of the kingdom after Solomon's death (1 Kings 12:16); and it asserted David's reign as being in rivalry with that of Saul's son, Ish-Bosheth, who succeeded his father in the North.

2:4b-11. David at once began to demonstrate his diplomatic skills. He first gained the friendship of the people **of Jabesh Gilead** by commending them for their treatment of Saul's remains (cf. 1 Sam. 31:11-13). David reminded them that now that **Saul** was **dead** he was their sovereign.

Next David began to deal with the problem of succession to **Saul. Abner . . . commander of** Israel's **army** now became the effective power behind the throne. **He** placed **Ish-Bosheth** (known otherwise and certainly originally as Esh-Baal; 1 Chron. 8:33; 9:39), apparently Saul's youngest and least effective **son,** in authority. The name Esh-Baal means "fire of Baal," so to avoid the pagan overtones the name was changed to Ish-Bosheth ("man of shame"). His age of **40 years** (2 Sam. 2:10) when his father died is an important chronological fact. Since he is not listed as one of the sons of **Saul** at the beginning of Saul's reign (1 Sam. 14:49) but is included in the total list of sons (1 Chron. 8:33), he must have been born after Saul became king, thus indicating at least a 40-year reign for Saul (see Acts 13:21; also see comments on 1 Sam. 13:1).

Reigning from **Mahanaim,** in the east-central part of the Transjordan, **Ish-Bosheth** had a brief tenure of only **two years.** The fact that **David** reigned for **seven** and one-half **years** at **Hebron** before he made Jerusalem his capital (2 Sam. 5:5) need not imply that Ish-Bosheth also reigned for seven and one-half years at Mahanaim. This would contradict 2:10. There may well have been an interregnum of some length between Saul and Ish-Bosheth, and clearly **David** reigned for some time over **Judah** from **Hebron** after Ish-Bosheth's death.

2:12-32. From the beginning of **David's** reign his real rival in the North was not **Ish-Bosheth** but **Abner.** As though to clear the air and settle the question of royal succession, **Abner** and David's military leader **Joab** appointed elite troops, **12 men** on a side, to engage in **hand-to-hand** combat at **Gibeon.** The winners would decide the issue. The nature of the contest is unclear. Perhaps it took the form of a wrestling match which ended up in swordplay. The irregular use of daggers is suggested by naming the **place** of the contest **Helkath Hazzurim** ("field of daggers").

The result was a victory for **David's men,** but they were not satisfied to end the contest there. Instead they made hot pursuit of **Abner** and his friends, a chase that resulted in the seasoned warrior **Abner** taking the life of **Asahel,** younger brother of David's leader **Joab** (v. 23). **Joab** and a surviving brother **Abishai** vowed to take revenge (v. 24) but when faced by immensely unfavorable odds gave up the chase (vv. 25-28). **Abner** then made his way home **to Mahanaim** (by way of **the Arabah,** i.e., the Jordan Valley, and **the whole Bithron,** a deep ravine leading to Mahanaim, v. 29), while **Joab returned** by **night** to **Hebron** (v. 32). David lost 20 soldiers, but **Abner** lost **360** (vv. 30-31). The battle was over but not the war.

C. Conflict between Joab and Abner (chap. 3)

3:1-11. The struggle was not limited to individuals but included dynasties. This is evident in verse 1: **The war between the house of Saul and the house of David lasted a long time** (cf. v. 6). The supporters of Saul's family were determined to resist David's designs and to limit him to Judah. But those of David's dynasty were convinced that it was time for "the man after God's own heart" to become ruler of the whole nation. The historian described these power plays by recounting the marriages of **David** to six wives (vv. 2-5; see the chart "David's Family"), especially **Maacah, daughter of Talmai, king of Geshur,** a state northeast of the Sea of Kinnereth (see 15:8). In the North, **Abner** took **Rizpah, a concubine** of **Saul,** as one of his own, a common practice in the ancient Near East when one wished to indicate his succession to a king. **Ish-Bosheth** understood the meaning of the act and rebuked **Abner** (3:7). In anger **Abner** responded that he would

now work to deliver **the kingdom** of **Saul** over to **David** (vv. 9-10). Abner would help **establish David's throne over Israel and Judah from Dan to Beersheba.** This ruptured the relationship between **Abner** and **Ish-Bosheth** (v. 11).

3:12-21. Abner then proposed **to David** that they **make an agreement** (a covenant) and that he would help David secure **Israel. David** demanded that Abner restore, as a sign of his good faith, his long-separated wife **Michal** to him (vv. 13-14; cf. 1 Sam. 18:20-27; 25:44). After this was accomplished (2 Sam. 3:15-16), **Abner** met with Israel's **elders,** especially those from **Benjamin,** Saul's own tribe, and persuaded them that the rule of **David** over them was in their best interest. This, of course, elevated **Abner** considerably in David's estimation, which greatly displeased David's loyal men.

3:22-39. Particularly incensed was **Joab.** When he found out that **David** had entertained **Abner** at a feast (v. 20) and made overtures of friendship to him (v. 22), he chided **the king,** saying that Abner's purpose was to spy on David (vv. 24-25). **Joab then** took measures to have **Abner** return to Hebron **from the well of Sirah** (site unknown). Pretending to whisper something of importance to **Abner . . . Joab** drew **him aside** and viciously assassinated him (**stabbed him in the stomach,** v. 27; cf. 4:5-6). This was in revenge for Abner's murder of Joab's **brother Asahel** (3:27, 30; 2:23). **When David** discovered what had happened, he did not rejoice but rather uttered a curse on **Joab** and his progeny (3:29). Joab's murder of Abner took place in Hebron, a city of refuge (Josh. 21:13), where such revenge was not permitted (Num. 35:22-25). **David** then proclaimed a public **mourning** (2 Sam. 3:31), **buried Abner in** honor at **Hebron** (v. 32), and composed a lamentation (vv. 33-34) in which he spoke of the shameful way in which **Abner** had died. David's compassion and forgiving spirit are evident here, qualities which separated him from ordinary men.

As a sign of his sincerity, **David took** a vow to fast. He also said that he was **weak** compared with Abner. Though he knew that the **sons of Zeruiah** (Joab and his brothers) must be punished, he did not know how to undertake it (vv. 35-39). Zeruiah was David's half sister (1 Chron.

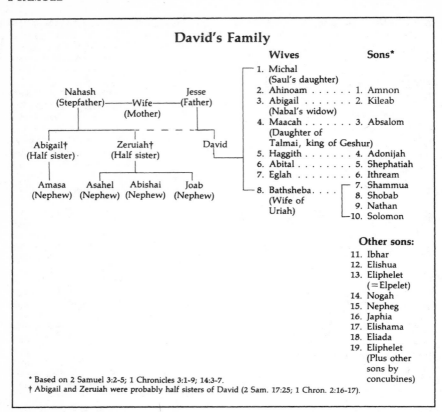

David's Family

	Wives	Sons*
	1. Michal (Saul's daughter)	
	2. Ahinoam	1. Amnon
	3. Abigail (Nabal's widow)	2. Kileab
	4. Maacah (Daughter of Talmai, king of Geshur)	3. Absalom
	5. Haggith	4. Adonijah
	6. Abital	5. Shephatiah
	7. Eglah	6. Ithream
	8. Bathsheba. (Wife of Uriah)	7. Shammua 8. Shobab 9. Nathan 10. Solomon

Nahash (Stepfather)——Wife——Jesse (Father) (Mother)

Abigail† (Half sister) · Zeruiah† (Half sister) David

Amasa (Nephew) Asahel (Nephew) Abishai (Nephew) Joab (Nephew)

Other sons:
11. Ibhar
12. Elishua
13. Eliphelet (=Elpelet)
14. Nogah
15. Nepheg
16. Japhia
17. Elishama
18. Eliada
19. Eliphelet
(Plus other sons by concubines)

* Based on 2 Samuel 3:2-5; 1 Chronicles 3:1-9; 14:3-7.
† Abigail and Zeruiah were probably half sisters of David (2 Sam. 17:25; 1 Chron. 2:16-17).

2:16; cf. 2 Sam. 2:18 and see the chart "David's Family").

D. Death of Ish-Bosheth (chap. 4)

4:1-8. News about Abner's death did not encourage **Ish-Bosheth** to reassert his own authority over **Israel**; on the contrary, it only increased his instability and brought a sense of panic to the nation (v. 1). Sensing that Ish-Bosheth was powerless, two Benjamite assassins—**Baanah** and **Recab** (vv. 2-3)—gained access to Ish-Bosheth's **house** at Mahanaim at midday and slew him in his **bed** (**stabbed him in the stomach,** v. 6; cf. the identical means of assassination of Abner by Joab, 3:27), beheaded him (4:7), and carried **his head** to **David at Hebron** (v. 8).

Within the narrative is a reference (v. 4) to Jonathan's son, **Mephibosheth** (otherwise and originally Merib-Baal, 1 Chron. 8:34). The name change is similar to that of Esh-Baal to Ish-Bosheth, but here the change was from "Baal contends" to "from the mouth of shamefulness." His lameness occurred when **his nurse,** who was carrying the young five-year-old lad out of danger after Jonathan's death, dropped him and injured him. Mephibosheth reappears later in the story as one in special need of protection (2 Sam. 9). Hence this parenthetical note prepares readers for what follows.

4:9-12. David's response to this deed, which was done obviously to gain his favor, was identical to his reaction when he learned of Saul's death (vv. 9-11; cf. 1:11-16). He ordered the two to be executed, their **hands and feet** to be **cut off,** and their corpses to be hanged publicly at **the pool** of **Hebron** (4:12). **David** regarded their act as an unjustified assault on a defenseless **man** (v. 11). No doubt David's stern measures of retribution also reflected his genuine love for Saul and his family, even though they had opposed him.

II. David's Prosperity (chaps. 5–10)
A. The capital at Jerusalem (chap. 5)

5:1-3. With Ish-Bosheth, Saul's son, now dead, the way was clear for **David** to assert his sovereignty over the Northern **tribes of Israel** as well as **over Judah.** There was a general recognition in the North that this should be done, so a delegation from all the tribes went to **Hebron** to encourage David's rule over them. They pointed out that they were his kinsmen, his **own flesh and blood,** that is, all were descendants of Jacob. They stated that he had distinguished himself as a hero of **Israel.** But furthermore they were conscious of the calling and anointing of **the** Lord in bringing **David** to power to shepherd them.

With no further hesitation they installed him as **king over** the entire nation. David reciprocated by entering into covenant **with them.** Samuel's earlier oil-anointing of David (1 Sam. 16:13) demonstrated God's choice of David. This third oil-anointing, like his second anointing in **Hebron** over Judah (2 Sam. 2:4), was the people's confirmation of that choice and a public installation. David's covenant probably involved an oath in which he pledged to follow the Mosaic requirements for kingship (Deut. 17:14-20).

5:4-5. **David** began his reign at age **30,** the age at which priests began to serve (Num. 4:3; 1 Chron. 23:3). After **seven** and one-half **years** at **Hebron,** David decided to relocate the capital. His reason was almost certainly political for he decided on **Jerusalem,** a city on the border between **Judah** and the Northern tribes. The distinction between **Israel and Judah** (2 Sam. 11:11; 12:8; 19:42-43; 24:1, 9) indicates that 2 Samuel was written after the nation was divided in 931 B.C. into the Northern and Southern Kingdoms.

5:6-9. Since **Jerusalem** had remained in Jebusite control ever since the days of Joshua (Josh. 15:63) it was considered neutral, so David's **residence** there would demonstrate tribal impartiality. But the very fact that Jerusalem had remained Jebusite indicated its security and defensibility. This is seen clearly in the taunting response of its citizens to David's siege of the city. **Even the blind and the lame can ward you off,** they said.

Taking up a position on Mount **Zion, the City of David,** which lay just south of the Jebusite city (Mount Ophel; see the map "Jerusalem in the Time of the Kings" near 1 Kings 9:15), David promised his men that whoever could discover a means of access to the city would be promoted to commander-in-chief (1 Chron. 11:6). The account in 1 Chronicles relates that Joab was able to do so, apparently by passing through the water tunnel which connected Jerusalem's water supply to its interior reservoirs (2 Sam. 5:8). The Hebrew word for **water shaft** (ṣinnôr) may refer instead to a sort of grappling hook (cf. NIV marg.). In any case, the city was entered and incorporated into the capital.

So galling to **David** was the Jebusite sarcasm about "the blind and lame," however, that it became proverbial to speak of his enemies in general as **the blind and lame.** After the city was captured, Mount Zion and Mount Ophel were consolidated into one entity described here and elsewhere as **the City of David** (5:7, 9; 6:12; 1 Kings 2:10). **The supporting terraces** (2 Sam. 5:9) were literally "the Millo" (NIV marg.). This Hebrew word means "filling"; thus this may have been the area between the hills which was filled in to level the whole city. It may also refer to embankments erected to protect the city from the North (1 Kings 9:15, 24).

5:10-12. David's capture, expansion, and occupation of Jerusalem made it clear to all Israel and to surrounding peoples as well that **God . . . was with him** and that he was not a renegade tribal chieftain but a political power with whom they must reckon. This is seen in the attention he received from **Hiram, king of** the Phoenician city-state of **Tyre,** who provided materials and men to build David **a palace** (cf. 1 Kings 5:1-11). Recognition by a person of such stature convinced **David** that God indeed **had established him** and **exalted his kingdom.**

5:13-16. One sign of such elevation in the ancient Near Eastern world was the acquisition of a large harem. Though David's action in this respect cannot be defended and eventually brought him untold sorrow, he nonetheless followed the prevailing custom.

5:17-25. **The Philistines** took special note of David's prosperity. Perhaps all through his years at Hebron they had

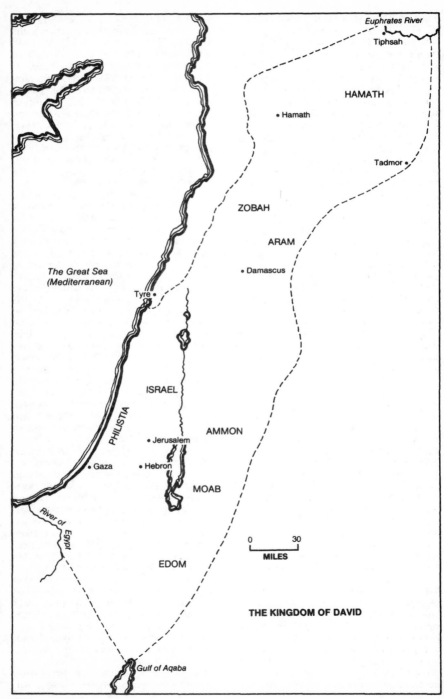

Euphrates River

Tiphsah

HAMATH

• Hamath

Tadmor •

ZOBAH

ARAM

*The Great Sea
(Mediterranean)*

• Damascus

Tyre •

ISRAEL

PHILISTIA

AMMON

• Jerusalem

• Gaza

• Hebron

MOAB

River of Egypt

```
0        30
MILES
```

EDOM

THE KINGDOM OF DAVID

Gulf of Aqaba

regarded him as a loyal vassal (1 Sam. 27:5-7; 29:3, 6-9). Now, however, they knew beyond question that David, as Saul's successor, was their implacable foe. After securing the promise of God's blessing (2 Sam. 5:19), **David** marched against **the Philistines** who had gathered for battle **in the Valley of Rephaim,** only three or four miles southwest of Jerusalem, and there he administered to them a resounding defeat. The result was that the **place** became known as **Baal Perazim,** "the Lord [here Israel's God] who breaks out." Ironically **the Philistines abandoned their idols** to the Israelites as Israel, in Samuel's early days, had surrendered the ark of the covenant, the token of God's presence, to the Philistines (1 Sam. 4:11).

But **the Philistines came up** to **Rephaim** again (2 Sam. 5:22). This time the divine strategy was different. Israel circled **behind** the Philistines and when they heard a **marching**-like rustle in **the balsam trees** they attacked and drove the Philistines **from Gibeon** (cf. 1 Chron. 14:16) **to Gezer,** a distance of 15 miles. Thus friend and foe could see the evidence of God's protection and power on **David** and his kingdom.

B. The return of the ark (chap. 6)

6:1-5. For 100 long years **the ark** of the covenant had been separated from the tabernacle and other places of worship. After its capture by the Philistines at Aphek (1 Sam. 4:11) it remained in Philistia for seven months, then briefly at Beth Shemesh, and the rest of the time at Kiriath Jearim. Now **David** had taken Jerusalem, a neutral place, and made it the political capital of the kingdom. All that remained was to retrieve **the ark,** place it in the tabernacle he would erect on Mount Zion, and declare Jerusalem the religious center of the nation as well.

David first went with **30,000** men to **Baalah of Judah** (the same as Kiriath Jearim; Josh. 15:9) to bring the ark **from the house of Abinadab,** its custodian. Described as that which bore **the name of** God Himself, **the ark** represented the presence of God who dwelled among His people in a special way (cf. Ex. 25:22). As such, it was to be handled with reverence, even in its transportation from place to place. The Law specified that it be carried by Levites who would bear it on their shoulders by means of poles passed through gold rings attached to the ark (Ex. 25:14; cf. Num. 4:15, 20). Even the Levites could not touch **the ark** or even look in it because of its holiness. Why David overlooked these requirements it is impossible to know, but he and **Uzzah and Ahio,** two descendants **of Abinadab,** placed the ark on a **cart** and proceeded, with great musical celebration, toward Jerusalem. The use of musical instruments (2 Sam. 6:5) was common in Israel's worship as may be seen, for example, in Psalm 150 where most of the same instruments are listed.

6:6-11. Along the way they passed over a rough outcropping of stone, a **threshing** place belonging to **Nacon** (or Kidon; 1 Chron. 13:9), and **the oxen stumbled,** threatening to throw **the ark** from the cart. Instinctively **Uzzah,** one of the attendants, laid **hold of the ark** to prevent its fall, an act of irreverence that cost him his life. The harshness of **the** LORD's discipline must be seen in the light of His absolute holiness which requires that sacred tasks be done in a sacred manner (cf. comments on 1 Sam. 6:19–7:2). Since God **had broken out** (*pāraṣ*) in **wrath** on **Uzzah,** David named that place **Perez** ("outbreak against") **Uzzah.** David learned his lesson. He would not move **the ark** again until the Lord gave him instruction. It **remained,** therefore, **in the house of Obed-Edom the Gittite** (a native of Gath) **for three months.**

6:12-15. At last the procession began again, this time according to divine requirement. As **the ark** was carried along, **David** offered sacrifice, dressed in priestly attire (**a linen ephod**), and dancing and shouting for joy with the Israelites. Here **trumpets** were played (cf. other instruments in v. 5). David was not a descendant of Aaron, and could not therefore ordinarily qualify to be a priest. He was, however, the anointed of the Lord, the founder of that messianic line that would be fulfilled in the King who would also embrace the offices of priest and prophet (7:12-16; 1 Sam. 2:35; Deut. 18:15-19). Some other Davidic kings functioned religiously as well, though not always properly (1 Kings 3:4; 8:62-63; 2 Chron. 26:16-19).

6:16-23. At length the procession made its way into Jerusalem itself. **Mi-**

chal, David's first wife and Saul's **daughter,** saw the **king . . . dancing** excitedly **before the LORD** and, chagrined and embarrassed by his celebrating, later rebuked him for it (v. 20). **David** defended his actions, affirming that he had done nothing wrong (vv. 21-22). **David** apparently separated from her and she never **had** any **children. Michal** had impugned his holy zeal to be nothing but exhibitionism, a charge which hurt him deeply. (See comments on 21:8.) **The ark** had been placed in a tabernacle which **David had** prepared (6:17). There the king continued his **burnt offerings and fellowship offerings** to the LORD and climaxed the festivities with food gifts, **a loaf of bread, a cake of dates, and a cake of raisins to each person in the** assembled **crowd.**

C. The Davidic Covenant (chap. 7)

7:1-2. After David had become well **settled** in Jerusalem and was enjoying a period of peace, his thoughts turned to the idea of building a more permanent structure in which the Lord could reside among His people. The **tent,** he felt, was no longer suitable, especially in comparison with his own elaborate **palace of cedar** (cf. 5:11).

7:3-17. Having communicated his desires to the Prophet **Nathan,** whose initial response was favorable, **David** soon learned that his intentions were premature. Since the Exodus **the LORD** had resided among the people in a temporary structure. There was no need now for anything different. In fact it was not God's will for **David** to **build** Him **a house;** instead God would build **a house** for David! (v. 11) God had called **David** from inauspicious beginnings **to be** a shepherd of God's **people** (v. 8). Likewise, God had gathered **Israel** to Himself and would **plant them** securely in their own land. The house to be built for David would be a royal house, a dynasty of kings. It would originate with him but would never end (v. 16). The **kingdom** and its **throne** would be permanent, a realm over which the Son of David would reign **forever** (cf. 23:5).

The promise that David and his seed would be kings fulfilled the even more ancient Abrahamic Covenant blessing that the patriarchs would be the fathers of kings (Gen. 17:6, 16; 35:11). To Judah,

great-grandson of Abraham, was given the explicit pledge that a promised ruler would come from Judah (Gen. 49:10). Samuel anointed this one from Judah, David himself, of whom the Lord said, "He is the one" (1 Sam. 16:12). David was aware of his election by God and of the theological significance of that election as part of the messianic line that would result in a divine Descendant and King (Pss. 2:6-7; 110; cf. Ethan's words in Ps. 89:3-4). The prophets also attested to the Davidic Messiah, the One who would rule over all and forever on His throne (Isa. 9:1-7; 11:1-5; Jer. 30:4-11; Ezek. 34:23-24; 37:24-25; Amos 9:11-15).

The promise that the people of the Lord, David's kingdom Israel, would have an enduring land of their own was also based on earlier commitments of the Lord. The seed of Abraham, God said, would be given Canaan as a home forever (Gen. 13:15; 15:18; 17:8; Deut. 34:4).

As for a temple, David would not be allowed to **build** it, but his son after him would have the honor of doing so (2 Sam. 7:12-13). That this refers to a literal house and not a dynasty is clear from the context, which speaks of the results that would follow if the **son** would be disobedient to the Lord (vv. 14-15). This could not be true of the King who is spoken of as the climactic figure of the Davidic dynastic line. These verses, then, are a good example of an Old Testament passage in which some elements find fulfillment in the immediate future (Solomon and other strictly human descendants of David), while other elements will be realized only in the more distant future (Jesus Christ, the Son of David; cf. Luke 1:31-33).

7:18-29. David's response to this magnificent revelation concerning the nature of his kingship was to acknowledge the Lord's goodness in bestowing it (vv. 18-21) and to extol God's incomparable sovereignty (**How great You are. . . ! There is no one like You,** v. 22). This, David said, was seen especially in God's selection of **Israel** and His redemptive grace on her behalf (vv. 23-24). Finally he prayed that **the promise** God had made might indeed find fulfillment to the glory of His own holy name—**so that** His **name** would **be great forever** (vv. 25-29). Interestingly David addressed God 7 times as **O Sovereign LORD** (vv. 18-20, 22, 28-29), words that translate the Hebrew *'ădōnāy* (lit., "Lord") *Yahweh*. **David** expressed his humility before God by referring to himself as **Your servant** 10 times (vv. 19-21, 25-29).

D. David's campaigns (chap. 8)

8:1-2. God had promised as part of His covenant with **David** that He would give Israel rest from all her enemies (7:11). He now began to do that very thing. First, **the Philistines**, Israel's perennial enemies for more than 125 years, were attacked and **defeated** at **Metheg Ammah**, a town otherwise unknown. Next **David** attacked **the Moabites**, putting **two** out of every three prisoners **to death**. The survivors he put in bondage to Israel, which implies that Moab became a vassal state **to David** as the great king. The reason for this harsh treatment is baffling since David had ancestral roots in Moab and relationships up until then appear to have been amicable (1 Sam. 22:3-4).

8:3-8. The Arameans then became David's objective. Consisting of a loose federation of city-states, the Arameans rose to prominence the same time Israel's monarchy rose under Saul and David. David first made an assault against **Hadadezer** (or Hadarezer), **king of Zobah,** an area just north of Damascus. Hadadezer had gone on a campaign to **the Euphrates River** to recover some territory, and in his absence **David** struck. His victory over these Arameans gained him prisoners (**7,000 charioteers and 20,000 foot soldiers**), 1,000 **chariots,** and **100 of the chariot horses,** the latter used for the first time to field a chariot corps in Israel. (Though the Heb. in v. 4 reads "1,700 charioteers," 1 Chron. 18:4, probably a better-preserved text, reads, as the NIV has it, "1,000 of his chariots [and] 7,000 charioteers.") Before David could return, he and his men were attacked by the Aramean troops **of Damascus**. Again **David** prevailed, and after slaying **22,000** of the enemy, he established an occupation force in **Damascus,** thus making Damascus another client state to Israel, required to pay **tribute.** Finally he returned **to Jerusalem** triumphantly, bringing **gold shields** and much **bronze** as trophies of conquest.

8:9-12. Having witnessed David's remarkable military successes, **Tou** (Heb.

Toi) king of the Aramean city-state of **Hamath,** decided to capitulate without struggle and become a vassal of Israel. To symbolize this move **he sent his son Joram** (or Hadoram, 1 Chron. 18:10) to **David** laden with precious **articles of silver and gold and bronze.** These **David** added to all the other spoils he had gained in previous campaigns (2 Sam. 8:11-12): **Edom** (cf. v. 14); **Moab** (cf. v. 2); **Ammonites** (cf. chap. 10); **Philistines** (cf. 8:1); **and Amalek** (David's conquest of Amalek is not narrated in the OT). All these spoils he **dedicated** to the service of **the LORD** (cf. 1 Kings 7:51).

8:13-14. Finally **David** gained far-flung fame by defeating an Aramean army of **18,000** in **the Valley of Salt,** a marshy plain south of the Dead Sea. Though "Aram" (i.e., "Arameans") is in most Hebrew manuscripts, the Septuagint and some other versions have "Edom," a reading that is also supported by a few Hebrew manuscripts and by 1 Chronicles 18:12. The difference in the original language is in only one letter: *d* (as in Edom) and *r* (as in Aram), easily confused in Hebrew. If "Aramean," it may be that the Edomites had solicited Aramean help against Israel. In any event, David again prevailed and brought Edom also under his hegemony. **The LORD gave David victory everywhere he went.**

8:15-18. The creation of an empire, though still small in comparison with the great powers of today, required the creation of a bureaucracy to administer its affairs. The principal officers were **Joab,** military commander; **Jehoshaphat,** record keeper; **Zadok** and **Ahimelech** chief **priests; Seraiah . . . secretary; Benaiah** (cf. 23:2-23), leader of the elite Kerethite and Pelethite troops (also mentioned in 1 Sam. 30:14; 2 Sam. 15:18; 20:7, 23; 1 Kings 1:38, 44; 1 Chron. 18:17; Ezek. 25:16; Zeph. 2:5, and possibly related to the Philistines in some way); **and David's own sons were royal advisers** (*kōhănîm*). This Hebrew word, usually rendered "priests," is explained in 1 Chronicles 18:17 as "chief officials" (cf. 2 Sam. 20:26). This no doubt is the better meaning since David's sons, as Judeans, were ineligible to serve as priests. The mention of Zadok and Ahimelech together (8:17) indicates the transition that was occurring in the office of priest. Ahimelech,

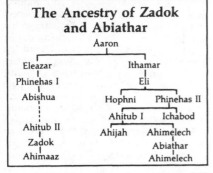

The Ancestry of Zadok and Abiathar

Aaron

Eleazar — Ithamar

Phinehas I — Eli

Abishua — Hophni, Phinehas II

Ahitub I — Ichabod

Ahitub II — Ahijah, Ahimelech

Zadok — Abiathar

Ahimaaz — Ahimelech

son of Abiathar, was a descendant of Eli (see the chart "The Ancestry of Zadok and Abiathar"), whose priestly line Samuel had said would come to an end (1 Sam. 3:10-14). Zadok was a descendant of Aaron through Eleazar (1 Chron. 6:4-8). Through Zadok the line of priests eventually continued through the remainder of Old Testament times.

E. David's kindness to Saul's family (chap. 9)

This chapter introduces what is sometimes called the "Succession Narrative," a literary piece which includes chapters 9–20. Its purpose is to show the steps David undertook to succeed Saul and to establish the permanence of his own dynasty. David's first step was to solicit the support of the Northern tribes by extending favor to the surviving members of Saul's household.

9:1-8. David had pledged to Jonathan that he would never forget the covenant of friendship that had bound them together (1 Sam. 20:14-17). He therefore called **Ziba,** a **servant** of Saul, and **asked** him if some member of Saul's family had special need (2 Sam. 9:2-3; cf. 1 Sam. 20:42). **Ziba** replied that **Mephibosheth,** the lame **son of Jonathan** (2 Sam. 4:4), was still alive and living at **Lo Debar** (just east of the Jordan, five miles south of the Wadi Yarmuk; cf. 17:27). **David** immediately sent for **him,** restored Saul's personal estate to him, and supported him on a royal pension (9:7). In humility **Mephibosheth** referred to himself as David's **servant** (v. 6) and as **a dead dog** (v. 8), that is, worthless (cf. 16:9).

9:9-13. David instructed Ziba and his **15 sons and 20 servants** to **farm** Mephibosheth's **land** and to treat him as

David's own son (9:9-11). David's provision for **Mephibosheth** and his letting him eat **at the king's table** (vv. 7, 10-11, 13) again demonstrated David's magnanimous heart. In all this David showed **kindness** (ḥeseḏ, "loyal love") **for Jonathan's sake** (v. 1; cf. v. 7).

F. David's ambassadors to Ammon abused (chap. 10)

10:1-5. Another aspect of David's succession was his international relationships. **David** had brought many of the surrounding nations under tribute to Israel (8:12). Included in these nations was Ammon, a kingdom directly east of the Jordan River. Since Saul's early years Ammon had been ruled by **Nahash.** In fact it was he who had attacked Jabesh Gilead in the beginning of Saul's tenure and was defeated by Saul (1 Sam. 11:1-11).

At last Nahash **died** and was succeeded by **his son Hanun.** Because Nahash had shown **David** some unspecified **kindness, David** sent an envoy to Ammon **to express his sympathy to Hanun** regarding **his father.** This, **David** no doubt hoped, would enable him to have a friendly ally on his eastern flank. But Hanun's advisers, perhaps recalling Saul's victory over Ammon 50 years before, counseled Hanun not to accept David's overtures but rather to view the Israelites as espionage agents. **David's** messengers were not only turned back but their beards were **half** shaved **off** and **their garments** cut away to an immodest length which, to those sensitive Semites, was an unbearable ignominy (cf. Isa. 15:2; 20:4).

10:6-14. Recognizing that his insult to David was, in effect, a declaration of war, Hanun engaged 33,000 mercenary troops from the three Aramean kingdoms of **Beth Rehob** (in northern Galilee), **Zobah** (see comment on 8:3), and **Maacah** (east of upper Galilee), and **from Tob,** a small kingdom on the western fringes of the Syro-Arabian desert. **David sent** his forces, led by **Joab** and **Abishai,** to encounter Hanun's own **army** and his mercenaries at Medeba (1 Chron. 19:7), 12 miles due east of the northern end of the Dead Sea. **Joab** directed his attention to the Aramean divisions and Abishai's troops to **the Ammonites,** with the understanding that one would help the other as circumstances required. The result was a smashing victory for Israel.

10:15-19. Though the Ammonites apparently learned their lesson, **the Arameans** determined to avenge the disaster of Medeba by recalling their occupation forces from **beyond the** Euphrates **River** and employing them against **Israel.** Under the command of **Shobach,** general of the **army** of Hadadezer of Zobah, they took up positions at **Helam,** a desert place 40 miles straight east of the Sea of Kinnereth. There **David** met them, and again the Lord gave **Israel** victory. David's men **killed 700 . . . charioteers and 40,000 . . . foot soldiers** and **struck down Shobach.** (Though the Heb. has 700 charioteers, the parallel passage in 1 Chron. 19:18 indicates that 7,000 charioteers were slain. The larger number is preferable since the Chron. account on the whole seems fuller and more comprehensive.) This broke the back of Aramean resistance and brought the Aramean confederates under Israel's domination. Never again did they side with Ammon against the people of Israel.

This is the second account of a subjugation of Hadadezer by David (cf. 2 Sam. 8:3-8). Apparently chapter 8 records an initial reduction of **the Arameans** of Zobah to Israelite vassaldom, while chapter 10 assumes an Aramean rebellion against David's overlordship, a rebellion which was squashed and which resulted in continued Aramean submission.

III. David's Sin and Domestic Problems (chaps. 11–21)

A. David's adultery (chap. 11)

11:1. Though the Arameans no longer came to their aid, **the Ammonites** stubbornly maintained their hostile posture toward Israel. In the context of David's ongoing problems with these inveterate foes occurred the turning point of his reign.

In the spring, after the latter rains were over and it was customary to resume military activity, **David** ordered **Joab** to launch an invasion of **Rabbah,** the capital of Ammon. Though **kings** usually led their armies personally, **David,** for reasons not related, **remained in Jerusalem.**

11:2-3. One evening, restless on his **bed . . . David** arose, went to a rooftop **of the palace,** and from there happened to observe **Bathsheba . . . the wife of** his neighbor **Uriah.** She was **bathing** out in the open. One may not fault **David** for perhaps seeking the cooler breezes of the late afternoon, but Bathsheba, knowing the proximity of her courtyard to the palace, probably harbored ulterior designs toward the king. Yet David's submission to her charms is inexcusable, for the deliberate steps he followed to bring her to the palace required more than enough time for him to resist the initial, impulsive temptation (cf. James 1:14-15).

11:4-5. Having discovered her identity, he **sent** for **her** at once and, assured of her ritual purity (cf. Lev. 12:2-5; 15:19-28), had intercourse with her. The bathing itself may have been for the purpose of ritual purification and would therefore not only advertise Bathsheba's charms but would serve as a notice to the king that she was available to him. In due time she found that she was **pregnant** by the king and, undoubtedly in great distress, informed him of her condition.

11:6-13. The crisis brought by the pregnancy required some kind of suitable resolution, so **David** determined to "legitimize" the impending birth by bringing **Uriah** back from the Ammonite campaign, thus making it possible for him to enjoy the intimacies of marriage. But the subterfuge did not work, for though **David** resorted to two schemes (vv. 8, 13) to induce **Uriah** to **go home** and be with his **wife,** the noble **Hittite** refused. (Though the Hittite Empire had ended by 1200 B.C., pockets of ethnic Hittites continued to exist in Syria and even Israel. **Uriah** was from one of these.) Why should he, he argued, be allowed the comforts of home and a conjugal visit while his friends in combat were deprived of them? Even after **David** plied him with wine, Uriah's sense of loyalty to his comrades prevailed over his desire for his wife.

11:14-21. In utter frustration **David** wrote a memo **to Joab** commanding that Uriah, when he returned to **the front line,** be abandoned to the enemy by an unexpected Israelite withdrawal. Ironically **Uriah** was the bearer of his own tidings of doom. This plan succeeded; **Uriah** was surrounded and slain. Ordinarily **David** would have been upset by the news of casualties. He would have wondered at Israel's indiscretion in fighting under Rabbah's **wall,** a blunder which had cost **Abimelech, son of** Gideon, his life long ago (Jud. 9:50-54). So **Joab** instructed the courier who bore the news to inform the king specifically that **Uriah** also had died. This he knew would mollify David's anguish.

11:22-27. David's response to the news was predictable. He **told the messenger** to tell **Joab** that in circumstances such as war, life and death were matters of blind chance. His instruction back to **Joab** was only that the siege of Rabbah be even more aggressive. Bathsheba soon learned of her husband's tragic death. **After the** customary **time of mourning,** she moved into the king's palace in time to bear their **son. The** LORD was **displeased,** however, and set events in motion that would trouble **David** till his death.

B. Nathan's rebuke and David's punishment (chap. 12)

12:1-6. Sometime after the birth of Bathsheba's son, **Nathan** the prophet told David a story of a **rich man** who, in spite of having everything, stole a **poor** neighbor's only **ewe** (i.e., female) **lamb** to provide a feast for a guest.

Enraged, **David** pronounced that **the man who** would do such a despicable thing ought **to die.** Though the Law contained no such penalty for the theft of property, kidnapping was a capital offense and it may be that David viewed the taking of a pet lamb in this light (Ex. 21:16). In addition, he said, **the rich man** must restore **four** lambs for the one stolen for not even the rich man's death could compensate the poor man's property loss (Ex. 22:1).

12:7-14. Nathan's reply to all this was a bombshell: **You are the man! The** LORD, he said, had given **David** everything, but he had taken, as it were, the pet lamb of a poor neighbor (v. 9). **David** now would suffer **the sword** as had **Uriah** and David's **wives** would be taken from him as Bathsheba had been stolen from **the Hittite.** This was fulfilled by Absalom (David's own son!) when he lay with David's concubines (16:22). But David's shame would be even greater because, in contrast with David's sin **in secret,** all these things would happen in the glare of the public eye, **in broad daylight.**

One may wonder, perhaps, why David was not punished with death as he had so sternly advocated for the guilty man. Adultery and murder both were sufficient cause for the execution of even a king (Ex. 21:12; Lev. 20:10). The answer surely lies in the genuine and contrite repentance which David expressed, not only in the presence of Nathan but more fully in Psalm 51. David's **sin** was heinous, but the grace of God was more than sufficient to forgive and restore him, as **Nathan** could testify. And yet, though David could be restored to fellowship with his God, the impact of his sin remained and would continue to work its sorrow in the nation as well as in the king's life.

12:15-23. Shortly **after** the interview with **Nathan . . . the child** became terminally **ill.** Despite David's intense fasting and prayer the baby **died** within a week. Only then did **David** cease his mourning, wash, worship, and eat, contrary to custom and much to the amazement of **his** servants. David's response is classic: **While the child was still alive, I fasted and wept. . . . But now that he is dead, why should I fast? Can I bring him back again?** David attested to the irrevocability of death—its finality renders further petition absurd. **I will go to him,** David said, **but he will not return to me.** This reflects his conviction that the dead cannot return to life as it was. Rather it is the living who go to the dead.

12:24-25. Eventually another **son** was born to David and Bathsheba, one who bore a double name. Called **Solomon** ("peace") by them, **the** LORD **. . . through Nathan** named **him Jedidiah** ("loved by the LORD").

12:26-31. In the meantime, the Ammonite war went well for **Joab.** He had all but captured the Ammonite capital, **Rabbah,** having taken **the royal citadel** and the city's **water supply.** And now, in order that **David** might gain the credit for its fall, **Joab** urged the king to lead the final assault himself. This **David** did. He sacked the city of its wealth, including the 75-pound (**a talent**) golden **crown** of the Ammonite **king** (malkām, which could also be a reference to "Molech," the Ammonite god). David also put the survivors to slave labor (using **saws**

... iron **picks, and axes** and working **at brickmaking)** and **returned** in triumph **to Jerusalem.**

C. Sin and murder of Amnon (chap. 13)

Because of his affair with Bathsheba David had been told by Nathan the prophet that the sword would never depart from his house (12:10). It was not long before he began to experience the heartbreaks of rape and murder within his own family.

13:1-6. Absalom, son of David by his wife Maacah (3:3), had a **beautiful sister** named **Tamar. Amnon,** David's firstborn by Ahinoam (3:2), **fell in love with Tamar. Frustrated** in his attempts to win her favor, **Amnon** sought the counsel of his **shrewd** cousin **Jonadab.** Jonadab advised Amnon to **pretend to be ill** and then to plead with his **father** to have **Tamar** bake him **bread** and bring it to him.

13:7-14. After **she** had prepared **the bread** before him, **Amnon** told her to dismiss all the servants. Then, despite her urgent pleading, **he grabbed her** and **raped her.** Such loss of a maiden's virginity was an unbearable curse **in Israel** (Deut. 22:13-21). Moreover, such relationships between half brothers and sisters were strictly forbidden in the Law. Those guilty of such things were to be cut off from the covenant community (Lev. 20:17). In this case, of course, **Tamar** was innocent since she had been assaulted (Deut. 22:25-29).

13:15-19. In revulsion at what he had done, **Amnon** now hated Tamar **more than he had** previously **loved her.** This indicates, of course, that his original feelings had not been love but only lust. To add insult to injury and in further violation of the Law, **Amnon** sent Tamar away. This suggests not only his desire to have her gone from his immediate presence but also his repudiation of her as a bride. He had humbled a **virgin** and the Law demanded that he marry her (Deut. 22:29). Tamar's reaction to all this—putting **ashes on her head and** tearing her royal robe (cf. 2 Sam. 13:31; Job 2:12)—shows the intensity of her sorrow at losing her purity and perhaps any further opportunity for marriage.

13:20-22. When **Tamar** got to the house of **her brother Absalom,** he suspected at once what had happened. No doubt he knew full well the propensities of **Amnon.** With plans for vengeance already developing in his own mind he counseled his **sister** to remain silent about the matter and to stay in his **house. David** somehow **heard** what had happened, and though **he was furious** he did not invoke the penalty prescribed by the Law. Perhaps this was because **Amnon** was his oldest son. But **Absalom . . . hated Amnon.**

13:23-29. Two long **years** passed before **Absalom** effected his plan for retaliation. He hosted a festival to celebrate the time of sheepshearing, a custom observed in Israel from earliest times (Gen. 38:12-13; 1 Sam. 25:2, 8). **He invited** and **urged** his father David to **join** him at **Baal Hazor** (ca. six miles south of Shiloh), the scene of the festivities, but David declined. **Absalom** then requested that **Amnon** attend in David's place, a request the **king** reluctantly granted. In the midst of the merriment the servants of **Absalom,** on a prearranged signal, attacked and murdered the unsuspecting **Amnon.** Thus a murder avenged a rape.

13:30-39. Having heard that **Absalom** had slain **all** of his other **sons . . . David** fell into inconsolable anguish. Even when he later knew that the report was unfounded and that **only Amnon** was **dead** he could not be comforted (v. 36). **Absalom** meanwhile **fled** from Baal Hazor and sought and found refuge with **Talmai,** his maternal grandfather, at **Geshur,** east of the Sea of Kinnereth. There **Absalom** remained for **three years** though his father, finally consoled, **longed to** have him return again.

D. Absalom's estrangement from David (chap. 14)

14:1-3. It was evident to all that David sorely missed his exiled son but no one knew how to achieve Absalom's return and a reconciliation. Finally **Joab,** always a tactician, convinced or commanded a clever **woman** from **Tekoa** (later the home of the Prophet Amos [Amos 1:1]; seven miles south of Bethlehem) to disguise herself as a mourner and **go to the king** with a story which he himself concocted and put **in her mouth.**

14:4-7. Having gained access **to the king,** the **woman** related to him that she had **had two sons,** one of whom had murdered **the other.** This meant that the surviving son was liable to blood vengeance at the hands of relatives. Since she was **a widow,** this would mean the elimination of her own source of support (expressed by the figure of speech, **They would put out the only burning coal I have left).** Perhaps even more important, she would have no **heir** to carry on the name and memory of her dead **husband.**

14:8-11. Obviously touched by her story, David told **the woman** to return **home** in peace. He would **issue an order** to resolve the matter. She was not convinced that she had fully made her point, however, and pressed her case even further. In the event of any miscarriage of justice, she said, she and her family would bear the responsibility. That is, if the circumstances really did require vengeance (Num. 35:9-21), she wanted **the king** to know that he would not be legally or morally culpable if he did not stop it from being carried out. Patiently David heard her out and again assured her that if anyone tried to prosecute the case he would have to answer to **the king.** Relentlessly she continued, however, till she elicited from David a formal oath that her accused **son** would suffer not even the slightest harm: **As surely as the LORD lives** (cf. comments on 1 Kings 1:29) **not one hair of your son's head will fall to the ground.**

14:12-14. Satisfied at last, **the woman** boldly accosted **the king** with the meaning of her parable. In granting amnesty to an unknown murderer it was now incumbent on him that he do the same for his own **son** Absalom. There are circumstances, she said, under which the death penalty need not be applied, particularly where premeditation was not involved (Num. 35:15). Though that was not relevant here, as Absalom had plotted Amnon's death long in advance, there was still the principle of mercy: **God does not take away life; instead, He devises ways so that a banished person may not remain estranged from Him.**

14:15-20. Then, to make David think that her remarks about Absalom were only incidental to her real purpose, **the woman** reminded **the king** of the fear that prompted her to come in the first place. She coupled this reminder with

effusive flattery of the king's wisdom (**My lord the king is like an angel of God in discerning good and evil,** v. 17; cf. v. 20). But David discerned that "the woman doth protest too much" and asked if **Joab** had something to do with **all this.** Found out in her treachery she had to admit it was true. David's recognition of **Joab** as the instigator lies no doubt not only in the general's recognized craftiness but in the fact that David was surely aware of Joab's interest in Absalom's return.

14:21-24. David had no alternative but to act on the sentiment he had expressed to the woman concerning forgiveness, even though he had been conned into doing so. He sent **Joab** to bring his alienated son **back.** But when **Absalom** returned David refused to meet him personally or to let him visit the palace. Perhaps David felt that too ready a reconciliation would lead the people to believe that he did not view Absalom's crime with sufficient seriousness.

14:25-27. In order to emphasize Absalom's attributes, features that should have made him attractive to David and which later proved irresistible to the people, the historian described **Absalom** as **handsome** in every way. The reference to his long **hair** (weighing **200 shekels,** i.e., about five pounds, when **he** infrequently **cut** it) is especially made to prepare for Absalom's peculiar undoing—later he was caught by his head (perhaps his hair) in the branches of an oak tree (18:9). His profound love for his violated sister **Tamar** also testifies to his attractiveness; he named his own **daughter** after her.

14:28-33. After **two** more **years** of estrangement from his father, **Absalom** twice sought Joab's aid in bringing about a final resolution of their differences. Rebuffed each time, **Absalom** resorted to dramatic action—he set **Joab's** barley **field on fire,** which did get the general's attention. **Joab** then intervened with **the king** and at last made it possible for **Absalom** to be reunited with his father. The meeting was at least superficially cordial, but as subsequent events demonstrated, David's long-delayed acceptance of his son came too late. **Absalom** was embittered and resolved to do whatever was necessary to make David pay for his intransigence.

E. Absalom's revolution (chaps. 15–18)

1. ABSALOM'S CAPTURE OF THE KINGDOM (CHAP. 15)

15:1-6. Absalom's first move to achieve his purposes of revenge was to make himself conveniently available (**by the side of the road leading to the city gate,** with his **chariot** and **50 men**) to hear the complaints of the citizens. Cleverly he insinuated that **the king** was too busy to hear them and that David had not even provided lesser judges to adjudicate their cases. If only he were chief **judge . . . Absalom** said, he would listen to one and all and deal impartially in every matter. **Absalom** showed the people great affection by kissing them when they came **to bow . . . before him.** Thus he gradually gained the support of the masses.

15:7-12. One day, feeling that his popular support was overwhelming, **Absalom** requested and received permission from **the king** to **go to Hebron,** allegedly to pay **a vow . . . to the LORD** which he had **made** while in exile in **Geshur** (cf. 13:37). For **4 years Absalom** had been weaning the people away from David. (The "4 years" appears in the Lucian recension of the LXX and the Syriac version [Peshitta], but the Heb. has "40 years," a figure which might refer to an event early in David's life, perhaps to his own anointing at Bethlehem, 1 Sam. 16:13.) Now the time was ripe for revolution. When **Absalom** reached **Hebron,** the very center of the Davidic dynasty, where David had begun his reign (2 Sam. 3:2-3), **Absalom** announced his usurpation of power (15:10). The **200 men** who **accompanied** him **from Jerusalem** were ignorant of his plans. Apparently they were won over as was **Ahithophel . . . David's** own chief **counselor.**

15:13-23. News quickly reached the capital that **Absalom** had effected a coup and that all was lost. **David,** convinced of the hopelessness of his cause and anxious to spare **the city** from destruction, made his plans to depart and head east for the Transjordan. He left behind **10** housekeeping **concubines. The people,** including **600 Gittites** (faithful men who had followed him from Gath in Philistia when he was pursued by Saul; 1 Sam. 23:13; 27:2; 30:9), fled with David. He tried to persuade his Philistine mercenary officer, **Ittai** of Gath, to remain behind since he had nothing to fear from **Absalom. But** to his credit **Ittai** refused, preferring to honor his commitment of loyalty by joining **the king** in banishment.

15:24-29. Zadok and Abiathar, the two chief priests, were sent **back to Jerusalem** by David. He knew that if it was God's will for him to return as king, he would do so. Hence there was no need to keep **the ark** away from the sanctuary. After all, it was David and not the Lord who was going into exile. Besides, the priests' two sons (**Ahimaaz,** Zadok's **son,** and **Jonathan,** Abiathar's **son;** see the chart "The Ancestry of Zadok and Abiathar," near 8:15-18) could carry to David any revelations which God might give their fathers.

15:30-37. David and his loyal supporters in the meantime made their way east across the Kidron Valley and **up the Mount of Olives.** His **covered** head and unshod feet indicated his depth of despair. To make matters worse **David** discovered that his trusted adviser **Ahithophel** had joined Absalom's cause. To contravene **Ahithophel's** effectiveness David recruited **Hushai,** a friend who asked to accompany the king on his way, and persuaded him to **return to** Jerusalem and attach himself to Absalom's court as a counselor. His mission would be to contradict the **advice** of Ahithophel and to communicate Absalom's plans to **Zadok and Abiathar** whose **sons** (cf. v. 27) in turn would relay them to David (cf. 17:21; 18:19). David then continued in his flight, but **Absalom** took firm control of **Jerusalem.**

2. ABSALOM'S SOLIDIFICATION OF POWER (CHAP. 16)

David's forced flight from Jerusalem not only put his own kingship in jeopardy, but it also opened the door to further contention for the throne between the dynasties of Saul and David. Absalom was apparently in the process of seizing power in Jerusalem but this by no means implied that he could also gain control over the Northern tribes. In fact the shakeup in David's own family began to revive hope among the Saulites that they might be able to recover the kingdom for themselves.

16:1-4. This is first evident in the reaction of Saul's grandson **Mephibosheth**

to David's withdrawal. While **the king** was heading east across the Judean hills, he was met by Mephibosheth's servant **Ziba** who, out of gratitude to David for his past kindness toward him (chap. 9), now provided the fugitive king **donkeys** and provisions for the journey. But **Ziba** also brought **David** the sad news that **Mephibosheth** had turned against the king, hoping that in the midst of the turmoil occasioned by the revolution he might be able to retrieve Saul's old throne (16:3; but cf. 19:24-30). David then stripped from Mephibosheth the generous pension he had given him earlier and bequeathed it all to **Ziba** (cf. 9:7, 13).

16:5-14. David next encountered **Shimei,** another relative of Saul, who greeted the fleeing monarch and his officials at **Bahurim** (east of the Mount of Olives) with curses and physical abuse, pelting them **with stones.** He taunted **David** with the observation that since he was **a man of blood** God was now avenging the death **of Saul** and his family by driving David from power. This was untrue, of course, for David had not raised his hand against Saul, whom he regarded as the anointed of the Lord, but had taken every measure to deal graciously with Saul's survivors. Shimei's real complaint, as is evident from his own admission, was that David sat on the throne of Saul (Saul, **in whose place you have reigned).**

Abishai, David's bodyguard and nephew, begged the king to let him decapitate Shimei (whom Abishai called a **dead dog,** i.e., worthless and despised; cf. 9:8). But **David** forbade him to do so, observing that it might well be that Shimei cursed as an instrument of God Himself. If Absalom, David's own **son,** was **trying to** kill him, why should the cursing of Shimei be of concern? God would someday vindicate, but for now there must be no recompense for Shimei's evil conduct. **Shimei** continued his **cursing,** stone-throwing, and dirt-tossing as David **continued** on **the road** to his **destination.**

16:15-23. Meanwhile Absalom arrived in **Jerusalem** and was immediately met by **Hushai,** a friend of David who was pretending to be loyal to Absalom. His mission as contradictor to the counsel of **Ahithophel,** Absalom's chief adviser, would be implemented later. When **Absalom** asked **Ahithophel** what he

should **do,** his adviser told him to **lie with** his **father's concubines,** an evidence of his succession (cf. 3:6-7), advice which **Absalom** quickly followed. The words of counsel which **Ahithophel** gave were given credence as though they came directly from **God,** so highly regarded was his wisdom. Hushai's assignment would be difficult indeed.

3. ABSALOM'S PURSUIT OF DAVID (CHAP. 17)

17:1-14. The second bit of advice which **Ahithophel** gave **Absalom** was that he, Ahithophel, should be delegated to pursue **David** in order to kill him and **return** everyone else. With their king dead his followers would certainly capitulate and return to Jerusalem peacefully.

Eager for a second opinion, **Absalom** called for **Hushai** and asked him if Ahithophel's counsel was wise. **Hushai** told **Absalom** that David and his men, far from being exhausted, would be more courageous and fearsome than ever. Like **a wild bear** whose **cubs** have been stolen, the king, Hushai said, would be enraged over the loss of his kingdom. To move against him now would be foolish. Initial casualties, which were certain to occur, would cause Absalom's men to despair of victory and thus his cause would be defeated. It would be far better, Hushai continued, for Absalom to wait until he could amass a huge army and then **attack.** David and his host could then be destroyed even if it meant dragging their place of refuge into **the Valley. Absalom** was at once struck with Hushai's sagacity and decided to follow his instruction and reject **that of Ahithophel.** Obviously this was the Lord's doing, to **frustrate** Ahithophel's **advice** and **bring disaster on Absalom.**

17:15-23. Hushai immediately communicated Ahithophel's advice and his own to **Zadok and Abiathar,** who then sent their sons **Jonathan and Ahimaaz** from **En Rogel** (south of Jerusalem; see the map "Jerusalem in the Time of the Kings," near 1 Kings 9:15) to **David** with the message that he must hasten his flight. But the young men were spotted and their errand was reported to **Absalom.** Thanks to the boldness and kindness of a **woman** in the village of **Bahurim** east of the Mount of Olives (cf. 16:5), they escaped detection by hiding in a dry **well.** Then they made their way to

David, who by now was at the Jordan. Without delay David and his followers crossed the river where they sought refuge at Mahanaim. Back at Jerusalem, Ahithophel, crushed because his counsel to Absalom had been spurned, committed suicide in his hometown by hanging himself.

17:24-29. Probably David chose to go to Mahanaim because it was fortified and also had served as the capital of Israel under Ish-Bosheth (2:8). There could well have been a residue of good feeling there toward David because of David's past favors to Saul's family, especially to Mephibosheth (9:10-13). While he was there, his meager provisions of food and supplies were augmented by Shobi son of Nahash (and brother of Hanun, 10:1), Makir of Lo Debar (see comments on 9:4), and Barzillai of Rogelim, 25 miles north of Mahanaim. They brought such items as bedding . . . bowls . . . pottery, and extensive food supplies including wheat and barley, flour and roasted grain, beans and lentils, honey, curds, and sheep, and cheese. These three men were chieftains tributary to David, bound to him by ties of loyalty and obligation. (Barzillai was old and wealthy, 19:32.) Besides, they may have preferred to cast their lot with David, a known quantity, as opposed to Absalom, an unknown.

4. ABSALOM'S DEFEAT AND DEATH (CHAP. 18)

18:1-5. David, now in security and with his supplies replenished, quickly took measures to reorganize his troops and prepare them for the inevitable encounter with Absalom. A third of his troops he assigned to Joab; a third to Abishai, Joab's brother; and a third to Ittai. David determined that he would lead the attack personally, but his comrades dissuaded him. He was worth 10,000 of them, they said. If half of them died all would go on. But if he died the whole cause would be lost. Reluctantly David agreed to remain behind but commanded his officers that they not harm Absalom in the battle.

18:6-18. The encounter soon followed in the forest of Ephraim, a deserted place in the vicinity of Mahanaim (cf. 17:24, 27) but otherwise unknown. As terrible as Absalom's losses were by the swords of David's heroes (18:7), they

were even greater from the elements of that inhospitable terrain (v. 8). Absalom himself, in a frantic attempt to escape on his mule, rode beneath a large oak tree and became tangled in its branches. He was suspended in midair. A soldier of David found him in this predicament but because David had ordered his men not to hurt Absalom, the soldier refused to harm him further. Bloodthirsty Joab was not so reluctant, however, and thrust Absalom in the heart with three javelins. Immediately 10 of his attendants struck Absalom to make sure he died. Absalom had already erected a memorial (a pillar called Absalom's Monument) to his own name in the King's Valley (traditionally the Kidron Valley immediately east of Jerusalem) because he had no son to carry on his name. Joab buried him in a pit in the forest and piled over it a memorial cairn.

18:19-23. When Ahimaaz, David's courier (cf. 15:36; 17:17), announced that he would set out to bear word to David of the army's victory Joab forbade him to do so, ostensibly to spare the king unnecessarily early grief over his son's death. Joab may also have been concerned for the well-being of the young messenger for the bearer of such bad news might not be well received. Instead Joab dispatched an unnamed Cushite (an Ethiopian) who was obviously known to David. He was either considered more knowledgeable as to what had happened to Absalom (see 18:29) or was more expendable. Ahimaaz was not to be denied, however, and finally received permission to go. Taking a shortcut, he outran the Cushite.

18:24-33. Both runners were seen from a distance, and when David understood that the nearer was Ahimaaz he assumed that the message he was conveying was good because Ahimaaz himself was good. The assumption was unfounded, however, for when Ahimaaz finally was able to deliver his message all he could do was speak in general terms of the victory over Absalom. The details were left to the Cushite who presently arrived and shared with the king the grisly news that Absalom and his confederates were dead. Overwhelmed, the king retired to an upper room where he privately poured out his heart before God in unremitting grief. The depths of his love for his rebel son are couched in his lament, **If only I had died instead of you.** Two of David's sons, Amnon (13:28-29) and Absalom (18:15), died violent deaths as a consequence of David's sin (12:10).

F. David's return to power (chaps. 19–20)

1. THE PREPARATIONS FOR RETURN (CHAP. 19)

19:1-3. What should have been a day of triumphant joy became to David a day of profound grief. His elation at having regained the kingdom was undercut by his despair at having lost a **son.** So chagrined were David's soldiers that they slipped out of Mahanaim as though they were losers instead of winners.

19:4-8a. Joab, who had known before the frustration of doing what he felt was right only to have **the king** turn it against him (cf. 3:27-39; 14:28-33), confronted David and rebuked him for his insensitivity toward his officers and people. It appeared, **Joab** said, that David would have been more satisfied **if Absalom** had lived **and all of** them had died. In order to salvage what little morale was left, Joab urged David to appear before the troops and assure them that he appreciated their selfless service to him.

19:8b-13. The remnants of Absalom's army had made their way home and together with the rest of **Israel** found themselves in a quandary. They had rallied behind **Absalom,** but now he was dead. Moreover, David had provided effective leadership in the past. **So why were the elders** not **bringing the king back?** Sensing the local officials' indecision, **David sent . . . Zadok and Abiathar, the priests,** to them to **ask** why they were so reluctant to restore David when it was clear that the people were willing and ready to do so. No doubt to shore up his support from Judah especially, David told the priests to promise **Amasa,** his nephew (cf. 17:25; 1 Chron. 2:17), that he would succeed **Joab** as **commander of** the **army** (2 Sam. 19:13). Joab, also David's nephew through another half sister (1 Chron. 2:16), had by now become completely discredited in David's eyes because of his open disagreements with David's policies.

19:14-23. The mission of Zadok and Abiathar was successful. With one accord (**as though they were one man**) the people **of Judah** not only invited David to return to rule over them but they also sent a delegation to **the Jordan** River to meet him and help him cross over the river. Included in the delegation were **Shimei** (v. 16), who had cursed David on his way into exile (16:5-8), and **Ziba** (19:17), Mephibosheth's servant who had refreshed David along the way (16:1-4). **Shimei,** realizing the peril in which he now found himself because of David's restoration, prostrated himself **before the king** and sought his forgiveness, a favor David temporarily granted over the objections of **Abishai** (19:21-23; but cf. David's last instruction to Solomon, 1 Kings 2:8-9). The large number of **Benjamites** who accompanied **Shimei** (2 Sam. 19:17) and who were identified by him (v. 20) as elements of **the whole house of Joseph** (i.e., Israel) indicates the first steps taken by the tribe of Benjamin to link itself with Judah.

19:24-30. Next came **Mephibosheth** who protested to David that **Ziba** had lied about Mephibosheth's motive for remaining in **Jerusalem** when **the king** was forced to leave. Saul's grandson said he had not tried to use the occasion as an opportunity to bring his grandfather's dynasty back into control as **Ziba** had reported (see 16:3). Whether this was true or not cannot be determined, but David at least was somewhat convinced by Mephibosheth and agreed to return at least half of the estate he had threatened to withdraw from him (19:29; cf. 16:4).

19:31-38. Then **Barzillai the Gileadite,** who had provided David with supplies when he had crossed into Transjordan (17:27-29), presented himself to **the king.** Grateful to the **80**-year-old for all his goodness, David urged him to move to **Jerusalem** and live out his days on government sustenance. **Barzillai** protested that he was too old to make such a move and preferred to die in his own land. He asked, however, that **Kimham,** perhaps his son, go in his place and be similarly rewarded. This David was more than happy to do.

19:39-43. At length David and his entourage **crossed the Jordan** and arrived at **Gilgal** where they were met by a throng of citizens from both **Judah** and **Israel.** The latter were upset that the Judeans claimed **David** as one of their own to the exclusion of the other tribes (v. 41). When the Judeans replied that David was part of their own flesh (v. 42), the Israelite counter-response was that there were 10 tribes of them and therefore their claim was much more weighty. **Besides,** they said, they had been **the first** to insist that David return to rule over the nation (v. 43), a claim for which, incidentally, there is an apparent basis in the preserved narrative (vv. 9-10). The argument reveals the fickleness of the people who had first acquiesced in, if not actively supported, the rebellion of Absalom and now clamored to be first to welcome David **back.** But it also indicates the depth of the schism which was developing between **Israel** and **Judah,** a rift which eventually produced two separate kingdoms.

2. THE REESTABLISHMENT OF AUTHORITY (CHAP. 20)

20:1-3. The contention between the Israelite and Judean delegations at Gilgal became so heated that **a Benjamite** by the name of **Sheba** announced a revolutionary movement against **David** and led the Israelites to desert the king. David and the Judeans then continued their homeward journey **to Jerusalem** alone. Once there, **David** reasserted his monarchical claims by, among other things, regathering his harem (cf. 15:16). **He provided for them, but** remained sexually aloof because they had been appropriated by his son Absalom (16:21-22).

20:4-10. The first matter of state was urgent. It was clear to **David** that he must overcome the rump movement that had been initiated by **Sheba** at Gilgal. So he ordered **Amasa,** his new commander (19:13), to reorganize the army **of Judah . . . within three days** so that Sheba might be brought to heel. **When Amasa** was unable to do so in the allotted **time . . . Abishai,** at David's command, took his own personal elite troops (cf. 18:2) and set out for the North (20:7). On the way they met **Amasa** at **Gibeon,** about five miles north of Jerusalem. **Joab,** though having been demoted and replaced by **Amasa,** was present. Pretending to greet **Amasa** warmly, **Joab** killed him with his **dagger.** Thus **Joab** gained revenge for his loss of rank. What is particularly heinous is the fact that **Joab** and **Amasa** were cousins, sons of two of Da-

vid's half sisters (1 Chron. 2:16-17). Again, then, the prophecy of Nathan came to pass: "The sword will never depart from your house" (2 Sam. 12:10).

20:11-22. Joab at once took command as though nothing had happened. **The troops** were stopping in **the road** to look at Amasa's corpse. So heartless Joab **dragged** Amasa's body to **a field and threw a garment over him,** without bothering to bury him. Summoning reinforcements, **Joab** marched as far north as **Abel Beth Maacah** (four miles west of Dan and north of the Sea of Kinnereth) through the territory **of the Berites** (site unknown). There he found **Sheba** safely ensconced behind **the city** wall, apparently prepared to face a long siege. While attempting to batter down **the walls** Joab was contacted by **a wise woman** from **the city** who yelled over the wall that she wanted to talk with him. She told **Joab** of her own fame as a purveyor of wisdom (v. 18) and then asked why he was destroying her **city** which had always been loyal to Israel. The city, as **a mother in Israel,** was a prominent one.

To this **Joab replied** that he was not attacking **the city** itself but only wanted **Sheba,** the rebel who had presumed to lead Israel away from its **king.** If she would assist in delivering Sheba **over** to him, he would end his siege. Soon **the head of Sheba** was thrown over the wall to **Joab.** Successful in his mission, Joab stopped the siege and returned to **Jerusalem.**

20:23-26. Apparently David tolerated Joab's assassination of Amasa for **Joab** appears in this list of **David's** royal administrators. Joab **was over Israel's entire army. Benaiah son of Jehoiada was** leader of David's special troops, **the Kerethites and Pelethites** (see comments on 8:15-18). Benaiah eventually replaced Joab at the beginning of Solomon's reign (1 Kings 2:35; 4:4). **Adoniram** (Heb. *"Adoram"*) **was in charge of** conscripted **labor** gangs, a position he retained in the government of Solomon. (In 1 Kings 4:6 and 5:14 the Heb. has *"Adoniram,"* a longer form of his name.) **Jehoshaphat . . . was** the **recorder** (or chronicler). **Sheva was** official scribe, evidently having succeeded Seraiah (2 Sam. 8:17). **Zadok and Abiathar** remained as chief **priests.** Finally **Ira the Jairite** was David's special minister, having succeeded the king's own sons in that capacity (see comments on 8:18 for the meaning of *kōhēn* in 20:26, usually rendered "priest").

G. Slaughter and burial of Saul's sons (chap. 21)

21:1-8. At some point in David's **reign,** probably toward the end, Israel was afflicted by a **three**-year drought. When he inquired of **the LORD** as to its cause, **the LORD** revealed that it came as punishment for Saul's violation of the covenant made with **the Gibeonites** back in the days of Joshua (Josh. 9:15-21). At that time Israel, under Joshua's leadership, had just destroyed Jericho and Ai and was about to attack the Amorite federation of the Canaanite hill country. The people of Gibeon, who were in the direct line of Joshua's conquest, pretended to be faraway aliens and so escaped annihilation. Moreover, they tricked Joshua into making a covenant with them whereby they would forever serve Israel in menial tasks but could never be harmed. Though the covenant was made deceitfully, its binding nature was recognized by both the Israelites and the Gibeonites.

Saul, in an action not recorded in the biblical account, had slain some Gibeonites during his tenure (2 Sam. 21:1). When David learned that the **famine** had come on Israel as punishment for that covenant violation, he asked the Gibeonite leaders **what** he should **do for** them. They responded by denying any interest in **silver or gold.** Nor, they said, could they, as Israel's vassals, take vengeance into their own hands. Instead they asked that **seven . . . male descendants** of **Saul** be **given over to** them so that they could practice the age-old tradition of *lex talionis*—eye for eye, tooth for tooth, and life for life (Ex. 21:23-25).

David recognized the propriety of their demand, but he also had to balance against it the pledge he had made to **Jonathan** that he would forever preserve his seed (1 Sam. 20:15-16). So David **spared Mephibosheth,** Jonathan's **son,** but singled out others of Saul's offspring for execution. These included **Armoni and** another **Mephibosheth,** sons of Saul's concubine **Rizpah** (cf. 2 Sam. 3:7). The other **five** were all **sons** of **Merab,** daughter of Saul, by her husband **Adriel**

(cf. 1 Sam. 18:19). (As stated in the NIV marg., many Heb. mss. have "Michal," but that reading makes 2 Sam: 21:8 contradict the statement in 6:23 that Michal died childless. Probably then, the NIV is correct in following the two Heb. mss. and a few other mss. that have "Merab.")

21:9-10. These **seven** sons and grandsons of Saul were publicly executed by **the Gibeonites** at the **beginning** of **barley harvest,** early in the spring (see the chart "Calendar in Israel," near Ex. 12:1). As their bodies hung suspended from their places of exposure, **Rizpah,** mother of the first two (v. 8), refused to take them down and bury them. In great grief she lamented for them on a rocky ledge until the coming of the drought-breaking rains. The reason for her action is not entirely clear unless she viewed the vengeance of the Gibeonites as being at the same time the vengeance of God against the land for Saul's sake. The fact that the bodies remained where they were until it rained suggests that God's curse had been on the land and now rested on the executed sons of Saul for "anyone who is hung on a tree is under God's curse" (Deut. 21:23). The coming of **the rain** meant that the curse was ended and the corpses could be taken down and buried. Though the Law stated that a body hung from a tree must be removed by sundown (Deut. 21:23), it implied punishment of an individual for his personal crime. This case had nothing to do with any personal act of murder but rather with violation of a covenant, the results of which brought God's displeasure on the whole nation and required vengeance of a public and extended nature.

21:11-14. When David saw the devotion of **Rizpah** in protecting the bodies of her sons from the carnivorous birds and beasts, he was reminded of the shameful exposure of the bodies of **Saul and his son Jonathan** on the walls of **Beth Shan where the Philistines had** displayed **them after** the battle of **Gilboa** (1 Sam. 31:11-13). Though the people of **Jabesh Gilead** had brought the bodies away for burial, the remains were interred far from Gibeah, Saul's family home. David resolved to bring their **bones** back from Jabesh Gilead and bury them in the sepulcher of **Saul's father Kish, at Zela in Benjamin. After** this was done **God** again **answered prayer** on behalf of the nation.

21:15-22. The chapter concludes with a final word about David's hostility toward **the Philistines.** No longer the robust young warrior of former days, **David** now was old and weak. A Philistine giant, **Ishbi-Benob,** advanced on **David** with a spear (with a **spearhead** weighing **300 shekels** or about seven and one-half pounds) and **a new sword** (the Heb. in v. 16 is lit., "armed with a new thing," without specifying the weapon), threatening to **kill** him. Just in time **Abishai . . . came to David's** aid **and killed** the giant. **David's** warriors advised him **never again** to take to the field of **battle.** His death would mean the end of his leadership, a tragedy synonymous with the snuffing out of Israel's illumination (**the lamp of Israel**) for in and through David were God's covenant blessings to be accomplished (1 Kings 11:36; 15:4; 2 Kings 8:19).

Other Philistine encounters, **at Gob** and **Gath,** followed the one just recorded. At Gob (Gezer in 1 Chron. 20:4), **Sibbecai,** a heroic Israelite, slew **Saph** (Sippai in 1 Chron. 20:4), another Philistine giant (**Rapha** is Heb. for "Rephaim," a race of giants; cf. 2 Sam. 21:16).

Again **at Gob, Elhanan** felled a giant, **Goliath.** Because Elhanan was from Bethlehem, some scholars believe that he was David and that the present passage recapitulates David's former exploit. Against this is the lack of evidence to equate Elhanan with David and the fact that the accounts in both verses 18-22 and 1 Chronicles 20:4-8 follow that of David's conquest of Goliath by many years. The chronicler in fact stated that the giant killed by Elhanan was Goliath's brother Lahmi (1 Chron. 20:5). The resolution of the problem might well be that two Philistines were named Goliath, one killed by David and the other by Elhanan. Perhaps the Chronicles version is an attempt to clear up the confusion of two giants with the same name.

A conflict **at Gath** involved a giant (**descended from Rapha;** cf. 2 Sam. 21:16, 18) **with six** digits **on each hand** and **foot.** The genetic strains which produced gigantism must also have caused this malformity. He was slain by **David's** nephew **Jonathan,** named, of course, for David's dear friend. With this giant's

death the terror caused by the Philistine giants came to an end.

IV. David's Final Years (chaps. 22–24)

A. David's song (chap. 22)

1. EXTOLLING OF THE LORD (22:1-4)

22:1. This composition, set between the account of David's Philistine wars (21:15-22) and his list of heroes (23:8-39), is a poem celebrating the providence of God in delivering him from **all his enemies** (cf. v. 4). It is found again in almost identical wording in Psalm 18, a piece that is generally classified from a literary standpoint as a royal hymn of thanksgiving.

22:2-4. In a manner characteristic of this literary form, the Psalmist David first acknowledged the greatness and glory of **the Lord** in a series of designations— **Rock . . . Fortress . . . Deliverer . . . Shield . . . Horn of . . . Salvation** (see comments on 1 Sam. 2:1), **Stronghold** (*miśgoḇ*; see comments on Ps. 9:9), **Refuge,** and **Savior.** All God's exploits in the past and promises for the future are predicated on who He is. These descriptions of **the Lord** are especially appropriate in light of the setting of the song, that of flight, conflict, and victory.

2. EXPLOITS OF THE LORD (22:5-20)

22:5-20. David was quite conscious of history and of God's providential arrangement of its particulars. He saw this in respect to his own peculiar circumstances (vv. 5-7) which he described hyperbolically as being akin to **death.** So desperate had been his peril that death was imminent. It was only the mercy of **God** in response to his prayer which brought David salvation from heaven (**His temple**).

From David, as a center of God's saving purposes, the exploits of the Lord ranged almost concentrically to the arena of **the** whole **earth** (vv. 8-9). With reference, perhaps, to prevailing pagan myths about Creation, David showed that it is the Lord who controls the earth. In His anger He **shook** the whole cosmos as an expression of His concern for David.

But the sovereignty of God goes even further. He is Lord also of **the heavens** (vv. 10-16). Though Baal, the Canaanite god, was known to his worship-

David's Mighty Men

2 Samuel 23	1 Chronicles 11

"The Three"

† 1. Josheb-Basshebeth, a Tahkemonite (23:8) — Jashobeam, a Hacmonite (11:11)

2. Eleazar son of Dodai the Ahohite (23:9) — (11:12)

3. Shammah son of Agee the Hararite (23:11) — *(Not mentioned in 1 Chron. 11, but implied in 11:15-19)*

Other honored men

4. Abishai the brother of Joab son of Zeruiah (23:18) — (11:20)

5. Benaiah son of Jehoiada (23:20) — (11:22)

*The "Thirty"**

6. Asahel the brother of Joab (23:24) — (11:26)

7. Elhanan son of Dodo (23:24) — (11:26)

†8. Shammah the Harodite (23:25) — Shammoth the Harorite (11:27)

9. Elika the Harodite (23:25) — *(Not mentioned in 1 Chron. 11)*

†10. Helez the Paltite (23:26) — Helez the Pelonite (11:27)

11. Ira son of Ikkesh (23:26) — (11:28)

12. Abiezer from Anathoth (23:27) — (11:28)

†13. Mebunnai the Hushathite (23:27) — Sibbecai the Hushathite (11:29)

†14. Zalmon the Ahohite (23:28) — Ilai the Ahohite (11:29)

15. Maharai the Netophathite (23:28) — (11:30)

16. Heled (or Heleb; cf. NIV marg.), son of Baanah (23:29) — (11:30)

17. Ithai son of Ribai (23:29) — (11:31)

18. Benaiah the Pirathonite (23:30) — (11:31)

†19. Hiddai from . . . Gaash (23:30) — Hurai from . . . Gaash (11:32)

†20. Abi-Albon the Arbathite (23:31) — Abiel the Arbathite (11:32)

†21. Azmaveth the Barhumite (23:31) — Azmaveth the Baharumite (11:33)

22. Eliahba the Shaalbonite (23:32) — (11:33)

†23. The sons of Jashen (23:32) (These words could be trans. Bene-Jashen, the proper name of one soldier.) — The sons of Hashem (11:34) (These words could be trans. Bene-Hashem, the proper name of one soldier.)

†24, 25. Jonathan son of Shammah the Hararite (23:32-33) (The Heb. could refer to two men, Jonathan, and Shammah; cf. NIV marg.) — Jonathan son of Shagee the Hararite (11:34)

†26. Ahiam son of Sharar the Hararite (23:33) — Ahiam son of Sacar the Hararite (11:35)

†27. Eliphelet son of Ahasbai (23:34) — Eliphal son of Ur (11:35) / Hepher the Mekerathite (11:36) / Ahijah the Pelonite (11:36)

28. Eliam son of Ahithophel (23:34) — *(Not mentioned in 1 Chron. 11)*

29. Hezro the Carmelite (23:35) — (11:37)

†30. Paarai the Arbite (23:35) — Naarai the son of Ezbai (11:37)

†31. Igal son of Nathan (23:36) — *(Not mentioned in 1 Chron. 11)* / Joel the brother of Nathan (11:38)

†32. The son of Hagri (23:36) (The Heb. could be trans. Bani the Gadite.) — Mibhar son of Hagri (11:38)

33. Zelek the Ammonite (23:37) — (11:39)

34. Naharai the Beerothite (23:37) (11:39)
35. Ira the Ithrite (23:38) (11:40)
36. Gareb the Ithrite (23:38) (11:40)
37. Uriah the Hittite (23:39) "There were (11:41)
37 in all" (23:39).*

Zabad son of Ahlai (11:41)

Adina son of Shiza (11:42)

Hanan son of Maacah (11:43)

Joshaphat the Mithnite (11:43)

Uzzia the Ashterathite (11:44)

Shama the son of Hotham (11:44)

Jeiel the son of Hotham (11:44)

Jediael son of Shimri (11:45)

Joha the Tizite (11:45)

Eliel the Mahavite (11:46)

Jeribai son of Elnaam (11:46)

Joshaviah son of Elnaam (11:46)

Ithmah the Moabite (11:46)

Eliel (11:47)

Obed (11:47)

Jaasiel the Mezobaite (11:47)

*The word "30" was either a technical term for David's select soldiers of approximately 30 men (here 32—nos. 6-37). Or the word "30" means exactly 30 men, with some men replacing others as they were killed in battle (e.g., Uriah, no. 37). This could account for the Chronicles list having several more men than the Samuel list.

†These soldiers' names and/or the words identifying their fathers or places of residence differ in the accounts in 2 Samuel and 1 Chronicles. (When the names are the same in both accounts, only the references are given in the right-hand column.) However, most of the changes are slight variations in spelling, an occasional practice in Hebrew. Some names may refer to different individuals (e.g., no. 13, Mebunnai and Sibbecai; and no. 14, Zalmon and Ilai). Perhaps Mebunnai died in battle and was replaced by Sibbecai, a fellow Hushathite.

ers as "the rider of the **clouds,**" it is Yahweh who is enthroned in the heavens and who reduces all Creation to His service. With **lightning** and a **voice** like thunder He cried out against His (and David's) **enemies,** terrifying them. The God of Creation rearranged Creation, as it were, on David's behalf.

That David refers to God's mighty works (vv. 8-16) as an expression not of His role of Creator as such, but as One **powerful** to save is clear from the conclusion of the passage (vv. 17-20): God had delivered him from his enemies because he was the object of God's mercy and grace. God's deliverance is expressed in several verbs: (a) **reached down,** (b) **took hold,** (c) **drew . . . out,** (d) **rescued** (vv. 18, 20), (e) **brought out.**

3. EQUITY OF THE LORD (22:21-30)

22:21-30. God's deliverance of David was followed by His blessings, divine rewards commensurate with David's own **righteousness.** David did not suggest that works are necessary for salvation, which is not the issue here. He was saying, however, that the benefits of God are often obtained in this life by faithful perseverance in godliness. He **kept** God's **ways** (v. 22), **law** (v. 23), and **decrees** (v. 23), and refrained from iniquity (v. 24; cf. vv. 21, 25). God therefore **rewarded** him (v. 25) and showed mercy to him as He does to all who are upright (**faithful . . . blameless . . . pure . . . humble;** vv. 26-28). The wicked, on the other hand, because of their pride cannot expect His favor (v. 28b). With God, who gives **light** as a **lamp** (v. 29), a righteous person is invincible. He can break through barricades (not **a troop**) or **scale** the highest walls (v. 30).

4. EXCELLENCE OF THE LORD (22:31-51)

22:31-51. In the final section of the psalm David turned once more to the attributes of **the LORD,** but he connected them now to specific ways in which **God** had worked and would work on his behalf. God was described first as a Strengthener (vv. 31-35), One who is a **Shield,** a **Rock,** a **Strength** (lit., "strong Refuge" or "Fortress"), One who gives speed and power to His own servants. He is also a **Shield** (v. 36), and He protects against slipping and falling (vv. 36-37). Again, He is a Subduer of **enemies**

(vv. 38-41). Through **the LORD,** David was able to pursue and destroy his **enemies** so that they could not rise again.

The Lord also is a Support (vv. 42-46). David's enemies called out to God **but** He would not answer them (v. 42). Instead He let David crush them (v. 43), and rule over them as well as over his own people (vv. 44-46).

Finally, David said that the Lord was his **Savior** (vv. 47-51). Though his enemies surrounded him and were about to destroy him, the Lord brought him through triumphantly. As a result David praised Him (v. 50) and acknowledged that all God's benefits of the past were tokens of His promised blessings on both **David and his descendants,** blessings which will endure **forever.**

B. David's heroes (chap. 23)

23:1-7. The list of David's mighty men is preceded by a short poem (vv. 1b-7) titled **the last words of David.** In the first stanza (v. 1) he identified himself as **son of Jesse . . . the man exalted by the Most High, the man anointed by the God of Jacob,** and **Israel's singer of songs.** There is a noticeable progress from the humble son of a Bethlehemite commoner to the poetically gifted king of Israel, a development which David attributed to his having been chosen and anointed by the Lord.

His consciousness of being God's instrument is clear from the second stanza (vv. 2-4), in which he acknowledged that God had spoken **to** him (v. 3) and **through him** (v. 2) to the nation, enabling him to rule righteously **in** the reverential **fear of God.** A king who rules as an agent of God is, he said, like the brilliance of the sun **on a cloudless morning** and like a clear day **after rain.**

In the third stanza (vv. 5-7) David centered on the Davidic **Covenant,** by which **God** chose and blessed him. God had made **an everlasting** commitment with him and his dynasty (**my house**), a covenant that guaranteed his ultimate well-being (cf. 7:8-16). In contrast, **evil men,** like so many **thorns,** will be cast aside to be consumed by the judgment of God (cf. Matt. 13:30, 41).

23:8-39. David's gallery of heroes consisted of **37** men (v. 39) who distinguished themselves by mighty exploits of service to God and Israel and who evidently made up his elite troops. These consisted of three **chief men** (vv. 8-17), two others of a second rank (vv. 18-23), and 32 in the longest list (vv. 24-39). (See the chart "David's Mighty Men.") Significant by its omission is any reference to **Joab.** Two of his brothers—**Abishai** and **Asahel**—are listed (vv. 18- 24). Neither the author of Samuel nor that of the Chronicles felt it necessary, perhaps, to list Joab since he was the commander of the whole army throughout most of David's reign (20:23).

Though the spellings of several of the names differ in the corresponding list in 1 Chronicles 11:11-47, the names can usually be equated. The chronicler does, however, add names beyond the 37 in 2 Samuel. Perhaps they were men of lower ranks than those listed in Samuel or perhaps they replaced others (already listed) who had fallen in battle.

The first **three** were (a) **Josheb-Basshebeth, a Tahkemonite,** who slew **800 men . . . in one encounter** (2 Sam. 23:8; on the "300" in 1 Chron. 11:11 see comments there); (b) **Eleazar, son of Dodai the Ahohite,** who **struck down the Philistines** (2 Sam. 23:9-10) **at Pas Dammim** (1 Chron. 11:13; cf. Ephes Dammim in 1 Sam. 17:1); and (c) **Shammah son of Agee the Hararite,** who brought **great victory** over **the Philistines** (2 Sam. 23:11-12).

These **three** also displayed their courage by obtaining **water** from **Bethlehem** for **David** while he was besieged in the summer (**harvesttime**) by **the Philistines** at **Adullam** (vv. 13-15; cf. 1 Sam. 22:1). So touched was **David** by their valor that he refused to **drink** the **water** but **poured it out** as an offering to **the LORD** (2 Sam. 23:16-17). Most scholars deny that the three involved are those just named since the word "three" has no definite article in the Hebrew text in verse 13. On the other hand verse 17 implies that all the foregoing had been done by these three and this time the definite article is used.

Included in the second rank were **Abishai . . . son of Zeruiah** (and nephew of David, 1 Chron. 2:15-16) who **was chief of the** second 3 (or "30," NIV marg.) but not as exalted as the first 3 previously listed (2 Sam. 23:18-19; cf. 1 Sam. 26:6-11; 2 Sam. 10:14; 21:16-17), and **Benaiah,** who achieved notable victories over both

men and **a lion** (23:20-23; cf. 8:18; 1 Kings 1:32, 36, 38; 2:35; 4:4).

The longest list consists of 32 men. Such a group normally consisted of 30 men but might have a few more or less and still be known as "the 30," a technical term for a small military contingent known in Hebrew as *haššᵉlošîm* ("the 30"). Or perhaps two had died in battle (including **Uriah the Hittite,** 2 Sam. 11:14-17) and were replaced.

C. David's sin in taking the census (chap. 24)

24:1-3. It is impossible to determine the date of this episode from 2 Samuel alone, but the parallel version in 1 Chronicles 21 places it just prior to David's instructions to Solomon about building the temple (1 Chron. 21:28–22:19). The census must have come late in David's reign, and may have been part of the plan of dynastic succession in anticipation of Solomon's coming to power.

For reasons not stated, **the LORD** was angry **against Israel** (the **again** of 2 Sam. 24:1 may refer to 21:1), and **He** led **David** to command that a census be taken. In 1 Chronicles 21:1 this motivation is attributed to (lit.) "a Satan" (or adversary). This is no contradiction for the Lord had simply allowed Satan to prompt David to an improper course of action in order that Israel might be punished and that David might be instructed. This is similar to the Lord's permitting Satan to trouble Job (Job 1:12; 2:6) and His allowing an evil spirit to torment Saul (1 Sam. 16:14; see comments there). In any case, the Lord Himself did not incite David to do evil for "God cannot be tempted by evil, nor does He tempt anyone" (James 1:13).

The reasons for David's desire for a census are not clear either, though the fact that he only had military **men** counted (2 Sam. 24:2, 9) suggests that he was interested in determining his military strength. And herein lay the sin—he probably did this so he could boast in human might. This may be implied in Joab's query as to **why** the census was to be undertaken. God was able, **Joab** said, to **multiply** their **troops** as much as necessary, so why did David feel the need to assess his strength?

24:4-9. David prevailed, however, and sent census takers throughout the realm. Beginning in the Transjordan they went counterclockwise north **to Dan Jaan** (a variation of Dan), then west and southwest of **Sidon** and **Tyre,** throughout the plains and valleys of Canaanite and Hivite (Horites or Hurrians) population, and south **to Beersheba.** Finally, after **nine months and 20 days,** the report was given; there were **800,000** eligible fighting **men** in **Israel** and **500,000** in **Judah** (v. 9). The figures in 1 Chronicles are 1,100,000 men in Israel and 470,000 in Judah, but the chronicler wrote that the Levites and Benjamites were not included (1 Chron. 21:5-6). The reconciliation of the data may lie in the possibility that 1,100,000 describes the grand total for Israel including the standing army which consisted of 12 units of 24,000 men each (288,000, 1 Chron. 27:1-15) plus 12,000 especially attached to Jerusalem and the chariot cities (2 Chron. 1:14). These 300,000 subtracted from 1,100,000 would yield the 800,000 figure in 2 Samuel 24:9. Also the chronicler may not have included the 30,000-man standing army of Judah (6:1) whereas they were included in chapter 24. This would raise the 470,000 total of Chronicles to the 500,000 of Samuel. This is only one solution, but with so little information available as to how the sums were obtained nothing further can be said with certainty.

24:10-25. After **David** received the report, he realized his sin of pride and self-sufficiency and confessed this sin (which he called **a very foolish thing) to the Lord** (1 Chron. 21:7 points out that the Lord punished Israel, thus indicating the evil of the census). The Lord then sent **Gad,** a **prophet,** to **David** with a list of **three** calamities from which he could **choose** and by which the Lord would register His displeasure and purge out the evil. The choices were **three years of famine . . . three months** of enemy pursuit, and **three days** of pestilence (2 Sam. 24:13). (Though the Heb. reads "seven" years of famine, 1 Chron. 21:12, probably a better-preserved text, reads "three," as the NIV has it.) **David** chose the third option, throwing himself on the **mercy** of God (2 Sam. 24:14).

The result was a **plague** which took the lives of **70,000** people. When **Jerusalem** itself was threatened, **the Lord** intervened and commanded His angelic destroyer to desist. **David** then confessed his own personal sin and urged **the Lord**

to spare His innocent people. Then, in order to make proper restitution and atonement, **David** arranged to construct **an altar to the Lord. Gad** told him that it must be built **on the threshing floor of Araunah,** a citizen of Jerusalem, since it was there that **the angel** had been commanded to cease his destruction of the city (v. 16).

According to well-founded tradition, this **threshing floor,** a wide, smooth, ledge-like surface, was on Mount Moriah, just outside the northern wall of David's Jerusalem. But David had no right to it because it was owned by a citizen. When **Araunah** learned of David's desire (v. 21), however, he was willing not only to give the threshing floor **to the king** but also to provide the **wood** and sacrifices needed (v. 22). To this gracious offer David could only give a negative response. How could he **sacrifice to the Lord** what **cost** him **nothing?** That would be a denial of the very meaning of sacrifice. **Araunah** therefore sold him the **threshing floor** and **oxen** for **50 shekels of silver** (the 600 shekels of gold in 1 Chron. 21:25 includes, however, "the site," more than just the threshing floor). Fifty shekels was about 1¼ pounds of silver. The silver David paid was only for the oxen and the threshing floor, and the 600 shekels (15 pounds of gold) mentioned in 1 Chronicles 21:25 was for the lot of land surrounding the threshing floor.

Having obtained the site, **David built** the **altar,** offered the sacrifices, and interceded on behalf of his people. God heard and **answered,** and the **land** was healed of **the plague.** This was where Abraham had offered Isaac (Gen. 22:2). And on this same spot Solomon later constructed his magnificent temple (1 Chron. 22:1; 2 Chron. 3:1).

BIBLIOGRAPHY

See the 14 entries in the *Bibliography* on 1 Samuel, in additon to these 3:

Ackroyd, Peter R. *The Second Book of Samuel.* New York: Cambridge University Press, 1977.

Kirkpatrick, A.F. *The Second Book of Samuel.* Cambridge: Cambridge University Press, 1886.

Moriarty, Fredrick. *The Second Book of Samuel.* New York: Paulist Press, 1971.

1 KINGS

Thomas L. Constable

INTRODUCTION

Title. The Books of 1 and 2 Kings were so named because they record and interpret the reigns of all the kings of Israel and Judah except Saul. (David's last days are mentioned [1 Kings 1:1–2:12] but the events in most of his reign are recorded in 2 Sam. 2–24 and 1 Chron. 11–29.) In the Hebrew Old Testament 1 and 2 Kings were one book and were regarded as a continuation of the historical narrative begun in 1 and 2 Samuel. The Septuagint, the Greek translation of the Old Testament, divided Kings into the two parts that constitute 1 and 2 Kings in English Bibles, though the Septuagint calls those two books "3 and 4 Kingdoms" (and calls 1 and 2 Sam. "1 and 2 Kingdoms"). The title "Kings" came from Jerome's Latin translation (the Vulgate) which was made about six centuries after the Septuagint; Jerome called the two books "The Book of the Kings."

Scope. First and 2 Kings provide a record of Israel's history from the beginning of the movement to place Solomon on David's throne through the end of the reign of Zedekiah, Judah's last king. Zedekiah ruled until the surviving Southern Kingdom was taken captive and Babylonian governors were placed in charge of affairs in Palestine.

Three major periods of Israel's history can be distinguished in Kings: (a) the united monarchy (during which time Israel and Judah remained united under Solomon as they had been under Saul and David); (b) the divided monarchy (from the rebellion of Israel against the rulership of Judean kings until Israel was carried off into captivity by the Assyrians); and (c) the surviving kingdom (the record of Judah's affairs from the deportation of Israel to Judah's own defeat and exile by the Babylonians).

First and 2 Kings were not divided as they are because a natural break occurs in the narrative, but because the large scroll of 1 and 2 Kings needed to be divided into two smaller, more easily manageable units. The result was two books which are almost equal in length.

Date. The release of Jehoiachin from prison is the last event recorded in 2 Kings. This took place in the 37th year of his imprisonment (560 B.C.). Therefore 1 and 2 Kings could not have been written before that event. It seems unlikely that the return of the Jews from the Babylonian Captivity in 538 B.C. had taken place when 1 and 2 Kings were written; had it occurred, the author would probably have referred to it. Probably 1 and 2 Kings were completed in their final form between 560 and 538 B.C.

Author. Though it is obvious that the author utilized various source materials in writing 1 and 2 Kings, the book bears the marks of single rather than multiple authorship. Some of those indicators are the choice of materials recorded (e.g., the records of the deeds and evaluations of the kings, and the ministries of several prophets), the emphases which run throughout the books (e.g., the ministries of the prophets and the evaluation of the kings in relation to the Mosaic Law, and the primacy of the Davidic dynasty), the method of expressing the beginnings and endings of the kings' reigns (e.g., 1 Kings 14:31; 15:1-3, 23-26), and phrases and terms that recur from beginning to end (e.g., "now the rest of the acts of . . . are they not written . . . " "evil in the sight of the Lord"; "he reigned . . . years and his mother's name was . . . " "As surely as the LORD lives").

The identity of the author is unknown, but he may have been an exile who lived in Babylon. Some commentators have pointed to his recording

Jehoiachin's release from captivity in Babylon in support of this conclusion since this event seems to them to have been specially significant for the Jews in captivity. This line of reasoning has led students of 1 and 2 Kings to suggest such notable exilic Jews as Ezra and Ezekiel as the author. Jeremiah has also been suggested. He of course was not a Babylonian exile; he died in Egypt. Ancient scholarship and tradition favor one of these three men above others who have been considered.

Purpose. The Books of 1 and 2 Kings were written to record history but, more importantly, to teach the *lessons* of history.

The author's chief historical concern was to preserve a record of the kings of both Israel and Judah. The emphasis in this record is on the royal actions and also on the actions of selected prophets that bear on the period in which they ministered.

More importantly the author sought to evaluate the monarchy by the standard of the Mosaic Law. Besides tracing the decline of the Northern and Southern Kingdoms, he pointed out the reasons for their decline in general and the fate of each king in particular. He may have intended to teach the exiles in Babylon the reasons for their plight so that they would learn from their past. In particular God's faithfulness to His covenant (blessing the obedient and punishing the disobedient) and the evils of idolatry receive strong emphasis.

Second Chronicles, of course, records the history of almost the same period as 1 and 2 Kings. (First Chron. includes the genealogies leading up to David [chaps. 1–9], Saul's death [chap. 10], and David's reign and death [chaps. 11–29].) The purposes and emphases of these two histories differ significantly. The kings of Judah were of more interest to the author of Chronicles whereas both the Israelite and Judean monarchs occupied the interest of the author of 1 and 2 Kings. The Books of 1 and 2 Chronicles emphasize especially the priestly elements in the nation's history, such as the temple and worship, while 1 and 2 Kings give attention to the royal and prophetic elements. In 2 Chronicles the kings of Judah after David are evaluated in reference to David and the worship of Yahweh; in 1 and 2 Kings the rulers of both kingdoms are evaluated in reference to the Mosiac Law. (For more on the purpose and emphases of 1 and 2 Chron. see the *Introduction* to 1 Chron.)

Historical Background. When Solomon came to the throne in 971 B.C. Israel had no strong military threat among its neighbors; Egypt and Assyria were both weak. Assyria grew stronger, however, and in 722 B.C. attacked and took Samaria, the capital of the Northern Kingdom of Israel. Assyria attacked Judah some time later and though it was able to take several southern cities, Jerusalem, the capital of the Southern Kingdom of Judah, did not fall. Assyria exerted control over Egypt too. In 609 B.C. Pharaoh Neco took his army north of Israel to Haran in Aram to assist Assyria in its threat from the Neo-Babylonian Empire. In 605 Babylon, under Nebuchadnezzar, defeated Egypt at Carchemish, moved south into Judah, and after three attacks (in 605, 597, and 586) completely destroyed Jerusalem, carrying all but the poorest Jews into captivity in 586 B.C.

Chronology. The major problem facing students of 1 and 2 Kings is the chronology of the rulers, especially those of Judah. In some cases the answer can be found in a coregency or vice-regency, periods during which two kings ruled. In other cases the problem can be solved after one establishes when a king began counting the years of his reign. Judah and Israel used two different methods to determine when a king's reign began, and each nation switched methods at least once during the period of history recorded in 1 and 2 Kings.

A third factor complicates the chronological problems further. Judah and Israel began their calendar years at different times. Space prohibits further explanation of the chronological problems in 1 and 2 Kings. (Some of the books listed in the *Bibliography* give more information.) Though exact dates are a problem, several different chronologies, worked out by conservative scholars, harmonize the narratives. In most cases these systems vary from each other by only one or two years.

The major dates for this period are as

follows: 931 B.C.—the division of the kingdom; 722 B.C.—the fall of Israel; 586 B.C.—the fall of Judah. (See the chart "An Overview of Old Testament History," p. 13. Also see the chart "Kings of Judah and Israel and the Preexilic Prophets," near 1 Kings 12:25.)

Theology. The Books of 1 and 2 Kings, like the other historical books of the Old Testament, were written not simply to record facts of historical significance, but to reveal and preserve spiritual lessons which have timeless value. This is evident in 1 and 2 Kings, for example, in the writer's interest in the prophets as well as the kings. God revealed Himself and His message by communicating to and through His servants the prophets. God also revealed Himself through events of history. People's decisions, made in faith and obedience or in unbelief and disobedience, led to inevitable consequences.

God intended that the nation Israel demonstrate to all people how glorious it can be to live under the government of God (Ex. 19:4-6). God chose Abraham to be the father of a family that would become a nation and be a blessing to the whole world (Gen. 12:1-3). This blessing would come to all mankind as Israel would allow the light of God's presence to dwell within her, transform her, and shine out from her as a light to the nations (Isa. 42:6).

The covenant God made with Abraham (Gen. 15:12-21) guaranteed him a land, descendants, and blessing. The promises of this covenant were repeated to his descendants at various times, but on certain significant occasions God amplified and elaborated one of these promises. As Israel prepared to enter the Promised Land God repeated His promise that the Israelites would possess a perpetual lease on the land from God, but that they would occupy this territory to the extent that they were faithful to God, its Owner (Deut. 28–30). In David's day God promised that Abraham's seed who descended through David would be blessed in a special way (2 Sam. 7:11-16). In particular, the king of the Israelites would always be one of one of David's descendants (2 Sam. 7:16). Later God promised Jeremiah that He would bless Israel in a specific way through the New Covenant (Jer. 31:31-34).

The Books of 1 and 2 Kings show that God is faithful to His promised word regarding Israel. Within this large purpose the writer showed how certain human activities affected God's dealings with His people and also how God accomplished His purposes in spite of the opposition of His enemies and the failures of His people.

Whereas Israel in 1 and 2 Kings functioned as a monarchy, it was more a theocracy. The kings of Israel were vice-regents under Yahweh, Israel's true Sovereign. To the extent that Israel's earthly kings faithfully led the nation under her heavenly King's direction, as revealed by God through the Mosaic Law and the prophets, the nation prospered as God intended. But when the earthly kings proved unfaithful, Israel inevitably failed to experience all God's good pleasure for her.

So 1 and 2 Kings reveal God's faithfulness to His Word, His ultimate sovereignty over His own and all other peoples, and His patience. These books also testify to the unbelief and disobedience of all people, even the beneficiaries of God's election and blessing. These books demonstrate that God has not cast off His disobedient people Israel whom He chose to enjoy a privileged relationship with Himself.

OUTLINE

COMMENTARY

I. The Reign of Solomon (chaps. 1–11)

First Kings continues the history of Israel's monarchy where 2 Samuel ends.

A. *The preparations for a new king (1:1–2:12)*

This section records the final events of David's rule that led to Solomon's becoming the next king.

1. DAVID'S OLD AGE (1:1-4)

1:1-2. King David died at or near the age of 70 (2 Sam. 5:4). From what is said of him in 1 Kings 1:1-4 it is obvious that he was in poor health and quite weak shortly before he died. His inability to retain body heat led his attendants to search for a way to keep David **warm.** Their decision to provide **a young** woman who could keep him warm by lying next to him in bed and also serve as his nurse was in harmony with medical customs of that day. Josephus (A.D. 37–ca. 100), a Jewish historian, and Galen (ca. A.D. 130–200), a Greek physician, refer to this therapeutic practice which continued into the Middle Ages.

The **covers** that David's **servants** placed **over him** to keep him warm were like sheets and blankets, not articles of clothing. That a **virgin** should be sought was reasonable since an unmarried young woman would likely be in vigorous health, free from domestic responsibilities, and able to wait on David continually as his needs might demand.

1:3. Since David was **the king** a woman who combined beauty with the other qualities needed in a nurse was sought. An attractive young woman was **found** in the town of Shunem, seven miles northwest of Nazareth, near the foot of Mount Tabor in the tribal territory of Issachar. Abishag's beauty is attested to by the attraction of Adonijah, David's son, to her (2:17). And if Abishag were the Shulammite (an alternate spelling of **Shunammite**) who captivated Solomon's heart (Song 6:13) her beauty apparently attracted many men. However, there is no definite way to link **Abishag** with the Shulammite of the Song of Songs.

1:4. The fact that David **had no intimate** (i.e., sexual) **relations with** his nurse Abishag shows that this was not her function and that David was very weak. The king's inability to withstand sexual temptation while in good health resulted in his committing adultery with Bathsheba. He also had had a harem. But now, due to poor health and advanced age, his vigor was gone.

Another reason Abishag is introduced by name in the narrative (v. 3) is because she figured significantly in Adonijah's attempt to capture the throne.

2. ADONIJAH'S PLOT (1:5-53)

David's domestic troubles followed him to his deathbed. In his hour of weakness another of his sons (Absalom; cf. 2 Sam. 15) rose up to snatch the kingdom from his grasp.

a. Adonijah's preparations (1:5-10)

1:5-6. Adonijah was the fourth son of David (2 Sam. 3:4) and probably the eldest of his brothers living at that time (see the chart "David's Family," near 2 Sam. 3:2-5). The description of Adonijah's decision to seek the throne strongly suggests a selfish motive: he **put himself forward and said** determinedly, **I will be king.**

Adonijah's preparation of **chariots** **. . . horses,** and **50 men to run ahead of him** was probably intended to give him prestige in the people's eyes. It also helped ready his coup d'etat against his father.

The author threw more light on Adonijah by recording that he was a spoiled, undisciplined young man who had apparently received much admiration for his good looks (**he was . . . very handsome**) more than for the quality of his character. Evidently Adonijah expected that his plot would succeed more because he was a popluar figure than because he was a capable person championing a worthy cause.

1:7. Among David's staff **Joab** and **Abiathar** forsook the king and sided with Adonijah. Joab was David's nephew, a **son of** his half sister, **Zeruiah** (1 Chron. 2:16). (See the chart "David's Family," near 2 Sam. 3:2-5.) He had served the king faithfully for many years—since David was pursued by Saul. David made Joab the commander-in-chief of his army, a position in which Joab distinguished himself as a brave warrior and intelligent strategist. However, Joab was brutal and used his position to murder at least two important men: Abner (2 Sam. 3:22-30), Saul's commander-in-chief, and Amasa (2 Sam. 20:8-10), who had slain Joab's brother fairly in battle. Joab had not remained completely loyal to David. When Absalom led a coup against David, Joab executed Absalom contrary to the king's orders (2 Sam. 18:5-15).

Abiathar **the priest** had joined David after Saul had Doeg kill all the other priests at Nob (1 Sam. 22:18-20). Because of his commitment to David, Abiathar became an adviser and friend of the king. This incident with Adonijah was Abiathar's first recorded act of disloyalty.

1:8. Zadok the priest had joined David after Saul was killed in battle (1 Chron. 12:28). He had supported David and had served as his spy during Absalom's rebellion. **Benaiah** (cf. 1 Kings 1:10) was one of David's mightiest warriors and commanders (2 Sam. 8:18; 20:23; 23:20-23). **Nathan the prophet** (cf. 1 Kings 1:10) brought the word of the Lord to the king on at least two occasions (2 Sam. 7:4-17; 12:1-14). If **Shimei** is the same man who cursed David (2 Sam. 16:5-13) and was later forgiven by David (2 Sam. 19:16-23), then Shimei's loyalty now to the king is understandable. However, he may have had his own sinister plot in mind (cf. comments on 1 Kings 2:36-38). Or this may have been another Shimei.

1:9-10. Adonijah held a feast for his supporters and tried to persuade others to join his cause. His sacrifice was evidently a feast rather than a religious offering. The **Stone of Zoheleth** has been identified on the steep rocky corner that overlooks the plain where the Valley of Hinnom joins the Kidron Valley just south of Mount Zion where the City of David was situated. **En Rogel** is one of the two main springs in the Kidron Valley that supplied water for Jerusalem (see the map "Jerusalem in the Time of the Kings," near 9:15).

Adonijah **invited** to his feast **all** the important people in the government who were not firmly allied with his father **or his brother Solomon,** who was David's and God's chosen prince. Adonijah's actions have been duplicated by aspiring politicians for centuries. In that culture, if Nathan and David's other supporters had been invited and eaten with Adonijah, he would have been bound to protect them, having extended them the fellowship of such a meal.

b. Nathan's plan (1:11-14)

1:11-12. The fact that **Nathan** took the initiative in countering Adonijah's rebellion suggests that God may have moved His prophet to this action as He had done previously (2 Sam. 12:1). **Bathsheba** enjoyed David's favor from the first moment he saw her on to the end of his life. **Adonijah** had **become king** in the sense that for all practical purposes he was the popular choice, though he had not been anointed or crowned. Nathan's choice of words seems designed to shock Bathsheba into realizing the seriousness of the situation. Apparently David was ignorant of the plot until now (cf. 1 Kings 1:18). Nathan was probably not overstating the danger to Bathsheba and **Solomon** by telling her that she needed to take steps to **save** her **own life and** Solomon's. Adonijah's not inviting them to share food at his feast freed him from the duty of an oriental host to protect their lives.

1:13-14. David's promise to Bathsheba that he would make **Solomon** . . .

king after him, to which Nathan referred, is not recorded in Scripture. But in view of what Nathan told Bathsheba to say here, obviously David had made such a promise (cf. 1 Chron. 22:8-10).

Nathan made sure that David's promise would be heard by two witnesses, Bathsheba and himself. Under Mosaic Law at least two witnesses were required to make a charge stick. If **David** was becoming forgetful in his old age a second witness (in this case Nathan) would also confirm that **the king** had indeed made such a pledge.

c. Bathsheba's report (1:15-21)

1:15-16. Evidently David was confined to his bed (vv. 15, 47). **Bathsheba** treated David like **the king** he was by bowing and kneeling **before** him. She intended to call on him to act as he must in view of the situation. David invited her to explain what she wanted.

1:17-21. Bathsheba stated the facts about Adonijah's uprising without exaggeration or embellishment. She called on David to announce publicly who his successor would be by appealing to his sense of duty (v. 20), and his love for her and **Solomon** (v. 21). She pointed out that she and **Solomon** would **be treated as** political **criminals** by **Adonijah.** Customarily in the ancient Near East a new monarch would purge his political enemies when he came to power, as Solomon did later (2:13-46).

d. Nathan's report (1:22-27)

1:22-26. Nathan sought an audience with **the king** while Bathsheba was talking with David. He was admitted and reported the same facts Bathsheba had announced, with a bit more detail as would have been appropriate for a man in his position. Nathan's statement that Adonijah's feast was taking place at that very moment would have encouraged David to act at once. Nathan knew David had promised Bathsheba that Solomon would succeed him (v. 13), but apparently the prophet had learned this from others, not from David.

1:27. Rather than reminding David of his promise regarding Solomon which might have annoyed **the king** who may not have wanted many people to know of his choice, Nathan diplomatically asked David if he had planned the present circumstances. The prophet left the initiative with David rather than putting him on the defensive.

e. David's promise (1:28-31)

1:28. Bathsheba had evidently left the room when Nathan entered as was customary in that culture. **David** called her to return, which she did.

1:29-30. The king invoked the sacred name of Yahweh, the living God **who** had **delivered** him from **every** one of his troubles. **As surely as the** LORD **lives** meant that David's intended action was as certain to take place as God's very existence. Those words occur frequently in the Old Testament including 14 times in 1 and 2 Kings (1 Kings 1:29; 2:24; 17:1, 12; 18:10, 15; 22:14; 2 Kings 2:2, 4, 6; 3:14; 4:30; 5:16, 20). David could not more forcefully have guaranteed that he would indeed do what he now said he would do. The God who had delivered David would now, through David, "deliver" Bathsheba and her son. David repeated his promise that **Solomon,** Bathsheba's son, would succeed him as **king** and **sit on** the **throne** that God had promised to bless.

1:31. With gratitude for his granting her request **Bathsheba bowed** before her **king.** The expression, **May my lord** the **king . . . live forever** (cf. v. 34), is a common expression found often in Scripture signifying a desire that God would bless a monarch by granting him long life. It is a complimentary wish; God had promised to bless the righteous with length of days. These words therefore implied that the king had acted righteously and was worthy of God's blessing.

f. David's instructions (1:32-37)

1:32. David's plans skillfully defused the rebellion which was building just south of Jerusalem at the spring of En Rogel (cf. v. 9). **Zadok . . . Nathan,** and **Benaiah** were the ranking priest, prophet, and soldier respectively (cf. v. 8), who had remained unallied with Adonijah. Their leadership in the events to follow would demonstrate to the general population that they were acting as the king's representatives.

1:33. Your lord's servants were the Kerethites and the Pelethites (v. 38; cf. 2 Sam. 8:18), David's special military guards under Benaiah (2 Sam. 23:22-23).

They were responsible to protect **the king,** his family, and his city. David told them to place **Solomon** on a **mule** and lead **him** through Jerusalem to the place of anointing. Kings rode on mules in the ancient Near East, symbolizing their role as the people's servants. The people would understand that Solomon's riding on a mule implied his kingship. The mule specified by David was to be his **own** personal animal. Perhaps the people would have recognized that mule by its trappings and concluded that David had given Solomon permission to ride it as his designated successor.

The officials were to lead Solomon **down to** the spring of **Gihon.** Two springs provided most of the water for Jerusalem: the En Rogel spring southeast of Jerusalem not far from the city wall where Adonijah was feasting his guests (cf. v. 9), and the Gihon spring about one-half mile north and directly east of Jerusalem also outside the city wall. On that day two processions, one by rebels and one by the king's men, were going to two neighboring springs.

1:34-35. At the Gihon spring both **Zadok the priest and Nathan the prophet** were to **anoint** Solomon. There was no prophet in Adonijah's camp. Nathan's presence symbolized the divine choice of Solomon as **king** in a way that Zadok's presence alone could not. Blowing **the trumpet** signaled the official nature of the anointing. Every king of Israel was anointed. The ceremony symbolized the coming of the Spirit of God on His chosen leader through pouring oil on his head.

The **shout, Long live King Solomon!** expressed the people's desire and prayer that the new king's reign would be long and prosperous. The leaders had been instructed to return **up** Mount Zion to the city of David and place Solomon **on** David's **throne.** This would be the ultimate proof of his election. Solomon was to commence his rule at that moment; the official seating on the throne was to be perceived not as simply a symbolic act. David clearly explained that he himself by the authority of his kingly office had **appointed** Solomon **ruler over Israel and Judah** effective immediately. Israel and Judah were distinguished (cf. 4:20, 25) because 1 Kings was written after the kingdom was divided in 931 B.C. and/or because a rift was already evident between the northern and southern parts of the kingdom (cf. 2 Sam. 19:41–20:2).

1:36-37. As military commander and the man responsible to execute these orders **Benaiah** responded to his commander in chief. His response, **Amen! May the LORD . . . so declare it,** means, "May what the king has said be what Yahweh has declared." Benaiah then requested that **God** would **be with Solomon** and bless his reign **even** more than He had blessed David's reign.

g. Solomon's anointing (1:38-40)

1:38-40. The Kerethites and the Pelethites were the royal bodyguard troops under Benaiah's personal, veteran command (cf. the "lord's [David's] servants," v. 33; 2 Sam. 8:18). **Gihon,** located east of the City of David in the Valley of Kidron just outside the city wall, was the main source of water for Jerusalem at this time (cf. comments on "Gihon," 1 Kings 1:33). **Zadok . . . took the horn** (perhaps an animal's horn used as a container) **of oil** that was used to anoint kings and priests **from the sacred tent** in Jerusalem and carried it to Gihon. Perhaps this tent, set up by David (1 Chron. 15:1), was similar to the Mosaic tabernacle. The olive oil symbolized the presence and power of God. A great throng of **people** followed the procession and witnessed the anointing. This was a glorious day in the history of Israel and the people celebrated enthusiastically, so much **so that the ground shook.**

h. The report of Solomon's anointing (1:41-48)

1:41-48. Adonijah's party was feasting only a half mile south of Gihon. They **heard** the celebration easily. But it was the blowing **of the trumpet,** the sign that an official function was taking place, that roused **Joab** to inquire about **all the noise in the city.**

Abiathar's son **Jonathan** had been in the city, and arriving at the feast just then, reported what was going on. Adonijah's optimism and complete ignorance of the plot to undercut his rebellion can be seen in his greeting of **Jonathan** (v. 42). Along with relaying the other events already recorded (vv. 43-46) Jonathan added that **the royal officials** had gone **to congratulate . . . David** and

wish God's blessing on **Solomon** (v. 47). Evidently David was confined to **his bed** and did not personally witness the anointing of Solomon.

Jonathan had apparently penetrated the palace or at least obtained information from within it since he reported to Adonijah what David had said in his bedroom (v. 48). Characteristically David praised **God** for one more blessing: allowing him to live long enough to **see** his **successor on** his **throne.**

i. Adonijah's fear (1:49-53)

1:49-51. Adonijah's guests scattered as far from the traitor and as fast as they could so they would not be linked with him and dealt with as they felt surely he would be. In the ancient Near East traitors could expect to be purged by a new king. Terror at this prospect drove **Adonijah** to the tabernacle where he claimed refuge by grasping **the horns** on **the** brazen **altar** in the tabernacle courtyard. Such a practice was common in Israel and in other neighboring nations (cf., e.g., Ex. 21:13-14). The symbolism of taking hold of the altar's horns seems to have meant that as God had been gracious to man, as seen in accepting man's offerings to atone for his sins, so one man should be gracious to another man who had offended him.

1:52-53. Solomon could have had Adonijah removed from the tabernacle and executed, but instead showed mercy. Solomon followed this pattern of graciousness throughout his reign. The new **king** simply asked for a promise from his half brother that he would not rebel again but would show **himself to be a worthy,** loyal subject. **Adonijah** promised and Solomon sent him **home.** But soon Adonijah conspired again and lost his life as a result (2:13-25).

3. DAVID'S CHARGE TO SOLOMON (2:1-9)

The amount of time that elapsed between the events of chapter 1 and this incident is not revealed, but in light of David's poor health and old age (1:1-4, 15, 47) his charge probably was given shortly after Solomon's anointing.

a. Solomon's relationship to God (2:1-4)

2:1-4. The first part of David's **charge** to **his son** concerned what was of primary importance.

To go the way of all the earth is a picturesque description of death. David was a realist; he knew he would soon die so he made plans which included counseling his successor. His charge is reminiscent of Moses' charge to Joshua (Deut. 31:23).

Solomon was encouraged to be strong to keep the Word of the Lord. He should show himself to be a man by being brave to stand for the right and against the wrong. He should observe what the LORD . . . requires in the sense of obeying Yahweh. What the Lord requires is to walk in His ways, namely, to keep His decrees (ordinances), commands . . . laws, and requirements (testimonies). These four words (decrees, commands, laws, requirements) refer to the different kinds of precepts in the Mosaic Law. Obedience to the propositional revelation of God would guarantee success, David said. God's blessing depended on His people's obedience to the Law of Moses. Solomon's personal obedience would result in God's fulfilling His promise that David's descendants would forever occupy the throne of Israel (2 Sam. 7:12-16).

b. Solomon's dealings with men (2:5-9)

2:5-6. David's instruction to put Joab to death did not manifest a vindictive spirit or a cowardly refusal to execute his commander himself. Joab had murdered two commanders . . . Abner and Amasa (cf. comments on 1:7). David described the blood of these two innocent victims as permanently staining Joab's belt and sandals; the blood clung to him to demonstrate his guilt. In mercy David had not executed the punishment that Joab's actions deserved, probably because Joab had shown David much loyalty and had served him well. But justice had to be done and Solomon had to do it. Joab had been living on borrowed time; soon he had to pay for his crimes.

2:7. Barzillai of Gilead (east of the Jordan River) had sustained David and his men when they were fleeing from . . . Absalom (2 Sam. 19:31-39). David charged Solomon to sustain Barzillai's sons at his table as Barzillai and his sons had provided sustenance for David in the wilderness. David wanted Barzillai's sons to reap what their father had sown.

2:8-9. Shimei a Benjamite had not only cursed David but, more seriously, had threatened David's life (2 Sam. 16:11). Evidently David had reason to believe that Shimei would again strike at his life. Solomon extended grace to Shimei, but later the Benjamite proved faithless and, like Adonijah, sealed his own doom (1 Kings 2:36-46).

4. DAVID'S DEATH (2:10-12)

2:10. The picturesque phrase rested with his fathers beautifully describes David's death and suggests that his activity did not cease forever. Indeed, the bodies of all believers who die simply "rest" until they are resurrected to live with God and serve Him eternally. The City of David (cf. 3:1; 8:1; 9:24; 11:27; 15:8, 24; 22:50) is Jerusalem which David captured from the Jebusites and made his capital. In his day Jerusalem was quite small and occupied a peninsula of high ground bounded on the east, south, and west by valleys. Solomon enlarged the city to the north later and other kings expanded it even farther.

2:11-12. David reigned 40 years over Israel (1011–971 B.C.). For 7 years his capital was Hebron until he moved to Jerusalem from which he ruled for 33 years. He was about 70 years old when he died (2 Sam. 5:4). David is remarkable in many respects: he was a warrior, poet, musician, military genius, administrator, and man of God. He experienced outstanding success and crushing failure. He extended the borders and influence of his nation greatly.

He was greatly loved and greatly hated during his lifetime. But perhaps his most significant characteristic was his heart for God. His son Solomon succeeded him and enjoyed a reign of peace.

B. The earlier years of Solomon's reign (2:13–4:34)

The wisdom for which Solomon became famous can be seen clearly in this section of Scripture. Solomon's wise decisions at the beginning of his reign resulted in 40 years (971–931) of peace and prosperity for Israel.

1. SOLOMON'S PURGES (2:13-46)

To lay a firm foundation for his reign Solomon had to deal with his and his father's enemies.

a. Adonijah's execution (2:13-25)

2:13-14. Adonijah had not abandoned his hope of becoming king (cf. 1:5). But to take the throne he would have to dispose of Solomon. The plot that he conceived was clever. He began his maneuvering by approaching **Bathsheba,** the queen **mother** (but not his own mother, who was **Haggith;** cf. 2 Sam. 3:4), through whom he hoped to receive a favorable decision from Solomon. In view of Adonijah's previous plotting **Bathsheba** initially expressed caution. But he convinced her that his intentions were peaceful; superficially they were, but ultimately they were not. He persuaded Bathsheba to listen to what he had **to say.**

2:15-16. Adonijah may have honestly believed that **all Israel looked to** him **as their king,** but this hardly seems to have been the case; Adonijah's wishful dreaming had convinced him of this. The throne had never been his. His saying that the present state of events had **come . . . from the LORD** seems to have been a pious ploy designed to convince Bathsheba that he had accepted Solomon's anointing as God's will and had submitted to it. There is no evidence that Adonijah was ever sincerely interested in what the Lord wanted. But there is much evidence that he was interested in what *Adonijah* wanted! His pious profession along with his apparent acquiescence to Solomon's anointing persuaded Bathsheba that Adonijah had no lingering aspirations to become king. So she gave him permission to proceed with his proposal.

2:17-18. Bathsheba apparently interpreted Adonijah's request for **Abishag** (cf. 1:3-4) as simply the desire of a handsome young man for the hand of a beautiful young woman. Bathsheba's excitement for this seemingly innocent love affair moved her to agree to present his request to **the king.** She probably relished the thought of having a part as a matchmaker.

2:19-21. Solomon respectfully greeted his mother by standing **up to meet her** and bowing **to her** when she entered the **throne** room. He gave her the seat of honor **at his right hand** so she could converse comfortably with him. She had only **one small request;** at least she perceived it as small. Assuming it was a small request, Solomon agreed to grant it.

2:22-25. However, he knew immediately that her proposal had far-reaching consequences that would threaten his throne. So he refused to agree to it. **Abishag** had become a member of King David's harem. Even though David never had sexual relations with her, Abishag's presence in the harem entitled her to part of David's inheritance. In the people's eyes she had been David's concubine. "Among the Israelites, just as with the ancient Persians (Herod. iii. 68), taking possession of the harem of a deceased king was equivalent to an establishment of the claim to the throne" (C.F. Keil, "The Books of the Kings," in *Commentary on the Old Testament in Ten Volumes,* 3:32).

Bathsheba may have thought that because Abishag was not really one of David's concubines this would be no problem. But **Solomon** in his wisdom realized that the people would regard Abishag as a concubine and therefore would interpret Adonijah's marriage to her as a claim to the throne. Also since **Adonijah** was **older** (v. 22) than Solomon (cf. 2 Sam. 3:4 with 2 Sam. 5:13-14) the people would assume that he had more right to be **king** than **Solomon.** The people generally did not recognize that God's purposes in election frequently violated the natural order of primogeniture. (For example, God chose the younger brother in His selection of Abraham, Isaac, Jacob, Joseph, and many others.) Solomon's perception of Adonijah's wicked intent led him to reply with much indignation to **his mother.** He had not executed his brother for his attempted coup before David died; **Solomon** had shown him mercy (1 Kings 1:52-53). But **Adonijah** was still plotting against the Lord and His anointed. Solomon was not only just in having **Adonijah . . . put to death,** but he also acted as a good steward of the kingdom that had been committed to him by God (**as He promised**). (On the words **As surely as the LORD lives** see comments on 1:29.) **Benaiah,** the captain of the guard, carried out the king's order immediately.

b. Abiathar's dismissal (2:26-27)

2:26-27. Abiathar, the priest who sided with Adonijah, could have been justly executed by Solomon for conspiracy. But because Abiathar was a priest of Yahweh who had **carried the ark** (served as high priest) during David's lifetime and because he had faithfully **shared all** of David's **hardships,** Solomon merely **removed** him from his office and restricted him to his hometown of **Anathoth** three miles northeast of Jerusalem. (Centuries later Jeremiah was born in Anathoth, Jer. 1:1.)

The author of 1 and 2 Kings noted that this act of Solomon fulfilled God's prophecy that Eli's line of priests, of which **Abiathar** was a member (see the chart "The Ancestry of Zadok and Abiathar," near 2 Sam. 8:15-18), would be cut off (1 Sam. 2:30-35). In this brief statement one of the 1 and 2 Kings' author's purposes can be seen clearly: to demonstrate the faithfulness of God to His **Word.**

c. Joab's execution (2:28-35)

2:28-30. The news that **reached Joab** was evidently what had befallen **Adonijah** and Abiathar (vv. 23-27), his fellow conspirators. Joab had been head of the army under David (2 Sam. 8:16). Now Joab, like Adonijah, sought the protection **of the horns of the** brazen **altar** in the courtyard of **the tent** (tabernacle) in Jerusalem (cf. 1 Kings 1:50). This was a place of refuge for those whose lives were in danger. The Mosaic Law provided refuge there for all but murderers (Ex. 21:13-14).

Why did Joab seek refuge there since he was a murderer? Perhaps he thought that Solomon was after him only because of his part in Adonijah's attempted coup and that **the king** did not know of or care about his murdering Abner and Amasa. But it was for all these sins that **Solomon** sought Joab. Solomon probably did not want to defile the tabernacle by shedding human blood there so he told **Benaiah** to order **Joab** to **come out.** But the commander refused. Joab would not let go of the altar's horns. **Solomon ordered** that he be treated like the murderer he was and struck **down** on the spot.

2:31-33. For his murders Joab was executed without mercy. As long as **Joab** remained alive, David's **house** (dynasty) bore some responsibility for Joab's action since he had murdered **Abner** and **Amasa** (cf. 2 Sam. 3:22-30; 20:8-10) in connection with his official duties. Solo-

mon (like David before him, 1 Kings 2:5-6) wanted to remove any obstacle to God's blessing on his reign and to identify Joab's **guilt** with **his** own **house** alone.

2:34-35. Benaiah, head of the royal bodyguard, returned to the tabernacle and carried out the king's order. **Joab** did not die in total disgrace, however, for **he was buried on his own land in the desert.** This was possibly the wilderness of Judea east of Bethlehem. To be buried in one's own land was an honor bestowed on Joab for his long service to David.

Solomon replaced Joab with **Benaiah,** promoting him to head of **the army. Zadok the priest** filled the place left by **Abiathar** (cf. v. 27).

d. Shimei's execution (2:36-46)

2:36-38. Shimei must have been a dangerous man. He was treated as such by both David and Solomon, though what is recorded of him here seems on the surface to be of minor importance. When David fled Jerusalem, being pursued by Absalom, Shimei verbally and physically attacked David and his officials. David's men recognized the danger Shimei posed for the king and asked David's permission to kill him then and there (2 Sam. 16:5-13).

But David did not allow this. He did not pardon Shimei's traitorous actions, but postponed Shimei's execution probably because of all that he was facing at the moment in view of Absalom's rebellion. Shimei was from the same clan as Saul's family (2 Sam. 16:5).

Solomon summoned **Shimei** and passed judgment on him: he was restricted to living **in Jerusalem;** the city would be his prison. In particular Shimei was not to **cross the Kidron Valley** just east of Jerusalem. If Shimei crossed the Kidron he would probably head home to stir up insurrection among the Benjamites. Solomon told Shimei that he would be executed if he disobeyed Solomon's orders. **Shimei** understood his sentence, agreed to abide by it, and did so **for a long time** (three years, 1 Kings 2:39).

2:39-40. After **three years . . . two of Shimei's slaves ran off** to **Gath** in Philistia, about 30 miles southwest of Jerusalem. Shimei's decision to leave Jerusalem to pursue **his slaves** revealed his low view of Solomon's authority.

2:41-46. Solomon then recognized that Shimei's attitude had not changed. Because Shimei had violated the terms of his sentence Solomon had every right to execute the punishment he had graciously postponed. Like Adonijah, **Shimei** had not changed. Solomon reviewed the terms of Shimei's sentence with him to justify his action (vv. 42-43). Solomon's chief concern was the security of **David's throne** (v. 45); this apparently had been David's concern too with respect to Shimei.

As David had commanded (vv. 8-9), **Solomon** put **Shimei** to death. But Solomon's prior mercy in dealing with Shimei (vv. 36-37) absolved **the king** from any charge of being vindictive or unfair.

In all Solomon's dealings with his political enemies—men who conspired against the will of God during David's reign—the young king's mercy and wisdom stand out. Because of his wise handling of these threats to the throne **the kingdom was** then **firmly established in Solomon's hands.**

2. SOLOMON'S PERSONAL WISDOM (CHAP. 3)

The wisdom of Solomon, already evident in the record of his dealings with his political enemies, is reeemphasized in chapter 3.

a. Solomon's attitudes (3:1-3)

The king's attitudes toward his office and his God are set forth and account for God's blessing.

3:1. This note by the author may be out of chronological sequence with the other events of Solomon's life. It is added here as an important historical fact and a portent of things to come. **Solomon made** a peace treaty **with Pharaoh king of Egypt** (probably Siamon of the 21st dynasty) and sealed it by marrying **his daughter.** The motivation for this marriage was obviously political. Solomon was not as careful about marrying non-Israelites as he should have been. But this union did result in peace with Israel's neighbor to the southwest who was weak during Solomon's reign. Solomon housed this bride in **Jerusalem.** After he **finished** several building projects including **his palace . . . the temple,** and other buildings (cf. 7:2-7), he prepared a special house (a palace) for her (cf. 7:8).

3:2-3. During the period of the Judges the Israelites adopted the Canaanite custom of offering sacrifices **at . . . high places.** These were on hilltops and other elevations. The pagan Canaanites felt that the closer they got to heaven the more likely was the possibility that their prayers and offerings would reach their gods. Offering sacrifices at places other than the tabernacle was prohibited in the Law (Lev. 17:3-4). Nevertheless this practice was commonly observed in Israel at this time, even by Solomon. The **temple** refers to Solomon's temple, not the tabernacle. In general, **Solomon** was careful to follow in David's godly footsteps thus demonstrating his love for Yahweh.

b. Solomon's prayer for wisdom (3:4-15)

3:4-5. The **most important** (popular or largest) **high place** was at **Gibeon** about five miles north of Jerusalem in the territory of Benjamin. There **Solomon** made a great sacrifice to the Lord. Evidently that very night **the LORD** revealed Himself to **the king. . . . in a dream.** Such revelations were not uncommon in ancient Israel (cf. Gen. 28:10-15; 37:5-7; etc.). **God** invited Solomon to **ask for whatever** he wanted. There seems to be a cause-and-effect relationship between Solomon's loving generosity in making his offering to the Lord and God's loving generosity in making him this offer.

3:6-9. Solomon recognized that God's **kindness** to **David** was due to his father's faithfulness to God which manifested itself in **righteous** actions and **upright** attitudes of **heart.** The king also acknowledged his own immaturity and need for God's wisdom. Solomon was about 20 years old when he took the throne.

In calling himself a **child,** he was admitting his inexperience (cf. 1 Chron. 22:5; 29:1). Solomon was concerned that he would be able to function effectively as the vice-regent of Yahweh. His responsibility as the leader and judge of God's **people** weighed heavily on him. So he requested a **discerning heart** (lit., "a hearing heart") tuned to the voice of **God** so he could lead Israel as God would want the nation to be led. He acknowledged his dependence on God by referring to himself as God's **servant** (1 Kings 3:7-8).

3:10-14. Solomon placed the good of God's people above his personal peace or prosperity and above any desire to become a powerful and popular king. His values were in the right place from God's perspective. Therefore **God** promised to give him what he requested. He would possess **a wise . . . heart** (v. 12) and be able to discern and render fair judgments (v. 11). Since Solomon sought what was most important God also promised to give him what was of secondary importance, **riches and honor,** to further enable him to govern God's people effectively. Solomon was to be the richest and most honored king of his day. If Solomon remained faithful to pursue the will of God, obeying the Law of Moses, God promised he would also live a **long life.**

3:15. As is often the case, a blessing from God drew the person blessed into a closer relationship with Himself. Inspired by this revelation **Solomon** turned from the high place and proceeded to the divinely appointed place of worship, the tabernacle. He did not enter the most holy place; only the high priest could enter there once a year (Lev. 16). But the king **stood before the ark of the** LORD's **covenant,** outside the tabernacle facing toward the ark. **Burnt offerings** expressed the complete dedication of oneself to God and **fellowship offerings** symbolized the fellowship people can enjoy with God and with others through God's grace. Solomon's **feast** expressed his joy and gratitude to the members of **his court.**

c. Solomon's demonstration of wisdom (3:16-28)

This incident was undoubtedly included at this point to show that God had indeed given Solomon the wisdom He promised (cf. v. 12). Significantly the essence of wisdom is revealed in Solomon's handling of this difficult case. The king had insight into basic human nature (in this case, maternal instincts) that enabled him to understand why people behave as they do and how they will respond in various situations. The opposite of this ability is seen in simply judging people's superficial words and actions.

3:16-23. Two **prostitutes** living **in the same house** each had **a baby** three days apart. One of the boy babies **died** during **the night** and his mother exchanged the dead child for the living child. In the **morning** when the other woman discov-

ered that the **dead** son was not hers, the guilty mother refused to admit her wrongdoing. Unable to settle their dispute they appeared before **the king,** each one claiming **the living** infant was hers.

3:24-27. Solomon ordered that the baby be **cut . . . in two.** As he had anticipated, the child's mother, not wanting it killed, volunteered to let the other woman have the **baby,** rather than have it killed. When **the other** woman argued that the baby should be **cut . . . in two,** it was evident that she, having no compassion for the child, was not the **living** son's **mother.**

3:28. Solomon's **wisdom** in this case became known throughout his kingdom so that he was admired as a wise administrator of **justice.**

3. SOLOMON'S POLITICAL ADMINISTRATION (CHAP. 4)

This chapter reflects the wisdom God gave Solomon (cf. 3:12) as manifested in his administrative leadership of Israel.

a. Solomon's chief officials (4:1-6)

4:1-3. Delegation of authority is a mark of wisdom. **Solomon** appointed 11 **chief officials** over his government. Three men are called priests: **Azariah** (v. 2), Zadok, and Abiathar (v. 4). Azariah, a **son of Zadok,** was Zadok's grandson (cf. 1 Chron. 6:8-9). "Son" often means descendant. **Elihoreph and Ahijah** were **secretaries** or scribes. This was an important office; the scribes prepared royal edicts affecting trade, commerce, and military alliances and kept official records. **Jehoshaphat** was the **recorder** who maintained the records of all important daily affairs in the kingdom. Jehoshaphat had also served in this capacity under David (2 Sam. 8:16; 20:24).

4:4. Benaiah was **commander in chief** of the whole army. **Zadok** and **Abiathar** had served as co-high **priests** under David (2 Sam. 15:35). But Abiathar had sided with Adonijah in the attempted coup so the priest was dismissed by Solomon (1 Kings 2:20-27). Zadok continued as high priest (2:35). Abiathar is listed here as one of Solomon's officials because even though he was fired from being high priest he retained the title and honor after he was deposed. Perhaps Azariah (4:2) and Zadok (v. 4) then

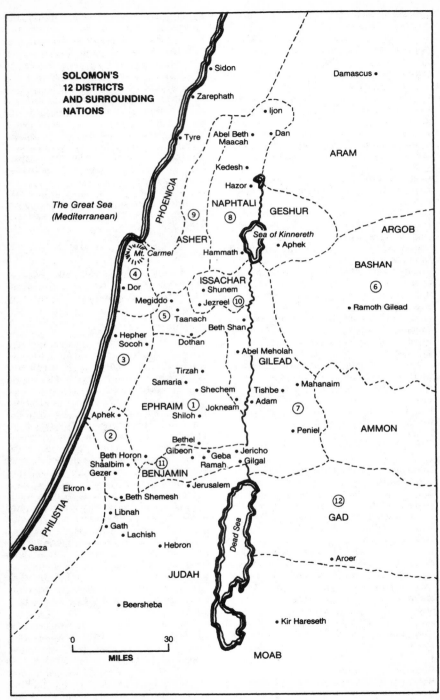

SOLOMON'S
12 DISTRICTS
AND SURROUNDING
NATIONS

• Sidon

Damascus •

• Zarephath

• Ijon

• Dan

ARAM

• Tyre

Abel Beth
Maacah •

Kedesh •

Hazor •

PHOENICIA

NAPHTALI

GESHUR

The Great Sea
(Mediterranean)

⑨

⑧

ASHER

Sea of Kinnereth

ARGOB

• Aphek

Mt. Carmel

Hammath •

BASHAN

④

ISSACHAR

⑥

• Dor

• Shunem

• Ramoth Gilead

Megiddo •

• Jezreel ⑩

⑤ • Taanach

• Hepher
Socoh •

Beth Shan

③

• Dothan

• Abel Meholah

GILEAD

• Tirzah

Samaria •

• Shechem

Tishbe
•

• Mahanaim

Aphek •

EPHRAIM ①

Jokneam •

• Adam

⑦

• Shiloh

②

• Peniel

AMMON

• Bethel

Beth Horon •

• Gibeon

• Geba • Jericho

Shaalbim •

Ramah •

• Gilgal

Gezer •

⑪

BENJAMIN

Ekron •

• Jerusalem

Dead Sea

⑫

• Beth Shemesh

GAD

• Libnah

• Gath

• Lachish

PHILISTIA

• Hebron

• Aroer

JUDAH

• Gaza

• Beersheba

• Kir Hareseth

0   30

MILES

MOAB

served together as Abiathar and Zadok had done previously.

4:5-6. Two men are listed as sons of **Nathan.** They may have been the sons of one man or the sons of different Nathans. **Azariah** (not the Azariah in v. 2) was **in charge of the** 12 district officers named in verses 8-19. **Zabud** was of the priestly line and served as the king's **personal adviser. Ahishar** was **in charge of the palace,** perhaps overseeing the servants and other workers there, and **Adoniram** (cf. 5:14) supervised the **forced labor,** non-Israelites living in Israel who were conscripted to work for **the king** (cf. 5:13-14; 9:15, 21; 2 Chron. 2:2; 8:8).

b. Solomon's district governors (4:7-19)

4:7-19. Solomon made each of his **12 district governors** responsible to supply **provisions** for **the royal household** (and for his thousands of horses, v. 28), one governor for each **month.** These provisions were huge (cf. vv. 22-28). This work doubtless kept these men busy. Interestingly two of the governors were sons-in-law of Solomon (vv. 11, 15). All 12 of them are mentioned only here in the Bible except for **Ahimaaz,** who possibly was a son of Zadok the priest (cf. 2 Sam. 15:27). On the boundaries of the districts see the map "Solomon's 12 Districts and Surrounding Nations." Judah, not included, was perhaps exempted by Solomon from the levy requirement.

c. Solomon's prosperity (4:20-28)

4:20. Solomon's kingdom was unified, secure, strong, and prosperous, with a large population. (On **Judah and Israel** see comments on 1:35.) The people became **as numerous as the sand on the seashore.**

The Israelites had enough to eat and drink, **and they were happy,** enjoying the basic comforts of life (cf. 4:25).

4:21. Solomon's domain stretched from **the Euphrates River** (cf. v. 24) on the east and north **to the land of the Philistines** on the west and **Egypt** to the southwest. This does not mean that the Abrahamic Covenant was fulfilled in Solomon's day (Gen. 15:18-20), for not all this territory was incorporated into the geographic boundaries of Israel; many of the subjected kingdoms retained their identity and territory but paid taxes (**tribute**) to Solomon. Israel's own geographic

limits were "from Dan to Beersheba" (1 Kings 4:25).

4:22-25. The ability of the nation to provide **Solomon's daily provisions** (cf. v. 7) testifies to its prosperity (vv. 22-23). Those provisions included **30 cors** (ca. 185 bushels; cf. NIV marg.) **of fine flour . . . 60 cors** (ca. 375 bushels; cf. NIV marg.) **of meal, 30 head** of **cattle . . . 100 sheep and goats,** and wild meat (**deer, gazelles, roebucks**) and fowl. These provisions were made possible by the great geographical extent of the kingdom—from the town of **Tiphsah** in the north (on the bank of the Euphrates) **to Gaza** in the south (cf. v. 21). **Each man** living **under his own vine and fig tree** (v. 25) is a figurative expression for peace and prosperity (cf. Micah 4:4; Zech. 3:10). The vine and fig tree were both symbols of the nation Israel and pictured the Promised Land's agricultural abundance.

4:26-28. Solomon's numerous **horses (12,000;** cf. 2 Chron. 1:14) and many chariots (1,400 according to 2 Chron. 1:14) were kept in several locations (called "chariot cities" in 2 Chron. 9:25; cf. 1 Kings 9:19). Though the Hebrew here has 40,000 **stalls** (cf. NIV marg.), this was probably the error of a copyist in transcribing the text which read **4,000,** the number in 2 Chronicles 9:25. The **horses** and chariots, used for national defense, served as a strong deterrent to potential foreign aggressors. **Barley and straw** for all Solomon's **horses** was supplied daily by **the district** governors.

d. Solomon's skill (4:29-34)

4:29. This additional information about Solomon's wisdom demonstrates God's faithfulness in blessing the king as He had promised (cf. 3:12; 5:12). **Wisdom** is the ability to live life successfully. While Solomon possessed this ability he did not always apply it to his own life. Thus the wisest man who ever lived (i.e., with the greatest wisdom) did not live as wisely as many others who preceded and followed him. Having insight into life does not guarantee that one will choose to do what is right. Solomon's **great insight** was his ability to see the core of issues (e.g., 3:16-27). His **understanding** was vast; today he would be described as a man of encyclopedic knowledge.

4:30-31. His **wisdom** exceeded that **of all the men of the East** (cf. Job 1:3) and **all the wisdom of** people in **Egypt,** both areas known for their wisdom. He was also superior to other men renowned for their wisdom, including **Ethan the Ezrahite** (whose name appears in the title to Ps. 89, which suggests that he wrote that psalm), **Heman** (both Ethan and Heman were musicians; cf. 1 Chron. 15:19), **Calcol, and Darda.** The last three of these four were **the sons of Mahol,** but in 1 Chronicles 2:6 they, along with Ethan and Zimri, are said to be "sons [descendants] of Zerah." Apparently Mahol was the father of the four (Ethan, Heman, Calcol, and Darda) and Zimri (whose father was Zerah) was an ancestor several generations earlier (cf. comments on 1 Chron. 2:6).

4:32-34. Several hundred of Solomon's **3,000 proverbs** have been preserved in the Book of Proverbs as well as a few in Ecclesiastes. One of his **1,005** songs is the Song of Songs. Solomon's literary output was extremely prolific. He became an authority in botany and zoology too. The statement in verse 34 is a hyperbole (an overstatement to make a point); obviously not every nation on earth **sent** a representative to visit Solomon. The point is that many important visitors from faraway places visited Solomon who received them openly at his court. He was recognized as the wisest man of his day as God had promised he would be.

C. Solomon's temple and palace (chaps. 5–8)

The author of 1 and 2 Kings was as interested in Solomon's temple as he was in Solomon himself. The provisions the king made for the spiritual strength of his nation were his outstanding contribution to Israel.

1. BUILDING PREPARATIONS (CHAP. 5)

a. Solomon's request of Hiram (5:1-6)

5:1. Tyre was an important port city on the Mediterranean Sea north of Israel. It was one of the chief cities of Phoenicia, one of Israel's friendly neighboring kingdoms. **Hiram, king of Tyre,** had been an ally and friend of King **David** and had supplied materials and laborers to build David's palace (2 Sam. 5:11). Hiram **sent his envoys to Solomon** to pay his respects to the new **king,** the son of his friend.

5:2-5. David had shared with his friend Hiram his desires to build a temple. But **because of the wars . . . David** had to fight, he was not allowed to construct it. **Now . . . peace** prevailed (cf. 4:24-25) and construction could begin. Solomon's assurance of peace would have encouraged Hiram to cooperate with his plans. His intention was **to build** the **temple** God Himself had approved.

5:6. Solomon called on Hiram to **give orders** that his subjects provide materials and craftsmen for the project. This may have been done with the authority of a superior but, more likely, Solomon made his words the request of a friend. **Cedars of Lebanon** grew profusely on the western slopes of the Lebanon Mountains east of Tyre, though few remain today. They were very old trees with hard, beautiful wood that was excellent for construction since it was not readily subject to decay or insect infestation. Solomon offered to supply workers to assist Hiram's men in felling the trees and to **pay** the Sidonian laborers whatever Hiram considered a fair wage. **The Sidonians** were indeed highly **skilled in felling timber;** doubtless Solomon's recognition of this ability impressed Hiram favorably. Sidon, another Phoenician city, was north of Tyre. Apparently Hiram hired workers from there.

b. Hiram's treaty with Solomon (5:7-12)

5:7-9. Solomon's suggestion met with an enthusiastic response. **Hiram** had regard for Yahweh, perhaps as a result of his contacts with **David.** Hiram perceived Solomon's wisdom at once. Apparently Solomon's total message to Hiram (vv. 3-6) was not recorded by the author of 1 and 2 Kings since Hiram agreed to provide **pine** as well as **cedar . . . logs.** Hiram suggested that the logs be transported to Solomon on **rafts** and offered to be responsible for this. However, Hiram wanted something in return: **food for** his **royal household.**

5:10-12. Solomon agreed to the arrangement and each year **gave** him **20,000 cors** (ca. 125,000 bushels; cf. NIV marg.) **of wheat** and **20,000 baths** (ca. 115,000 gallons) **of . . . olive oil.** Barley and wine were also included (2 Chron. 2:10). Obviously **Hiram** had a large household, which no doubt included his courtiers as well as family members. Apparently wheat and olive oil were not plentifully available in or near Tyre. Due to Solomon's wise initiative (**the LORD gave Solomon wisdom**; cf. 1 Kings 3:12, 28; 4:29) this **treaty** arrangement continued for many years and contributed to **peaceful relations between** the **two kings.**

c. Solomon's conscription of laborers (5:13-18)

5:13-18. Solomon's conscription touched the lives of many non-Israelite (cf. 2 Chron. 8:7-8) males in Israel (183,300 are referred to here). The **king** drafted them for temporary government service which they worked into their schedules along with their private responsibilities. This method of conscripting **forced labor** eventually proved exceedingly distasteful to the Israelites, perhaps because of the way it was administered (cf. 1 Kings 12:18). The **3,300 foremen** plus an additional 550 (9:23) equal 3,850 (cf. the 3,600 foremen in 2 Chron. 2:18 plus 250 in 2 Chron. 8:10).

Working under **Adoniram** (cf. 1 Kings 4:6), the **carriers** transported materials from place to place and the **stone-cutters** cut massive limestone blocks out of **the quarry** in **the hills** north of Jerusalem. **The men of Gebal** (modern Byblos, 13 miles north of Beirut, and 60 miles north of Tyre) made a significant contribution by preparing **timber and stone** along with Solomon's and Hiram's **craftsmen.**

2. TEMPLE CONSTRUCTION (CHAP. 6)

a. The dimensions of the structure (6:1-10)

6:1. This verse is one of the most important in the Old Testament chronologically because it enables one to fix certain dates in Israel's history. The dates of Solomon's reign have been quite definitely established through references in ancient writings. They were 971–931 B.C. According to this verse, **in the fourth year of** his **reign** Solomon **began to build the temple.** That was in 966 B.C. The Exodus took place **480 years** earlier (1446 B.C.). The month **Ziv** is April-May (see the chart "Calendar in Israel," near Ex. 12:2). Interestingly the rebuilding of the temple, 430 years later under Zerubbabel (536), also began in the second month (Ezra 3:8).

6:2-3. A cubit was about 18 inches. So **the temple** was 90 feet **long,** 30 feet **wide,** and 45 feet **high.** It was not large; it had only 2,700 square feet of floor space. But it was strikingly beautiful in appearance because of its white limestone, cedar, and gold exterior. It had a large open front porch (**portico**) that added 15 more feet to its length.

6:4-6. The **narrow clerestory windows** were evidently high on the walls above the three stories of **side rooms** that surrounded **the temple** on two or three sides. The temple's **main hall and** the **inner sanctuary** were the holy place and the most holy place, respectively. The **structure around the building** was built against the outer sides and perhaps the back of the temple. This structure was probably about 25-30 feet high and was divided into three stories of side rooms each of which was 7½ feet high on the inside. These rooms were used by the priests for storage and service. The rooms were smallest (7½' wide) on the first floor which also contained hallways and stairways (cf. v. 8), larger on the second floor (9' wide) with some space also given to halls and stairs, and largest on the third floor (10½' wide). The **offset ledges** were apparently the supports for the upper floor which were built into the walls of this surrounding structure. The measurements are probably inside dimensions.

6:7. Apparently Solomon felt that the noise of construction was not appropriate for this **temple** in view of its purpose. So he had all the building parts cut and fitted **at the quarry** so that they could be assembled quietly on the **site.**

6:8-10. The temple faced east, but the entrance to the surrounding structure (v. 5) was **on the south. The side rooms** on all floors were connected by internal staircases and passageways. Though no **beams** of this side structure were "inserted into the temple walls" (v. 6), the inner walls of the side rooms **were attached to the temple by** cedar beams (v. 10).

b. The Lord's promise to bless Solomon's obedience (6:11-13)

6:11-13. During the **temple** construction God reaffirmed **to Solomon . . . the promise** He had previously made **to David.** "The promise" given David to which God referred (v. 12) was that He would

PLAN OF SOLOMON'S TEMPLE

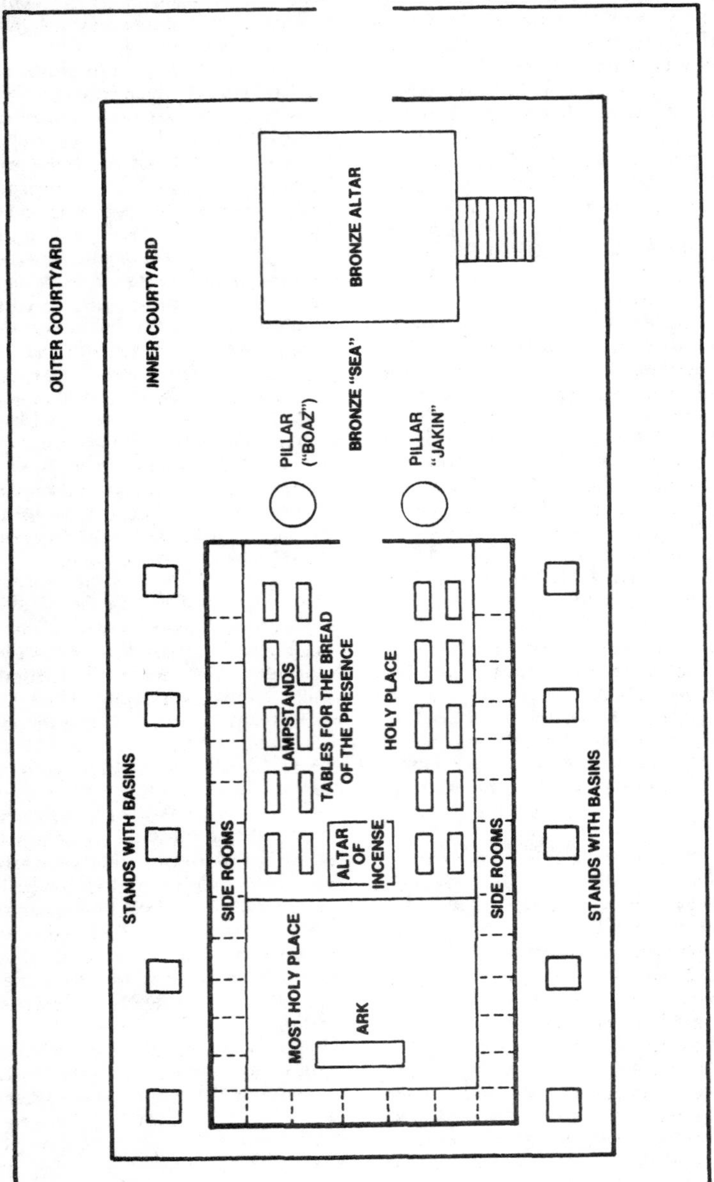

OUTER COURTYARD

INNER COURTYARD

BRONZE ALTAR

PILLAR ("BOAZ")

BRONZE "SEA"

PILLAR "JAKIN"

STANDS WITH BASINS

SIDE ROOMS

LAMPSTANDS

TABLES FOR THE BREAD OF THE PRESENCE

HOLY PLACE

ALTAR OF INCENSE

MOST HOLY PLACE

ARK

SIDE ROOMS

STANDS WITH BASINS

Note: The exact positions and size of the lampstands and golden tables for the bread of the Presence in the holy place are uncertain.

"establish the throne of [David's] kingdom forever" (2 Sam. 7:13). God would do this through Solomon if Solomon would **obey** Him (1 Kings 6:12). Later Solomon's disobedience resulted in God's removing part of the nation from the control of his son Rehoboam. God also promised that if Solomon obeyed the Lord his nation would enjoy God's fellowship and protection. Israel experienced this only partially because of Solomon's later apostasy.

c. The completion of construction (6:14-36)

6:14-18. The entire **interior** of **the temple** was covered **with cedar boards** (on the **walls**) and with **pine** boards (on **the floor**), all overlaid with gold (vv. 22, 30). **The main hall** (cf. v. 5) in front of the **inner sanctuary (the most holy place)** was the holy place. The main hall was 60 feet long, twice the length of the most holy place. (See the sketch "Plan of Solomon's Temple.") The interior was decorated with carved **gourds** and **flowers.**

6:19-22. Inside the most holy place (a 30-foot cube, all **overlaid . . . with . . . gold**) was **the ark of the covenant. The altar of cedar** was the altar of incense located in the holy place. Solomon's incense altar was made of cedar and **overlaid with gold**; it was also called "the golden altar" (7:48). **Gold chains** were hung in the holy place across the doors that led into the most holy place. First Kings 6:22a recapitulates part of what was stated in verses 14-21. **The altar** (v. 22) is the incense altar located in the holy place.

6:23-28. The **cherubim** were sculptured angels, carved from **olive wood. Their wings** were **spread out** so that side by side they extended 30 feet (from the north to the south walls of the most holy place; cf. 2 Chron. 3:13). **Gold** covered **the cherubim** too.

6:29-35. The walls of **the inner and outer rooms,** the most holy place and the holy place, respectively, were decorated with **carved cherubim, palm trees, and open flowers.** The olive wood **doors** leading from the holy place were framed **with five-sided jambs** (frames). Some commentators believe they were sliding doors. The **doors** leading from the porch into **the main hall** (the holy place) were made of **pine** (v. 34). They hung on **four-sided jambs** and were bifold (**each hav-**ing **two leaves** hinged together that folded open against each other and **turned** on **sockets** or pivot points). All the doors were decorated like the walls (vv. 32, 35; cf. v. 29).

6:36. The inner courtyard was an open plaza surrounding the temple. There was also an outer courtyard not mentioned here (cf. 2 Chron. 4:9), which was somewhat lower in elevation than the inner courtyard (cf. "upper courtyard" in Jer. 36:10). This inner courtyard (also called the "courtyard of the priests," 2 Chron. 4:9) was separated from the outer (great) court by the wall described here. This wall consisted of **three courses** (rows) **of dressed** (cut) **stone** (limestone) **and one course** (row) of **cedar beams.** (The outer courtyard was also surrounded by a wall.) The size of the inner courtyard is not given, but if the dimensions of the courtyards of the temple are proportionate to those of the tabernacle courtyard, as the dimensions of the temple and tabernacle structures are, the inner courtyard was about 150 feet wide and 400 feet long.

d. The time spent in construction (6:37-38)

6:37-38. Seven years were **spent** building **the temple,** from **the 4th year** of Solomon's reign (966 B.C.; cf. comments on 6:1) to his **11th year** (959 B.C.). More precisely, this was seven and one-half years. **Ziv** is April-May and **Bul,** the eighth month, is October-November.

3. SOLOMON'S PALACE (7:1-12)

7:1-6. The description of Solomon's **palace** in verses 1-12 raises a question as to whether one building or several were constructed. Probably one palace complex was built that contained several separate but interconnected buildings. The arrangement harmonizes with the style of other large oriental mansions and palaces.

The palace **took** longer to build than the temple (**13 years** compared with 7½; cf. 6:37-38) because it was larger. **The Palace of the Forest of Lebanon** (cf. 10:17, 21; Isa. 22:8) was probably given its name because of the extensive use of Lebanese **cedar** throughout (cf. 1 Kings 7:2-3); it was located not in Lebanon but in Jerusalem. It measured 150 feet by 75 feet and was 45 feet high. The floor space was 11,250 square feet, more than four times the 2,700 square feet of the temple floor (cf. 6:2).

The palace evidently served as an armory (10:17; cf. Isa. 22:8). Apparently next to it was a pillared **colonnade** (a covered walkway surrounding a patio) that had a front **portico** (porch) with a **roof** and supporting **pillars**.

7:7-11. Solomon's **throne hall, the Hall of Justice,** was attached to the Palace of the Forest of Lebanon, as were his own residence (v. 8a) and a separate residence **(palace) for Pharaoh's daughter, whom he had married** (v. 8b), all of harmonious **design.** A **great courtyard** (v. 9) united all these buildings into one palace complex. The **structures** were all built of **stone** (except the roofs) and they rested on stone **foundations.** Each stone was **cut to size . . . with a saw.** Palestinian limestone can be cut with a saw when freshly quarried, but hardens when exposed to the elements.

7:12. The great palace **courtyard** was protected **by a wall** similar in design to that around **the inner courtyard of the temple** (cf. 6:36). The palace was probably built close to (perhaps south of) the temple, though none of its remains have been found by archeologists.

4. THE TEMPLE FURNISHINGS (7:13-51)

a. The work of Huram (7:13-47)

7:13-14. Huram (a variant spelling of the Heb. Hiram) should not be confused with Hiram, the king of Tyre (5:1). Huram was a **skilled** craftsman, also from **Tyre . . . whose mother was** an Israelite **widow from . . . Naphtali, and whose father was a** Phoenician of Tyre. According to 2 Chronicles 2:14 Huram's mother was from Dan. Perhaps Dan was the tribe into which she was born and Naphtali was her residence, or vice versa. Huram's special talent was working with **bronze** (a copper alloy).

7:15-22. Huram **cast two** huge **bronze pillars, each** 27 feet high and 18 feet in circumference. With their **capitals** the pillars were over 34 feet high. (On the alleged discrepancy between verse 15 and 2 Chron. 3:15, see comments there.) Much detail is given in 1 Kings 7:17-20, 22 (cf. comments on 2 Chron. 3:16) to demonstrate the beauty and intricacy of these free-standing monuments.

The pillars were **erected** on either side of the temple **portico** (the roofless front porch). **Jakin,** the name of the **south** pillar, means "He [Yahweh] establishes," and **Boaz,** the name of the **north** pillar, means "In Him [Yahweh] is strength." These stood as a testimony to God's security and strength available to the nation as she obeyed Him.

7:23-26. The Sea corresponded to the laver of the tabernacle. It too was gigantic in size: 15 feet across its circular rim and 7½ feet high. On the three-to-one ratio of the circumference (45') to the diameter (15') compared with the geometric π (*pi*), see comments on 2 Chronicles 4:2. The "Sea" looked like a huge basin resting on the backs of the **12** sculptured **bulls** that supported it, and it could contain **2,000 baths** (ca. 11,500 gallons; cf. NIV marg.) of water. This basin served as a reservoir for the temple courtyard. Second Chronicles 4:5 includes the statement that the laver "held 3,000 baths" (ca. 17,500 gallons). Perhaps this was its total capacity but it actually contained 2,000 baths.

7:27-40a. The **10** bronze **movable stands** were evidently used for butchering sacrificial animals. Each was six feet square and five and one-half feet high at its highest point. On the surface of each stand was a **basin** (v. 38) that held about 230 gallons **(40 baths)** of water. Apparently another **basin** (v. 30) drained into a **circular frame** (perhaps a tank) below through an **opening. Each stand had** decorated **panels** on each side, and **four bronze wheels.** These **10 . . . identical** work tables could be wheeled around the inner courtyard (though with difficulty) as needed. **Five were stationed on the south side of the temple and five on the north.**

7:40b-47. This summary of Huram's handiwork excludes the bronze altar which he also fashioned (2 Chron. 4:1). Recording the crafting of these furnishings in so much detail emphasizes the magnificent beauty, symmetry, and glory of **the temple.** The **bronze** objects were **cast in clay molds in the . . . Jordan** Valley **between Succoth and Zarethan,** about 35 miles north of the Dead Sea and east of the Jordan River. **Bronze** was so abundant that it was **not** even weighed.

b. The furniture and accessories (7:48-50)

7:48-50. Bronze was used for the furnishings outside the **temple** (vv. 40-45), but the furniture on the inside was made of **gold.** The **golden altar** was the altar of incense. The **table** for **the bread of the Presence** ("showbread," KJV) was possibly one larger table with nine others with it, which, though not mentioned here, are mentioned in 2 Chronicles 4:8 ("10 tables") and 2 Chronicles 4:19 ("tables"). Whereas the tabernacle had one lampstand, the temple had 10 **lampstands** in the holy place (**the main hall**). Other items were all of **gold** as well, including even the door **sockets.**

c. *The furnishings dedicated by David (7:51)*

7:51. To all these items were added **the furnishings** King **David** had prepared and dedicated for **temple** service (2 Sam. 8:11; 1 Chron. 22:14; 29:1-9). The **treasuries of the LORD's temple** were probably the rooms of the temple in the surrounding "structure" (1 Kings 6:5-6).

5. THE TEMPLE DEDICATION (CHAP. 8)

a. *The placing of the ark (8:1-11)*

8:1-2. After all the new furnishings, utensils, and accessories had been made and placed in position (chap. 6; 7:13-51), **Solomon summoned** the people for the installation of **the ark** and the dedication of the temple. **All the heads of . . . tribes and . . . families** in **Israel** received special invitations. The ceremony was scheduled for **the festival in the month of Ethanim** (the Feast of Tabernacles in September-October [Lev. 23:33-36]; see the chart "Calendar in Israel," near Ex. 12:1). Formerly the ark had rested in the tabernacle David pitched (2 Sam. 6:17) on Mount **Zion,** the southeast portion of Jerusalem called the **City of David** (cf. 2 Sam. 5:7). (See the map "Jerusalem in the Time of the Kings," near 1 Kings 9:15.)

8:3-5. As God had prescribed, **the ark** was carried by **the priests** by means of long poles that passed through rings on its sides. It must have been a great day when the ark and the other **furnishings** of David's tabernacle were **carried** through the crowded streets of Jerusalem to their new home. Apparently the tabernacle and its utensils were set aside. The only piece of furniture installed in the temple that was not new was **the ark.** The temple courtyard buzzed with busy priests **sacrificing** more animals than **could** be **counted** as the people joyfully worshiped **the LORD.**

8:6-9. The priests put **the ark** in **its place** under the outstretched **wings of the** golden **cherubim** in **the most holy place.** As God had commanded they left the **carrying poles** in the rings (Ex. 25:15). When the doors into the most holy place were open the **poles . . . could be seen from the holy place . . . but not from outside.** The statement that the poles **are still there today** suggests that this part of 1 Kings was written before the temple was destroyed in 586 B.C. **The two stone tablets** of the Law **placed in** the ark by **Moses** were still there. They served to remind Israel that the nation was still under the blessings and responsibilities of the Mosaic Covenant. The pot of manna and Aaron's rod that budded, which had been preserved in the ark (Heb. 9:4) for many years, were no longer there. They may have been removed by the Philistines or some other enemy. Or perhaps the objects, being in front of the tabernacle, not in the ark (cf. Ex. 16:33-34; Num. 17:10), were added to the ark sometime later than Solomon and then eventually were lost.

8:10-11. The cloud that **filled the temple** was a visible representation of the Lord's **glory.** A similar manifestation took place when the tabernacle was dedicated (Ex. 40:34-35).

b. *Solomon's address to the people (8:12-21)*

8:12-14. Solomon explained to the people that God had **said . . . He would dwell in** the **cloud** over the temple. A cloud often symbolized God's presence (cf. Ex. 19:9; 34:5; Lev. 16:2; Deut. 4:11; 31:15). It was Solomon's intention that God should abide in the **temple** he had built as God had dwelt within the tabernacle. Solomon had sought to reflect the magnificence of Yahweh in the temple. **Forever** should be interpreted to mean "as long as possible." Turning from addressing **the LORD,** Solomon spoke to the people **standing** reverently before him.

8:15-21. With His own hand means Himself (cf. v. 24). The promise Solomon referred to was that God would place His **Name** in Jerusalem (cf. comments on 2 Chron. 6:6). "Name" occurs in Solomon's prayer 14 times (1 Kings 8:16-20, 29, 33, 35, 41-44 [twice in v. 43], 48). The **temple** was not to be a "container" for God (v. 27) but a place for his **Name** to dwell (vv. 16-17, 19-20), that is, a place where His presence and character would be evident.

Solomon gave **David** the credit due him for purposing to build the **temple** (vv. 17-18). Solomon explained that **God** had promised David that his **son** would **build the temple** (cf. 2 Sam. 7:12-13). God had been faithful, and Solomon glorified Him for it. The temple was primarily **a place . . . for the ark,** the throne of God on earth and the repository of God's covenant promises to His redeemed people. In this address Solomon demonstrated humility and thankfulness.

c. Solomon's prayer of dedication (8:22-53)

8:22-24. Solomon stood and then kneeled (v. 54) on a special bronze platform that had been built in the temple courtyard for the dedication service (2 Chron. 6:13). Solomon began his prayer with worship and praise to God for His uniqueness and His faithfulness in keeping His promises. **Love** translates *hesed,* meaning loyal love (cf. 1 Kings 10:9).

The king then proceeded to petition God and to intercede for His people. Nine requests may be noted in this prayer:

(1) God's presence and protection. **8:25-30.** Solomon called on God to continue to be faithful to His **promises** to **David** (vv. 25-26; cf. 2:4) and to continue to **hear** the prayers of His **people** (8:28-30; **hear** occurs five times in these three verses). Of course no temple or even **the heavens** could **contain** the omnipresent God (v. 27). **Heaven** itself is His **dwelling place** (cf. vv. 39, 49; Ps. 11:4; Hab. 2:20). Yet in His majesty He is interested in His people's prayers.

(2) Forgiveness of trespasses. **8:31-32.** Solomon asked God to **judge** righteously in interpersonal disputes among the Israelites.

(3) Forgiveness of sins that had caused defeat in battle. **8:33-34.** The king asked the Lord to **forgive** His **people** when they confessed their sins that caused defeat in combat.

(4) Forgiveness of sins that had brought on drought. **8:35-36.** Solomon also asked God to **forgive** His **people** if they confessed sins that resulted in **rain** being withheld (cf. Lev. 26:18-19; Deut. 11:16-17; 28:23-24).

(5) Forgiveness of sins that had re-

sulted in other calamities. **8:37-40. Famine . . . plague . . . blight . . . mildew, locusts . . . grasshoppers,** enemies, **disaster,** and **disease** were all instruments God used to chasten His sinning people. (See the chart "The Covenant Chastenings," near Amos 4:6.) Again the king asked God to **forgive** those who repented of sin that led to these calamities. Solomon affirmed God's knowledge of people's motives (**hearts**).

(6) Mercy for God-fearing foreigners. **8:41-43.** Solomon interceded on behalf of non-Israelites who would trust Yahweh and pray to Him. By hearing them, God's fame would spread worldwide.

(7) Victory in battle. **8:44-45.** Solomon asked God to **uphold** His **people** when they prayed to Him in times of physical distress in combat.

(8) Restoration after captivity. **8:46-51.** The king seemed to have prophetic insight into the fate of God's people. They did indeed go into captivity because of their sins against God; they called on Him for forgiveness, and they experienced restoration to their land. Centuries later Daniel prayed **toward the land** when he was in Babylon (Dan. 6:10).

(9) Attention to every prayer. **8:52-53.** Solomon summarized his petitions by calling on God to hear His people **whenever they cry out** in prayer. These calamities were all listed in Deuteronomy as curses on Israel for her breaking the covenant (Deut. 28:22, 25, 38, 42, 59; 31:17, 29; 32:24).

In this whole prayer (1 Kings 8:23-53) Solomon called on God, who had been faithful to His promises in the past, to continue to be faithful and to show mercy to His people (His chosen **inheritance,** vv. 36, 51, 53) in the future. Confession and forsaking of sin would result in God's hearing His people's prayers ("hear" occurs 13 times in this prayer, and in the first eight of the nine petitions) and God's forgiving them ("forgive" occurs 6 times).

d. Solomon's blessing of the people (8:54-61)

8:54-55. Solomon . . . had been kneeling in prayer **with his hands spread out toward heaven** in a posture of supplication. Then he arose to pronounce a benediction on the people.

8:56-61. God had **given rest** (peace)

to His people and had kept all the good promises He Had given through . . . Moses. Solomon reminded the people of this. Then he expressed his desire for three things: That the LORD would be with Solomon's generation as He had been with his forefathers, that God would give His people the will to walk in all His ways, and that the requests Solomon had made in his prayer would remain close to the heart of God day by day. Solomon ultimately desired that all the peoples of the earth (cf. v. 43) might know that Yahweh is the only true God (cf. 18:39). In order for all this to take place Solomon reminded the people that they must be fully committed to the LORD and obedient to His Word. Solomon himself eventually failed to do this.

As the king finished speaking, "fire came down from heaven and consumed the burnt offering and the sacrifices, and the glory of the LORD filled the temple" (2 Chron. 7:1) as it had earlier filled the tabernacle (Ex. 40:34-35; Lev. 9:23-24).

e. Solomon's sacrifices (8:62-66)

8:62-63. The number of animals sacrificed (22,000 cattle and 120,000 sheep and goats) seems incredibly large. But records of other sacrifices that involved thousands of animals are extant. One must remember that thousands of priests sacrificed on many auxiliary altars, and the celebration lasted for two weeks.

8:64-66. The same day Solomon dedicated the temple he also consecrated . . . the courtyard in front of the temple with his offerings. This dedication took place at the beginning of the festival of Tabernacles which normally lasted one week, but was extended to two weeks on this special occasion. The Feast of Tabernacles commemorated Israel's years of wandering in the wilderness (Lev. 23:33, 41-43). It was fitting that the temple should be dedicated at this feast since that permanent sanctuary now symbolized the end of Israel's wanderings. People from as far away as Lebo Hamath in northern Israel toward the Euphrates River and the Wadi of Egypt (modern Wadi el-Arish) far to the south attended the festivities; all Israel participated. The people returned home at the end of the feast joyful and thankful to God for His goodness to them.

D. The later years of Solomon's reign (chaps. 9–11)

1. GOD'S COVENANT WITH SOLOMON (9:1-9)

9:1-3. As God had revealed Himself to Solomon . . . at Gibeon (3:4-5), so He did again, probably in Jerusalem. First, the LORD assured Solomon that He had heard his prayer of dedication and that He would always abide in the temple in a special sense. His people could always count on His eyes resting on them and His heart compassionately responding to their needs as Solomon had requested.

9:4-9. But the LORD also warned the king. If he would walk before God, manifesting attitudes and actions that expressed obedience to the Lord's Word, God would provide an unceasing line of descendants for Solomon who would always rule over Israel. But if Solomon or any of his descendants did not follow the LORD faithfully, but instead turned aside to worship and serve other gods, then the LORD would do two things: remove Israel from her land and abandon the temple. The Davidic dynasty, though interrupted for centuries starting with the Babylonian Captivity, will be restored by the Messiah when He sits on David's throne in the Millennium (Ps. 89:30-37). This judgment would cause other peoples to marvel at and ridicule Israel. Scoff (1 Kings 9:8) literally means "whistle in amazement." People would know that Israel fell because of her idolatry. Not only did later kings lead Israel away from Yahweh to false gods, but also Solomon himself did (11:4-8), and the nation was on the path toward exile (2 Kings 25:1-21).

2. SOLOMON'S ACHIEVEMENTS (9:10-28)

a. His gifts to Hiram (9:10-14)

9:10-14. Near the mid-point of Solomon's reign (after 20 of his 40 years), after he had finished building the temple (7 years, 6:38) and his palace complex (13 years, 7:1), Solomon gave 20 villages in Galilee to his old friend King Hiram . . . of Tyre. Hiram had previously given Solomon cedar and pine (cf. 5:10) and much gold as well. The amount of gold was 120 talents (9:14; ca. 9,000 pounds). But when Hiram visited the 20 towns . . . he was disappointed; they were apparently located near unproductive land. Hiram called them the Land of Cabul

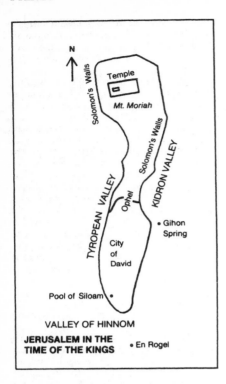

N

Temple

Mt. Moriah

Solomon's Walls

Solomon's Walls

KIDRON VALLEY

TYROPEAN VALLEY

Ophel

• Gihon
Spring

City
of
David

Pool of Siloam •

VALLEY OF HINNOM

**JERUSALEM IN THE
TIME OF THE KINGS**   • En Rogel

("Cabul" sounds like the Heb. for "good-for-nothing").

b. His public works (9:15-19)

9:15. In addition to the **temple** (chap. 6) and his **palace** (7:1-12) **Solomon** built **supporting terraces** (probably large level areas between hills made by filling in land), and **the wall of Jerusalem** which he extended farther to the north, more than doubling the size of the city. His wall surrounded the temple and probably the palace which were built to the north of the old City of David (see the map "Jerusalem in the Time of the Kings"). **Hazor, Meggido, and Gezer** were fortress cities. Hazor, north of the Sea of Kinnereth, guarded the northern part of the kingdom. Meggido protected the Valley of Jezreel that stretched from west to east in the central sector of Israel. And Gezer served as a site of defense in western Judah where it discouraged potential southern and western aggressors from attacking Israel. Israel was stronger and wealthier under Solomon than under

any of its other kings.

9:16-19. Gezer had previously been **captured** and burned by Egypt's **king,** its residents had been executed, and the town had been given by **Pharaoh** as a part of his dowry for **his daughter** who had married Solomon. **Solomon** then **rebuilt** and fortified **Gezer. Lower Beth Horon** (as well as Upper Beth Horon) and Gezer were important defense towns for protection against attacks from Israel's southwest. **Baalath** stood near Gezer. **Tadmor** (later named Palmyra) was located on a caravan route between Damascus and the Euphrates River to Israel's northeast.

Solomon's **store cities,** scattered throughout Israel, were fortified towns in which surplus food was stockpiled. **The towns** where he kept **his chariots and . . . horses** were ready to defend Israel against any invader. Solomon also built up other towns throughout his kingdom for various other purposes.

c. His labor force (9:20-23)

9:20-23. Solomon used **slave labor** for his building projects. The **descendants** of the conquered native tribes did the hardest manual labor. (On the various population elements not conquered in the Conquest see comments on 2 Chron. 8:7.) **The Israelites** served as soldiers and supervisors. The labor force was obviously very large. (On the **550** supervisors along with the 3,300 foremen mentioned in 1 Kings 5:16, see comments there.)

d. His house for Pharaoh's daughter (9:24)

9:24. Solomon also built **terraces** by filling in land near the residence he had built for **Pharaoh's daughter** in his **palace** complex (cf. 7:8). She moved there from her other residence in the **City of David** after the palace was completed.

e. His annual offerings (9:25)

9:25. All the offerings mentioned were for worship (on the **burnt offerings** cf. Lev. 1, and on the **fellowship offerings** cf. Lev. 3). The **three** annual occasions were perhaps the Feast of Unleavened Bread, the Feast of Harvest (also called Weeks and Pentecost), and the Feast of Tabernacles (also called Ingathering) since these were the major feasts of Israel (cf. Ex. 23:14-16).

f. His navy (9:26-28)

9:26-28. Archeologists have discovered the remains of **Ezion Geber** at the northern tip of the Gulf of Aqaba. This site, on the east arm of **the Red Sea,** gave Israel access to the east and south by water. Hiram's Phoenician **sailors,** who joined **Solomon's,** were some of the most skillful of their day. **Ophir** was probably in southwestern Arabia (cf. 10:11; Job 22:24; 28:16). The vast amounts **of gold** brought in from expeditions to these lands helped finance and decorate Solomon's vast building projects. While 1 Kings 9:28 has **420 talents** (ca. 16 tons, or 32,000 pounds), 2 Chronicles 8:18 has 450 (see comments on that verse).

3. SOLOMON'S GLORY (CHAP. 10)

a. The queen of Sheba's visit (10:1-13)

This incident seems to have been included here to support the statements made previously that Solomon's reign was so glorious that rulers from all over the world came to see his kingdom and observe his wisdom (4:34). Its function is similar to the story of the two prostitutes (3:16-28) which also illustrated Solomon's wisdom. Interestingly both stories pertain to women, though of different social strata.

10:1-5. Sheba is modern Yemen (not Ethiopia), in Arabia, about 1,200 miles from Jerusalem. Sheba may be the land of the Sabeans (cf. Job 1:15; Ezek. 23:42; Joel 3:8). Solomon's expeditions to the east by sea (cf. 1 Kings 9:26-28) would have brought him news of this prosperous and important Arabian kingdom. The queen's primary purpose in visiting **Solomon** seems to have been to see if he was really as wise and wealthy as she had heard (**she came to test him**). Such testing was a sport among ancient Near Eastern monarchs. Probably **the queen** was interested in discussing trade and perhaps defense arrangements as well. Her **very great caravan** reflected her own prestige and also carried her money and expensive gifts for **Solomon.** Visiting heads of state still commonly bring costly gifts to their hosts. **The queen** was especially impressed with Solomon's **wisdom . . . palace . . . food . . . officials . . . servants,** and **burnt offerings** to Yahweh.

10:6-9. Originally skeptical, the queen admitted that Solomon's **wisdom**

and wealth . . . far exceeded what she had been told. Though probably a pagan, she was willing to credit the LORD with giving Israel a wise **king** in whom He **delighted.**

10:10. The queen was quite wealthy herself. **She gave** Solomon **120 talents of gold** (ca. 4½ tons), great **quantities of spices, and precious stones** (cf. v. 2).

10:11-12. These verses, which seem out of place here, may reflect a trade arrangement that resulted from the queen's visit. **Ophir** may have been close to or a part of the queen's kingdom of Sheba (cf. 9:28). **Almugwood** is strong, beautiful (black outside, ruby red inside), and long-lasting. Solomon used it in the **temple** steps (cf. 2 Chron. 9:11) as well as for the other purposes mentioned here.

10:13. Solomon gave the queen gifts, **all she desired and asked for** from him. She **then** began the long trip back home **to her** people.

b. Solomon's riches (10:14-29)

This section summarizes Solomon's wealth.

10:14-15. The revenue of **gold** recorded as being **received** annually (almost 25 tons, or 50,000 pounds) did not include what must have been vast quantities required from trading with **all the Arabian kings** and taxes brought in by **the governors** of Israel. God had told His kings not to multiply gold (Deut. 17:17), but Solomon disobeyed.

10:16-17. The Palace of the Forest of Lebanon (cf. 7:2-5; 10:21) must have served as an armory among other things. Each **large . . . shield** was made of **600 bekas** (7½ pounds) **of gold** and each **small . . . shield** had **three minas** (3¾ pounds) **of gold.** (In 2 Chron. 9:16 the small shields are said to be made of 300 bekas of gold. But that is the same amount expressed in a different unit of measure.) Evidently these 500 shields were intended for parade use rather than for battle as **gold** is a soft metal.

10:18-22. Solomon's **throne . . . overlaid with gold** reflected the king's glory. The **12 lions,** one on each end of **the six steps** to the throne, may have been intended to represent the 12 tribes of Israel. The wealth of Solomon's kingdom could be seen in the abundance of **gold** which made **silver of** comparatively **little value** even though it was a precious metal. Solomon's **fleet** of traders brought riches from distant lands. The **apes and baboons** may have been pets in vogue at the time.

10:23-25. God's promise to make **Solomon** the richest and wisest king of his time was fulfilled. His wealth continued to increase as people (**the whole world** is a hyperbole) who came **to hear** his **wisdom** brought him **gold** and silver **articles . . . spices,** and animals.

10:26-29. Chariots were the most effective and dreaded military machines of that day. Their mobility and versatility gave Israel a great military advantage and discouraged enemies from invading the wealthy nation. Solomon's **chariot cities,** some have suggested, were Gezer, Hazor, and Megiddo. He purchased **horses . . . from Egypt** (or perhaps Musri, in Asia Minor) **and from Kue** (probably Cilicia in modern-day Turkey). He bought **a chariot** for **600** silver **shekels** (ca. 15 pounds) and **a horse** cost **150** silver shekels (ca. 3¾ pounds). In exporting some of them to **the Hittites** and the **Arameans** he presumably made a profit on them.

Though Solomon's wealth enabled him to purchase large quantities of **horses** and **chariots,** this practice was specifically prohibited in the Mosaic Law (Deut. 17:16). The reason for this prohibition was that the Lord wanted His people to depend on Him for their protection. The presence of strong physical defenses in Israel turned the hearts of Solomon and the people away from the Lord with a false sense of security. As is often the case, an abundance of material benefits leads people to think they have no needs when in reality their need for God never diminishes.

4. SOLOMON'S APOSTASY (CHAP. 11)

The internal weaknesses of Solomon's reign which have been only hinted at so far come into full view in this chapter.

a. His foreign wives (11:1-8)

11:1-8. Besides a **king** being forbidden by God to increase the number of his horses (Deut. 17:16; cf. comments on 1 Kings 10:26-29), a king was also forbidden by God to marry **many** wives "or his heart will be led astray" (Deut. 17:17). This is precisely what happened to **Solomon.** His palace apparently included a harem; **He had 700 wives** and **300 concubines.** Solomon's pagan **wives** led him into idolatry just as God had warned (Ex. 23:31-33; 34:15-16; Deut. 7:1-4). **Solomon** did not abandon Yahweh but he worshiped other gods as well. **His heart was not fully devoted to the** LORD; he compromised his affections. Apparently he concluded that since he was a great king he should live like the other great kings of the world even though it meant disobeying God's Word.

As Solomon grew older he got farther away from God (cf. 1 Kings 11:33). **Ashtoreth** was a **goddess of** sex and fertility whose worship involved licentious rites and worship of the stars. She was a vile goddess (cf. 2 Kings 23:13). **Molech** worship involved human sacrifices, especially children, which was strictly prohibited by the Law (Lev. 18:21; 20:1-5). **Chemosh** worship was equally cruel and licentious. The **hill east of Jerusalem** on which **Solomon built . . . high** places may have been the Mount of Olives (cf. 2 Kings 23:13).

b. His sentence from God (11:9-13)

11:9-13. The reason for God's judgment of Solomon is clear: **his heart had turned away from the** LORD (cf. v. 4). Solomon's great sin was a change in his **attitude** toward **God** (v. 11). This happened despite the two times God had revealed Himself to Solomon, making promises to him (3:5; 9:2). His decision to pursue **other gods** led to his disobeying (11:10) God's specific command against idolatry (9:6-7).

One of Solomon's **subordinates** (11:11) was Jeroboam, who tore **the kingdom . . . from** Solomon's **son.** The **one tribe** (v. 13) that God left in Rehoboam's hand was Judah. Actually two tribes were left (Judah and Benjamin) but Benjamin was small and the two became known as the Southern Kingdom of Judah. The tribe of Simeon had been given territory south of Judah but later at least part of Simeon moved north (see comments on Josh. 19:1-9). It was **for** David's **sake** that God tempered His judgment with mercy, and did not allow the split in Solomon's day. Whereas David had sinned against God deliberately, his heart remained devoted to the Lord, which is why his sin was not so serious as Solo-

Kings of Aram in 1 and 2 Kings

Kings	Dates	Scripture References
Rezon (=Hezion)	ca. 940–915	1 Kings 11:23, 25; 15:18
Tabrimmon	ca. 915–900	1 Kings 15:18
Ben-Hadad I	ca. 900–860	1 Kings 15:18, 20
Ben-Hadad II	ca. 860–841	1 Kings 20; 2 Kings 6:24; 8:7, 9, 14
Hazael	841–801	1 Kings 19:15, 17; 2 Kings 8; 9:14-15; 10:32; 12:17-18; 13:3, 22, 24-25
Ben-Hadad III	ca. 801–?	2 Kings 13:3, 24-25
Rezin	?–732	2 Kings 15:37; 16:5-6, 9 (cf. Isa. 7:1, 4, 8; 8:6; 9:11)

mon's. The greatest commandment is to love God with all one's heart (Deut. 6:5).

c. His external adversaries (11:14-25)

11:14-22. Hadad was a prince of **Edom,** Israel's ancient enemy to the southeast. **When David was** at war **with Edom,** Hadad, then a boy, escaped to Egypt. On the way he went **from Midian,** a kingdom south of Edom and east of the modern-day Gulf of Aqaba, **to Paran,** an area in the Sinai Peninsula between Midian and **Egypt. Pharaoh** took him in and even **gave him a** sister-in-law **in marriage.**

The ancient hostility of the Edomites toward the Israelites must have been aggravated in Hadad's mind by David's slaughter of the Edomites, and **Hadad** lived for the day he could take revenge. Hearing **that David** had died (in 971 B.C.) and that **Joab** was also dead **Hadad** asked **Pharaoh** for permission to go back to Edom. Apparently he caused trouble for Solomon militarily (cf. v. 25).

11:23-25. Another enemy of **Solomon** was the rebel **Rezon** (see the chart "Kings of Aram in 1 and 2 Kings"). He was from **Zobah,** a kingdom just south of Damascus (cf. 2 Sam. 8:3-6). Rezon went with some other **rebels** to **Damascus,** the capital of Aram, and **took control** there.

d. His internal adversary (11:26-40)

11:26-28. Jeroboam was from Ephra-

im, the leading tribe of Israel's Northern Kingdom. Apparently he had worked for **Solomon** when the king **built the supporting terraces and . . . filled in the gap in the wall of the City of David.** As a result of his good work **Solomon** promoted him over **the whole** forced **labor force** of the tribes of Ephraim and Manasseh (the house of Joseph).

11:29-33. Ahijah the prophet (who was sought out later by Jeroboam, 14:1-18) graphically demonstrated to **Jeroboam** the division of **the kingdom** by tearing his own **new cloak** in **12 pieces** and giving 10 to **Jeroboam.** This must have impressed Jeroboam greatly. The **one tribe** (11:32) to be left with Solomon was Judah (cf. comments on v. 13). Actually two were left—Judah and Benjamin—which were often regarded as one tribe and referred to as Judah. This portrayal by **Ahijah** demonstrated what God had said earlier to Solomon (vv. 11-13). Not only Solomon but also the people of Israel (**they,** v. 33) had **forsaken** Yahweh by worshiping idols (cf. comments on **Ashtoreth . . . Chemosh,** and **Molech** in vv. 5-7).

11:34-39. Solomon's **son** (v. 35) was Rehoboam to whom would be given **one tribe** (cf. vv. 13, 32). Like a **lamp** kept burning perpetually in a tent or home, Judah would be a perpetual testimony to God's choice of **David,** who was of the tribe of Judah (cf. 15:4; 2 Sam. 21:17;

2 Kings 8:19).

Jeroboam was told that he would **rule over all that** his **heart** desired (1 Kings 11:37) in **Israel,** that is, he would have freedom to rule as he saw fit. It is remarkable that God's conditional promise to establish Jeroboam's line (v. 38) was similar to His unconditional promise to establish David's line (v. 38). Unfortunately Jeroboam did not value this promise but forfeited it. God prophesied that He would **humble David's descendants . . . but not forever.** This ending of the humbling was fulfilled in the birth of Jesus Christ, David's greatest Son (i.e., Descendant). All that Ahijah prophesied came to pass.

11:40. The reason **Solomon tried to kill Jeroboam** is not stated. Perhaps **Jeroboam** tried to take matters into his own hands and seize the kingdom. Or he may have done something else that made it necessary for him to flee **to Shishak the king** (Pharaoh) of **Egypt** (cf. Hadad's escape to Egypt, vv. 14-22). Shishak (945–924), also known as Sheshonk I, later invaded Judah (2 Chron. 12:2-4) and Jerusalem (1 Kings 14:25-26) in Rehoboam's reign.

e. His death (11:41-43)

11:41-43. The writer of 1 and 2 Kings was led by the Spirit of God to record no more **events of Solomon's reign** though others were preserved in **the book of the annals of Solomon,** which is not extant today (cf. comments on 14:19). This is the first of several such sources mentioned in 1 Kings (cf. 14:19, 29) and 2 Chronicles (cf. 2 Chron. 9:29; 12:15; 26:22; 32:32). **Solomon reigned** for **40 years** (971–931 B.C.). After he died he was given an honorable burial **in the City of David** (cf. comments on 1 Kings 2:10).

Solomon's life ended in tragedy. Solomon was greatly blessed by God but he allowed God's gifts to dominate his affections. The fault lay not with God for giving Solomon so much, but with Solomon who, though he had the wisdom to deal with such temptations, chose to set his affections on the gifts and not on the Giver. The man best qualified to live life successfully chose not to do so. Success in life in the eyes of God does not come automatically with the possession of wisdom but with the applicaton of wisdom to one's life. Spiritual success depends not only on insight but also on choices.

II. The Earlier History of the Divided Kingdom (chaps. 12–22)

The fatal division of the kingdom of Israel into two nations resulted from a foolish decision by Solomon's son, Rehoboam. However, the tribes that separated had a long history of antagonism that had threatened for many years to split Israel. Judah, the largest tribe in population, enjoyed prominence as the leader of the other tribes in the wilderness march. Judah received the largest area in the Promised Land because of its large population. But Ephraim was the preferred son of Joseph, and though that tribe was not large, it demonstrated a feeling of superiority on occasion (cf. Jud. 9:1-3 [Shechem was in Ephraim]; 12:1-6). The Northern tribes led by Ephraim separated from their brethren to the south briefly during David's reign (2 Sam. 19:41–20:22). So a fault line had developed between these two groups of tribes that opened up and split the monarchy at this stressful time in its history.

A. The division of the kingdom (12:1-24)

The date when Israel passed from a united to a divided monarchy was 931 B.C.

1. REHOBOAM'S DILEMMA (12:1-5)

12:1. Shechem afforded a fitting site for the coronation of a **king** of Israel. At Shechem Yahweh first appeared to Abraham in the land and promised to give him all of Canaan (Gen. 12:6-7). Jacob later settled there (Gen. 33:18-20) and Joseph was buried there (Josh. 24:32). After they had entered the Promised Land the Israelites, at Shechem in the valley between Mount Ebal and Mount Gerizim, dedicated themselves to keep the Mosaic Law (Josh. 24:1-27). This sacred spot now reminded **the Israelites** of their divinely revealed destiny as a nation and of God's faithfulness.

12:2-5. Evidently the heads of the Northern tribes under the leadership of the Ephraimites **sent for Jeroboam,** who apparently had just returned from exile in **Egypt** after Solomon's death (cf. 11:40). They wanted him to present their plea for lower taxes **to Rehoboam.** They did this sometime during the coronation festivities. Perhaps **Jeroboam** served as their spokesman. Jeroboam had, of course, been told by the Prophet Ahijah that the kingdom would be divided and that he would rule 10 of the tribes (11:31-39). But he seems to have decided to let events take their course rather than initiating an unprovoked revolution. By reducing the tax load and by lightening the **labor** conscription requirements on his people, King **Rehoboam** could have won the support of his petitioners. But he said that he wanted **three days** to think about their suggestion.

2. REHOBOAM'S COUNSELORS (12:6-11)

12:6-7. The king asked two groups of counselors for their advice. **The elders** were probably about the same age as **his father Solomon,** having **served** as the former king's official advisers; they were elders both by reason of years and by their office in the government. This group's counsel was wise—to lighten the tax and work load, as the people asked. If taken, this advice would have resulted in peace, at least for a time.

12:8-11. Perhaps to appear in control **Rehoboam rejected** this good **advice** and turned to his contemporaries for their opinions. The younger men's counsel was the opposite from what **the elders** had given, but just what Rehoboam wanted to hear. The king was no child at this time; he was 41 years old (14:21). Nor was his decision made on the spur of the moment; he had three days to think it over (12:5). It was a deliberate choice possibly based on what he believed was needed most in the nation at that time.

The wording of Rehoboam's reply to his petitioners, as suggested by his younger advisers, seems almost designed to provoke hostility: he would be far more harsh than his **father,** for his **little finger** was **thicker than** his **father's waist** (an obvious hyperbole intended to express his greater power) and he would **scourge . . . with scorpions** not with his father's **whips.** Perhaps the king and his counselors thought intimidation would send the potential rebels scurrying for cover and would drive any ideas of insurrection far from their minds. "Scorpions" refers to a particularly cruel kind of whip used in that day, with sharp pieces of metal.

3. REHOBOAM'S DECISION (12:12-15)

12:12-15. The king followed through with his decision and delivered his insulting threat to his petitioners (vv. 13-14; cf. vv. 10-11). Rather than listening **to the people** Rehoboam put his own interests first. **This turn of events,** the writer noted, **was from the** LORD (v. 15) in fulfillment of His prophecy through Ahijah (11:31-39). God's judgment because of Solomon's apostasy was being carried out (11:11-13).

4. ISRAEL'S REBELLION (12:16-20)

12:16-17. Rehoboam's insensitivity to the Israelites' hardships extinguished any hope they may have entertained of economic recovery. His dictatorial threat alienated his suffering subjects. Then and there they seceded and broke the union of the 12 tribes. Only Rehoboam's closest countrymen from **Judah** did not abandon him. The reply of the Israelites (v. 16) evidently had become a battle cry; it was used years earlier by Sheba who rebelled against David (2 Sam. 20:1).

12:18-19. What could have motivated **Rehoboam** to send **Adoniram** (a variant spelling of the Heb. Adoram; cf. NIV marg.), the personification of oppression, (the foreman **of forced labor**), to meet with the rebels at that crucial moment? Perhaps Adoniram was the best-qualified ambassador. Whatever the reason, Rehoboam's "wisdom" proved foolish again. Adoniram died as the target of the rebels' wrath. And **Rehoboam** barely escaped with his own life. What should have been a glorious national celebration (v. 1) turned into a humiliating rout for Judah's new king who fled his own coronation to **escape** assassination by his infuriated subjects. The writer noted that the Israelites were really rebelling **against the house of David,** God's appointed dynasty, which they did **to this day** (i.e., the time this section of the book was written).

12:20. Rehoboam's coronation turned into Jeroboam's coronation. The people brought **Jeroboam** forward and **made him king** then and there. This action suggests that plotting had been involved in the rebellion. **Only . . . Judah** (and Benjamin, v. 21) **remained loyal to the** ruler from David's **house** (dynasty).

5. REHOBOAM'S REPRISAL (12:21-24)

12:21. Having failed to preserve unity through diplomacy **Rehoboam** sought to restore it by force. **The tribe of Benjamin** was Judah's immediate neighbor to the north. The capital city of **Jerusalem** lay almost on the Judah-Benjamin border. Probably for the sake of their close neighbors and the capital, the Benjamites sided with **Judah.** Together these tribes called up **180,000** soldiers to fight their brothers in the 10 tribes to the north. **12:22-24.** Rehoboam's battle plans were interrupted by a prophet of Yahweh, **Shemaiah. The man of God** made a public announcement that civil war was definitely not God's will and he convinced **Rehoboam** and **the people** to go back **home.** To his credit Rehoboam **obeyed the word of the LORD** and did not proceed into battle. Again the writer pointed out the overruling hand of **God** in these affairs (**as the LORD had ordered,** v. 24; cf. v. 15).

B. Jeroboam's evil reign in Israel (12:25–14:20)

Jeroboam could have been an instrument of blessing for Israel. He was divinely chosen and given promises that his dynasty would continue and prosper if he obeyed the Lord (11:38-39). But Jeroboam did not trust or obey the Lord; he committed many serious sins that resulted in the Israelites turning *from* God rather than *to* Him. He planted seeds that bore bitter fruit for Israel as long as it continued as a nation. Twenty kings ruled the Northern Kingdom and not one of them turned the people back to the Lord. Instead of one stable dynasty, Israel experienced several dynasties (see the chart "Kings of Judah and Israel and the Preexilic Prophets").

1. JEROBOAM'S IDOLATRY (12:25-33)

12:25. Jeroboam chose **Shechem** (where Rehoboam had been crowned, v. 1) as his capital and began at once to fortify it as his stronghold. During its history the Northern Kingdom had three capitals: Shechem, Tirzah (14:17; 15:33), and Samaria (16:23-24). (See the map "Solomon's 12 Districts and Surrounding Nations," near 4:17-19.) Jeroboam also **built up Peniel** (see the map) as a fortress east of the Jordan River, probably to protect Israel from invasion from the east by the Gileadites, who had been consistently loyal to David.

12:26-27. Jeroboam's musings reveal an evil heart of unbelief. Rather than believing God's promise to establish his dynasty (cf. 11:31, 37-38), the king sought security by turning the people away from God. His fears that the **people** might **revert to the house** (dynasty) **of David,** that is, to **Rehoboam,** were understandable, but God had told him that He would keep Israel for the house of **Jeroboam.** Fear for his personal safety crept in when he stopped trusting God.

12:28. The king's "reforms" all involved religious apostasy. This is why he was such an evil influence in **Israel.** His changes struck at the heart of Israel's strength, her relationship with God. They polluted Israel for generations. Jeroboam researched his ideas; he sought **advice** about how to maintain the secession effectively.

The first change involved new religious symbols. To prevent the Israelites from returning to their magnificent temple and the ark in **Jerusalem** (cf. v. 27) Jeroboam offered substitute objects: **two golden calves** or bulls. Perhaps he actually intended the people to turn from worshiping Yahweh to worshiping his golden idols. His words, **Here are your gods . . . who** delivered **you** from **Egypt,** suggest this.

It is probable, however, that the king may have set up these calves as aids to the worship of Yahweh (W.F. Albright, *From the Stone Age to Christianity.* Rev. ed. Baltimore: Johns Hopkins University Press, 1957, p. 299). This suggestion has the support of ancient Near Eastern tradition which conceived of an image as a support or pedestal for one's god. Jeroboam's decision may have been influenced by what he had seen in Egypt where a bull was commonly used to represent or support a god. Or perhaps more likely, his action was influenced by the Canaanites' similar practice regarding Baal. He seems to have been poorly informed concerning Israel's history, however, since a former golden calf had brought God's wrath down on the Israelites in the wilderness (Ex. 32). Whatever their original purpose these calves became the objects of Israel's worship (cf. Hosea 8:5-6; 13:2-3).

12:29-30. New sanctuaries were also

Kings of Judah and Israel and the Preexilic Prophets

JUDAH

Kings*	Dates	Years
Rehoboam	931–913	17
Abijah	913–911	3
Asa Coregency† with Jehoshaphat	911–870 873–870	41 (3)
Jehoshaphat Coregency with Jehoram	873–848 853–848	25 (5)
Jehoram OBADIAH**	848–841	8
Ahaziah‡	841	1
Queen Athaliah‡	841–835	6
Joash‡ JOEL**	835–796	40
Amaziah‡ Azariah's vice-regency under Amaziah	796–767 790–767	29 (23)
Azariah (Uzziah) Coregency with Jotham	790–739 750–739	52 (11)
Jotham Ahaz's vice-regency under Jotham Coregency of Jotham with Ahaz	750–735 744–735 735–732	16 (9) 4
Ahaz Hezekiah's vice-regency under Ahaz	732–715 729–715	16 (14)
Hezekiah Manasseh's vice-regency under Hezekiah	715–686 697–686	29 (11)
Manasseh NAHUM	697–642	55
Amon‡	642–640	2
Josiah ZEPHANIAH	640–609	31
Jehoahaz	609	1/4
Jehoiakim HABAKKUK	609–598	11
Jehoiachin	598–597	1/4
Zedekiah	597–586	11

(Prophet brackets along left margin: MICAH, ISAIAH, JEREMIAH)

ISRAEL

Dynasty§	Kings	Dates	Years
1st Dynasty	Jeroboam I	931–910	22
"	Nadab‡	910–909	2
2nd Dynasty	Baasha	909–886	24
"	Elah‡	886–885	2
3rd Dynasty	Zimri	885	7 days
—	Tibni Overlapping reign† with Omri	885–880 885–880	6 (6)
4th Dynasty	Omri	885–874	12
"	Ahab	874–853	22
"	Ahaziah	853–852	2
"	Jehoram (Joram)‡	852–841	12
5th Dynasty	Jehu	841–814	28
"	Jehoahaz	814–798	17
"	Jehoash (Joash) Coregency with Jeroboam II	798–782 793–782	16 (11)
"	Jeroboam II JONAH AMOS	793–753	41
"	Zechariah‡	753–752	1/2
6th Dynasty	Shallum‡	752	1/12
7th Dynasty	Menahem Overlapping reign with Pekah	752–742 752–742	10 (10)
"	Pekahiah‡ Overlapping reign with Pekah	742–742 742–740	(2) (2)
8th Dynasty	Pekah‡	752–732	20
9th Dynasty	Hoshea	732–722	9

(Prophet brackets along left of Israel kings: ELIJAH, ELISHA, HOSEA)

---

*Includes one queen (Athaliah).

†In a coregency the kings ruled together; in overlapping reigns they reigned separately; in a vice-regency a son ruled with his father in a subordinate position.

‡These kings and one queen were assassinated.

§A dynasty is a succession of rulers who are members of the same family or a single ruler of a family different from those before and after him. (The kings of Judah were all of one dynasty because they were all descendants of David.)

**Evangelical scholars differ on the dates of Obadiah and Joel. Some place them at later dates (see the *Introductions* to Joel and Obad.).

Note: In some kings' reigns the dates (e.g., Rehoboam, 931–913), when subtracted, may vary from the number in the "Years" column for that king. This is because the beginning and ending dates for a given king may include only portions of those years in the Gregorian calendar.

The dates of the kings are adapted from Edwin R. Thiele, *The Mysterious Numbers of the Hebrew Kings.* 3rd ed. Grand Rapids: Zondervan Publishing House, 1983.

built to house these calves to replace the temple that contained the ark with its golden cherubim. These were located in the towns of **Dan** in far northern Israel and **Bethel** just north of the Judean border in southern Israel (see the map "Solomon's 12 Districts and Surrounding Nations," near 4:17-19). **The people** were told to conduct pilgrimages to these places rather than traveling to Jerusalem. Thus the Israelites could find a sense of fulfillment in going through similar forms of **worship** (rituals) though they were being disobedient to God.

12:31. New **priests** were **appointed . . . from all sorts of people. . . not** from the **Levites** as God had directed. Jeroboam dismissed the Levitical priests who then migrated to Judah (2 Chron. 11:14). The new priests conducted religious rites for the people at **shrines** Jeroboam **built** at various **high places** convenient to them. This accommodation again gave the people a feeling that they could worship as much as they pleased so they felt less longing for their former ways of worship.

12:32-33. Jeroboam **instituted a** new **festival . . . like the festival held in Judah,** a carefully designed counterfeit of the Day of Atonement. Israel's festival was held **in Bethel** and in **the eighth month** (October-November) exactly one month later than Judah's, **a month of** Jeroboam's **own choosing. Priests . . . sacrifices,** and an **altar** were all provided to make Israel's festival just as good as if not "better" than Judah's. But Israel's feast was designed by Jeroboam whereas Judah's feasts had been decreed by God. Jeroboam set the example for his people; he personally **went up to the altar** at Bethel **to make offerings.**

2. THE MAN OF GOD FROM JUDAH (13:1-32)

Jeroboam's idolatrous system of worship (12:28-33) was soon condemned by a prophet of the Lord. This man's experiences point out the evil of what Jeroboam did and how deceptive it was. Then the prophet himself fell into a trap.

a. His prophecy (13:1-10)

13:1-3. The mission of this anonymous **man of God** had its origin in **the word of the LORD** (vv. 1-2, 9); this was a prophecy of judgment fully authorized by God. The prophet was sent **from** the Southern Kingdom of **Judah to Bethel;** he lived under the authority of God's Davidic ruler rather than under the influence of the apostate Jeroboam. He uttered his prophecy publicly at the altar **as Jeroboam was standing** near it **offering** a sacrifice.

This man's prophecy is one of the most remarkable in Scripture because it predicted the name and actions of a king who would not appear on the scene for 290 years. **Josiah,** who reigned from 640 to 609 B.C., fulfilled this prophecy just as the man of God predicted (2 Kings 23:15-20). Josiah demolished the Bethel **altar** built by Jeroboam and slaughtered the false **priests** there. **A sign** was often given in prophecies of this kind when the fulfillment would take place many years later. The man of God predicted that **the sign,** a miracle to verify the prophecy, would be performed then. The sign, he said, was that **the altar** would **split apart** that very **day** (cf. 1 Kings 13:5).

13:4-6. Jeroboam's reaction to the prophecy was to order the arrest of the prophet. When the king's outstretched **hand,** symbolizing his authority, withered, this illustrated that God's authority was greater than Jeroboam's. **God** could paralyze Jeroboam's might and render it completely useless. The sign (**the altar** splitting **apart**; cf. v. 3) also left no doubt in the minds of those present that the prophecy came from the **God** who controlled Jeroboam and who would judge his wickedness.

The king acknowledged God's power and asked **the man of God** to ask **God** to restore his **hand,** which God graciously did. Jeroboam referred to Yahweh as **your God,** not "my God," thereby testifying to his own idolatry.

13:7-10. Receiving an immediate cure for his hand's paralysis (cf. v. 6), **the king** extended a great favor and privilege to the prophet. He offered the shelter of his royal palace, a meal, and **a gift.** In the ancient Near East hospitality was a sacred custom. **To eat** a meal with an invited guest under one's roof was to give him a promise of continuing personal protection. **But the man of God** wanted no treaty with wicked Jeroboam. He had been instructed by God not to accept even a meal, which would have placed him in Jeroboam's debt.

Returning home by a different route

would have further illustrated the official nature of the prophet's visit; this was not a pleasure trip, but he was in **Bethel** on business for God. The prophet had obeyed God faithfully up to this point.

b. His seduction (13:11-19)

This somewhat confusing story may appear at first to contribute nothing to the advancement of the narrative or the writer's purpose. But careful study clarifies its value.

13:11-14. A second **prophet** was **living in Bethel** and was **old.** These are important clues. Old age sometimes tends to make one lazy and complacent. This man's complacency is further suggested by his willingness not only to live in the territory of the apostate king but at the very center of the king's false system of worship.

Why the old prophet **rode after** the prophet **from Judah** is not stated. Perhaps he simply wanted to visit with a younger, more faithful servant of the Lord. Or his motive from the beginning could have been jealousy and his intent could have been to destroy the younger prophet's ministry.

13:15-19. In response to the faithful prophet's refusal, **the old** man claimed direct revelation from God through **an angel** who had told him, he said, that the young man should forget his former instructions from **the Lord.** So the prophet of Judah, not suspecting that the old prophet **was lying to him . . . returned** to Bethel and ate **with him.** The apostasy of Jeroboam had infected even a prophet who seems to have had the same selfish motives and practiced the same brazen disobedience as the king. The spirit of apostasy was spreading quickly and was already reaping a grim harvest in Israel.

c. His death and burial (13:20-32)

13:20-22. Even though **the old prophet** had sinned, **the word of the Lord came to** him again, as it did to many other prophets of the Lord who sinned (e.g., Jonah, Elijah). The old man announced the fate of his brother prophet then and there. The younger prophet, because he had disobeyed the Lord's **command,** would not be given an honorable burial. The severity of God's judgment on this man, compared with His dealings with the older prophet who was

also disobedient, seems unfair. But the severity of God's judgment was proportionate to the importance of the younger man's mission. All Israel would have heard about his prophecy of God's judgment on Jeroboam for his disobedience to the word of the Lord through Moses. If God had not judged His own prophet for *his* disobedience to the word given him by God and which he had announced publicly, doubt would have been cast on his prophecy and on God's credibility. By comparison the older prophet's sins were private and were judged privately by God.

13:23-32. Lions **on the road** were not common in Israel, but neither were they unknown. Wild animals roamed the land (cf. Jud. 14:5) and occasionally **killed** people. That this beast was divinely sent to judge the younger prophet is clear in that after the **lion** killed the man he stood **beside** the **body** and **neither** ate the corpse nor **mauled the donkey** (1 Kings 13:28). The death of the prophet became public knowledge (v. 25). Out of reverence for **the man of God** the **old prophet . . . picked up** his **body,** mourned **for him, and** buried **him** (v. 29) **in his own tomb** (v. 30). The old prophet undoubtedly suffered the pains of a guilty conscience for having had a part in the man of God's death. He was convinced the prophecy about Josiah would come to pass (v. 32; cf. v. 2).

This story clarifies the importance of consistent and complete obedience to the Word of God, the lesson God was seeking to impress on Jeroboam and His people at that time. It also illustrates that added privilege brings increased responsibility; God dealt with the prophet who had the greater responsibility more severely than he did with the man who had less. The effects of spiritual apostasy even on God's servants can be seen too, especially in the behavior of the older prophet.

3. JEROBOAM'S PERSISTENT APOSTASY (13:33-34)

13:33-34. That the preceding incident was intended to teach Jeroboam and the Israelites the danger of disregarding the word of the Lord seems clear from this brief passage. The king's sins had been recounted (12:25-33), then he was warned (13:1-32), but still **Jeroboam did**

not change his evil ways. Though the appointing of just **anyone** to the priestly office is singled out (v. 33; cf. 12:31) and was perhaps the most serious aspect of his apostasy, it was his total disregard for the will of God as expressed in the Law of Moses that resulted in Jeroboam's **downfall** and **destruction. This was the sin** (i.e., apostasy) from which many others grew. Though God used political situations and social conditions to bring about His ends, this sin by **Jeroboam** was the root cause of Israel's fall.

4. AHIJAH'S PROPHECY AGAINST JEROBOAM (14:1-18)

Whereas the prophecy of the man of God (13:2) dealt primarily with the destruction of Jeroboam's religious system, Ahijah's prophecy addressed Jeroboam's house (dynasty).

a. The sickness of Jeroboam's son (14:1-5)

14:1-5. At that time probably refers to a time shortly after the incident recorded in chapter 13. Jeroboam's son, **Abijah,** should not be confused with Rehoboam's son of the same name (15:1). Jeroboam's **son** was just a **boy** at this time (14:3, 12, 17). It is not possible to determine what ailed the lad, nor is this information essential to the narrative.

Jeroboam obviously did not believe that Yahweh could or would reveal his wife's identity to the prophet. Perhaps the **king** asked her to **disguise** herself because he did not want other people to observe her visiting a prophet of **the LORD. Ahijah the prophet** was living at **Shiloh,** the former site of the tabernacle in Israel. Jeroboam's allusion to Ahijah's prediction of his coronation (cf. 11:29-39) suggests that perhaps the king hoped to receive another welcome prophecy, this time that his son would recover. The gifts of food sent to **Ahijah** may have been simply customary, but in light of Jeroboam's other actions they seem designed to win a positive word from the prophet. **Ahijah** was old and blind, but God gave him a message and insight into the king's plan.

b. The fate of Jeroboam's dynasty (14:6-18)

14:6-7a. Jeroboam's **wife** hoped to hear a message of deliverance for her boy, but instead she heard a message of doom for her husband, herself, and her son. The prophet quickly unmasked the actress (**Why this pretense?**). The king's wife thought she had been sent to **Ahijah,** but the prophet said he had **been sent to** her. **The LORD** is **the God of Israel,** not the idols **Jeroboam** had set up. The message he had for her came from Him.

14:7b-9. God reminded the king through the prophet that it was He who had **made** him **a leader over** His **people.** But Jeroboam had not followed in David's footsteps as he should have done. In fact God said Jeroboam had **done more evil than all who lived before** him. Whether Jeroboam intended his golden calves to be idols or aids in the worship of Yahweh, God called them **other gods** and **idols.** They were only pieces **of metal.** The king's idolatry had angered the Lord who regarded it as a rejection of Himself.

14:10-11. Because **Jeroboam** had led God's people away from God his **house** (dynasty) would be **cut off.** No **male** would be able to perpetuate his line which God compared to **dung.** Jeroboam's family would not be buried but would be eaten by **dogs** and **birds,** a terrible disgrace in the minds of Semites. (This would also be true of Baasha's family, 16:4, and Ahab's family, 21:24.)

14:12-13. The **only** male descendant of **Jeroboam** to **be buried** would be Abijah, who would die very soon. His death on the return of the queen to her **home** would signify the sure fulfillment of the more distant aspects of Ahijah's prophecy.

14:14-15. Ahijah the prophet said **a king** would be raised up **who** would **cut off** Jeroboam's **family.** This was Baasha (15:27-29). The last part of 14:14, which is subject to several interpretations, probably means that this would surely come to pass. Moreover, the whole nation would experience instability and waver like **a reed. Jeroboam** had planted Israel not in the solid soil of God's Word but in the unsubstantial waters of idolatry, like Egyptian rushes or papyrus reeds. God promised to **uproot** the nation **from the good land that He gave to their forefathers** and to **scatter them beyond the River** Euphrates, which He did in 722 B.C. by the hands of the Assyrians. The Israelites' idolatry was the reason for this judgment. **Asherah poles** (cf. v. 23; 15:13;

16:33) were wooden shafts carved to encourage worship of the Canaanite goddess Asherah.

14:16. God's giving **Israel up** must be understood in a limited sense. He promised Abraham that his descendants would be blessed forever (Gen. 12:2-3; 18:17-18; 22:17-18). Later God brought Israel back from captivity but still has not fulfilled all His promises of blessing which they will yet experience (Isa. 62). God did give them up to judgment in captivity, however, which is the forsaking that is in view here.

14:17-18. These verses record the exact fulfillment of Ahijah's prophecy of the death of Prince Abijah. The queen must have traveled from Shiloh (v. 2) back to her home in **Tirzah** with a heavy heart. Jeroboam had moved to Tirzah from Shechem (cf. 12:25).

As the Lord's word came to pass immediately in the death of the prince, His long-range prophecies also began to take shape in Jeroboam's reign. One may safely assume that all the territory Solomon ruled except Judah came under Jeroboam's control. Much of this was lost during his reign. This lost area included the land around Damascus to the north which became an independent Aramean state. In the southwest the Philistines repossessed some of their former territory and grew stronger (cf. 15:27). On the east Moab was apparently lost. Ironically Jeroboam's protector in Egypt (11:40), Shishak (Sheshonk I), invaded Judah (14:25) during Jeroboam's reign. This resulted in heavy damage and widespread destruction. Jeroboam was also defeated by King Abijah of Judah (2 Chron. 13:13-20). Israel suffered both in military strength and in territorial holdings during Jeroboam's reign.

5. JEROBOAM'S DEATH (14:19-20)

14:19-20. Starting with Jeroboam the events of the reigns of 18 of the 20 kings of the Northern Kingdom are said in 1 and 2 Kings to have been recorded in **the book of the annals of the kings of Israel** (all except Tibni, 1 Kings 16:21-22, and Hoshea, 2 Kings 17:1-6). Similarly the events of the reigns of 14 of the 19 kings of the Southern Kingdom are said in 1 and 2 Kings to be recorded in "the book of the annals of the kings of Judah" (starting with Rehoboam, 1 Kings 14:29).

These books were historical documents, perhaps kept in the royal archives. They are no longer extant. (Also cf. 1 Chron. 27:24, "the book of the annals of King David," and 1 Kings 11:41, "the book of the annals of Solomon," and see "Authorship" in the *Introduction* to 1 Chron.) The writer of 1 Kings selected his material under the inspiration of the Holy Spirit to emphasize the unspiritual aspects of Jeroboam's **22-year** rule over Israel. **Nadab his son succeeded him** on the throne.

Jeroboam must have been a powerful man to have separated Israel from Judah and ruled it for so long a time. But he lacked the commitment to the Lord that would have made him a great and successful king.

C. Rehoboam's evil reign in Judah (14:21-31)

The scene shifts now to the southern monarchy of Judah.

1. REHOBOAM'S WICKEDNESS (14:21-24)

14:21. Rehoboam . . . reigned 17 years (931–913 B.C.). He and all succeeding kings of Judah reigned **in Jerusalem.** Perhaps to contrast this city with the capitals of the Northern Kingdom (Shechem, Tirzah, and Samaria; cf. comments on 12:25) the writer described it as **the city the LORD had chosen,** not like the northern capitals that were chosen by men. The king's mother **Naamah** was one of Solomon's foreign wives. As **an Ammonite** she worshiped the detestable idol-god Molech (cf. 11:5, 33). Probably she was partially responsible for the revival of Canaanite paganism that took place during Rehoboam's reign.

14:22-24. Rehoboam turned from the Lord after he had become established on the throne and was strong (2 Chron. 12:1, 14). This revival of idolatry reintroduced conditions that had prevailed in the days of the Judges before David turned the nation to **the LORD.** The Lord's **jealous anger** was directed at those responsible for the sins that destroyed His beloved people. The **high places** were sometimes places where Yahweh was worshiped but not as He had commanded. The **sacred stones** or pillars **and Asherah poles** (cf. 1 Kings 14:15) were aids to the worship of male and female Canaanite idols. The **high**

hills and **spreading** trees were favorite locations for these cultic shrines. **Male shrine prostitutes** (sodomites) were used in pagan worship. The same practices that moved God to purge the land of the moral cancer that plagued it in Joshua's day were those to which the Israelites returned under Rehoboam's leadership.

2. SHISHAK'S INVASION (14:25-28)

14:25-28. Shishak (cf. 11:40), **king (pharaoh) of Egypt** (945–924 B.C.), also known as Sheshonk I, was the founder of her 22nd dynasty. He had given asylum to Jeroboam earlier (cf. 11:40). In Rehoboam's **fifth year** Shishak tried to establish Egyptian supremacy over Palestine. His military campaign into Judah, Israel, Edom, and Philistia netted him control of 156 cities. The record of his campaigns is inscribed on the exterior of the Amon temple's south wall at Karnak in Egypt. Shishak captured cities in Judah and threatened to besiege **Jerusalem.** This resulted in **Rehoboam** and the leaders humbling themselves before the Lord and God spared Jerusalem from destruction (2 Chron. 12:2-12). Rehoboam bought Shishak off by giving him many of the **treasures of the temple** and **of the . . . palace** (1 Kings 14:26). These included the 500 **gold shields** made by **Solomon** (cf. 10:16-17). These were replaced by less expensive **bronze shields** which were kept locked up and used mainly in escorting **the king** to the **temple.** Shishak's invasion was the first serious attack against Judah by any foreign power since Saul's days. The Egyptian king was not able to subdue Palestine as he had hoped.

3. REHOBOAM'S DEATH (14:29-31)

14:29-30. In addition to **the book of the annals of the kings of Judah** the chronicler noted other contemporary sources where more of Rehoboam's deeds were recorded (2 Chron. 12:13-16). The **continual warfare** mentioned here (1 Kings 14:30) is mentioned briefly again (15:6; cf. 2 Chron. 12:15) but is not explained. In view of Rehoboam's initial plan to regain Israel by force (1 Kings 12:21; which he abandoned after the Prophet Shemaiah reported God's prohibition of civil war, 2 Chron. 11:1-4), these constant wars probably involved border disputes in the territory of Benjamin. It appears that **Rehoboam** was more successful in these border disputes since he won both the hearts and the land of the Benjamites. The exact border probably changed many times in these early years of the divided monarchy.

The 15 cities Rehoboam fortified were located in Judah and Benjamin, south and west of Jerusalem (see the map "Fifteen Judean Cities Fortified by Rehoboam," near 2 Chron. 11:5-10). Probably after Shishak's invasion they were strengthened to defend Judah against future attacks from Egypt and Philistia.

14:31. Rehoboam died **and was buried** in the old **City of David** (cf. comments on 2:10) in Jerusalem. **His mother's name** is given again (cf. 14:21) as part of the regular summary of the kings' reigns. His son **Abijah . . . succeeded him.**

D. Abijah's evil reign in Judah (15:1-8)

1. ABIJAH'S WICKEDNESS (15:1-6)

15:1-2. Abijah's **three**-year reign in **Judah** (913–911 B.C.) was within Jeroboam's **reign** in Israel (931–910 B.C.). **Abijah** was a son of Rehoboam and **Maacah,** a **daughter of** Absalom (**Abishalom** is a variant spelling), David's son. "Daughter" or son does not always mean a descendant in the very next generation; it is often used of a descendant two or more generations removed.

15:3-6. All the sins of Rehoboam refer to the same kinds of idolatrous offenses (cf. 14:23-24). The importance of one's affections is emphasized by the reference to Abijah's **heart**; one's affections often determine his actions. God's patience with Abijah was because of His promises to **David** more than to Abijah's own character. (**Him,** v. 4, refers to **David,** not Abijah.) **A lamp** is a picturesque way of describing a successor or successors who would dispel all kinds of darkness; the figure refers to the whole of David's dynasty (cf. comments on 11:36; also see 2 Sam. 21:17; 2 Kings 8:19).

The **war between Rehoboam and Jeroboam** (cf. 1 Kings 14:30) continued **throughout Abijah's lifetime.** One episode is recorded in 2 Chronicles 13:2-20 where Abijah's trust in God resulted in victory in spite of his being outnumbered. Abijah did not abandon the Lord even though he tolerated idolatry.

2. ABIJAH'S DEATH (15:7-8)

15:7-8. On **the book of the annals of the kings of Judah** see comments on 14:29. The second reference to **war** with **Jeroboam** (cf. 15:6) suggests that the antagonism between Israel and Judah at this time was intense. **Rested with his fathers** is a euphemism for death.

E. Asa's good reign in Judah (15:9-24)

Eight of the 19 kings of Judah were good. That is, their whole reign was evaluated by God as good even though some of their recorded deeds were evil. Four of these good kings led Judah in religious reforms designed to restore the nation to a purer form of worship and to return the people to obeying the Mosaic Law. Asa was the first good king of Judah (v. 11) and the first reformer.

1. ASA'S GOODNESS (15:9-15)

15:9-10. Asa **became king** just shortly before Jeroboam's reign in Israel ended in 910 B.C. Asa **reigned . . . 41 years** (911–870 B.C.). **Maacah** was his grandmother (not "mother" as in some versions; cf. v. 2).

15:11-13. The divine assessment of Asa's rule was that he **did what was right in the eyes of the LORD,** generally speaking. **David,** of course, was Asa's ancestor, not his immediate **father.**

The writer of 2 Chronicles gave much more information about Asa's reign than is found in 1 Kings. Asa's reign began with 10 years of peace (2 Chron. 14:1). It was probably during this period that he instituted his first series of religious reforms (2 Chron. 14:2-5). At that time he also fortified Judah's defenses (2 Chron. 14:6-8). The peace was broken by an invasion by Zerah the Ethiopian, a commander of the Egyptian King Osarkon I. But Asa defeated the Egyptians, though Judah was greatly outnumbered, by relying on the Lord (2 Chron. 14:9-15). The Prophet Azariah warned Asa to continue to trust in God and not to think that his own power had saved him (2 Chron. 15:1-7). More years of peace followed (2 Chron. 15:19).

Encouraged by God's prophet, Asa embarked on a second period of reformation (1 Kings 15:12-15; 2 Chron. 15:8-18). The expulsion of the sodomites and the destruction of **idols** introduced by Rehoboam and Abijah were part of this re-

form, as was Asa's deposing of **his grandmother Maacah** from the official position of **queen mother because of** her **repulsive Asherah pole,** which he **burned . . . in the Kidron Valley** east of Jerusalem.

15:14-15. Asa removed some of **the high places** (2 Chron. 14:3) but not all of them (1 Kings 15:14). Nevertheless his **heart was fully committed to the LORD all his life.** In view of **Asa's** self-reliance later in his life this statement probably means that he did not tolerate idolatry but worshiped only the true God. **The silver . . . gold,** and **articles that he and his father had dedicated** probably refer to the booty that Abijah had taken in his war with Jeroboam (2 Chron. 13:16-17) and what Asa had acquired in defeating the Egyptians (2 Chron. 14:12-13). Second Chronicles adds other details of Asa's reform including an account of the formal renewal of the Mosaic Covenant (2 Chron. 15:9-17).

2. ASA'S VICTORY OVER BAASHA (15:16-22)

15:16-17. Baasha king of Israel (909–886 B.C.) was a perennial enemy of **Asa. Baasha . . . fortified Ramah,** on the Judah-Israel border just four miles north of Jerusalem, so he could maintain control of the traffic between Israel and **Judah.**

15:18-21. Asa's plan to divert **Baasha** from strengthening **Ramah** included emptying his treasuries to buy **a treaty** with **Ben-Hadad** I, **the king of Aram . . . in Damascus** (see the chart "Kings of Aram in 1 and 2 Kings," near 1 Kings 11:23-25). **Asa** tried to induce Ben-Hadad to **break** his **treaty with Baasha,** and Asa's plan succeeded. **Ben-Hadad** invaded **Israel** and took some towns near the Sea of **Kinnereth** (later known as the Sea of Galilee), forcing Baasha to move his forces from Ramah to the north. Baasha himself went **to Tirzah,** the capital of Israel at that time (cf. 14:17).

15:22. Asa then proceeded to confiscate the building materials (**stones and timber**) Baasha left behind to fortify **Ramah** and used them to strengthen his own defense cities of **Geba** and **Mizpah** near Israel's border. Asa's plan was clever and successful, but it demonstrated lack of trust in God. For getting help from Aram's king, the Prophet Hanani rebuked Asa (2 Chron. 16:7-9). **Asa** resented the rebuke and put Hanani in prison (2 Chron. 16:10). Perhaps Asa's successes against Egypt and Israel made him think too highly of himself.

3. ASA'S DEATH (15:23-24)

15:23-24. Asa's achievements were recorded in **the book of the annals of the kings of Judah** (cf. 14:29; 15:7). At the end of his life Asa again failed to seek the Lord. When **his feet became diseased** he did not ask for the Lord's help but relied only on the physicians (2 Chron. 16:12). Though Asa's faith was not what it might have been, all in all his relationship with God was characterized by fidelity and blessing during his long reign. Perhaps because of Asa's poor health his son **Jehoshaphat** reigned as coregent with him during the last years of his life (873–870 B.C.). When Asa died, Ahab (874–853 B.C.) was reigning in Israel.

F. Nadab's evil reign in Israel (15:25-32)

The scene reverts to the Northern Kingdom and shifts back in time to the early years of Asa's reign over Judah.

1. NADAB'S ACHIEVEMENTS (15:25-28)

15:25-26. **Nadab** was the brother of Abijah who had died in childhood (14:17). Whether Nadab was older or younger than Abijah is not known. He was the second ruler of the **Jeroboam** dynasty, and **reigned** for **two years** (910–909 B.C.). Nadab continued the policies begun by **his father** which the LORD regarded as **evil**. The seriousness of Jeroboam's sins can be seen in that **he had caused Israel to commit** sin as well as sinning himself.

15:27-28. **Baasha killed Nadab** at **Gibbethon, a** strong **Philistine town** southwest of Israel, between Ekron and Gezer. Evidently **Israel** did not capture this town (cf. 16:15-17). Perhaps the siege ended when **Nadab** was killed. His assassin **Baasha** then became **king** of Israel (15:33–16:7).

2. THE END OF ISRAEL'S FIRST DYNASTY (15:29-32)

15:29-32. Baasha's destruction of the house of **Jeroboam** was intended to secure his own throne. It fulfilled Ahijah's prophecy of the destruction of **Jeroboam's** dynasty (14:14). The reason for this severe judgment is reiterated by the writer here (15:30). Specifically the worship at

the golden-calf shrines is in view. This worship was continued by all of Jeroboam's successors and was frequently condemned by the writer of 1 and 2 Kings (cf. 1 Kings 15:34; 16:19, 26, 31; 22:52; etc.). The reference to the continual warfare in Baasha's day (15:32; cf. vv. 16-22) forms a bridge to the next section.

G. Baasha's evil reign in Israel (15:33–16:7)

1. BAASHA'S ASSESSMENT (15:33-34)

15:33-34. **Baasha** took the throne of Israel **in the third year of Asa** and **reigned** in **Tirzah** the capital (cf. 14:17; 15:21) for **24 years** (909–886 B.C.). His was the third-longest reign of the Israelite kings. However, the brevity of his history as recorded here suggests that his reign was comparatively insignificant. He continued the religious policies begun by **Jeroboam.**

2. JEHU'S PROPHECY (16:1-4)

16:1-4. **Jehu** the prophet must be distinguished from Jehu the king of Israel (841–814 B.C.). This prophet was the **son of Hanani.** This Hanani may or may not have been the prophet who warned King Asa of Judah (2 Chron. 16:7-9). God said He had **lifted** Baasha **up from the dust and made** him **leader of** the Israelites. This implies that **Baasha** had a lowly origin. Almost the same words used to describe Baasha's future judgment (1 Kings 16:4) had been given to Jeroboam by the Prophet Ahijah (cf. 14:7, 10-11) and were given later by Elijah to Ahab (21:24). The fact that **Baasha** did not turn to the Lord in spite of his being God's instrument of judgment on the house of Jeroboam suggests his complete blindness to the importance of spiritual matters in his own life and in that of his nation. **Baasha** committed the same sins himself. This indicates that the level of his apostasy was deep.

3. BAASHA'S DEATH (16:5-7)

16:5-7. The writer followed his regular recording of the facts surrounding the king's death (vv. 5-6) with an additional reemphasis on the reasons for Baasha's judgment by God (v. 7). Baasha's destruction of Jeroboam's **house** (family or dynasty) was one reason. Even though God determined that Jeroboam's dynasty would be destroyed and announced this beforehand through Ahijah, God held Baasha responsible for killing Jeroboam's descendants. In doing so Baasha had not acted under God's direction, but only to gain his own ends.

H. Elah's evil reign in Israel (16:8-14)

16:8-10. Elah assumed the throne **of Israel and . . . reigned in Tirzah,** the capital, for **two years** (886-885 B.C.). He continued the wicked policies of his predecessors (v. 13). No specific accomplishments are recorded for him. He is infamous as the king who was murdered while **getting drunk** (v. 10). As commander **of half** of Elah's **chariots . . . Zimri** was a powerful military officer.

16:11-14. Zimri completely **destroyed** Israel's second ruling **family** plus friends of the family in order to avoid retaliation against his coup d'etat. Thus Jehu's prophecy (cf. v. 3) was fulfilled. Again the writer identified the spiritual root of the judgment (v. 13).

I. Zimri's evil reign in Israel (16:15-20)

16:15-20. Zimri's **seven**-day reign (885 B.C.) proved to be the shortest of any Israelite **king. Gibbethon** in Philistia was again under siege by Israel's **army** (cf. 15:27). It probably took a runner two days to reach the army at Gibbethon after the assassination of Elah. The troops immediately heralded **Omri, the commander of the army** (16:16), as the new **king** even though **Zimri** had declared himself king **in Tirzah.** Zimri was not an acceptable candidate for the throne in the minds of **Omri** and his men as they marched back to the capital. They appeared at the city walls (probably after marching about four or five days) and took control of **the city. Zimri** apparently knew he could not retain his throne or save his life, so he did as much damage to **the palace** as he could while taking his life. His death resulted ultimately from his **sins** (v. 19).

J. Omri's evil reign in Israel (16:21-28)

16:21-24. The death of Zimri (vv. 17-18) did not automatically place the kingdom in Omri's hands. **Half** the population including the army sided with him, but the other half preferred **Tibni.** Tibni's strength can be seen in that he was able to oppose Omri successfully for six years (885-880 B.C.). During this time civil war

ravaged **Israel** and threatened to **split** the Northern Kingdom **into two** parts. But eventually **Omri** overpowered **Tibni** and became the sole ruler (880-874 B.C.). Omri's army support apparently proved decisive and **Tibni died** (v. 22), probably by being executed.

For the first **six** years of his reign (885-880 B.C.) **Omri** ruled in the old capital of **Tirzah** (cf. 14:17; 15:21, 33; 16:6, 8-9, 15, 17). But then he moved into his brand new capital, **Samaria.** He **built** this **city** on a hill, well situated for defense, seven miles west of Tirzah. Omri paid **Shemer . . . two talents** (ca. 150 pounds) **of silver** for **the hill.** (Samaria was named after Shemer; cf. v. 24.) Archeologists have unearthed evidence that Samaria was built by skillful craftsmen. The site dominated the north-south trade routes. Samaria proved to be almost impregnable as a stronghold against alien attacks because of its elevated position.

Omri was probably the strongest leader of the Northern Kingdom up to that time. Assyrian records dating from over a century later refer to Israel as "the land of Omri." During Omri's reign Ben-Hadad I, king of the Arameans in Damascus (see the chart "Kings of Aram in 1 and 2 Kings," near 1 Kings 11:23-25), continued to add to his holdings to the north of Israel. Omri's son, Ahab, had difficulty containing these Aramean aggressors. Also the Assyrian Empire was growing stronger and farther to the northeast under Ashurnasirpal II (883-859; see the chart "Kings of Assyria in the Middle and New Assyrian Kingdoms," near Jonah 1:2) and proceeded to expand its territory as far west as the Mediterranean Sea. Faced by these threats on his north, Omri was able to protect Israel well enough to attack and defeat Moab to the southeast at the same time. This victory is referred to on the famous Moabite Stone. Another of Omri's significant achievements was his alliance with the Phoenicians which was sealed with the marriage of his son Ahab to Jezebel, a daughter of the Phoenician king, Ethbaal (cf. 1 Kings 16:31).

16:25-28. Though **Omri** is passed over quickly in 1 Kings, he was a powerful and politically effective king. But the major concern of the writer of 1 Kings was Omri's spiritual condition. In this he was the worst Israelite king so far (vv. 25-26). Omri's 12-year reign ended with his death and burial in his new capital city. His rule passed to his son, **Ahab. Omri** was the founder of the fourth dynasty of Israelite kings.

K. Ahab's evil reign in Israel (16:29–22:40)

1. AHAB'S WICKEDNESS (16:29-34)

16:29-31. Ahab ruled **Israel** from **Samaria** for **22 years** (874–853 B.C.). He was the most wicked king Israel had experienced, even worse than his father Omri who was worse than all before him (v. 25). Ahab's wickedness consisted of perpetuating all **the sins of Jeroboam**; he even **considered** them **trivial.** In addition Ahab **married** a pagan princess, **Jezebel,** who zealously tried to promote her depraved cult as the exclusive religion of Israel. Jezebel's father, **Ethbaal,** was **king of the Sidonians** (Phoenicians), with his capital in Tyre. **Baal** (meaning "lord") is a name used generally in the Old Testament for the male deity the native Canaanite tribes worshiped under various other titles. The Tyrians called him Baal Melqart, but their religion was only a cultic variation of the standard Baal worship common throughout Palestine. Evidently **Ahab** was not forced to marry Jezebel; his choice to marry her is something for which the writer held him responsible.

16:32-33. Ahab built a temple for **Baal** in the capital of Israel and constructed an **altar for Baal** in it. **Asherah** poles (cf. 14:15, 23; 15:13) were idols carved to stimulate worship of Baal's female counterpart. The writer repeated the seriousness of Ahab's sins for emphasis (16:33; cf. v. 30).

16:34. The refortification of **Jericho** was specifically forbidden by **Joshua** after God supernaturally destroyed it (Josh. 6:26). Though the city had been occupied since Joshua's day, Hiel's reconstruction seems to have been the first serious attempt to restore it to its former condition. Joshua's prophecy was fulfilled literally when two of Hiel's sons perished. Perhaps this reference, which seems unrelated to Ahab's accomplishments, was included to show that as God's word was fulfilled in this instance so it would be in Ahab's case. Ahab was setting up a system of worship that God said He would judge, as Hiel had tried to **set up** a city that God had said He would judge.

2. AHAB'S PUNISHMENT (CHAPS. 17–18)

Because of his wickedness Ahab was disciplined by God, who used the Prophet Elijah in a remarkable way to bring Israel back to Himself.

a. Elijah's announcement of drought (17:1-6)

17:1. Elijah had been and was being prepared by the Lord to demonstrate to all Israel that Yahweh, not Baal, is still the only true God. Even Elijah's name, which means "Yahweh is my God," conveyed that fact! Elijah lived **in Gilead** east of the Jordan River near a community called **Tishbe.** Perhaps as Elijah heard reports of Jezebel's increasing maneuverings to replace the worship of the Lord with Baal worship his godly heart was stirred up. God gave him a mission. Armed with God's promise he walked westward to Samaria. Bursting into the palace, he hurled his ultimatum at King **Ahab.** He claimed that **the LORD** is **the God of Israel,** that He is alive (cf. v. 12; 18:10), and that he, Elijah, was God's servant. (On the words "**As** the LORD . . . **lives**" see comments on 1:29.) Elijah could confidently declare that there would be neither **dew nor rain** because God had promised to withhold these from the land if His people turned from Him to other gods (Lev. 26:18-19; Deut. 11:16-17; 28:23-24). God had apparently revealed to Elijah that He would honor that promise in Elijah's day. This would have struck at the heart of Baalism, for Baal-worshipers believed that their god was the god of rain! The drought, brought on by the true God, showed that He, not Baal, controls the weather. This was a remarkable demonstration of God's superiority and of the total inadequacy and falsehood of Baal worship.

17:2-4. Having made his dramatic announcement, **Elijah** was told by **the LORD** to **leave** Samaria, return **eastward, and hide in** a **ravine** by the wadi **Kerith, east of the Jordan** River. Elijah had to hide because he would soon be hunted by the king (cf. 18:10). The exact location of this seasonal **brook** is not known; it was one of many streams that flowed during the rainy season but dried up when the weather turned hot. God promised to provide food and **drink** for His servant at this unlikely spot.

17:5-6. Elijah obeyed **the LORD,** who

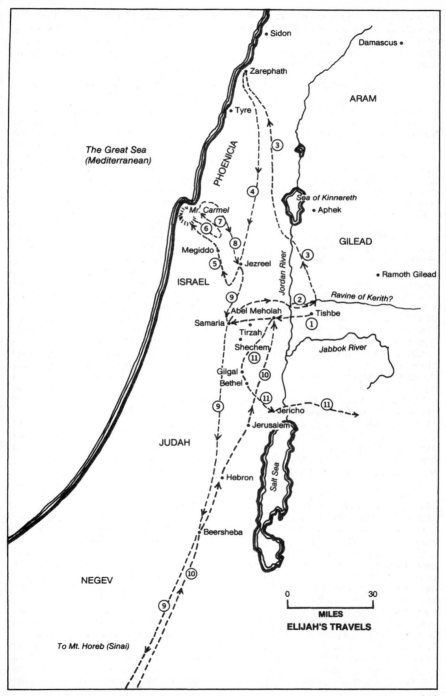

ELIJAH'S TRAVELS

miraculously provided for him as He had promised. God directed **ravens,** birds that normally neglect their own young (cf. Job. 38:41), to bring **bread and meat** faithfully to Elijah every **morning** and **evening.** And **he drank** water **from the brook.** The Hebrew word for "bread" (*leḥem*) means food in general, possibly including berries, fruit, nuts, eggs, etc. Perhaps they were brought from a distance where the drought had not yet affected the vegetation. Through this unusual manner of nourishing His prophet physically, God was also nourishing Elijah's faith for later feats of spiritual strength (see the list "God's Miracles through Elijah and Elisha," near 2 Kings 2:13-14).

b. Elijah's ministry at Zarephath (17:7-24)

17:7. How long Elijah stayed at **the brook** is not revealed. **Some time later** it **dried up** because of the drought which lasted three and one-half years in all (Luke 4:25; James 5:17). Elijah had learned that God would miraculously provide for him, but now he would learn that God could do the same for others— even Gentiles—as well. God was preparing His servant for a great showdown on Mount Carmel.

17:8-11. Elijah was directed to **Zarephath,** a town on the Mediterranean coast between Tyre and **Sidon** in Phoenicia, the homeland of Jezebel (cf. 16:31) and the heart of Baal-Melqart territory (see the map "Elijah's Travels"). Zarephath was 80-90 miles from Kerith. God told Elijah that **a widow** would feed him (cf. Luke 4:25-26). Widows were usually poor people; normally they ran out of food first in a famine. This famine had been created by the drought. Therefore going to a widow for food was a strange directive. God was again using an unusual source to feed His prophet.

Obediently Elijah made his way **to Zarephath.** When he entered **the town** he tested the first **widow** he saw by asking her for **a drink.** Her favorable response led him to request **a piece of bread.**

17:12-16. The widow recognized **Elijah** as an Israelite and appealed to Yahweh in affirming that she had no **bread;** she had **only a** little **flour** and **oil,** enough for a last **meal for** her **son** and herself. Here was a Gentile woman in Phoenicia who believed in the Lord; she

said she believed He is alive (**As surely as the** LORD **your God lives;** cf. v. 1; 18:10).

Elijah calmed her fears of himself, her hunger, and her imminent death. He asked her to feed him **first . . . and then** use what was left to feed herself and her **son.** Then he gave her a promise on the authority of the word of **God:** she would have **food** until the drought ended.

Her obedient response demonstrated her faith in **the word of the** LORD. The Lord honored her faith by fulfilling His promise miraculously. This miracle of God's continually supplying **flour** and olive **oil** was another polemic (protest) against Baal, just as was the drought. Baal-worshipers believed he was a fertility god, giving rain to make crops grow. But he could not overcome the drought to make wheat and olive trees grow. Only the true God could provide flour and oil in a drought!

17:17-18. Some time later (cf. v. 7)— again the exact time is not given—tragedy befell Elijah's hostess. **The woman who owned the house** was the widow. Her young **son** fell **ill** and **finally stopped breathing.** Some Bible critics say the boy was only unconscious, not dead, and that his restoration was therefore not a miracle. However, verses 18, 20, 22-23 make it clear that he had actually died.

The woman had a guilty conscience and immediately concluded that **God** was punishing her for her **sin** by killing her **son.** This is a common reaction among many people who do not know God's ways well when personal tragedy enters their lives (cf. John 9:2-3). What sin she was referring to is not stated.

17:19-21. The boy was small enough to be carried in his mother's **arms.** Many homes in Palestine at that time had guest rooms built on their roofs. It was in one such **upper room** that Elijah **was staying.** Elijah's first prayer (v. 20) simply expressed his compassion for the woman who, in addition to the trials of the famine, now **also** had to bear this tragedy. Implicit in the prayer was the desire that **God** relieve her of this added burden. Often in cases of miraculous restoration and healing, God's servant placed his hand on the afflicted one to indicate that the power of God in him was passing to the needy individual (e.g., Matt. 8:3). In this instance **Elijah** out of heartfelt concern **stretched himself out** placing the whole body of the lad in contact with his own. **Three times** Elijah did this, praying each time that **God** would restore the **boy's life.** Persistence in prayer is a fundamental requisite for obtaining one's petitions (cf. Matt. 7:7-8; Luke 11:5-13). It proved effective in this case.

17:22-24. God miraculously restored **the boy's life.** This is the first recorded instance in Scripture of restoration to life of one who had died. **Elijah . . . carried** the lad downstairs (the boy was apparently weak) and presented **him to his mother.** This miracle proved to the woman that **Elijah** was indeed a **man of God** and that **the word of the** LORD that Elijah claimed to speak was indeed **the truth.**

This incident showed the widow and others that the power of the Lord as the true God contrasted greatly with the impotency of Baal.

c. Obadiah's search (18:1-15)

18:1-6. **In the third** and last **year of** the famine God directed **Elijah to present** himself **to** King **Ahab.** Elijah had God's word that He would soon end the drought.

The famine in the land was particularly **severe in** the capital, **Samaria.** (Cf. the famine[s] in Elisha's days, 2 Kings 4:38; 6:25; 7:4; 8:1.) God was directing this calamity especially at the guilty parties, Ahab and Jezebel. This situation prompted **Ahab** and his trusted servant, **Obadiah,** to go in different directions, looking for **some grass** in the **valleys** or near **the springs** where the most necessary **animals** (**horses and mules**) might graze. **Obadiah** had great responsibility in Ahab's court (**in charge of** Ahab's **palace**). **Obadiah was** also a **devout believer in the** LORD (but not the writer of the Bible book of that name). Whether **Jezebel** knew of Obadiah's commitment to the Lord is not clear, but undoubtedly he and the queen were not close friends. Jezebel's aim was to replace the worship of Yahweh with Baal-Melqart worship. Her plan included **killing off the** LORD's **prophets** (1 Kings 18:4). **Obadiah,** aware of her strategy, had hidden **100 prophets** of the Lord in **caves** and was supplying **them with food and water**—a difficult task in days of extreme famine and drought. Obviously there were many in Israel (cf. 19:18) and probably also in Judah at that time who believed in the

Lord, though Israel as a whole had apostatized.

18:7-12a. Obadiah recognized Elijah when they met somewhere outside Samaria; **Elijah** was a "wanted" man in Israel. Out of respect for the prophet, Obadiah **bowed down to the ground.** He could hardly believe he had found **Elijah.** Elijah, wanting to talk with Ahab (vv. 1-2), asked Obadiah to announce him to his **master. Obadiah,** however, was afraid that **Elijah** would disappear again. **Obadiah** explained to the prophet how **Ahab** had searched for him at home and abroad (v. 10) to no avail. Obadiah affirmed that fact by the familiar words, **As surely as the** LORD **your God lives** (cf. 17:1, 12). If he reported to his king that **Elijah** had been found, and then could not produce him (**the Spirit of the** LORD **may carry you** away; cf. 2 Kings 2:16), **Ahab** would regard Obadiah's words as a mocking trick and would probably execute him.

18:12b-15. To convince Elijah that his concern was sincere, Obadiah related proof that he was a devout believer in **the** LORD (cf. v. 3) **since** his **youth.** Obadiah seemed to think **Elijah** would have **heard** about his hiding and feeding the **prophets of the** LORD. Perhaps this was known among many of the faithful in Israel, especially the prophets, though of course not by **Jezebel** or her sympathizers. **Elijah** assured Obadiah that he would not disappear but would indeed stand before **Ahab** that same day. Elijah's description of God as **the** LORD (Yahweh) **Almighty** who **lives** and whom Elijah served (cf. 17:1; 18:36) indicates that he was confident in God's ability to handle the physical and spiritual situation in Israel, an assurance that had grown as a result of his experiences at Kerith and Zarephath.

d. Elijah's vindication of the Lord on Mount Carmel (18:16-46)

This popular story of Elijah's contest with the prophets of Baal is both exciting and extremely significant in the history of Israel. The first part of this narrative (vv. 16-24) clarifies the reason for the dramatic encounter.

(1) The issue at stake. **18:16-18.** When **Ahab** heard Obadiah's message the king **went to meet** the prophet; **Elijah** maintained the initiative as the spokesman of God to whom the king must sub-

mit. In Ahab's eyes **Elijah** was the **troubler of Israel. Elijah** set the record straight and instructed the king who did not perceive or was not willing to admit that *he* and his **father's** (Omri's) **family** (cf. 16:25-26) were the real reason for Israel's troubles. **Ahab** had **abandoned the LORD's commands** in His Law **and** had instead **followed the Baals.** The plural "Baals" refers to local idols of Baal (cf. Jud. 2:11) sometimes with differing names (e.g., Baal-Berith, Jud. 8:33; Baal-Zebub, 2 Kings 1:2-3, 6, 16). This was the real issue and the root cause of all the trouble in Israel, spiritual as well as physical.

(2) The proposed test (18:19-24). **18:19.** In view of Elijah's directive that Ahab **summon the people from all over Israel,** it is likely that hundreds, if not thousands, congregated **on Mount Carmel.** The Carmel range of mountains, 1,742 feet in elevation at its highest point, extends about 30 miles to the southeast of modern-day Haifa from the shores of the Mediterranean Sea. It is a beautiful series of rounded peaks and valleys from which the sea can easily be seen. It is not known exactly where along this ridge Elijah staged this test; any of several sites is possible; Muḥraka is suggested by many as one of the more probable sites.

The extent of **Baal** worship in Israel can be estimated by the number of priests Jezebel regularly fed: **450 prophets** of the male god and **400 . . . of the** female goddess **Asherah,** Baal's consort.

18:20-21. Mount Carmel was agreed on by **Ahab.** It would be a fitting site since it lay between Israel and Phoenicia, the lands of the deities in question. Also Mount Carmel was regarded by the Phoenicians as the sacred dwelling place of Baal. No doubt Ahab was highly pleased with this suggested site for the contest because it would have given the Baal prophets a definite advantage; but this did not worry Elijah. It was also a geographically prominent location and thus a fit setting for Elijah's contest.

When **all** the **people** had **assembled. . . . Elijah** stood before them and challenged them to end their double-mindedness, wavering **between two opinions.** It was not good to try to "walk the fence" worshiping two gods. Apparently the Israelites thought that if Yahweh let them down they could turn to

Baal, and vice versa. Elijah was saying that if One is the true God and the other false they should follow the true One wholeheartedly and forget about the impotent impostor. **The people** could not argue with this statement, so they **said nothing.**

18:22-24. Elijah then pointed out that in this contest the odds would be **450 prophets** to 1—a humanly impossible situation in which to win! Elijah knew there were other prophets of Yahweh besides himself (cf. v. 13), but as far as this contest was concerned he was **the only one** of the **LORD's prophets** left.

Of the **two bulls** required, Elijah **let** his adversaries select their favorite. Each side would prepare to sacrifice its **bull** as a burnt offering to its god. **Then** they would each **call on** their **god** and **the god who** answered **by fire** would be shown to be the true **God.** Baal was supposedly a fertility god, the one who sent rain, caused the crops to grow, and provided food for his people. He was the one who supposedly sent fire (lightning) from heaven. The three-and-one-half-year drought and famine had been a great embarrassment to the worshipers of Baal. It seemed as if Elijah and his God rather than Baal were in control of the fertility of Israel. So Elijah's test to Baal's followers seemed like a good opportunity to vindicate their god and they readily agreed to it. When the preparations were completed, the test began.

(3) The false prophets' failure. **18:25-29.** All **morning** Baal's **prophets . . . called on** their god and **danced around** his **altar** to arouse him to action. **At noon** Elijah **began to taunt them,** mocking their ineffectiveness. Sarcastically he suggested that Baal was thinking about other things, or **busy** (lit., relieving himself), away on a trip (the Phoenician sailors believed Baal traveled with them on the Mediterranean Sea and elsewhere), or even **sleeping!** Surprisingly Baal's prophets responded by increasing the fervor of their appeals, working themselves into a frenzy. To propitiate their god they mutilated their own bodies as the **custom** of pagan worshipers has been for centuries. This continued for three hours (**the time for the** Israelites' **evening sacrifice;** cf. v. 36, was 3 P.M.), **but still there was no response. No one answered** or **paid attention;** that is, Baal did not respond to

their six-hour chanting for lightning, though rain and lightning often come readily to the Carmel mountain range near the Mediterranean Sea.

(4) Elijah's success (18:30-39). **18:30-32.** When it was obvious to all that the prophets of Baal had failed, **Elijah** invited **all the people** to draw near and observe what he would do. An **altar to the LORD** had been built on the site long before but it was in disrepair. **Elijah** selected **12 stones, one for each of the tribes.** Though the tribes had been divided into two nations they were still one people in God's purposes—with a single Lord, a single covenant, and a single destiny. **With** these **stones he built an altar . . . and . . . dug a trench around it . . . to hold** about one-third of a bushel **of seed (two seahs** equaled about 13 quarts; cf. NIV marg., and a bushel has 32 quarts). Perhaps the trench on each side of the altar could hold that much seed.

18:33-35. After **the bull** had been slain and **laid . . . on the wood,** Elijah gave another strange directive. He called for the whole sacrifice and its **wood** to be soaked with **water** three separate times. The excess **water . . . even filled the trench.** The water—**four large jars** filled three times each!—probably was collected from a spring on the mountain or in the Kishon Valley below (v. 40), or from the Mediterranean Sea. The purpose of this soaking, of course, was to show everyone present that the burning of the sacrifice that was to take place was not a natural phenomenon or a trick but was a miracle. Also the time involved in securing the water would have added to the tension of the hour.

18:36-39. At the time of the Israelites' evening **sacrifice** (3 P.M.; cf. v. 29), **Elijah stepped forward and prayed.** Without any of the theatrics of his adversaries Elijah simply addressed **God** as one addresses another living person. His words were designed to demonstrate to the onlookers that all he had done as God's **servant** (cf. 17:1; 18:15) had been in obedience to God's **command** and not on the prophet's own initiative. Elijah simply asked God to show the **people** that He is the true **God** and to turn the **hearts** of the people **back** to Himself.

Instantly **fire . . . fell** from heaven (lightning), consuming **the sacrifice . . . wood,** altar, and even the surrounding

soil and **water.** Spontaneously the crowd **cried** out in amazement. Since **the LORD** (Yahweh) had answered by fire (cf. v. 24); they acknowledged that **He is** the true **God.**

(5) The consequences (18:40-46). **18:40-42.** **The Kishon Valley** ran parallel to the Carmel range on its north side. There the people **slaughtered** the false **prophets** in obedience to the command of God through Moses (Deut. 13:12-15) and **Elijah.** Previously **Elijah** had predicted the drought **to Ahab** (1 Kings 17:1); now the prophet told the king there would be **a heavy rain. Ahab** rode off down the mountain to celebrate the end of the drought by eating and drinking, **but Elijah** walked back up the mountain to pray for rain. His posture as he prayed reflected the earnestness of his petition, again for the glory of the Lord.

18:43-46. Rains normally came from the west off the Mediterannean **Sea,** so Elijah instructed **his servant** to **look** in that direction. God answered Elijah's petition as he persevered in prayer. At first the rain **cloud** was **small** (like **a man's hand**), but soon **the** whole **sky grew black** and **heavy rain** descended. The torrent evidently overtook **Ahab** as he **rode** in his **chariot . . . to Jezreel,** his winter capital about midway between Mount Carmel and Samaria. **Elijah** overtook him, running the approximate 25 miles with divinely given energy. **Tucking his cloak into his belt** enabled him to run without tripping over the long garment (cf. comments on "Brace yourself like a man" in Job 38:3; 40:7).

Because of Mount Carmel Elijah had discredited Baal and his worshipers, but he had also humiliated vindictive Queen Jezebel.

3. AHAB'S WICKED WIFE (CHAP. 19)

a. *Elijah's flight (19:1-8)*

19:1-5a. Jezebel had not been present on Mount Carmel; her husband reported to her what had taken place. Infuriated by Elijah's treatment of her **prophets . . . Jezebel sent a** message to him. He was evidently still in the city of Jezreel as she was (cf. 18:46) when he received her warning. She threatened to take his **life** in 24 hours in retaliation for his slaughtering the 450 Baal prophets.

It is remarkable that her threat terrified **Elijah** as it did. Ironically by contrast he had told the widow in Zarephath not to be afraid (17:13). He had just demonstrated that the gods to whom she now appealed in her curse had no power at all. (Her statement that she was willing to be dealt with severely by the gods [cf. 2:23; 20:10; 2 Kings 6:31] points up the seriousness of her threat. She was so certain she would kill Elijah that she willingly put her own welfare "on the line.") Evidently Elijah's fear sprang from the power Jezebel possessed. Rather than resting in God for His protection as he had for the past three and one-half years, Elijah ran for his life. He ran all the way through the kingdom of Judah to the southernmost town in the land, Beersheba.

Still fearful he might be discovered by Jezebel's spies he told his servant to stay behind and he traveled alone one more day's journey (about 15 miles) into the Negev desert. Finally he sat down under a broom tree (a desert bush that grows to a height of 12 feet and provides some, though not much, shade) and rested. He was so discouraged he prayed that he might die. Elijah had forgotten the lessons God had been teaching him at Kerith, Zarephath, and Carmel. His eyes were on his circumstances rather than on the LORD. His statement that he was no better than his ancestors (19:4) suggests that he was no more successful than his forefathers in ousting Baal-worship from Israel. Exhausted and discouraged, Elijah lay down . . . and fell asleep.

19:5b-8. Elijah woke at the touch of a divinely sent messenger. This angel had prepared freshly baked bread, still warm, and plenty of water, which he invited Elijah to consume. The prophet did so and then returned to his rest. The angel probably appeared as a human being as was common in the Old Testament.

Again the angel woke Elijah, perhaps after he had slept for some time, and urged him to eat more food since the journey before him would require much energy. Moses and the Israelites had traveled in that wilderness for 40 years, sustained by the manna God had provided for them and learned lessons of His faithful care and provision. Now Elijah would traverse the same desert for 40 days and . . . nights, sustained by the bread God provided and would learn the same lessons. A direct trip from Beersheba to Mount Horeb (the ancient name for Mount Sinai; cf. Ex. 3:1; 17:6; 33:6; Deut. 5:2; 1 Kings 8:9; Ps. 106:19; Mal. 4:4) would have taken Elijah only about 14 days on foot (a distance of ca. 200 miles). God was reminding him and teaching him during those 40 days and nights. Finally He went to the mountain of God, the very place where God had revealed Himself to Moses and the Israelites and where He had entered into a covenant with His Chosen People.

b. Elijah's revelation (19:9-18)

19:9-10. Arriving at one of the mountains in the Sinai range Elijah found a cave and took refuge in it. There he received a revelation from God. The LORD began this lesson with the question, What are you doing here, Elijah? (cf. v. 13; Gen. 3:9) God had not sent him here as He had directed him to other places (cf. 1 Kings 17:3, 9; 18:1). Elijah had run out because of fear (19:3). Elijah's response revealed that he felt he was standing completely alone and defenseless against the ungodly forces that threatened to overpower him (cf. v. 14). Of course he knew that he was not the only one left of all the faithful remnant (cf. 18:13), but he felt all alone. Interestingly Elijah spoke only of the Lord's prophets being killed (cf. 18:13a); he made no mention of Baal's 450 prophets who were killed. Fear and discouragement caused him to see only the dark side. He sensed failure in spite of his being zealous. Mercifully God did not lecture Elijah or chasten His chafed prophet. God simply gave him a demonstration of His ways.

19:11-14. Standing on the mountainside outside his cave (cf. v. 9) Elijah witnessed what Moses had seen in those mountains centuries before (Ex. 19:16-18) and what he himself had seen on Mount Carmel only a few days earlier (1 Kings 18:38, 45), namely, a spectacular demonstration of the power of God, this time in wind, an earthquake, and fire. But on this occasion the LORD was not in any of these, that is, they were not His instruments of self-revelation.

Evidently some time later when Elijah was back in his cave (19:13) he heard the sound of a gentle whisper. Recognizing this as a revelation of God he pulled his cloak over part of his face, walked out to the mouth of the cave, and stood there waiting for God to act. God asked the same question He asked earlier (cf. v. 9): **What are you doing here, Elijah?** The prophet's response was identical to his first reply (cf. v. 10), suggesting that even though he may have understood the point of God's display of natural forces for his benefit he still felt the same way about himself.

The message God seems to have intended for Elijah is that whereas He had revealed Himself in spectacular demonstrations of His power in the past at Kerith, Zarephath, and Carmel, He would now use Elijah in gentler, less dramatic ways. These ways God proceeded to explain to His servant (vv. 15-18). God would deal with Elijah's personal feelings about himself later in a gentle way too.

19:15-17. The LORD told Elijah to leave there, to **go back the way** he **came** (i.e., through Israel) to **Damascus.** (Cf. God's commands "leave" and "go" to Elijah in 17:3, 9; 18:1; 21:18; 2 Kings 1:3, 15.) The Lord then gave him three assignments: to **anoint Hazael king** of the Arameans in Damascus (see the chart "Kings of Aram in 1 and 2 Kings," near 1 Kings 11:23-25), to **anoint Jehu . . . king** of **Israel,** and to **anoint Elisha . . . from Abel Meholah** (cf. Jud. 7:22) as his own successor. Through these three men God would complete the purge of Baal worship that Elijah had begun. Actually Elijah did only the last of these three directly, but he did the other two indirectly through Elisha, his protegé. Elisha was involved, though strangely, in Hazael's becoming Aram's king (2 Kings 8:7-14) and one of Elisha's associates anointed Jehu (2 Kings 9:1-3).

19:18. God then revealed to Elijah that He had preserved **7,000** faithful followers **in Israel** who had **not bowed** before or **kissed** the emblems of idolatry in worship. Such news undoubtedly cheered Elijah. Were it not for the insight into his feelings of fear and discouragement given in this chapter, one might not believe that Elijah was indeed "a man just like us" (James 5:17).

c. Elijah's successor (19:19-21)

19:19-20. Elijah returned from the Sinai peninsula to find **Elisha** (whose name

means "My God is salvation") near his hometown of Abel Meholah (v. 16) in the Jordan Valley about halfway between the Dead Sea and the Sea of Kinnereth in the Northern Kingdom of Israel. Elisha evidently came from a family that owned lots of land (as implied by the 12 yoke of oxen). He himself **was plowing** when Elijah **found** him. Throwing a prophet's **cloak around** a person symbolized the passing of the power and authority of the office to that individual. That **Elisha** realized the meaning of this act is obvious from his reaction. Immediately he started to abandon his former occupation and follow **Elijah. Elijah** gave him permission to say farewell to his family. The unusual reply, **What have I done to you?** is an idiom meaning, "Do as you please" or "What have I done to stop you?"

19:21. Elisha sealed his decision by slaughtering **his yoke of oxen** and burning his **plowing** implements. He evidently hosted a farewell banquet, serving his sacrificed animals to his guests for supper. **Then he set out to** accompany **Elijah** as **his attendant.**

4. AHAB'S ARAMEAN ADVERSARY (CHAP. 20)

In this chapter the focus is again on Ahab rather than on Elijah.

a. The battle over Samaria (20:1-25)

This was the first of three battles recorded in 1 Kings (cf. 20:26-43; 22:1-38) between Ahab and Ben-Hadad II, king of Aram, Israel's northern neighbor.

(1) Ben-Hadad's attack (20:1-12). **20:1-4.** Ben-Hadad II was evidently the son of Ben-Hadad I whom Asa had hired to attack Baasha some years earlier (cf. 15:18, 20; 20:34). Allied with Ben-Hadad II were **32 kings,** probably rulers of neighboring city-states. Together they **went up** the hill of **Samaria and attacked it,** placing it under siege. Ben-Hadad then **sent messengers . . . to Ahab** with his demands for withdrawal. He demanded Ahab's **silver . . . gold . . . wives, and children.** Greatly outnumbered, Ahab submitted to these terms.

20:5-9. Evidently **Ben-Hadad** regretted that he had demanded such "easy" terms after Ahab had accepted them. He felt he could get much more than that. So he sent his **messengers** back with a new demand, namely, that Ben-Hadad's men be allowed to enter the **palace** and the officials' **houses** and plunder them. Ahab assembled **the elders of the land** and pointed out that Ben-Hadad was **looking for trouble. The king** had **not** refused Ben-Hadad's **demands** for his own most valued possessions, but now the Aramean enemy wanted everything of value he could lay his hands on. **The elders and the people** who had also become aware of these demands counseled resistance. Ahab sent his decision back to Ben-Hadad through the **messengers**: he would hold to his **first** promise but not to **this demand.**

20:10-12. Shortly thereafter Ahab received a third **message** from his adversary. The Arameans now threatened to destroy **Samaria** totally. Like Jezebel with Elijah, **Ben-Hadad** risked his life in an oath (cf. 19:2; also note 2:23). Ahab replied that Ben-Hadad should not **boast** of victory till he had obtained it. Ben-Hadad's greed and boasting seem to have been heightened since he and his kings were under the influence of strong drink. Since negotiations had broken down **Ben-Hadad . . . prepared to attack** Samaria.

(2) Ben-Hadad's defeat (20:13-25). **20:13. Meanwhile,** as Ben-Hadad was preparing to attack, **a prophet,** whose name is not given, went **to Ahab** with a message from **the LORD.** God, he said, was going to deliver the huge Aramean **army** into Ahab's **hand** so Ahab would **know** that He is **the LORD.** God's goodness on this occasion obviously was prompted not by Ahab's godliness but by God's own grace. This was another step in His seeking to get His people to acknowledge that He **is the LORD.**

20:14-16. Ahab asked **the prophet** what strategy should be employed. He responded that **the LORD** would use **the young officers of the provincial commanders** of the army. The king himself was to lead them into **battle. Ahab** prepared the troops as instructed and **at noon,** when **Ben-Hadad and** his **32 kings** were resting and **getting drunk,** he launched his surprise attack. Even today little is done in the middle of the day in the Near East because the weather is usually so hot.

20:17-21. Evidently it was not clear to **Ben-Hadad** if the 232 **men** (cf. v. 15) approaching him were coming to talk **peace** or whether they were intending to fight.

This probably resulted in his being unprepared for their attack. The Israelite **army** (of 7,000; cf. v. 15) followed along **behind the young officers. Ben-Hadad** was able to escape **on horseback,** but Ahab **overpowered** his cavalry troops and the **chariots,** inflicting **heavy losses on the** surprised **Arameans.**

20:22-25. After Ahab had returned to Samaria **the prophet** went to him again. He warned **the king,** undoubtedly by the word of the Lord, that he should expect Ben-Hadad to **attack . . . again** in the **spring,** the most popular time of the year for kings to wage war (cf. 2 Sam. 11:1). In view of this Ahab was warned to build up his defenses.

In the camp of the Arameans, Ben-Hadad was also receiving advice. His counselors concluded that they had lost the battle because Israel's **gods** were **gods of the hills.** If they would **fight** Israel **on the plains** these gods would not help them and the Arameans would win. They also advised the king to **replace** the 32 allied kings with regular **army** commanders and to build up his forces to their former numbers. Ben-Hadad followed this advice and prepared to return to Samaria the following spring.

b. The battle of Aphek (20:26-43)

(1) Ahab's victory (20:26-34). **20:26-27.** As the Lord had revealed (v. 22), **the next spring** (856 B.C.) **Ben-Hadad** assembled his troops and proceeded **to Aphek.** Several towns in **Israel** bore this name (meaning "a fortress"). This one may have been located on the tablelands east of the Sea of Kinnereth between Samaria and Damascus. Ben-Hadad chose a flat battleground this time as his counselors had advised. Ahab led the Israelite army **to meet them.** In comparison with the vast host of the Arameans the Israelite forces looked like **two small flocks of goats.** That Israel was arranged in two groups may indicate that Ahab had in mind a certain battle strategy.

20:28-30a. The man of God, evidently the same prophet (vv. 13, 22), informed Ahab that **Israel** would win this battle. Again he said that the Lord's purpose was to prove to Ahab (as well as, perhaps, **the Arameans** and the Israelites) that He is **the LORD** (cf. v. 13). **Seven days** passed before **the battle**

began. On the very first day of combat the Israelites inflicted 100,000 casualties on the . . . foot soldiers of the enemy. The rest of their troops took refuge within the city walls of Aphek. But God killed an additional 27,000 by causing the city wall to collapse on them.

20:30b-34. While **Ben-Hadad** was hiding **in an inner room** of a city building, his officials advised him to give himself up and plead for mercy. **The kings of . . . Israel** were indeed **merciful** compared with other ancient Near Eastern kings. **Sackcloth** and **ropes** were signs of penitential submission.

Ben-Hadad's agents waited on Ahab and pleaded for Ben-Hadad's life. They called him Ahab's **servant,** indicating the position he was willing to take if he could **live.** Ahab seemed surprised that the Aramean king was **still alive.** Ahab said he was willing to receive **Ben-Hadad** as his **brother,** not as a servant. He was, of course, not his real brother; Ahab had in mind a treaty for defense against Assyria in which he and Ben-Hadad would join as brothers.

Quick to pick up this ray of hope, Ben-Hadad's ambassadors affirmed that Ahab's **brother** was alive. They escorted the defeated king to **Ahab** as they had been ordered, and as a gesture of friendship **Ahab** invited Ben-Hadad **up into his chariot,** a position of favor. Quick to placate his enemy, **Ben-Hadad** pledged to **return the cities** his **father** Ben-Hadad I had taken from Ahab's **father** (predecessor) Baasha (cf. 15:20). In addition, the Aramean king offered trade privileges to Ahab **in Damascus** which Ben-Hadad's **father** had enjoyed **in Samaria.** The two kings formalized the **treaty** and with this promise of nonaggression Ahab let Ben-Hadad **go** back home.

Three years later (853 B.C.) Ahab and Ben-Hadad faced their mutual foe, Assyria, led by mighty King Shalmaneser III (859–824 B.C.) and repelled him at Qarqar on the Orontes River in Aram. Ahab supplied 10,000 troops and 2,000 chariots for this coalition. This battle is not referred to in Scripture but a record of it written by Shalmaneser has survived. It is now in the British Museum. (See James B. Pritchard, ed., *Ancient Near Eastern Texts Relating to the Old Testament.* Princeton, N.J.: Princeton University Press, 1955, pp. 278-9.)

(2) Ahab's disobedience (20:35-43). **20:35-36.** **The sons of the prophets** were students in the schools of the prophets, well-established institutions in Israel designed to perpetuate the Law of Moses and the Word of the Lord. **One of** these young men received an assignment from the Lord. His unusual request that **his companion** injure him with a **weapon** was **by the word of the LORD.** The friend's refusal, though understandable, was an act of disobedient rebellion against the Lord. It was for this reason and the importance of the man of God's mission that the compassionate companion suffered death. Again **the LORD** used **a lion** to execute his will (cf. 13:24).

20:37-40a. **The prophet** then **found** a more willing accomplice who did wound **him.** Playing the part of a wounded soldier **the prophet** waited by the roadside for **King** Ahab to pass on his way back to Samaria. The prophet **disguised himself** using a **headband over his eyes.** Without this the king would have recognized him immediately as a prophet (cf. 20:41). Interestingly this is the second time in 1 Kings when a person disguised himself (cf. 14:2). Later Ahab disguised himself in battle (22:30).

Apparently Ahab thought he had met this man before. **The prophet** told the king that he, the prophet, was told in combat to **guard** a prisoner who got away. The prophet added that either his own **life** was to have been taken **or** he had to **pay a talent** (ca. 75 pounds) **of silver.**

20:40b-43. Ahab quickly assessed the storyteller's guilt; this was an obvious case of negligence. As in Nathan's story to David (2 Sam. 12:1-7) the king responded to the prophet in words that judged himself. **The prophet,** immediately revealing his identity, told **the king** he had been negligent in his responsibility to obey the order received from God to execute Ben-Hadad. Though this order is not recorded in the biblical text it is clear that Ahab had received it. Rather than obeying the Lord which probably would have resulted in a final end of the conflict with the vexing Aramean army, Ahab chose to follow his own plan. He believed Ben-Hadad's help against Assyria would be more valuable to Israel than Ben-Hadad's death.

Therefore Ahab would forfeit his

own **life** in exchange for Ben-Hadad's (cf. 1 Kings 22:37). Also Ahab's **people,** the Israelites, would die in place of Ben-Hadad's **people.** Ahab returned to **Samaria** sullen because of this prophecy and angry (cf. 21:4) at himself as well as at God's prophet.

5. AHAB'S CRIMES AGAINST NABOTH (CHAP. 21)

a. Ahab's proposal (21:1-4)

21:1-2. A period of peace followed the battle of Aphek (20:26-34). **Some time** after the battle the events recorded in chapter 21 took place. This **incident** further illustrates the evil characters of **Ahab** and Jezebel and enables readers to understand God's dealings with them. It also shows God's faithfulness in fulfilling the prophecies given by Elijah (21:20-24).

Naboth was Ahab's near neighbor in **Jezreel;** they apparently owned adjoining property. **Ahab** offered to buy Naboth's **vineyard** because it was a suitable piece of ground **for a vegetable garden** he wished to plant. Ahab offered to **pay** for it with **a better vineyard** elsewhere or with cash, whichever Naboth might prefer.

21:3-4. **Naboth** was a God-fearing Israelite. In obedience to the Mosaic Law he refused to sell his paternal **inheritance** (cf. Lev. 25:23-28; Num. 36:7). Evidently Ahab wanted this to be a permanent transaction. Again **Ahab** returned **home sullen and angry** (cf. 1 Kings 20:43). Ahab behaved in a childish manner. Rather than accepting Naboth's decision, Ahab **lay on his bed sulking and** even **refused to eat.**

b. Jezebel's plot (21:5-10)

21:5-7. When **his wife** asked Ahab why he was behaving strangely, he told her about Naboth's refusal. She had grown up in a culture where the rights of individuals were not honored as they were in **Israel.** It seemed incredible to her that Ahab would not just take what he wanted. That was how a **king** should **act,** according to her way of thinking. If he would not do what was necessary *she* would do so and without hesitation.

21:8-10. Knowing how to use the laws of Israel to gain her ends, Jezebel sent **letters** to leaders in **Naboth's** town, asking them to declare a fast and to have **two scoundrels** accuse **Naboth** of cursing

God and Ahab so that the people would **stone** Naboth. At least two witnesses were required to condemn a person in Israel (Deut. 17:6-7). Cursing God was a crime punishable by stoning (Lev. 24:16). Cursing the king was not punishable in that way. Jezebel may have added that part of her orders because she may have thought it was also punishable by death.

c. Naboth's murder (21:11-16)

21:11-14. The leading men of Jezreel obviously feared **Jezebel** more than they feared the Lord because they carried out her orders exactly. When **Naboth** (and his sons; cf. 2 Kings 9:26) were **dead** the **scoundrels** dutifully reported that the job was done.

21:15-16. **Jezebel** then announced **to Ahab** that he could **take possession** of Naboth's **vineyard** because its former owner was now **dead.** The king **got up** from his bed **and went down to take possession of** this property he coveted.

d. Elijah's prophecies (21:17-26)

21:17-19. Again God chose **Elijah** to bear a message of judgment to **Ahab,** who was then **in Naboth's vineyard.** God told Elijah just what to say (cf. v. 19). Jezebel was directly responsible for Naboth's death but Ahab was ultimately responsible since Jezebel's letter to the elders ordering Naboth's murder had been sent out over Ahab's name (v. 8). Elijah said Ahab had committed the crime of seizing **property** not his own as well as killing Naboth. **The place where dogs licked up Naboth's blood** was in Jezreel. Dogs licking up one's blood was a disgraceful death, especially for a king whose body would normally be carefully guarded and buried with great respect. Elijah left no doubt in Ahab's mind concerning whose **blood** he referred to: **yes, yours!**

21:20-22. When **Elijah** approached **Ahab** in the stolen vineyard, the king greeted him with the words, **So you have found me, my enemy.** This suggests that Ahab may have concluded that it would be only a matter of time till Elijah or some other man of God hunted him down. Elijah was not now the "troubler of Israel" (18:17), but the king's "enemy." Ahab had made himself the enemy of the Lord and His people by doing **evil in the eyes of the** LORD (cf. 21:25). When Elijah said the king had **sold** himself, he meant the king had sacrificed his principles to obtain what he wanted, which included a comparatively worthless vineyard. God promised **to bring disaster on** Ahab personally and to **consume** his **descendants,** cutting **off from** him every . . . **male in Israel.** He would have to stand alone without allies (cf. 14:10; 16:3). Ahab's dynasty would be cut off as Jeroboam's and Baasha's had been (cf. 2 Kings 9:9).

21:23-24. As for **Jezebel . . . dogs** would eat her **by the wall of Jezreel,** hardly a fitting end for a powerful queen (cf. 2 Kings 9:10, 36-37). Wild dogs lived off the garbage in cities such as Jezreel. Ahab's descendants would not receive honorable burials either but would be consumed by **dogs** and **birds** (cf. 1 Kings 14:11; 16:4).

21:25-26. The writer at this point inserted his own evaluation of **Ahab** and **Jezebel** into the narrative of Elijah and Ahab's conversation. Ahab was unique in his wickedness. He **sold himself to do evil in the** Lord's **eyes** (cf. v. 20). **Jezebel,** being void of any spiritual sensitivity and conscience, **urged** him **on** in evil. In pursuing idolatry Ahab **behaved in the vilest manner** by following the sinful ways of **the Amorites** whom God had driven **out** of Palestine when the Israelites entered the land in Joshua's day (Josh. 10:12-13).

e. Ahab's repentance (21:27-29)

21:27-29. Elijah's predicted judgment crushed **Ahab.** In sincere repentance he **humbled himself** before the Lord. Tearing one's **clothes** (Es. 4:1; Job 1:20), wearing **sackcloth** (Gen. 37:34; 1 Kings 20:31-32; Es. 4:1; Neh. 9:1; Dan. 9:3), and fasting (Neh. 9:1; Dan. 9:3) all manifested a spirit of grief and contrition. God noticed Ahab's change of mind and behavior. Ahab's life was deep-dyed with sin, but in response to his self-humbling, God showed him some mercy. The destruction to come on Ahab's **house** would not be carried out in his own **days** but **in** those **of his son** Joram (2 Kings 9:24-26; 10:17). Jezebel, however, did not repent. She suffered all that God promised she would suffer without mercy (2 Kings 9:30-37).

6. AHAB'S DEATH (22:1-40)

a. Ahab's alliance with Jehoshaphat (22:1-4)

22:1-4. For **three years** after the battle of Aphek (cf. 1 Kings 20:26-34) **there was**

no war between the Israelites and the Arameans. However, **in the third year** (853 B.C.), shortly after Ahab and Ben-Hadad had fought Shalmaneser at the Battle of Qarqar, Ahab decided that he needed to **retake** the important city of **Ramoth in Gilead** from the Arameans who had taken it from Israel earlier. Ramoth was one of the chief cities of the tribe of Gad, 28 miles east of the Jordan and 15 miles south of the Sea of Kinnereth, almost directly east of Jezreel. To field an army large enough to defeat the Arameans Ahab asked **Jehoshaphat** the **king of Judah** to ally with him against Ben-Hadad II. **Jehoshaphat** agreed for political reasons though he should have done so for spiritual reasons; he was a godly king, faithful to the Lord.

b. Ahab's prophets' counsel (22:5-12)

22:5-7. **Jehoshaphat** wanted divine counsel from **the** Lord before he and Ahab embarked on their mission. Ahab apparently could not have cared less. But to satisfy Jehoshaphat, Ahab called for **the prophets, about 400** of them. These were evidently prophets of the Lord; Baal prophets would have been unacceptable to Jehoshaphat. But they were apostate prophets. They had no concern about obtaining and relating the true word of the Lord. Their desire was to give their king the kind of advice they thought he wanted to hear. This would please him and he would favor them. Their answer to Ahab's question somehow led **Jehoshaphat** to believe that they did not have the mind of the Lord. So he requested **a prophet** true to **the** Lord of whom they could **inquire** (cf. 2 Kings 3:11).

22:8-12. Ahab replied that there was **one man** of God remaining whom they could contact. However, that one always prophesied evil for Ahab and for that reason Ahab said he hated **him.** Obviously Ahab was more concerned about feeling good than he was about knowing the truth. **Micaiah,** like Elijah, was one of the comparatively few faithful prophets in Israel in that day. Urged on by Jehoshaphat's continuing interest in hearing from **Micaiah,** Ahab sent for him.

Perhaps Micaiah lived in or near **Samaria** where this conversation took place. **The threshing floor** was usually an elevated area; it would have been a good place for Ahab and **Jehoshaphat** to prepare themselves for battle. **The gate of the city** was the most popular place to assemble, so a large crowd was gathered including the 400 **prophets.** One of these prophets, **Zedekiah** (cf. v. 24), had even fashioned some **horns** out of **iron** and claimed blasphemously that God had told him that the two allied kings with the horns would **gore the Arameans** to destruction. With this prediction **all the other prophets** agreed, adding their own optimistic promises of victory.

c. Micaiah's prophecy (22:13-28)

22:13-14. The messenger who was sent to get **Micaiah** urged him to **agree with the other prophets in giving an optimistic prediction. But Micaiah** told him that he would utter whatever words **the LORD** gave him regardless of what **others** might say. Like Elijah, Micaiah was prepared to stand alone.

22:15-16. The king, probably Ahab the host, **asked . . . Micaiah** the same question he had asked the other prophets (v. 6). Micaiah seems to have been familiar with this procedure; he had probably been through it several times before. His reply was sarcastic, though probably not delivered in a sarcastic tone which would have been inappropriate for a man of his character. Ahab recognized at once what **Micaiah** was doing. His own reply was equally sarcastic. He had probably never told Micaiah to **swear to tell** him **nothing but the truth** before, as he did not need to. But Ahab's saying that probably sounded good.

22:17-18. The time for sarcasm was over. **Micaiah** related the burden of the Lord in all its devastating simplicity and force. Micaiah said he had seen, perhaps in a vision, **all Israel scattered** over **the hills** of Gilead **like sheep without a shepherd,** wandering and in need of leadership. **The LORD** had told the prophet that **these** sheep had **no master,** obviously a reference to Ahab. After the shepherd would be killed in battle the sheep would return **home** without being pursued by the enemy, Aram. Ahab reacted to this sober warning offhandedly (v. 18; cf. v. 8), unwilling to consider it seriously.

22:19-23. Micaiah proceeded to explain the rest of what God had shown him, not about the battle but about the advice both kings had been receiving

from the 400 prophets. He called on the two kings to **hear the word of the LORD.** Micaiah **saw . . . the host of heaven,** the angelic armies of God, assembled **around** God's heavenly **throne.** Whether the conversation Micaiah then described (vv. 20-23) actually took place in heaven or whether it was a revelation given in anthropomorphic terms to help Micaiah and his audience visualize what was taking place on the threshing floor before them, the point was clear to all: The 400 **prophets** spoke with **a lying spirit** (vv. 22-23) to deceive, and to lead Ahab to **disaster** in battle and **to his death** (v. 20). Micaiah, however, spoke the truth. The Lord had apparently permitted a "lying spirit" (i.e., a demon) to speak through the 400 prophets as a means of bringing **Ahab** to his death.

22:24-25. Zedekiah (cf. v. 11) certainly understood Micaiah's message as did everyone else. A slap **in the face** was a great insult (cf. Job 16:10; Lam. 3:30; Micah 5:1), greater then than it is today. The false prophet brazenly or innocently claimed that he had not invented his prophecy himself but that it had been given to him by the Lord.

Micaiah did not need to argue about whose prophecy had come **from the LORD** and whose had come from the lying spirit; time would tell. He was not trying to scare people when there was no real cause for fear. Zedekiah would **find out** who had the true word from the Lord when he fled **to hide in an inner room** (i.e., after Ahab had been killed the false prophets would flee in terror).

22:26-28. Ahab's reaction evidences the blindness and folly that overtakes those who disregard the Word of the Lord. Rather than repenting, as he had done previously (21:27), now hardened in sin to the point of insensibility, Ahab ordered that **Micaiah** be given to **Amon,** the **city** mayor, **and to Joash, the king's son.** "King's son" is apparently a title of a royal official and is not to be taken as the literal son of Ahab (cf. 2 Chron. 28:7; Jer. 36:26; 38:6). Ahab told Amon and Joash to **put** the prophet who had warned him of impending doom **in prison. Micaiah** had the final word, however, and it was another gracious but strong warning for Ahab, indicating that the king would not **return** from battle **safely.** The prophet also called on **all**

present to remember his **words** for they would prove that **the** LORD had **spoken through** him when his prophecy came to pass.

d. The battle of Ramoth Gilead (22:29-40)

22:29-33. Despite Micaiah's warning Ahab, **the king of Israel, and Jehoshaphat,** his ally, **went up to Ramoth Gilead** to face Ben-Hadad II, **the king of Aram.** Perhaps Ahab suggested his plan to **enter the battle . . . disguised** (probably as a regular soldier or officer) out of fear for his life in view of what Micaiah had said.

Jehoshaphat did not realize that this tactic would put him in greater danger until the battle began. He may not have been aware of Ben-Hadad's anger against Ahab that led the king of Aram to concentrate his attack on **the king of Israel.** Ben-Hadad may have wanted to kill Ahab alone because he knew that without their king the soldiers of Israel would not fight effectively. Probably the fact that Ahab was now breaking his treaty with Ben-Hadad (cf. 20:34) angered the Aramean king too. Dressed in his royal attire **Jehoshaphat** became the target of the whole Aramean army. Under attack he **cried out** something that told the Arameans **he was not** the man they sought. Perhaps he cried out to God as well as to the soldiers since he trusted in and prayed to the Lord.

22:34-36. The manner in which Ahab was fatally wounded is one of many examples in Scripture of God using an incident that would have been regarded as accidental to accomplish His purpose. Ahab was injured by an arrow shot **at random.** The man who shot the arrow did not knowingly aim it at the chink in the king's **armor,** but God directed him and guided the fatal missile to its mark. The king's **chariot** was large enough to accommodate Ahab as he sat **propped up in** it to watch the battle until sunset.

The reference to Ahab's **blood** running down **onto the floor of** his **chariot** sets the stage for the later word about the fulfillment of the prophecy of Ahab's death (v. 38). The battle broke up when Ahab died; Ben-Hadad had achieved his objective as the Israelites could not take Ramoth Gilead.

22:37-38. The body of Ahab was returned **to Samaria** where he was **buried.** Had he not repented earlier (21:27) Ahab

would not have been buried at all (21:28-29). Ahab's **chariot** was then driven around to an out-of-the-way **pool** where it was **washed.** Ahab was despised by God for his wickedness. The story of Ahab concludes with his **blood** being desecrated in the company of Samaria's despised **prostitutes** and **dogs.** Ahab died as God had predicted he would (20:42; 21:19, 21).

22:39-40. In excavating Samaria archeologists discovered more than 200 **ivory** figures, panels, and plaques in one storeroom. Ahab used large quantities of ivory to beautify his **palace** in various ways. He also **fortified** several **cities** in **Israel.**

In addition to the projects just mentioned, Ahab ruled capably in spite of the gross spiritual apostasy that characterized his administration. He was generally successful militarily because of his own native ability and God's mercy on Israel. His alliance with Judah under Jehoshaphat began the first real period of peace between the Northern and Southern Kingdoms since the monarchy had split and it lasted about 30 years until the reign of Jehu began in 841. But in spite of Ahab's other accomplishments his building a Baal altar and temple and encouraging Baal worship (16:32-33) weakened Israel as never before.

L. Jehoshaphat's good reign in Judah (22:41-50)

22:41-43a. Asa's son, **Jehoshaphat,** began his reign in Judah in 873 B.C. as coregent with his father. This coregency existed because of Asa's poor health (15:23) and it continued for three years until Asa's death in 870 B.C. when Jehoshaphat became sole ruler. This was the first instance of coregency since Solomon had ruled jointly with David for a brief time. **Jehoshaphat** was **king** for **25 years** altogether (873–848 B.C.). He was one of Judah's eight good kings and one of its four reformers like **his father Asa.**

22:43b-44. According to 2 Chronicles 17:6 Jehoshaphat removed **the high places,** but 1 Kings 22:43 and 2 Chronicles 20:33 indicate that he did not remove them. Apparently he did, but when the people restored them he did not again obliterate the restored high places. Other kings of Judah who did not remove the high places were Joash (2 Kings 12:3),

Amaziah (2 Kings 14:4), Azariah (2 Kings 15:4), and Jotham (2 Kings 15:35). Ahaz sacrificed at the high places (2 Kings 16:4), perhaps ones he restored. Those were then removed by Hezekiah (2 Kings 18:4), rebuilt by Manasseh (2 Kings 21:3), and demolished again by Josiah (2 Kings 23:8, 13, 15, 19).

As mentioned previously (cf. comments on 1 Kings 22:39-40), Jehoshaphat and Ahab united in a treaty which resulted in **peace** between Judah and **Israel** during his reign. Unfortunately this treaty involved the marriage of Jehoshaphat's son Jehoram to Ahab's daughter Athaliah who followed Jezebel's example and caused Judah problems later (cf. 2 Kings 11).

22:45-47. Jehoshaphat's achievements and attitudes are more fully expounded in 2 Chronicles 17–20. These included ordering the teaching of the Law of Moses throughout Judah. God miraculously delivered Judah from the united armies of Moab, Ammon, and **Edom** in response to the king's prayers and his obedience to the Lord. He was a strong ruler whose favor Philistia and Arabia courted. Jehoshaphat instituted many judicial reforms in Judah also. The writer of Kings noted his purge of the remaining **male shrine prostitutes** (cf. 1 Kings 14:24; 15:12) in particular.

22:48-50. As a result of the unstable political situation in Edom in his day (cf. v. 47) **Jehoshaphat** was able to build **a fleet of trading ships . . . at Ezion Geber** on the northern tip of the Gulf of Aqaba with Israel's king **Ahaziah,** Ahab's eldest **son** (cf. 2 Chron. 20:36). The plan was to bring back **gold** from **Ophir,** in southwestern Arabia (cf. 1 Kings 9:28; 10:11) as Solomon had done. But in some way the fleet was **wrecked** and never fulfilled its mission. **Jehoshaphat** had **refused** to let Ahaziah's **men sail with** his own. This venture resulted in failure and frustration for Jehoshaphat as did all his other joint efforts with Israel.

Jehoshaphat's son **Jehoram** began reigning as coregent with his father in 853 B.C. When Jehoshaphat died in 848 B.C., Jehoram continued to reign till 841.

M. The beginning of Ahaziah's evil reign in Israel (22:51-53)

22:51-53. A short summary of Ahaziah's reign concludes 1 Kings, but the events of his rule follow in 2 Kings.

Ahaziah . . . of Israel began his reign of **two** official **years** (one actual year) in 853 B.C. and he ruled until 852, during Jehoshaphat's reign in Judah. Ahaziah was the elder **son of Ahab.** Since Ahaziah had no son his brother Joram (also called Jehoram) succeeded him when he died. His **mother** was Jezebel. Ahaziah followed his parents' evil **ways** and those **of Jeroboam. Baal** worship continued in Israel under his protection and encouragement.

BIBLIOGRAPHY

Davis, John J., and Whitcomb, John C., Jr. *A History of Israel*. Grand Rapids: Baker Book House, 1980.

Finegan, Jack. *Light from the Ancient Past*. 2nd ed. Princeton, N.J.: Princeton University Press, 1959.

Gray, John. *I & II Kings: A Commentary*. 2nd ed. Philadelphia: Westminster Press, 1970.

Jamieson, Robert. "I and II Kings." In *A Commentary, Critical, Experimental and Practical on the Old and New Testaments*. 3rd ed. Grand Rapids: Zondervan Publishing House, 1983.

Keil, C.F. "The Books of Kings." In *Commentary on the Old Testament in Ten Volumes*. Vol. 3. Reprint (25 vols. in 10). Grand Rapids: Wm. B. Eerdmans Publishing Co., 1982.

McNeely, Richard I. *First and Second Kings*. Chicago: Moody Press, 1978.

Montgomery, James A. *A Critical and Exegetical Commentary on the Books of Kings*. The International Critical Commentary. Edinburgh: T. & T. Clark, 1951.

Thiele, Edwin R. *A Chronology of the Hebrew Kings*. Grand Rapids: Zondervan Publishing House, 1977.

_____. *The Mysterious Numbers of the Hebrew Kings*. Rev. ed. Chicago: University of Chicago Press, 1983.

Wood, Leon J. *A Survey of Israel's History*. Grand Rapids: Zondervan Publishing House, 1970.

2 KINGS

Thomas L. Constable

INTRODUCTION

See the *Introduction* to 1 Kings.

OUTLINE

COMMENTARY

I. The Later History of the Divided Kingdom (chaps. 1–17)

This section of 2 Kings continues the history of Israel and Judah begun in 1 Kings 12. It ends with the Assyrian Captivity of the Northern Kingdom in 722 B.C.

A. The remainder of Ahaziah's evil reign in Israel (chap. 1)

The account of the rule of Ahab's elder son Ahaziah continues from 1 Kings 22:51-53.

1. AHAZIAH'S INQUIRY (1:1-2)

1:1. Moab, under Mesha its king, **rebelled against Israel** after Ahab died. The death of the Israelite king encouraged Mesha to throw off the burden of taxation that Omri (Ahaziah's grandfather) had imposed when he had brought Moab under Israel's control (cf. comments on 1 Kings 16:21-24). This rebellion was not effective at first but the fact that it began in Ahaziah's reign may suggest that Mesha considered Ahaziah a weaker king than Ahab.

1:2. This verse begins a new incident

in Ahaziah's life which occupies the remainder of chapter 1. The king had suffered an injury from falling **through the lattice** covering of a window in **his upper story room,** probably to the ground below. His serious injury later proved fatal. The king's veneration of Baal can be seen in his sending **messengers** to **Ekron,** a Philistine city about 40 miles away (see the map "Elijah's Travels," near 1 Kings 17:8-11), to inquire of a pagan idol whether he would recover. **Baal-Zebub** was one of the many local male fertility gods which bore some form of the name Baal (meaning "lord"). Baal-Zebub means "Lord of the flies," but the original spelling in Philistia was probably Baal-Zebul, which means "Exalted lord." He was credited with healing powers. Ahaziah sought some prophetic word of encouragement from the oracle of Baal-Zebub. His failure to inquire of Yahweh, the God of Israel, reveals the depth of his apostasy.

2. ELIJAH'S PROPHECY (1:3-8)

1:3-4. The Angel of the LORD (the preincarnate Christ; cf. comments on Gen. 16:9) appeared **to Elijah** as He had appeared to many other Old Testament leaders in the past (e.g., Abraham, Moses, Gideon). His appearances always identified an important revelation. The angel gave Elijah a prophecy to pass on to the king through the royal **messengers** whom Elijah intercepted as they traveled south from Samaria to **Ekron.** Though Ahaziah sought a message from **Baal-Zebub,** he got an answer from the true and living **God.** Perhaps Ahaziah, like his father Ahab, did not want to inquire of a faithful prophet of the Lord since those prophets were consistently opposing rather than supporting **the king** because of his wickedness. God's punishment for consulting a pagan idol rather than Himself was that Ahaziah would fail to recover from his injuries (cf. 2 Kings 1:6, 16).

1:5-8. The messengers returned to Ahaziah and reported their meeting with Elijah and his prophecy. Ahaziah knew who Elijah was, of course, since Elijah had consistently opposed his parents, Ahab and Jezebel, for their **Baal** worship. The hairy **garment** (probably made from goats' dark **hair)** and large **leather belt** were part of the dress of prophets at that time. Cloth woven from hair, as rough as burlap, was sometimes called sackcloth. Since sackcloth symbolized distress or self-affliction (cf. 6:30; Gen. 37:34; 2 Sam. 3:31), Elijah's garb probably visualized the repentance to which the prophets called the people (cf. penitence and sackcloth in Neh. 9:1; Jer. 6:26). Ahaziah recognized his messengers' description of **Elijah** immediately.

3. THE CAPTAINS AND THEIR 50S (1:9-16)

1:9. To many readers this story seems like an unnecessarily cruel demonstration of God's power. However, the issues at stake justified severe action. Ahaziah showed complete contempt for **Elijah** and the God he represented by sending a band of soldiers to arrest the prophet like an outlaw and drag him before the throne. Perhaps Elijah's position **on the top of a hill** should have reminded **the captain** of Elijah's victory over the prophets of Baal on Mount Carmel (1 Kings 18:20-40) and of his great God-given power. Either the captain did not make this connection or decided to disregard it. He acknowledged that **Elijah** was a **man of God** (cf. 2 Kings 1:11), but ordered him to **come down** to him in Ahaziah's name.

In 1 and 2 Kings the term "man of God" is a synonym for a prophet. It is used of Shemaiah (1 Kings 12:22), of Elijah seven times (1 Kings 17:18, 24; 2 Kings 1:9, 10-13), of Elisha more than two dozen times in 2 Kings (the first occurrence is in 4:7 and the last is in 13:19), and of two other anonymous prophets (one is mentioned frequently in 1 Kings 13 and in 2 Kings 23:16-17; the other is referred to in 1 Kings 20:28).

1:10. Elijah's repetition of the fact that he was indeed **a man of God** (cf. v. 12) shows that this was an important issue; God's reputation was at stake. Was Ahaziah in charge, able to command God's servants to obey *him?* Or was God in charge, able to command Ahaziah's servants to obey *Him?* By sending **fire . . . from heaven** (cf. v. 12) to **consume** the soldiers of the king, God was reminding Ahaziah that He was Israel's Ruler and that the king should submit to His sovereignty. In a play on similar-sounding Hebrew words **Elijah** said that because he was a man ('îš) of God, fire ('ēš) would consume them.

1:11-12. Ahaziah disregarded this tragedy and tried again to force **Elijah** to submit to him. This time **the captain** ordered the prophet, **Come down** (cf. v. 9) **at once!** Again **Elijah** reminded the **captain,** undoubtedly for the benefit of those looking on who would report the incident as well as for the officer, that he was indeed God's **man.** The **fire** of judgment **fell** again (cf. v. 10), proving that the first miracle was not just an accident but was the hand **of God** at work in judgment.

1:13-14. Still Ahaziah hardened his heart. The **third captain** he sent had more respect for Yahweh and His representative than Ahaziah did. Rather than demanding surrender from a position of assumed superiority this man submitted to Elijah's authority, falling to **his knees before** him. He too recognized **Elijah** as a **man of God,** but unlike the first two captains (cf. vv. 9, 11) he pleaded for mercy. He acknowledged that the **fire** that had **fallen** had come **from heaven** (i.e., was caused by God).

1:15-16. The Angel of the LORD directed **Elijah** to **go down with him . . . to the king** and **not be afraid of him;** God had superior power and would control the situation. (This was the sixth time God told **Elijah** to "go" or "leave"; cf. 1 Kings 17:3, 9; 18:1; 21:18; 2 Kings 1:3.) This whole incident, like the contest on Mount Carmel, was designed to demonstrate God's sovereignty to the king and the people of Israel.

Standing before **the king,** Elijah fearlessly delivered the message **God** had given him. Because of Ahaziah's failure **to consult** Israel's God (cf. v. 2) and his determination to lead independently, God would depose him. This is the same message Elijah had given earlier to the king's **messengers** on their way to **Ekron** (vv. 3-4).

4. AHAZIAH'S DEATH (1:17-18)

1:17-18. Just as **Elijah** had announced (vv. 4, 16), Ahaziah never recovered from his injuries and **died** shortly thereafter. Since **Ahaziah had no son** his brother **Joram** (a variant of the Heb. "Jehoram"; cf. NIV marg.) **succeeded him as king** of Israel. This accession took place **in the second year of Jehoram . . . king of Judah** (i.e., the second year of his coregency with his father **Jehoshaphat,** viz., 852 B.C.). The kings of Israel

and Judah at this time had the same name. (The NIV keeps the two kings distinct by spelling the king of Israel's name "Joram" and the king of Judah's "Jehoram.")

B. Joram's evil reign in Israel (2:1–8:15)

Much space is devoted to the years when Joram reigned because of Elisha's important ministry which took place then. As always the interest of the writer of 1 and 2 Kings was primarily spiritual rather than political.

1. ELISHA'S INAUGURATION (CHAP. 2)

This chapter records the transition that took place in the spiritual leadership of Israel with the assumption of Elijah into heaven. Elisha's miracles here have to do mainly with his inauguration as Elijah's spiritual successor.

a. Elijah's assumption into heaven (2:1-12)

2:1-3. Departing **from Gilgal** in Israel **Elijah** and his younger fellow prophet **Elisha** headed for **Bethel** on a mission from God. This Gilgal may be modern Jiljiliah (seven miles northwest of Bethel), different from the Gilgal near the Jordan River (see the map "Elijah's Travels," near 1 Kings 17:8-11). **Elisha** had learned somehow (perhaps from **Elijah** himself) that this would be Elijah's last day on earth. Determined to be with his father in the faith till the very end **Elisha** refused Elijah's suggestion that he remain comfortably in Gilgal. A dying person often pronounced blessings on others (cf. Gen. 49) and **Elisha** did not want to miss out on this opportunity to receive God's blessings on his life and ministry.

Some **prophets** of the LORD living at **Bethel** also knew of Elijah's departure and told **Elisha.** These groups or schools of the prophets had been established to teach the Israelites the revealed Word of God. Elijah was Elisha's **master** in the sense of his being the younger prophet's mentor. Elisha's response, **Do not speak of it,** means, "Do not add to my sorrow at this prospect by reminding me of it."

2:4-5. Testing Elisha's commitment again, **Elijah** suggested that **Elisha** stay in Bethel rather than accompanying him to his next stop, **Jericho.** Elisha showed his zeal by refusing to leave Elijah. **So they** continued on **to Jericho. The company of the prophets** at Jericho repeated what their brethren in Bethel had said. **Elisha** gave them the same reply (cf. v. 3).

2:6-8. **Elijah** tested **Elisha** a third time, and Elisha again refused to put his own comfort ahead of the possibility of receiving a special blessing from God. So they went toward **the Jordan** River. As the day wore on **50 . . . of the** young **prophets** from Jericho, realizing that Elijah's departure was imminent, followed **at a distance** to observe what would happen to him. At the bank of **the Jordan** River **Elijah . . . rolled** up **his cloak** and, using it as a symbol of God's power, **struck the water with it** (cf. Ex. 14:16, 21-22). A prophet's cloak symbolized his authority under God (cf. 1 Kings 19:19) with which God clothed and empowered him. Miraculously **the water divided** and the riverbed dried up so that **the two** men **crossed over** as the Israelites had crossed the Red Sea and the Jordan River hundreds of years earlier. (This is one of many similarities between the ministries of Moses and Elijah.) Elisha was reminded that the same God with the same power was still alive and active in Israel.

2:9-10. **Elijah** then invited **Elisha** to ask what he wanted from him **before** he would be **taken** away. **Elisha** requested the blessing of the firstborn, **a double portion.** But Elisha wanted spiritual rather than material blessing. He was not asking to be twice as popular as Elijah or to perform twice as many miracles. Elisha was asking to be the successor of Elijah and to be privileged to carry on his ministry under God (cf. "double share of," Deut. 21:17).

However, this was not Elijah's to give; for that reason it was **a difficult thing.** Elijah did not know if God would grant Elisha's request. The sign that He would grant it would be Elisha's actually seeing Elijah being **taken from** him. This was not a condition for Elisha to receive the double portion but the evidence that he would.

2:11-12. **Suddenly a** fast-approaching **chariot . . . and horses of fire . . . separated** Elijah from Elisha. These did not bear **Elijah** into **heaven;** a **whirlwind** did that. The fiery horses and chariot were symbols of God's power in battle. Horses and chariots were the mightiest means of warfare in that day. God was saying in this event that His power was far greater than any military might. It was this power that Elijah had demonstrated and which **Elisha** in his wisdom valued so highly (cf. Ex. 14:9, 17; 1 Kings 10:29; Ps. 104:3-4; Isa. 31:1). The whirlwind was actually a storm with lightning and thunder. Like the pillar of cloud that led the Israelites in the wilderness (Ex. 13:21), it represented God's presence.

God swept Elijah off the face of the earth into His very presence. And **Elisha** did see the event. Elijah had been Elisha's spiritual **father,** his predecessor in the ministry of calling people back to God. Elisha's reference to **the chariots and horsemen of Israel** shows that he regarded Elijah as a powerful instrument whom God had used to wage war against the idolatry in Israel. He would be greatly missed. Elisha **tore** his **own clothes** as an act of mourning (cf. Gen. 37:29, 34; 44:13; Josh. 7:6; Es. 4:1; Job 1:20; 2:12) over the loss of this great spiritual warrior. From then on Elisha would wear Elijah's cloak and would serve with the authority and power it symbolized.

b. The parting of the Jordan (2:13-14)

2:13-14. Elijah's **cloak . . . had fallen from** him as he was taken up into heaven. Using it as **Elijah** had done, Elisha **struck the water** of the Jordan and the river parted again (cf. v. 8). Obviously then he possessed the power of Elijah. His words, **Where now is the LORD, the God of Elijah?** were a call to God to demonstrate His power through him as He had done through Elijah.

c. The search for Elijah (2:15-18)

2:15-18. The 50 **prophets from Jericho** (cf. v. 7), observing the whirlwind and the parting of the Jordan both times, concluded that Elijah's spiritual gifts had been passed **on** to **Elisha.** Out of respect for his special calling they **bowed . . . before him.**

They did not realize as **Elisha** did that **Elijah** had been taken into the presence of God and had not returned to the earth. So they requested permission to send out search parties to locate Elijah. They, like Obadiah, thought he might have been transported by **the Spirit of the LORD** (cf. 1 Kings 18:12), perhaps to **some** remote **mountain or . . . valley.** Knowing their search would be futile, **Elisha** tried to dissuade them. But they

God's Miracles through Elijah and Elisha

ELIJAH		ELISHA	
Miracle	Some of the Elements Involved*	Miracle	Some of the Elements Involved*
1. Elijah fed by ravens	Water and food	1. Jordan River parted	Water
2. Widow's food multiplied	Flour and oil	2. Jericho spring water purified	Water
3. Widow's dead son raised to life	Life	3. Widow's oil multiplied	Oil
4. Elijah's altar and sacrifice consumed	Water and fire	4. Shunammite's dead son raised to life	Life
5. Ahaziah's 102 soldiers consumed	Fire	5. Poisonous stew purified	Flour
6. Jordan River parted	Water	6. Prophets' food multiplied	Bread and grain
7. Elijah's transport to heaven	Fire and wind	7. Naaman healed of leprosy	Water
		8. Gehazi's leprosy	—
		9. Axhead floated	Water
		10. Horses and chariots surrounded the city of Dothan	Fire
		11. Aramean soldiers blinded	—

*Many of these elements—water, flour, oil, fire, and wind—were polemics against Baal, the god of rain, lightning (fire), and vegetation. Even the restoration of two boys back to life (one by Elijah and one by Elisha) was a polemic against the practice of child sacrifice and against the myth that Baal was dead six months each year and then was raised annually. Baal's restoration to life was only mythical; the boys' restoration to life was real.

insisted and in order to avoid appearing heartless Elisha finally gave them permission. They returned **three days** later without Elijah as Elisha had predicted. Elisha's word was thereafter more readily accepted and respected by them.

d. The purifying of the waters (2:19-22)

2:19. The incident recorded in verses 19-22 evidently followed soon after the one in verses 15-18. **Elisha** was still in Jericho. Apparently word about him had spread for now all **the** citizens **of the city** knew of Elisha's power. The leading **men** came to him with a practical problem that gave him opportunity to demonstrate the Lord's desire and ability to bless the people. Jericho had many natural advantages since it was located in a fertile area of the Jordan Valley. **But the water** from a major spring had turned **bad,** perhaps brackish, and when used for irrigation it killed the crops rather than nourishing them. The parallelism between this physical situation and the spiritually polluting influences of Baal worship in Israel is obvious.

2:20-22. Elisha's solution, given by **the LORD,** was designed to teach the peo-

ple as well as to relieve their immediate distress. The **new bowl** represented himself, the new instrument in God's hand. **Salt** was known by the Israelites to preserve and purify; it was used in each of their daily grain offerings to the Lord (cf. Lev. 2:13). But adding salt to water normally makes water worse, not better. When **the salt** was put into **the** Jericho **water** the situation miraculously improved. This miracle showed the people of Jericho that the Lord, not Baal, the so-called god of fertility, could heal their barrenness. God's permanent work on the spring would serve as a perpetual reminder of His ability to bring fruitfulness and blessing out of the barrenness and sterility caused by idolatry.

e. The cursing young men (2:23-25)

2:23. As **Elisha** was traveling from Jericho **to Bethel** several dozen **youths** (young men, not children) confronted him. Perhaps they were young false prophets of Baal. Their jeering, recorded in the slang of their day, implied that if Elisha were a great prophet of the Lord, as Elijah was, he should **go on up** into heaven as Elijah reportedly had done.

The epithet **baldhead** may allude to lepers who had to shave their heads and were considered detestable outcasts. Or it may simply have been a form of scorn, for baldness was undesirable (cf. Isa. 3:17, 24). Since it was customary for men to cover their heads, the young men probably could not tell if Elisha was bald or not. They regarded God's prophet with contempt.

2:24. Elisha then **called down a curse on** the villains. This cursing stemmed not from Elisha's pride but from their disrespect for **the LORD** as reflected in their treatment of His spokesman (cf. 1:9-14). Again God used wild animals to execute His judgment (cf., e.g., 1 Kings 13:24). That **42** men were **mauled** by the **two bears** suggests that a mass demonstration had been organized against God and Elisha.

2:25. Elisha journeyed on from Bethel **to Mount Carmel.** There among other activities he undoubtedly reviewed God's mighty vindication of Himself through Elijah (1 Kings 18:19-46). Elisha's ministry would continue what Elijah had begun (1 Kings 19:16).

From Mount Carmel Elisha **returned to Samaria.** This city, capital of the Northern Kingdom of Israel, was to be the site of many of Elisha's mighty deeds.

These early miracles in Elisha's ministry identified him as a unique spokesman for God with the authority and power of Elijah, one worthy of the greatest respect as a representative of the living God.

2. JORAM'S WICKEDNESS (3:1-3)

3:1-3. Joram was the second **son of Ahab** to rule **Israel. In the 18th year** after Jehoshaphat began reigning as sole **king of Judah,** Joram **became king** over Israel **and . . . reigned 12 years** (852–841 B.C.). Though wicked, he was less **evil** than his **father** Ahab and his **mother** Jezebel. **The sacred stone of Baal . . . made** by Ahab, was evidently an image of that god. Though Joram did get **rid of** this idol he remained sympathetic to and supportive of Baal worship in **Israel** (cf. 10:19-28). For some reason he removed this important image, but continued the religious policies of his parents and his predecessor **Jeroboam** (cf. 1 Kings 12:26-33; 13:33).

3. ELISHA'S MINISTRY (3:4–8:15)

The great ministry of Elisha, already begun and revealed in part, is recorded in this large section of stories.

a. The battle against Moab (3:4-27)

3:4-8. The Moabites **raised** many **sheep.** When Omri subjugated **Moab** he imposed a tribute of **lambs and . . . wool** which the Moabites grudgingly provided for many years. When **Ahab died** in battle, **Mesha** the Moabite **king . . . rebelled against . . . King** Ahaziah (1:1). This rebellion seems to have been ineffective since Mesha also rebelled against Ahaziah's successor, Joram (3:4-27). Eager to suppress this uprising **Joram . . . mobilized all . . . Israel.** Seeking permission to march through Judah to fight Moab from the south, Joram asked **Jehoshaphat** of **Judah** to join him as an ally in battle. Jehoshaphat agreed and pledged his support to Joram. Joram suggested attacking from the south **through the Desert of Edom** rather than from the north, the more normal though heavily defended frontier, and Jehoshaphat agreed.

3:9-12. Edom at this time was under Judah's authority and joined the alliance. After marching through Judah down the southwestern coast of the Dead Sea, around the southern end, and into Edom, **the army** ran out of **water.** Joram's expression of dismay (v. 10) indicates that he considered **the LORD** responsible for their predicament. As on an earlier occasion (1 Kings 22:7) **Jehoshaphat** suggested they find a **prophet of the LORD** who could obtain instructions for them. One of Joram's officers volunteered that **Elisha** was nearby. Probably the Lord had directed him there to be ready for this mission; it is unlikely that he was traveling with the army. Pouring **water on the hands** of another for washing was a servant's work; Elisha had been Elijah's minister (cf. 1 Kings 19:21). Evidently the officer thought Joram did not know Elisha, which may have been the case. Whether Joram knew of Elisha or not, **Jehoshaphat** did. Humbling themselves before the prophet, the three kings paid him a visit.

3:13-19. Elisha's question, **What do we have to do with each other?** is probably an idiom meaning "Why should I obey you?" The prophet's suggestion that Joram go to his parents' **prophets** implies that since the king promoted Baal worship he should seek his own god. This barb forced Joram to face up to the impotency of Baal. Joram's rejoinder placed the blame for the army's predicament on **the LORD.** He had come to Elisha because now it was up to Yahweh to get them out of their trouble.

Elisha was not intimidated by Joram's charge. He knew God had not directed Israel into its difficulty but that the army was there on the king's initiative. Nevertheless for Jehoshaphat's sake **Elisha** consented to seek a word from the Lord. (His words **As surely as the LORD Almighty lives, whom I serve** are strikingly similar to Elijah's words to Joram's father Ahab (1 Kings 17:1; cf. 2 Kings 5:16). Harp music helped put **Elisha** into a frame of mind in which he could readily discern the Lord's direction. (David's harp-playing also helped soothe Saul, 1 Sam. 16:23.)

Elisha received a direct revelation and proceeded to explain God's plan. The **valley** was probably the valley of the Zered on Moab's southern boundary. God would provide **water** enough in an unnatural way so that everyone would know that it was He who had provided. This would be **an easy thing in the** Lord's **eyes.** Ultimate victory would be theirs. Cutting **down** all the **good** trees would make it difficult for the Moabites to have fruit to eat and would mean they would have little shade. Stopping **up all the springs** would limit the Moabites' water supply, and putting large **stones** in the fields would retard cultivation and lessen their productivity.

3:20-25. Evidently God caused the **water** from rains in **Edom** to flow down into the valley and fill the trenches that had been dug. This **water** was an expression of God's love for His people. The fact that it had not rained locally probably caused **the Moabites** to think that having water in the valley was impossible. The **morning . . . sacrifice** included a lamb and a grain and drink offering (Ex. 29:38-43).

The border where **the Moabites** were stationed **early in the morning** was the boundary between Moab and Edom east and south of the Dead Sea. Not expecting water, the Moabites assumed that **the water** shining in the sunlight

was **blood.** So the Moabite army erroneously concluded that the Israelites, Judahites, and Edomites had had a falling out and had **slaughtered each other**— not an unrealistic possiblity. Rather than advancing with weapons drawn for battle they ran to **plunder** the "dead" soldiers' armor and weaponry. **But** instead, they ran into the waiting ranks of their enemies. Defenseless, **the Moabites . . . fled** before **the Israelites. The Israelites,** and presumably their allies with them, **invaded** Moab, **slaughtered** the people, **destroyed** many **towns,** and did to the fields, **springs,** and trees what God had instructed (cf. 2 Kings 3:19). But **Kir Hareseth,** the major city, could not be taken. It was situated at the end of a valley and successfully resisted the attacks of the stone slingers surrounding it.

3:26-27. The city of Kir Hareseth (v. 25) was King Mesha's refuge. Courageously he assembled **700 swordsmen,** broke out of the city, and attacked **the king of Edom,** whom he apparently concluded was the weakest link in the three-nation alliance. He was not successful, however, and was forced back behind the walls. Defeat in battle was regarded by pagan Near Eastern warriors as a sign that their gods were angry with them. To propitiate his god, Chemosh (1 Kings 11:7, 33; 2 Kings 23:13), Mesha offered **his firstborn son,** the heir to his throne, **as a** human **sacrifice on** top of **the city wall.** He was fighting with all his might. It was not Israel's intent to annihilate the Moabites; they only wanted to keep their neighbors from rebelling against their sovereignty to keep them under their control. So offensive to the allies was Mesha's act of sacrificing his son that **they withdrew and returned** home. Israel had won the battle even though they had not destroyed Kir Hareseth or captured Mesha.

Some say **the fury against Israel,** which **was great,** may refer to God's anger. More likely it refers to Judah's anger against Israel for invading Moab in a battle that resulted in their seeing such a repulsive act.

A remarkable archeological discovery, the Moabite Stone, contains Mesha's own record of this battle and other battles with Israel. On this stone the Moabite king claimed to have been delivered from the Israelites by his god

Chemosh on this day. Though it is true that he was not captured at Kir Hareseth and the Israelites withdrew, Israel and her allies were the real victors in this campaign.

The account of this battle provides further proof of the sovereignty of Yahweh and of the complete vanity of idols and idolatry. But even with so many proofs Israel continued to spurn the Lord and foolishly worshiped pagan deities.

b. The oil for the prophet's widow (4:1-7)

4:1. The place where this incident took place is not stated but probably the widow lived in one of the cities where the schools of the prophets were situated, perhaps Bethel, Gilgal, or Jericho. Since the prophet had a **wife** it is clear that **the company of the prophets** was not a monastic settlement (or settlements) of celibates. This widow turned **to Elisha** for help in her hour of need. She appealed to him on the basis that her **husband** had been faithful to the Lord (**he revered the LORD**). The taking of **boys as . . . slaves** in payment for debts was not uncommon in the ancient Near East.

4:2-7. Elisha was eager to **help** the widow. His miracles, as contrasted with Elijah's, frequently involved meeting the needs of individuals. Her **little** bit of **oil** was olive oil used for food and fuel. **Elisha** told her to collect **empty jars**; they would be **filled** with oil God would provide. The widow's faith can be "measured" by the number of **jars** she collected in response to the prophet's instructions. Shutting **the door** provided privacy for the task of pouring the **oil**. Not everyone was to see the miracle take place; only the widow **and her sons,** the direct beneficiaries of God's grace, should see it. But later she probably told all her friends about God's miraculous provision. God provided oil enough to fill **all the jars** the woman had collected, all she felt she needed. She returned to Elisha with a report of the miracle and he told her to **sell the oil and pay** her **debts.** There was enough money **left** over for her to **live on** after all her financial obligations had been met. Elisha is called a **man of God,** a term used of several prophets in 1 and 2 Kings (cf. comments on 1:9).

This story demonstrates God's care for His faithful ones who lived in apostate Israel at this time. Widows were always vulnerable and the widow of a prophet would have been even more needy. Yet God miraculously cared for this faithful, dependent believer.

c. The Shunammite woman (4:8-37)

God's concern for women and their special needs can be seen clearly in both the preceding and this incident. Whereas women were regarded as inferior to men in most ancient Near Eastern societies, God showed His concern for them here as well as in many other portions of Scripture.

(1) The Lord's gift (4:8-16). **4:8-10.** In contrast with the poor widow in the previous story this **woman** in **Shunem** (near Jezreel) was **well-to-do** and had a **husband. Elisha** evidently **stopped** at her house regularly at her invitation as he traveled between Samaria, Jezreel, and other cities. The woman's faith in Yahweh is seen in her desire to be a blessing to the **man of God.** Apparently she was more spiritually sensitive and outgoing then her husband (cf. comments on v. 23). He did, however, consent to his wife's proposal to build a guest **room on the** typically flat **roof** of their house and to furnish it for Elisha's comfort.

4:11-13. After Elisha had enjoyed this couple's hospitality for some time he desired to do something for them in return. He asked **his servant Gehazi** to express his offer to the woman. Perhaps this was to make the woman feel more inclined to ask for something than she would have if the prophet addressed her. God's grace to His faithful ones can be seen in Elisha's offer (v. 13; cf. v. 2). Elisha obviously enjoyed a position of some influence in the palace even though he opposed Joram's religious policies. The woman's reply (**I have a home among my own people**) expressed contentment with her lot in life; she was at peace and felt no special needs.

4:14-16. Determined to return her favors, **Elisha** discussed with **Gehazi** after she left his room what he might do **for her.** Gehazi observed that **she** had **no son** and probably never would have one since **her husband** was old. **Elisha** called **her** back and told **her** that she would have **a son** in **about** a year. This miraculous birth would be God's gift to her for her goodness to His servant. The woman's response to this announcement does not mean that she did not want a son; every Israelite woman did. To be childless was regarded in Israel as a great personal tragedy. Her reply indicates that she felt having a son was impossible. She urged Elisha not to build up her hopes only to disappoint her later.

(2) The child's birth and death. 4:17-23. Like Sarah (cf. Gen. 18:12-13; 21:2) the Shunammite did bear a son as God promised. However, one morning while the child, evidently still quite young, was out in the fields with his father in the heat of harvesttime a violent headache overtook him. He was carried back to his mother but failed to improve and died shortly thereafter, perhaps from sunstroke. Clearly the lad was dead, not just sick (cf. 2 Kings 4:32), and his mother knew it. Her thoughts turned immediately to Elisha and she prepared to seek his help. Perhaps she did not tell her husband that her son had died because she feared he would not let her go if he knew the boy was dead. When she told him she wanted to see Elisha (the man of God; cf. vv. 9, 16, 21, 25 [twice], 27 [twice]), he questioned the need since it was not the New Moon or the Sabbath, occasions for religious festivals. The husband's spiritual concerns seem to have been superficial and ritualistic. Her words, It's all right (v. 23), were designed to avoid further explanation and delay.

(3) The mother's plea (4:24-31). 4:24-26. Quickly the woman rode her donkey, while her servant led. Elisha was only a few miles away at Mount Carmel. Interestingly she knew where to find him. When the prophet saw her coming he sent Gehazi to intercept her. But she would not be delayed with explanations; she hurried on to Elisha. Her confidence lay in Elisha's ability as a man of God, not in his servant.

4:27-28. Arriving where Elisha was, she grasped his feet, a gesture indicating extreme humility, need, and desperation. Gehazi felt that her behavior was improper, but Elisha recognized it as the expression of deepest grief. The LORD sometimes informed his prophets beforehand of situations they would face (e.g., 1 Kings 14:5), but this time He did not.

As is common under extreme stress the woman's first words to Elisha did not tell him why she had come but how she felt about what had happened. She referred to the fact that having a son who died was a loss of her hopes, much like never having a son at all. She was so heartbroken at her son's death that at the moment she felt it would have been better if he had never been born.

4:29-31. Elisha probably understood that the lad had died; he probably would not have done anything without first learning what had happened. He sent Gehazi with his staff, the symbol of his authority as a prophet of the Lord, and instructed him to lay it on the boy's face. Either Elisha believed God would honor this method or he wanted to teach a lesson. Gehazi was to go immediately to Shunem; he was not to greet anyone he met on the way or return their greetings. (People in the East lost much time giving and returning prolonged greetings.) The mother told Elisha that she would not leave him. (Cf. comments on words similar to As surely as the LORD lives, in 1 Kings 17:1. That same and similar phrases occur seven times in 1 Kings and seven in 2 Kings.)

So Elisha got up and followed her back to Shunem. Gehazi went on ahead of Elisha who apparently followed his servant at a slower pace. Gehazi followed Elisha's instructions but the boy did not awaken to life. So Gehazi returned to his master and reported what had happened.

(4) The prophet's miracle (4:32-37). 4:32-35. That the boy was indeed dead is stated again (cf. v. 20). Elisha. . . . shut the door of the room so that he could concentrate in prayer on the object of his petition, while Gehazi and the woman stayed outside the room. The earnestness of Elisha's entreaty to the LORD is reflected in his prone posture. The boy's body grew warm from contact with Elisha; God was beginning to answer the prophet's prayer.

Elisha then paced back and forth in the room, apparently continuing to pour out his soul in fervent, persistent prayer. He returned to prostrate himself on the body of the lad once again. These actions were not some kind of magic; they were the natural physical expressions of a man engaged in earnest prayer. God restored the lad's life, air returned to his lungs, he **sneezed seven times** (seven indicating a work of God; cf. 5:14), **and opened his eyes.** These were the first signs that God had restored his life.

4:36-37. Then the prophet told **Gehazi** to **call the Shunammite,** who also was probably praying in some private place. **When she** entered the room and saw her son alive she first **fell at** Elisha's **feet** out of respect and gratitude (cf. v. 27), **and bowed to the ground** before the Lord in worship. **Then she took her son,** probably in her arms, and left the room full of joy and gratitude for what God had done for her.

Throughout this story evidences of the woman's faith keep shining through (cf. vv. 8-10, 16, 21-22, 24-25, 27, 30, 37). God rewarded her trust with a miraculous birth and a miraculous restoration to life. Gehazi's failure to restore the boy to life by using Elisha's staff shows that the living God works in response to the requests of trusting people rather than magically through a fetish (Elisha's staff). Baal, a god of fertility, undoubtedly suffered ignominy as this story of Yahweh's provision of life circulated in Israel (cf. 1 Kings 17:21-22).

d. The deadly stew (4:38-41)

4:38-41. On one of Elisha's trips to **the company of the prophets** located at **Gilgal** a situation developed that provided an object lesson of what **Elisha** was teaching. The fact that this incident took place in a time of **famine** is important to a correct understanding of the story. This famine may have been the same one(s) referred to later (6:25; 7:4; 8:1) or a different one (cf. the famine in Elijah's days, 1 Kings 18:2). (These stories of Elisha's ministry are evidently not in strict chronological order but were arranged by the writer in sequence for a variety of reasons: similar subject matter, related lessons, geographical connections, etc.) Though there was a famine Elisha prepared to feed the prophets with whatever could be collected. He asked **his servant** (Gehazi or another person) to prepare the **stew** pot for a meal.

One of the prophets **went out . . . to gather** whatever he could find growing wild to put in the stew. Finding **a wild vine, he gathered some of its gourds. . . . cut them up,** and put them **into the pot.** The unknown gourds had a horrible taste and may have caused some violent physical reactions in those who tasted **the stew.** The prophets concluded that the gourds had poisoned the stew. **Elisha** added some **flour** to the stew. Not much of it could have been available in a famine. But with this additive the stew became quite palatable and the prophets ate it without harm.

In Elisha's day a spiritual famine had resulted from the people's turning from God and His Law. The people were hungry spiritually. In an effort to satisfy their need they had imbibed a false religion called Baalism. It looked harmless enough but proved disgusting and deadly. God's prophets helped counteract the deadly effects of Baalism in Israel.

e. The multiplication of bread (4:42-44)

4:42-44. Baal Shalishah was a town close to Gilgal so this incident may have taken place about the same time as the preceding one. Evidently the famine still persisted. The **man** who brought the **bread** and **grain** to **the man of God** (Elisha; cf. v. 21) was apparently a believer in the Lord, taking these items as the firstfruits offering of his harvest to God (cf. Num. 18:13; Deut. 18:4). When **Elisha** suggested to **his servant** (Gehazi) that the food be given to feed the **100 men** assembled (probably the company of the prophets; cf. 2 Kings 4:38), the servant's response indicated that it was far too little. Nevertheless **Elisha** ordered him to distribute it and assured him that **the Lord** had promised there would be plenty and **some** would be **left over.** The servant obeyed and God multiplied the food as He had promised.

This miracle instructed all who heard of it that God could multiply the limited resources (cf. 1 Kings 17:7-16) that were dedicated to Him and with them nourish and sustain a large multitude. Baal, a god of fertility known as "the lord of the earth," had no such power.

f. Naaman the Aramean (chap. 5)

Elisha's ministry expanded beyond the borders of Israel as recorded in this story of another miracle he performed.

(1) Naaman's disease (5:1-6). **5:1. Naaman was commander of the army of the king of Aram,** Ben-Hadad II (860–841

B.C.; see the chart "Kings of Aram in 1 and 2 Kings," near 1 Kings 11:23-25). Naaman was a successful and courageous warrior, **highly regarded because** of the victories God **had given** the Arameans under his leadership. However, **he had leprosy** (perhaps this was not leprosy as it is known today; cf. NIV marg.). This dreaded disease degenerated its victims and eventually proved fatal. No cure for it was known. In Israel lepers were normally isolated from nonlepers, but this was not always the custom in other nations including Aram. Naaman was able to carry on his duties as long as the disease permitted him to do so.

5:2-3. In the course of their occasional battles with **Israel,** Naaman's forces had captured some Israelites whom they made slaves. One of these was **a young girl** whom Naaman had given to his **wife** as a servant. Evidently Naaman and his wife were kind to this girl because she sought **Naaman's** welfare. **She** told **her mistress,** who told her husband, that a **prophet** living **in Samaria** could cure . . . **leprosy.** This was Elisha; he lived in a house in the capital city (6:24, 32). Probably the girl had heard of Elisha before she was carried off as a slave. Apparently she assumed he could cleanse leprosy in view of his supernatural power. No leper in Israel, though, was healed in Elisha's day (Luke 4:27). Later the slave girl's faith in the Lord may have been an indirect rebuke to Israel's King Joram who had no faith in God.

5:4-6. The Aramean **king** was anxious for his valuable commander to be cleansed, not only because he was a trusted friend but because the dreaded disease would eventually rob the king of his top military commander. **Naaman** set out to visit **King** Joram who he assumed would order the prophet to cure him. **With him** the commander took gifts of **10 talents** (ca. 750 pounds) **of silver, 600 shekels** (ca. 150 pounds) **of gold, and 10 sets of clothing,** all prized gifts in the Near East. He also carried a **letter** from his king to Joram requesting in matter-of-fact terms that **Naaman** be cured.

(2) *Naaman's cure* (5:7-14). **5:7.** Joram was dismayed when he **read the letter** from Ben-Hadad II. Tearing one's **robes** indicated great anxiety and distress (cf. 2:12; 6:30; 11:14). Israel and Aram had

been at peace, but it appeared to Joram that Ben-Hadad was trying to **pick a** fight again as he had done with Joram's father Ahab (cf. 1 Kings 20:1-3). Joram did not realize that Naaman did not expect *him* to cure the leprosy. Elisha did not even enter Joram's mind. The Israelite king had no use for that prophet who constantly opposed him. Joram wanted as little contact with him as possible.

5:8-10. When Elisha learned of Joram's anxiety over Ben-Hadad's letter he sent the king a **message** not to worry. If Joram would send Naaman to him the prophet would cure him. Naaman would learn, even if Joram had not, **that there** was a true **prophet in Israel.** Before long **Naaman** and his whole retinue arrived at **Elisha's** door.

Not at all awed by the great general, **Elisha** did not even go out to meet him; instead he **sent a messenger to** convey his simple "prescription." Naaman was told to dip **seven times in the Jordan** River and he would be free of his disease. The cure lay not in the water of the Jordan but in obedient faith in God's promise through His prophet.

5:11-14. Naaman turned from Elisha's house **angry** for two reasons: (1) His pride had been offended by Elisha's offhanded treatment of him; he had expected a cleansing ceremony in keeping with his own dignity. (2) He resented having been told to wash in a muddy river that he considered inferior to the **Abana and Pharpar . . . rivers** in his hometown; the water of the Jordan, he thought, could not possibly do him any good.

The commander's **servants,** however, had not been personally put down as their master had, and could view the situation more objectively. Approaching him tenderly they appealed to him as a **father** to be reasonable. They pointed out that it was not as though Elisha had requested something difficult (**some great thing**). What harm would there be in giving his remedy a try? Undoubtedly feeling rather ashamed Naaman humbled himself and obeyed the word of the Lord. As he obeyed in faith he was **cleansed.** God did even more for him and **restored** his flesh to its soft boyhood texture. God had prescribed that he wash **seven times** (cf. 4:35) to indicate that the healing was completely a work of God, "for seven is the stamp of the works of God" (C.F. Keil, "1 & 2 Kings," in *Commentary on the Old Testament in Ten Volumes*, 3:319). The fact that in Elisha's day an Aramean leper was healed whereas no Israelite leper was (Luke 4:27) points up Israel's apostasy.

(3) Naaman's gratitude (5:15-18). **5:15-16.** **Naaman** returned from the Jordan to Elisha's house in Samaria (about 25 miles) with a heart full of gratitude and hands full of gifts. Rather than expecting Elisha to come to him he willingly **stood before** the prophet and testified to his belief that Israel's **God** is the only true God. (Unfortunately many in Israel, including her king, had not come to the same realization.) This was the highest purpose of Naaman's healing from God's point of view. Elisha agreed that **the LORD** whom he served **lives** (cf. comments on 1 Kings 17:1; 2 Kings 4:30). But the prophet **refused** to accept any reward for his ministry. Naaman's urging did not budge Elisha. The man of God had not performed his miracle for reward but at the word of the Lord and he did not want anyone to think otherwise. The false prophets could easily be bought, but not Elisha.

5:17-18. Since Elisha would not take anything, **Naaman** asked him to give **as much earth** as he could carry back to Damascus on two **mules**. He intended to use this in making an altar to the Lord. Many polytheists believed that no god could be worshiped except in its own land or on an altar built with the dirt of that land.

Naaman proposed to worship only Yahweh Himself (**the LORD**), but superstition shaped his thinking. In the course of his official duties, however, he would have to give token respect to the god of his **master** the king. The god of Damascus was Hadad-Rimmon, a god of rain and thunder, here shortened to **Rimmon**. It was Naaman's duty to participate in this official worship with the king and probably other officials of state. The commander was not prepared to risk his life, as Daniel's three friends would (Dan. 3:12), by refusing to bow before an idol. But one must remember that Naaman was not an Israelite with the advantage of knowledge of the revealed Word of God. Perhaps his responsibility therefore was not as great as an Israelite's would

have been. **Leaning on my arm** (cf. 2 Kings 7:2) is a figurative expression for relying on an assistant for help.

(4) Gehazi's greed (5:19-27). **5:19-21.** Elisha's departing benediction (**Go in peace**) probably was a blessing on the journey ahead of **Naaman** rather than on the compromising behavior the general had outlined (vv. 17-18), which the prophet neither approved nor disapproved verbally.

Gehazi became greedy of what Naaman had offered to give Elisha. Evidently he justified his greed by reasoning that since **Naaman** was an **Aramean**, a natural enemy of Israel, he should at least be taken advantage of. So **Gehazi** pursued **Naaman** to **get something from him.** Gehazi was able to overtake the large slow-moving caravan on foot. Naaman **got down from** his chariot (cf. 4:26) and **asked** if **everything** was **all right.**

5:22-24. Gehazi said **everything** was **all right** but then lied to the commander. He said his **master** had received unexpected guests (**two . . . prophets**) and wanted to give them some **silver** and a change **of clothing** each. Gehazi put this lie in Elisha's mouth and made the request sound very unselfish. **Naaman** was happy to oblige and urged Gehazi to accept twice as much **silver** as well as the clothing. He even provided **two . . . servants** to carry these gifts back to Elisha. **Gehazi** followed **the servants** and when they arrived at **the hill** (on which Samaria was built) **he took the** gifts **from** them **and put them . . . in** his **house.**

5:25-27. Shortly thereafter **Gehazi** returned to **Elisha.** He did not realize that God had revealed his whereabouts to **his master.** So to cover one lie he told another. Elisha then explained that he was aware of everything **Gehazi** had done. **Elisha** added that true servants of the Lord should not **take** personal rewards from people, especially influential non-Israelites, in return for blessings that God, not His servant, had given them. False prophets were selfishly lining their own pockets and bringing contempt on the prophetic office; true prophets should avoid conduct that might be misunderstood as self-seeking.

Naaman's leprosy had been removed from him for his trust in and obedience to God. Now, ironically, leprosy would **cling to** Gehazi for his lack of trust in and obedience to God. The servant had brought dishonor to Yahweh's name. A bad case of leprosy turned one's skin and hair white as snow. Gehazi's judgment was serious because his sin had far-reaching consequences; this story was probably told all over Aram and Israel. As a servant of God Gehazi had more privilege than most people and therefore more responsibility than most people.

This story contains many lessons. Naaman's healing was another great proof of the Lord's power to restore health, power which only Baal supposedly possessed. This incident also helped spread the fame of Yahweh to another part of the ancient world. The contrasting behaviors of Elisha and Gehazi also model positive and negative attitudes and actions for God's servants of all ages.

g. The floating axhead (6:1-7)

6:1-4a. Another incident involving **the company of the prophets** follows. At one of their schools their accommodations had become inadequate because of the growing number of young men, a tribute to the effectiveness of Elisha's ministry. This may have been the school at Jericho since the young men went to the nearby **Jordan** River for their wood. They intended to **build** new facilities at a new site **there.** Elisha gave his permission for this project and agreed to accompany the workmen.

6:4b-7. In the process of cutting **down trees** an **iron axhead** flew off its handle and **fell into the** river. The man wielding the ax **cried out** to his **lord** (i.e., to Elisha) in dismay because his tool had been **borrowed.** Ascertaining **where** the axhead had fallen into the water **Elisha** threw **a stick** into the river. Miraculously **the iron** implement floated to the surface. The workman was able to retrieve it easily.

Certainly this miracle encouraged the group of faithful followers of the Lord that their God really is alive and that He would supernaturally provide for their needs even though many Israelites in that day had turned from the true God to Baal.

h. The blinding of the Aramean army (6:8-23)

6:8-10. As mentioned previously the Arameans were sometimes **at war** and sometimes at peace **with Israel** during the years of Elisha's ministry. At the time of this particular incident **the Arameans** were making profitable surprise raids into Israel. **The king of Aram** (cf. 5:1) was probably Ben-Hadad II. (Of the major persons in this narrative only Elisha is mentioned by name. This may suggest that readers should focus on the Lord and His prophet.) In preparation for another raid Ben-Hadad planned to pitch his **camp** on the border of Israel from which he could strike unexpectedly. However, **God** informed **Elisha** of the place and the prophet passed his information on **to the king of Israel** (Joram) with a warning to **beware.** Joram **checked** Elisha's information, found it to be correct, prepared for the encounter, and frustrated Ben-Hadad's secret attack. This happened several times.

6:11-14. **Enraged** by his continual failure to surprise the Israelites Ben-Hadad concluded that one of his men was tipping off the enemy. An officer assured **the king** that there were no traitors in his camp but that it was **Elisha** who had supernatural knowledge of all his plans. **The very words you speak in your bedroom** mean even his most private conversations were known to the prophet. Obviously this officer had somehow learned of Elisha and his powers.

As long as Elisha remained free the army of Aram would be unsuccessful, so Ben-Hadad ordered that he be located and captured. He stealthily sent a strong contingent of soldiers with **horses and chariots. . . . by night** and completely surrounded **Dothan** (12 miles north of Samaria), where Elisha was staying. The fact that Ben-Hadad would try to take Elisha by surprise even after the prophet had repeatedly anticipated the Arameans' moves indicates the king's lack of faith in the supernatural origin of Elisha's ability. Therefore he needed to be convinced that Yahweh is the living and true God.

6:15-17. Since Gehazi had been dismissed as a disobedient servant and "leper" (5:27), the Naaman story must follow this one if Elisha's **servant** here is Gehazi. Or this servant may be someone who replaced Gehazi. **Early the next morning** the servant was terrified to see that **the whole city** was under the Arameans' control, or so he thought. He returned in a frenzy to Elisha and nervously asked, **What shall we do?** The servant's anxiety reflected his lack of understanding and trust in the Lord which, one would think, Elisha's previous revelations would have changed.

Elisha was not at all disturbed by the present situation. He encouraged his aide to stop fearing, and assured him that they had behind them a force superior to that of the enemy. **Elisha** then asked the Lord to enable his servant to see this host and the Lord did so. He gave the servant the ability to **see** the normally unseen world of invisible spirits (angels) that are constantly ready to do God's bidding (cf. Gen. 28:12). The **hills** around Dothan were filled with superior **horses and chariots.** These appeared as fiery agents of God suggesting to the servant their superterrestrial origin (cf. 2 Kings 2:11). **The Lord** had surrounded the armies of Aram and was in control.

6:18-20. Proceeding with a divinely revealed strategy **Elisha** called on God to blind the Arameans as they began to converge on Dothan, and God did so.

Elisha said, **This is not the road and this is not the city** for that road and **city** were not where God intended them to go. They unknowingly followed Elisha **inside** the walls of **Samaria,** the capital of Israel. What the Israelite army might not have been able to do except with much fighting and loss of life, God did peacefully through one man. In response to Elisha's prayer God opened **the eyes of** the Arameans and they discovered that they were surrounded and helpless captives at the mercy of the king of Israel.

6:21-23. Joram, realizing that **Elisha** was in control, and almost hysterical because of his good fortune, **asked** the prophet, whom he respectfully addressed as his **father** (cf. 5:13), if he should **kill** his prisoners. Elisha said no. Joram probably would not have killed soldiers captured in battle and furthermore God's purpose was not to destroy the Arameans' lives but to save the Israelites' lives. The king then assured them of this in an unusual way. By setting **a great feast** before the soldiers he was expressing confidence in God's ability to control the enemy; Israel had absolutely nothing to fear and could even treat these soldiers as friends because God had

them in His sovereign power. In the ancient Near East eating together under one's roof constituted making a covenant of peace (J. Herbert Livingston, *The Pentateuch in Its Cultural Environment.* Grand Rapids: Baker Book House, 1974, p. 157). The Arameans were now bound by social custom not to attack the friend who had extended his gift of hospitality and protection. For these reasons the Arameans **stopped raiding Israel's territory** for a time.

The reference to the soldiers returning **to their master** suggests that King Ben-Hadad II was not part of the force that had been sent to capture Elisha (cf. 6:13). Evidently this was just part of the total Aramean army.

This incident demonstrates Yahweh is His people's defense. So to depart from Him was the height of folly. Israel's victory by means of God's prophet rather than by warriors undoubtedly encouraged many in Israel and Aram to fear the Almighty God.

i. The famine in Samaria (6:24–7:20)

Joram and the nation of Israel failed to turn back to the Lord as a result of the previous incident. Consequently God sent a more severe situation to draw them back to Himself.

(1) The desperate condition (6:24-31). **6:24-25.** **Some time** after the events narrated in verses 1-23 **Ben-Hadad** II tried again to defeat Israel. This time instead of sending raiding parties (cf. "bands" in v. 23), he **mobilized his entire army** and besieged **Samaria.** Since no one could leave or enter the capital, **a great famine** resulted. It was so severe that one **donkey's head,** one of the least nourishing and most repulsive parts of this animal, unclean to the Israelites, became a highly valued commodity selling **for 80 shekels** (ca. two pounds) **of silver.** Approximately a half pint **of seed pods,** normally considered animal fodder, cost **5 shekels** (ca. two ounces) of silver.

6:26-27. Joram's reply (**Where can I get help for you?**) to **a woman** who called **to him** revealed his frustration. He was angry with **the Lord** for permitting this situation (cf. v. 33). God had promised that such conditions would discipline His people if they turned from Him (Lev. 26:29; Deut. 28:53, 57). Joram sarcastically told the woman that he could not provide bread **from the** grain on the **thresh-ing floor** or wine **from the** grapes in the **winepress;** he was not greater than God was supposed to be.

6:28-31. Having vented his frustration with these words the king then invited the woman to explain her problem. She said that a friend had persuaded her to cook her **son** but **the next day,** when the friend was to cook **her . . . son . . . she had hidden him.** Learning the desperate extent to which the siege had driven his people, **the king** angrily **tore his robes,** an expression of deep distress and sorrow (cf. 2:12; 5:7; 11:14). **Sack-cloth,** coarse material made from black goat's hair, was worn as a symbol of repentance and self-affliction. But Joram's repentance seems to have been rather shallow in view of his attitude toward God's servant **Elisha.** Rather than dealing with the real cause of God's discipline, his own apostasy, Joram blamed Elisha who had perhaps only explained the reason for Israel's condition. In oath (**May God deal with me, be it ever so severely;** cf. 1 Kings 2:23; 20:10) the king swore to put the prophet to death that very day (cf. Elijah's experience, 1 Kings 19:2).

(2) The prophecies of deliverance (6:32–7:2). **6:32. The elders** who **were sitting with** Elisha **in his house** (cf. 5:9) were the officials of the land. Perhaps they were meeting with the prophet to discuss what should be done. Warned by God, **Elisha** announced that the king was **sending someone to** have him beheaded. Joram did not realize that **Elisha** was the solution to his problems rather than their source. The prophet's instruction to **the elders** to bar **the door** against the executioner was evidently intended to postpone any violence until Joram himself would arrive. (**Is not the sound of his master's footsteps behind him?**) The instruction would also give Elisha opportunity to announce God's message of imminent deliverance.

6:33. When Joram did arrive he asked Elisha why he should **wait . . . any longer** for God to act. Apparently Elisha had told Joram that God had said he should not surrender to Ben-Hadad but should wait for divine deliverance. Since that help was not forthcoming Joram had decided to take matters into his own hands. As he had done many times be-

fore he was disobeying the orders of his Lord through Elisha, acting as an unfaithful administrator (cf. 1 Sam. 15:11). Since, as Joram stated, the **disaster** (the siege and the famine) was **from the** LORD, the king should have obeyed Him.

7:1-2. Elisha then announced a prophecy. Within 24 hours the siege would be over and there would be plenty to eat. **A seah** (ca. seven quarts) **of flour** would **sell for a shekel** (about two-fifths of an ounce) **and two seahs** (ca. 13-14 quarts) **of barley** (for cattle to eat) would sell for the same price (cf. v. 16) **at the gate of** the city where business of this sort was normally transacted. These prices were not unusually low but compared with what the people had been paying during the famine (cf. 6:25) they were great bargains.

The officer assisting Joram (cf. 7:17 and the comments on 5:8) found this prophecy incredible. His retort expressed his utter disbelief that **God** would or could do this. **Elisha** replied that the officer would **see** the miracle **with his own eyes;** it would indeed take place. But because of his unbelief he would not experience the blessing (cf. 7:17).

(3) The lepers' discovery (7:3-9). **7:3-4.** The **four** lepers may have been housed in huts just outside **the city gate;** they were isolated from contact with non-lepers in Israel. Of their three options, they correctly concluded that their best choice lay in giving themselves up to **the Arameans.** They might be killed but, they reasoned, that would be better than dying gradually of starvation.

7:5-7. Entering **the camp of the Arameans** (apparently at night; cf. **dusk,** v. 7, "daylight," v. 9, and "night," v. 12) the lepers found that the enemy soldiers had **fled.** The writer explained the reason for the soldiers' departure. **The Lord had caused** them **to hear** noises from the north and the south that made them think the armies of the Hittites (who earlier had lived in the area now called Turkey but were now living in enclaves in Aram) and the Egyptians were descending on them. They supposed these were reinforcements **hired** by the Israelites. So at **dusk** they retreated eastward toward their homeland. So great was their haste that **they left** many of their animals and supplies behind.

7:8-9. At first the lepers filled their

own stomachs and pockets and even **hid** some of their treasure so that they could retrieve it later. But gradually their sense of duty to their fellow Samaritans convicted them. Also they reasoned that if they failed to **report** the situation, others would discover in the morning that the enemy had fled and they would be punished for not announcing the situation to the starving population. Rather than suffer as criminals they preferred to be treated as heroes. So they decided to return to Samaria and proclaim their **good news.**

(4) The cautious investigation (7:10-15). **7:10-12.** The lepers returned to Samaria and told **the city gatekeepers** their story. The news spread like wildfire through the city during **the night** (cf. vv. 9, 11). But **the king** suspected a trap. He calculated that since **the Arameans** had not been able to break into Samaria they had planned this apparent retreat to draw the Samaritans **out,** leaving **the city** open to invasion.

7:13-15. One of Joram's **officers** proposed sending only **five** horsemen out to scout **the Aramean** camp. If these soldiers were caught their deaths would **only be** hastened; he thought death was inescapable for all the people in Samaria. Joram liked this plan. So he ordered **two chariots with their horses,** risking four horses (not five as had been suggested) to follow the supposedly fleeing Aramean **army.** The chariot **drivers** followed a trail of discarded **clothing and equipment** all the way to **the Jordan** River, about 25 miles from Samaria. Israel's enemy then had crossed the Jordan and was far away. The drivers **returned** to Samaria and announced the good news **to the king.**

(5) The fulfillment of Elisha's predictions. **7:16-20. The king** apparently threw the gates open before the excited multitudes who streamed out to find food and booty. Those who found the food first were able to sell it to their neighbors for the same prices **the LORD had** predicted through Elisha (cf. v. 1). So heavy was the traffic through the **gate** that **the officer** who assisted the king (cf. v. 2 and the comment on 5:18) and who had been stationed there to insure an orderly departure was **trampled** to death. This man had ridiculed God's ability to do what He said He would do (cf. v. 2). The fate that Elisha had predicted overtook him.

Yahweh, not Baal, provides food; in fact God even foretold exactly when He would provide it. The remarkable way in which God kept the Samaritans safe and sustained them should have turned them and **the king** back to Him. God's future discipline of the Israelites can be understood better in the light of their rejection of His many gracious and miraculous provisions for them.

j. The preservation of the Shunammite woman (8:1-6)

This story illustrates God's marvelous care of those who trust in Him even in times of popular apostasy.

8:1-3. These verses relate background information. **Elisha** had directed his benefactress and her **family** (cf. 4:8-37) to leave Israel temporarily. **The LORD** had revealed to His prophet that He would bring a **seven**-year **famine** on **the land** (cf. 4:38; 6:25; 7:4). This was a punishment for apostasy (cf. Deut. 11:16-17; 28:38-40; 1 Kings 18:2). Trusting in the word of the **man of God. . . . she and her family** left their home and lived in Philistia for **seven years.** Returning to Israel, the woman appeared before **King** Joram **to beg for her** former property which has been taken over by someone else in her absence. She may not have been asking that her property be given to her but that she be permitted to buy it back since it was apparently her paternal inheritance, guaranteed to each Israelite family by the Law of Moses.

8:4-5. Since **King** Joram **was talking to Gehazi** (Elisha's **servant**) when **the woman** called on the king, this incident must have taken place before **Gehazi** became a leper (5:27). Joram's interest in **Elisha** seems to have been motivated by curiosity rather than conviction; there is no evidence that Joram ever abandoned his apostate ways and became a faithful follower of the Lord. Elisha's resuscitation of the Shunammite's **son** (4:32-37) was a great event to recount. Amazingly Gehazi's **telling** of it was interrupted by **the woman** herself who had come to present her request to **the king.**

8:6. The woman and her son's timely appearance so impressed Joram that he **asked the woman** to fill in some details of Gehazi's story, which she did. Besides permitting her to return to her former homestead, **the king** even ordered that the proceeds **from** the **land,** since she had **left** it, be paid to her.

The perfect timing of God's actions stands out in this brief narrative. God preserved His faithful Shunammite believer by removing her from the famine before it began and by bringing her before the king at a uniquely propitious moment. Joram had been uniquely prepared by Gehazi to help her. In view of the woman's faith in the Lord, it was remarkable that Joram showed her any favor at all.

k. Hazael's murder of Ben-Hadad II (8:7-15)

8:7-8. Elisha visited **Damascus,** the capital of **Aram,** and **Ben-Hadad,** as the old enemy of Israel **was ill.** (He died in 841 B.C.) Elisha was well known to the king for the prophet had performed many miracles that affected the Arameans. It was unusual for Elisha to go **all the way up** to Damascus from Israel. The king instructed his official **Hazael** to greet Elisha by taking him **a gift.** Having respect for **the Lord** Ben-Hadad asked Hazael to **ask** God's prophet if he would **recover from** his **illness** (cf. King Ahaziah's similar request, in Elijah's day, which the king planned to ask of the false god Baal-Zebub, 1:2).

8:9. The **40-camel** caravan may not have carried as much wealth as one might suppose. It was customary in the ancient Near East to make a great show of giving gifts and it was fairly common to have one camel carry only one gift. Referring to **Ben-Hadad** as Elisha's **son,** Hazael was courteously deferring to **Elisha** (cf. "father" in 5:13; 6:21). Elisha was evidently staying at some house or inn in **Damascus.**

8:10-11. In response to Ben-Hadad's question, **Elisha** told Hazael to tell the king that he would **certainly recover** (as he would have if Hazael would not have interfered). Elisha then told Hazael that his master would **in fact die.** Elisha evidently knew that Hazael would murder his master though he did not tell Hazael this. **With a fixed gaze** Elisha **stared** at **Hazael** perhaps hoping to embarrass him out of the deed. Hazael, secretly glad at the news of Ben-Hadad's fate, could not help feeling **ashamed** because Elisha seemed to read his mind. God's revelation to His prophet of what Hazael would do to Israel brought tears to Eli-

sha's eyes and he **began to weep.**

8:12-13. In response to Hazael's inquiry Elisha told him he knew the destruction Hazael would cause in Israel. **Hazael** pretended to be offended at the very suggestion of such cruelty. He feigned humility by calling himself **a mere dog,** incapable of **such a feat.** **Elisha** then explained that **Hazael** would **become king of Aram**; God had revealed this to the prophet.

8:14-15. Hazael . . . returned to **Ben-Hadad** and reported the encouraging prediction of his recovery. Rather than waiting for the Lord to arrange his accession to the throne through natural processes, as David had done, Hazael decided to seize the crown. So **the next day** he suffocated his master in a manner that made it look as if Ben-Hadad had **died** of natural causes. As Elisha had predicted **Hazael** was elevated to the throne (cf. v. 13).

Elijah may have previously anointed **Hazael . . . as king** (1 Kings 19:15) or the event just reported may have constituted that act with Elisha carrying out Elijah's assignment. Hazael's cruel domination of Israel was part of God's discipline of His people for their idolatry. Hazael did not come from noble stock; on one Assyrian record Shalmaneser III called him "the son of a nobody" (David Luckenbill, *Ancient Records of Assyria and Babylonia.* 2 vols. Chicago: University of Chicago Press, 1926–1927, 1:246). Hazael reigned as king of Aram from 841 to 801 B.C. during the reigns of Joram, Jehu, and Jehoahaz in Israel, and Ahaziah, Athaliah, and Joash in Judah.

C. Jehoram's evil reign in Judah (8:16-24)

The scene shifts once again to the Southern Kingdom of Judah as the writer continued his narrative with Jehoshaphat's son Jehoram.

1. JEHORAM'S WICKEDNESS (8:16-19)

8:16-19. Jehoshaphat appointed **Jehoram** his coregent the year he went off to battle with Ahab at Ramoth Gilead (853 B.C.). He may have thought he would be involved in wars out of the country for many months. Jehoram evidently remained in Jerusalem to run the nation. The 18th year of Jehoshaphat's sole reign in Judah (852) when Ahab's son Joram began to rule in **Israel** (3:1) was the second year of Jehoram's coregency with Jehoshaphat (1:17). **The fifth year of Joram** of Israel was the year Jehoram **began his reign** in Judah alone (848 B.C.). The length of Jehoram's reign, including his coregency was 13 years (853–841) while his sole reign was **8 years** (848–841).

Unfortunately Jehoram's godly father had less of an influence on him than his ungodly wife did. The **daughter of Ahab,** whom Jehoram **married** as part of Jehoshaphat's treaty with Ahab, was Athaliah. Jehoram was one of Judah's **evil** kings. But because of God's covenant with **David** (2 Sam. 7) He did not cut off the Davidic dynasty or **destroy** the Judean nation. (On a Davidic king as a **lamp,** see comments on 1 Kings 11:36; also cf. 2 Sam. 21:17; 1 Kings 15:4.)

2. THE REVOLTS OF EDOM AND LIBNAH (8:20-24)

The writer of 2 Kings mentioned only two of the unfortunate events that marked the reign of Jehoram. One not included was his slaughter of six of his brothers, all sons of Jehoshaphat (2 Chron. 21:2-4). This purge seems to have been Athaliah's idea since no other Judean king practiced such a thing, but Athaliah herself did when she ruled (2 Kings 11:1).

8:20-22. Edom had come under Judah's control when Jehoshaphat had defeated a coalition of kingdoms that included Edom (2 Chron. 20:1-29). At that time an Edomite deputy may have been placed on the throne in place of an Edomite king (1 Kings 22:47). Edom had helped Israel and Judah in their campaign against King Mesha of Moab (2 Kings 3:4-27). But in Jehoram's day **Edom** rebelled . . . **and set up its own king. Jehoram** took his army **to Zair** (probably Seir, another name for Edom) to put down the **rebellion,** but he was unsuccessful and barely escaped with his life. His army retreated **back home.**

Libnah was located southwest of Jerusalem near the border of Philistia. Its rebellion seems to have been precipitated by Philistine influence (cf. 2 Chron. 21:16). The Philistines invaded Judah in Jehoram's day and Judah suffered heavy losses at their hands (2 Chron. 21:16-17). The Arabians also rebelled. Both Phi-

listia and Arabia had feared and paid tribute to Jehoram's father (2 Chron. 17:11). Obviously **Judah** was weaker under **Jehoram,** partly because of his wickedness.

8:23-24. Jehoram died of a painful disease of the intestines (2 Chron. 21:18-19). Jehoram had been warned by Elijah early in his reign because of his wickedness (2 Chron. 21:12-15), but he did not change his ways and died as Elijah had prophesied. On **the book of the annals of the kings of Judah** see comments on 1 Kings 14:29, and on **the City of David** see comments on 1 Kings 2:10.

D. Ahaziah's evil reign in Judah (8:25–9:29)

Most of what is recorded about Ahaziah's brief reign in Judah concerned the activities of Jehu.

1. AHAZIAH'S WICKEDNESS (8:25-29)

8:25-27. Ahaziah of Israel should not be confused with Ahaziah of Judah; they were two different kings. Each ruled only one year and their reigns did not coincide. **Ahaziah . . . of Judah** reigned during the last **year of Joram** (Jehoram) **king of** Israel (841 B.C.). His reign commenced while he **was 22 years old** when his father **Jehoram** died. **His** mother **was Athaliah,** the daughter of Ahab and **granddaughter of Omri.** Influenced by his evil mother (2 Chron. 22:3) he followed the wicked **ways** of his ancestors in the Northern Kingdom.

8:28-29. Israel and Judah were still allied in Ahaziah's day. That is why he joined his uncle **Joram** in battle **against Hazael king of Aram at Ramoth Gilead.** (This was not the battle at Ramoth Gilead in which Ahab was fatally wounded; 1 Kings 22:29-40. That battle took place 12 years earlier.) **Joram** was **wounded** in this battle and **returned to Jezreel** (cf. 1 Kings 21:1), probably where his winter palace was located, **to recover** (cf. 2 Kings 9:14-15). **Ahaziah . . . went down** from Jerusalem to visit him there. While he was there Jehu attacked and killed Joram (9:14-26) and **Ahaziah** fled to Megiddo (9:27).

2. JEHU'S RISE (9:1-29)

Elijah and Elisha were God's instruments to warn Ahab and many of his relatives of the consequences of apostasy. Jehu was God's instrument to judge that dynasty when the kings failed to repent.

a. Jehu's anointing (9:1-10)

9:1-3. Elijah had been commissioned by God to anoint Jehu king over Israel (1 Kings 19:16). This assignment fell to his successor **Elisha** who delegated it to one of the young **prophets** under his tutelage. Tucking one's long **cloak into** his **belt** (cf. 2 Kings 4:29) enabled a person to move swiftly. The **flask** held the **oil** the young **man** would use to anoint **Jehu** who was still in **Ramoth Gilead** on the east side of the Jordan after the battle there (cf. 8:28-29). Jehu was the commander of Joram's army (9:5). The anointing was to be done privately, as was normal. Pouring the olive **oil** on the **head** was a symbolic way of illustrating the coming of the Spirit of God on a man to enable him to function as king (cf. 1 Sam. 16:13). An announcement of God's will for the king accompanied the ritual. The words are related briefly here (2 Kings 9:3) but more fully later (vv. 6-10).

9:4-10. The young . . . prophet. . . . **found** Jehu outdoors in the company of his fellow **officers.** He explained that he had a private **message for** the **commander** who then led the prophet **into** a building where they could talk confidentially. **The prophet** anointed **Jehu** and explained the purpose for which **God** had chosen him. Jehu was **to destroy** Ahab's dynasty. This would **avenge the blood of the Lord's prophets and . . . servants** which had been **shed** as a result of Jezebel's influence. God would thoroughly annihilate Ahab's line as Elijah had prophesied (1 Kings 21:21-22, 29), and **Jezebel** would also die as Elijah had foretold (1 Kings 21:23). Jeroboam's dynasty and Baasha's dynasty had ended violently (cf. 1 Kings 15:25, 28-29; 16:3-4) and so would Ahab's.

Jezebel, the young prophet said, would be eaten by **dogs,** and not be buried; both facts were ignominious to Semites. The young prophet's mission completed, he **ran** away from **Jehu** and friends as Elisha had told him to do (2 Kings 9:3). Perhaps this was in view of the coup that would soon begin and the accompanying recriminations that often trap innocent victims.

b. The announcement of Jehu's anointing (9:11-13)

9:11-13. The officer's calling the prophet a **madman** probably refers to the prophet's behavior in running away so quickly (v. 10). **Jehu** tried to change the subject when his friends asked him what the prophet had said. He implied that his companions knew the prophet was a little odd. Perhaps the young man's clothing identified him as a prophet. Jehu's friends would not be put off, however. Sensing that the prophet's mission was important, they wanted to know what had happened. So **Jehu** explained that the prophet had anointed him **king over Israel.** Immediately the **officers** arranged a little ceremony (cf. 1 Kings 16:16). They **spread** their **cloaks . . . under him on the bare steps. . . . blew the trumpet, and shouted, Jehu is king!** These were customary rituals for announcing a king (cf. 2 Sam. 15:10; 1 Kings 1:34, 39; Matt. 21:7-9).

c. Jehu's conspiracy against Joram (9:14-16)

9:14-16. Jehu's father **Jehoshaphat** was not the king of Judah by the same name. **Jehu** proceeded with plans to carry out God's will against the house of Ahab. **Israel** had regained **Ramoth in Gilead** from **the Arameans** since Ahab had been defeated there by Ben-Hadad II (1 Kings 22:29-40). While **defending** it from Aramean aggressors under Hazael's command, **King Joram** had been wounded. He **had returned to Jezreel** to recuperate. Jehu probably made his statement (2 Kings 9:15) in the context of his being proclaimed king (v. 13). He wanted to arrive **in Jezreel** and execute **Joram** before the king had heard of Jehu's being hailed as king by his men and before Joram could prepare to defend himself.

d. Jehu's ride to Jezreel (9:17-20)

9:17-20. A **lookout** spotted **Jehu's troops . . . coming** long before he could identify them as Jehu's. He probably saw a cloud of dust on the horizon and concluded that many horsemen were approaching. Fearful that these might be Arameans or bad news from Ramoth, **Joram** ordered a **horseman** to go intercept the convoy and find out who they were. **The horseman** met **Jehu** and posed his question. Jehu's reply was conciliatory. **What do you have to do with**

peace? means "Do not worry about the situation." **Jehu** told the messenger to follow him to Jezreel.

The king sent out a second messenger when the first did not speed back to Jezreel with news. His message and Jehu's response were the same as with the first **horseman.** As the troops drew closer to Jezreel **the lookout** observed that the officer leading the convoy was **driving** his chariot very fast, **like a madman** (cf. "madman" in v. 11). This was Jehu's characteristic style and it identified him to the scout on the tower. Jehu was the descendant but not the direct **son of Nimshi** (cf. v. 14).

e. Jehu's execution of Joram (9:21-26)

9:21-23. Thinking that Jehu brought bad news of the fighting at Ramoth Gilead (the messengers would have hurried back to Jezreel if their news had been good), **Joram** prepared to ride out **to meet Jehu** and get the news himself as quickly as possible. He suspected no rebellion but was so concerned about the war that he did this in spite of his injuries. **Ahaziah,** his guest, joined his uncle **in his own chariot. They met** Jehu **at the plot of ground that had belonged to Naboth** (1 Kings 21).

Joram's question (**Have you come in peace, Jehu?**) meant, "Is there peace at Ramoth?" As yet the king had no inkling of Jehu's plans. Jehu's reply, however, revealed that he was returning to Jezreel as Joram's adversary. He gave a different meaning to the word **peace.** It was Jezebel's **idolatry and witchcraft** that had ruined Israel's peace with God and for which Jehu was setting himself against her son (cf. Ex. 22:18; Deut. 18:10-12). As **Joram** wheeled his chariot around to flee he shouted a warning **to Ahaziah.** "Witchcraft" translates *kᵉšāpîm* (lit., "sorceries"), which is used in the Old Testament only here and in Isaiah 47:9, 12; Micah 5:12; Nahum 3:4. It suggests seeking information from demonic forces. No wonder Jezebel's influence in Israel was so devastating!

9:24-26. Jehu took Joram completely by surprise; apparently the king was not wearing his armor. Jehu easily **shot** him fatally with an **arrow.** Jehu reminded **Bidkar, his chariot officer,** of the **prophecy** they both had heard Elijah make (cf. 1 Kings 21:17-19). They were fulfilling that prediction. Jehu's free quotation added a fact not revealed previously: Jezebel had also had Naboth's **sons** killed. Jehu was careful to obey and to fulfill the Lord's word, thus ending Israel's fourth royal dynasty.

f. Jehu's execution of Ahaziah (9:27-29)

9:27-29. The two accounts of Ahaziah's fate (2 Kings 9:27-29; 2 Chron. 22:9) seem contradictory, but they can be harmonized. Evidently **Ahaziah . . . fled** from Jezreel south by way of **Beth Haggan.** Jehu and his men pursued **him** and **wounded him . . . near Ibleam.** Apparently Ahaziah reached Samaria where he hid for some time (2 Chron. 22:9). Jehu's men sought him, found him, and brought him to Jehu probably in Jezreel. Jehu may have wounded him again there. Then Ahaziah **escaped** and fled west **to Megiddo** where he **died** (2 Kings 9:27). **His servants took** his body back **to Jerusalem** where he was **buried** in the royal cemetery. **The 11th year of Joram** was 841 B.C.

E. Jehu's evil reign in Israel (9:30–10:36)

Since Jehu's coronation before the whole nation is not recorded, his reign may be regarded as beginning when Joram died (in 841 B.C.).

1. JEHU'S EXECUTION OF JEZEBEL (9:30-37)

9:30-31. By the time **Jehu** returned **to Jezreel. . . . Jezebel** had learned of her son's death. Hearing of Jehu's return **she painted her eyes** and **arranged her hair.** Evidently she anticipated her fate, and wanted to present an imposing appearance to Jehu and to die as a queen. She called out to **Jehu** and he **entered the** city **gate** beneath her window. Her words were sarcastic; she was arrogant to the end of her life. Perhaps she sought to shame Jehu by asking if he came **in peace** (cf. vv. 18-19). Obviously he had not. **Zimri,** of course, also rebelled against his master, Elah (1 Kings 16:9), and he himself died only seven days later by the influence of Omri, the founder of Ahab's dynasty (1 Kings 16:18-19). Jezebel implied that Jehu's rebellion would destroy him as Zimri's had. This implication is clearer in another translation of Jezebel's words: "Did Zimri have peace, who murdered his master?" (Cf. NIV marg.)

9:32-33. Jezebel's household was not loyal to her. Several **eunuchs** who waited on the queen were willing to help **Jehu** and pitched their mistress out her **window** at Jehu's command. Probably the window was on a second story or higher. When Jezebel hit the ground **her blood splattered the wall** (evidently the city wall; cf. 1 Kings 21:23) and Jehu's **horses.**

9:34-37. After **Jehu** drove his horses and chariot over her corpse, he then went farther into the city where he obtained a meal. He was so satisfied with his accomplishments that his gory act did not affect his appetite. Evidently at first Jehu did not remember Elijah's prophecy about Jezebel's fate. He later ordered that she be buried since **she was a king's daughter** (1 Kings 16:31) though she was also a **cursed woman**—cursed by God for her wickedness. By the time Jehu's gravediggers arrived on the scene, the wild **dogs** had already torn her corpse apart and had carried off all but the **skull . . . feet, and . . . hands.** When they reported this to **Jehu** he remembered Elijah's prophecy (1 Kings 21:23). Ironically she who had caused Naboth and his sons to die undeservedly now died an ignominious death—deservedly—on the ground that had been Naboth's vineyard. This was part of the same plot of ground where Bidkar had thrown the corpse of her son Joram (2 Kings 9:25-26).

Jehu's commentary on the prophecy (v. 37) is in harmony with Elijah's words. The king's complete lack of respect for Jezebel in her death reflects how he and God, as well as the godly in Israel, viewed this callous sinner who had been directly and indirectly responsible for so much apostasy and wickedness among God's people.

2. JEHU'S EXECUTION OF AHAB'S RELATIVES AND FRIENDS (10:1-11)

10:1-3. Seventy sons (i.e., descendants) **of Ahab** and his ancestors lived in **Samaria,** the capital of Israel. **Jehu,** planning to execute every relative who could possibly succeed Ahab, **wrote letters** to the chief administrators of Israel who were not Ahab's relatives. These included **the officials of Jezreel** (possibly those responsible for the winter palace in Jezreel; cf. 1 Kings 21:1; 2 Kings 8:29), **elders** of Samaria, and others who had been

assigned by Ahab to guard the young male members of the royal family and to rear them properly (cf. 10:6). Jehu proposed that these leaders, whom he assumed would remain loyal to Ahab's dynasty and oppose himself, select a new king from Ahab's **sons.** Jehu challenged them to have this new king and his city **fight** him. Rather than fielding large armies, ancient Near Eastern leaders sometimes proposed that only two individuals join battle and so decide which family would rule (cf. 1 Sam. 17:8-9; 2 Sam. 2:9). This may have been what Jehu was suggesting, or he may have intended to go to war against the whole **house** of Ahab and the city of Samaria.

10:4-8. In either case the officials, elders, and guardians **were terrified.** They knew Jehu would win such a contest; he was a powerful and successful army commander who had already killed **two kings,** Joram (9:24-26) and Ahaziah (9:27). Being state officials with no personal connections to the Omride dynasty, they decided to transfer their allegiance **to Jehu.** They said they would **do anything** he told them to do.

Jehu sent directions immediately. He commanded them to execute each of Ahab's **70** heirs and to bring their **heads** to him **in Jezreel** within the next day. The officials did exactly as Jehu had commanded. When the **heads of the royal princes** had been collected Jehu had them **put . . . in two piles at the entrance of the . . . gate** of Jezreel where they remained overnight. In the ancient Near East the practice of piling the heads of conquered subjects at the city gate was an effective way of demonstrating subjugation.

10:9-11. In the **morning Jehu** assembled **the people** of Jezreel at the city gate. He relieved them of any responsibility for the death of King Joram (**my master**) by admitting that he alone was responsible. This statement would have given Jehu a psychological advantage with the people; he was confessing to them and was not implicating them in his act.

This was all a part of Jehu's strategy which then became clear. He claimed innocence of and implied ignorance of the execution of Ahab's sons. This had been done by Ahab's chief officials but Jehu did not tell the people it had been done at *his* command. Since he had been honest with the people about his own responsibility in killing Joram, the people assumed he was being honest with them about his innocence in this mass murder. Jehu further ingratiated himself with the people by identifying himself with God and His prophet, claiming (rightly so) to be the fulfiller of Elijah's prophecy that Ahab's **house** (dynasty) would be destroyed. In this way Jehu gained popular support for his plot to massacre the officials of Samaria who had murdered Ahab's sons (cf. 2 Sam. 1:14-15). **Jehu** wiped out Ahab's heirs in Samaria and **Jezreel,** which God approved. But he also executed **all** Ahab's **chief men** (officials, v. 1), **close friends,** and **priests,** which God did not approve and for which God judged Jehu's own dynasty later (cf. Hosea 1:4). Jehu got carried away in his zeal and killed many innocent people who could have helped him be a more effective king than he proved to be.

3. JEHU'S EXECUTION OF AHAZIAH'S
RELATIVES (10:12-14)

10:12-14. Traveling south from Jezreel **toward Samaria** Jehu and his men **met** a party of **42 men** on the road. He learned that they were **relatives of Ahaziah, king of Judah** who were going from Jerusalem to visit other relatives of **the king** including **the queen mother,** Jezebel. Obviously they had not heard of Jehu's coup. **Jehu** seized them at once since they were part of the house of Ahab and executed them near a **well,** leaving **no survivor.** Not all 42 travelers were necessarily blood relatives of Ahab; some may have been related by marriage. But that would not have mattered to Jehu (cf. v. 11). In 2 Chronicles 22:8 they are called "princes of Judah" and "the sons of Ahaziah's relatives, who had been attending Ahaziah."

4. JEHU'S EXECUTION OF THE REST OF
AHAB'S RELATIVES (10:15-17)

10:15-17. Continuing his journey, Jehu met **Jehonadab son of Recab.** This man was a faithful follower of the Lord and a strict observer of the Mosaic Law (cf. Jer. 35:6-7, where his name is spelled Jonadab). He **was on his way to meet** Jehu. Meeting Jehonadab, **Jehu** learned that he was a supporter of his policy to purge the land of Ahab's apostate influ-

ence. Joining hands and sharing a **chariot** were signs of agreement and mutual commitment. The new king invited his ally to accompany him to Samaria to witness his **zeal for the Lord.** After they arrived Jehu proceeded to kill all the remaining members of **Ahab's family** in fulfillment of Elijah's prophecy (cf. 1 Kings 21:21).

5. JEHU'S EXECUTION OF THE BAAL
PROPHETS (10:18-28)

10:18-23. Jehu called a special convocation of **the people** of Israel under the pretense that he would **sacrifice** to and **honor . . . Baal.** It was to take place at the central **temple of Baal** that **Ahab** had built in Samaria (1 Kings 16:32). Every leader of the **Baal** cult was required to attend. Obviously Jehu's true religious preferences had not yet become known in Israel. **Jehonadab** (cf. 2 Kings 10:15) accompanied **Jehu** and observed his preparations. **Jehu** carefully guarded against the possibility of any worshipers of the **Lord** being present and slain. He also made sure that none of the **Baal** worshipers would escape.

10:24-28. Presumably **Jehu** did not personally participate in the **sacrifices and burnt offerings** of the priests **of** Baal; to have done so would have undermined his attempts to win the support of the faithful in Israel. However, he did offer a **burnt offering,** perhaps to set a trap for the priests **of Baal. Jehu** then **ordered** his **guards and officers** (80 of them) to enter **the temple** and slaughter all Baal ministers. Then **they brought** out **the sacred stone . . . burned** it, probably to dishonor it, and then **demolished** it. However, perhaps two stones were involved, because two different Hebrew words are used for the stones in verses 26 and 27. If the first "stone" was actually a wooden idol, then the second "stone" was the main image **of Baal,** probably a conical stone dedicated to **Baal.**

Jehu's massacre completed the destruction of **Baal worship in Israel** which Elijah had begun. The king was God's instrument of judgment.

6. JEHU'S ASSESSMENT (10:29-31)

10:29-31. Though **Jehu** killed the Baal priests, he did not completely obey the Lord. He continued the idolatrous policies **of Jeroboam** with **worship of the**

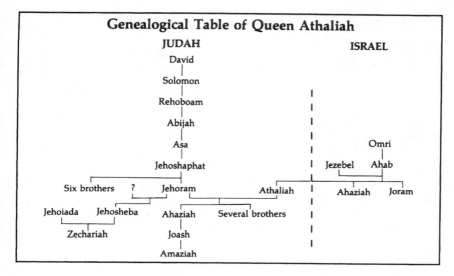

Genealogical Table of Queen Athaliah

JUDAH

David
|
Solomon
|
Rehoboam
|
Abijah
|
Asa
|
Jehoshaphat
|
Six brothers — ? — Jehoram — Athaliah

Jehoiada — Jehosheba — Ahaziah — Several brothers

Zechariah — Joash

Amaziah

ISRAEL

Omri
|
Jezebel — Ahab

Ahaziah — Joram

---

golden calves at Bethel and Dan.

Because he obeyed the Lord in the matter of judging Ahab's dynasty, **God** promised **Jehu** that four generations of his **descendants** would reign as kings over **Israel.** These were Jehoahaz, Jehoash (Joash), Jeroboam II, and Zechariah. No doubt God's blessing would have been greater if Jehu's **heart** had been more completely devoted to Him. But he did become the head of Israel's fifth royal dynasty.

7. JEHU'S LOSSES (10:32-36)

10:32-36. God's discipline on Israel for Jehu's incomplete devotion (cf. v. 31) came in the form of territorial losses. Jehu's reign was characterized by turmoil and unrest. He was not a strong ruler. Social and economic abuses marked his administration. Both the Arameans and the Assyrians humiliated Israel during his leadership. **Hazael,** king of Aram, seized all of Transjordan from **Israel** and later even made inroads into Israel's territory west **of the Jordan** (cf. 12:17-18; 13:7). Before Hazael's attacks, Assyria under Shalmaneser III had forced Jehu to bow before him and pay tribute. A bas relief on Shalmaneser's so-called "Black Obelisk" shows Jehu doing this. This is the only picture of an Israelite king that has been found so far.

Jehu could have used the experience of the seasoned officials he unnecessarily

slew (cf. 10:11). His ruthlessness and deception probably made even his closest allies suspicious of him. The alliance that had united and provided some strength for both Judah and Israel was broken when Jehu killed Judah's king Ahaziah. Israel's treaty with Phoenicia also ended when Jehu killed Joram, Jezebel, and the prophets of Baal. This is how God **began to reduce the size of Israel** in Jehu's reign. In all Jehu **reigned . . . 28 years** (841–814 B.C.).

F. Athaliah's evil reign in Judah (11:1-20)

Athaliah usurped the throne of Judah. She was Judah's only reigning queen and the strongest Baal advocate among Judah's rulers.

1. JOASH'S PRESERVATION (11:1-3)

11:1. Athaliah was **the mother** of the Judean king **Ahaziah,** whom Jehu had slain (9:27-29; 2 Chron. 22:9) in 841 B.C. Athaliah was a daughter of Ahab and Jezebel, and a sister of Ahaziah and Joram who had reigned successively in Israel after Ahab's death. She was the wife of King Jehoram of Judah who had died of an intestinal illness (2 Chron. 21:18-19). Her other sons had all been killed by the raiding Philistines and Arabians (2 Chron. 21:17). Now she saw the opportunity to seize the throne for herself. So she proceeded to have all her grandsons killed in total disregard for God's will that the descendants of David should rule over Judah forever (2 Sam. 7:16).

11:2-3. Jehosheba, a daughter of Athaliah's husband **King Jehoram** (though perhaps not Athaliah's own daughter), was a **sister of** King **Ahaziah** of Judah. She took one of Ahaziah's sons, **Joash,** and hid him so that he was not put to death with the other children. During Athaliah's **six-**year reign (841–835 B.C.) this aunt kept the prince safe by hiding him in **the temple of the LORD** where her husband, Jehoiada, served as high priest (2 Chron. 22:11). (See the chart "Genealogical Table of Queen Athaliah.") Joash was a one-year-old when he was taken by Jehosheba because he was hidden for six years and then was made king at the age of seven (cf. 2 Kings 11:21).

2. JEHOIADA'S PLANS (11:4-8)

11:4-8. As Athaliah began **the seventh year** of her reign, **Jehoiada** the high priest assembled the military **commanders** at a certain level of authority (those commanding **100** soldiers each), **the Carites** (also called Kerethites [see comments on 2 Sam. 8:18] and possibly Phoenician mercenaries who guarded the city), **and the guards** (lit., "runners," probably royal bodyguards) secretly in Solomon's **temple.** These were all loyalists who did not support the queen. **He showed them** little Joash, then seven years old (cf. 2 Kings 11:21), to assure them that there was indeed a living legitimate heir to the throne. He then outlined his plan to crown Joash as **the king.** The guards (consisting of priests and Levites, 2 Chron. 23:4) were to divide into **three** groups **on the Sabbath,** one group at the **palace,** another at **the Sur Gate** near the temple, and another group **at the gate behind the guard** through which opposition might come. The others, who were going **off . . . duty,** were to **guard the temple.** A ceremony would take place at the changing of the guard on the Sabbath when the temple area would be busy, perhaps on a feast day. The boy was to be fenced off by the soldiers and **anyone who** came near their **ranks** was to be killed. The soldiers were to guard Joash with their lives as he was conducted from the temple to his place of coronation in the temple courtyard.

3. JOASH'S CORONATION (11:9-12)

11:9-11. On the appointed day **the commanders** did as they had been instructed. **Jehoiada** gave them the special **spears and shields** that were kept in **the temple** and used for state occasions. Their use would have helped the people recognize that the coronation was official as well as important. Since the temple faced east **the guards** evidently made a semicircular arc in front of the building from its northeast to its southeast corners, creating a shielded area in **the temple** courtyard where the anointing would take place.

11:12. Jehoiada then **brought** Joash **out** of the temple where he had been living into this protected area of the courtyard, placed the royal **crown on** his young head, **presented him with a copy of the covenant** (the Mosaic Law or a part of it; cf. Deut. 17:18-19), **and proclaimed him king.** At some time in the ceremony, probably near the beginning, the high priest also **anointed** Joash with oil, symbolizing enduement with divine power (cf. 2 Kings 9:6). Undoubtedly Jehoiada had scheduled this coronation for a time when as many people as possible would witness it. When the king had been crowned **the people** raised a roar of approval, **clapped . . . and shouted, Long live the king!**

4. ATHALIAH'S EXECUTION (11:13-16)

11:13-14. The first that **Athaliah** knew of Jehoiada's plan was when she **heard the noise** of the celebration. **She went** from her palace to **the temple** to find out what was happening. To her amazement, she saw little Joash (**the king**) with the royal crown on his head **standing by the pillar** at the eastern gate of the inner courtyard of the temple, the place the king customarily occupied when he addressed the people in the temple area (cf. 2 Chron. 23:13). An elevated platform was provided for the king to stand on when he visited the temple on festive occasions (cf. 2 Kings 23:3; 2 Chron. 6:13). This is where Joash stood. The queen immediately understood what was taking place, **tore her robes** signifying her great distress (cf. 2 Kings 2:12; 5:7; 6:30), and cried, **Treason! Treason! 11:15-16.** What Jehoiada had done was not treasonous because Joash was a legitimate heir to the throne. Athaliah was not a legitimate heir since she was not a blood descendant of David. *She* was the one guilty of treason. For this reason **Jehoiada the priest ordered the commanders** to arrest her, to lead her out of **the temple** area under guard, and to kill anyone who tried to help her. It was not appropriate to execute anyone in the temple area since it was a place of worship (cf. 2 Chron. 24:20-22). Athaliah **was put to death** with the sword at the place **where the horses** entered **the palace grounds** (the Horse Gate; cf. 2 Chron. 23:15, not the Horse Gate into the city). So ended the life of one of the most wicked women in Scripture, a true daughter of Jezebel.

5. JEHOIADA'S PURGE OF BAALISM (11:17-20)

11:17. Jehoiada led the **people** in a rededication of themselves to **the Lord** and His **covenant** given through Moses (cf. Deut. 4:20; 27:9-10) from which they had departed since the days of Jehoshaphat. **He also made a** new **covenant between the king and the people** that the king would lead the people according to the Mosaic Law and the people would obey the king (cf. 2 Sam. 5:3).

11:18-20. The people then **tore . . . down** the **temple of Baal** that had been built in Jerusalem and used by Athaliah to promote Baal worship in Judah. They also destroyed **the altars and idols** which this temple contained, **and killed Mattan the** chief **priest of Baal in front of the altars.** This showed deliberate disrespect for the pagan worshipers' false belief that the temple area was a sacred place of sanctuary.

To avoid recriminations by the devotees of Baal, **Jehoiada . . . posted guards at** Solomon's **temple.** At the end of the coronation ceremonies the people led by Jehoiada and his guards conducted **the new king** to his **palace** where he sat down **on** his **throne.** The people of Judah as a whole **rejoiced** greatly that once again a descendant of David ruled and that the worship of Yahweh was again made official. The turmoil that had existed in Jerusalem during Athaliah's reign subsided and **the city was quiet** once again. (For more details on the reign of Athaliah, see 2 Chron. 22:10-23:15.) As Jezebel had promoted Baalism in

Israel, her daughter **Athaliah** had encouraged it in Judah. During Athaliah's reign as queen, Baalism gained its strongest foothold in the Southern Kingdom. However, it was never as influential in Judah as it was in Israel, because of the stronger commitment of some kings of Judah to the Lord.

G. Joash's good reign in Judah (11:21-12:21)

The beginning of Joash's reign marks the commencement of over 100 years of consecutive rule by four men who were all judged as good kings. None of these four—Joash, Amaziah, Azariah (Uzziah), and Jotham—was as good for Judah as Jehoshaphat, Hezekiah, or Josiah, but together they did provide the longest continuous span of God-approved leadership in Judah's history.

1. JOASH'S GOODNESS (11:21-12:3)

11:21-12:3. Joash was the youngest king to mount the throne of Judah; he **was seven years old.** His **reign** began in 835 B.C. and ended in 796 B.C., **40 years** later. He was the son of King Ahaziah and a woman named **Zibiah** from **Beersheba** in southern Judah.

Joash did the Lord's will as long as his mentor **Jehoiada the priest** lived. But after Jehoiada died Joash turned away from following the Lord. During his years of faithfulness Joash ruled well, but he did **not** remove **the high places** (as was true of most kings of Judah; see comments on 1 Kings 22:43), where **the people** made **sacrifices** and burned **incense** contrary to the Mosaic Law (cf. Deut. 12:2-7, 13-14). These high places may have been regarded by Joash as relatively unimportant as they apparently were considered by his predecessors.

2. JOASH'S TEMPLE RESTORATION (12:4-16)

12:4-8. Joash purposed to restore Solomon's **temple** which had fallen into disrepair and had suffered major damage during Athaliah's reign (cf. 2 Chron. 24:7). This was the first temple restoration project recorded in 1 or 2 Kings. The king planned to use the money **brought** by the people in regular **census** offerings (Ex. 30:11-16), vow offerings (Lev. 27; Num. 30), and free-will offerings. But this plan did not work. Apparently revenue from these regular sources was insufficient to support the priests and Levites and also to pay for the temple repairs.

Joash's impatience with **the priests** who were responsible for collecting **the money** (1 Kings 12:7; 2 Chron. 24:5) suggests that they may not have wanted to divert any funds from their own support. They had been using the money given them by the priestly **treasurers** for the regular expenses of temple service, which was probably legitimate. So **Joash** told them to stop taking **money** from the offerings for this purpose since he was instituting a new procedure. Instead they were to **hand . . . over** what would be collected in a new way to other men who would be responsible to supervise the renovations. **The priests agreed** to separate this project from the regular **temple** service and to let other men be responsible for it.

12:9-16. At Joash's instructions **Jehoiada . . . bored a hole** in the top of a large wooden **chest** and **placed it** on the north **side** of **the altar** of burnt offering in **the temple** courtyard. **The priests** then **put into the chest all the money** the people **brought** for **the temple** renovation project. **Whenever . . . the chest** filled up **the royal secretary and the high priest . . . counted the money . . . and put it into bags** where it was stored until needed to pay for materials, labor, and other expenses connected with the project.

This **money** was **not** used for **temple** furnishings at first (v. 13), but later the excess money received was used for that purpose (2 Chron. 24:14). The paymasters, serving **with complete honesty,** were trusted to **pay** out all **the money** due to **the workers.** (Integrity had returned to Judah with her rededication to the Lord.) **The money** received **from** the people as part of their **guilt . . . and sin offerings was** used for the support of **the priests,** not for **the temple** building project. (See 2 Chron. 24:4-14 for the parallel passage.)

Several events transpired during the reign of Joash that are not recorded in 2 Kings but do appear in 2 Chronicles. Jehoiada the high priest died at the uncommonly advanced age of 130 years (2 Chron. 24:15-16). After Jehoiada's voice was silenced Joash followed the counsel of certain Judean officials who advised him to do things that resulted in his turning from the Lord. When the king did this God sent prophets to warn the nation (2 Chron. 24:17-19). Jehoiada's son, Zechariah, who had replaced his father as high priest, also sounded a prophetic warning. But Joash had him stoned to death for his rebuke (2 Chron. 24:20-22).

3. JOASH'S RANSOM TO HAZAEL (12:17-18)

12:17-18. Hazael king of Aram had defeated Israel during the reigns of Israel's kings Jehu and Jehoahaz (13:3, 22) and then pressed south along the coast into Judah. He captured **Gath,** the Philistine city that had been taken by Judah (cf. 2 Chron. 11:8). **Then he** sent a contingent of soldiers against **Jerusalem.** This unit destroyed "all the leaders of the people" (2 Chron. 24:3). To buy Hazael off, **Joash** gave him **all the sacred objects** and **gifts** that his forefathers and **he . . . had dedicated** to the Lord as well as **all the gold** in the temple and the palace **treasuries** (cf. 2 Chron. 24:23). This ransom caused **Hazael** to withdraw his troops. The whole incident illustrates the weakness of Judah at this time which resulted from Joash's apostasy.

4. JOASH'S DEATH (12:19-21)

12:19-21. The Arameans had severely wounded **Joash** (2 Chron. 24:25). Evidently he went for recovery to **Beth Millo,** a town **on the road down to Silla.** (The locations of these towns are now unknown.) Several of **his officials,** conspiring against him because he had slain the high priest Zechariah (2 Chron. 24:20-22), **murdered** Joash in his bed. The assassins were **Jozabad** and **Jehozabad,** whose mothers, according to 2 Chronicles 24:26 (see comments there), were an Ammonitess and a Moabitess, respectively. Joash **was buried** in the royal **city** (Jerusalem) but not in the royal tombs (cf. 2 Chron. 24:25) because he was not as respected as some of his ancestors. His son **Amaziah . . . succeeded him as king.**

H. Jehoahaz's evil reign in Israel (13:1-9)

The scene shifts once again to the Northern Kingdom.

13:1-3. Jehoahaz began reigning **in the 23rd year** of Joash's reign in **Judah** and **reigned** for **17 years** (814–798 B.C.).

(The 23rd year of Joash would seemingly mean Joash began reigning in 837. Actually he began in 835 [see the chart "Kings of Judah and Israel and the Preexilic Prophets," near 1 Kings 12:25-33]; different systems of dating began to be used in both Judah and Israel, thus making for a two-year deviation in the dating system.) Jehoahaz was Jehu's **son** and his capital was **Samaria.** Jehoahaz followed **the sins of Jeroboam** throughout his career (cf. Jehu, 2 Kings 10:29). As discipline against Israel for her disobedience to the Mosaic Law, God allowed the Arameans to dominate her. Jehoahaz reigned during the last years of Hazael's administration and early years of his son **Ben-Hadad III's** reign.

13:4-6. Because of Aram's distressing oppression King **Jehoahaz sought the LORD's** help. Out of compassion for His people and in spite of the king's idolatry **the LORD provided a deliverer.** This deliverer probably was King Adad-nirāri III of Assyria (811–783 B.C.; see the chart "Kings of Assyria in the Middle and New Assyrian Kingdoms," near Jonah 1:2) who fought against Damascus (as well as against Tyre, Sidon, Media, Edom, and Egypt) and defeated it in 803 B.C. The Arameans consequently turned their attention from attacking **Israel** to defending themselves against the Assyrians. Thus Israel **escaped** Aram's **power** and the people were able to return to **their . . . homes** and live in peace. Israel had to pay tribute to Assyria, but the nation was free from Aram's attacks. This answer to prayer did **not** result in the people repenting of their idolatry, however. Even **the Asherah pole,** a symbol of the pagan goddess Asherah, Baal's consort, **remained** conspicuously **in Samaria.**

13:7-9. Jehoahaz's **army** had been decimated by his wars with the Arameans, though some of the Israelite army was lost during the reign of Jehu (cf. comments on 10:32-36). **Dust at threshing time** was blown away and never seen again.

When **Jehoahaz** died he **was buried in Samaria,** and his son **Jehoash** followed him to the throne.

I. Jehoash's evil reign in Israel (13:10-25)

Jehoash was the third king of Jehu's dynasty to rule over Israel.

1. JEHOASH'S ASSESSMENT (13:10-13)

13:10-11. When **Jehoash** (a variant of the Heb. Joash; cf. NIV marg.) took the reins of power in **Israel** a king by the name of **Joash** ruled in **Judah.** (The NIV translators have rendered the name of Israel's king Jehoash and that of Judah's king Joash consistently so these men are not so easily confused.) Jehoash began reigning in Israel in 798 B.C. and served for a total of **16 years** until 782 B.C. However, after five years (in 793 B.C.) Jehoash's son Jeroboam II began to reign as coregent with him. The king continued the religious policies of his predecessors and **did evil in the eyes of the LORD.**

13:12-13. The statement that normally concludes the writer's history of a particular king occurs here early in the story of Jehoash. These words about Jehoash are repeated almost verbatim in the history of Amaziah of Judah (14:15-16). Jehoash's **war against Amaziah** is described by the writer as a part of the Judean king's reign (14:8-14). **Jeroboam** II **succeeded. . . . Jehoash,** but the son actually began reigning as coregent 11 years before his father's death.

2. ELISHA'S PROPHECY (13:14-21)

13:14. **Elisha** the prophet now reenters the narrative. He was **suffering from** a terminal **illness.** Out of respect for this man of God, King **Jehoash** paid him a visit. The fact that the king **wept over him** reveals that though Jehoash followed in the ways of Jeroboam I (v. 11) he also revered Yahweh. He anticipated the great loss that the death of this servant of God would be to Israel. He regarded Elisha as superior to himself, calling him **my father** in true humility. By the phrase **the chariots and horsemen of Israel,** he showed that he recognized in Elisha, and behind him in the Lord, the real defense and power of Israel against all her adversaries. Elisha had used the same expressions himself when Elijah's ministry was terminated by God (2:12).

13:15-17. In view of Jehoash's evidence of faith **Elisha** blessed him with a promise of victory. The **bow and . . . arrows** were symbols of strength and victory that God was going to give Jehoash. By taking **the bow in his hands** the **king** was symbolically becoming the agent of God's power. **Elisha put his own hands on** Jehoash's **hands** to symbolize that the power the king would exert came from the Lord through His prophet.

Jehoash was to **open** an **east window,** which faced toward the enemy Aramean hosts at Aphek, so that he could **shoot.** Obeying the prophet, the king **shot** an arrow out the window toward Aram. By actually shooting the arrow the king was appropriating the victory symbolized by the arrow. As the king shot, **Elisha** said that **the arrow** represented **victory over Aram. . . . at Aphek** (cf. 1 Kings 20:30) in the Transjordan.

13:18-19. Elisha then instructed **the king** to **take the arrows** that remained and to shoot them at the ground. (The Heb. which is trans. **Strike the ground** probably means that the king was to shoot these arrows as he had shot the first one rather than to grasp them together in his hand and strike the ground with them.) The king fired off **three** more arrows **and** then **stopped.** Elisha **was angry with him** for stopping because the king was manifesting failure to trust God to give him as many victories as there were arrows. Jehoash understood what shooting the first arrow symbolized; Elisha had explained it. By letting the king shoot more arrows God was inviting him through Elisha to claim as many victories as he had arrows. God assured him that he would have victory by divine enablement. But perhaps Jehoash felt that God could not or would not do as much for him as Elisha implied. This unbelief explains why Elisha became angry. Jehoash had failed to trust God even though he knew what God had promised. The prophet told the king that had he shot more arrows God would have honored his faith and given him additional victories resulting in Aram's complete destruction. As it was he would now win **only three** victories (v. 25).

13:20-21. Shortly thereafter **Elisha died.** Elisha's ministry spanned at least 56 years (including his years of serving as Elijah's servant) since he was called by Elijah during Ahab's reign (which ended in 853 B.C.) and Elisha died in Jehoash's reign (which began in 798 B.C.). The prophet was probably **buried** as most of the early Israelites were in a cave or tomb (v. 21) hewn out of a rock, after his body was wrapped in linen cloths.

Some time later some men were laying another **man's body** to rest near Elisha's tomb. They were surprised by a group of **Moabite raiders** who were apparently going to rob whomever they met. To flee quickly, the Israelite pallbearers removed the stone in front of **Elisha's** tomb, **threw** the corpse of their friend in the **tomb,** and retreated. **When the** new corpse **touched Elisha's** he **came to life and stood up on his feet.** Evidently the men who placed the body in Elisha's tomb observed this. Doubtless they told their story far and wide, and it probably reached the ears of Jehoash for whom this miracle seems to have been intended primarily. Such a sign of the power of God working even through His prophet's corpse may have both encouraged the king as he anticipated his battles with the Arameans and rebuked him for his lack of faith (cf. comments on vv. 18-19).

3. JEHOASH'S VICTORIES (13:22-25)

13:22-23. Even though **Hazael** had his hands full combating his Assyrian foe he kept his foot on Israel's neck too, during **the reign** of Jehoash's **father Jehoahaz. But** because of the Lord's **covenant with** the patriarchs He graciously and compassionately cared for the Israelites, refusing **to destroy them or** cast **them** out of **His presence.** It was God's promise, not the Israelites' goodness, that moved God to be merciful as the writer notes, **to this day,** that is, right to the time 1 and 2 Kings were written.

13:24-25. After **Hazael . . . died** (801 B.C.) **Jehoash** engaged the new Aramean king, **Ben-Hadad III** in battle and **defeated** him **three times,** as prophesied by Elisha (v. 19). The battle of Aphek (v. 17), though not mentioned here, may have been one of the three battles. **Jehoash . . . recaptured** the Israelite **towns . . . Jehoahaz** had lost in battle to Hazael in these three encounters (cf. v. 3).

J. Amaziah's good reign in Judah (14:1-22)

1. AMAZIAH'S POLICIES (14:1-6)

14:1-6. Amaziah . . . began to reign in **Judah** about a year after **Jehoash** had become **king of Israel.** Amaziah was fairly young, **25 years old, when he became king,** and ruled a long time, **29 years** (796–767 B.C.). Much of this time his son Azariah's reign overlapped with his own

(790–767 B.C.). The king followed his father Joash's example; he upheld the worship of the LORD but did not remove the high places (cf. comments on 1 Kings 22:43), where the people worshiped God in disobedience to the Mosaic Law (Deut. 12:2-7, 13-14). Compared with David, the founder of his dynasty and Judah's greatest king, Amaziah fell short.

In obedience to God's Law (Deut. 24:16) Amaziah did not execute the children of his father's assassins as was customarily done by Near Eastern monarchs. He trusted God to control these potential rebels.

2. AMAZIAH'S WAR WITH EDOM (14:7)

14:7. This war with Edom is described more fully in 2 Chronicles 25:5-16. Edom had revolted from Judean control during the reign of Jehoram. Amaziah wanted to regain control of this neighbor because Edom gave Judah access to southern trade routes. The battle took place in the Valley of Salt, a marshy plain at the south end of the Dead Sea (cf. 2 Sam. 8:13). Sela, renamed Joktheel by Amaziah, was later named Petra, the stronghold city of Edom carved out of sheer mountain walls.

3. AMAZIAH'S WAR WITH ISRAEL (14:8-14)

14:8-10. Riding high after his victory over Edom, Amaziah decided to challenge Israel which had recently suffered defeats by Hazael (13:22). Amaziah's invitation to Jehoash constituted a declaration of war.

The Israelite king responded to this challenge by sending a warning to Amaziah in the form of a parable. Thistles and cedars were common in Lebanon. Amaziah was the thistle and Jehoash the cedar. As a wild beast could easily squash a thistle, so anyone could easily defeat Judah. Jehoash's advice that Amaziah stay at home was good, but Amaziah's pride had been hurt by the story. So he committed himself even more strongly to war. His decision was of the Lord who intended that he should suffer defeat because after conquering the Edomites, Amaziah had brought Edomite idols into Judah and had worshiped them (cf. 2 Chron. 25:14, 20).

14:11-14. Jehoash seized the initiative and attacked Judah. He faced Amaziah in battle at Beth Shemesh,

about 15 miles west of Jerusalem. Judah was defeated, its troops retreated, and Amaziah was captured. Jehoash then proceeded to Jerusalem where he broke down . . . 600 feet of the city wall. He took the remaining gold . . . silver, and other articles of value from the temple and palace, as well as hostages, and returned to Samaria. Apparently when Amaziah was taken prisoner his son Azariah began to reign as Judah's king in Jerusalem (790 B.C.).

4. JEHOASH'S DEATH (14:15-16)

14:15-16. This second mention of Jehoash's death (cf. 13:12-13) seems to be added here because of the unusual situation that existed with Amaziah being held prisoner in Israel. When Jehoash died (782 B.C.) Amaziah was released and returned to Judah. Jehoash's successor was his son Jeroboam II.

5. AMAZIAH'S DEATH (14:17-22)

14:17-20. Amaziah (who died in 767) outlived Jehoash (who died in 782) by at least 15 years. After Amaziah returned to Judah he made his son Azariah his vice-regent. They shared the throne (790–767) until Amaziah's death.

The people who conspired against Amaziah are not identified but may have been some of his own officials. The king fled to Lachish, a former royal city on the southern border of Judah, from which he could have fled the country if his enemies had not caught up with him first. He received a royal burial in the ancient City of David section of Jerusalem.

14:21-22. In 790 B.C. Azariah had begun to reign at the age of 16 when his father Amaziah was taken prisoner to Israel. Then when his father died in 767, Azariah began his sole reign. His restoration of Elath on the coast of the Gulf of Aqaba was probably mentioned here because it was one of Azariah's most significant accomplishments. More information about Azariah is given in 15:1-7.

K. Jeroboam II's evil reign in Israel (14:23-29)

14:23-24. Jeroboam II had served as coregent with his father Jehoash from 793 to 782 B.C. The 15th year of Amaziah . . . king of Judah marked the beginning of his sole reign (782 B.C.). In all, he reigned 41 years (793–753 B.C.), longer than any other **king of Israel** before him.

Spiritually Jeroboam II followed in the footsteps of his predecessors in Israel. However, politically he was Israel's strongest king. Only a few of Jeroboam II's accomplishments are recorded; these were of lesser importance in view of the writer's emphasis on the spiritually significant aspects of Israel's history.

14:25-27. Jeroboam II **restored** Israel's **boundaries** to approximately their extent in Solomon's time (excluding of course the Southern Kingdom's territory belonging to Judah and Benjamin). **Lebo Hamath** (cf. 1 Kings 8:65) was over 150 miles northeast of the Sea of Kinnereth. **The Sea of the Arabah** was the Dead Sea. This territorial extension had been prophesied by **Jonah,** who ministered in Jeroboam II's reign (see the chart "Kings of Judah and Israel and the Preexilic Prophets," near 1 Kings 12:25-33). This prophecy of Jonah is not recorded elsewhere in Scripture. This is the same Jonah who traveled to Nineveh with God's message of repentance for the Assyrians (cf. Jonah 1:1). His hometown, **Gath Hepher,** was located a few miles north of Nazareth in Israel.

The **suffering** of the Israelites came as a result of the oppressive influence of Hazael of Damascus. Out of compassion for His people **the LORD** began to relieve their distress under Jehoash (cf. 2 Kings 13:22-25) and continued to do so under **Jeroboam** II.

14:28-29. How God granted the Israelites relief is not explained. Only a few particulars are revealed in these verses. Jeroboam II took **Damascus,** the Aramean capital, **and Hamath.** These cities (and their surrounding territory) **had belonged to Yaudi** (Judah) in the days of David and Solomon but not since that time. By controlling this area Jeroboam II undoubtedly also recovered all of Israel's Transjordanian territory which Hazael had seized (cf. 10:32-33), thus making Israel the largest country on the eastern Mediterranean coast.

Jeroboam II's victories were accomplished because Damascus had been weakened by attacks from the Assyrians to their northeast under Adad-nirāri III (cf. 13:5). Also Assyria herself was weak at this time, suffering from the threat of attack from the Urartu people on their northern frontier, internal dissension,

and a series of weak rulers. Jehoash had been a successful military strategist (cf. 14:11-14), and his son Jeroboam II evidently inherited his father's abilities and even surpassed him.

During Jeroboam II's reign the Prophets Amos and Hosea ministered in Israel (Amos 1:1; Hosea 1:1). Their prophecies give additional insights into life in Israel during Jeroboam's reign. **Jeroboam** II died in 753 B.C. and his son **Zechariah . . . succeeded him** (cf. 2 Kings 15:8-12).

L. Azariah's good reign in Judah (15:1-7)

15:1-4. Azariah ("Yahweh has helped") is also called Uzziah ("Yahweh is my strength") in the Old Testament (cf. vv. 13, 30, 32, 34; 2 Chron. 26; Isa. 1:1; Hosea 1:1; Amos 1:1; Zech. 14:5; etc.). **The 27th year of Jeroboam** II's coregency with Jehoash was 767 B.C. In that year Azariah **began to reign** over **Judah** as sole ruler. He had previously served as **king** in his father's place while Amaziah was imprisoned in Israel and as coregent with him after Amaziah returned to Judah. Azariah **was 16 years old when he** began his coregency (in 790 B.C.) **and he reigned** a total of **52 years** (790–739 B.C.) **in Jerusalem.** Up to that time this was the longest reign of any king of Judah or Israel. Azariah was a good king like **his father** (cf. 2 Chron. 26:4-5), but he too failed to remove **the high places** (cf. comments on 1 Kings 22:43) where the people worshiped Yahweh in disobedience to the Mosaic Law (cf. Deut. 12:2-7, 13-14).

15:5. The writer of 2 Chronicles gave a fuller explanation of the sin that led to Azariah's becoming a leper (2 Chron. 26:16-21). When Azariah became a leper (in 750 B.C.) he shared the throne with his son **Jotham** as coregent until **he died** in 739. Azariah **lived** a life of limited seclusion as required of lepers in Israel, but still played a part in leading the nation, with his son Jotham serving as executor of **the palace.**

15:6-7. In addition to **Azariah's** history being recorded in **the book of the annals of the kings of Judah,** the chronicler added that Isaiah wrote his story (2 Chron. 26:22). Perhaps Isaiah wrote the annals of some of Judah's kings, or there may have been two separate documents.

When the king died he **was buried . . . in the City of David,** undoubtedly in the royal tombs, **and Jotham his son** continued reigning in his place.

Azariah was one of Judah's most effective and influential kings. He expanded Judah's territories southward to Elath (2 Kings 14:22), eastward so that the Ammonites paid him tribute (2 Chron. 26:8), and westward by defeating the Philistines (2 Chron. 26:6-7). He fortified Jerusalem and other parts of Judah (2 Chron. 26:9-10, 15), and reorganized the army (2 Chron. 26:11-14). The combined territories of Azariah and Jeroboam II approximated those of David and Solomon. After Jeroboam II's death Azariah became even more powerful and was looked to for leadership by his neighbors who formed a coalition with him to resist the threat of Assyria. Unfortunately he became proud, intruded into the priest's office, and was tragically humbled by God (2 Chron. 26:16-21).

M. Zechariah's evil reign in Israel (15:8-12)

15:8-12. Zechariah succeeded **Jeroboam** II in Azariah's **38th year** (753 B.C.), but **he reigned** only **six months.** Like all his predecessors in Israel, he continued the worship of the golden calves at Dan and Bethel that **Jeroboam** I had begun. He was **assassinated** publicly by **Shallum.** The fact that Shallum was allowed to assume the throne suggests that Zechariah did not enjoy strong public support. Zechariah's death fulfilled God's **word** to **Jehu** that four generations would succeed him on Israel's **throne** (10:30). Thus Israel's fifth dynasty came to an end.

N. Shallum's evil reign in Israel (15:13-16)

15:13-16. Shallum's **one-month** reign in 752 B.C. was the second shortest in Israel's history (after Zimri's seven-day reign, 1 Kings 16:15-20). **Menahem** was the commander in chief of Jeroboam II's army (Josephus *The Antiquities of the Jews* 9. 11. 1). He was stationed in **Tirzah,** the former capital of Israel (cf. 1 Kings 15:21, 33; 16:6, 8-9, 15, 17, 23). Menahem, who regarded Shallum as a usurper to the throne, believed that he as commander of the army should succeed Zechariah. Menahem apparently **attacked Tiphsah,**

perhaps near Tirzah and Samaria, **because** its inhabitants, who **refused to** acknowledge him as king, shut **their gates** against him. His violent destruction of the city, even down to murdering **all the pregnant women,** was probably intended to intimidate other Israelite towns into supporting him.

O. Menahem's evil reign in Israel (15:17-22)

15:17-18. Menahem began ruling **in the 39th year of Azariah** and **reigned . . . 10 years** (752–742 B.C.). Menahem instituted Israel's seventh dynasty. His apostasy was as bad as that of many of his predecessors.

15:19-22. Pul has been identified from Assyrian inscriptions as Tiglath-Pileser III (745–727 B.C.; cf. v. 29; 16:7, 10; 1 Chron. 5:26). This is the first mention of **Assyria** in 2 Kings. Pul was one of Assyria's strongest rulers. This invasion of **Israel** took place in 743 B.C. and resulted in Menahem's paying tribute to Pul. In return for the **1,000 talents** (ca. 37 tons) **of silver** Menahem raised from the **wealthy** men of Israel, the Assyrian **king** gave Menahem **his support** and helped him retain his crown.

After **Menahem** died, he was **succeeded** by his son **Pekahiah.**

P. Pekahiah's evil reign in Israel (15:23-26)

15:23-26. Pekahiah . . . reigned two years in **Samaria** (742–740 B.C.). He too followed Jeroboam's apostate ways. His reign ended when **one of his** military **officers, Pekah,** led **50 men,** under his command from **Gilead** in Transjordan, to Samaria and there **assassinated** the king. **Argob and Arieh,** possibly princes, were also **killed.** This took place **in the citadel,** the most secure part of the **palace,** in **Samaria. Pekah** then assumed the throne of Israel.

Q. Pekah's evil reign in Israel (15:27-31)

15:27-28. The **52nd year of Azariah** was 740 B.C. (His 52nd year, his last, extended into part of 739.) At this time **Pekah** began to rule over **Israel** from **Samaria.** However, he had apparently never accepted Menahem's claim to the throne and had set up a rival government east of the Jordan River in Gilead. There Pekah lived as a military officer under the Samarian government, till the time was right for him to assert himself. His **20**-year reign means that he began ruling in Gilead at the same time Menahem took the throne in Samaria (752 B.C.). His reign overlapped Menahem's and Pekahiah's (752–740 B.C.). In 740 B.C. he assassinated Pekahiah and started ruling in Samaria where he remained until he was overthrown in 732 B.C.

Pekah continued in the sinful ways of his predecessors on the throne of **Israel.**

15:29. Part of Pekah's reason for opposing Menahem and his son Pekahiah seems to have been a different conviction regarding Israel's foreign policy toward **Assyria.** Menahem was conciliatory and willing to submit to Assyrian control (cf. vv. 19-20). **Pekah** apparently favored a harder line of resistance. Popular reaction against Menahem's taxing of the people may have encouraged Pekah to make his move. When Pekah had taken power in Samaria he made a treaty with Rezin, king of Damascus, against Assyria. This resulted in **Tiglath-Pileser** III (Pul) leading a campaign into Philistia, Israel, and later Aram in 734–732 B.C. (cf. 2 Chron. 28:5-8). In these battles he **took Ijon,** a town in Naphtali, **Abel Beth Maacah,** just south of Ijon, **Janoah,** another neighboring village, **Kedesh,** just west and north of Lake Huleh, **and Hazor,** south of Kedesh. **He took** all of **Gilead** east of the Jordan River and **Galilee,** the northern portion of Israel, including the territory **of Naphtali,** and he **deported the people to Assyria.** This first deportation of the Israelites probably took place in 733 B.C. A second deportation followed 11 years later in 722 B.C.

15:30-31. As a result of Israel's defeat **Hoshea . . . conspired against Pekah . . . assassinated him, and . . . succeeded him as king** of Israel in 732 B.C. On one of the Assyrian inscriptions Tiglath-Pileser III claims to have had a hand in establishing Hoshea on the throne (James B. Pritchard, ed., *Ancient Near Eastern Texts Relating to the Old Testament.* 3rd ed. Princeton, N.J.: Princeton University Press, 1969, p. 284). Evidently Hoshea submitted to being a pawn of Assyria as Menahem and Pekahiah had done.

R. Jotham's good reign in Judah (15:32-38)

15:32-35. The **second year of Pekah** was 750 B.C. when **Jotham . . . began to reign** as coregent with his father Azariah **(Uzziah).** Jotham's **16**-year reign was from 750 to 735 B.C. Actually Jotham continued as coregent with his son Ahaz until 732 B.C., but during this time Ahaz was regarded as the official king.

Jotham was a good king, but he did not remove **the high places** (cf. comments on 1 Kings 22:43).

Only one of Jotham's accomplishments is recorded in 2 Kings. He **rebuilt the Upper** (north) **Gate of the temple,** perhaps to encourage the worship of Yahweh. Jotham's other building projects and his subjection of the Ammonites are recorded in 2 Chronicles 27:3-5. The reason he became a powerful king is that "he walked steadfastly before the LORD his God" (2 Chron. 27:6).

15:36-38. Rezin, king of Aram, and Pekah, king of Israel, united **against Judah** to force Jotham and Ahaz to join with them in taking a hard line of resistance against the Assyrian threat. **In those days** refers specifically to the time when Jotham and Ahaz were coregents (735–732; see comments on 16:1). This pressure was from the Lord and proved to be a test of faith for the Judean king (cf. 16:5-8; Isa. 7:1-17). **His father** (2 Kings 15:38) may refer to Jotham's father Azariah who had controlled Jerusalem for 52 years, or to his ancestor David.

S. Ahaz's evil reign in Judah (chap. 16)

1. AHAZ'S ASSESSMENT (16:1-4)

16:1-2a. The **17th year of Pekah** was 735 B.C. It was not until 732, however, that **Ahaz . . . began** his **16**-year reign, which continued to 715. As shown on the chart "Kings of Judah and Israel and the Preexilic Prophets," near 1 Kings 12:25-33, the reign of Ahaz's father Jotham was 16 years (2 Chron. 27:1), 750–735. But Jotham did not die until 732. Apparently, then, in the four years from 735 to 732 neither Jotham nor Ahaz was credited with independent rule; they were coregents. In another sense Ahaz's rule began in 744 (see 2 Kings 17:1 and comments there). Therefore he may have been a vice-regent under his father

Jotham from 744 to 735.

16:2b-4. Unlike his ancestor **David,** with whom many of the Judean kings were compared, Ahaz **did not do** the will of **God.** Instead he followed the examples of the wicked **kings of** the Northern Kingdom. He went so far as to sacrifice **his son** (obviously not Hezekiah who succeeded him as king) as a burnt offering to an idol. This heinous sin (cf. 17:17) was a common practice of the Ammonites and the other native pagan Canaanite nations that Israel under Joshua **had** partially **driven out** of the land. Ahaz also promoted worship **at the high places** (cf. comments on 1 Kings 22:43), on **hilltops and under** large trees. These places of worship were so numerous that the writer said hyperbolically that they could be found **under every spreading tree** (cf. 2 Kings 17:10).

2. AHAZ'S ENEMIES (16:5-9)

16:5-6. Rezin . . . and Pekah had formed an alliance to resist Assyrian aggression and they wanted Ahaz to join them. Ahaz, however, did not feel Assyria's threat as keenly as did his neighbors who were situated between Judah and Assyria. Ahaz preferred a conciliatory policy with Assyria. Consequently Rezin and Pekah attacked **Ahaz** hoping to force him to join them. **But they** were unsuccessful in this attempt for reasons stated in verses 7-9.

The writer inserted parenthetically here (v. 6) that **Rezin** was successful in taking **Elath** at the northern tip of the Gulf of Aqaba which Azariah had recently made a Judean city (14:22). This important port town thus passed into Aramean control. Judah never was able to recapture it. It later fell to the **Edomites.**

16:7-9. Rather than joining Rezin and Pekah **Ahaz** appealed for help **to Tiglath-Pileser** III. Ahaz voluntarily submitted as a **vassal** to Assyrian control and sent a gift of **silver and gold** from **the temple** and **palace** in Jerusalem to encourage Tiglath-Pileser to get his harassing neighbors away from his walls. Tiglath-Pileser obliged **by attacking** and **capturing** Rezin's capital **Damascus.**

This diverted the Arameans from besieging Jerusalem; they had to return home to defend their own territory. Damascus fell to Assyria, **Rezin** was executed, and many of the Arameans were

deported . . . to Kir, an area of Assyria, in keeping with the Assyrians' policy of relocating conquered peoples (cf. 15:29; 17:23). Ahaz's decision to appeal to Assyria for help was a foolish one (cf. Isa. 7). Besides losing many of his people to Pekah in the siege (2 Chron. 28:5-8), Ahaz encouraged further Assyrian advancement into Palestine. The chronicler also recorded successful invasions of Judah by the Edomites and the Philistines at that time (2 Chron. 28:17-19). All these losses resulted ultimately from Ahaz's apostasy (2 Chron. 28:19).

3. AHAZ'S APOSTASY (16:10-18)

16:10-14. Ahaz traveled **to Damascus to meet Tiglath-Pileser** III. There **he saw an altar** (a large one; cf. v. 15) which was Aramean or, more likely, Assyrian. Ahaz sent **Uriah the** high **priest** in Jerusalem **a sketch of** this **altar** with instructions to have one **built** just like it. The apostasy of the priesthood at that time can be seen in Uriah's speedy acquiescence. When **Ahaz returned** home he had **the** Lord's **bronze altar** of burnt offering moved aside to give a prominent place to **the new altar.** On it he offered the traditional **offerings** of Judah.

16:15-18. Ahaz then commanded that all regular **offerings** be made **on the . . . new altar.** He would **use the bronze altar** only **for seeking guidance** probably from the Lord. **Uriah** cooperated with the king's wishes.

Ahaz also **took** the **basins from the** 10 bronze **movable stands** (cf. 1 Kings 7:27-40), **removed** the massive bronze **. . . base** from under **the Sea** (cf. 1 Kings 7:23-26) and substituted **a stone** stand. He also **took** down **the Sabbath canopy** (evidently a covering erected in the courtyard to shade the king and his retinue when they visited the temple), **and removed the royal entryway outside the temple** (a special ramp or stairway that only the king used to enter the temple). What Ahaz did with the pieces of furniture he removed is not explained. It is clear, however, that he willingly disobeyed God who had approved the use and arrangement of the bronze altar and the other furnishings and deferred to Tiglath-Pileser III in order not to offend or anger the Assyrian ruler. Ahaz's other acts of idolatry are recorded in 2 Chronicles 28:2-3, 22-25.

2 KINGS

4. AHAZ'S DEATH (16:19-20)

16:19-20. Ahaz . . . was buried in Jerusalem, but not laid in the royal sepulchres with the other godly kings of Judah (2 Chron. 28:27). This shows that there were influential people in Judah who did not approve of Ahaz's policies.

T. *Hoshea's evil reign in Israel (17:1-6)*

17:1-2. Hoshea became **king** in 732 B.C., **the 12th year of Ahaz.** Ahaz's reign, which began in 744, included 9 years as vice-regent (744–735), 4 years as coregent with his father Jotham (735–732), and 16 years as principal king (732–715). (Cf. comments on 16:1-2a.) Hoshea began his reign of **9 years** in the 20th year of Jotham (15:30), which was 732 B.C. Jotham's 20 years (750–732) included his 16-year reign (750–735) and 4 years as coregent with Ahaz (735–732). Jotham's reign from 750 to 732 appears to be 18 or 19 years, but it was considered 20 years because he reigned 18 full years and parts of two other years (see note at the bottom of the chart "Kings of Judah and Israel and the Preexilic Prophets," near 1 Kings 12:25-33).

The sins of Jeroboam I are not mentioned in connection with Hoshea. He was a wicked king but perhaps as a result of the tumultuous times in which he lived he did not promote the policies of Jeroboam. According to some Jewish tradition he allowed the Israelites to go to Jerusalem to worship the Lord.

17:3-6. Shalmaneser V (727–722 B.C.; see the chart "Kings of Assyria in the Middle and New Assyrian Kingdoms," near Jonah 1:2) had succeeded his father Tiglath-Pileser III on the throne **of Assyria.** He attacked Samaria because **Hoshea** had failed to pay the yearly **tribute** he owed as a **vassal.** Instead of paying his taxes **Hoshea** tried to make a treaty with **So** (Osorkon IV, ca. 727–716 B.C.) **king of Egypt.** This was a foolish mistake because Egypt did not and apparently could not help **Hoshea. Shalmaneser** discovered Hoshea's plan to revolt, **marched** on Israel, and took Hoshea prisoner. Shalmaneser then subdued the remaining territory of the Northern Kingdom: Galilee and Transjordan (the northern and western portions of Israel) had already fallen to Tiglath-Pileser (cf. 2 Kings 15:29). It took Shalmaneser **three years** to capture **Samaria.** He took it in

Hoshea's **ninth year** (722 B.C.) **and deported** many of the people to Assyria (cf. 18:9-11). **The Israelites** were sent to various parts of the Assyrian Empire: the town of **Halah in** the area of **Gozan on the Habor** (modern Khabur) **River** that flows into the Euphrates, and various **towns of the Medes** northeast of Nineveh.

U. *Israel's Captivity (17:7-41)*

After just over two centuries the Northern Kingdom of Israel ceased to exist as a nation (931–722 B.C.). Seven of her 20 kings were assassinated. All were judged to be evil by God.

1. REASONS FOR THE CAPTIVITY (17:7-23)

17:7-13. The defeat and deportation of Israel **took place because the Israelites . . . sinned against** God. In view of His miraculous liberating redemption of the nation from Egyptian bondage, their sin was even more serious. How ironic that the last king Hoshea had sought help from Egypt (v. 4) when 724 years earlier (1446 B.C.) Israel had finally escaped from **Egypt.**

Israel did not forsake **the LORD** completely but **worshiped other gods (idols;** cf. v. 12) also (cf. Ex. 20:3). They compromised with their pagan neighbors **and followed the practices** of the very **nations** God dispossessed because of their wickedness. They followed the apostate **practices which** their own **kings,** especially Jeroboam I, **had introduced** into their national life. Though many of their sins were practiced **secretly** they were open to **the LORD.**

Throughout the land the people **built . . . high places** of worship **in all their towns** rather than worship God where and as He had specified for their own good (cf. Deut. 12:2-7, 13-14). They erected **stones** that they regarded as **sacred** (cf. 2 Kings 18:4) **and** wooden **Asherah** poles representing the pagan goddess Asherah at virtually **every** site (cf. 16:4) regarded by the pagans as having special power. Israel also **burned incense** on the heights hoping to placate the gods as their pagan predecessors, whom God **had driven out** of the land for their idolatry, **had done.** Their worship involved **wicked** behavior that angered **the LORD** (cf. 13:3; 17:17). Their idolatry involved disobeying a plainly revealed prohibition by God. The LORD had sent **prophets and seers** with special warnings in addition to those contained in the Mosaic **Law.** These messengers (God's **servants**) had warned (cf. 17:23) both kingdoms to repent and observe God's commandments in the Law.

17:14-15. The Israelites, however, refused to **listen** to the prophets (cf. vv. 13-14) **and were as** obstinate as their forefathers who lived before the divided kingdom came into existence. This rebellion manifested lack of confidence **in** Yahweh **their God.** The Israelites deliberately **rejected . . . the covenant** God **had made with their** ancestors as well as **His decrees** (cf. v. 13). They also disregarded **the warnings** God **had given** their forefathers. Choosing instead to follow vain **idols** (cf. v. 12), **they became** vain and **worthless** themselves. They took on the characteristics of the idols, which they put first in their lives. **They imitated the** godless **nations around them** in spite of God's order **not** to follow their example. **They** practiced **the things** God had told them not to do.

17:16-17. Forsaking all God's **commands,** they fashioned **two . . . calves** out of metal and worshiped them at Dan and Bethel (cf. 1 Kings 12:28-29; Deut. 4:15-18). In Samaria, their capital city, Israel set up a **pole** that symbolized the Canaanite fertility goddess **Asherah** (2 Kings 13:6). They worshiped the planets and stellar constellations (cf. 21:5; 23:4-5) with their neighbors and practiced astrology (cf. Deut. 4:19). **They** also **worshiped Baal,** the male fertility god of the Near East. They even followed the brutal practice of offering their children as human sacrifices to placate the gods (cf. 2 Kings 16:3; Deut. 18:10). **They practiced divination** (witchcraft) **and sorcery** (consulted evil spirits; cf. Deut. 18:10-11). In doing all these things the Israelites **sold themselves** to sin, thereby provoking **the LORD . . . to anger** (cf. 2 Kings 13:3; 17:11). In all these things the Israelites were disobeying specific commands in the Mosaic Covenant.

17:18-20. Because they were so rebellious, God in anger at their attitude disciplined His people by deporting **them from His presence** (i.e., out of the land; cf. v. 23, where He had promised to dwell with them). Exile was one of the curses (judgments) God said He would

bring on the nation if the people disobeyed Him (Deut. 28:45-48). **Only the tribe of Judah** remained. Though Benjamin was part of the Southern Kingdom, it often was not mentioned with Judah because of its small size. **Even** the Southern Kingdom disobeyed **the LORD.** Many Judahites imitated the Israelites and adopted **the practices** their brethren **had introduced.** Because of this God punished the Southern Kingdom too. He sent Judah affliction and let **the people** suffer at the hands of other nations that plundered them till they too were led captive out of their land. (These statements in vv. 18b-20 are editorial comments inserted by the writer of 2 Kings after Judah had been taken into captivity.)

17:21-23. God **tore Israel away from** Judah (**the house** or dynasty **of David**) in Rehoboam's day because of the sins of Solomon (1 Kings 11:9-13). The Israelites then **made Jeroboam . . . their king.** He **enticed** the nation **away from** God **and caused them to** worship two golden calves (cf. 2 Kings 17:16). The Israelites followed this form of worship consistently **until** they were **removed . . . from His presence** (i.e., from the land) through captivity in spite of the persistent warnings of **the prophets,** God's **servants** (cf. v. 13). For these reasons—flagrant idolatry, obstinate disobedience, star-worship, child sacrifices, and occult practices—the Israelites were removed **from** the land God had given them as their home **into exile in Assyria. They** were **still there** when the writer penned these words.

2. RESULTS OF THE CAPTIVITY (17:24-41)

a. Immediate results (17:24-33)

17:24. The king of Assyria was probably Sargon II (722–705 B.C.). Shalmaneser V died either during or shortly after the siege of Samaria. The policy of Assyria toward conquered lands was to deport many of the most influential inhabitants and then import many leading Assyrians to take their places. Sargon **brought people from Babylon, Cuthah** (a city northeast of Babylon), **Avva** (between Anah and the Habor River; cf. v. 6, on the Euphrates River), **Hamath** (a city in Aram on the Orontes River), and **Sepharvaim** (people from Sippar on the Euphrates above Babylon) **and settled them in the**

towns of Israel, now called the Assyrian province of Samaria. These Assyrians took the leadership in the province and settled down in various towns.

17:25-28. Because the people did not worship the LORD . . . He sent lions among them. The lions already in Israel may have multiplied more quickly because of the reduced human population. God sometimes used these wild animals as His agents of judgment (cf. 1 Kings 13:23-26; 20:36); they killed some of the people. The Assyrians interpreted this as a punishment from the God of Israel whom they viewed as a deity who needed to be placated. Since they did not know how to appease Him they reported the situation to Sargon.

The king responded by sending an Israelite priest back to Samaria from Assyria. He was to teach the people about Yahweh and how to worship Him. The priest moved to Bethel. If this had been his former dwelling place he was probably one of the priests involved in worshiping the golden calf there.

17:29-33. Each national group of Assyrian immigrants set . . . up . . . shrines for the worship of their own pagan gods wherever they settled, using the high places the Israelites had frequented. The national groups (cf. v. 24) and their idols are listed (vv. 30-31) along with some of their pagan practices. Nergal was the Babylonian god of the underworld; the exact identity of the other gods is uncertain. As polytheists the foreigners did not hesitate to add Yahweh to their pantheon of gods. They had no priestly caste but appointed all sorts of their own people to serve as priests. For emphasis the writer wrote twice that these people worshiped the LORD and also . . . their gods. This syncretism was forbidden by the Lord (Ex. 20:3).

Second Kings 17:24-33 shows how the Samaritan people came into being. The Samaritans, racially a mixture of Israelites and various other ancient Near Eastern peoples, were despised by full-blooded Jews (cf. John 4:9). Possibly, however, the Samaritans were the pure descendants of the Israelites who remained in the land.

b. Continuing results (17:34-41)

17:34-41. To the day of the writing of 2 Kings (and long after, as just noted)

these Samaritans maintained their ways. They did not worship God. Though in verses 32-33 they are said to worship the Lord, verse 34 is not contradictory because they did not worship God from the heart and in the ways He specified. Nor did the people keep the laws He gave to Jacob's descendants. God had changed Jacob's name to Israel to show that he and his descendants were to become a distinct people in the world. This distinctiveness was being broken down by the Samaritans. This distinctiveness is further highlighted by a loose quotation in verses 35-39 of several commands from the Mosaic Law (Ex. 6:6; 20:4-5, 23; Deut. 4:23, 34; 5:6, 15, 32; 6:12; 7:11, 25; etc.). All this again underscored the Israelites' disobedience to their gracious God. God's people would not listen to Him but persisted in their former sinful ways (2 Kings 17:40). Syncretistic worship continued for generations, to the days of the writer.

II. The History of the Surviving Kingdom of Judah (chaps. 18–25)

The rest of the Book of 2 Kings records the reigns of the remaining kings of Judah as well as events in Judah immediately after the Babylonian Captivity which started in 586 B.C.

A. Hezekiah's good reign (chaps. 18–20)

The writer of 1 and 2 Kings devoted more space and gave more commendation to Hezekiah for his accomplishments than to any king except Solomon.

1. HEZEKIAH'S GOODNESS (18:1-8)

18:1-2. Evidently Hezekiah reigned as coregent with his father Ahaz for 14 years (729–715 B.C.) The third year of Hoshea was the year in which Hezekiah is said to have begun reigning (as coregent with Ahaz), namely, 729 B.C. He reigned alone for 18 years (715–697) and then as coregent with his son Manasseh for 11 years (697–686). Together these two reigns were 29 years (715–686 B.C.). (See the chart, "Kings of Judah and Israel and the Preexilic Prophets," near 1 Kings 12:25-33.)

18:3-4. The commendation that Hezekiah did . . . right as David had done is made of only three other kings of Judah: Asa (1 Kings 15:11), Jehoshaphat

(2 Chron. 17:3), and Josiah (2 Kings 22:2). Like Jehoshaphat before him Hezekiah **removed the high places** (2 Chron. 17:6) where the Lord was worshiped contrary to the Mosaic Law (cf. Deut. 12:2-7, 13-14). (Later, however, Jehoshaphat did not remove the high places, 1 Kings 22:43; 2 Chron. 20:33. Apparently the people rebuilt them and Jehoshaphat did not remove them again.) Josiah also destroyed the idols used to aid in the worship of Baal and **Asherah** (2 Chron. 31:1). **The bronze snake** that **Moses . . . made** in the wilderness (Num. 21:5-9) had been preserved and had become a religious fetish. Hezekiah **broke** it up since it was a spiritually unclean thing; it had become a stumbling block to the Israelites. (**Nehushtan** was the name of the snake, a word that sounded like the Heb. for "bronze," "snake," and "unclean thing"; cf. NIV marg.)

18:5-7a. Hezekiah's best quality was that he **trusted in the LORD.** He was the greatest of **all the kings of** the Southern Kingdom in this respect. Unlike some of the other kings he did **not apostasize later in life but kept** the Mosaic Covenant faithfully. As a result **the LORD was with him** and blessed him with success in all **he undertook.** Whereas the writer of 2 Kings gave only a brief record of Hezekiah's spiritual reforms and activities the chronicler recorded many more, including his cleansing and reconsecration of the temple (2 Chron. 29:3-36), his celebration of the Passover and other feast days (2 Chron. 30), and other religious reforms (2 Chron. 31:2-21).

18:7b. Hezekiah's rebellion **against** Sennacherib (705–681 B.C.), **king of Assyria,** precipitated the Assyrian invasion recorded later (18:13–19:36). Hezekiah was anti-Assyrian in contrast with his father Ahaz. But so long as Sargon II remained on the throne Hezekiah wisely did not antagonize the Assyrians. With the accession of Sennacherib, Sargon's son, Hezekiah judged that Assyria was not so strong. He decided to join an alliance with neighboring nations to oppose the northern foe and began making preparations for Assyria's anticipated retaliation.

18:8. Hezekiah was successful in defeating **the Philistines** who had taken several cities from Judah during Ahaz's reign (2 Chron. 28:18). **Gaza** was the southernmost city in Philistia. **From watchtower to fortified city** means wherever he turned.

2. SAMARIA'S CAPTURE (18:9-12)

18:9-12. This second account of the fall of **Samaria** (cf. 17:3-6) was added as a historical reference point in view of its great importance in the life of Judah as well as Israel. **Hezekiah's fourth year,** beginning with his vice-regency, was 725 B.C. **At the end of three years** (in 722) Shalmaneser V captured Israel's capital. The places to which the Israelites were deported for resettlement are the same as those mentioned in 17:6. The summary statement in 18:12 states why Israel fell: she was disobedient to the Mosaic Law (cf. 17:7-23).

3. JERUSALEM'S SIEGE BY ASSYRIA (18:13–19:37)

The following section is recorded also in the Book of Isaiah (chaps. 36–37) with only a few changes.

a. Sennacherib's campaigns (18:13-16)

18:13. Sennacherib's predecessor Sargon II had continued to expand Assyrian territory and to strengthen her hold on conquered peoples. He put down a revolt headed by Hamath (a city north of Damascus; cf. 14:28), fought successfully in Asia Minor, squelched a revolution at Carchemish north of Hamath and deported its population, broke the power of Assyria's hated northern neighboring kingdom Urartu, and moved down into Philistia where he crushed a rebellion led by the city of Ashdod, then the leading city in Philistia.

Sennacherib was a less capable ruler than his father. During Sennacherib's first four years on the throne he was occupied with controlling Babylon. During this time an alliance had formed in which cities of Phoenicia and Philistia as well as Egypt (under Shaboka) and Judah (under Hezekiah) joined together to resist **Assyria.** Certain that Sennacherib would try to put down this uprising, as Sargon had done, Hezekiah prepared for an Assyrian invasion by fortifying Jerusalem (cf. 2 Chron. 32:1-8).

Sennacherib led his armies into Judah as expected. This was in 701 B.C., **the 14th year of . . . Hezekiah's** sole **reign** which began in 715 B.C. On their way to

Judah the Assyrians defeated the rebels in Phoenicia, which caused several other members of the alliance to withdraw. Then Sennacherib marched his armies down the coast into Philistia where he brought the Philistine cities into line. Next he **attacked all the fortified cities of Judah** except Jerusalem **and captured** the people. Sennacherib's inscriptions refer to his conquest of 46 strong cities of Hezekiah plus many villages.

18:14-16. The Assyrian **king** then set up his headquarters at Lachish, a well-fortified city near the Philistine border in central Judah, in preparation for his siege of Jerusalem.

Understandably **Hezekiah** did not want to fight Sennacherib, whose armies had been consistently successful against other members of the now severely weakened alliance. So Hezekiah **sent a message to** Sennacherib **at Lachish.** Judah's king admitted that he had **done wrong** in allying with the other nations against **Assyria.** He offered to **pay whatever** the Assyrian king demanded if he would **withdraw** and not attack Jerusalem. Sennacherib asked for **300 talents** (ca. 11 tons) **of silver and 30 talents** (ca. 1 ton) **of gold. Hezekiah** paid **him all the silver in the treasuries of the temple and palace.** To gather all the gold the king had to strip **off** all **the gold** plating on the temple **doors and** door frames.

b. Sennacherib's threat (18:17-37)

The ransom did not satisfy Sennacherib, however, so he sent messengers to demand a complete surrender. At first they presented their claims only to Hezekiah's representatives (vv. 17-27) but then to all the people of Jerusalem (vv. 28-37).

18:17-18. The three officers **sent** by Sennacherib were his top men. They went **with a large army** to intimidate **Hezekiah** so he would capitulate without resistance. They advanced by way of **the road to the Washerman's Field** to the **aqueduct of the Upper Pool** that extended from the spring of Gihon to the field where the people washed their clothes. This was within earshot of the wall of **Jerusalem** (cf. v. 26) and was a busy location. The messengers wanted to speak to **the king,** but Hezekiah sent three of his deputies—**Eliakim . . . Shebna,** and **Joah**—to negotiate with Sennacherib's

three representatives.

18:19-22. Sennacherib's **field commander** spoke for his side and repeated his king's message to **Hezekiah.** What he said was designed to impress Hezekiah with Sennacherib's power and glory, and to intimidate him into surrendering. He asked the basis of Hezekiah's **confidence** that he could possibly withstand the **great king . . . of Assyria.**

Assuming Judah was depending on **strategy** and force, the commander pointed out the weakness of both these resources. **Egypt** was the only member of the alliance yet remaining, and she would splinter like a weak **reed** if any weight of confidence were placed on her. Rather than helping Judah, **Egypt** would hurt her by both failing and frustrating Hezekiah. The commander was correct; Egypt was not strong at that time and could not be counted on for help. If the Judahites' strategy was to rely **on the** LORD, the commander said they should remember that **Hezekiah** had incurred His wrath (he supposed) by removing the **high places and altars** (cf. v. 4) where the Lord had been worshiped throughout the land. The Assyrians obviously had information about what had been going on in **Judah,** but they did not understand that Hezekiah's actions had been carried out in obedience to God's commands, not out of disrespect for Him.

18:23-24. The commander called on Hezekiah to strike **a bargain** and surrender. This, the commander reasoned, would be wise. The Judahites had few horses; this was part of the help Hezekiah had hoped to get from Egypt. Even if Sennacherib were to **give** Judah **2,000 horses** Hezekiah could not **put** trained cavalrymen **on them.** Judah's army was probably not really that small, but it was small in comparison with Assyria's. From the commander's viewpoint even 2,000 Judean horsemen were no match for **one** Assyrian **officer.** In other words Judah's army was inferior in both quantity and quality.

18:25. The commander's final appeal was a strong one. He claimed that **the** LORD had commanded his master **to attack and destroy** Jerusalem. Though this is improbable it is not impossible (cf. Isa. 45:1-6). The people of Judah had seen Israel fall to Assyria. Might not God's plan be the same for Judah?

18:26-27. Hezekiah's three representatives realized that these arguments could make the people lose heart. Since many Jews were perched on the city wall and were overhearing what was being said the three Judean ambassadors asked the Assyrians to speak only in the Aramaic language which only the educated leaders of Israel understood.

The commander refused; he realized the importance of destroying the people's confidence in their ability to succeed in any military encounter against the Assyrian army. The commander replied that he had been sent with this message to all the people, not just the leaders of Judah. After all, it was the common people who would suffer most from a long siege and the resulting famine. They would be reduced to eating their own excrement and drinking their own urine. Nothing could be more repulsive to the residents of Jerusalem than this possibility. The commander wanted the people to conclude that surrender would be better than resistance.

18:28-31. Now the Assyrian top officer called out to the common people standing around, listening in, and peering over the wall. His words were designed to undermine their confidence in their king and to encourage them to oppose Hezekiah's decision to resist. He claimed Hezekiah did not have the power or ability to deliver the city and that the LORD would not deliver it either.

It would be better for the people, the commander promised, if they surrendered. Rather than siege and starvation there would be peace and plenty to eat and drink. Each person having his own vine and fig tree is a figure of speech for enjoying peace and prosperity (cf. 1 Kings 4:25; Micah 4:4; Zech. 3:10).

When under a siege one of the first needs people faced was water. Hezekiah had provided for this need by cutting a tunnel from the spring of Gihon under the wall of the city to the Pool of Siloam (cf. 2 Kings 20:20) but the Assyrians did not know about this or chose to ignore it.

18:32-35. In time, the commander said, the Assyrians would transport them to other cities. The people had heard that this was Assyrian policy. But he assured them that they would be sent to a land like their own where they would have

plenty of their favorite foods and drink. The commander punctuated his eloquent and attractive appeal with a call to choose surrender and life rather than resistance and certain death. He next focused on Hezekiah's promise to the people that the LORD would deliver them if they trusted in Him. His ideas reflect a polytheistic and pagan concept of God but his words could not help but raise questions in his hearers' minds. No other gods had been able to deliver their worshipers from the might of Assyria. The places mentioned (v. 34) were probably known to the Judahites. Arpad was 13 miles north of Aleppo in Aram. Hena and Ivvah were north of the Euphrates River east of Hamath. (On Hamath and Sepharvaim see 17:24.) The commander's reference to the inability of the gods of Samaria to deliver the Israelites would have been especially effective since Israel's God was also Judah's God.

18:36-37. The Assyrian commander's six rhetorical questions (vv. 33-35) needed no answer and the people gave him none; they remained silent. Hezekiah had previously instructed the people not to reply to the cunning general's statements. Undoubtedly those forceful arguments aroused much heated discussion among the common people after the Assyrian messengers departed.

The summit conference broke up and Hezekiah's three representatives (cf. v. 18) returned to the king. He could see that they had torn their clothes out of great distress (cf. Gen. 37:29, 34; Josh. 7:6; 2 Kings 5:7; 6:30; 11:14; 22:11; Es. 4:1; Job 1:20; 2:12); they faced a most serious situation. Then they told him what the Assyrians had said.

c. The Lord's promise (19:1-7)

19:1-2. When the king had heard the report of his messengers he too tore his clothes. He put on sackcloth, coarse goats'-hair clothing that symbolized self-affliction and despair (cf. Gen. 37:34; 1 Kings 21:27; Neh. 9:1; Es. 4:1-4; Dan. 9:3). He then went into the temple to seek God's face in prayer. He also sent Eliakim and Shebna (cf. 18:18) and the leading priests, who were also mourning in sackcloth, to the Prophet Isaiah who lived in Jerusalem. Isaiah and Hezekiah knew and respected each other.

19:3-4. The king's representatives

conveyed Hezekiah's message that this was indeed a black day in Judah's history. They were distressed, rebuked by God for their sins, and disgraced before their enemies. A crisis had come to a head but now there was not adequate strength to resist the Assyrian invasion. It was like a pregnant woman who finally goes into labor but cannot deliver her child for lack of strength. It seemed as if the whole nation would die. Hezekiah's hope was that God, having been ridiculed by the Assyrians, would act on behalf of His people and prove that He was the true and living God by granting a miraculous deliverance to His people. The king called on the prophet to pray for the small remnant of people left in Jerusalem and Judah.

19:5-7. Isaiah responded to the king's request with a message of hope from the Lord. The Lord encouraged the king not to fear the blasphemous words of Sennacherib's underlings. God would cause Sennacherib to decide to return home when he heard a report (of something God had arranged), and there the Assyrian king would die a violent death.

d. The Lord's diversion (19:8-13)

19:8. Evidently Sennacherib's field commander pitched his tents near Jerusalem and waited for Hezekiah to send him a message of surrender. While the commander was there, word reached him that Sennacherib had left Lachish (cf. 18:14). He withdrew from Jerusalem and located his master near Libnah where he was engaged in battle. Libnah was just a few miles north of Lachish. This is why the field commander removed his large army (18:17) from the walls of Jerusalem.

19:9-13. Evidently while Sennacherib was at Libnah (or perhaps Lachish) he received a report (cf. v. 7) that Tirhakah, the king of Egypt, who was from Cush (modern-day southern Egypt, Sudan, and northern Ethiopia), and an ally of Hezekiah, was marching up to fight Sennacherib. There is insufficient evidence to support the contention by some scholars that Tirhakah was only a boy at this time, incapable of leading such an attack and that this whole campaign of Sennacherib's (18:17–19:36) therefore must have taken place in 686 B.C. rather than in 701 B.C.

Somehow Sennacherib knew that the king of Judah had been told (by Isaiah) that Yahweh would deliver Jerusalem from the Assyrians. He sent a message to Hezekiah not to believe this prophecy even though it looked as if the Assyrians were withdrawing. He boasted of previous victories in all the surrounding countries. His armies had destroyed many of them completely. Surely Jerusalem would not be spared, he claimed.

None of the gods of the defeated peoples had been able to deliver them, had they? Sennacherib obviously granted the Lord no greater respect than the idols of the nations. To reinforce his warning the Assyrian king mentioned 10 cities and nations, 5 of which had not been referred to previously. Gozan was located on the Habur River east of Haran, the town where Abraham lived for some time. Rezeph was probably Rusafah (or Risafe) northeast of Palmyra and south of Haran. Eden was a small kingdom in the Euphrates basin west of the Balikh River, and Tel Assar was one of the cities in this area. The 5 other sites were mentioned in 18:11, 34.

e. Hezekiah's prayer (19:14-19)

19:14-16. When the king had received . . . and read Sennacherib's message which had been carried to him by messengers (cf. v. 9) he returned to the temple to pray again (cf. v. 1). His prayer included a recognition of God's sovereignty (v. 15), mention of the defiance of the Assyrians (vv. 16-18), and a request for deliverance (v. 19). Spreading the letter. . . . before the Lord, Hezekiah addressed Him as Israel's God, whose throne was the atonement cover ("mercy seat," KJV) on the ark of the covenant between the cherubim. God had said He would dwell between the cherubim in a unique sense (1 Sam. 4:4; 2 Sam. 6:2; 1 Chron. 13:6). The king recognized that God is a Spirit, not a piece of wood or stone (cf. 2 Kings 19:18). He alone (cf. v. 19) was the real Ruler of Judah, the Sovereign over all the kingdoms of the earth including Assyria, and the all-powerful Creator of heaven and earth. Hezekiah besought God to listen carefully to what he would say and to view closely what was happening. He then reported Sennacherib's blasphemous insults.

19:17-19. Hezekiah could easily understand why Assyria had successfully defeated her foes; the **gods** in which those nations trusted for protection were mere pieces of **wood and stone.** They were created objects, not the Creator (cf. v. 15). So they had no power and were easily **destroyed.** But Hezekiah appealed to the living God to **deliver** His people **from** Sennacherib's **hand.** Hezekiah believed He could; this was a prayer of faith. And the objective of the king's petition was God's glory, not primarily his own survival. He asked God to vindicate Himself and to demonstrate that He was not just an impotent idol **so that** the whole world would acknowledge Him.

Hezekiah's petition is one of the finest prayers in Scripture.

f. The Lord's answer (19:20-34)

19:20. The Lord's answer to Hezekiah's request (vv. 15-19) came through **Isaiah,** and was delivered to the king by a messenger. God assured **Hezekiah** that his **prayer** had been **heard.** God then announced a message of judgment against **Sennacherib** for his blasphemy.

19:21-24. The first part of God's answer (vv. 20-28) gave the reason for His judgment on Sennacherib. The figurative, poetic language was probably used to stress the importance and divine source of the answer.

The Virgin Daughter of Zion suggests that Jerusalem had never been conquered since it had passed into Israelite control. Jerusalem would despise and mock Sennacherib, shaking **her head as** the Assyrian king fled from her. Sennacherib had **raised** his insulting **voice** in blasphemy and **pride,** not against the city but **against** her God, **the Holy One of Israel** (see comments on this title under "Internal Evidence" in the section on "Unity" in the *Introduction* to Isa.). This was his great sin and his undoing. He and his **messengers** had insulted **the Lord** by claiming their victories were a result of their own might.

Though Sennacherib may have literally cut down the trees **of Lebanon** the description (v. 23) probably represents his destruction of various nations' leaders. "Lebanon" probably refers especially to the Northern Kingdom of Israel. Its **choicest** trees were its leaders. Assyria had dominated Israel and had killed many of its best citizens. Sennacherib boasted that he had **dug** up many for-

eign lands and had taken for himself what satisfied him at their expense. He had done this to the Southern Kingdom of Judah, here referred to figuratively as **Egypt.** (Or perhaps Egypt refers to his defeat of an Egyptian army at the Judean town of Eltekeh.) He boasted that his siege had kept her life-giving resources from flowing.

19:25-26. Addressing Sennacherib in this prophecy, God said that king was not responsible for Assyria's success. Instead God had **ordained . . . planned,** and **brought . . . to pass** all that had happened (cf. Isa. 10:5). The **fortified cities** were those the Assyrians had destroyed. The conquered **people** had no **power** to resist and in fact could not even attain normal full strength, like the shallow-rooted **grass** that grew **on the housetops** but died prematurely. This had been God's doing.

19:27-28. The Lord knew all about Sennacherib and his proud raging in rebellion **against** Himself. Because the Assyrian monarch hated God and had spoken insolently against Him, God would take the king captive as Sennacherib had taken so many other people captive.

The **hook** and the **bit,** which portray catching a fish and controlling a horse, are uniquely appropriate. On some ancient monuments the Assyrian conquerors pictured themselves as leading their captives with a line that passed through rings that had been placed in the victims' noses. God promised to do to them as they had done to others. He would lead them back from where they had come and reduce them to their former humble state.

19:29-31. Through Isaiah God then promised **Hezekiah** a **sign** that these predictions (vv. 26, 28) would indeed come to pass. The sign was a near-future miracle that would confirm the fulfillment of the more distant aspects of the prophecy.

For two years the people of Jerusalem would be able to **eat** the produce of their land. It would not be stolen by the Assyrians who would have lived off the land if they had returned to besiege the capital. The Judeans had not been able to plant crops outside the city walls because of the Assyrians' presence. But God promised that He would feed them for two years by causing the seed that had been sown naturally to grow up into an adequate crop. **The third year** people could return to their normal cycle of sowing and reaping.

This provision of multiplied food was further designed to illustrate God's plan to multiply miraculously the people of Judah who had been reduced to small numbers. Sennacherib claimed to have taken 200,150 prisoners from Judah. However, though Judah seemingly might cease to be a nation through attrition, God promised to revive it. Like the crops, **a remnant** of people would **take root . . . and bear fruit,** that is, be established and prosperous. God's **zeal** on behalf of His people would perform this (cf. Isa. 9:7).

19:32-34. Sennacherib's fate was then revealed. He would **not** forcefully take Jerusalem, besiege it, **or** even **shoot an arrow** against it. Instead **he** would **return** to his own homeland without even entering Jerusalem. God promised to **defend** Jerusalem **and save it** from Sennacherib's wrath. God would do this **for the sake of** His own reputation (cf. v. 19) and because of His promise to His servant **David** (cf. 1 Kings 11:13).

g. Sennacherib's departure (19:35-36)

19:35-36. **That** very **night** while the **Assyrian** army lay sprawled across the Judean countryside **the Angel of the Lord** (cf. comments on Gen. 16:9) executed **185,000** of their soldiers. **When the** Jerusalemites arose in **the . . . morning** they discovered the extent of the catastrophe. **Sennacherib** probably recognized this as a supernatural event. In any case he concluded he should return to **Nineveh** where he **stayed** for some time.

h. Sennacherib's death (19:37)

19:37. Years later (in 681 B.C.) Sennacherib **was worshiping in the temple of his god Nisroch.** This Assyrian deity was represented as being part eagle and part human. The temple was probably in Nineveh, Assyria's capital. There the king fell prey to the plot of assassins, two of **his** own **sons.** Ironically his god was not able to deliver him even in its temple. The murdering sons fled **to the land of Ararat** (Armenia), about 300 miles north of Nineveh. Armenia is now divided between Russia, Turkey, and Iran. Another son, **Esarhaddon** (681–669 B.C.), **succeeded** Sennacherib **as king.** Thus the word

of the Lord (v. 7) came to pass.

4. HEZEKIAH'S ILLNESS (20:1-11)

a. Hezekiah's petition (20:1-7)

20:1. In those days refers to days of the invasion of Jerusalem by Sennacherib, recorded in 18:13–19:36. God added 15 years to Hezekiah's life in response to his petition for mercy (20:6). Hezekiah died in 686 B.C. which would place this incident in 701 B.C., the year of Sennacherib's invasion (cf. Isa. 38).

Hezekiah's serious illness (with some kind of boil, v. 7) may or may not have been directly connected with the invasion by Sennacherib. God sent **Isaiah** to announce to **Hezekiah** that he would **die.** The prophet instructed him to prepare for this by setting his **house** (affairs) **in order.**

20:2-3. **Hezekiah** responded to this bad news by praying earnestly **to the** Lord. The king reminded God of his faithfulness to Him, his **wholehearted devotion,** and his **good** behavior as God's vice-regent. He **wept bitterly** perhaps because he felt his death would give Sennacherib something to boast about, perhaps because his heir, Manasseh, was still very young, and perhaps because he wanted to continue living and reigning.

20:4-6. The king's appeal in prayer was effective with **God. Before Isaiah had left** the palace on his way home **the** Lord gave him a second message: to return to the king with word announcing a postponement of his death. **Hezekiah** had behaved like a true son of **David** in the way he reacted to God's first message. Hezekiah's **prayer** (what he said) **and** his **tears** (how he felt about what he said) moved God to **heal** him. Isaiah announced that in three days the king would be well enough to worship God in **the temple.** God promised to **add 15 years to** Hezekiah's **life** (from 701 to 686). The Lord also promised to **deliver** Hezekiah and Jerusalem from Sennacherib's siege and to defend Jerusalem for His own **sake and for** David's **sake** (cf. 19:34).

20:7. Isaiah then gave Hezekiah a treatment for his illness. The **poultice of figs** was well known in the ancient world as a means of helping to heal boils and ulcers, but Hezekiah's physicians had not prescribed it. Some think the remedy was designed to demonstrate God's supernatural power at work in granting the king's recovery.

b. Hezekiah's sign (20:8-11)

20:8. Requesting a **sign** that God would indeed do what He had promised was common among the Israelites (cf. Jud. 6:17, 36-40; 1 Cor. 1:22). God did not object to such a request if the sign were requested to strengthen the faith of the person seeking it. Signs were miracles that signified that what God had said He would indeed do. Perhaps the imminent danger that Hezekiah faced from Sennacherib led him to ask for this sign.

20:9-11. God let the king choose whether **the shadow** would **go forward,** as it normally would, or backward. Ahaz's **stairway** (v. 11) was evidently a stairway King **Ahaz** had built. It may have been constructed as a sundial to measure the time of day or it may have simply been a regular staircase used by God on this occasion to provide the sign Hezekiah had requested.

By offering to advance **the shadow** God undoubtedly intended to advance it faster than was normal since the usual rate would have been no sign at all. **Hezekiah** requested the most obvious and dramatic alternative: that the sun's shadow be reversed **10 steps.** It is not necessary to insist that God reversed the rotation of the earth to effect this miracle. Some similar miracles were evidently limited in their scope, being local rather than universal (cf. Ex. 10:21-23; Josh. 10:12-13).

5. HEZEKIAH'S VISITORS (20:12-19)

This incident evidently took place shortly after Hezekiah recovered from his illness (cf. Isa. 39:1-2).

a. Hezekiah's reception (20:12-15)

20:12-13. **Merodach-Baladan** reigned as **king of Babylon** for two periods of time, 721–710 and 703–702 B.C. In 702 B.C. he fled to the country of Elam where he continued his efforts to resist Assyrian control as a refugee. It was probably during this period that he sought the support of Judah as an ally by sending this embassy. (See comments on Isa. 39:1 on the sequence of these events: Hezekiah's illness, Merodach-Baladan's visit, and Sennacherib's attack.) He courted **Hezekiah's** favor by sending a **gift** when he

heard that **Hezekiah** had become sick. Merodach-Baladan also wanted to ask about the miracle that had occurred in the land (2 Chron. 32:31).

Hezekiah . . . showed his Babylonian visitors the full extent of his wealth and armaments partly because he concluded his ally should know how much Judah would be able to contribute to their joint anti-Assyrian effort.

20:14-15. **Hezekiah** made no attempt to hide what he had done from **Isaiah** who had been sent by God to inquire about the visitors. The king of Judah likely did not think that his desire to form an alliance with **Babylon** was either an expression of lack of confidence in God or a foolish move politically.

b. Hezekiah's judgment (20:16-19)

20:16-18. Because Hezekiah's heart was proud (2 Chron. 32:25), God announced through **Isaiah** that the Babylonians would carry away **all** that **Hezekiah** had shown them. **Some of** the royal family who had not yet been **born** would also **be taken** captive and be made **eunuchs in the palace** in **Babylon.** Eunuchs were often high-ranking officials (*sārîs;* see comments on Dan. 1:3).

20:19. Hezekiah repented of his pride (2 Chron. 32:26) and humbly accepted the fact that God's judgment would come on the nation (**the word of the LORD . . . is good**). He was also grateful for the **peace and security** Judah would enjoy by God's mercy in his **lifetime.**

6. HEZEKIAH'S DEATH (20:20-21)

20:20-21. The building of **the tunnel** from the Gihon spring to **the Pool** of Siloam was singled out by the writer as one of **Hezekiah's** more important achievements (cf. 2 Chron. 32:30). Hezekiah had this 1,777-foot tunnel dug from the oldest source of **water,** just outside the wall of Jerusalem, under the wall to a reservoir inside **the city.** He then covered up the spring so the Assyrian invaders would not discover it and cut off Jerusalem's water supply. This tunnel, dug from both ends to the middle, was a remarkable engineering feat which still can be seen today.

Years before **Hezekiah** died he made his son **Manasseh** vice-regent in 697 B.C. The father and **son** ruled together until

Hezekiah died in 686 B.C. Then Manasseh **succeeded** Hezekiah and ruled **as sole king.**

B. Manasseh's evil reign (21:1-18)

Though Manasseh reigned longer than any other king of Judah or Israel, the record of his reign is brief.

1. MANASSEH'S WICKEDNESS (21:1-9)

21:1-6. When **Manasseh was 12 years old** . . . he began ruling as vice-regent with his father Hezekiah (697 B.C.). In all **he reigned . . . 55 years.**

Rather than continuing the God-honoring policies of his father, Manasseh reverted to those of his grandfather Ahaz and reestablished **the detestable practices of the** native Canaanite peoples. **He** also **rebuilt the high places** which had been so common in the nation (cf. comments on 1 Kings 22:43; also note 1 Kings 3:2-3) until **Hezekiah** had purged the land of them (2 Kings 18:4). Manasseh reerected **altars to Baal and made** a **pole** to represent **Asherah** (cf. 21:7) as Ahab had done in Samaria (1 Kings 16:33). Manasseh defiantly **built altars** to idols right **in the temple, and** its courtyards which God had said were to be reserved for worship of the true and living God (1 Kings 8:29). Manasseh also opened the doors of the nation to Assyrian astral worship again (2 Kings 17:16; 23:4-5).

Manasseh also practiced human sacrifice and offered one of **his own** sons to the Ammonite god Molech in the Valley of Hinnom (cf. 1 Kings 11:7, 33; 2 Kings 23:10, 13). **Sorcery . . . divination . . . mediums, and spiritists** were all part of Manasseh's religious system even though these were prohibited in the Mosaic Law (cf. comments on 17:17). The king believed that all forms of worship were better for the people than the exclusive worship of Yahweh prescribed in the Law. His policies provoked the LORD . . . **to anger** (cf. 21:15; 22:13, 17; 23:19, 26; 24:20) and were **evil** (cf. 21:2) **in His eyes.**

21:7-9. Manasseh further desecrated **the temple** by placing in it **the carved Asherah pole he had made** (cf. v. 3). By so doing he gave an idol the place that God alone deserved (cf. v. 4 and comments on God's **name** in 1 Kings 8:16-20; 2 Chron. 6:6). This act showed no respect for God's promises to the king's **forefa-**

thers or His faithfulness to His promises. Manasseh treated the **Law of Moses** with contempt and **led** the **people** of God away from His commandments. Amazingly the people under Manasseh practiced **more evil** (cf. 2 Kings 21:15-16) **than** the Canaanites before them.

2. JERUSALEM'S FATE (21:10-15)

21:10-13. God's judgment against Manasseh and **Judah** came **through . . . the prophets** (probably Isaiah and perhaps others). **The Amorites** were one of the most wicked people of Palestine in Joshua's day. Besides practicing idolatry himself Manasseh compounded his wickedness by leading the Judeans **into sin** with him. Therefore God promised that the news of **Jerusalem** and Judah's **disaster** would shock all who heard it. He said He would **stretch** the straight **plumb line** (symbolizing destruction) against **Jerusalem** and Manasseh as He had done to **Samaria** and **the house** (family or dynasty) **of Ahab.** God would cleanse Judah of all her corruption as a dishwasher scours a **dish.**

21:14-15. God also said He would **forsake** what remained of His **inheritance** (i.e., Judah) **and** cause **their enemies** to discipline them. The Judeans would be robbed and spoiled **by their** enemies. This judgment would come on them for all their **evil** (cf. vv. 9, 16) since their birth as a nation when God led them **out of Egypt.** Though Judah had undergone other judgments, this one would be the most severe.

3. MANASSEH'S DEATH (21:16-18)

21:16-17. The **innocent blood** Manasseh **shed** included that of his own son (v. 6) and the sons and daughters of those who followed his examples of worship. According to Jewish tradition Isaiah was put to death by Manasseh by being sawed in two (Heb. 11:37 may refer to Isaiah).

The chronicler reported that Manasseh for his sins was taken captive to Babylon (2 Chron. 33:11) by the king of Assyria, probably Ashurbanipal (669–626 B.C.). There Manasseh repented of his sins and God in His grace allowed Manasseh to return to Jerusalem after a period of captivity (2 Chron. 33:12-13; cf. 2 Chron. 33:18-19). After his restoration the king cleaned up much of the idolatry in Judah (2 Chron. 33:15-17). Manasseh's sins had stained Judah deeply, however, and even later reforms under Josiah could not avert God's judgment (2 Kings 23:26).

21:18. When **Manasseh** died he was not **buried** in the royal tombs with the good kings of Judah but was laid to rest **in his palace garden** instead. His son **Amon . . . succeeded him.**

C. Amon's evil reign (21:19-26)

21:19-22. Amon began ruling when he **was 22 years old,** but he lived only **two** more **years** (642–640 B.C.). Amon did not continue the policies of his father's later rule but reverted to the syncretistic, idolatrous worship that had characterized Manasseh's earlier reign (cf. vv. 2-7). Amon abandoned **the LORD** completely.

21:23-26. Fearing a continuation of the havoc that **Amon's** policies were sure to bring, some of the king's **officials . . . assassinated** him. A popular uprising followed, however, in which Amon's murderers were brought to justice and executed.

On Amon's death his son **Josiah** was placed on the throne. Amon was buried with his father **in the** palace **garden** (cf. v. 18).

D. Josiah's good reign (22:1–23:30)

1. JOSIAH'S GOODNESS (22:1-2)

22:1. Josiah was one of Judah's best kings. Peace, prosperity, and reform characterized his reign. Josiah was only a lad of **eight . . . when he** was crowned **king,** and **reigned** over Judah **31 years** (640–609 B.C.). During his reign world power passed from Assyrian to Babylonian leadership. Nineveh, the capital of Assyria, was destroyed in 612 B.C., and the Assyrian Empire fell in 609.

22:2. Like Asa and Hezekiah before him Josiah **did what was right in the** sight **of the LORD and** followed the good **ways of his** ancestor **David.** He did not deviate from this course at any time during his reign.

The chronicler added that Josiah began to seek after the Lord when he was 16 and he began his religious reforms when he was 20 (2 Chron. 34:3-7).

2. JOSIAH'S REFORMATION (22:3–23:25)

Josiah was the fourth and final reformer among Judah's kings, following Asa, Jehoshaphat, and Hezekiah. But Josiah's reforms were more extensive than those of any of his predecessors.

a. Josiah's repairs (22:3-7)

22:3-7. The temple had fallen into disrepair and had been desecrated by Manasseh who had built pagan altars and images in it (cf. 21:4-5, 7, 21). In Josiah's **18th year** as king, at age 26, he began to **repair the temple** and restore it to its former condition. He **sent the secretary, Shaphan** (perhaps like a secretary of state) along with other high government officials (cf. 2 Chron. 34:8) to begin **the temple** renovations. (On Shaphan's immediate descendants see the chart "The Line of Shaphan," near Jer. 26:24.) For some time **money** had been **collected** for this purpose. Now enough was in hand to begin the work. The procedure was similar to that followed by Joash (cf. 2 Kings 12:10). As then, the supervisors proved trustworthy. (See 2 Chron. 34:8-13 for more details of this aspect of Josiah's reform.)

b. Hilkiah's discovery (22:8-13)

22:8-10. In the process of renovating **the temple** a copy of **the Book of the Law** (either the Book of Deut. or, more likely, the entire Pentateuch, the first five books of the Bible) was **found.** Evidently Manasseh or Amon had destroyed other copies so that the discovery of this one constituted an important find. **Hilkiah the high priest** shared his discovery with **Shaphan who** also **read it.** After reporting progress on the restoration to Josiah, **Shaphan . . . informed the king** of this important discovery and **read from it** to him.

22:11-13. In distress Josiah **tore his robes** (cf. Gen. 37:29, 34; Josh. 7:6; 2 Kings 5:7; 6:30; 11:14; 19:1; Es. 4:1; Job 1:20; 2:12) and wept (2 Kings 22:19) on hearing what God required of His people as he compared that with how far they had departed from His will. He then sent five of his top officials to **inquire of the LORD** what should be done. Josiah feared the **anger** of the Lord and wanted to turn it away from all **the people** of **Judah,** not just himself. The shock expressed by **the king** at the contents of **the Law** reveals that Judah had not consulted the Law for a long time.

c. Huldah's prophecy (22:14-20)

22:14. The fact that the king's five officers (cf. v. 12) sought out **the Prophetess Huldah** suggests that she was highly regarded for her prophetic gift. Other prophets also lived in and around Jerusalem at this time including Jeremiah (Jer. 1:2), and Zephaniah (Zeph. 1:1), and perhaps Nahum and Habakkuk. But the five consulted Huldah for reasons unexplained. This woman **was the wife of Shallum** who was responsible for the royal or priestly **wardrobe. She lived in . . . the Second District** of Jerusalem which was the part of the city lower in elevation than the rest.

22:15-18. After consulting **the LORD** Huldah sent His message back to **the king. God** would surely send **disaster on** Jerusalem and the **people** of **Judah** as He had warned in the Law of Moses. This judgment would come **because they** had **forsaken** Him and made **idols** and **burned incense** to them. God's **anger** burned **against** His people (cf. v. 13) basically because they had forsaken His appointed way whereby they could experience blessing, enjoy life, and demonstrate to all other peoples how glorious it was to live under the Lord's leadership.

22:19-20. Josiah would experience God's mercy personally, however, because he had responded to God's Word and had **humbled** himself **before the LORD** when he **heard** the Law of Moses. God said that the king would die and **be buried** before judgment would descend on Judah. His death in 609 was four years before Nebuchadnezzar's first attack on Jerusalem in 605.

d. The reading of the Law (23:1-3)

23:1-2. The king did not wait for the temple renovation to be completed before he **called** the assembly described here; this convocation took place soon after the Law was discovered. To this important **temple** ceremony he summoned **all the elders . . . the priests,** and **prophets** (no doubt including Jeremiah and Zephaniah) and **all the people from the least to the greatest.** The king **read . . . all the words of the Book.** Perhaps this was the whole Pentateuch but more likely it was the sections promising blessing for obedience and discipline for disobedience (Deut. 27:15–28:68).

23:3. Standing **by the pillar** (cf. 11:14) in the temple courtyard **the king** led the people in a rededication of themselves to **the LORD** and His Word. He first pledged himself **to follow the LORD** faithfully and to carry out the words **written in** the Law of Moses (cf. 1 Kings 2:3). **Then all the people** promised to do the same (cf. Ex. 19:8; Josh. 24:21-24).

e. Josiah's reforms (23:4-14)

23:4-7. Josiah then removed everything connected with the worship of false gods that his ancestors had set up in Judah and Jerusalem. **The doorkeepers** were Levites responsible for controlling who entered **the temple.** This house of worship was cleansed of all the paraphernalia that had been brought inside to be used in the worship of **Baal . . . Asherah,** and the astrological deities (cf. 21:3-5). Josiah had these **burned** (cf. Deut. 7:25) **in the . . . Kidron Valley** (cf. 2 Kings 23:6, 12) just east of **Jerusalem.** To desecrate the very center of pagan worship he **took the ashes** of these relics **to Bethel.** He also drove **away the pagan priests** who had led the people in various forms of idolatry. The Hebrew word rendered "pagan priests" is $k^e m\bar{a}r\hat{\imath}m$, used elsewhere only in Hosea 10:5 and Zephaniah 1:4. It refers to idol-priests, priests who prostrated themselves before idols. The king then removed **the Asherah pole from the temple** (cf. 2 Kings 21:7), **burned it in the Kidron Valley** (cf. 23:4), and scattered its ashes (cf. v. 4) **over the graves of** the idolatrous **common people. Male shrine prostitutes,** who served as part of the pagan worship, had set up tents in **the temple** courtyard. These Josiah **tore down** as he did the shelters that had been erected there where female idolaters wove materials used in some way in the worship of **Asherah.**

23:8-9. Josiah reassembled **all the** Levitical **priests** and proceeded to desecrate **the high places** (cf. comments on 1 Kings 22:43) where the Lord had been worshiped contrary to the Law of Moses (Deut. 12:2-7, 13-14). Hezekiah had demolished them also (2 Kings 18:4), but Manasseh rebuilt them (21:3). Josiah destroyed those pagan places of worship **from Geba** on Judah's northern frontier **to Beersheba** on its southern border. He also destroyed **the shrines** (high places) located at the gates near the residency of Joshua, the governor of Jerusalem, and at the other gates of the city. These altars had been placed to the left of the gate as people entered the city. The Levitical priests who had offered sacrifices on the high places were not allowed to serve at the rededicated altar in the temple, but Josiah did permit them to eat the unleavened bread brought to the temple (cf. Lev. 6:9-10, 16).

23:10-11. Topheth was the place where worshipers of Molech, the god of Ammon (cf. v. 13), burned their children as sacrifices. This was in the Valley of Ben Hinnom at the south side of Mount Zion (cf. Josh. 15:8). Josiah desecrated this site so that no idolater would worship there again. He also removed the sacred horses that were used in formal processions honoring the sun. These animals had been dedicated by the kings of Judah (probably Ahaz, Manasseh, and Amon) and were stabled in the temple courtyard. Josiah also burned up the ceremonial chariots used in these idolatrous processions.

23:12-14. Ahaz had evidently built an upper room on one of the buildings at the gate of the temple. On the roof near that structure Ahaz had built altars, probably to the stars and planets (cf. Zeph. 1:5; Jer. 19:13; 32:29). Hezekiah undoubtedly destroyed these altars but apparently Manasseh or Amon had rebuilt them.

Manasseh also had built altars in the temple courtyards (2 Kings 21:5). All these Josiah destroyed and tossed into the Kidron Valley (cf. 23:6). He also desecrated the altars that had been erected on the southern hill of the Mount of Olives which became known as the Hill of Corruption. These altars dated back to Solomon's reign (1 Kings 11:5, 7). Josiah removed all the pagan sacred stones and Asherah poles (cf. 2 Kings 23:6, 15) at that site also. Human bones rendered those sites unclean and unsuitable as places of worship thereafter.

f. Jeroboam's altar (23:15-20)

23:15-16. The ancient altar that Jeroboam I had erected (cf. 1 Kings 12:28-29) at Bethel (ca. 931 B.C.) also toppled in Josiah's purge. To desecrate (cf. 2 Kings 23:10, 13) the site forever Josiah removed the bones of the people who had been buried in the tombs cut out of a hillside nearby and burned them on the altar (obviously before the altar was demolished). These bones probably belonged to the priests (cf. 1 Kings 12:31-32) who out of reverence for the altar had been buried near it. This act by the king fulfilled the prophecy of the man of God from Judah who had predicted it in the days of Jeroboam, even calling Josiah by name (1 Kings 13:2-3).

23:17-18. Learning that a certain tombstone marked the grave of the man of God from Judah who had predicted Josiah's action (cf. comments on v. 16), the king ordered that his grave not be disturbed out of respect for him. The bones of the old prophet from Bethel (in Samaria, the Northern Kingdom, not the city of Samaria which had not yet been built) who had been buried next to the younger prophet (1 Kings 13:31-32) were left undisturbed too.

23:19-20. Josiah even extended his purge into the territory of the old Northern Kingdom. His ability to do so reflects the weakness of the Assyrian Empire which controlled Israel at this time. Some of the Israelites who remained in their land after the fall of Samaria still worshiped at the high places that Josiah now destroyed. The priests whom Josiah executed in Israel were probably not Levites but idolatrous priests like those Jeroboam had appointed (cf. 1 Kings 12:31).

g. Josiah's Passover (23:21-23)

23:21-23. Josiah did more than simply eliminate idolatry. He also reestablished the divinely ordained Passover feast. This important feast commemorated God's redemption of His people from their bondage in Egypt. It was also Israel's oldest feast. (On this Book of the Covenant, cf. v. 2.) This observance by Josiah was conducted with more careful attention to the Law than any Passover since the days of the Judges. It also was unusual because people from both the kingdom of Judah and the old kingdom of Israel participated together (2 Chron. 35:18). The observance of this feast is described in detail in 2 Chronicles 35:1-19. It took place in Josiah's 18th year of reign. Apparently all the reforms just described (2 Kings 22:3–23:20) took place that same year (cf. 22:3).

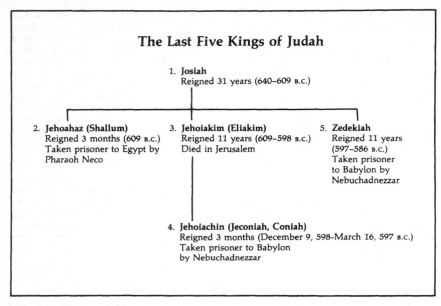

The Last Five Kings of Judah

1. Josiah
Reigned 31 years (640–609 B.C.)

2. Jehoahaz (Shallum)
Reigned 3 months (609 B.C.)
Taken prisoner to Egypt by
Pharaoh Neco

3. Jehoiakim (Eliakim)
Reigned 11 years (609–598 B.C.)
Died in Jerusalem

5. Zedekiah
Reigned 11 years
(597–586 B.C.)
Taken prisoner
to Babylon by
Nebuchadnezzar

4. Jehoiachin (Jeconiah, Coniah)
Reigned 3 months (December 9, 598–March 16, 597 B.C.)
Taken prisoner to Babylon
by Nebuchadnezzar

h. Josiah's greatness (23:24-25)

23:24-25. Josiah's purge weeded out even the informal practitioners (**mediums and spiritists**; cf. 21:6) of rites God had condemned (Lev. 20:27; Deut. 18:9-12). **Household gods** were worshiped as sources of prosperity and as oracles. These were destroyed as well as all other **idols** throughout **Judah and Jerusalem.** Josiah **did** all this in direct obedience to the Mosaic **Law.** There was not a king **before** or **after** him who so conscientiously observed the Word of **the LORD** (cf. Deut. 6:5; Jer. 22:15-16).

3. JUDAH'S JUDGMENT (23:26-27)

23:26-27. Even Josiah's reformation, as great as it was, could not dispel the accumulated wrath of God **against Judah** for her years of rebellion, especially under Manasseh's leadership (cf. 22:16-17). The Lord's words in 23:27 may be a direct quotation of a prophecy given through an unnamed prophet at that time, or a free quotation taken from God's previous words of warning. God would reject His people, their **city,** and His **temple** in the sense of handing them over to their enemies for discipline. To be removed **from** His **presence** (cf. 24:3, 20) meant being **removed** from the land (cf. 17:18, 20, 23).

4. JOSIAH'S DEATH (23:28-30)

23:28-30. Other events of Josiah's reign were recorded in the source noted by the writer.

Josiah's death is explained more fully in 2 Chronicles 35:20-27. **Josiah** seems to have been motivated to fight **Pharaoh Neco** II (610–595 B.C.) **of Egypt** in the desire to frustrate any hope **Assyria** or Egypt might have had of regaining strength and attacking Judah. Egypt and Assyria were allies and were trying to stop Babylonia from becoming the new world leader. Josiah evidently regarded Babylonia as a lesser threat than Assyria or Egypt. As Pharaoh Neco marched his troops up the Mediterranean coastline in 609 B.C., **Josiah** headed northwest with his army, determined to stop Neco **at Megiddo,** a well-fortified stronghold in old Israel. Unfortunately for Judah, Josiah died in the ensuing battle. **His body** was returned **to Jerusalem** where it was given a royal burial. The officials of Judah placed his son **Jehoahaz** on the throne.

Josiah was a strong influence for righteousness in his day and also a most capable ruler. The success of his sweeping reforms indicates that he had the ability to overcome strong popular opinion which undoubtedly opposed his convictions. His influence even extended into the territory of the fallen Northern Kingdom. Tragically his reign ended prematurely.

E. Jehoahaz's evil reign (23:31-35)

23:31-32. Josiah had four sons, three of whom ruled over Judah after their father's death (1 Chron. 3:15; see the chart "The Last Five Kings of Judah"). **Jehoahaz** was the middle son agewise and was chosen by the people to succeed Josiah. He **was 23 years old when he** acceded, but he **reigned** only **three months** (in 609 B.C.). His grandfather **Jeremiah** was not the prophet of the same name since that prophet was not permitted by God to marry (Jer. 16:2). In the brief time Jehoahaz ruled he determined to revert to the ways of his idolatrous ancestors rather than follow his father's good example.

23:33. When **Pharaoh Neco** defeated Josiah at Megiddo (cf. v. 29) Judah fell under Egyptian control. Neco summoned the newly appointed king of Judah to **Riblah** on the Orontes River about 65 miles north of Damascus. The Egyptian king later continued marching northward toward his encounter with Nabopolassar the Babylonian at Haran even farther north. Evidently Neco judged Jehoahaz to be an uncooperative vassal so he imprisoned him and sent him to Egypt (v. 34) where Jehoahaz eventually died (cf. Jer. 22:10-12). Neco also **imposed** a heavy tax **on Judah . . . of 100 talents** (ca. 3¾ tons) **of silver and a talent** (ca. 75 pounds) **of gold.**

23:34-35. **Neco** then placed Jehoahaz's older brother **Eliakim** on the throne of Judah and **changed** his **name to Jehoiakim** (from "God has established" to "Yahweh has established"). The naming of a person was regarded in the ancient Near East as a sovereign prerogative; by doing this Neco was demonstrating that he controlled Judah. **Jehoiakim** submitted to Neco's lordship and provided the tribute of **silver and gold** the Egyptian king required by taxing **the people** of Judah.

F. Jehoiakim's evil reign (23:36–24:7)

1. JEHOIAKIM'S WICKEDNESS (23:36-37)

23:36-37. Jehoiakim was two years older than his brother Jehoahaz (cf. Jehoiakim's age of **25** with Jehoahaz's age of 23, in 609 B.C.). Jehoiakim **reigned . . . 11 years** (609–598 B.C.) as a puppet

king. His mother's hometown **Rumah** was near Shechem (cf. Jud. 9:41). Jehoiakim too failed to follow his father's good example but chose the path of idolatry and self-reliance. Jehoiakim was a weak ruler. This can be deduced by the fact that even though he was the eldest son of Josiah he was not chosen by the people of Judah to succeed his father. Also Neco sensed that Jehoiakim would be easier to control than his brother Jehoahaz.

2. JUDAH'S ENEMIES (24:1-7)

24:1-4. Nebuchadnezzar had succeeded his father Nabopolassar as king of Babylon in 605 B.C. Earlier that year **Nebuchadnezzar** had led his father's army against the Egyptians under Pharaoh Neco and had defeated them at Carchemish on the Euphrates River in northern Aramea. This battle established Babylonia as the strongest nation in the Near East. Egypt and its vassals, including Judah, passed under Babylonian control with this victory.

Nebuchadnezzar **invaded the land** of Judah later the same year (605 B.C.) in order to bring Judah securely under his rule. At that time he took some captives to Babylon including Daniel and others (cf. Dan. 1:1-3). **Jehoiakim** submitted to Nebuchadnezzar **for three years,** but then Jehoiakim revolted and unsuccessfully appealed to Egypt for help. He was eventually taken prisoner to Babylon (2 Chron. 36:6), but apparently was released or escaped because he died in Jerusalem (Jer. 22:19; cf. comments on 2 Kings 24:10-11). **Judah** was plagued by raiding bands from Babylonia, Aramea, Moab, and Ammon, who took advantage of Judah's weakened condition later in Jehoiakim's reign. God **sent** these enemies against **Judah** to punish her for her sins according to the words of **the Prophets** Isaiah, Micah, Jeremiah, Habakkuk, and others. God was removing the people **from His presence** (cf. 17:18, 20, 23; 23:27) **because of the sins of Manasseh** (cf. 21:1-16).

24:5-7. Jeremiah the prophet despised **Jehoiakim** for his wickedness (cf. Jer. 22:18-19; 26:20-23; 36). When Jehoiakim died in 598 B.C. in Jerusalem his son **Jehoiachin . . . succeeded him** on the throne of Judah. Jehoiakim did not receive a royal burial (Jer. 22:19).

Pharaoh Neco **did not** again assert

2 KINGS

himself to regain the territory he had lost
to Nebuchadnezzar between the Wadi of
Egypt (Wadi el-Arish) in the south to the
Euphrates River in the north which included all of Palestine. This too was part
of God's sovereign plan to discipline His
people and illustrates the strength of
Babylonia at this time.

G. Jehoiachin's evil reign (24:8-17)

1. JEHOIACHIN'S WICKEDNESS (24:8-9)

24:8-9. Jehoiachin began reigning
when his father Jehoiakim died. He ruled
Judah only three months while he was 18
years old and, like Jehoiakim, he did evil
in the sight of the LORD.

2. THE SECOND DEPORTATION (24:10-17)

24:10-12. Nebuchadnezzar had sent
troops against Jerusalem late in Jehoiakim's reign because the Judean king
continued to resist Babylonian control
and to look to Egypt for help in throwing
off the Babylonian yoke. Jehoiakim may
have died in the siege of Jerusalem, or he
may have been killed by raiders from
some other country that harassed Judah
(v. 2). Nebuchadnezzar himself decided
to go up against Jerusalem but by the
time he arrived (in 597 B.C.) Jehoiakim
had died and Jehoiachin had replaced
him as king. Jehoiachin . . . surrendered
to Nebuchadnezzar along with the queen
mother and all his attendants . . .
nobles, and officials. Nebuchadnezzar
then took the king prisoner to Babylon.

24:13-16. Nebuchadnezzar also took
all the treasures of the temple and palace
including the gold articles that remained
from Solomon's days. This invasion took
place in fulfillment of God's Word
(1 Kings 9:6-9). Nebuchadnezzaar also
took captive virtually all the officers and
7,000 soldiers (2 Kings 24:16) as well as
1,000 craftsmen and artisans. In all,
10,000 people were taken captive including the Prophet Ezekiel (Ezek. 1:1-3).
Only the most poor people remained in
Judah. This was the second time Judahites had been deported to Babylon; the
first deportation followed Nebuchadnezzar's victory in 605.

24:17. None of Jehoiachin's sons sat
on Judah's throne, as Jeremiah had predicted (Jer. 22:30). The Babylonian king
set up Jehoiachin's uncle Mattaniah as
king. This man was the third son of Josiah to rule Judah (see the chart "The Last

Five Kings of Judah," near 2 Kings 23:31-
32); he was the younger brother of Jehoahaz and Jehoiakim. Nebuchadnezzar exercised his sovereign prerogative and
changed Mattaniah's name to Zedekiah
(see comments on 23:34).

H. Zedekiah's evil reign (24:18–25:7)

Though Zedekiah was king of the
Southern Kingdom the people of Judah
apparently did not recognize him as such
at the time. This may have been due in
part to his being placed on the throne by
a foreign king (2 Chron. 36:10-13). This
explains why inscriptions from the time
refer to Jehoiachin as Judah's last king
(Pritchard, ed., Ancient Near Eastern Texts
Relating to the Old Testament, p. 308).

1. ZEDEKIAH'S WICKEDNESS (24:18-20)

24:18-20. Zedekiah was 21 years old
when he began his rule, and he reigned
. . . 11 years (597–586 B.C.). He did evil
as his brother Jehoiakim had done. Jehoiakim is mentioned probably because
he reigned 11 years whereas Zedekiah's
immediate predecessor Jehoiachin
reigned only three months. Again the
reason for Judah's troubles is said to be
the LORD's anger with His people for
their apostasy (cf. 21:6, 15; 22:13, 17;
23:19, 26). Therefore He cast them from
His presence (i.e., out of the land; cf.
17:18, 20, 23; 23:27; 24:3).

For several years Zedekiah submitted obediently to his master in Babylon.
But finally under continuing pressure
from nationalists at home (cf. Jer. 37–38)
the king foolishly rebelled. He made an
alliance with Pharaoh Hophra (589–570
B.C.) who was anti-Babylonian and
aggressive.

2. JERUSALEM'S FINAL SIEGE (25:1-7)

25:1-3. In January 588 B.C. (in the
10th month of Zedekiah's ninth year)
Nebuchadnezzar again marched against
and besieged Jerusalem. The siege was
lifted briefly when Egypt attacked Nebuchadnezzar (Jer. 37:5) but the Babylonians defeated Judah's ally easily and resumed the siege. The Jerusalemites
suffered the consequences of this extended siege: famine and fear.

25:4-7. Finally the Babylonians broke
through the wall of Jerusalem. This was
on July 16, 586 B.C., the fourth month of
Zedekiah's 11th year (vv. 2-3). The few

remaining soldiers (cf. 24:16) **fled** by **night through** a gate in a section of the wall where it was double. They headed east **toward the Arabah** (the Jordan Valley) but were overtaken and captured near Jericho. Zedekiah fled the city with the **soldiers** (Jer. 39:4) and **was** also **captured.** He was taken to Nebuchadnezzar's field headquarters **at Riblah** (cf. 2 Kings 23:33) on the Orontes River north of Damascus. (Nebuchadnezzar was also conducting campaigns against Tyre and other Judean cities according to the Lachish Letters [D. Winton Thomas, ed., *Documents from Old Testament Times.* New York: Harper and Brothers, 1958, pp. 212-7].) There Nebuchadnezzar **killed** Zedekiah's **sons** (to cut off the heirs to the throne) **before his eyes,** blinded **Zedekiah** (to make further rebellion virtually impossible; cf. Ezek. 12:3), placed **him** in **shackles,** and transported **him to Babylon** (cf. Jer. 32:4; 34:1-3; 39).

I. Judah under Babylonian government (25:8-30)

1. JERUSALEM'S BURNING (25:8-12)

25:8-12. About four weeks after the breakthrough into the city (cf. vv. 3, 8) **Nebuchadnezzar** sent **Nebuzaradan, commander of** his **imperial guard,** to burn **Jerusalem.** This was **on the 7th day of the fifth month** of Nebuchadnezzar's **19th year** (August 14, 586 B.C.). However, Jeremiah 52:12 reads "the 10th day" (cf. comments there). This officer led his troops in burning down **every important building** in Jerusalem including **the temple** and **the royal palace** which had stood for almost four centuries. Then **the whole . . . army** proceeded to break **down** vast sections of the city wall so that the remaining inhabitants could not defend themselves against their Babylonian conquerors. **Nebuzaradan** also removed all but **the poorest people,** carrying the majority off to **Babylon.** Some of these captives had surrendered to the Babylonians but others had not. The remaining farmers were intended by Nebuchadnezzar to keep **the land** from growing completely wild.

2. THE TEMPLE'S DESTRUCTION (25:13-17)

25:13-17. The Babylonians broke . . . the large **bronze pillars** and pieces of furniture in **the temple** area to make **the bronze** easier to transport. The smaller furnishings of **bronze . . . gold,** and **silver** were simply packed up and carted off to **Babylon.**

The two pillars on the temple porch were so huge that the amount of **bronze** in them **could** not **be weighed** (cf. 1 Kings 7:15-22; Jer. 52:20-23).

3. THE LEADER'S EXECUTION (25:18-21)

25:18-21. Seraiah, an ancestor of Ezra (Ezra 7:1), and other priests were taken captive to preclude their leading another revolt. For the same reason the **chief** officer and **advisers** were arrested. Nebuchadnezzar **executed** all 72 of these leaders **at Riblah,** his field headquarters (cf. 2 Kings 25:6).

4. GEDALIAH'S MURDER (25:22-26)

25:22-24. Gedaliah was a descendant of **Shaphan,** Josiah's secretary of state who had implemented that king's reforms (22:3). **Gedaliah** was a friend of Jeremiah (Jer. 39:14) who followed that prophet's counsel to cooperate with the Babylonians. Since **Gedaliah** assumed a pro-Babylonian stance Nebuchadnezzar **appointed** him **governor** of **Judah. Gedaliah** set up his headquarters **at Mizpah** (about eight miles north of Jerusalem) since Jerusalem lay in ruins. In Mizpah a party of pro-Egyptian leaders and their followers who had escaped execution by the Babylonians called on him. The governor tried to convince these men to remain **in the land** and **serve** Nebuchadnezzar for their own good.

25:25-26. Some time later, however, **Ishmael . . . who was of royal** descent and apparently wanted to govern **Judah,** conspired against **Gedaliah** and slew him (cf. Jer. 41:2). Gedaliah had been warned of this possibility but had refused to take it seriously (Jer. 40:13-16). Gedaliah's associates were **also** slain. Fearing reprisals from Nebuchadnezzar, **all** the Judahites including **the army officers** who had failed to prevent this assassination **fled to Egypt** for safety, forcing Jeremiah to go with them (Jer. 41:1–43:7).

5. JEHOIACHIN'S BLESSING (25:27-30)

25:27-30. The 12th month of **the 37th year** of Jehoiachin's captivity in **Babylon** was March 560 B.C. (he was taken captive in 597; cf. 24:15). Earlier, in 562, a new king, **Evil-Merodach,** had become ruler **of Babylon.** (Evil-Merodach's rule was from 562 to 560; see the chart "Kings of the Neo-Babylonian Empire," in the *Introduction* to Dan.) He changed the former policy of treating the Judean king like a criminal and gave him privileges because he was a king. **Jehoiachin** was treated with greater respect **than the other** conquered **kings who were** also prisoners **in Babylon.** This treatment may have been a result of Jehoiachin's repentance before the Lord, though such a change of heart is not mentioned in the text. **For the rest of his life** Jehoiachin lived in minimum security **prison** conditions and **ate regularly** the food Evil-Merodach provided for him (cf. Jer. 52:31-34).

The positive note on which 2 Kings ends reveals again the Lord's mercy, which stands out repeatedly in 1 and 2 Kings. This notation also points to the continuation of the Davidic dynasty which God had promised would lead His people forever (2 Sam. 7:16). Evil-Merodach's attitude toward Jehoiachin was followed by policies that allowed the Israelites more freedom. When Cyrus overthrew Babylonia he allowed the Jews to return to their land (Ezra 1:1-4).

BIBLIOGRAPHY

See *Bibliography* on 1 Kings.

1 CHRONICLES

Eugene H. Merrill

INTRODUCTION

In the early Hebrew manuscripts 1 and 2 Chronicles were one scroll. The earliest evidence of the division of the book into two is the Septuagint, the Greek version of the Old Testament, of about 200 B.C. Since the original material presented the historical record in one unbroken account, one should read and study 1 and 2 Chronicles together in order to appreciate the unity and progressive development of the argument of the books.

Authorship. The author of 1 and 2 Chronicles is not mentioned in the Old Testament but Jewish tradition has suggested that it was Ezra. However, there is no way to be certain in the matter. So it has become customary to refer to the author as "the chronicler," a term which may not be entirely satisfactory but which is accurate enough in the absence of more precise information. Scholars generally agree that the work's uniformity of style, flavor, and viewpoint necessitate a single author. Yet 1 and 2 Chronicles, more than any other Old Testament books, testify to their dependence on several earlier written sources. More than half of 1 and 2 Chronicles has parallels in 1 and 2 Samuel and 1 and 2 Kings, for example. This does not mean that the chronicler used these books as direct sources, however. Most scholars agree that there is little or no evidence that 1 and 2 Chronicles has any quotations from them. On the other hand there are references to "the book of the annals of King David" (1 Chron. 27:24), "the book of the kings of Israel and Judah" (2 Chron. 27:7; 35:27; 36:8), "the book of the kings of Judah and Israel" (2 Chron. 16:11; 25:26; 28:26; 32:32), "the book of the kings of Israel" (1 Chron. 9:1; 2 Chron. 20:34), "the annals of the kings of Israel" (2 Chron. 33:18), "the records

of Samuel the seer" (1 Chron. 29:29), "the records of Nathan the prophet" (29:29; 2 Chron. 9:29), "the records of Gad the seer" (1 Chron. 29:29), and others (see, e.g., 2 Chron. 9:29). Whoever the author was, he was a meticulous historian who carefully utilized official and unofficial documents.

Date. Nearly all biblical scholars agree that 1 and 2 Chronicles could not have been written later than the end of the fifth century B.C., perhaps around 400. Liberal critics maintained at one time that a date around 300–250 B.C. was more suitable because of allegedly late characteristics such as references to the highly developed organization of priests and Levites, the use of vocal and instrumental music in worship, the anti-Samaritan polemic, the midrashic type of scriptural interpretation (narratives setting forth or illustrating religious teachings), and the mention of the Persian word *daric* (1 Chron. 29:7). All these features are now known to have been used as early as the fifth century; in addition such factors as the character of the Hebrew language in 1 and 2 Chronicles argue for an earlier rather than later date. The latest person named in 1 and 2 Chronicles is Anani, of the eighth generation from Jehoiachin (1 Chron. 3:24). Jehoiachin was taken captive by the Babylonians in 598 B.C. If 25 years are allotted for each generation, Anani would have been born between 425 and 400 B.C. If David's posterity was so important to the chronicler, a point that cannot be denied, it is incredible that he did not list any descendants after about 400 if the book were written later than that time. This genealogical datum is also helpful in determining the *earliest* possible time of composition as well, since eight generations could not lie between 598 B.C. and any time much earlier than 400 B.C. That is, the book could not have been written before 400 B.C.

Purpose and Structure. These two elements will be considered together since the one explains the other. In Hebrew, the name of the one scroll for 1 and 2 Chronicles was known as *diḇᵉrē hayyāmîm,* "the words concerning the days." This is a historical account of the "days" of the Davidic kings of Israel and Judah. The Greek title *Paraleipomena* ("Things omitted") in the Septuagint wrongly implies that the only purpose of 1 and 2 Chronicles is to preserve information not given in Samuel or Kings.

It is obvious that 1 and 2 Chronicles take the form of a history commencing with Adam (1 Chron. 1:1) and ending with the decree of Cyrus of Persia (2 Chron. 36:23) in 538 B.C. This view must be tempered by the fact that the period from Adam through the death of Saul is related only in genealogical registers interspersed with fragmentary narrative sections that especially emphasize the lineage of David and the priestly and Levitical orders. In His elective purposes God chose Israel—and her supreme king, David—from among all the nations on the earth. So David and Judah are the focal points of 1 and 2 Chronicles.

The emphasis on the Davidic and political history and the priestly and Levitical religious institutions intimated in the genealogical section (1 Chron. 1–9) finds confirmation in the remainder of 1 and 2 Chronicles. The reign of Saul is described in only one chapter (1 Chron. 10) and this is merely a record of his death. The purpose of this narration of Saul's death is to prepare for David's succession. David's reign is then the subject of the last 19 chapters of 1 Chronicles (chaps. 11–29). The reign of Solomon is described in 2 Chronicles 1–9 and the rest of the dynastic history is given in chapters 10–36. Though there are sporadic references to Israel, the Northern Kingdom, the whole thrust of 2 Chronicles 11–36 is centered on the Southern Kingdom. The history of the divided kingdom is always viewed in that light. David and the Davidic descent is the great theme.

The subsidiary but significant strand of the book—its preoccupation with religious matters—also is incipient in the genealogical section (1 Chron. 1–9). The priestly and Levitical lines of origin and descent prepare the way for the unusual attention to the temple and temple worship, evident from the time of David onward. Since Chronicles was composed in the postexilic period long after the monarchy had ceased as a viable institution, political as well as religious power became more and more the priesthood's responsibility. This could well account for the emphasis on the priests and their associates. More important, however, was the need to prepare the people for a heightened understanding of the messianic implications of the priesthood. David's intense interest and involvement in worship was not without design. As king, he was a type of the messianic King (cf. Pss. 2; 110; etc.), and as a priest (1 Chron. 15:25-28; cf. 2 Sam. 6:12-15), David was also a type of Christ, the messianic Priest. The twin emphases of 1 and 2 Chronicles—on David as king and on the priesthood as a royal function with messianic implications—are central to a theological understanding of these books.

Some writers believe that the chronicler is guilty of biased historiography. He failed, they say, to report David's adulterous affair with Bathsheba, for example, but was careful to detail the repentance of the evil King Manasseh, a feature missing in 2 Kings. While these examples, along with many others, could be cited as instances of supposedly "slanted" history writing, one must not make the mistake of interpreting them as errors of fact. It is incorrect to charge the chronicler with prejudicial reporting.

One cannot deny that as a whole David and the monarchy appear in a better light in Chronicles than in Samuel and in Kings. But this has been generally overstated. Though David's adultery is omitted in 1 Chronicles, other episodes that are recorded certainly place him in less than a favorable light. A few examples are his mishandling of the ark (1 Chron. 13:9-14), his polygamy (14:3-7), and his premature request to build a temple for the Lord (chap. 17). Furthermore since all scholars admit that the account of David's adultery in 2 Samuel 11 was well known and written long before 1 and 2 Chronicles were composed, there was no need to repeat it.

The best resolution of the charge of bias seems to be that the elements in 1 and 2 Samuel and 1 and 2 Kings which do not directly and positively contribute to the purpose of 1 and 2 Chronicles were not included since they would have been extraneous. The purpose of 1 and 2 Chronicles is to show God's elective and preserving grace in His covenant people through David, the messianic king and priest. The purposes of 1 and 2 Kings are different. These books explain the fall and destruction of Samaria and Jerusalem as evidence of divine judgment of God's people who had forsaken His covenant requirements. The Books of 1 and 2 Chronicles, though not avoiding this theme, show that the gracious God of all the earth and all the ages has a better plan by which He will achieve redemptive reconciliation. That plan does not do away with David; on the contrary, it eventuates in a greater "David" (the Messiah) who is both King and Priest.

The chronicler's emphasis on David, the priesthood, and the temple would have been a source of great encouragement to postexilic Judah. The nation had fallen into captivity, a comparatively small remnant had returned, and the restored temple was meager compared with its former splendor (cf. Hag. 2:3). But God's promises will not fail. In His time the temple will be filled with His own glory. And the Davidic line once more will be established and the Messiah will rule on David's throne in the kingdom. The religious and political sides of the covenant sovereignty of the Lord will be reestablished. This assurance would have instilled fervent joy and anticipation in the hearts of the remnant of God's people who otherwise saw all about them only a vague reminiscence of the glory their fathers had known in former years.

OUTLINE

COMMENTARY

I. Genealogies (chaps. 1–9)

As suggested under "Purpose and Structure" in the *Introduction*, the emphasis in 1 and 2 Chronicles is on the Davidic dynasty in Judah and the Levitical line. The genealogies are given to show how David and Judah were chosen by God. That divine selection is traced back to patriarchal and even prepatriarchal times.

A. Patriarchal genealogies (chap. 1)

Careful comparison of this passage with the genealogical lists in Genesis reveals little difference in substance. The author either cited Genesis directly (though not always in the form of the Heb. text) or used sources which in turn depended on Genesis. His purposes, however, precluded a mere copying of the Genesis texts. Rather he used those texts selectively to include nations, tribes, and individuals that were relevant to his overall design.

1. GENEALOGY OF ADAM (1:1-4)

1:1-4. The names here, based on Genesis 5:3-32, trace the ancestry of the human race from the first man, **Adam**, through **Noah** and his three **sons**. This enabled the chronicler not only to root the Chosen People in Israel and the Davidic line but also to show how they derived from only one of the three sons of Noah, that one through whom redemptive blessing would come, namely, **Shem** (cf. Gen. 9:26-27).

2. GENEALOGY OF JAPHETH (1:5-7)

1:5-7. In the reverse order in which the names of Noah's sons are usually given, **Japheth** is mentioned here first. For the identification of these names and the others as ethnic or geographic names, see the comments on Genesis 10:2-4.

3. GENEALOGY OF HAM (1:8-16)

1:8-16. This list is almost identical to Genesis 10:6-8, 13-18. There is even an abbreviated narrative concerning **Nimrod** (1 Chron. 1:10; cf. Gen. 10:8-12), a fact that points decidedly to the view that the chronicler had the Genesis genealogies before him.

4. GENEALOGY OF SHEM (1:17-27)

1:17-23. The tracing of the line of **Shem** follows that of Japheth's and Ham's lines because it is most important theologically. The Shemites (i.e., Semites) are the Noahic line from which Abraham, Israel, and hence David originated. The basis for this first part of the list is Genesis 10:22-29.

1:24-27. This genealogy of Shem has the added feature of a brief summation of names in which the first five names (**Shem** through **Peleg**), which are central to the line of descent, are repeated (cf. vv. 17-19). In addition five other names are given (**Reu** through **Abram**; cf. Gen. 11:18-26). Striking by omission are the names of Abram's brothers, Nahor and Haran (which are found in Gen. 11:26). (The **Nahor** in 1 Chron. 1:26 is Abraham's grandfather, not his brother.)

Abraham's brothers were left out by the chronicler because they were not in the line from Adam to David.

5. GENEALOGY OF ABRAHAM (1:28-34)

1:28-31. This section is arranged around the descendants of **Abraham** according to their mothers. First, the descent of **Ishmael,** son of Hagar, appears (cf. Gen. 25:12-16). As founder of the various Ishmaelite and, ultimately, Arabic tribes he was important to the chronicler's own historical situation (cf. 1 Chron. 27:30; 2 Chron. 17:11; 21:16; 22:1; 26:7; also cf. Neh. 2:19; 4:7; 6:1). **1:32-33.** This second section lists the offspring of **Keturah, Abraham's concubine,** all of whom are listed in Genesis 25:2-4. Of interest is the chronicler's omission of the descendants of **Dedan** (who *are* given in Gen. 25:3b), probably because of the geographic distance of the "Dedanites" from Judah (cf. Jer. 25:23).

1:34. This third section merely introduces Abraham's line through Sarah, his wife, and **Isaac,** son of Sarah. It mentions Isaac's two **sons . . . Esau and Israel** (Jacob), whose own genealogies then follow in verses 35-54 (Esau's line) and chapters 2–7 (Jacob's line).

6. GENEALOGY OF ESAU (1:35-54)

1:35-42. The descendants of Esau, who settled in the land of Edom, east and south of the Dead Sea (cf. Gen. 36:8), are listed in two divisions here, as they are in Genesis. First are **the sons of Esau** (1 Chron. 1:35-37) and then "the kings who reigned in Edom" (vv. 43-54). Some Bible versions read as if **Timna** (v. 36) was a son of **Eliphaz.** But in Hebrew the name Timna is feminine, and in Genesis 36:12 she is said to be a concubine of Eliphaz (son of Esau), and mother of **Amalek.** Having mentioned Timna, the chronicler then identified her as a native "Seirite" (1 Chron. 1:38-39; she was a daughter of **Seir**), a pre-Edomite. Then the chronicler spoke of her family connections (vv. 38-42). This corresponds to the order in Genesis 36:20-29 except that in most Hebrew manuscripts there are minor spelling variations in four names (cf. NIV marg. for the names **Alvan,** 1 Chron. 1:40, **Hemdan,** v. 41, **Akan,** v. 42, and **Dishan,** v. 42). Moreover, the wives of Esau are mentioned in Genesis 36 but are not listed in 1 Chronicles 1.

Why this was done is not known.

1:43-54. The lists of Edomite **kings,** apart from minor spelling differences are identical here with Genesis 36:31-43. These Edomite kings are not otherwise known but the relationship of the Edomites to Israel and Judah was so close and of such long duration that the chronicler's interest in them is not surprising.

B. Genealogy of Judah (chap. 2)

1. SONS OF JUDAH (2:1-4)

2:1-2. At last the author arrived at the people who were the focus of interest in his theological history. David and the Davidic dynasty were Judeans so it is fitting that Judah's genealogy is traced first (2:3–4:23) after listing Israel's 12 **sons** (2:1-2).

2:3-4. The details of the sordid story (Gen. 38) of Judah's sons, two of whom (**Er** and **Onan**) were slain by the Lord and the third (**Shelah**) withheld from **Tamar,** are not discussed here. The chronicler wanted to introduce the two sons of **Judah (Perez and Zerah)** in order to follow the line through Perez to the Davidic family.

2. GENEALOGIES OF PEREZ AND ZERAH (2:5-8)

2:5-8. These verses mention only selective and representative descendants (**sons** often means descendants of later generations) of **Perez** and **Zerah** as is clear from the fact that **Achar** (or Achan) is here noted as **the son of Carmi** (v. 7) and Carmi's father is not mentioned at all. Perhaps **Zimri** (v. 6) is a variant spelling of Zabdi because in the story of Achan's sin (Josh. 7) Achan was a son of Carmi, who was a son of Zabdi (Josh. 7:1, marg.), son of Zerah. Even so, the period from Zerah (born ca. 1877 B.C.) to Achan (an adult in 1406, Josh. 7) was almost 500 years, much too long for four generations. The chronicler's reference to Zerah, then, is primarily to introduce **Ethan, Heman, Calcol, and Darda** (Dara in most Heb. mss.; cf. marg.), all actually the sons of Mahol, whose ancestor was Zerah (cf. comments on 1 Kings 4:31), and celebrated sages to whom Solomon was compared (1 Kings 4:31; Ps. 89, title).

3. GENEALOGY OF HEZRON (2:9-41)

2:9-20. The chosen line now continues through **Hezron,** son of Perez, Judah's son. In line with Ruth 4:18-21, the descent goes on to **David** (1 Chron. 2:9-15; see the chart "David's Ancestry from Abraham" near 1 Sam. 16:1-13). The lineage also includes David's immediate family and half sisters (1 Chron. 2:16-17; see the chart "David's Family" near 2 Sam. 3:2-5). **Caleb,** another son of Hezron, was not the Caleb who was Joshua's associate. (In 1 Chron. 2:9 the Heb. has "Kelubai"; cf. marg., a variant spelling of **Caleb;** cf. v. 42.) His lineage follows in verses 18-20 and is expanded later in verses 42-55.

2:21-24. Segub, another son of Hezron, was born of **the daughter of Makir,** a son of Manasseh (Gen. 50:23) and **father of Gilead** (Num. 26:29). The name of Gilead was given to the upper Transjordan district. The incident of the taking of **60** Gilead **towns** by **Geshur and Aram** (areas northeast of Gilead) is otherwise unknown in the Old Testament. Another son, born posthumously to **Hezron** by his wife **Abijah,** was **Ashhur.**

2:25-41. The oldest son of **Hezron, Jerahmeel** (cf. v. 9), is mentioned last. His family detail appears only here, though Jerahmeelites were viewed as a clan closely related to Judah in David's time (1 Sam. 27:10).

4. GENEALOGY OF CALEB (2:42-55)

2:42-55. The line of **Caleb,** Hezron's third son (cf. v. 9), introduced briefly in verses 18-20, is expanded here. Many of these names appear elsewhere as placenames (e.g., **Ziph,** Josh. 15:24; **Mareshah,** Josh. 15:44; **Hebron,** Josh. 15:54; **Tappuah,** Josh. 15:34; **Rekem,** Josh. 18:27; **Shema,** Josh. 15:26; etc.). This does not prove a connection, but since most of these places lay in Judah they were probably founded by the various Calebites listed here.

Of particular interest are the references to **Bethlehem** (1 Chron. 2:51, 54), birthplace of both David and Jesus. The town was founded by or named after the great-grandson of Caleb through Caleb's wife **Ephrathah** (v. 50, spelled Ephrath in v. 19). The combination of Bethlehem and Ephrath(ah) appears also in the story of Rachel's death in childbirth (Gen. 35:19), where it is used anachronistically; in Ruth 4:11 in reference to blessing on Ruth; and in Micah 5:2 with respect to the birth of the Messiah.

C. Genealogy of David (chap. 3)

Almost like an interruption in the grand sweep of the genealogy of Judah, the line of David appears. This is in order to make clear that he succeeded in the Perez-Hezron line and that his own descent could be traced to the very end of Judah's history (from the chronicler's historical vantage point).

1. SONS OF DAVID (3:1-9)

3:1-9. Though Solomon was the son in the promised line of succession from David (22:9-10), for completeness David's other sons were included (3:1-9). This list should be compared to 2 Samuel 3:2-5, where one notes correspondence except in the name of the **second** son by **Abigail** (see the chart "David's Family" near 2 Sam. 3:2-5). The chronicler calls him **Daniel,** while he is Kileab in 2 Samuel 3:3. Though he may have had two names it is obvious that the chronicler is not, here at least, slavishly following 2 Samuel. The names of the **six** sons born in **Hebron** (1 Chron. 3:1-4a) are followed by those of David's **nine** sons born in **Jerusalem** (vv. 4b-8; cf. the corresponding list in 2 Sam. 5:14-16). Four of these were sons by **Bathsheba** (the Heb. has Bathshua, a variant spelling; cf. NIV marg.). This is the only place she is mentioned in Chronicles. (For comments on this see the *Introduction.*) Also **Eliphelet** (the one in 1 Chron. 3:6) and **Nogah** (v. 7) are not included in 2 Samuel but are mentioned again in 1 Chronicles 14:4-7 (see comments there). Perhaps the occurrence of two Eliphelets (3:6, 8) means that one died and another, born later, took his name. Perhaps Nogah also had died and 2 Samuel preserves only the names of surviving sons.

2. DESCENDANTS OF SOLOMON (3:10-24)

3:10-24. This list of **Solomon's** descendants is in effect a list of Judah's kings from Solomon through **Zedekiah** (vv. 10-16) and their exilic and postexilic continuation (vv. 17-24). Athaliah, the queen who ruled between **Ahaziah** and **Joash,** is not mentioned (v. 11). That is because she was only a political usurper and was not in the true dynastic succession (cf. 2 Kings 11). Of the sons of **Josiah, Johanan** (1 Chron. 3:15) is otherwise unknown. He cannot be Jehoahaz (2 Kings 23:31) because Jehoahaz was younger than **Jehoiakim** (cf. 2 Kings 23:36). This means that **Shallum** (1 Chron. 3:15) is identical to Jehoahaz who, though the next-to-youngest son of Josiah, preceded his brothers on the throne (cf. Jer. 22:11-12).

The remainder of the succession followed by the chronicler is Jeconiah (Heb.; cf. NIV marg. of 1 Chron. 3:16; also known as **Jehoiachin**; cf. v. 17 and 2 Kings 24:8, and Coniah, Jer. 22:24, marg.). Then came **Pedaiah** (1 Chron. 3:18), **Zerubbabel** (v. 19), **Hananiah** (v. 19), **Shecaniah** (v. 21), **Shemaiah** (v. 22), **Elioenai** (v. 23), and **Hodaviah** (v. 24).

Three difficulties here must be addressed. First, Zerubbabel (v. 19) is elsewhere called the son of **Shealtiel,** not the son of Pedaiah (Ezra 3:2, 8; 5:2; Neh. 12:1; Hag. 1:12, 14; 2:2, 23; Matt. 1:12; Luke 3:27). Since Shealtiel and Pedaiah were brothers (1 Chron. 3:17-18) the best solution seems to be that Shealtiel died early on and his role of dynastic succession was assumed by his younger brother Pedaiah. The second problem concerns Luke's account of the genealogy in which he identifies Shealtiel as the son of Neri, whose descent is not from Solomon but from David's son Nathan (Luke 3:27-31). The answer may lie in the possibility that since Jeconiah had no male heir to sit on the throne (cf. Jer. 22:30), a daughter of Jeconiah married Neri, son of Melki (Luke 3:27-28; not the Melki of Luke 3:24), of the line of Nathan. Legally Shealtiel, as grandson of Jeconiah, would continue the Davidic dynasty through Solomon, a viewpoint espoused by Matthew (Matt. 1:6-12).

The third conflict appears in Zerubbabel's line. The chronicler lists Zerubbabel's seven sons and one daughter (1 Chron. 3:19b-20). But none of them is mentioned in the genealogies of either Matthew or Luke. Matthew, who traces Jesus' descent from David through Solomon, wrote that the son of Zerubbabel was Abiud (Matt. 1:13). Luke, viewing it through Nathan, said Rhesa was that son (Luke 3:27). It is entirely possible, of course, that the Shealtiel and Zerubbabel of Luke are not the same as those of 1 Chronicles and that Luke preserves a genealogy of Mary straight from David through Nathan, a line of succession that has no other connection with the chronicler's genealogy (cf. comments on Luke 3:27). This would preclude the suggested solution to the second problem previously mentioned (and would, in fact, eliminate the problem altogether). This still leaves the variance between 1 Chronicles 3:19b-20 and Matthew 1:13. One may conjecture that Abiud is another name for one of the seven sons of Zerubbabel listed in Chronicles or that his name is missing from that list to begin with. That such a thing is possible may be seen in 1 Chronicles 3:22 where the historian wrote that **Shemaiah** had six sons but listed only five names.

D. Genealogy of Judah (4:1-23)

Having traced the Davidic line specifically and in detail (chap. 3), the chronicler returned to that of Judah generally. His intent here was: (a) to provide genealogical and geographical information and (b) to show the preeminence of the role of the Davidic tribe of Judah among the tribes by dealing with Judah first and by appealing to the antiquity of her residence in her allotted area (4:22b).

4:1-7. Verse 1 is a heading for the whole list, a matter that is clear from observing that the five named **descendants of Judah** are, in fact, sequential generations (cf. chap. 2). **Reaiah** (4:2) was no doubt identical to Haroeh (2:52) and was founder of **the Zorathites**, better known as the family from which Samson came (Jud. 13:2). The Hurites (**descendants of Hur**, 1 Chron. 4:3-4; cf. 2:19-20, 50-51) were distinguished as the family of the Bethlehemites. The Ashhurites (4:5-7) were the clan which produced **Tekoa**, the village of a wise woman (2 Sam. 14:2) and of Amos the prophet (Amos 1:1).

4:8-15. **Jabez** (vv. 8-10; cf. 2:55), whose ancestral roots are not delineated, prayed for God's blessing and received it. The village named after him was celebrated as the home of scribes. The Recahites (**men of Recah**, 4:11-12) are not otherwise identified. The Kenazites (vv. 13-15), however, were the prominent clan from which came both **Caleb,** Joshua's colleague, and his son-in-law, **Othniel,** Israel's first judge. Caleb was called a Kenizzite in the Conquest story (Josh. 14:6) and Othniel was called the "son of **Kenaz,** Caleb's younger brother" (Jud. 1:13), obviously a different **Kenaz** from the founder of the clan and to be distinguished also from Caleb's grandson of that name (1 Chron. 4:15).

4:16-20. The descendants of **Jehallelel** (v. 16) of **Ezrah** (vv. 17-18), of Hodiah (v. 19), and of **Shimon** (v. 20) are mentioned in the Bible only here. Verse 18 contains the interesting information that **Mered,** a son of Ezrah (v. 17) had married a **daughter** of an Egyptian Pharaoh. This would date the origins of this clan well before Moses' time, when Israel was still in favor with Egypt (cf. Ex. 1:8).

4:21-23. The genealogy of Judah closes with a brief summation of the family **of Shelah** (vv. 21-23), the youngest son **of Judah** by Bathshua (2:3). Shelah had been promised as husband to Tamar (cf. Gen. 38:5, 11, 14). His descendants were busy in **linen** manufacture (1 Chron. 4:21) and ceramics (v. 23) and also **ruled** over **Moab** in **ancient times.**

E. Genealogy of Simeon (4:24-43)

4:24. **Simeon** is listed after Judah because it received no tribal allotment of its own and was eventually assimilated into Judah (cf. Josh. 19:1-9). The list of sons in 1 Chronicles 4:24 differs somewhat from the list in Genesis 46:10 where there are six names (Ohad being added) and there are variations in spelling. The names in Exodus 6:15 agree perfectly with those in Genesis 46:10. The list in Numbers 26:12-13, on the other hand, is almost identical to the chronicler's rendition, with only Jakin for **Jarib** as the third son being different.

4:25-43. The remainder of Simeon's genealogy has no Old Testament parallels. Of interest is the note that the Simeonites did not increase much in population (v. 27) but were limited to certain restricted areas of **Judah,** primarily in the south-central Negev (vv. 28-33). Eventually they prospered, however, particularly by means of the **rich** pasturelands they had appropriated from the original Hamitic settlers (vv. 39-40). If **Gedor** (v. 39) should be read Gerar (Gerara in the LXX) this locates them in the west part of the upper Negev, not far from modern Gaza. This would explain why the **Hamites** (v. 40), people of Egypt, were there, for Egypt was not many miles away. The chronicler indicates that a violent removal of the Hamites occurred in the time of **Hezekiah** (715–686 B.C.) and involved the **Meunites** as well (v. 41). These people are mentioned again in reference to

Uzziah's exploits in the Negev (2 Chron. 26:7) but cannot be further identified.

In Hezekiah's day **500 . . . Simeonites** spread to the east, to the **hill country of Seir** (the same as Edom), where they displaced a remnant of the **Amalekites** who had **lived there,** possibly from the time of David (1 Chron. 4:42-43; cf. 1 Sam. 30:16-20).

F. Genealogies of the Transjordan tribes (chap. 5)

The rationale for the order in which the remaining tribal genealogies appear is somewhat elusive but possibly Reuben is introduced next because that tribe is named after the eldest son of Israel. Gad (vv. 11-22) and the eastern half of Manasseh (vv. 23-26) are listed after Reuben because all were located east of the Jordan River.

1. REUBEN (5:1-10)

5:1-2. The lineage of **Reuben** is introduced by an explanation of that tribe's fall from divine favor and replacement by **Judah.** As Jacob's **firstborn,** Reuben would ordinarily expect to be the son through whom the leadership and covenant blessing would be transmitted. But Reuben committed adultery with his father's concubine Bilhah (Gen. 35:22), and so forfeited his privileges. The right of primogeniture then fell to **Joseph** (i.e., Joseph's **sons,** Ephraim and Manasseh, Gen. 48:15-22), **though** through Judah came **a ruler** (David), and through him *the* Ruler, Jesus Christ (cf. comments on Gen. 49:8-12).

5:3-10. The genealogy of **Reuben** includes his four **sons** (cf. Num. 26:5-11) and selected generations thereafter. From a certain **Joel** (1 Chron. 5:4) eventually came **Beerah** (v. 6) **whom Tiglath-Pileser** III (745–727 B.C.) **took** captive when he conquered Samaria. By that time **the Reubenites** occupied all the Transjordan, including not only the area from the Arnon River (**Aroer** was on that river) **to Nebo** in the north but also **Gilead** (east of the Jordan River) and on north and northeast **to the Euphrates River.** On the **war** with **the Hagrites** see comments on verses 18-22.

2. GAD (5:11-17)

5:11-17. **The Gadites** settled in **Bashan,** south and east of the Sea of

Kinnereth and north of the Yarmuk River. There was no clearly defined border between **Gilead** and **Bashan** (v. 16) so no doubt the Eastern tribes mingled rather freely. The descendants of Gad listed here appear nowhere else, the names evidently having been compiled from documents of the period of **Jeroboam** II **of Israel** (793–753 B.C.) and **Jotham . . . of Judah** (750–735 B.C.).

3. EXPLOITS OF THE EASTERN TRIBES (5:18-22)

5:18-22. The chronicler interrupted the genealogies to comment on military matters common to the Eastern tribes. He recounted their **war** with **the Hagrites** (cf. v. 10) and their allies. The Transjordanian tribes, with their **44,760** soldiers, achieved a signal triumph by God's help in answer to **their prayers.** The number of captured **livestock** was huge (v. 21), revealing that that land area was fertile for **sheep** grazing. This occurred in the days of Saul (v. 10), perhaps in connection with Saul's Ammonite wars (cf. 1 Sam. 11:1-11). **The Hagrites,** known now from Assyrian inscriptions, were replaced by the victorious Israelites **until the Exile** (1 Chron. 5:22), perhaps the Assyrian Captivity of some Israelites led by Tiglath-Pileser III in 734 B.C. (not to be confused with the final Assyrian Captivity of Israel in 722 B.C.).

4. THE HALF-TRIBE OF MANASSEH (5:23-26)

5:23-26. The **half-tribe** mentioned here had been allocated a territory east of the Jordan, from Gad in the south to **Mount Hermon** in the north (cf. Num. 32:39-42; Deut. 3:12-17; Josh. 13:29-31). Though their leaders were celebrated for military exploits, they led the people into idolatry. As a result they were deported along with **the Reubenites** and **Gadites,** by **Pul (Tiglath-Pileser** III) **of** Assyria. For the places where they were sent, see comments on 2 Kings 17:6. The site of **Hara,** not mentioned in 2 Kings, has not yet been identified.

G. Genealogy of Levi (chap. 6)

1. DESCENDANTS OF LEVI (6:1-15)

6:1-3a. Levi's genealogy begins by referring to the line of which **Moses** and **Aaron** were a part because of their obvious importance. After the reference to the three **sons of Levi,** the chronicler concentrated on **Kohath** and his offspring through **Amram.** The length of time between Levi's death and Moses' birth (ca. 1800–1526 B.C.) requires that the sequence (Levi—Kohath—Amram—Moses) represents a much longer list of names (see comments on Num. 26:58-59). The names here probably refer to tribe, clan, family, and individual respectively (cf. Josh. 7:16-18). Moses is mentioned no further here because the purpose of this list is to trace the high priestly line.

6:3b-15. Aaron was the first high priest (Ex. 28:1) and his descendants followed after in their respective generations. The list here agrees with that in Ezra 7:1-5 except for minor spelling variations and Ezra's omission of six names, from **Meraioth** to **Azariah** (1 Chron. 6:7-10). Also the chronicler indicated that **Jehozadak** was the son of **Seraiah** who was captured by Nebuchadnezzar (vv. 14-15). Ezra identified *himself* as a son of Seraiah, however (Ezra 7:1). Since Ezra could not have been born much before 500 B.C. and the Babylonian Captivity was in 586 B.C., he must have meant that he was not the son of Seraiah in the strict sense but a more distant descendant. The additions and omissions in these parallel lists should caution Bible students not to assume that genealogical lists are always complete. The compilers always had their special reasons for including some names and not others. The chronicler's theological view of Israel reveals itself in his comment that the last of the Aaronic priests **was deported when the LORD sent Judah and Jerusalem into exile by the hand of Nebuchadnezzar** (1 Chron. 6:15; cf. the Exile of the Northern Kingdom, 5:22, 26).

2. OTHER DESCENDANTS OF LEVI (6:16-30)

6:16-21. The historian next recapitulated the tribal descent of Levi by listing **the sons** and grandsons **of Levi** (vv. 16-19) and their subsequent generations of prominent persons (vv. 20-30). He began with **Gershon** whose line he traced for seven generations (vv. 20-21). (The Heb. here has Gershom, a variant spelling; cf. marg., though the name is usually Gershon; cf. Ex. 6:16.)

6:22-30. Next is **Kohath,** Levi's son who was not only an ancestor of Aaron (vv. 2-3) but also an ancestor of the prophet-priest **Samuel.** Kohath's son

Amminadab (v. 22) is otherwise known as Izhar (cf. vv. 2, 18, 38). Whereas Aaron, then, was a Kohathite and founder of the priestly line, Samuel, though a Kohathite, could not function as a high priest. Samuel could (and did), however, officiate at the tabernacle and performed other ministries which evidently included sacrifice (Num. 3:27-32; cf. 1 Sam. 1:21; 2:11; 9:11-14; etc.). Finally, **the descendants of Merari,** Levi's third **son,** are noted, especially the descent through **Mahli** (1 Chron. 6:29-30).

3. LEVITICAL MUSICIANS (6:31-48)

6:31-38. This section contains the names of **the tabernacle** musicians whom **David** appointed from the three Levitical families (vv. 31-32). The Kohathite list (vv. 33-38) begins with **Heman** (not the Heman in 2:6), **son of Joel** and grandson **of Samuel** (6:33). Samuel's ancestry is then retraced (cf. vv. 27-28; and cf. 1 Sam. 1:1, where the same names appear back to **Zuph;** cf. 1 Chron. 6:35, with slight spelling variations: Elihu for **Eliel,** and Tohu [called Nahath in v. 26] for **Toah).** Though this version of the Kohathite lineage agrees essentially with that in verses 22-28, the differences are significant enough to suggest that the chronicler may have used two different sources in his own compilations. Two people (Assir and **Elkanah,** vv. 22-23) between **Korah** and **Ebiasaph** are not listed in verse 37. And spelling variations (or different individuals) occur in six instances; Eliel (v. 34) for Eliab (v. 27), Toah (v. 34) for Nahath (v. 26), **Zuph** (v. 35) for Zophai (v. 26), **Joel** (v. 36) for Shaul (v. 24), **Azariah** (v. 36) for Uzziah (v. 24), and **Zephaniah** (v. 36) for Uriel (v. 24). Interestingly four Elkanahs are in this genealogy (vv. 23, 25 [the same as the one in v. 36], 34-35).

6:39-43. The Gershonite order begins with **Asaph,** famous as a singer and psalmist (cf. titles of Pss. 50; 73–83). The remainder of the list contains many names not found in the preceding section (1 Chron. 6:20-21).

6:44-48. The Merarite singers begin with **Ethan** (called Jeduthun in 9:16) and are traced back to **Merari** through **Mushi** (6:47). This list is not a repetition of the earlier list (vv. 29-30) because the names simply do not match. Mahli, son of Merari (v. 29), is not the same as **Mahli,**

son of Mushi (v. 47). Merari had two sons, Mahli and Mushi (v. 19); Mahli's succession appears in verses 29-30 and Mushi's in verses 47-48. The purpose of this entire section (vv. 31-47) is to justify the ministry of David's chief musicians—Heman, Asaph, and Ethan—by describing their pure Levitical lineage.

4. AARONIC PRIESTS (6:49-53)

6:49-53. In distinction from the ministry of music carried out by the Levitical orders (vv. 31-48) was that of the sacrifices for **atonement** carried out by **the descendants of Aaron.** To emphasize the propriety of David's Zadokite priesthood, the chronicler again (cf. vv. 3-8) traced the Aaronic lineage from **Aaron** to **Ahimaaz,** son of **Zadok.**

5. SETTLEMENTS OF THE LEVITES (6:54-81)

6:54-81. The places where the Levites settled are described by **clans** with Kohath again appearing first. (See the chart "Levite Towns Listed in Joshua 21 and 1 Chronicles 6.") Some of the towns were for Kohathites who were priests (vv. 57-60) and others were for Kohathites in nonpriestly roles (vv. 61, 64-70). One of the towns in **Benjamin** was **Anathoth** (v. 60). The Prophet Jeremiah was a son of a priest from Anathoth and hence must have been a Kohathite (Jer. 1:1).

The Gershonites settled in **13 towns** in **Issachar, Asher, Naphtali,** and eastern **Manasseh** (1 Chron. 6:62). These towns are named in verses 71-76 and include the important city **Kedesh** of **Naphtali** (v. 76), as well as a **Kedesh** in the **Issachar** tribe (v. 72).

To **the Merarites** fell cities in **Zebulun . . . Reuben,** and **Gad** (vv. 77-81). In all, 48 cities were designed for the use of Levi (cf. Josh. 21:41) since that tribe had been assigned no tribal allotment (cf. Num. 35:1-8).

H. Genealogies of six Northern tribes (chap. 7)

1. ISSACHAR (7:1-5)

7:1-5. The descent of this tribe is not traced fully. In agreement with Genesis 46:13 and Numbers 26:23-25 there were four **sons of Issachar,** but the chronicler went on to feature the line **of Tola.** For some reason he also gave population figures: **22,600** military **men in** David's era

Levite Towns Listed in Joshua 21 and 1 Chronicles 6

	Joshua 21:9-42	*1 Chronicles 6:54-81*
Towns for Kohathites Who Were Priests		
In Judah and Simeon	1. Hebron	1. Hebron
	2. Libnah	2. Libnah
	3. Jattir	3. Jattir
	4. Eshtemoa	4. Eshtemoa
	5. Holon*	5. Hilen*
	6. Debir	6. Debir
	7. Ain*	7. Ashan*
	8. Juttah	(Juttah)†
	9. Beth Shemesh	8. Beth Shemesh
In Benjamin	10. Gibeon	(Gibeon)†
	11. Geba	9. Geba
	12. Anathoth	10. Alemeth*
	13. Almon*	11. Anathoth
Towns for Kohathites Who Were Not Priests		
In Ephraim	14. Shechem	12. Shechem
	15. Gezer	13. Gezer
	16. Kibzaim‡	14. Jokmeam‡
	17. Beth Horon	15. Beth Horon
In Dan	18. Eltekeh	—
	19. Gibbethon	—
	20. Aijalon	16. Aijalon
	21. Gath Rimmon	17. Gath Rimmon
In western Manasseh	22. Taanach‡	18. Aner‡
	23. Gath Rimmon‡	19. Bileam‡
Towns for Gershonites		
In eastern Manasseh	24. Golan	20. Golan
	25. Be Eshtarah*	21. Ashtaroth*
In Issachar	26. Kishion‡	22. Kedesh‡
	27. Daberath	23. Daberath
	28. Jarmuth*	24. Ramoth*
	29. En Gannim*	25. Anem*
In Asher	30. Mishal*	26. Mashal*
	31. Abdon	27. Abdon
	32. Helkath*	28. Hukok*
	33. Rehob	29. Rehob
In Naphtali	34. Kedesh	30. Kedesh
	35. Hammoth Dor*	31. Hammon*
	36. Kartan*	32. Kiriathaim*
Towns for Merarites		
In Zebulun	37. Jokneam	(Jokneam)†
	38. Kartah	(Kartah)†
	39. Dimnah*	33. Rimmono*
	40. Nahalal‡	34. Tabor‡
In Reuben	41. Bezer	35. Bezer
	42. Jahaz*	36. Jahzah*
	43. Kedemoth	37. Kedemoth
	44. Mephaath	38. Mephaath
In Gad	45. Ramoth	39. Ramoth
	46. Mahanaim	40. Mahanaim
	47. Heshbon	41. Heshbon
	48. Jazer	42. Jazer

* The two cities in each of these 12 pairs have only minor spelling variations.
† These four cities are not included in the Hebrew manuscripts of 1 Chronicles (see NIV margs.).
   Perhaps these cities, though assigned by Joshua, were not conquered by the Israelites.
‡ The two cities in each of these five pairs differ in name. The cities originally assigned by Joshua (ca. 1399 B.C.) may
   have changed names by the chronicler's time (ca. 400 B.C., after the exiles' return), almost 1000 years later. Or five
   of the cities assigned may have never been conquered by the Israelites.

(1 Chron. 7:2; cf. 2 Sam. 24:1-9) who descended from Tola, **36,000** who came from **Uzzi** (1 Chron. 7:4), and a total of **87,000** (v. 5), which included 28,400 others from unnamed families.

2. BENJAMIN (7:6-12)

7:6-12. This genealogy is greatly expanded in chapter 8 as a climax to the pre-Davidic history, but appears here in a succinct form characteristic of the other Northern tribes. Though Genesis 46:21 lists 10 **sons of Benjamin,** Numbers 26:38-41 names 5 and the chronicler names 3 (1 Chron. 7:6-7) and 5 (8:1-2). (See comments on 8:1-5 for an explanation that Benjamin's 10 "sons" [Gen. 46:21] probably included some grandsons.) The first 2, **Bela** and **Beker,** are mentioned in Genesis 46:21, but **Jediael** is mentioned nowhere else unless he was the same as Ashbel (Gen. 46:21; Num. 26:38; 1 Chron. 8:1). The truncated nature of this list in 1 Chronicles 7:6-12 is also clear in that Bela here had 5 sons whereas in 8:3-5 he had 9. On the other hand Beker had 9 sons (7:8) but is not mentioned at all in chapter 8. Similarly, Jediael's son **Bilhan** (7:10) does not appear in chapter 8. The reason Bela's descent was traced in chapter 8 to the exclusion of the others is clear, of course: Saul was in his succession (8:33).

The **Shuppites and Huppites** descended from **Ir** (7:12), a son of Bela (v. 7, assuming Ir = Iri). The **Hushites** descended from **Aher,** son of Benjamin (if Aher = Ahiram = Aharah, Num. 26:38; 1 Chron. 8:1, and if Ahiram/Aharah is a son of Benjamin).

The census figures were **22,034** for **the sons of Bela** (7:7), **20,200** for **the sons of Beker** (v. 9), and **17,200** for **the sons of Jediael** (v. 11). This grand total of 59,434 fighting men is thought by many scholars to be far too many for David's time since the tribe of Benjamin had been decimated by civil war and reduced to 600 men in the time of the Judges (Jud. 20:44-48). However, since that event was early in the era of the Judges, probably 400 years before David's census (cf. 1 Chron. 21:1-7), the 600 families could easily have multiplied to that extent.

3. NAPHTALI (7:13)

7:13. The names of the four **sons of Naphtali** listed here correspond with those in Genesis 46:24 and Numbers 26:48-49 (except that **Jahziel** in 1 Chron. 7:13 is spelled Jahzeel in Num. 26:48).

4. MANASSEH (7:14-19)

7:14-15a. The genealogy **of Manasseh** does not appear in Genesis since Manasseh was at that time part of Joseph. Manasseh and **his** Aramean concubine had a son **Makir** (cf v. 17b; Num. 26:29; Josh. 17:1), who was Gilead's **father** (cf. Num 26:29; 36:1). **Asriel,** descended from Manasseh, is not mentioned in Numbers 26:29. The dual reference to **Maacah** (1 Chron. 7:15-16) is best explained by the coincidence that this was the name of Makir's sister as well as his **wife.**

7:15b-19. A second prominent **descendant** of Manasseh through Makir was **Zelophehad,** who was distinguished because he had no sons (cf. Num. 36:1-9; his five **daughters** are named in Josh. 17:3). Though this genealogy centers in Makir and his offspring (inhabitants of the Manasseh territory in the Transjordan), the Manasseh elements west of the Jordan were represented by **Hammoleketh,** Makir's **sister,** the four **sons of Shemida** (1 Chron. 7:18-19); Zelophehad and his daughters; and perhaps Asriel (v. 14; cf. Josh. 17:2-6).

5. EPHRAIM (7:20-29)

7:20-24. The descent **of Ephraim,** second son of Joseph, culminates here in Joshua (v. 27), Moses' illustrious successor. Ephraim's first son, **Shuthelah,** produced a line which several generations later included a second **Shuthelah** (vv. 20-21). Two other sons of Ephraim, **Ezer and Elead,** were slain by the early (pre-1200 B.C.) Philistines of Gath, a tragedy that caused **their father** much sorrow (vv. 21-22). Since **Ephraim** himself was born in Egypt before the famine (cf. Gen. 41:50-52), this episode may have occurred in Egypt (in which case the **men of Gath** went down to Egypt to kill Ephraim's sons). Or, more likely, some Israelites, though living in Egypt, continued to have access to Canaan, even maintaining agricultural pursuits there. In support of this is the statement that Ephraim had a **daughter . . . Sheerah,** who founded two settlements in Canaan, **Beth Horon** and **Uzzen Sheerah.** Again, this could only have been in the period of Egyptian sojourn.

7:25-29. Through Ephraim's son **Rephah** eventually came **Joshua.** The fact that eight generations lay between Ephraim and Joshua would also argue for the Egyptian sojourn setting for the previous two incidents concerning Ephraim's sons and daughter (vv. 21-24). The post-Conquest **settlements** of Ephraim follow in verses 28-29. The territory is roughly from **Bethel** on northward to the Valley of Jezreel and from the Jordan River to the Mediterranean Sea.

6. ASHER (7:30-40)

7:30-40. The first part of this list is paralleled by Genesis 46:17 and Numbers 26:44-46, but the names from **Birzaith** (1 Chron. 7:31) through **Rizia** (v. 39) appear only here. The **men** of war (**26,000,** v. 40) were descendants from **Asher** (v. 30). (**Helem** in v. 35 may be the same person as **Hotham** in v. 32.)

I. Genealogy of Benjamin (chap. 8)

8:1-5. Benjamin and his descendants were briefly introduced earlier (7:6-12) but now a full genealogy is given. Its purpose was obviously to trace the lineage of Saul and his immediate family. As noted, not all the names of Benjamin's **sons** listed here are the same as those in 7:6 (see comments there). There are five here, of whom only two, **Bela** and **Ashbel** (perhaps the same as Jediael) are mentioned in 7:6. On the other hand Genesis 46:21 lists Bela, Beker, and Ashbel, and also lists as sons (Gera, Naaman, and Ard) those whom the chronicler viewed as Benjamin's grandsons. (Ard of Gen. 46:21 is possibly the same as Addar of 1 Chron. 8:3; cf. Num. 26:40.) Similarly Numbers 26:38-39 counts Shupham and Hupham as Benjamin's sons while the chronicler (1 Chron. 8:5) calls them grandsons (**Shephuphan** is a variant spelling of Shupham and **Huram** a variation of Hupham). However, Numbers agrees with the chronicler that Ard and Naaman were grandsons of Benjamin (Num. 26:40). What all this suggests is that "son" frequently means grandson or even a more remote descendant and that not every list is complete. Since 1 Chronicles 8 is longer and more comprehensive than the other lists (Gen. 46:21; Num. 26:38-40), one may assume that Benjamin had five sons (1 Chron.

8:1-2) and that the other lists were editorially selective.

8:6-28. Ehud had already been identified as a grandson of Jediael (7:10), probably otherwise known as Ashbel. Ehud's family (8:6) engaged in hostility against other Benjamites (**Naaman, Ahijah, and Gera,** v. 7a) events otherwise unattested. **Shaharaim** (v. 8) is probably the same as Ahishahar (7:10), a son of Bilhan, so the line is still traced through Ashbel (= Jediael), Bilan, and others. Shaharaim lived for a time in Moab, where he **divorced his wives Hushim and Baara.** Through a third **wife Hodesh** (8:9) he had seven other **sons,** but the chronicler's interest was in the descent through **Hushim** (v. 11a). It passed from Shaharaim through **Elpaal** (v. 11b) **and Beriah** (v. 13). This list concludes with **sons of Shimei** (vv. 19-21), **of Shashak** (vv. 22-25), and **of Jeroham** (vv. 26-27), none of whom can be otherwise identified. **All these** descendants of Benjamin, the chronicler wrote, **lived in Jerusalem** (v. 28), which was possible, of course, only after Jerusalem was taken by David and made Israel's capital (cf. 2 Sam. 5:1-10).

8:29-40. In the second major city of Benjamin, namely, **Gibeon,** lived a line of Benjamites to which **Saul** was related. It is impossible to discover the linkage between this line and any of those of the previous section because this line begins only with Saul's great-grandfather **Jeiel,** a period much later than that presupposed by most of verses 1-28.

The descent appears to be: (a) Jeiel (v. 29), (b) **Ner** (v. 30; cf. 9:36), (c) **Kish** (8:33), and (d) **Saul** (v. 33). (Cf. comments on Ner, Kish, and Saul in 1 Sam. 14:50-51.) Next are the sons of Saul: **Jonathan, Malki-Shua, Abinadab** (= Ishvi; cf. comments on 1 Sam. 14:49), **and Esh-Baal** (= Ish-Bosheth; cf. 1 Sam. 14:49; 2 Sam. 2:8). A grandson of Saul, **Merib-Baal** (1 Chron. 8:34), also known as Mephibosheth (2 Sam. 4:4), is prominent in the annals of history as are his father **Jonathan,** his uncle Ish-Bosheth, and his grandfather Saul. Following Mephibosheth's (Merib-Baal's) son **Micah** (1 Chron. 8:34; cf. 2 Sam. 9:12), however, are names (1 Chron. 8:35-40) which do not appear elsewhere in the Bible except in another genealogy of Saul (9:41-44).

J. Citizens of Jerusalem (9:1-34)

1. POLITICAL LEADERS (9:1-9)

9:1. No doubt verse 1a is a summary statement concerning **the genealogies** of **all Israel** which also includes **Judah** before the Babylonian deportation. The purpose of the remainder of chapter 9 is to identify **the people** who settled in Jerusalem and Gibeon after their return from the Exile.

9:2-9. After a brief mention of the return of the various groups in general (v. 2), the chronicler went into some detail with each group. By **Israelites** he meant the people of **Judah . . . Benjamin . . . Ephraim, and Manasseh** who settled in **Jerusalem** (v. 3). The descendants of Judah represent all three lines—that of his sons **Perez** (v. 4), Shelah (**the Shilonites,** v. 5; cf. Gen. 38:5), and Zerah (1 Chron. 9:6; cf. Gen. 38:30).

Benjamin's descendants were traced through four lines—**Hassenuah** (1 Chron. 9:7), **Jeroham** (v. 8), **Micri** (v. 8), and **Ibnijah** (v. 8)—none of whom was an immediate son of Benjamin.

The list of settlers here should be compared with the list in Nehemiah 11:4-9, the structure of which is essentially the same as the chronicler's. The names of the lineage of **Judah,** however, do not correspond unless **Uthai** (1 Chron. 9:4) is Athaiah (Neh. 11:4) and **Asaiah** (1 Chron. 9:5) is Maaseiah (Neh. 11:5). If so, one must assume a different selection of ancestors from these men back to Judah. Also Nehemiah does not mention the line through Zerah. This no doubt explains the different census figures—**690** in 1 Chronicles 9:6 and 468 in Nehemiah 11:6. The Benjamite lists agree more closely, at least at the beginning, where **Sallu** is **son of Meshullam,** in both cases (1 Chron. 9:7; Neh. 11:7). However, the chronicler named four lines of descent and Nehemiah only one, that of Sallu back to Jeshaiah (Neh. 11:7). Chronicles has a total of **956** Benjamite men (1 Chron. 9:9) while Nehemiah (11:8) has 928. Since there is no way of knowing the basis for these respective figures, one cannot account for their differences.

2. PRIESTS (9:10-13)

9:10-13. The six priestly families here—**Jedaiah, Jehoiarib, Jakin, Azariah . . . Adaiah,** and **Maasai**—correspond (with some spelling variations)

to the six in Nehemiah 11:10-14 except that (in Neh. 11:10) Jedaiah is the son of Joiarib (= Jehoiarib). Moreover, Nehemiah's list is evidently more comprehensive since it includes more names. Finally, the chronicler's total of **1,760** persons (1 Chron. 9:13) differs from Nehemiah's total of 1,192. Since there is no hint of the basis for these figures, it is impossible to know what accounts for their differences.

3. LEVITES (9:14-16)

9:14-16. The seven families of **Levites** who lived in Jerusalem (v. 34; cf. "the Holy City," Neh. 11:18) and vicinity (Netophah; cf. 1 Chron. 9:16, was a suburb of Jerusalem) are the same as those of Nehemiah 11:15-18, though there is considerable variation in the spelling of some names and additions and omissions of still others. The reasons for these differences are unclear.

4. GATEKEEPERS AND OTHERS (9:17-34)

9:17-27. The tasks of the Levites in the preceding list (vv. 14-16) are not spelled out, so it may be assumed that they were primarily of a sacrificial nature. But the Levites of this section (vv. 17-27) were responsible to open and close the temple **gates** at the appropriate times and to **guard** them against improper intrusion. The names here are paralleled in Nehemiah to some extent (Neh. 11:19-23), though Nehemiah's account is shorter. Strangely **Shallum,** described by the chronicler as the **chief** gatekeeper (1 Chron. 9:17), was not mentioned by Nehemiah. (On Shallum's grandfather's name Ebiasaph, v. 19, see comments on 26:1.) Shallum's position was especially important as he was in charge of **the King's Gate,** which led to the main, eastern entrance to the temple (cf. Ezek. 46:1-2). That had been his ancestors' role even back to the time of the tabernacle when **Phinehas son of Eleazar** had been their supervisor (1 Chron. 9:19-20; cf. Num. 3:32). The enigmatic reference to **Zechariah** (1 Chron. 9:21; cf. 26:2) suggests that in Davidic times the role of the ancestors of Shallum was shared by another Levitical family whose responsibility was the gate of **the Tent of Meeting** (the tabernacle) proper.

In all, the chronicler wrote, the Levite **gatekeepers** in Jerusalem and the surrounding **villages** totaled **212.** (In

Neh. 11:19 the gatekeepers totaled 172, but that verse implies that only the families of Akkub and Talmon were counted while 1 Chron. 9:17 adds the names Shallum and Ahiman.) This evidently was the pool from which the manpower was drawn since 22 were needed each day (26:17-18). They each served for a **seven-day** period (9:25) at which time they were relieved for an indeterminate period of time.

9:28-34. Besides the gatekeepers **some** Levites were responsible for **the articles** and foodstuffs **in the temple service.** This included **the furnishings,** vessels, **flour. . . wine. . . oil, incense . . . spices,** and **bread** (vv. 28-32; cf. Lev. 24:5-9). Other Levites **were musicians** who were free from all other duties and for convenience were assigned living quarters in **the temple** complex itself.

K. Genealogy of Saul (9:35-44)

9:35-44. This genealogical record is almost identical to that of 8:29-40 (which adds the family of Eshek, brother of Azel, 8:39). But because the chronicler was about to narrate the death of **Saul** (chap. 10) and the succession of David (11:1-3) he repeated Saul's genealogy (9:35-44).

II. The Reign of David (chaps. 10–29)

A. Death of Saul (chap. 10)

Chapter 10. As pointed out in the *Introduction,* the major objective of 1 and 2 Chronicles is to enhance the reign of David and his dynasty by showing it to be divinely ordained and directed. One effective way of achieving this was to set the beginnings of that reign against the tragic end of Saul's reign (cf. Saul's 40 years [1051–1011 B.C.] with David's dynasty of 425 years [1011–586]). The chronicler assumed, of course, that the life and tenure of **Saul** were well known to his readers, having occupied most of 1 Samuel. So he turned immediately to the point at issue—the **death** of **Saul** as an act of God's judgment.

The narrative of the Philistines' conquest of **Israel** at **Mount Gilboa** (1 Chron. 10:1-12) is practically identical to 1 Samuel 31 (see comments there). For some reason Chronicles adds the item that the Philistines **hung** Saul's **head in the temple of Dagon** (1 Chron. 10:10) but

omits the fact that they hung his body on the wall of Beth Shan (1 Sam. 31:10).

In 1 Samuel 31 there is no moral or theological observation about the death of **Saul** and the transference of his **kingdom** to **David.** The chronicler, however, pointed out (1 Chron. 10:13-14) that God's judgment fell because of Saul's disobedience to His **word** (cf. 1 Sam. 13:13-14; 15:23). Another reason was Saul's recourse to demonic spirits (1 Sam. 28:7).

B. David's heroes (chaps. 11–12)

11:1-3. The story of David's reign from **Hebron** and the steps taken by him and others to gain control over **all Israel** is briefly recounted in 1 Chronicles. The reason, again, is that the details were well known from 2 Samuel. Only those nuances necessary to the chronicler's special emphases need be repeated. On the other hand those men God used to help establish David's kingdom play a significant role in Chronicles. The chronicler did not refer to any factors (such as Abner's machinations, 2 Sam. 2:8-32) that might tend to overemphasize the human element, giving Saul's family a hand in David's success. The narration opens, then, with an appeal to David by the men of **Israel** that he be **their ruler.** They recognized that his kingship was a matter of divine appointment (1 Chron. 11:2).

David responded by making a covenant (**compact**) with **the elders,** a pact that probably consisted of an oath in which he pledged his loyalty to the requirements of the Law of Moses for human kingship (cf. Deut. 17:14-20).

11:4-9. David next **marched to Jerusalem, that is, Jebus** (cf. Josh. 18:16, 28; Jud. 19:10-11), centrally and neutrally located between Israel and Judah, which he proceeded to conquer and occupy. This was possible because **Joab** breached the walls of the Jebusite fortress, possibly by locating the water tunnel and gaining entrance thereby (cf. 2 Sam. 5:8). **The fortress of Zion** was evidently a hill overlooking the Jebusite **city** which **David** added to the original settlement. He himself **took up residence** on Zion (1 Chron. 11:5, 7) and extended the whole city north to the terraces, encompassing the entirety with walls. This **was called the City of David** (cf. 2 Sam. 5:7, 9; 6:12; 1 Kings 2:10). **The supporting terraces** (1 Chron. 11:8) is literally, "the Millo"

(NIV marg.). This Hebrew word means "filling," so this may have been the area between the two hills (Jebus and Zion) which was filled in to level the whole city. The chronicler's account of the capture of Jerusalem singles out **Joab** as the hero, a point not made in 2 Samuel. This assured Joab the position of **commander-in-chief** (1 Chron. 11:6).

11:10-14. The narrator then introduced the rest **of David's mighty men.** First, Joab and three others—**Jashobeam . . . Eleazar** (vv. 11-12), and Shammah (2 Sam. 23:11)—comprised the inner circle of the commander and three mighty men. Joab was David's nephew, son of his half sister Zeruiah (cf. 1 Chron. 2:16; also cf. 18:15; 26:28; 27:24). Jashobeam, **chief of the officers** (or "chief of 30" [or "of 3"], LXX; cf. NIV marg.) was famous for slaying **300** at once (11:11). Second Samuel 23:8 has 800. The difference may be due to a scribal error in copying Chronicles for the Hebrew numerical symbols 300 and 800 look much alike. Eleazar distinguished himself by defending **Pas Dammim,** with David, against **the Philistines** (1 Chron. 11:12-14). The third great hero, Shammah, is not included in this list; his exploits are recounted in 2 Samuel 23:11-12.

11:15-25. A second group of **three** mighty men is introduced by the story of their risking **their lives** to get **David . . . water** from **Bethlehem** when he was hiding from the **Philistines** at **Adullam.** David was so moved by their self-sacrifice that **he refused to drink** the water; **instead, he poured it out** on the ground as a sacrificial offering. This event, paralleled in 2 Samuel 23:13-17, may have occurred at the time of David's first encounter with the Philistines (2 Sam. 5:17-21) after his capture of Jerusalem.

Abishai . . . brother of Joab (cf. 1 Chron. 2:16) is named among this second group of **three.** Because of his courage in slaying **300** of the enemy he was counted as head of this second group of **three** (11:20-21). Yet he was not promoted to the level of the first **three.**

Benaiah became known because of his slaughter of two mighty Moabites, **a lion** in **a pit,** and **an Egyptian . . . seven and a half feet tall.** Benaiah was put **in charge of** David's **bodyguard** (vv. 22-25). Later Solomon advanced him to Joab's place as commander-in-chief (cf.

1 Kings 2:35).

11:26-47. The list of remaining heroes is nearly identical to the list in 2 Samuel 23:24-39 except for spelling variations and other minor differences. The Chronicles list does, however, include (in 1 Chron. 11:41-47) 16 names after **Uriah the Hittite** which are not in 2 Samuel. If the five named members of the two groups of three (1 Chron. 11:10-14 and vv. 15-25; cf. comments on 2 Chron. 11:10-21) are not counted, the Chronicles list (1 Chron. 11:26-41a) has 30 heroes from **Asahel** (v. 26) through Uriah the Hittite (v. 41a), not counting **the sons of Hashem** (v. 34). "The sons of Hashem" could refer to (a) an undesignated number of unnamed soldiers, (b) the previously listed two or three men (vv. 32b-33), or (c) perhaps to an individual ("the sons of Hashem" could be trans. "Bene-Hashem"). The extra 16 after Uriah, then, are an addendum to the original list. (According to 2 Sam. 23:39 there were 37 men in all. For an explanation of this total, see the comments on 2 Sam. 23:8-39 and the chart "David's Mighty Men" near that passage.)

12:1-7. Most of the mighty men of David listed in 11:26-47 were his fellow tribesmen of Judah. In addition to these, defectors went **to David** from many other tribes. While he was in exile from **Saul** at **Ziklag** (cf. 1 Sam. 27:1-7), David was joined by several of Saul's own kin **from . . . Benjamin.** These 23 **men** are listed in 1 Chronicles 12:3-7.

12:8-18. The next group of men to join David were 11 **Gadites** (vv. 8-15) who lived on the east side of the Jordan (v. 15). They came to David's aid in **his stronghold, in the desert,** apparently during his years of pursuit by Saul. They **crossed the Jordan in the first month,** probably April-May, **when** the river **was overflowing** (cf. Josh. 3:15; 4:19). They were fierce, capable **warriors** (**their faces were the faces of lions**), and amazingly quick-footed (**swift as gazelles**).

With the Gadites came many others from Benjamin and **Judah** (1 Chron. 12:16-17). As their leader **Amasai** said, they knew that **God** was with **David** and would **help** him, so they wished to associate themselves with him (v. 18).

12:19-22. When **David . . . went with the Philistines to** engage Israel in battle at Gilboa (cf. 1 Sam. 28:1-4) some men of Manasseh came to his aid. But along with David they were dismissed from the battlefield lest they would defect to Saul (1 Chron. 12:19). When David returned to Ziklag the seven Manasseh men accompanied him, and even helped him pursue and defeat the Amalekites who had pillaged his town in his absence (cf. 1 Sam. 30).

12:23-40. The chronicler also enumerated the soldiers (many of them brave and experienced) who made up the delegations seeking to encourage David to expand his rule beyond Hebron. They came from Judah . . . Simeon . . . Levi . . . Benjamin . . . Ephraim, western Manasseh . . . Issachar . . . Zebulun . . . Naphtali . . . Dan . . . Asher . . . Reuben, Gad, and eastern Manasseh—a total of well over 300,000 men of war (vv. 23-37). All the tribes were named in order to show that David's support was broad-based, a point not made in 2 Samuel. This point is also made by describing their meeting with David at Hebron as a time of great festivity and joy (1 Chron. 12:38-40).

C. Transporting the ark (chap. 13)

13:1-6. After David had taken Jerusalem from the Jebusites and made it the capital of the then-united Israel and Judah, he was eager to make it the religious center as well. This could not be done, however, till the ark of the covenant was returned to a permanent resting place in Jerusalem. The Philistines had captured the ark at Shiloh (1 Sam. 4:4, 11), exhibited it for several months in Philistia (1 Sam. 6:1), and then returned it to Israel (1 Sam. 6:2-12) where it was housed at Beth Shemesh (1 Sam. 6:13-15) and Kiriath Jearim for about 100 years, from about 1104 to 1003 B.C. (see comments on 1 Sam. 7:2).

Early in David's reign at Jerusalem he commissioned priests and Levites from throughout the land (from the Shihor River, Josh. 13:3; Isa. 23:3; Jer. 2:18, a stream at Israel's southern border at Egypt, to Lebo Hamath; cf. 2 Chron. 7:8, Israel's northern boundary) to bring the ark back from Kiriath Jearim (also called Baalah) to Jerusalem (1 Chron. 13:1-6, see the map "The Wanderings of the Ark of the Covenant" near 1 Sam. 6). The ark was referred to as the ark that is called by the name. This identification of

God's presence with His name was common in later portions of the Old Testament, especially in Chronicles, but was also known in Moses' time (cf. Deut. 12:5, 11, 21; 14:23-24; 16:2, 6, 11; 26:2).

13:7-14. With great pageantry the procession with the ark made its way (vv. 7-8) till it hit a rough place in the road and the cart on which the ark was riding began to jostle and tip. Instinctively Uzzah reached out to keep the ark from falling, and for his sacrilege he was struck dead (vv. 9-10). The reason, of course, was not only the intrinsic holiness of the ark but the fact that it was being transported improperly. The Law of Moses stipulated that the ark was to be carried by the Levites using poles inserted through its corner rings (Ex. 25:13-14; cf. 1 Chron. 15:2, 13, 15).

The impropriety of David's action and its subsequent punishment by the LORD resulted in a delay of three months in the movement of the ark, a time when it was sheltered in the house of a certain Obed-Edom (13:13). Because of its presence God blessed Obed-Edom and his family (v. 14). A proper attitude toward the things of God brings blessing while a cavalier spirit brings divine displeasure.

D. David's establishment in Jerusalem (chaps. 14–16)

1. HIS PALACE (14:1-2)

14:1-2. At about the time David was arranging for the arrival of the ark (chap. 13) he was also undertaking several building projects (15:1). Chief among these was the construction of his own royal palace, a task that was considered essential in the ancient Near East in order to authenticate the reign of a new king. Having entered into a friendly alliance with the Phoenician King Hiram, David engaged him and his artisans in the project of providing cedar logs and doing the work of construction, using skills for which the Phoenicians were famous (cf. 2 Chron. 2:8-9). David recognized that he had been elevated by the LORD to great prominence.

2. HIS FAMILY (14:3-7)

14:3-7. Another symbol of oriental regal splendor was the accumulation of a large harem of wives and concubines. Though the Lord forbade polygamy (cf. Deut. 17:17), David succumbed to the custom of the day. The list of 13 sons here, those born **in Jerusalem,** differs from the list in 2 Samuel 5:14-16 by adding **Elpelet** (spelled Eliphelet in 1 Chron. 3:6) and **Nogah** (14:5-6). These two—Elpelet (alias Eliphelet) and Nogah—are also in the genealogy in 3:5-9 (cf. comments there). In another spelling variation, **Beeliada** in 14:7 is Eliada in 3:8. (Cf. the chart "David's Family" near 2 Sam. 3:2-5.)

3. HIS VICTORIES OVER THE PHILISTINES (14:8-17)

14:8-12. Another evidence of David's newly found power and grandeur was his successful encounter with Israel's perennial enemies, **the Philistines.** When they saw **that David** was no longer a trusted ally or perhaps even a vassal (see comments on 2 Sam. 5:17-25), **the Philistines** attacked Israel in **the Valley of Rephaim,** a few miles southwest of Jerusalem. God gave Israel victory by breaking **out against** the enemy (cf. NIV marg.) like a flood so the battle site became known as **Baal Perazim.** Ironically, more than a century earlier **the Philistines** had captured the ark of the Lord (1 Sam. 4:11), but now in panic they left **their** own idols.

14:13-17. After **the Philistines** were defeated by **David** they did not lose heart altogether; they returned again to Rephaim. This time the Lord instructed David to set an ambush. When Israel would **hear** a **sound of marching in the . . . balsam trees** (i.e., a loud rustling of the leaves) this would be their signal that the Lord was already leading their army into **battle** and they should follow. **David** had such a victory (pursuing the enemy **from Gibeon to Gezer,** about 15 miles) that **all** other **nations** heard of it and feared **him.**

4. ARRIVAL OF THE ARK (CHAP. 15)

15:1-13. At last **David . . . prepared** once more to relocate and house **the ark** of the covenant **in Jerusalem.** Though he planned to place the ark in a substantial temple (17:1-4), for the present he set up **a tent** (15:1), perhaps similar to the Mosaic tabernacle. Then, careful to observe proper protocol (vv. 2, 13, 15), he gathered **the priests** and **Levites** and commanded them to transport **the ark** from the house of Obed-Edom (cf. 13:14) to its new shrine in Jerusalem. The priests

were **Zadok and Abiathar** (15:11; see the chart "The Ancestry of Zadok and Abiathar" near 2 Sam. 8:15-18) and **the Levites** came from the three Levitical families of **Kohath . . . Merari,** and **Gershon** (1 Chron. 15:5-7). They were **Uriel** (vv. 5, 11; cf. 6:24), **Asaiah** (15:6, 11; cf. 6:30), and **Joel** (15:7, 11; cf. Joah, 6:21).

In addition, there were three other **Levites,** all from the family of Kohath. **Shemaiah** was of the clan of **Elizaphan** (15:8, 11; cf. Ex. 6:22), **Eliel** of the clan of **Hebron** (1 Chron. 15:9, 11; cf. Ex. 6:18), and **Amminadab** of the clan of **Uzziel** (1 Chron. 15:10-11; cf. Ex. 6:18). There were thus four Levites of Kohath and one each of the other two branches, plus 862 assistants.

15:14-24. After the prescribed consecration (Num. 8:5-13) all these set about the task of transporting **the ark** (1 Chron. 15:14-15). This included more than merely moving the object, however. It was accompanied by great religious celebration. So **David** ordered the Levitical leaders to **appoint** musicians who would join in the great procession (v. 16). The chief of these were **Heman, son of Joel** (and grandson of Samuel, 6:33), **Asaph,** and **Ethan** (15:17), who sounded **the bronze cymbals.** Eight other musicians (v. 20) played **lyres according to** *alamoth* (probably a musical term; cf. NIV marg. and the title to Ps. 46). Six others (1 Chron. 15:21) played **harps** set to *sheminith* (also a musical term; cf. NIV marg. and title to Ps. 6). **Kenaniah, the head Levite, was in charge of the** vocal music since he had special expertise in that area (1 Chron. 15:22). Four others **were to** protect **the ark,** probably two in front of it (v. 23) and two behind it (v. 24b); between them was a contingent of seven trumpeters (v. 24).

15:25-29. Somewhere in the procession, perhaps at its head, **David** danced (v. 29), **clothed in** the garments of a priest (a **robe of fine linen** and **a linen ephod,** v. 27). **Michal,** his wife, watching **from a window . . . despised him** for she mistook his holy zeal for exhibitionism (cf. comments on 2 Sam. 6:20).

5. APPOINTMENT OF RELIGIOUS PERSONNEL (CHAP. 16)

16:1-6. Having **brought the ark** into **the tent . . . pitched for it** and having completed the sacrifices of **burnt offer-**

ings and fellowship offerings, David blessed the people of Israel and distributed bread and cakes of dates and raisins to each one (vv. 1-3). He then appointed . . . Asaph to be in charge of the ark in its new surroundings (vv. 4-5; cf. v. 37) and to offer prayers and praises to the LORD (v. 5). With Asaph were certain other Levites, all mentioned in 15:17-18, who were to accompany the praises with musical instruments. A model of such praise, a piece undoubtedly composed by David for this occasion, follows (16:8-36).

16:7-36. This hymn of thanksgiving is actually a compilation of passages from other psalms, a fact which suggests the priority of those psalms. David then must have excerpted parts from his earlier poetry and woven them together into this beautiful piece. The parallels are as follows:

1 Chronicles	Psalms
16:8-22	105:1-15
16:23-33	96:1b-13a
16:34-36	106:1b-c, 47-48

For an explanation of the contents of this hymn in 1 Chronicles see the comments on the respective psalms.

16:37-38. Others who served with Asaph included two Obed-Edoms. One (v. 38a) was a musician and minister of the ark (15:21, 24; 16:5), who may be the same man who looked after the ark in his own home (13:14). The other Obed-Edom was a gatekeeper identified as a son of Jeduthun (16:38b); he is also mentioned in 26:4, 8, 15. This Jeduthun should not be confused with the chief musician Jeduthun (16:41-42; 25:1, 3; 2 Chron. 5:12) who was also known as Ethan (1 Chron. 6:44; 15:17) and was a descendant of Merari. The Jeduthun in 16:38, whose son was Obed-Edom, was a descendant of Korah (26:1, 4), a grandson of Kohath.

16:39-43. The reference to Zadok as priest of the tabernacle at Gibeon reveals the reason for the retention of two high priests. Zadok, of the Aaronic line of Eleazar (6:4-8), was in charge of the Gibeon sanctuary, while Abiathar, of the line of Ithamar (24:6), officiated at the new tent-shrine in Jerusalem. The origin of Gibeon as the site of a tabernacle is not known but it must not have been deemed illicit since David appointed Zadok as priest there and later on Solomon

offered sacrifices there with God's approval (cf. 1 Kings 3:4-10). In fact it appears that sometime after the ark was taken from Shiloh the tabernacle was moved also, eventually ending up at Gibeon (1 Chron. 21:29). Zadok thus was ministering at the original Mosaic house of worship. While Asaph was with Abiathar in David's tabernacle which housed the ark, Heman and Jeduthun (also called Ethan; cf. 6:44; 15:17) functioned with Zadok at the original Mosaic tabernacle of Gibeon.

E. David's desire for a temple (chap. 17)

17:1-15. After David's palace was completed and he was living comfortably in it, he was struck by the disparity of his sturdy surroundings and the relatively flimsy temporality of the tent for the ark. Expressing a desire to provide the Lord with a temple (suggested by the word house, v. 4), David found Nathan the prophet to be encouraging at first (v. 2). But after the Lord appeared to Nathan in a dream and forbade such a project, David learned that God would build a house for David instead! (v. 10; cf. vv. 25, 27) "House" here means dynasty.

The divine message to David through Nathan is almost identical here in its wording to 2 Samuel 7:1-17 (see comments there). Whereas 2 Samuel 7:15 refers to Saul by name, the chronicler simply called him David's predecessor (1 Chron. 17:13). This may reflect a certain abhorrence toward Saul on the chronicler's part. (For the content of Nathan's message, vv. 4-14, see comments on 2 Sam. 7:4-17.)

17:16-27. David's prayer of response to the covenant promise is also virtually the same in Chronicles and Samuel (cf. 2 Sam. 7:18-29). Notable in Chronicles is an emphasis on David's exalted position (1 Chron. 17:17), a theme which is in keeping with the general tenor of the book. (For the content of David's prayer, vv. 16-27, see comments on 2 Sam. 7:18-29.)

F. David's foreign affairs (18:1–20:8)

1. THE PHILISTINES AND MOABITES (18:1-2)

18:1-2. The chronicler, like the author of Samuel (2 Sam. 8:1), put the Philistines at the head of his list of peoples conquered by David. The reference to Gath may indicate the limit of David's conquest, and perhaps suggests that the enigmatic "Metheg Ammah" in 2 Samuel 8:1 is another name for Gath.

The description of Moab's defeat is much milder in tone than that in 2 Samuel 8:2. The chronicler merely mentioned that Moab became a vassal state, whereas Samuel spoke of David's systematic slaughter of two thirds of the population. The reason may be the chronicler's overall purpose to extol the Davidic dynasty, the roots of which are at least partially found in Moab with his great-grandmother Ruth (Ruth 4:13, 21).

2. THE ARAMEANS (18:3-11)

18:3-11. The chronicler's narrative of David's dealings with **the Arameans** of **Zobah** (vv. 3-4), **Damascus** (vv. 5-8), and **Hamath** (vv. 9-11) is in all essentials the same as that in 2 Samuel 8:3-12. (See comments on 2 Sam. 8:4 for an explanation of the differences in numbers in that verse and those in 1 Chron. 18:4.) The cities belonging to **Hadadezer** ("Hadarezer" in Heb.) were called **Tebah** ("Betah" in Heb., a variant spelling; cf. NIV marg.) and **Berothai**. Apparently then David took bronze from three cities: Tebah (also known as Tibhath), **Cun,** and Berothai. Tou's **son Hadoram** is spelled Joram in 2 Samuel 8:10. David **dedicated . . . to the LORD** (for the temple construction) the wealth acquired from the **nations** he conquered (cf. 2 Sam. 8:7-13; 1 Chron. 22:14; 26:26; 29:2-5).

3. THE EDOMITES (18:12-13)

18:12-13. In his recounting of the Edomite conquest, the chronicler gave credit for its success to David's nephew **Abishai** (**Zeruiah** was a half sister of David, 2:16), who killed 18,000 Edomites, rather than to David himself (cf. 2 Sam. 8:13). This is unusual in that the chronicler generally promoted **David** rather than his underlings. **The Valley of Salt** is evidently in **Edom,** near the Dead Sea.

The superscription to Psalm 60 states, on the other hand, that *Joab,* Abishai's brother, killed *12,000* Edomites in the Valley of Salt. Perhaps this difference is explainable by noting that the entire campaign was under Abishai's direct command, and that Joab was responsible (with the soldiers in his contingency) for killing two thirds of the Edomites.

4. THE ROYAL ADMINISTRATION (18:14-17)

18:14-17. Possibly Abishai (rather than David) was mentioned in verse 12 because the chronicler was about to list other figures prominent in David's administration. **Shavsa** (v. 16) is spelled Seraiah in 2 Samuel 8:17. **David's sons,** his **chief officials** (*rî'šônîm,* "chief ones"), are called royal advisers in 2 Samuel 8:18 (see comments there).

5. THE AMMONITES (19:1–20:3)

19:1-5. The war with **the Ammonites** was introduced by the chronicler the same way it was introduced in 2 Samuel—the **king** of Ammon had **died** and **David** had **sent a delegation** to comfort the king's **son** and successor, **Hanun** (1 Chron. 19:1-2; cf. 2 Sam. 10:1-2). But David's messengers were humiliated by the Ammonites, with the result that they returned to Israel in embarrassing ignominy (1 Chron. 19:3-5).

19:6-7. The ensuing account of the preparations for war and the battle itself differs in several ways from the details of wording and fact in 2 Samuel 10. The chronicler mentioned that **Hanun** hired the Arameans of Mesopotamia (**Aram Naharaim**), **Aram Maacah, and Zobah** for **1,000 talents of silver** (ca. 37 tons; cf. NIV marg.), while 2 Samuel 10:6-7 lists Arameans of Beth Rehob, Zobah, Maacah, and Tob. There is no contradiction here; the two historians merely mentioned those Arameans of special interest to them, for whatever reason. Likewise, the Samuel report omits the information about the price paid to the mercenaries. The chronicler also pointed out that the total Aramean chariot force consisted of **32,000** units (1 Chron. 19:7), but the author of 2 Samuel gave the number of infantrymen ("foot soldiers"), which was 33,000 (2 Sam. 10:6).

19:8-19. The account of the strategy for preparation is practically the same in 2 Samuel and 1 Chronicles. **The Ammonites** guarded the gate of **their** capital **city** (Rabbah; cf. 20:1) and the Arameans took to the surrounding fields (**the open country**). This meant that **Joab,** David's commander, would have to defeat the Arameans on the outer perimeter before he could even get close to the Ammonites themselves. In order to effect this, **Joab** divided his **troops** into two units, one of which he led **against the**

Arameans and the other he entrusted to his brother **Abishai** to engage **the Ammonites** (19:10-11). After agreeing to come to each other's aid if need be (v. 12), Joab and Abishai undertook the campaign. Confident in **the LORD** (v. 13), they achieved success. **The Arameans** were routed, and **the Ammonites** retreated to the security of the fortifications of their **city,** Rabbah (vv. 14-16).

Meantime **the Arameans** called for reinforcements from across the Euphrates **(the River)** and with **Shophach** (spelled Shobach in 2 Sam. 10:15) as their leader engaged David's troops at Helam (2 Sam. 10:16-17) in the Transjordan. Again **David** was victorious, killing **7,000** . . . **charioteers** (cf. comments on 2 Sam. 10:18), **40,000** infantrymen, and **Shopach** himself (1 Chron. 19:16-18). This squelched any further desire of **the Arameans** to confront **David;** in fact the Arameans made themselves **vassals** to Israel (v. 19).

20:1-3. **The Ammonites** remained in **Rabbah** until the next **spring** when **Joab** once again took up the siege of the city. The chronicler wrote that **David remained in Jerusalem** and in line with his overall design wrote nothing of David's adulterous and murderous activities (cf. 2 Sam. 11:2–12:25). Reasons for the omission of the stories of Bathsheba and Uriah are discussed in the *Introduction*. Chronicles also omitted the report of how **David,** who **took** the great **crown** of **gold** (weighing ca. 75 pounds) from the Ammonite king, happened to be at Rabbah. (The words **their** king could also be trans. "of Milcom," the name of the Ammonite god; cf. NIV marg.) According to 2 Samuel 12:26-29, after Joab had taken the city's water supply, he invited David to come and personally lead the attack on the citadel or inner fortification. Having captured the city, David reduced its population to slave **labor** involving **saws** . . . **picks** . . . **axes,** and brickmaking (cf. 2 Sam. 12:31). Thus the Ammonites also came under David's authority.

6. THE PHILISTINES (20:4-8)

The chronicler's record of David's conquests begins and ends with references to wars against the Philistines (18:1; 20:4-8). Israel had no more inveterate and persistent foe than the Philistines and Israel was never able to dominate

them completely.

The author of 2 Samuel also recounted the series of Philistine wars (2 Sam. 21:15-22) but placed his record several chapters after the Ammonite wars narrative (2 Sam. 10–12). He had at least two reasons for this: (1) He first discussed in detail the involved stories of David's personal and family tragedies which befell him because of his affair with Bathsheba (2 Sam. 13:1–21:14), none of which occupied the interest of the chronicler. (2) In 2 Samuel 22–23 are David's hymn of praise and his catalog of heroes, many of whom were prominent in the Philistine hostilities. It may well be then that the Philistine war annals (2 Sam. 21:15-22) were placed immediately before 2 Samuel 22–23 because they dealt with a common theme. Also Chronicles treats the Philistine campaigns more briefly than 2 Samuel. For example, the latter refers to David's hand-to-hand fight with the giant Ishbi-Benob (2 Sam. 21:15-17), in which David nearly lost his life and was then advised by Abishai not to take part in further combat. But the chronicler passed over that episode. Perhaps he did so because of his interest in emphasizing the positive aspects of David's reign, a pervasive theme in his writings.

20:4-5. Chronicles includes three instances paralleled in 2 Samuel 21:18-22, though with some differences. First was the battle of **Gezer** (Gob in 2 Sam. 21:18), 20 miles northwest of Jerusalem, in which **Sibbecai** (cf. 1 Chron. 11:29) slew **Sippai,** a Philistine giant. Next **Elhanan son of Jair** slew **Lahmi,** Goliath's **brother** (20:5). In 2 Samuel 21:19 Elhanan is identified as the son of Jaare-Oregim of Bethlehem. This is no problem, however, because Jair may be identified with Jaare-Oregim; the latter name may actually be translated "Jair the weaver" (cf. NIV marg.; 2 Sam. 21:19). But in 2 Samuel 21:19 Elhanan is said to have slain Goliath, not Lahmi. A further complication is introduced by the reference in 1 Chronicles 11:26 to a certain "Elhanan son of Dodo from Bethlehem." Since nothing more is known of this Elhanan one may assume he is different from Elhanan son of Jaare-Oregim.

The major problem of harmonization between 2 Samuel 21:19 and 1 Chronicles 20:5 has to do with who was slain. Was Lahmi slain or was it his brother Goliath?

It is common knowledge that David himself killed Goliath (1 Sam. 17), so some scholars suggest that Elhanan was none other than David. According to this view, David killed *both* Goliath (2 Sam. 21:19) and the brother of Goliath (1 Chron. 20:5). However, there is no evidence that David was also known as Elhanan or is it possible to equate Jesse, David's father, with Jair or Jaare-Oregim. Much more likely is the probability that the original manuscript of 2 Samuel 21:19 read "the brother of Goliath" and that in scribal transmission the words "the brother of" were somehow omitted.

20:6-8. The third Philistine war narrative reveals that a mutant Philistine giant met death at the hands of **David's** nephew **Jonathan** (cf. 2 Sam. 21:20-21). There follows a succinct summary of the defeat of the Philistines, epitomized in the deaths of **descendants of Rapha** (1 Chron. 20:8). Rapha was the ancestral father of a race of giants, known as Rephaites, who coexisted with the early Philistines and perhaps even intermarried with them (cf. Gen. 14:5; Deut. 2:11, 20; 3:11; 1 Chron. 20:4).

G. David's census and the Lord's punishment (21:1–22:1)

21:1-7. The chronicler did not state David's motivation for taking **a census of Israel** except to say **Satan . . . incited** him to do so and David wanted to **know how many . . . fighting men** there were. In 2 Samuel 24:1, however, the historian revealed that the Lord was angry with His people and used David's census as an occasion to punish him and them. No contradiction is here for the Lord simply let Satan tempt David to undertake the census, much as He permitted Satan to attack Job (cf. Job 1:12 and comments on 2 Sam. 24:1-3). In His sovereignty God's ultimate authority extends even to the workings of Satan. David's immediate purpose was to assess his military strength (1 Chron. 21:5). This incurred divine displeasure because it suggested that he was relying more on military capabilities than on God's power. Probably that is why David admitted that his action was sin (v. 8).

Joab, despite his objections to David's edict (v. 3), had to undertake the census (v. 4) and reported the totals of **1,100,000 men** of Israel and **470,000** of **Judah** (v. 5). **Joab did not** count the Levites or Benjamites, however, since **Levi** could not participate militarily (cf. Num. 1:47-49) and the attempt to complete the census was frustrated apparently before **Benjamin** could be counted (cf. 1 Chron. 27:24). Also David's command was repulsive to Joab (21:6). The Samuel account indicates that 800,000 combat troops were available in Israel and 500,000 in Judah (2 Sam. 24:9). The NIV suggests that the 1,100,000 (**in all Israel**) *included* the 470,000 of Judah (1 Chron. 21:5), thus giving a total of 630,000 for Israel proper. The 800,000 of 2 Samuel 24:9 might then include an *estimate* of 170,000 Levites plus 630,000 other Israelites, though such a large number of Levites is difficult to imagine. The 500,000 Judeans of 2 Samuel could also include an *estimated* 30,000 Benjamites who were not counted by the chronicler.

Another possible solution (cf. comments on 2 Sam. 24:9) is that the chronicler's grand total of 1,100,000 included a standing army of 300,000, thus reducing the total to 800,000 given in 2 Samuel. Also the 500,000 Judeans (in the 2 Sam. account) may have included the 470,000 of 1 Chronicles along with a standing army of 30,000 (2 Sam. 6:1).

21:8-15a. At some point **David** realized the evil of his project and sought the Lord's forgiveness. This no doubt was granted but the purposes of **the LORD** had to be served—**Israel** had to be chastened. So the message came **to David** through the Prophet **Gad** that David was to **choose one of** three judgments **God** would bring on the people. There could be **three years of famine,** or **three months of** pursuit by the enemy, or **three days of** direct divine retribution by a **plague** (vv. 11-12).

Rather than choosing one of the three options, **David** placed himself in God's **hands,** who then destroyed **70,000 men** by **a plague.** Satisfied, **the LORD** turned from His judgment.

21:15b-25. The Angel of the LORD, elsewhere identified with God Himself, was probably the preincarnate Christ (cf. Gen. 16:13; 18:1-2; 22:11-12; 48:16; Jud. 6:16, 22; 13:22-23; Zech. 3:1; cf. comments on Gen. 16:7). He appeared to David near **the threshing floor of Araunah** (cf. 2 Sam. 24:16; the Heb. in 1 Chron. 21:15

has the variant spelling Ornan; cf. NIV marg.) **with a . . . sword in His hand. David and the elders** repented publicly and **David** pleaded that the rest of the **people** might be spared and that further punishment be meted only to him and his **family.**

The **Angel** then commanded **Gad to tell David to . . . build an altar . . . on the threshing floor** so he might offer appropriate propitiatory sacrifices. To do this it was necessary to acquire the threshing floor from **Araunah,** a **Jebusite** who lived just north of Jerusalem. Meanwhile **Araunah** had seen the **Angel** (v. 20) so when **David approached** him **Araunah . . . bowed down** and offered to **give the threshing floor** to David without price (vv. 21, 23). **David** refused his kind offer, however, and insisted that he could not offer anything to **the LORD** that had cost him **nothing** (vv. 22, 24). So the king **paid Araunah 600 shekels of gold** (ca. 15 pounds). However, according to 2 Samuel 24:24 David paid a much smaller amount (50 shekels of silver, ca. 1¼ pounds). This problem is explained by noting that the silver paid for the threshing floor and oxen (2 Sam. 24:24) and that the gold paid **for the site,** a large plot of ground apparently adjacent to the threshing floor.

21:26–22:1. After David **built the altar** he **offered** up **burnt offerings and fellowship offerings,** the former to plead God's forgiveness of his sin and the latter to speak of the renewal of unbroken covenant relationship which would follow. God's response was favorable as indicated by His answering **with fire from heaven.**

It was too late to save the 70,000 who had perished (21:14) but Jerusalem itself was spared by David's intercession (v. 27; cf. v. 16).

The chronicler noted that **David** took this response from **the LORD** as a sign that that place was now one of special significance. As a result he began to worship there regularly instead of going to **Gibeon** where the Mosaic **tabernacle** was located (cf. 16:39). **David** did not go to Gibeon, the historian says, **because he was afraid of the sword of the Angel of the LORD** (21:30). This probably means that David, as a result of this whole experience, now knew that Araunah's threshing floor, not Gibeon, was God's choice

for the location of central worship. This is confirmed by the next verse (22:1): **David** solemnly proclaimed that this new site would now be **the house of the LORD.** When Solomon later built the temple it was on this same piece of land (cf. 2 Chron. 3:1), a place hallowed also because it was the Mount Moriah on which Abraham offered to sacrifice his son (Gen. 22).

H. David's plans for a temple (22:2-19)

The plan and purpose of the chronicler are both clear in this passage. He had preceded his narrative on David's intention to build a temple by telling the story of the acquisition of its site (21:1–22:1). Now the chronicler stressed David's importance in connection with the temple by elaborating on the king's desire to build a temple and establish a systematic program of worship. Samuel's version mentioned only David's wish to build a temple (2 Sam. 7:2, 5) and left the matter once David's request had been denied. Even 1 Kings is silent about any further steps David might have taken to prepare Solomon for the construction of a temple. But the chronicler, while not denying the fact that God said David was not to build the temple (1 Chron. 17:4-12), was aware that David was permitted to prepare plans and materials for the project. There follows then a description of these steps.

22:2-5. David first selected **stone-cutters** from among **the aliens** of the land to quarry and prepare stones for the temple (**the house of God**). These aliens may have included Phoenicians as they were particularly adept at masonry. In addition, **iron-** and **bronze-**workers undertook the manufacture of **nails** and other metal **fittings.** Also David secured a countless number of **cedar logs** from Lebanon. He made all these **preparations,** he said, because his **son Solomon** was so **young** (cf. 29:1) he did not have the expertise necessary to provide a temple suitable for the great God of Israel.

22:6-10. When all was ready David **called . . . his son** and told him that it had been his own desire **to build** the **house** of the **LORD** but **the LORD** had forbidden it because David was a man of war. In the eyes of God the shedding of **blood** in war was incompatible with building a place of worship. It was therefore to be left to **Solomon, a man of peace**

(whose name is related to the word for "peace"), to oversee the actual building. Remarkably the Lord, through David, said that Solomon would be His **son** and that Solomon's dynasty (i.e., his **kingdom**) would last **forever** (cf. 28:7). The kings of the Davidic dynasty as sons of God in a special sense is an important theme in the Bible. Psalm 2, for example, refers to the king ("His anointed," Ps. 2:2) as God's son (Ps. 2:7). And the author of Hebrews, citing Psalm 2, applied it to Jesus Christ (Heb. 1:5; 5:5). The Davidic kings were not only physical ancestors of Christ but also their role as "sons of God" prepared the way for the concept of Jesus' divine sonship.

22:11-16. David then charged Solomon to obey in the matter of the temple and to **keep the Law of the Lord** in every way. To do so would bring blessing (**success**, v. 13). Finally David pointed out to Solomon the extent of David's preparation. The king had accumulated **100,000 talents of gold** (3,750 tons) and 1 **million talents of silver** (37,500 tons)—together, 41,250 tons (or 82½ million pounds)—a staggering amount of weight and value! Probably this accumulation was largely plunder from conquering surrounding nations (2 Sam. 8:7-13; 1 Chron. 18:11). David had also gathered tradesmen skilled in **every** necessary **kind of work.** All that was needed was for Solomon to **begin the work.**

22:17-19. Turning to **the leaders of** the nation, **David** instructed them to seek **the Lord** and also to assist Solomon in every way **to build** the temple (**the sanctuary of the Lord**) and place within it the holy **ark** which symbolized the presence of **God.**

I. David's theocratic organization (chaps. 23–27)

1. THE LEVITES IN GENERAL (CHAPS. 23–24)

23:1-6. At the end of David's life, after he had already effectively turned the reins of government over to **Solomon** (v. 1), he undertook the task of organizing and ensuring the perpetuation of a religious and political structure that would best meet the nation's needs. David took a count of **the Levites** from **30 years** of age (the legal age for their ministry; cf. Num. 4:3) upward. The total of **38,000** was then divided into **24,000** for **the work of the temple . . . 6,000** as officials and judges . . . **4,000** as **gatekeepers,** and **4,000** musicians (1 Chron. 23:3-5). Each of these was in turn **divided . . . into groups** according to their familial descent from **Levi** (v. 6).

23:7-11. The list of **Gershonites** begins with the sons of Gershon, **Ladan** ("Libni" in 6:17) **and Shimei.** The names that follow were not immediate descendants but were men in David's time who sprang from these two branches and became leaders of the various Levitical groups. The **Shimei** in 23:9 is not the same as the Shimei in verses 7 and 10. The summary statement in verse 9b makes this clear (vv. 8-9 list the descendants of **Ladan,** not Ladan's brother). The line of Ladan, then, produced a total of six leaders. Three were traced directly to Ladan (v. 8) and three others were through a Ladanite descendant, Shimei (v. 9).

Shimei, son of Gershon (v. 7), gave rise to **four** leaders (v. 10), but since the second two (**Jeush and Beriah**) had small families they combined to make **one** group (v. 11).

23:12-20. One of Kohath's descendants (**Amram**) fathered **Aaron and Moses** (see comments on Num. 27:57-65). **Aaron,** of course, **was set apart** for priestly service (v. 13) but Moses' descendants were limited to lesser Levitical duties (v. 14). Through Moses' two sons **Gershom and Eliezer** arose leaders such as **Shubael** (v. 16) and **Rehabiah** (v. 17).

A second son of Kohath, **Izhar,** was the source of the line which produced **Shelomith** (v. 18). A third son, **Hebron,** sired four Levitical leaders (v. 19). Kohath's last son, **Uzziel,** fathered the line of **Micah** and **Isshiah** (v. 20).

23:21-32. As for Levi's third son, **Merari,** his two sons, **Mahli and Mushi,** gave rise, respectively, to **Eleazar and Kish** on the one hand (vv. 21-22) and to **Mahli, Eder, and Jeremoth** on the other (v. 23). The chronicler concluded the lists by reiterating David's purposes in allocating the Levites' assignments. Since these purposes presupposed a much larger ecclesiastical burden, David lowered the age of Levitical service to **20** from the previously designated 30 (vv. 24, 27; cf. v. 3). This would permit many more men to function.

The Levites' principal tasks were to assist the priests (**Aaron's descendants**) in the **temple** precincts (v. 28), to prepare the **bread** of the Presence and **grain offerings** (v. 29), and **to thank and praise** God at the times of **burnt** offerings (vv. 30-31).

24:1-3. To implement the foregoing plan, David enlisted **Zadok** and **Ahimelech,** the two chief **priests,** to help him divide first the priests and then the Levites **into** the **divisions** in which they would serve. As the chronicler pointed out, Zadok was **a descendant of** Aaron's son **Eleazar** and Ahimelech (son of Abiathar; cf. v. 6) descended from Aaron's son **Ithamar** (v. 3). (On the death of **Nadab and Abihu** see Lev. 10.) Though it is impossible elsewhere to establish Ahimelech's descent from Ithamar, it is interesting to note that Ahimelech was a direct successor of Eli, the high priest during Samuel's childhood. (According to 1 Sam. 22:9, 11, 20 Ahimelech was son of Ahitub, son of Phinehas, son of Eli.)

24:4-5. Since there were more **descendants** of **Eleazar** than of **Ithamar,** the result of the apportionment was **16** divisions of the former and **8** of the latter. By having 24 divisions, each would serve about two weeks a year. Gradually then, their service would move around the calendar. The phrase **officials of the sanctuary and officials of God** can be rendered "officials of the sanctuary, that is, officials of God," to distinguish them from civil officials.

24:6-19. The priests' and Levites' **names** were recorded by **the scribe Shemaiah . . . in the presence of** David and the kingdom rulers. **Zadok** and **Ahimelech** were listed first and then their **family** members, descendants of **Eleazar** and of **Ithamar,** were listed (vv. 7-18) in an apparently alternating fashion (v. 6b). These are names of individuals, but they also became attached to the divisions which they founded. For example, **Jehoiarib** and **Jedaiah** (v. 7) are also listed among those who returned from the Babylonian Exile (9:10; cf. Neh. 7:39). Zechariah, father of John the Baptist, was from the division of **Abijah** (1 Chron. 24:10; cf. Luke 1:5). Most of the remaining names are nowhere else attested as priests.

24:20-31. The Levites who were not priests were divided into ministering groups. Their roster begins with **Amram** and his descendant **Shubael** (v. 20), and

Shubael's descendant **Jehdeiah.** The second Amramite was **Rehabiah** and his son **Isshiah** (v. 21; cf. 23:16-20). The **sons of** Izhar were listed next (24:22; cf. 23:18), then those **of Hebron** (24:23; cf. 23:19), and of **Uzziel** (24:24-25; cf. 23:20). These were all Kohathites (cf. 23:12).

The chronicler next listed the line **of Merari,** third son of Levi (24:26-30). The names are the same as those in 23:21-23 except for the addition of **Jerahmeel** to **Kish** (24:29) and an entirely new line— that of **Jaaziah** (vv. 26-27). For some unknown reason the Gershonite line is omitted though it was given in 23:7-11. By means of **lots** the various divisions undertook their service (24:31; cf. v. 5; Luke 1:9) so that all were **treated** alike in the kinds of service they rendered (cf. 1 Chron. 23:28-32).

2. THE LEVITICAL MUSICIANS (CHAP. 25)

25:1. The temple ministry of vocal and instrumental music had previously been assigned to **Asaph, Heman, and Jeduthun** (also known as Ethan; cf. 15:17, 19), but chapter 25 lists the names of their kin who performed this ministry with them and those who succeeded them. It is called a **ministry of prophesying** (25:1) which no doubt meant a sort of musical proclamation of divine revelation and expressions of hymnic praise and worship (cf. 1 Sam. 10:5; 2 Kings 3:15). Their appointment by **David** and the military **commanders** perhaps suggests a close connection between the religious and military establishments. This may suggest overtones of the ancient concept of holy war in which music and the ark of the Lord accompanied His armies in battle (cf. Josh. 6:1-11).

25:2-31. The sons of Asaph are listed in verses 2, 9a, 10-11, 14 (**Jesarelah,** v. 14, is another spelling for **Asarelah,** v. 2; cf. NIV marg. for v. 14). With their **sons and relatives** they made up 4 of the 24 divisions of musicians. The **sons** of **Jeduthun** (v. 3) with their **sons and relatives,** constituted 6 divisions (vv. 9b, 11 [**Izri** is spelled **Zeri** in v. 3; cf. NIV marg. for v. 11], 15, 17, 19, 21). The **sons** of **Heman** (v. 4) consisted of 14 divisions in all, each of whom is named in the list of lots (vv. 13, 16, 18 [**Azarel** is a variant of **Uzziel** in v. 4; cf. NIV marg. for v. 18], 20, 22-31). The 24 divisions, each with 12 men, totaled **288** men (v. 7). The appointments of specific responsibilities by **lots** guaranteed that there would be no favoritism in assigning **their duties** (v. 8).

3. THE LEVITICAL GATEKEEPERS (26:1-19)

26:1-3. The **gatekeepers** were evidently closely related to the musicians in function since they too were affiliated with **Asaph.** The first major division was that of **Meshelemiah** (vv. 1-3), whose seven sons are said to be **Korahites,** that is, descendants of Korah, son of Izhar, son of Kohath, son of Levi (cf. Ex. 6:16, 18, 21). Meshelemiah himself was a **son of Kore, one of** Asaph's **sons.** On the other hand since Asaph is elsewhere (1 Chron. 6:39-43) listed as a descendant of Gershon (Kohath's brother), it may be better to understand Asaph here as a shorter form of Ebiasaph, the spelling given in 9:19 (and spelled Abiasaph in Ex. 6:24).

26:4-5. The second division was that of the family of **Obed-Edom.** The statement that **God had blessed Obed-Edom** seems to identify him with the Obed-Edom who had sheltered the ark in his house and was blessed by God for so doing (13:14). However, as suggested earlier (see comments on 16:38), the Obed-Edom who protected the ark went on to be a minister before the ark in the temple. Obed-Edom the gatekeeper of this present passage must be the Obed-Edom of 16:38 who is identified as a son of Jeduthun.

The observation that Jeduthun (also called Ethan) was a descendant of Merari (6:44-47) and the fact that Obed-Edom here (26:4) was of the line of Kohath raises no difficulty if Obed-Edom the gatekeeper was the son of a different Jeduthun. There were, then, Obed-Edom the musician and minister of the ark (13:14; 15:21; 16:38a) and Obed-Edom the regular gatekeeper (16:38b; 26:4, 8, 15). Apparently the first Obed-Edom was also an occasional gatekeeper (15:18) or doorkeeper (15:24; cf. 16:4-5).

26:6-11. The third division of gatekeepers consisted of a subdivision of the family of Obed-Edom headed by **Shemaiah.** All three divisions of the Kohathite branch of Levites totaled 80 persons (vv. 8-9). **The Merarite** branch was represented by **Hosah** and his family which provided **13** men. In all, therefore, there were three Kohathite divisions (vv. 2-3,

9, 4-5, 6-8) and one of Merari (vv. 10-11).

26:12-19. All these **gatekeepers** were assigned their stations by **lots** (v. 13) as were the musicians and other priests and Levites (24:5, 31; 25:8). **The East Gate** became the responsibility of the family of **Shelemiah** (the same as Meshelemiah, 26:1). **His son Zechariah** manned the **North Gate** (v. 14). **The South Gate** and **storehouse** fell by **lot** to **Obed-Edom** and **his sons** (v. 15). Finally **the West Gate** and **Shalleketh Gate** (otherwise unknown) were presided over by **Shuppim and Hosah** (v. 16). The meaning of Shuppim is unclear since, as a personal name, it appears only here and in 7:12 ("Shuppites," clearly not relevant to 26:16). There were to be 22 gatekeepers in all at any one time (vv. 17-18), though certainly this means leaders only (cf. v. 12) for there were 4,000 gatekeepers altogether (cf. 23:5).

4. THE LEVITICAL TREASURERS (26:20-28)

26:20-25. As noted in the NIV margin, the words **Their fellow Levites were** come from the Septuagint. The Hebrew reads, "As for the Levites, Ahijah was." This makes good sense and should be followed here. Admittedly the name Ahijah does not occur elsewhere in chapters 23–26 and he is not otherwise identified, but this is insufficient grounds for rejecting the Hebrew text in favor of the Septuagint. Ahijah, then, was **in charge of** all **the treasuries of the** temple. The treasuries consisted of the revenues from tithes, offerings, and other sources which were presented to the Lord by His people (cf. Ezra 2:69).

The management **of the treasuries** was the responsibility of (a) Levites descended from Gershon, son of Levi, through the line **of Ladan** (also spelled Libni; cf. Ex. 6:17; 1 Chron. 6:17) and headed by the family of **Jehieli** (26:21-22), and (b) Levites descended from Kohath (the clans of which are listed in v. 23; cf. 23:12) through the line **of Moses** and headed by **Shubael** and his descendants (26:24-25; cf. 23:16).

26:26-28. The portion of the treasury which had accumulated through military **plunder** (v. 27) and the other special dedicatory offerings of **David** (v. 26), **Samuel . . . Saul . . . Abner,** and **Joab** (v. 28) was under the jurisdiction **of Shelomith,** a descendant of Moses' second son

Eliezer (v. 25; cf. 23:17 [the Shelomith in 23:18 was not the Shelomith of 26:25]).

5. THE LEVITICAL ADMINISTRATORS (26:29-32)

26:29-32. The Amramites were over the treasury, as verses 23-28 indicate, but their brethren **the Izharites** provided external leadership; that is, they were charged with duties in outlying areas **away from the temple** (v. 29). Descendants of Hebron, the third son of Kohath, were also assigned to such work throughout the kingdom: **1,700** of their number, under **Hashabiah**, served in the Western tribes (v. 30) while **2,700** more, under **Jerijah**, were in Transjordania (vv. 31-32). The implementation of this arrangement took place in David's **40th** (and last) **year.** The 6,000 officials and judges of 23:4 may be the 1,700 and 2,700 "external" Levites (26:30, 32) plus the Levites in charge of the temple treasuries (vv. 20-22).

6. THE MILITARY AND POLITICAL STRUCTURE (CHAP. 27)

27:1-15. David's organization of the army of Israel consisted of 12 **divisions** of **24,000 men** each, each division serving on active **duty** one **month** each **year.** It is impossible to determine the geographic entities involved but perhaps the monthly musters corresponded roughly to tribal patterns (cf. 1 Kings 4:7-19). Most of the names of David's divisional commanders appear in the lists of his heroes. The prowess of **Jashobeam** (1 Chron. 27:2), a Judean (**descendant of Perez,** v. 3), was described in 11:11 (cf. 2 Sam. 23:8, NIV marg.). **Dodai** was father of Eleazar, a mighty man (1 Chron. 11:12). Dodai's assistant was **Mikloth** (1 Chron. 27:4). **Benaiah,** assisted by his son **Ammizabad** (27:5-6), was a famous warrior of the "second three" (11:22-25) and **was over the Thirty.** Asahel, of course, was David's own nephew and Joab's **brother** (27:7; cf. 11:26). **Shamhuth** (spelled Shammoth in 11:27) was in charge on **the fifth month.** Ira (27:9) of Tekoa also was listed in 11:28.

Helez . . . an Ephraimite (27:10), was listed only as a **Pelonite** earlier (11:27). **Sibbecai** (27:11) was also a Judean (Zerah, cf. v. 13, was a son of Judah; cf. 2:4) and is on the hero list (11:29). **Abiezer** (27:12), **a Benjamite** of the village of Anathoth (cf. Jer. 1:1), is also

mentioned in 1 Chronicles 11:28. **Maharai** (27:13), another Judean descended from Zerah (cf. v. 11), is in 11:30. **Benaiah the Pirathonite** (27:14), not to be confused with the Benaiah of verse 5, is listed in 11:31. Finally, **Heled,** a descendant of Israel's first judge **Othniel** (27:15), was commander of the **12th** division. His connection with Othniel is not mentioned in the hero lists (11:30; cf. 2 Sam. 23:29, where his name is spelled Heldai).

27:16-24. The officials **over the tribes** may have been of a quasi-military nature. Most of these leaders are mentioned only here, though **Zadok** (v. 17) and **Elihu** (v. 18; called Eliab in 1 Sam. 16:6) are well known elsewhere. Conspicuous by their omission are the tribes of Gad and Asher. The ideal total of 12 tribes survives, however, by the inclusion of **Levi** (1 Chron. 27:17) and two parts **of Manasseh,** east and west (vv. 20-21). Having given the roster of tribal **officers** the chronicler again mentioned David's ill-conceived census, a tabulation that remained incomplete because of the Lord's obvious displeasure (vv. 23-24; cf. 21:2-5). Having counted only **the men** of military age, **David** left off and once again trusted in the hand of God to bring deliverance. (On **the book of the annals of King David,** see comments on 1 Kings 14:19.)

27:25-34. This final list records the names of supervisors over various aspects of David's bureaucracy. **Azmaveth** was over the king's **storehouses** in Jerusalem while **Jonathan** oversaw royal assets elsewhere (v. 25). **Ezri** was in charge of farm labor (v. 26), **Shimei** of **the vineyards** (v. 27), **Zabdi** of the vintage (v. 27), Baal-Hanan of **the olive and sycamore-fig trees,** and **Joash** of the olive oil supplies (v. 28). **Shitrai** was over the **herds . . . in Sharon** (v. 29; Sharon was west of the central hill country along the Mediterranean), **Shaphat** over the valley **herds** (v. 29), **Obil** over **the camels** (v. 30), **Jehdeiah** over **the donkeys** (v. 30), and **Jaziz** over **the flocks** (v. 31). **Jonathan, David's uncle** (perhaps nephew is the meaning of the word here; cf. 2 Sam. 21:21), was **a counselor** and **Jehiel** was the tutor(?) of David's **sons** (1 Chron. 27:32). **Ahithophel was** another **counselor** (cf. 2 Sam. 15:12) and **Hushai** a close confidant (1 Chron. 27:33). Though the chronicler did not relate the story of

Ahithophel's disloyalty to David in Absalom's rebellion (2 Sam. 15:31), he did mention Ahithophel's succession **by Jehoiada** and **Abiathar** (2 Sam. 15:35). The list ends with **Joab . . . the commander of the royal army** (1 Chron. 27:34).

J. David's farewell address (28:1–29:22a)

1. DAVID'S INSTRUCTIONS CONCERNING THE TEMPLE (28:1-10)

28:1-10. David had already communicated to Israel's leaders (who are all enumerated in chap. 27) his desire to construct a temple for **the Lord.** In fact he had already started collecting the building materials (chap. 22). Now, with the end of his life imminent, he summoned all the leaders again to encourage them to recognize Solomon's leadership and to follow him in this magnificent enterprise. In the temple, David said, would be placed **the ark of the covenant,** a holy object which symbolized the earthly throne of the heavenly King.

David then reviewed the history of his own attempts to build the temple, attempts that did not come to fruition because God had ordained that **Solomon** (a man of peace, 22:9) would be its builder (28:2-7). **Solomon** was qualified because he was the **chosen** son of David, who was himself chosen from the elect tribe of **Judah** (v. 4). Solomon was said to be the "son of God" (**My son,** v. 6) in a peculiar way (cf. 17:13 and comments on 22:10). If Solomon remained true to the **Lord** his **kingdom** would endure (28:6-7; cf. 22:10).

David concluded his instructions with a **charge** both to the people (28:8) and **Solomon** (vv. 9-10) to keep the divine covenant and to trust God to bring the temple project to a happy conclusion. David told Solomon to **serve** God completely (cf. v. 9) and willingly, aware that **the Lord** knows every person's **thoughts** and motives.

2. DAVID'S PLANS FOR THE TEMPLE (28:11-21)

28:11-21. In a most remarkable declaration David shared with **Solomon the plans** and specifications for **the temple** and its furnishings which **the Spirit** of God had revealed to him (vv. 11-12, 19). The construction would be done by human hands but **the plan** and significance

of **the temple** were from **God.** This also included the ministry of **the priests and Levites** (v. 13) and **the weight of** the **gold** and **silver** from which the sacred temple furnishings were to be made (vv. 14-18). Not wanting to leave anything to chance, **David** wrote down every detail of the heavenly revelation (v. 19). He encouraged Solomon to **be strong** for the task (cf. v. 10), **courageous,** and not fearful because **God** was **with** him (v. 20) and the workers would willingly assist him (v. 21).

3. DAVID'S APPEAL FOR OFFERINGS (29:1-9)

29:1-5a. Turning to the assembled crowd **David** again stressed the inexperience of young **Solomon** (cf. 22:5) and the importance of realizing that they were about to build not a palace for a mere human king but the **temple** of the Almighty **God.** Therefore the **task** was **great** and required an extensive amount of materials. Then, by way of example, he pointed out that he had already made official contributions of **gold . . . silver . . . bronze . . . iron . . . wood,** precious stones, and other materials necessary for **the temple** (28:2). **Besides** this he pledged to give of his own **personal** resources **3,000 talents of gold** (ca. 110 tons) from **Ophir** (cf. 1 Kings 9:28; 10:11; 22:48; 2 Chron. 8:18; 9:10; Isa. 13:12) on the east African coast or the western coast of Arabia, and **7,000 talents of . . . silver** (ca. 260 tons). These amounts were **over and above** the large amounts he had already given (see comments on 1 Chron. 22:14).

29:5b-9. On the basis of his own commitment (vv. 2-5) David then urged the other **leaders** to participate in the giving, an invitation they gladly accepted. They **willingly** (cf. v. 9) contributed in all **5,000 talents** of gold (ca. 190 tons), **10,000 darics of gold** (ca. 185 pounds), **10,000 talents of silver** (ca. 375 tons), **18,000 talents of bronze** (ca. 675 tons), and **100,000 talents of iron** (ca. 3,750 tons). In addition they gave **precious stones** as they were able. The result was great joy on the part of the masses and **David** himself. The gold, silver, and bronze David and the leaders gave (22:14; 29:4, 7) weighed a massive total of more than 46,610 tons (or 93.22 million pounds), not counting the other metals, stones, and lumber!

4. DAVID'S PRAYER AND SACRIFICES OF
   DEDICATION (29:10-22a)

29:10-20. After the almost spontaneous reaction of generosity by the people, **David** turned to the LORD in worship. He first extolled Him as the **God of . . . Israel** (v. 10) and spoke of God's attributes of eternality, omnipotence, **glory,** and sovereignty (vv. 10b-11). David then acknowledged Him as the One able to provide people's needs (v. 12b). Next he offered thanksgiving and **praise** (v. 13) with a confession that even the gifts which had just been presented were possible because the Lord was their original Giver (cf. James 1:17) of all things **from** His **hand** (1 Chron. 29:14-16). Moreover, David prayed, the gifts were of no avail if given insincerely, so he said that he and the others, had **given** from purest motives (v. 17; cf. 28:9).

Finally, referring to **God** as the One who had made a covenant in the past with the nation's ancestors **Abraham, Isaac, and Israel,** he prayed that the Lord would **keep** the people willing and **loyal** (29:18) and would continue His blessing, especially in enabling **Solomon** to have complete **devotion** to God and to the building of the temple (v. 19; cf. 28:9). After his prayer, **David** asked the **assembly** to **praise the** LORD (29:20).

29:21-22a. Next **day** the prayers of dedication were confirmed by the offering of an enormous number of sacrificial animals (3,000 in all), the giving of which brought the people **great joy** before **the** LORD.

K. David's successor to the throne (29:22b-30)

29:22b-23. The last recorded act of **David** was his acceptance of the co-regency of **Solomon . . . as king** (cf. 1 Kings 1:38-40; 2:1). How long they ruled together cannot be known but it must have been only briefly. **Zadok** also was anointed (again).

29:24-25. With Solomon's succession came the recognition by the people that he now was the king in **David's** stead.

Divine confirmation of this was apparent in the Lord's great blessing on **Solomon.** God **exalted** him, gave him unprecedented **royal splendor** (v. 25; cf. v. 23, "he prospered").

29:26-30. These last verses summarize David's reign from his accession at **Hebron** (2 Sam. 5:1-5) till his death. A complete record of his reign, the chronicler wrote, could be found **in the records of Samuel** (perhaps referring to 1 Sam. 1–24), **Nathan,** and **Gad** (perhaps 1 Sam. 25–2 Sam. 24 is the record of Nathan and Gad). To these accounts the chronicler added his own record (1 Chron.) with his particular purposes in view.

BIBLIOGRAPHY

Ackroyd, Peter R. *I and II Chronicles, Ezra, Nehemiah.* Torch Bible Commentaries. London: SCM Press, 1973.

Coggins, R.J. *The First and Second Book of the Chronicles.* New York: Cambridge University Press, 1976.

Curtis, Edward Lewis, and Madsen, Albert Alonzo. *A Critical and Exegetical Commentary on the Books of Chronicles.* The International Critical Commentary. Edinburgh: T. & T. Clark, 1910.

Keil, C.F. "The Books of the Chronicles." In *Commentary on the Old Testament in Ten Volumes.* Vol. 3. Reprint (25 vols. in 10). Grand Rapids: Wm. B. Eerdmans Publishing Co., 1982.

Myers, Jacob M. *I Chronicles.* The Anchor Bible. Garden City, N.Y.: Doubleday & Co., 1965.

Sailhamer, John. *First and Second Chronicles.* Chicago: Moody Press, 1983.

Slotki, I.W. *Chronicles: Hebrew Text and English Translation with an Introduction and Commentary.* London: Soncino Press, 1952.

Zöckler, Otto. "The Books of the Chronicles." In *Commentary on the Holy Scriptures, Critical, Doctrinal, and Homiletical.* Vol. 4. Reprint (24 vols. in 12). Grand Rapids: Zondervan Publishing House, 1960.

2 CHRONICLES

Eugene H. Merrill

INTRODUCTION

See the *Introduction* to 1 Chronicles.

OUTLINE

COMMENTARY

I. The Reign of Solomon (chaps. 1–9)

A. Solomon's wisdom and prosperity (chap. 1)

1:1-6. From the beginning of his reign **Solomon** established firm control **over his kingdom.** This was made possible by God's presence and blessing (v. 1).

Solomon and Israel's **leaders** made a pilgrimage to the tabernacle (the **Tent of Meeting) at Gibeon** to offer sacrifices on the great **bronze altar (made** by **Bezalel;** cf. Ex. 31:11, under Moses' direction, Ex. 38:17) that was still located **there** (cf. 1 Chron. 16:39-40; Ex. 38:1-7). **The ark,** however, was still **in Jerusalem** (2 Chron. 1:4; cf. 1 Chron. 15:1), where it had been brought **from Kiriath Jearim** by **David** (see the map "The Wanderings of the Ark of the Covenant" near 1 Sam. 6). Along with the other national leaders Solomon expressed his devotion to **the LORD** by offering **1,000 burnt offerings** on that one occasion (2 Chron. 1:6).

1:7-13. **That night** the Lord responded to Solomon's expression of worship by appearing to him (in a dream; cf. 1 Kings 3:5) and inviting him to request **whatever** he wanted. Because **Solomon** was young and inexperienced (1 Chron. 22:5; 29:1) he was apprehensive about his ability to rule the great nation (**as numerous as the dust of the earth**; cf. Gen. 13:16) **over** which **God** had placed him. So he requested that he might receive **wisdom and knowledge** to **lead** the **people** (2 Chron. 1:8-10). "Wisdom" (*ḥokmâh*) refers to discernment and judgment while "knowledge" (*maddā'*) means practical know-how in everyday affairs.

The unselfish character of Solomon's choice prompted the Lord to grant not only what **Solomon . . . asked for** but also more. God said He would **also give** Solomon **wealth, riches, and honor** unlike any other **king** of Israel (vv. 11-12; cf. 1 Chron. 29:25).

1:14-17. To show God's faithfulness to His promise, the chronicler itemized the material blessings that came to **Solomon.** The king acquired **1,400 chariots** and **12,000 horses** (or charioteers; cf. NIV marg.; the Heb. word *pārāšîm* can mean either horses or charioteers), which he stationed in **chariot cities** (cf. 1 Kings 9:19) and **in Jerusalem.** It is not possible to identify the chariot cities today though some have suggested Gezer, Hazor, and Megiddo, based on 1 Kings 9:15.

Silver and gold, the chronicler wrote in hyperbole, became **as common** as the ubiquitous **stones** of Israel, and **cedar** was like the common **sycamore-fig trees** of **the** western **foothills.**

Also Solomon **imported** (by trade) **horses** and chariots with great profit. He brought them **from Egypt** (or perhaps Muṣri, in Asia Minor) **and . . . Kue** (*qᵉwē*; not "in droves" as in KJV), probably Cilicia in the south portion of modern-day Turkey (cf. NIV marg.). No doubt Solomon kept some and **exported** the rest, especially to **the Hittites and . . . Arameans.** A chariot cost **600 shekels of silver** (ca. 15 pounds) and a **horse** cost **150** silver shekels (3¾ pounds). Presumably Solomon realized a handsome profit on each one as he traded them. Yet he should not have **accumulated** such great numbers of **horses** and amassed so much silver and gold (Deut. 17:16-17) because of the temptation to trust in those material things rather than in God.

B. Building of the temple (2:1–5:1)

1. THE PREPARATIONS (CHAP. 2)

God had denied David the opportunity to build the temple. However, David had received detailed instructions about its erection and furnishings and had purchased the site and gathered together materials and workmen to bring it to pass (1 Chron. 21:18–22:19; 28–29). It now fell to his son and successor Solomon to bring the dream to reality.

2:1-6. **Solomon** first drafted aliens to provide the labor. They consisted of **70,000 . . . carriers** and **80,000** stonemasons, and **3,600 . . . foremen** (v. 2; cf. v. 18). **Solomon** then notified **Hiram** (the Heb. here has Huram, a variant spelling; cf. NIV marg.), **king of** the Phoenician city-state of **Tyre,** that he was ready to begin the **temple** about which his **father David** had probably informed Hiram (cf. 1 Kings 5:3). This **temple** would be the **place** for offering **sacrifices,** and it would be grand and glorious to befit the **God** who is above **all other gods** (2 Chron. 2:5). Solomon's reference to other gods does not imply that he believed in their existence. It was a way of setting forth to Hiram, a polytheistic pagan king, the uniqueness and incomparability of the Lord God of Israel (cf. Isa. 40:18-26; 46:3-7). Of course such a God cannot be housed in a mere earthly **temple,** Solomon confessed, since **even the highest heavens cannot contain Him.**

2:7-10. Nonetheless the temple was to be as appropriate as human creativity could make it. Since the Phoenicians were famous the world over for their architectural and building skills, Solomon solicited Hiram to **send . . . a man** of requisite abilities **to work** with his own **craftsmen** (v. 7). Hiram should also provide **timber** (on **algum** and its uses see comments on 9:10-11), the hewers of which would receive **20,000 cors** (ca. 125,000 bushels) **of ground wheat, 20,000 cors of barley, 20,000 baths** (ca. 115,000 gallons) **of wine, and 20,000 baths of olive oil** (2:8-10).

2:11-12. This appeal was readily received by **Hiram,** who recognized the legitimacy and divine origin of Solomon's succession as **king,** so he proceeded to comply. Hiram's acknowledgment of **the Lord** (*Yahweh*), **the God of Israel,** as the Creator of **heaven and earth** (v. 12) was just a formal courtesy and tells nothing of his own personal faith.

2:13-16. The man whom Hiram chose to send to Solomon was **Huram-Abi,** a half-Israelite **whose mother was from** the tribe of **Dan.** According to 1 Kings 7:14, his "mother was a widow from the tribe of Naphtali." This difference may be explained by understanding Dan to be her tribe by birth and Naphtali her residence, or vice versa. The terms and conditions Solomon set were acceptable to Hiram in every way. He would immediately **cut** and ship the timber **by sea** to the Israelite port of **Joppa** (cf. Jonah 1:3; Acts 9:36-43; 10:32; 11:5) from where it would be transported overland **to Jerusalem.**

2:17-18. With the arrangements now complete, **Solomon** gathered his work gangs, drawing them not from Israelites but from resident **aliens** (v. 17; cf. 1 Chron. 22:2). This presupposes class structures in which non-Israelites were sometimes forced into public service projects such as this project of temple building (cf. Josh. 9:22-27). The numbers in 2 Chronicles 2:18 correspond with those given in verse 2 (cf. comments on 8:10).

2. THE TEMPLE PROPER (CHAP. 3)

3:1. At last the work **began** at **Mount Moriah,** just north of the old Jebusite city of Ophel, on the spot marked by **the threshing floor of Araunah** (Heb., Ornan; cf. NIV marg.). This was **the place** designated by **the Lord** and purchased **by David** as a site for sacrifice at the time of David's illicit census (cf. 1 Chron. 21) and as a site for the temple (1 Chron. 22:1). Also the place was holy to Israel as the place where Abraham started to offer Isaac to the Lord in obedience to God's command (cf. Gen. 22). Known today as the Temple Mount, it is occupied by a Moslem mosque called the Dome of the Rock. Recent excavations, however, suggest that the site of **the temple** (and thus that of Araunah's threshing floor) may have been immediately north of the Dome of the Rock (see Asher S. Kaufman, "Where the Ancient Temple of Jerusalem Stood," *Biblical Archaeology Review* 9. March-April 1983: 40-59).

3:2. The construction commenced **on the second day of the second month** of Solomon's **fourth year.** According to the best chronological calculations this would be 966 B.C. The author of 1 and 2 Kings added the interesting fact that this was 480 years after the Exodus, an event which would then be dated at 1446 B.C. (1 Kings 6:1).

3:3-4. The main **temple** structure rested on a **foundation** of **60 x 20 cubits,** or 90 x 30 feet, on the basis of 18-inch **cubits. The portico** (porch) on **the front** was **20 cubits** (30 feet) **long,** thus extending **across the** entire **width of the** main **building.** According to 1 Kings 6:3, the portico was 10 cubits (15 feet) wide. The entire edifice, then, was 105 feet long and 30 feet wide.

The height of the temple was 30 cubits (1 Kings 6:2) but the portico was **20 cubits** (30 feet) **high.** (See the sketch "Plan of Solomon's Temple" near 1 Kings 6:1-10.) The entire interior of the portico was gilded with **gold.**

3:5-7. The main hall, the room known in the tabernacle as "the holy place" (cf. Ex. 26:33), was **paneled** with **pine** (or perhaps the Heb. word means cypress) and **covered** with **gold** decorations. This consisted of engraved **designs** of **palm** trees and chains. The meaning of this symbolism is not clear though the palm may represent the tree of life (cf. Gen. 2:9; 3:20, 22; Rev. 2:7; 22:2, 19) or something similar. **Precious stones** were inset here and there. **The gold** was from **Parvaim.** Though this land cannot yet be identified, it must have been a source of unusually **fine gold.** With this **gold** the artisans veneered every surface of **the temple** interior. They then engraved figures of **cherubim** in the gold of **the walls.** These creatures symbolized the awesome presence and glory of God. The angelic beings which these carvings represented had their wings outspread ("covering ones," as the Heb. word *kerûbîm* may suggest). The Lord was said to dwell between the cherubim (cf. Num. 7:89; 2 Kings 19:15; Pss. 80:1; 99:1).

3:8-14. The smaller chamber, **the most holy place,** was **20 x 20 cubits** (30 x 30 feet). Its interior was also plated **with gold—600 talents** (ca. 23 tons; cf. NIV marg.) of it—fastened with **gold nails** which **weighed 50 shekels** (1¼ pounds; cf. NIV marg.).

Within this room was the ark of the covenant (1 Kings 6:19) which apparently, as in the tabernacle, was placed in the most holy place between the two **cherubim** (cf. Ex. 25:10-22). The ark represented or symbolized the Lord's dwelling among His people. The **cherubim** evidently faced **the main hall** (2 Chron. 3:13), from within the **most holy place,** each with a total wingspan of 10 cubits (15 feet). From one wingtip to another they thus stretched from one side **wall** of the **temple** to the other (vv. 11-12).

Just before the two **cherubim** and hiding them and the most holy place from the main hall was the veil or **curtain** with its various colors (**blue, purple, and crimson**) and fabrics (**yarn and . . . linen**) with representations of **cherubim** woven **into it** (v. 14). Thus the temple proper had two rooms, the main hall (the holy place) and the most holy place, the former being exactly twice the size of the latter. The curtain served as a partition between them.

3:15. In front of the temple were **two** free-standing **pillars . . . 35 cubits** (52½ feet) tall including a 5-cubit (7½ feet) **capital.** But according to 1 Kings 7:15 these pillars, made of bronze, stood 18 cubits (27 feet) high. One explanation of this alleged discrepancy is suggested by the NIV which supplies the word

together in 2 Chronicles 3:15. The thought is that when the heights of the two pillars are added together they total 35 cubits. This is a close (though not exact) harmonization because two pillars of 18 cubits each total 36, not 35. Perhaps a better solution is to recognize that the Hebrew figures for 18 and 35 are so similar that a scribe copying verse 15 could easily have read 35 when the text actually said 18. Architecturally it seems more reasonable that the pillars would be in line with or less than the height of the temple, not towering far above it. The temple height was 30 cubits (45 feet, 1 Kings 6:2), so each pillar was probably 18 cubits (27 feet) not 35 cubits (52½ feet).

3:16. The Hebrew word rendered **interwoven** is translated "in the inner sanctuary" in the NASB (cf. NIV marg.). In copying the text, scribes probably transposed some Hebrew letters so that the original *brbd* ("interwoven") became *bdbr* ("in the inner sanctuary"). The reading "interwoven" is supported by 1 Kings 7:17 which speaks of interwoven **chains.**

Above the band of **chains** at the **top** of each pillar was a band of **100** engraved **pomegranates.** Actually 200 pomegranates were on each pillar (2 Chron. 4:13), thus suggesting that there were two bands or rows (1 Kings 7:18) of 100 each. The pomegranates on each pillar were interwoven among the chainlike lattice, with seven chains on each pillar (1 Kings 7:17). Since the capitals on top of the pillars were five cubits high (2 Chron. 3:15) and since each capital's top portion, shaped like lilies, was four cubits high (1 Kings 7:19) that left one cubit for the chains and pomegranates.

3:17. The pillars stood before **the temple,** which faced east. So **one** pillar was on **the south** side and **one on the north.** The pillar on **the south** was **named Jakin** ("He establishes"; cf. NIV marg.) and the other was **Boaz** ("in Him is strength"; cf. NIV marg.). So the pillars symbolized the fact that the Lord had established His house and would maintain it forever (cf. 7:16).

3. THE TEMPLE FURNISHINGS (4:1–5:1)

4:1. Along with or after the temple's construction Solomon commissioned the manufacture of the furnishings of the temple and its precincts. The first article listed is the great **bronze altar** which measured **20 cubits long, 20 cubits wide, and 10 cubits high** (30 feet x 30 feet x 15 feet). Though the steps are not mentioned here, they must have led to the top of the altar (cf. the altar in the millennial temple, Ezek. 43:17). The bronze altar stood in the courtyard directly in front of the temple (cf. Ex. 40:6; 2 Kings 16:14).

4:2-6, 10. The Sea of cast metal was a huge round basin **10 cubits** (15 feet) in diameter and **5 cubits** (7½ feet) in depth. Its circumference of **30 cubits** (45 feet) comports well with its 10-cubit diameter according to the formula of C (circumference) = π (3.14159) x D (diameter), a discovery of much later geometricians. The slight difference between 30 cubits and 31.4159 cubits (3.14159 x 10 cubits diameter) can be explained by noting the common practice of giving approximate figures. Even today people speak of a circle's circumference being three times its diameter. Another explanation is that the *inside* circumference of the basin may have been exactly 30 cubits and the outer circumference 31.4159 cubits.

Under the basin's **rim** was a frieze consisting of **two rows** of engraved **bulls, 10** bulls per **cubit** (18 inches). These engravings were obviously highly stylized since the Hebrew here says literally, "bull-like forms," whereas 1 Kings 7:24 has "gourd-like forms" as though there were room for interpretation.

The basin rested on the back of **12** manufactured **bulls, 3 facing** each of four directions. These probably represented Israel's 12 tribes and their arrangement in the wilderness camps (cf. Num. 2). The capacity of the Sea was **3,000 baths** (ca. 17,500 gallons; cf. NIV marg.), though 1 Kings 7:26 says 2,000 baths. Many scholars suggest that this difference may be explained by the view that the chronicler considered the basin as cylindrical and the author of Kings as hemispherical. This explanation, however, presumes that the respective authors could not agree on the actual shape of the vessel, an unlikely possibility. Perhaps the best reconciliation is that the Sea had a capacity of 3,000 baths but actually contained only 2,000.

The basin was **placed** east of the temple, **south** of the bronze altar (2 Chron. 4:10), and served as a wash basin for **the priests** as they underwent their ceremonial cleansings (v. 6b). There were also **10** wash **basins . . . 5** on each **side** of the temple in which the items **used for . . . burnt offerings** were washed (v. 6; cf. 1 Kings 7:38).

4:7-8. Inside the main hall of **the temple** were **10 gold lampstands . . . 5 on the south** wall **and 5 on the north.** (The former tabernacle had only one lampstand.) In the same locations were **10 tables** (possibly for the "bread of the Presence"; cf. comments on v. 19) and in unspecified places **100** golden basins.

4:9, 11a. The courtyard of the priests was probably "the inner courtyard" mentioned in 1 Kings 6:36, and **the large court** was, of course, "the great courtyard" of 1 Kings 7:12. The first of these was no doubt the area immediately around the temple and the other was in the vicinity of the temple complex. The **bronze** doors of the large court must have been gates in the walls surrounding the entire temple area.

Listed last are the various utensils used in conjunction with the bronze altar: **the pots and shovels** to remove ashes and the **sprinkling bowls** to contain the blood (2 Chron. 4:11a).

4:11b-18. The work of **Huram** (called Huram-Abi in 2:13), described in detail in 3:3–4:11a, is summarized in 4:11b-16a. To this summation is added the information that these **bronze** objects (v. 16) were **cast** by use of **clay molds** in **the Jordan** Valley **between Succoth and Zarethan** (v. 17). Recent exploration has revealed the probable location of this industry, about 35 miles north of the Dead Sea and east of the Jordan River, just north of the Jabbok River. So abundant was **the bronze** used that it was **not** even weighed (v. 18). Much if not all of the bronze came from David's conquest of the Arameans (1 Chron. 18:3-8).

4:19-22. These verses describe the remaining **furnishings** and utensils, some of which were mentioned already. These are **the golden altar,** on which incense was burned (cf. the tabernacle's gold-covered altar of incense, Ex. 37:25-29); **the tables** for **the bread of the Presence** ("showbread," KJV), probably the 10 tables mentioned in 2 Chronicles 4:8; **the** 10 gold **lampstands** (cf. v. 7); the various parts and attachments of the lampstands such as the **lamps and tongs** of **solid gold**

(v. 21); and miscellaneous items such as **gold wick trimmers, sprinkling bowls** (cf. v. 8), **ladles** (or spoons), **and censers** (for burning incense).

The emphasis here is not merely on the articles, since there is some obvious repetition with previous verses, but on the fact that they were made of **pure gold.** So extensive was its use that the **doors** both to **the main hall** (the holy place) and **the most holy place** were made of **gold** (v. 22). According to 1 Kings 7:50 even the door sockets were made of gold. All this points up the richness and lavishness of the **temple** as a fitting tribute to the God who manifested Himself there.

5:1. When all . . . the temple was completed (a construction project that lasted seven years; cf. 1 Kings 6:38), **Solomon** directed that **the furnishings** be brought into the **temple** and also that the offerings **David had** previously gathered (cf. 1 Chron. 22:14; 29:1-9) be **placed** within the temple **treasuries.** So great were David's and the leaders' contributions that Solomon's craftsmen had not used all those metals.

C. Dedication of the temple (5:2–7:10)

1. HOUSING OF THE ARK (5:2-14)

5:2-6. The only object which had not been put in the temple, but which was indispensable to its true function, was **the ark.** It had remained in a tabernacle **David** had built on Mount Zion (1 Chron. 15:1) but all was ready now for its removal to Solomon's temple. The time chosen for this momentous event was **the festival in the seventh month,** the Feast of Tabernacles in September-October (Lev. 23:33-36). This was in 959 B.C. With great fanfare the tribal leaders gathered to witness the procession **from Zion** (here the southeast portion of Jerusalem; cf. 2 Sam. 5:7, just south of Moriah where the temple was built). Apparently **the ark** had been temporarily removed from Moriah while the temple was under construction there. **The priests who were Levites,** bore not only **the ark** but also David's tabernacle and all its **furnishings** (2 Chron. 5:2-5). Like David before him, **Solomon** celebrated the transporting of the ark by **sacrificing** innumerable animals (v. 6).

5:7-10. When **the ark** arrived at the temple, **the priests,** the only persons authorized to do so, took it into **the most holy place** and placed it **beneath the** overarching **cherubim** (vv. 7-8). When the doors to the most holy place were open the **poles . . . could be seen** from **the holy place,** but **not from the outside.** The only contents in **the ark** were the **two** stone **tablets** of the Law (v. 10). The author of Hebrews wrote that the ark also contained Aaron's rod and a pot of manna (Heb. 9:4). This is nowhere attested in the Old Testament (Ex. 16:33-34 and Num. 17:10 state that the rod and manna were placed in front of the tabernacle, not in the ark). But these extra objects may have been added to the original contents sometime later than Solomon. Or perhaps they had been lost by Solomon's time.

5:11-14. After **the priests . . . withdrew from** the temple, they were joined by other priests and Levitical **musicians** who **stood** to **the east . . . of** the great **altar** (i.e., in front of it) and lifted up their voices and instruments (**120 . . . trumpets,** plus **cymbals and other instruments**) in loud and joyous **praise to** God. On this special occasion all 24 priestly and Levitical **divisions** (v. 11) were represented. They did not follow the prescribed order of ministry (cf. 1 Chron. 24:1-19) because of the unique significance of this celebration. In their praise the musicians sang of the Lord's goodness and **love** (ḥeseḏ, "loyal love"; cf. 2 Chron. 6:14; 7:3, 6; 20:21). The LORD showed His approval by filling **the temple** with the **cloud of glory,** which represented His presence in **the temple** (cf. Ex. 40:34-35; Ezek. 10:3-4).

2. SOLOMON'S BLESSING AND PRAYER (CHAP. 6)

6:1-11. The appearance of the glory of God in the cloud (5:13-14) reminded **Solomon** that God had made His presence known to Moses in the same way though in a much more modest tent, or tabernacle. Now, however, **the LORD . . . would dwell** in a more permanent magnificence (vv. 1-2). Solomon addressed the people in a blessing (vv. 4-11). First he praised **God** for having **fulfilled** His promises **to . . . David** by choosing him and his dynasty, selecting **Jerusalem** as the divine "residence," and permitting the erection of **a temple** (vv. 4-6). The term **name,** which occurs 14 times in this chapter and 14 times elsewhere in 2 Chronicles, refers to God's attributes or presence (cf. 1 Chron. 13:6). **David** had not been allowed to build **the temple** but God in His infinite grace had ordained that Solomon, David's **son,** do so and now that **promise** had come to pass (2 Chron. 6:7-11).

6:12-21. After blessing the people, **Solomon** offered a dedicatory prayer (vv. 14-42). Kneeling on a specially constructed **bronze platform . . . in the center of the outer court** (vv. 12-13), he extolled **the LORD** for His **covenant**-keeping faithfulness (vv. 14-15). **Love** translates *ḥesed,* meaning God's loyal love (cf. 5:13; 7:3, 6; 20:21). The king then implored the **LORD** to continue His favor on David's dynasty as the people continued to serve Him **according to** the Law (6:16-17). In one of the finest statements of divine transcendence found in the Scriptures, Solomon acknowledged the insufficiency of a mere **temple,** no matter how grand and commodious, to **contain** the Lord of **the heavens** (v. 18). Yet Solomon was persuaded of God's interest in human affairs. He besought the **LORD** to recognize the **temple** as a focal point of His communion with **Israel** (**hear** occurs five times in vv. 19-21) and to respond **from heaven** (cf. vv. 23, 25, 27, 30, 33, 35, 39), His true **dwelling place** (cf. vv. 30, 33, 39; 30:27). Because Solomon spoke of the Israelites praying **toward this place** (6:21; cf. vv. 34, 38), centuries later Daniel faced Jerusalem as he prayed (Dan. 6:10).

6:22-31. Solomon also prayed that the **temple** might be the place where God would adjudicate **wrongs** between individuals (vv. 22-23), where He would forgive the nation when it was **defeated** in battle because of **sin** (vv. 24-25), and where He would hear their prayers of repentance when drought (vv. 26-27) and other disasters would befall them as a result of divine judgment (vv. 28-31).

6:32-39. In a spirit of magnanimity, Solomon also entreated the Lord to **hear** the prayers of foreigners who might go to the **temple** to seek His face (vv. 32-33). Solomon prayed that in times of **war** the Lord would bless His people in battle (vv. 34-35). If, however, they sinned and were taken **captive to** a foreign **land** and there repented, Solomon prayed

that they would be forgiven (vv. 36-39).

6:40-42. In a closing hymnic refrain, Solomon interceded for the temple (God's **resting place**), the **priests,** the people (**saints**), and himself as the **anointed** successor to David (cf. Ps. 132:8-11). God should do these things, Solomon suggested, because of His **kindnesses** (pl. of *ḥesed,* "loyal love"· cf. 2 Chron. 5:13; 6:14; 7:3, 6; 20:21), which He had **promised to David** and to his dynasty.

3. SOLOMON'S SACRIFICES (7:1-10)

7:1-3. As though to dramatize His answer to Solomon's prayer visually, **the LORD** sent down **fire** to consume **the sacrifices** that had been prepared (cf. Lev. 9:24; 1 Chron. 21:26), and the cloud of His **glory . . . filled the temple** once again (cf. 2 Chron. 5:13-14). So overwhelmed were the people by God's theophanic presence that they fell to **their faces** and acclaimed His covenant faithfulness (**love,** *ḥesed,* "loyal love"; cf. 5:13; 6:14; 7:6; 20:21).

7:4-7. Then the assembled worshipers **offered** more **sacrifices**—with **Solomon** alone offering **22,000 . . . cattle** and **120,000 sheep and goats.** In praise the **priests** and **Levites** played their **musical instruments** (v. 6). So numerous were the sacrifices that Solomon instructed that they be made in a specially constructed and dedicated area in **the courtyard** before **the temple.**

7:8-10. For **seven days** the festivities went on with the **people** of **the LORD** gathered **from Lebo Hamath** (Israel's northern boundary toward the Euphrates River) **to the Wadi of Egypt** (modern Wadi el-Arish, south of Gaza). Finally, **on the eighth day,** which followed the seven-day Feast of Tabernacles (Lev. 23:36), the people assembled once **more** just before returning **to their homes.** In all, the temple celebration lasted 15 days, for having begun in the seventh month (2 Chron. 5:3) and probably on the 15th day (cf. Lev. 23:39), the Feast of Tabernacles extended through the 22nd day. The **festival** mentioned in 2 Chronicles 7:9b is certainly the Tabernacles feast, so **the dedication of the altar** (v. 9a), which also lasted **seven days,** preceded the Tabernacles festival and began on the eighth day of that **month.**

D. God's blessings and curses (7:11-22)

7:11-12. Included in every covenant text in the ancient Near East as well as in many of those in the Old Testament was a section containing blessings and curses. The blessings would become effective if the subservient party would stay loyal to the great king while the curses would be expected to fall on the disobedient (cf. Deut. 27–28). In line with God's covenant with David and Solomon such a section now follows. **The LORD appeared to** Solomon and assured him that his work on **the temple** and its dedication pleased Him (2 Chron. 7:11-12). (Interestingly, chap. 7 has only a passing reference to Solomon's building of **the royal palace,** no doubt because of the chronicler's planned emphasis on the **temple** [see the *Introduction* to 1 Chron.]. In 1 Kings 7:1-12 details are given on Solomon's **palace** construction.)

7:13-22. God then encouraged Solomon by the promise that if His judgment (by drought, **locusts,** or a **plague**) should fall on the nation for **their sin,** they need only **turn** to the Lord in earnest humility and repentance and they would find forgiveness and restoration (vv. 13-15). This promise, in answer to Solomon's prayer (6:26-31), was given because God's presence among His people Israel is eternal, focused particularly on the **temple** (7:16). The covenant theme comes through clearly in the Lord's declaration that if Solomon would obey Him (v. 17) he could be assured of God's reciprocal blessing in the perpetuation of his dynastic **rule** (v. 18; cf. 1 Chron. 17:11-14). Conversely, if Solomon and the nation should fall **away** from the Lord and **serve other gods** they would be exiled and their magnificent **temple** destroyed (2 Chron. 7:19-20). This does not suggest that the Davidic Covenant is conditional from God's standpoint. He had said it would be forever (2 Sam. 7:13, 15-16). But Solomon's (or any king's) enjoyment of it would depend on his obedience to **God.**

Later Solomon did worship **other gods** (1 Kings 11:4-8), as did many of his successors, so the nation was exiled (2 Chron. 6:36; 36:17-18, 20) to Babylon and the temple destroyed (36:19). Everyone who would witness the desolation of the **land** and the **temple** would know that it was a mark of God's judgment on His people because of their sin (7:21-22).

E. Solomon's successes (chaps. 8–9)

1. POLITICAL SUCCESS (8:1-11)

8:1-2. Within **20 years** of his accession (i.e., by 951 B.C.) **Solomon** had completed **the temple . . . and his own palace** and had **rebuilt** certain **villages that** Hiram had ceded to Israel. According to 1 Kings 9:10-14, these towns, 20 in all, had originally been given by Solomon to Hiram but Hiram was displeased with them. The chronicler was possibly referring to the return of these rejected towns to Solomon who then restored them.

8:3-6. At that time **Solomon** began his conquest of foreign states, commencing with the Aramean city of **Hamath Zobah,** almost 300 miles north of Jerusalem. He then refortified **Tadmor** (later known as Palmyra), a **desert** oasis trading center on the main highway from Mesopotamia, about 150 miles northeast of Damascus. He did the same with the newly acquired **cities** around **Hamath.** In Israel proper **he rebuilt Upper . . . and Lower Beth Horon** to make them strong fortresses, and undertook similar projects at **Baalath** and other storage **cities** and military centers. **Beth Horon** was about 10 miles northwest of Jerusalem on the border between Judah and the Northern tribes (Josh. 18:13). Baalath was in the territory of Dan (Josh. 19:44). The other unnamed cities probably include Hazor, Megiddo, and Gezer (cf. 1 Kings 9:15).

8:7-10. **Solomon conscripted** his forced **labor** from among non-Israelite population groups still living **in the land.** These included **Hittites** (originally from central Anatolia, in modern-day Turkey), **Amorites** (early hill-dwellers in Canaan), **Perizzites** (a Canaanite subtribe), **Hivites** (perhaps the same as the Indo-Aryan Hurrians), **and Jebusites** (the original Canaanite inhabitants of Jerusalem)—peoples not fully subjugated by Israel in the Conquest (Jud. 3:1-6). **The Israelites** were exempted from such drudgery, serving instead in the army and as labor foremen. The **250** supervisors were only Israelites whereas the 550 officials in 1 Kings 9:23 probably included Canaanite foremen as well. In addition to the 250 Solomon had 3,600 other foremen (2 Chron. 2:18), a total of 3,850 (which equals 3,300, 1 Kings 5:16, plus 550, 1 Kings 9:23).

8:11. A final political achievement

by **Solomon** was his relocation of his wife, the **daughter** of the Pharaoh of Egypt, **from** David's old **palace** on Mount Zion (**the City of David**; cf. 5:2; 1 Kings 3:1; 1 Chron. 11:5) **to** her new **palace** on the temple mount (cf. 1 Kings 7:8; 9:24). The reason given is that she, an Egyptian, would profane David's palace which at one time had had such close connection with **the ark** of the covenant. Though the chronicler did not relate how the daughter of the Egyptian king (Pharaoh Siamun of Dynasty 21?) had become Solomon's **wife,** the fact that she had implies the political strength and status of Israel's king for he must have been regarded by Pharaoh as at least his equal.

2. RELIGIOUS SUCCESS (8:12-16)

8:12-16. Solomon's spiritual devotion, evidenced by the many sacrifices he gave at the dedication of the temple (7:5), was typical of his religious commitment, in the view of the chronicler. True, 2 Chronicles does not mention Solomon's introduction of pagan shrines and worship, a point stressed in 1 Kings 11:1-13. But the chronicler, though he surely knew those things, did narrate what must have been Solomon's general practice of fulfilling Mosaic sacrificial requirements (2 Chron. 8:12-13). **Solomon** also maintained the priestly and Levitical **divisions** established by **his father** (vv. 14-15). Last but not least, Solomon had begun and had completed **the temple,** his highest religious achievement.

3. ECONOMIC SUCCESS (8:17–9:31)

8:17-18. Much of Solomon's prosperity was due to his maritime industry, an enterprise he was able to undertake with Phoenician help. Operating out of **Ezion Geber and Elath,** seaports on the eastern arm of the Red Sea (known today as the Gulf of Aqaba or Gulf of Eilat), his and Hiram's sailors **sailed to** distant points such as the land of **Ophir** (cf. comments on 1 Chron. 29:4) whence they imported **450 talents of gold** (ca. 17 tons, or 34,000 pounds), apparently on one voyage. (First Kings 9:28 has 420 talents, ca. 16 tons. One of the two figures may be due to a copyist confusing the two similar-looking Heb. letters for 450 and 420.)

9:1-8. Another source of revenue came to **Solomon** from **the queen of She-** ba, possibly the land of the Sabeans (cf. Job 1:15; Ezek. 23:42; Joel 3:8) in southwestern Arabia. Having **heard of** his **wisdom** (cf. 1 Kings 10:1-13), she traveled over 1,200 miles **to test him.** In her camel **caravan** she brought **spices . . . gold, and precious stones** as tokens of her friendship. So impressed was she with Solomon's **wisdom** and prosperity **she was overwhelmed. She** said that what she saw **far exceeded the report** she had **heard.** Surely, she said, Solomon's workmen must be **happy,** and the **God** who could bless in all these ways was to be praised. Like Hiram's words of **praise** (2 Chron. 2:12), hers too were probably a formal courtesy, not an indication of her conversion to Yahweh.

9:9-12. Then the queen of Sheba bestowed her gifts, the **gold** alone amounting to **120 talents** (4½ tons, or 9,000 pounds), **spices, and precious stones.** The **spices** exceeded in quality (and quantity?) anything ever seen before in Israel. The land of **Ophir** (cf. comments on 1 Chron. 29:4) yielded not only **gold** but also **algumwood** (cf. algum in 2 Chron. 2:8; perhaps a name for sandalwood) **and precious stones.** The **algumwood** was employed in the **steps** of **the temple** and **the royal palace** and as frames for **harps and lyres. Solomon** also gave gifts to **the queen.**

9:13-16. Other evidences of Solomon's prosperity follow. His annual income in **gold** was **666 talents** (25 tons, or 50,000 pounds). This did not include profits through taxation or tolls on caravans and other **merchants.** The source of this massive wealth of **gold and silver** was both external (from **all the kings of Arabia**) and internal (**governors of the land**). With the **gold** he **made 200 large shields,** each containing **600 bekas** (7½ pounds) of **gold,** and **300 small shields . . . each** with half that amount (**300 bekas**) **of gold.** (In 1 Kings 10:17 the amount of gold in each of the small shields is said to be three minas each. That is the same amount, expressed in a different unit of measure.)

These shields were only ornamental for they were placed **in the Palace of the Forest of Lebanon,** one of Solomon's public buildings in Jerusalem, probably built mostly of cedar (cf. 1 Kings 7:2; Lebanon was the major source of cedar). The royal palace was a separate building (cf. 1 Kings 7:2 with 1 Kings 7:8).

9:17-24. Solomon's **throne** was decorated **with ivory and overlaid with . . . gold.** With great detail the chronicler described its **six steps,** gold **footstool,** arms, and **12** guardian **lions,** one on each **end of each step.** His drinking vessels and other table service were of **gold** only, for **silver** was thought, by comparison, to be of insufficient **value. Every three years** the king sent out merchant **ships** in order to acquire exotica such as **gold, silver . . . ivory . . . apes, and baboons!** As a result he was regarded as the wealthiest monarch of his day. And his wealth increased as visitors came regularly **to hear** his God-given **wisdom,** bringing, of course, their extravagant tokens of appreciation, including **articles of silver and gold . . . robes,** weaponry, **spices . . . horses, and mules.**

9:25-28. In summation, the historian wrote of Solomon's military (v. 25) and political (v. 26) power (his rule extended **from the** Euphrates **River to** Egypt's **border;** cf. 1 Kings 4:21, 24) as well as his incalculable wealth, produced largely through his trading expertise (2 Chron. 9:27-28). (Vv. 25, 27-28 are similar to 1:14-16.) The extent of Solomon's kingdom did not fulfill the Abrahamic Covenant (Gen. 15:18) because many countries in that territory only paid tribute to Solomon (1 Kings 4:21) and were not assimilated into the nation Israel.

9:29-31. Then the chronicler appended the note that information on **other** affairs of **Solomon's reign** could be found in the writings of the Prophets **Nathan** (cf. 1 Kings 1:11-13), **Ahijah** (cf. 1 Kings 11:29), and **Iddo** (cf. 2 Chron. 12:15; 13:22). **Solomon reigned . . . 40 years** (971–931 B.C.) and was **succeeded** by his son **Rehoboam.**

II. The Reign of the Davidic Dynasty (chaps. 10–36)

A. Rehoboam (chaps. 10–12)

1. DIVISION OF THE NATION INTO ISRAEL AND JUDAH (CHAP. 10)

10:1. Strangely, though Solomon must have had many sons, none is mentioned except **Rehoboam** whom he begot by Naamah the Ammonitess (cf. 1 Kings 14:21). Having no doubt sensed the increasing spirit of alienation on the part of **Israelites** in the northern part of the kingdom against his father, Rehoboam **went to Shechem** to be formally coronated. This city had held an important part in Israel's life since the time of Abraham. Joshua had reaffirmed the Mosaic Covenant there and from that time Shechem had been more or less the unofficial capital of the north (cf. Josh. 24:1-28).

10:2-11. Jeroboam was formerly the foreman of labor in Ephraim, in which Shechem was located. When he **heard** that Solomon had died, **he returned from Egypt** where **he had fled** from **Solomon** sometime previously (v. 2; cf. 1 Kings 11:26-28, 40). By popular demand **Jeroboam** headed a delegation which appealed **to Rehoboam** to **lighten** their load of **labor** and taxation (2 Chron. 10:3-4). Asking for **three days** to consider the matter, **Rehoboam consulted** with the old advisers of **his father,** who counseled him to listen to the Israelites. Then he turned to his own **young** peers who urged him not to relent but rather to make the people's **yoke** all the **heavier** (vv. 5-11). Rehoboam's young advisers said his heavier burden would be like his **little finger** being **thicker than** his **father's waist** and like **scorpions** (a cruel kind of whip with sharp pieces of metal) compared with his father's **whips.**

10:12-16. When **Rehoboam** again confronted **Jeroboam** and the people, he repeated the policy advocated by his **young** cohorts (vv. 12-14). This, the chronicler wrote (v. 15), **was** of **God,** however, for He had already promised **Jeroboam** that he would rule over the Northern tribes (cf. 1 Kings 11:29-39). Surely enough, when the assembly heard the words of Rehoboam they disassociated themselves from the house of **David** (**To your tents, O Israel!** cf. 2 Sam. 20:1) and, in effect, declared their independence of Judah (2 Chron. 10:16).

10:17-19. This left only **Judah** to Rehoboam. So serious was the cleavage that **Adoniram** (Heb. has Hadoram, a variant spelling), perhaps the new work manager over Ephraim (cf. 1 Kings 4:6), was **stoned . . . to death** by **the Israelites** when **Rehoboam sent** him to them to arbitrate their differences. Finally realizing the hopelessness of gaining unified control, **Rehoboam** fled for his life **to Jerusalem.**

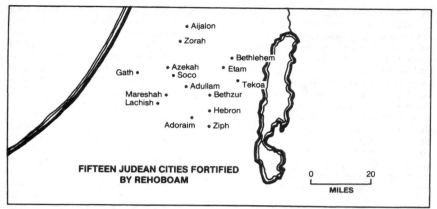

FIFTEEN JUDEAN CITIES FORTIFIED
BY REHOBOAM

0   20
MILES

Aijalon
Zorah
Bethlehem
Azekah · Etam
Gath · · Soco
Adullam · Tekoa
Mareshah · · Bethzur
Lachish ·
· Hebron
Adoraim · Ziph

2. REHOBOAM'S FORTIFICATIONS AND FAMILY (CHAP. 11)

11:1-12. When Rehoboam arrived in Jerusalem he amassed an army of **180,000 . . . men** from **Judah and Benjamin** (Benjamin had become part of Judah politically) and made plans to launch an attack on the rebel tribes. His plans were interrupted, however, by **the word of the LORD** through **Shemaiah** the prophet (cf. 12:5, 15) who proclaimed that the rupture of the kingdom was in the plan **of God** (11:2-4). **Rehoboam** nonetheless **built** defensive outposts in a number of places throughout **Judah and Benjamin,** the 15 cities listed here forming pretty much a circular defense all around **Judah** (vv. 5-12; see the map "Fifteen Judean Cities Fortified by Rehoboam").

11:13-17. Meantime **the priests and Levites** of the North came south to join Rehoboam **because Jeroboam** (as the 1 Kings 12:25–14:16 account relates in detail) had removed them from office and replaced them with an illegitimate priesthood (2 Chron. 11:13-15). The devout populace of the North also recognized the impropriety of the new Jeroboam cult and for at least **three years** made their pilgrimages **to Jerusalem to offer** worship **to the LORD** (vv. 16-17).

11:18-23. In keeping with the chronicler's purpose to magnify the Davidic dynasty, it is interesting that he, unlike the author of 1 and 2 Kings, related that Rehoboam's wife was a descendant of David from two sides (2 Chron. 11:18-19). Her father **Jerimoth** is otherwise unknown but here is identified as a **son** of David. Her mother was **Abihail, daughter of** David's brother **Eliab.** (So Jerimoth married his cousin Abihail.)

Rehoboam's second wife, **Maacah,** was a **daughter of Absalom** (v. 20). This may not be David's son Absalom, however, for he apparently left no children who achieved adulthood except a daughter Tamar (cf. 2 Sam. 14:27; 18:18). Moreover, Maacah's father is otherwise named Abishalom (1 Kings 15:10) and Uriel (2 Chron. 13:2).

By this second wife of Rehoboam, **Abijah** was born. **Rehoboam loved** his second wife **more than any** other **of his. . . . 18 wives and 60 concubines** (11:20-21). Like his father Solomon and his grandfather David he was guilty of polygamy (cf. Deut. 17:16-17). **Abijah** was his father's choice to succeed him as **king** so **Rehoboam** made him crown **prince** (cf. 2 Chron. 13:1). To palliate the other **sons,** however, Rehoboam gave them political appointments, with handsome remunerations (11:23).

3. EGYPT'S ATTACK ON JERUSALEM (CHAP. 12)

12:1-4. Rehoboam had not been ruling long when it became apparent that his border fortifications were inadequate to guard **Judah** against the invasion of the Egyptian army under King **Shishak** I (who ruled ca. 935–914 B.C.). Shishak had earlier given asylum to Jeroboam (cf. 1 Kings 11:40). Shishak, also known as Sheshonk, was the founder of Egypt's 22nd dynasty. On the walls of the temple of Amon at Karnak, Egypt he carved the names of Israelite cities he conquered.

In Rehoboam's **fifth year** (926 B.C.) the Lord brought Shishak as a punishment for Rehoboam's sin of abandoning the Law of the LORD (cf. 1 Kings 14:22-24). With 1,200 chariots and 60,000 cavalry and aided by his Libyan, Sukkite (Egyptian foreign mercenaries), and Cushite allies, the Egyptian king had no difficulty in overrunning the fortresses and was ready to attack Jerusalem itself.

12:5-8. At that point the Prophet Shemaiah (cf. 11:2; 12:15) told Rehoboam that the Egyptian invasion was a divine retribution for Judah's sin and that only sincere repentance would turn it aside. Recognizing the justice of their punishment the leaders humbly turned to the LORD who therefore promised to deliver them from destruction but would allow them to become vassals of the king of Egypt. In this way they would come to appreciate the merciful rule of the Lord in contrast with the cruel ways of human kings. How long this relationship lasted is unknown though it surely did not outlast the reign of Rehoboam.

12:9-11. Before Shishak withdrew from Jerusalem, he plundered the temple and the royal palace of all their gold. The gold supply was so diminished that Rehoboam had to replace the golden ornamental shields (cf. 9:15-16) with bronze. To protect the new shields from theft, guards carried them from the guardroom to the temple and back, whenever Rehoboam went to the temple.

12:12-16. In later years Rehoboam regained his power and wealth, at least to some degree. He died at age 58 and was buried in Jerusalem (the city of David) with his kingly ancestors. His reign, characterized by an evil heart toward the LORD and incessant war with Jeroboam, was chronicled, the historian said, in the annals of the Prophets Shemaiah (cf. 11:2; 12:5) and Iddo (cf. 9:29; 13:22).

B. Abijah (chap. 13)

13:1-2a. By a different chronological system at use in Judah from that in Israel, Abijah began his reign in the 18th year . . . of Jeroboam of Israel but only in the 17th year of his father Rehoboam, though both began to rule at the same time. Thus Abijah came to power in 913 B.C. and reigned until 911 (see comments on his mother Maacah at 11:20-21).

13:2b-12. Abijah took up the hostilities with Jeroboam which had prevailed in the days of Abijah's father. So massive

had the strife between them become that Judah fielded 400,000 . . . men and Israel 800,000 during some point of their antagonism at least (vv. 2b-3). Hoping to forestall a bloody encounter, Abijah addressed his Israelite brothers from Mount Zemaraim, perhaps a short distance east of Bethel (cf. Josh. 18:22). He reminded them that the true kingship lay with David's dynasty, not with Jeroboam. God had made with David . . . a covenant of salt, suggesting durability (cf. comments on Lev. 2:13; Num. 18:19). In fact Jeroboam's rebellious action was possible only because Rehoboam . . . young (i.e., relatively so, for he began reigning at age 41; cf. 2 Chron. 12:13) and naive as he was, had been duped by his counselors (13:7).

The Israelites indeed had a vast army, Abijah said, but since they had exiled the true priests and Levites (cf. 11:14b-15) and chosen other gods (golden calves; cf. goat- and calf-idols, 11:15) they could have no hope of victory for the Lord God was on the side of Judah. God is with us; He is our Leader, Abijah affirmed (13:8-12). (However, cf. Abijah's sins, 13:21; 1 Kings 15:3.) Abijah referred to only 1 lampstand, though Solomon's temple had 10 (2 Chron. 4:7). Perhaps this 1 was the original lampstand Moses made for the tabernacle.

13:13-18. While Abijah's warning was being sounded, Jeroboam set up an ambush . . . behind the troops of Judah. Then Israel attacked from both front and rear. But Judah cried out to the LORD. . . . the priests blew their trumpets (cf. Num. 10:9), and the soldiers raised their battle cry. God then delivered Israel into Judah's hands (2 Chron. 13:16). Judah was victorious because of her reliance on the LORD (v. 18). Altogether Israel suffered 500,000 casualties (v. 17) out of 800,000 men (cf. v. 3).

13:19-22. Thus defeated, Israel retreated and left Judah to occupy (a) Bethel, where Jeroboam had set up a golden calf for worship (1 Kings 12:26-29, 33), (b) Jeshanah (now Burj el-Isaneh, four miles south of Shiloh), and (c) Ephron (four miles northeast of Bethel). Jeroboam never recovered from this blow and died at about the same time as Abijah (910 B.C.). Abijah, like his father and grandfather, was strong politically. Like them he too was involved in polygamy (cf. 2 Chron. 11:21), having 14 wives and 38 children. Other details on Abijah, the chronicler noted, were **written by the Prophet Iddo** (cf. 9:29; 12:15).

C. Asa (chaps. 14–16)

As has been stressed repeatedly, one of the chronicler's major purposes was to provide a comprehensive and systematic account of the divine selection of David and his dynasty and its historical development. This is why the kings of Judah dominate the record and those of Israel appear only when they relate to affairs in the Southern Kingdom. This is contrary to the approach in 1 and 2 Kings where, if anything, the rulers of Israel are pivotal and those of Judah, at least till the fall of Samaria, are almost incidental. So it is not surprising that little is said of Jeroboam in 2 Chronicles 10–13. This neglect of Israel's kings continues to be the rule in the remainder of 2 Chronicles. So the chronicler proceeded to discuss the reign of Asa (chaps. 14–16), Judah's next king, with no mention of Jeroboam's successor in Israel.

1. ASA'S OBEDIENCE TO THE LORD (CHAP. 14)

14:1-5. Asa, son of **Abijah,** occupied the Davidic throne for 41 years (911–870 B.C.; cf. 16:13). His **10 years** of peace (cf. 14:6) preceded the attack by Zerah (vv. 9-15). Asa was assessed as a generally **good** ruler who destroyed pagan objects of worship and urged compliance with the covenant of the LORD. The **sacred stones and . . . Asherah poles** (v. 3) were Canaanite fertility symbols which played an important role in the people's depraved nature religion. (On **the high places** see comments on Num. 33:52.) The Asherah poles were probably images of Asherah, Baal's mother and El's consort, and may have served as incense stands in Baal worship.

14:6-10. Militarily Asa refortified Judah's defensive posts (vv. 6-7), apparently the ones his grandfather Rehoboam had **fortified** (11:5-12) and which Shishak had captured (12:2-4). **Asa** raised **an army . . . from Judah** and **Benjamin** of 580,000 **brave** spearmen and bowmen (14:8). This he did perhaps in anticipation of the invasion by **Zerah the Cushite** (from Cush, modern-day southern Egypt, Sudan, and northern Ethiopia), apparently the mercenary general under Osorkon I of Egypt (914–874 B.C.), suc-

cessor to Shishak. With a vast army (see NIV marg.) **and 300 chariots,** Zerah met **Asa** at **Mareshah** (ca. 25 miles southwest of Jerusalem; cf. 11:8; Micah 1:15). **Zephathah** is mentioned only here in the Bible. Libyans were included in Zerah's army (cf. 2 Chron. 16:8). Whereas Shishak had been successful in his invasion of Judah (12:2, 4, 9), Zerah was not. Shishak's success was probably because of Rehoboam's sins (11:21; 12:1-2) whereas Zerah's defeat was because of Asa's faithfulness (cf. 14:2).

14:11-15. Asa turned to **the** LORD in urgent prayer and was granted a smashing victory. Falling in uncounted numbers, **the Cushites fled** to Gerar (ca. 20 miles farther southwest of Mareshah), to an area that may have already been in Egyptian hands. When **Asa** got there he plundered **Gerar** and the surrounding **villages** and **returned to Jerusalem** in triumph, with **plunder** that included many animals as well as other material goods. Judah had no more war with Egypt till Josiah and Neco met in battle in 609 B.C. (35:20-24).

2. ASA'S REFORMS (CHAP. 15)

15:1-7. In due course **Azariah son of Oded,** a prophet of **the** LORD mentioned only here, **went . . . to . . . Asa** and challenged him to remain true to **the** LORD so that he could continue to enjoy God's blessing. He was told not to lead the people into lawlessness (**without the true God** means without His presence and blessing, **and without the Law,** v. 3, probably means without knowledge of or obedience to it) and anarchy (**great turmoil,** v. 5, and **distress,** v. 6) such as they had experienced in the past, probably in the time of the Judges. Instead Azariah told Asa to **be strong.**

15:8-15. Asa responded to this message from **the prophet** by intensifying his destruction of **idols** (cf. 14:3-5) and repairing the great bronze **altar** of the LORD's **temple** which, for some unspecified reason, had suffered damage. **Then he assembled . . . the people** of his kingdom, including defectors **from Ephraim, Manasseh, and Simeon. . . . in the third month** (May-June) of his **15th year** (896 B.C.). (Apparently some Simeonites, who had not been assimilated into the tribe of Judah, had migrated north.) Asa's purpose was to renew the **covenant** made between the LORD and their fathers under Moses (15:12). Using some of the livestock they had seized from the villages around Gerar (cf. 14:15), the priests offered up a sacrifice of **700 . . . cattle and 7,000 sheep and goats** (15:11). Those refusing to renew the covenant **were to be put to death** for by their refusal they indicated their enmity to **the LORD** and acceptance of other gods (v. 13; cf. Deut. 13:6-9). The people **wholeheartedly** pledged their continued faithfulness (2 Chron. 15:14-15).

15:16-19. Perhaps the most striking evidence of Asa's reformation was his removal of **his** own **grandmother Maacah from** being **queen mother.** (The Heb. '*ēm* can mean either mother, NASB, or "grandmother," NIV.) As "queen mother" she may have been Asa's mother; if so it is coincidental that his grandmother was also named Maacah (cf. 11:20). **She had made** an **Asherah pole,** a Canaanite fertility symbol (cf. comments on 14:3), which **Asa** destroyed **and burned . . . in the Kidron Valley** (cf. 29:16; 30:14), just east of Jerusalem. So Asa eradicated foreign worship from Judah, except for some **high places** that remained (cf. 14:3)—usually sites of pagan altars.

He also enriched **the temple** with **silver and gold** given by Abijah and himself, presumably to help replace some of what Shishak had plundered in Asa's grandfather's day (12:9). Finally, God gave **Asa** a period of peace **until** his **35th year** (876 B.C.; but see comments on 16:1).

3. ASA'S TREATY WITH ARAM (CHAP. 16)

16:1. In Asa's **36th year** he was confronted by **Baasha, king of Israel,** who built a fortress at the Israel-Judah border at **Ramah,** about six miles north of Jerusalem. Baasha's purpose was to prevent further movement of Israelites south to **Judah.** A problem surfaces here in that the dates of Baasha (909–886 B.C.; cf. 1 Kings 15:33) necessitate his death 10 years before the 36th year of Asa. This has led some scholars to conclude that the 35th year (2 Chron. 15:19) refers to the 35th year of the kingdom of Judah since its division from Israel in 931 B.C. This would be 896 B.C. But this is unlikely for the 35th year of the kingdom would hardly be called "the 35th year of Asa's reign." More likely is the suggestion that the numbers may rest on a copyist's mis-

reading of Hebrew figures whereby 35th (15:19) and 36th (16:1) may have been misread for 15th and 16th. This would push the date of the events of chapter 16 back to 895, within Baasha's reign.

16:2-6. Asa felt so threatened by this turn of events that he bribed **Ben-Hadad** the Aramean **king** of **Damascus** to make a defense **treaty** with him and to **break** his (Ben-Hadad's) **treaty with Baasha. Ben-Hadad** did so and invaded northern **Israel,** taking several important **towns. Dan** and **Abel Maim** (or Abel Bethmaacah, 1 Kings 15:20) were about 10 miles north of Lake Huleh, and **Ijon** (modern Merj Ayyun) was just north of Abel Maim. This diverted **Baasha** from barricading **Ramah** so that **Asa** dismantled Baasha's work there and used the materials (**stones and timber**) to build his own defenses at **Geba and Mizpah,** both on the border of Judah and Israel. Geba is probably Gibeah (the city of Saul); Mizpah may be modern Nebi Samwil.

16:7-10. Asa's reliance on Ben-Hadad brought the rebuke of **Hanani the seer** (i.e., prophet) who chided the **king** for having forgotten that it was **the LORD,** not mere soldiers, who had given victory over the **Cushites** (14:12) **and Libyans.** As a result of this **foolish** action, **Asa** would experience **war** to the end of his days. This so angered **Asa** that he cast the prophet into **prison** and took out his frustrations on **the people.**

16:11-14. The book of the kings of Judah and Israel (not 1 and 2 Kings) recorded more details on **Asa's reign.** Later, when **Asa** suffered a foot **disease** in his **39th year** of rule (872 B.C.) he refused to **seek** God's **help** but **only** turned to **the physicians.** Two years later (870) he **died** and was **buried** with an impressive state funeral. The **fire** was not a cremation.

Though **Asa** was generally an upright king, his reign was marred by his reliance on the ungodly Ben-Hadad and his failure to trust the Lord in his illness. The dates of Jehoshaphat, Asa's son (873–848), reveal a coregency of some three years. This may reflect the period of Asa's incapacity.

D. Jehoshaphat (chaps. 17–20)

1. JEHOSHAPHAT'S POWERFUL KINGDOM (CHAP. 17)

17:1-9. Asa was **succeeded** by **Jehoshaphat his son,** a man whose reign was generally complimented by the chronicler. The **king** built up Judah's defenses **against Israel (including towns in Ephraim . . . his father Asa had captured;** cf. 15:8); he **followed** the LORD, removing heathen worship and its accoutrements (17:3-4, 6; on the **Baals** [pl.] see comments on Jud. 2:11, and on **the Asherah poles** see comments on 2 Chron. 14:3); he received **gifts** which brought him **wealth and honor** (17:5); and he **sent** out teachers (**officials. . . . Levites,** and **priests**) all over **Judah** to instruct **the people** in the Law (vv. 7-9). This last act he did in his **third year** (v. 7), perhaps after the death of Asa.

17:10-19. Jehoshaphat also enjoyed the respect of **surrounding** nations, so much so that they left him in peace and **some** (including **Philistines** and **the Arabs**) even **brought** him **tribute** as a sign of his sovereignty over them. The reason for this respect was the vast military might which **Jehoshaphat** amassed. He fortified and supplied defense emplacements **in Judah** (vv. 12-13) and enrolled an army of 780,000 men of **Judah** and 380,000 of **Benjamin** (vv. 14-18). This did not include those **stationed in the** fortifications (v. 19). These numbers seem unusually large. His father Asa had 300,000 from Judah and 280,000 from Benjamin (14:8). Some suggest that Jehoshaphat's troops consisted of military units whose composition is now unclear (e.g., the Heb. word for "thousands" might be, it is suggested, a technical term for a unit of perhaps no more than 100 men, so Judah would have had 780 such units). However, since David, more than 100 years earlier, had 500,000 Judean soldiers (2 Sam. 24:9), Jehoshaphat's roster of 780,000 may not be excessive.

2. JEHOSHAPHAT'S ALLIANCE WITH AHAB (18:1–19:3)

18:1-3a. One result of Jehoshaphat's formidable strength was his attractiveness to **Ahab, king of Israel,** who both feared him and wished to use him as an ally. **Ahab** was the second king of the Omride dynasty of Israel, the most illustrious family in the Northern Kingdom's history. He had come to power at about the same time as **Jehoshaphat** (Ahab reigned from 874 to 853 B.C.) and was related to Jehoshaphat **by a marriage** alliance (Jehoshaphat's son Jehoram had

married Athaliah, Ahab and Jezebel's daughter, 21:6; 22:2b). Toward the end of Ahab's life (in 853) he was engaged in bitter hostilities with the Arameans in the Transjordan (cf. 1 Kings 22:1-4). **Jehoshaphat** went to **Samaria,** Israel's capital, to see **Ahab.** After flattering Jehoshaphat with an elaborate banquet **Ahab** urged him to go to **Ramoth Gilead** to join him in war against the Arameans.

18:3b-7. Jehoshaphat agreed to go to war with Ahab on condition that **the** LORD give His approval. Ahab then gathered his **400** false and mercenary **prophets** (perhaps prophets of Asherah; cf. 1 Kings 18:19b) who gave their blessing to his plans. **Jehoshaphat,** however, knew the prophets were charlatans so he asked for a true **prophet** of the LORD. The only **one** available was **Micaiah son of Imlah,** but Ahab hated **him because** he would not compromise his integrity and give Ahab any **good** words (cf. 2 Chron. 18:17).

18:8-11. While **Micaiah** was being summoned, **the** other **prophets** continued to predict victory. **Zedekiah** was especially dramatic in his approach, holding in his hands some **iron horns** which he said symbolized Ahab's ability to thrust through the enemy.

18:12-17. Then **Micaiah** arrived, having been instructed to tell King Ahab what he wanted to hear. Micaiah declined to do so. But when he was first asked the outcome of the campaign he pretended to give assurance of victory (v. 14b). But he soon gave the true message of **the** LORD, predicting a defeat for **Israel.** He compared **Israel** to **sheep** whose **shepherd** (Ahab) is taken away.

18:18-27. Then **Micaiah** related a vision in which he **saw** God commission a demonic **spirit** to inspire the **prophets** of Ahab to lie to him (vv. 18-22). On hearing that, **Zedekiah** (cf. v. 10) **slapped Micaiah,** who then predicted that Zedekiah would suffer calamity in the day of Israel's defeat (vv. 23-24). Ahab then returned **Micaiah** to **Amon,** the mayor of Samaria, **and to Joash the king's son** (v. 25). "King's son" is apparently a title of a royal official, not a literal son of Ahab (cf. Jer. 36:26; 38:6; 2 Chron. 28:7). Ahab also commanded that **Micaiah** be imprisoned, but as Ahab left, the man of God once more promised that **the king** would not **return** whole (18:25-27).

The vision of Micaiah is troublesome to some as it seems to suggest that God is the author of deceit (vv. 18-21). However, it is clearly just one of many examples of the sovereignty of God who does not initiate evil but sometimes allows it to occur for His own purposes (cf. 1 Sam. 16:14; Job 1:12; 2:5-6; 2 Cor. 12:7).

18:28–19:3. Having disregarded Micaiah (18:25), Ahab **and Jehoshaphat** went forth to **battle.** Despite being **in disguise,** Ahab was struck mortally by an enemy arrow and **died** at the close of the **day. Jehoshaphat** was spared by the goodness of **God** and managed to escape unscathed. When he got back to **Jerusalem,** however, he was met by the Prophet **Jehu** (cf. 20:34) **the son of Hanani** (cf. Hanani and Asa in 16:7) who rebuked him for his ungodly alliance with Ahab (19:1-2). The prophet did praise him, though, for his removal of paganism in Judah (cf. 17:6) and his love for **the LORD** (19:3).

3. JEHOSHAPHAT'S APPOINTMENT OF JUDGES (19:4-11)

19:4-11. Part of Jehoshaphat's program of reform was his personally traveling through **Judah** to encourage **people** to turn **back to the LORD.** He also **appointed** godly **judges** throughout **the land,** arbiters whose task it was to judge without **partiality or bribery** (cf. Deut. 16:18-20). He did the same **in Jerusalem** with a kind of supreme court charged with hearing the matters referred to them from outlying districts. **Over** this court he selected **Amariah the chief priest** to oversee religious cases and **Zebadiah** (not the same Zebadiah as in 2 Chron. 17:8, who was a Levite) to be **over** civil cases. **The Levites** would **serve** as officers to implement the work of the judges as a whole.

4. JEHOSHAPHAT'S DEFEAT OF A FOREIGN ALLIANCE (20:1-30)

20:1-2. Shortly after the disastrous adventure at Ramoth Gilead (chap. 18), **Moabites . . . Ammonites,** and **Meunites** launched an attack **on Jehoshaphat** from across the Jordan. The Meunites (cf. 1 Chron. 4:41; 2 Chron. 26:7) were an Arabian tribe living in Edom and elsewhere east and south of the Dead Sea. The **army** mentioned in 20:2, then, was from Edom (cf. Mount Seir [Edom] in vv. 10, 22-23), not from Aram (Heb.; cf. NIV

marg., v. 2). **Jehoshaphat** learned that this great host was **already** at **Hazazon Tamar (En Gedi;** cf. 1 Sam. 23:29), on the west shore of the Dead Sea, and would soon head for Jerusalem.

20:3-12. This situation prompted the king to proclaim a national **fast** (perhaps to show the people's sincerity; cf. 1 Sam. 7:6) and to **seek** God. He then addressed **the LORD** in prayer before **the temple . . . courtyard** (cf. 2 Chron. 4:9). **Jehoshaphat** first extolled **God** for His sovereign **power** (20:6) and then recalled God's grace in giving them, Abraham's **descendants,** the **land** (v. 7; cf. Gen. 15:18-21) and temple (**sanctuary,** 2 Chron. 20:8). (**Abraham** was also called God's **friend** in Isa. 41:8 and James 2:23.)

Next Jehoshaphat reminded the Lord of His promise to deliver them if they would only seek Him before His **temple** (2 Chron. 20:9; cf. 6:28-31). The prayer closed by referring to the immediate need—Judah was being assaulted by the same nations they had spared en route to Canaan **from Egypt.** They now needed the Lord's help (**we have no power to face this vast army** and **we do not know what to do**) to deliver them from their ungrateful attackers (20:10-12).

20:13-19. After Jehoshaphat's moving prayer, **the Spirit of the LORD came** on the Levite **Jahaziel** and empowered him to address **the assembly.** His message was one of comfort. (Twice he said, **Do not be afraid or discouraged,** vv. 15, 17.) **The battle,** he said, was **not** theirs **but God's.** David had spoken similar words when facing Goliath (1 Sam. 17:47). The next day they should depart and meet the enemy in the narrow mountain **pass** called **Ziz,** somewhere in the wilderness of Judah southeast of Jerusalem. But when the enemy was in sight they need only **stand** and watch what God would do. The assembly then **fell down in worship to the LORD,** and **some Levites** gave **loud** praise to Him.

20:20-26. Next day **Jehoshaphat** and the singers led the way to the conflict in **the Desert of Tekoa.** (Tekoa, Amos' hometown, Amos 1:1, was ca. 12 miles south of Jerusalem.) The singers inspired **the people** with their words of encouragement to trust **the LORD.** Then, at the moment of encounter, **the LORD** caused such confusion among the enemy troops that they turned on **one another.** The

Ammonites and the Moabites fought against the Meunites until the latter were annihilated, and after that the Ammonites fought against the Moabites. The slaughter was so great that **the men of Judah** could not **carry** away all the **plunder.** With thanksgiving to God they gathered **in the Valley of Beracah** ("praise") and offered their praise to God for His enduring **love** (2 Chron. 20:21; ḥesed, "loyal love"; cf. 5:13; 6:14; 7:3, 6).

20:27-30. The soldiers then **returned** home to praise **God** at **the temple** with musical instruments. So obvious was God's hand on His people that **all** other nations feared Him. From then on **Jehoshaphat** enjoyed **peace.**

5. JEHOSHAPHAT'S LAST DAYS (20:31-37)

20:31-33. The chronicler concluded the annals of **Jehoshaphat** by mentioning his age **(35)** at accession, his length of reign **(25 years),** and the **name** of his mother **(Azubah).** His final assessment of the king was positive for the most part— **he walked in the ways of . . . the LORD** as had **his father.** Yet Jehoshaphat had allowed **the high places** to remain and had not brought his **people** to a steadfast commitment to the Lord. Earlier he had removed the practice of pagan worship at the high places (17:6), but apparently some people had restored them and the king did nothing about it.

20:34-37. Besides the details of **Jehoshaphat's reign** preserved in the records of the Prophet **Jehu** (cf. 19:2; also note comments on 33:18; 1 Kings 14:19; and comments under "Authorship" in the *Introduction* to 1 Chron.), the chronicler added a note about the king's ill-fated venture **with Ahaziah,** son of Ahab (cf. 1 Kings 22:49), the two of whom attempted **to construct** merchant **ships** at **Ezion Geber** (cf. comments on 2 Chron. 8:17). The plan was frustrated by the **LORD** because, as the Prophet **Eliezer** (from **Mareshah,** where the Cushites were defeated by Asa, 14:9-15) announced, **Jehoshaphat** had sinned by his temporary ungodly **alliance** (cf. chap. 19) **with** the Omride dynasty. Somehow **the ships were wrecked** before they ever sailed.

E. *Jehoram (chap. 21)*

21:1-3. Jehoshaphat was succeeded by his son **Jehoram,** the oldest of his seven sons. **Jehoshaphat** gave to each of the others properties and goods.

21:4-7. When **Jehoram** came to power, however, he killed **his brothers** along with others of the royal family, perhaps because of his close ties with the wicked rulers of Israel (vv. 4, 6). He too would suffer a cruel death after a brief reign of only **eight years** (v. 5, 848–841 B.C.). Like his father, **Jehoram** had a close tie with the Omrides, going so far as to marry Athaliah, **daughter** of Ahab (v. 6; cf. 22:2). Despite Jehoram's personal **evil,** however, **the LORD** did not **destroy** the nation, for he remembered his everlasting **covenant** with **David** (21:7; cf. 1 Chron. 17:4-14). Like **a lamp** that was kept burning in one's tent or house, so David's line would continue (cf. 2 Sam. 21:17; 1 Kings 11:36; 15:4; 2 Kings 8:19).

21:8-11. Since the time of David and Solomon, Israel and **Judah** had held certain foreign provinces, including **Edom.** Moab had finally revolted from Israel's King Joram, in the last years of Jehoshaphat and, in an action not recounted by the chronicler, the two kings had attempted, apparently unsuccessfully, to regain their tribute state (cf. 2 Kings 3). Now **Edom** revolted from **Judah,** an action which called forth a futile response from **Jehoram** (2 Chron. 21:8-10a). **Libnah** also **revolted** (v. 10b), probably as a result of renewed Philistine pressure against the lowlands region where Libnah was located (cf. v. 16). All these setbacks occurred, the narrator wrote, **because Jehoram had** led **the people** away from **the LORD** and into pagan practices (vv. 10b-11).

21:12-15. In a final word of condemnation the Prophet **Elijah** sent **a letter** to **Jehoram** in which he charged the king with behaving like an Israelite and not like his godly fathers (vv. 12-13). **Now the LORD** would **strike** the nation and Jehoram's family **with a heavy blow** and would afflict him with an incurable **disease of the bowels** (vv. 14-15).

This letter from Elijah is of more than passing interest because it is the only known written message from the great prophet. Some scholars allege that it could not be authentic since, they say, Elijah was translated to heaven before Jehoram began to reign. But Elijah was still living on earth in the days of Joram, son of Ahab, who succeeded his

2 CHRONICLES

brother Ahaziah in 852 B.C. (cf. 2 Kings 1:17).

This event, the author of 2 Kings wrote, occurred "in the second year of Jehoram . . . king of Judah." Though Jehoram's sole regency in Judah began in the year of Jehoshaphat's death (848), he co-reigned with his father from 853 to 848. It is still true, of course, that Jehoram could not have murdered his brothers until after 848 so the matter of Elijah's knowledge of this fact still remains. Since there is no certain way to date Elijah's translation perhaps it did not take place until 848 or even later.

21:16-20. The prophecies of Elijah came to pass. Judah was invaded by **the Philistines** and South Arabians **who lived near the Cushites** (of the Cush that was in southern Arabia, not the Cush in northeastern Africa). They looted the royal **palace** and **carried off** the **king's** family except **the youngest** son. **Jehoram** was afflicted by the promised **disease** (cf. v. 15), diagnosis of which is impossible in view of the scant information in verses 15, 18-19. His burial was without fanfare (**no funeral fire** was burned **in his honor** as was done for Asa, 16:14). Jehoram's death was **to no one's regret** because he had brought such misery on the nation. Like several other Judean kings he **was buried** in Jerusalem **but not in the tombs of the kings** (cf. 24:25; 26:23; 28:27).

F. Ahaziah (22:1-9)

22:1-5a. Ahaziah was **Jehoram's youngest** and only surviving **son** (cf. 21:17). **He became king** and **reigned** for **one year** (841 B.C.). He **was 22 years old** at the time. The Hebrew has "42" (cf. NIV marg.) but that is probably a copyist's error for 22 (cf. 2 Kings 8:26). Since his father was dead and **his mother** was **Athaliah,** daughter **of Ahab** (and **granddaughter of Omri**), it is little wonder that Ahaziah's brief tenure was **evil.** He followed his father's **advisers** in every respect including **their counsel** that he go **to war** with **Hazael king of Aram** in league with **Joram,** Ahab's **son** and **king of Israel.** Ahab had died **at Ramoth Gilead** (2 Chron. 18:34), and now **Hazael,** having murdered Ben-Hadad, was **king of Aram** (2 Kings 8:14-15).

22:5b-9. Joram, Israel's king, was **wounded** in the battle near Ramoth Gilead and **returned to** his secondary residence at **Jezreel to recover. Ahaziah** then went to **visit . . . Joram,** probably because of their close family ties (Joram was Athaliah's brother and thus Ahaziah's uncle). While both were at Jezreel, **Jehu son of Nimshi,** an Israelite military officer whom **the LORD had** chosen to be Israel's next king (cf. 2 Kings 9:1-13), met them. After **Jehu** killed Joram (2 Kings 9:24), he pursued **Ahaziah** (who had fled to **Samaria,** about 20 miles south) and **brought** him back to Jezreel.

The chronicler seems to have implied that **Ahaziah** died at Jezreel (2 Chron. 22:9) while the author of Kings wrote that Ahaziah died at Megiddo (2 Kings 9:27). Probably the two accounts are supplementary. Ahaziah fled to Samaria and was **captured** there by Jehu's **men,** who brought him back **to Jehu.** Meanwhile Jehu left Jezreel and met Ahaziah as he was being returned. Jehu's men wounded him and Ahaziah escaped to Megiddo where he died (2 Kings 9:27).

The king's servants **buried him** in Jerusalem (2 Kings 9:28). In addition to murdering the two kings, **Jehu** almost annihilated the royal families of both Israel and **Judah** (2 Chron. 22:8; cf. 2 Kings 10:1-14). This left Jehu in power in the north; and **there was no** male survivor in the Davidic dynasty except Joash, an infant son **of Ahaziah** back in Jerusalem (cf. 2 Chron. 22:11).

G. Athaliah (22:10–23:21)

22:10-12. The empty throne of Judah was left by default to **Athaliah,** Ahaziah's wicked Israelite **mother,** who finished the bloody massacre begun by Jehu and destroyed all remaining members of the Judean **royal family** she could find. This meant, of course, that she put to the sword many of her own flesh and blood since she was the queen mother! Thanks to **Jehosheba,** sister of **Ahaziah,** the infant **Joash,** her nephew, was spared and placed under close security during the **six years** of Athaliah's reign (841–835 B.C.).

23:1-3. In the **year** 835 **Jehoiada** the priest (and husband of Jehosheba, 22:11) made his move. Eager to restore the Davidic family, and specifically Joash, to the throne, he engineered a plot with five army officers to assemble the **Levites** and leaders of **Judah** in **Jerusalem** and persuaded them to support the young **king** in a formal **covenant** ceremony.

23:4-7. Jehoiada then divided the **priests and Levites** up by thirds and stationed them at **the temple,** the **palace,** and **the Foundation Gate** (the Sur Gate in 2 Kings 11:6 is perhaps just another name for the same gate). The lay leaders were stationed **in the** temple **courtyards.** Since only **the priests and Levites** who were then **on duty** were authorized to **enter the temple,** the others were to remain outside to protect **the king.**

23:8-15. All the assembly then took up **spears** and **shields** from **the temple** storerooms and awaited the appearance of young Joash. When all was ready **Jehoiada . . . presented him** to the crowd, crowned him, gave him **a copy of the covenant** (i.e., the Law) as protocol required (cf. Deut. 17:18-20), **anointed him,** and led the acclamation, **Long live the king!**

When Athaliah heard the clamor **she** rushed out to **the temple** and saw in a moment that she had been the victim of a coup. In grief over her loss she **tore her robes** (cf. Gen. 37:29, 34; Josh. 7:6; Job 1:20; 2:12) **and shouted, Treason!** This was not a bloodless coup, for **Jehoiada** ordered Athaliah and her followers dragged from the temple area and had her executed at **the Horse Gate** of the **palace** complex.

23:16-21. Jehoiada then led the whole populace in **a covenant** oath that **he . . . the people, and the king** would **be** loyal to **the Lord.** In keeping with this vow they **went to the temple of Baal** and destroyed it and its **altars and idols** and slew **Mattan the priest of Baal** (in compliance with the Law, Deut. 13:5-10). **Jehoiada** then restored the regular priestly and Levitical assignments just as **David** had prescribed they be carried out. Finally, he took **the king** with all the entourage of leaders to **the palace and seated** him **on the throne** officially. At last Judah knew peace once more.

H. Joash (chap. 24)

1. JOASH'S TEMPLE RESTORATION
(24:1-16)

24:1-3. Joash, apparently the only surviving son of Ahaziah, began to reign at the age of **seven** and held the kingship for **40 years** (835–796). He was under the tutelage of **Jehoiada the priest** for the first several **years** and Joash remained

righteous before **the Lord** all that time. **Jehoiada** even selected **two wives** for **Joash.**

24:4-7. Eventually (perhaps as much as 20 years later; cf. 2 Kings 12:6) the young monarch **decided to restore the temple** which had deteriorated during the apostate days of Athaliah. To do so required the raising of funds, so he ordered **the priests and Levites** to go throughout the land and **collect** the temple taxes required by the Law of Moses (cf. Ex. 30:12-16). Presumably these had not been gathered for many years. When **the Levites** were slow to **act,** Joash rebuked **Jehoiada** for not having seen the task to completion (2 Chron. 24:4-6). Part of the reason for the need of temple restoration was the fact that God's house had been looted and its contents used for the worship of **the Baals.**

24:8-16. Having given up on the Levites, Joash **issued** a formal **proclamation** that **all the people** of the kingdom must **bring** their taxes to **the temple** and put them in a specially prepared **chest** near the temple **gate** (vv. 8-9). The response was so generous that the **chest** was filled and had to be emptied over and over again (vv. 10-11). The money was then used to pay the workmen commissioned to do **the temple** restoration (v. 12). They did **the work** quickly, carefully, and well within the budget for when the job was **finished** the workers had **money** left over with which to provide furnishings and utensils for the **temple** worship (vv. 13-14). Unfortunately, however, **Jehoiada . . . died** and with him died the spirit of reformation (vv. 15-16).

2. JOASH'S WICKEDNESS AND ASSASSINATION
(24:17-27)

24:17-20. Joash seemingly was as easily influenced to do evil **after the** priest's **death** as he was to do good before. He began to listen to **officials** who pandered to him and he allowed **the temple** worship to decline and be replaced by Canaanite fertility rites (vv. 17-18a). This naturally displeased **the Lord** so **He sent prophets** to protest this evil but to no avail (vv. 18b-19). Finally **God** sent **Zechariah,** Jehoiada's **son,** to tell the **people** that because they had **forsaken** God **He** had **forsaken** them (v. 20).

24:21-22. This so infuriated the mob that they **stoned** Zechariah **to death in,** of all places, the temple **courtyard**! Even **Joash**, forgetting **the kindness** of **Jehoiada** to him, took part in the murder of Zechariah. Perhaps this was the Zechariah Jesus referred to in Matthew 23:34-35. If so, Zechariah may have been the son of Berekiah and also the "son" (i.e., grandson) of Jehoiada (cf. comments on Matt. 23:35). However, Jesus may have been referring not to this Zechariah in 2 Chronicles but to the Zechariah who wrote the Old Testament book that bears his name, for he *was* the son of Berekiah. As Zechariah expired he pronounced a divine curse on the **king**.

24:23-27. Soon the prophet was vindicated. The very next **year** (in the spring) the Arameans **invaded Judah . . . killed** her **leaders,** and took away great **plunder.** (Other battles between Judah and the Arameans occurred in the reigns of Ahaziah, 22:5, and Ahaz, 28:5.) The Arameans did this even though they were greatly outnumbered. It was clear that this was God's **judgment . . . on Joash.**

After **the Arameans withdrew,** leaving the king **wounded,** Joash's confidants **killed him** because of what he had done to Zechariah. No doubt they thought this would allay the divine wrath. Even in death Joash was dishonored for he, like several other Judean kings, was **not** buried in the royal **tombs** with his ancestors (cf. 21:20; 26:23; 28:27) and Jehoiada the righteous priest (24:16). The names of the two assassins are also given in 2 Kings 12:21, but the chronicler added that they were **an Ammonite** and **a Moabite.** Apparently this was his way of blaming foreigners for this deed against an anointed son of David. **The book of the kings** may be the Old Testament Books of 1 and 2 Kings.

I. Amaziah (chap. 25)

25:1-4. Joash was succeeded by his son **Amaziah,** who enjoyed a reign of **29 years** (796–767 B.C.). The chronicler's summary of his character is that he pleased **the LORD, but not wholeheartedly.** One of his first official acts was the avenging of his father's murder (cf. 24:25-26) but his heart for God is seen by his sparing the assassins' **sons** in accord with Moses' principle that **children** must not be punished for the **sins** of **their fathers** (cf. Deut. 24:16).

25:5-10. Amaziah's interest in military affairs was manifested by his conscripting an army of **300,000 men.** He even went so far as to hire **100,000** Israelites for **100 talents of silver** (ca. 3¾ tons; cf. NIV marg.). However, this was tantamount to making an ungodly alliance, which was made pointedly clear to him by **a man of God** (whose name is unknown), who reminded the **king** that **the LORD** was **not with Israel,** so He would not be with Judah **in battle** if Israel went along. **Amaziah** was convinced of the correctness of this advice but wondered how he would get back the silver he had already **paid.** To this the prophet responded that **God** could **more than** make it up to Amaziah. **So Amaziah** sent the Israelites **home,** but they became angry (**furious** and **in a great rage**) that they were prevented from participation. No doubt they felt gypped out of their plunder.

25:11-16. Judah then marched against the **men of Seir** (Edomites; cf. Gen. 36:9; 2 Chron. 20:2 with 20:22) in **the Valley of Salt** (probably the salt plains south of the Dead Sea) and **killed 10,000** of them. (For other battles fought there see Gen. 14:3; 1 Chron. 18:12.) With unusual brutality the Judeans took an additional **10,000 men** as prisoners and **threw them** over **a cliff** to their deaths. (High cliffs were in that area; cf. Obad. 1, 3.)

Meanwhile the frustrated Israelite **troops** (cf. 2 Chron. 25:6, 10) **raided Judean** outposts in central and southern Israel (see comments about **Beth Horon** in 8:5), **killed 3,000** persons, and took **great** amounts of their possessions.

When Amaziah returned from his victory over **the Edomites,** he **brought** as a part of the spoils the idols of that land. He went so far as to **set them up** and worship them, a blasphemous act that prompted **the LORD** to send **a prophet** (also anonymous; cf. 25:7) **to rebuke him. Why,** the man of God asked, should **Amaziah** worship **gods which could not** even save their own people? **The king** was cut to the quick and threatened to kill the man of God on the spot if he would not desist. In his last words to the king **the prophet** announced that Amaziah would come to know God's punishment because of his idolatry and rejection of the prophet's **counsel.**

25:17-19. Amaziah then turned his attention to the Israelite raids on his outposts. He in effect challenged **Jehoash . . . king of Israel** (grandson of Jehu) to wage war. But **Jehoash** answered in the form of a parable or fable. It concerned a **thistle** (Amaziah) who demanded of a **cedar** (Jehoash) that the cedar **give** his **daughter** as a wife for the thistle's **son.** The thistle was rewarded for his presumptuousness by being overrun by a **wild beast** (Israel's army). Jehoash interpreted his own story by comparing Amaziah to a mere bush who, because he **defeated** the minor power of **Edom,** thought he was equal to a mighty tree. He ought to know better and refrain from conflict.

25:20-24. Amaziah paid no heed, **however,** to Jehoash's belligerent refusal, **for God** had determined to use **Jehoash** as His punishing rod for Amaziah's idolatry. As a result **Israel attacked** Judah, achieved a smashing victory, and **captured Amaziah** himself at **Beth Shemesh** (ca. 15 miles southwest of Jerusalem). From there he **brought** the humiliated king **to Jerusalem** itself, **broke down** a long **section (600 feet)** of its walls **from the Ephraim Gate** (cf. Neh. 8:16; 12:39) on the north to the northwest **Corner Gate** (cf. Jer. 31:38, Zech. 14:10; see the map "Jerusalem in the Time of Nehemiah," near Neh. 2), and **took all** the temple **articles** that were under **the care of** the family of **Obed-Edom** (cf. 1 Chron. 26:4-8) and the **palace treasures** and prisoners back **to Samaria.**

25:25-28. Amaziah either remained alive at Jerusalem or was returned there later for he outlived **Jehoash** by **15 years.** He had become unpopular with his own people **in Jerusalem,** however, and was forced finally to go into exile at **Lachish** (ca. 30 miles southwest of Jerusalem). He was not safe even there, for a band of assassins found him, **killed him,** and **brought** his body **back** for burial. His father Joash had been assassinated too (cf. 24:25-26).

J. Uzziah (chap. 26)

26:1. Amaziah apparently had made no plans for his succession, for after his untimely death **the people** took his young son **Uzziah** (Azariah in 2 Kings 14:21 is a variant spelling) and elevated him to kingship. Only **16 years old** at the time, Uzziah reigned for the extraordinarily long period of 52 years (cf. 2 Chron. 26:3; 790–739 B.C.). A serious chronological problem emerges here. Amaziah reigned from 796 to 767, so if Uzziah commenced his reign in 790 he co-reigned with his father for 23 years. Yet the chronicler (and the author of 2 Kings as well) seemed to indicate that Uzziah's tenure *followed* that of Amaziah and that Uzziah was only 16 years old at the time. How then could his coregency be for 23 years?

The chronological data for both kings are very well established on grounds too complicated to be considered here. (For a full discussion see Edwin R. Thiele, *The Mysterious Numbers of the Hebrew Kings.* Rev. ed. Grand Rapids: Wm. B. Eerdmans Publishing Co., 1983, pp. 113-23.) The narratives can be viewed in a way that legitimately comports with the dates mentioned earlier. The best solution appears to be that the leadership of Judah, fearing early in Amaziah's reign that he was unstable and incompetent, made his young son Uzziah viceregent. In other words after Amaziah had reigned only six years (796–790) Uzziah, *then* (in 790) 16 years old, was appointed second to the king. From then until Amaziah's death (767) they reigned together for 23 years (790–767). Then Uzziah reigned alone for 29 years until his own death.

This would require, of course, that the chronicler meant that the people of Judah had made Uzziah vice-regent at the age of 16 (2 Chron. 26:1). In support of this reconstruction is the fact that Uzziah received religious instruction from Zechariah (v. 5). Zechariah, however, was stoned to death by some Judeans before the death of Amaziah's predecessor Joash (24:21-22), who died in 796. Uzziah, then, obviously was of a teachable age before 796 (by 796 he would have been 10 years old). His major independent accomplishments could not have come about until his sole regency began in 767 so these are the ones with which the historian is particularly concerned.

26:2. Uzziah recovered **Elath** from Edom and **rebuilt** it. (On Elath's location see comments on 8:17.) Apparently Edom repossessed Elath when Edom rebelled from **Judah** in the reign of Jehoram

(21:8-10), Uzziah's great-great-grandfather. Later in the reign of Ahaz, Uzziah's grandson, Edom regained Elath (2 Kings 16:6).

26:3-8. God rewarded Uzziah's godliness with **success** in several areas, including military adventures. He destroyed the Philistine towns of **Gath, Jabneh, and Ashdod** and rebuilt others in the region. He was successful also in campaigns **against the Arabs** of Gur Baal (site now unknown) and **the Meunites** (cf. 1 Chron. 4:41). **The Ammonites** recognized his sovereignty over them and **his fame** (cf. 2 Chron. 26:15) **spread** to Egypt's borders.

26:9-15. Internally **Uzziah** masterminded the construction of fortress **towers in Jerusalem** at various points on the walls, perhaps including the portion of wall Jehoash had destroyed (cf. 25:23). (On **the Corner Gate** see comments on 25:23; on **the Valley Gate,** probably on Jerusalem's western wall, see Neh. 2:13, 15; 3:13; and on **the angle of the wall** see Neh. 3:19-20, 24-25.) He also undertook massive agricultural projects in the desert as well as **the foothills** and plains. He reorganized **an army of 307,500** men (similar in size to Amaziah's army, 2 Chron. 25:5) into **well-trained** and well-equipped **divisions** under **2,600** leaders. He pioneered the use of certain advanced weapons such as catapults to hurl **arrows** and **large stones** a great distance. All this enhanced his reputation (cf. 26:8) and increased his strength.

26:16-20. Uzziah's great power led to pride, which proved to be **his downfall** (cf. Prov. 16:18; 18:12). Apparently he began to depend on men and weapons rather than on **the Lord.** He even presumed to offer **incense** in **the temple,** a sacrilege for which **Azariah the priest** and **80 other . . . priests** roundly condemned him. He was **unfaithful** to the Law (2 Chron. 26:16-18), which limited this function to the priest (Ex. 30:7-8). Uzziah responded in rage but the propriety of the priests' rebuke was immediately evident when the king's **forehead** broke out with **leprosy.** This rendered the king ceremonially unclean so that he had to **leave** the **temple** at once (2 Chron. 26:19-20; cf. Lev. 13).

26:21-23. Until **the day** of his death **Uzziah** was **leprous** to such an extent that he had to be quarantined and had to

yield the reins of government to **Jotham his son.** Even in death he was ostracized because of his disease and was buried **near** his **fathers** (ancestors), not *with* them (cf. 21:20; 24:25; 28:27). Other information on **Uzziah** may be found, the chronicler indicated, in the writings of **the Prophet Isaiah** (cf. Isa. 1:1; 6:1).

K. Jotham (chap. 27)

27:1. The reign of Uzziah's son **Jotham** began in 750 B.C. and hence overlapped Uzziah's by about 11 years (till Uzziah died in 739). This fact is understandable in light of Uzziah's incapacity in the last years of his life (26:21). But Jotham also co-reigned with his son for four years (735–731) so that the reference to his length of reign as **16 years** (cf. 27:8) does not include that period. His dates as principal ruler were the 16-year period of 750–735.

27:2-4. His record was nearly blameless (cf. v. 6) but **the people** were still unfaithful to **the Lord** (cf. 2 Kings 15:35). His building projects included repairing **the Upper Gate** (cf. 2 Chron. 23:20) **of the temple** (i.e., the north side of the outer court) and reconstructing the **Ophel** wall which encompassed the old city of Jerusalem (cf. 33:14). Jotham also followed up Uzziah's projects in the **hills** and forest **areas.**

27:5-9. Evidently **the Ammonites** had slacked off in their payment of tribute (cf. 26:8) so **Jotham** brought them to heel by conquering **them.** They now were required to pay **100 talents of silver** (3¾ tons), **10,000 cors of wheat** (62,000 bushels), **and 10,000 cors of barley.** This they did for three successive **years,** after which perhaps the burden was lessened. The rest of **Jotham's** affairs could be found in the records of **the kings of Israel and Judah,** perhaps some of which are preserved in the Books of 1 and 2 Kings (cf. 2 Kings 15:32-38).

L. Ahaz (chap. 28)

28:1-4. **Ahaz** co-reigned for four years with Jotham (cf. comments on 27:1). So, as the historian noted, Ahaz **reigned** (alone) for **16 years** (731–715). **Unlike David his father** (i.e., ancestor), Ahaz was evil, walking in the pattern **of the kings of Israel** (those in the Northern Kingdom, all of whom were wicked). He **made** Baal idols, offered **sacrifices in the**

Valley of Ben Hinnom (cf. 33:6), which included human victims (even his own sons!); and practiced the Canaanite cult on the high places (cf. comments on 14:3) and in the sacred groves (cf. other comments about his sins in 28:19, 22-25).

Human sacrifice was particularly associated with the Ammonite god Molech and was vehemently condemned in the Law (cf. Lev. 18:21; 20:2-5; Deut. 12:31). It was practiced especially in the Hinnom Valley, just south and west of Jerusalem, a place later known as Gehenna (from gê, "valley," and the proper name Hinnom). Because of the fires which burned there both in these sacrificial orgies and to consume garbage, Gehenna became a term for hell (cf. comments on Matt. 5:22).

28:5-8. Because of Ahaz's gross sins against God, he fell into the hands of the Arameans (whose king was Rezin, 2 Kings 16:5), who took many Judeans as prisoners . . . to Damascus. This was the third time the Arameans fought Judah (cf. 22:5; 24:23). Ahaz also suffered defeat by the armies of Israel under their King Pekah, who killed 120,000 Judean soldiers in one day. These included several casualties within Ahaz's own family and court. Also Israel took . . . 200,000 wives, sons, and daughters of Judah off to Samaria.

28:9-15. As 2 Kings 16:5 indicates, Ahaz was not totally overcome but he clearly was in great jeopardy. Meanwhile Oded, a prophet in Samaria, persuaded the leaders of Israel that God was displeased (angry) with Israel's taking these prisoners of Judah to make them slaves. The leaders (four of them are named in 2 Chron. 28:12) therefore ordered the returning army not to bring the prisoners to Samaria. So the leaders gave the prisoners food and clothing and led the prisoners to Jericho where they could be repatriated to their own country. Ironically Israel listened to the Lord whereas Judah did not.

28:16-18. Not satisfied that Israel's kind overtures were signals of a new and friendly era, Ahaz entered into negotiations with the king of Assyria, who at that time was Tiglath-Pileser III (745–727 B.C.). Isaiah had tried to prevent Ahaz from turning to Assyria (cf. Isa. 7:4-9). This move was necessary, Ahaz thought, because of intensifying pressure from the Edomites (cf. comments on 2 Chron.

26:2) to the east and the Philistines to the west (the foothills) and south (the Negev, the desert south of Judah). In addition, of course, was the continuing threat from the Arameans and Israelites (cf. 28:5-8), a factor mentioned in 2 Kings 16:5-9 and Isaiah 7:1-17.

28:19-27. Tiglath-Pileser proved to be a curse rather than a blessing for despite receiving a generous bribe from Ahaz . . . from the temple and the palace, the Assyrian king gave no help. The author of Kings wrote that Tiglath-Pileser heeded Ahaz and went on to attack and defeat Damascus, the Aramean capital (2 Kings 16:9). But this does not contradict the chronicler, who was more concerned with spiritual than military repercussions. Ahaz's entanglements with the Assyrians led eventually to disaster. This may be seen in his adoption of Aramean gods, whom he sought to placate because the Arameans had defeated Judah (2 Chron. 28:5).

This Aramean victory signified to Ahaz that these gods must be superior to Israel's God (Yahweh). What Ahaz failed to note was that these same Arameans (and their gods) had been vanquished by the Assyrians. Logically, then, should not Ahaz have embraced the Assyrian gods? In any case, Ahaz abandoned the LORD and robbed and barred the temple. In their place he established pagan worship centers throughout Jerusalem and the entire land (cf. vv. 2-4). As a final indictment of this evil king the author remarked that on his death he was buried in . . . Jerusalem but . . . not . . . in the tombs of the kings (cf. 21:20; 24:25; 26:23). Repeatedly the chronicler noted that Judah's troubles were God's judgment (in anger) on Ahaz's and Judah's sins (28:9, 19, 25b).

M. Hezekiah (chaps. 29–32)

1. CLEANSING OF THE TEMPLE (CHAP. 29)

29:1-9. Hezekiah, whose independent reign lasted 29 years (715–686 B.C.), also apparently co-reigned with his father Ahaz for 14 years (729–715). The account of his life in 2 Chronicles covers his 29-year period after 715. Israel, the Northern Kingdom, had already fallen to the Assyrians in 722 B.C. and its people had been deported in large numbers (cf. 2 Kings 17:1-6).

Hezekiah was one of Judah's greatest kings (2 Kings 18:5). **In the very first month** of **his** sole **reign** (in 715) **he opened** the temple **doors** to repair **them** and restore the Lord's house, since Ahaz, his wicked father, had barred **the temple** (2 Chron. 28:24). Hezekiah gathered **the priests and the Levites** before the temple **(on the east side)** and commanded them to **consecrate** themselves to the work of purifying and repairing **the temple,** which, in the years of Ahaz especially, had fallen into a sorry state of deterioration. **The LORD** in His **anger** (cf. 28:9, 25) had therefore sent judgment on the nation, so much so that some of them had gone into **captivity** to the Arameans, Israelites, and Edomites (cf. 28:5-8, 17).

29:10-14. Hezekiah now intended to renew the ancient Mosaic **Covenant with the LORD** so that He might once again bless the nation. To this call the **Levites** assented and by their allotted divisions began to do the **work. The Gershonites** and **Merarites** evidently made up the smaller groups (v. 12) while **the Kohathites** were further subdivided by the clans of **Elizaphan** (v. 13; cf. 1 Chron. 15:8) and **Heman** (2 Chron. 29:14; cf. 1 Chron. 15:17). **Asaph,** however, was a Gershonite and **Jeduthun** was a Merarite (2 Chron. 29:13-14). Of the 14 Levites in all, 6 were descended from Kohath and 4 each were of Gershon and Merari.

29:15-19. They, with their comrades, began to remove **to the Kidron Valley** (cf. 15:16; 30:14) **everything** impure from **the temple.** In this action **Hezekiah** was **following the word of the LORD,** as given in Deuteronomy 12:2-4. Then for eight **days,** they reconsecrated everything outside **the temple** and **for eight more** everything inside. When the Levites had finished, they **reported** to Hezekiah that they had not only reconsecrated **the temple** and all its contents but had retrieved **all** the objects **Ahaz** had carried away to use in his pagan services (2 Chron. 29:18-19; cf. 28:24).

29:20-30. The next day **Hezekiah** led the people in a great festival of sacrifice (including 28 animals **as a sin offering;** cf. Lev. 4:1–5:13) to make atonement for their sins (2 Chron. 29:20-24). With the musicians in their prescribed places, the sacrifices, including also a **burnt offering** (cf. Lev. 1), began to the accompaniment of vocal and instrumental music (2 Chron. 29:25-28). **The Levites** played

cymbals, harps, and lyres, as **David** had prescribed when he moved the ark to Jerusalem (cf. 1 Chron. 15:16, 19; 16:4-5). Why **Gad** and **Nathan** are mentioned here is not clear. Also **the priests** played **trumpets,** as was done when Solomon took the ark to the temple (2 Chron. 5:12-13). Then **the king** and the people prostrated themselves before **the LORD** while psalms of **David** and **Asaph** were sung (29:29-30).

29:31-36. Since the **offerings** just made were for the kingdom, **the temple,** and the collective covenant community (v. 21), **Hezekiah** now gave individuals an opportunity to participate. The people **brought. . . . 70 bulls, 100 rams, and 200 male lambs** as **burnt offerings** (v. 32). The people also brought **600 bulls, and 3,000 sheep and goats** as **sacrifices** (v. 33) for burnt offerings and **thank offerings** (v. 31). The thank offerings were called **fellowship offerings** in Leviticus 3; 7:11-21. These burnt and thank offerings were expressions of personal piety above and beyond those offered on behalf of the nation as a whole. **Drink offerings** were included for they were part of the daily **burnt offerings** (Ex. 29:38-41). Because of a shortage of **priests . . . the Levites** assisted in slaughtering the animals. Thus in his first month **Hezekiah** had reestablished proper **temple** worship, an accomplishment that **brought** great rejoicing (2 Chron. 29:35b-36).

2. HEZEKIAH'S GREAT PASSOVER (30:1–31:1)

30:1-5. In anticipation of what must have been the first **Passover** of his reign, **Hezekiah sent** out invitations throughout all **Israel and Judah** including even **Ephraim and Manasseh** to encourage the faithful to attend. Some of the people in those two Northern tribes had apparently not been taken captive by Assyria. This feast was usually held in the first month (of the religious calendar; cf. Ex. 12:1-2), but Hezekiah had not been able to recruit sufficient priestly personnel that early (cf. 2 Chron. 29:34) nor had **the people** been able to arrive from distant points (30:3). So it was decided to hold it **in the second month,** that is, April-May (cf. Num. 9:10-11).

The plan was acceptable to **the king** and **the people,** so an announcement was sent out **from Beersheba to Dan** (the southernmost and northernmost cities in

Judah and Israel) with the expectation of great attendance (cf. 2 Chron. 30:13).

30:6-14. Hezekiah's proclamation (vv. 6-9) was to the effect that those Israelites who had **escaped** Assyrian deportation should repent of their sins and turn **to the LORD . . . submit to** Him, and **serve** Him. They should express the genuineness of their contrition by assembling at the temple in **Jerusalem (come to the sanctuary)** to celebrate the Passover. This was one of the three annual festivals which every adult male was supposed to attend in Jerusalem (Deut. 16:16). By assembling for the Passover, they would bring God's forgiveness and could even expect the return of their captured loved ones. Their repentance would divert God's **fierce anger,** for He **is gracious and compassionate.**

Alas, the message was spurned except for a few who came from **Asher, Manasseh . . . Zebulun** (2 Chron. 30:10-11), **Ephraim,** and Issachar (v. 18). In addition, of course, **the people** of **Judah** came with united purpose and commitment (v. 12) **to celebrate the Feast of Unleavened Bread** (v. 13). This seven-day festival followed immediately after the Passover (cf. Ex. 12:11-20; Lev. 23:4-8; and comments on Mark 14:1a). Indicative of the people's dedication was their disavowal once more of heathen **altars** (2 Chron. 30:14), discarding **them into the Kidron Valley** (cf. 15:16; 29:16).

30:15-20. When **the priests and the Levites** saw the dedication of the throngs of people they were chagrined and quickly **consecrated themselves** (by **burnt offerings)** for the service of **Passover** (vv. 15-16). Ordinarily the laity could offer their own **Passover lambs** in sacrifice (cf. Ex. 12:3). But because of the laxity of many of the Israelites in those apostate days, especially in the Northern Kingdom, they were **ceremonially** unclean and thus **could not** slaughter their own Passover lambs. Nonetheless they did eat of **the Passover** even though they were ritually disqualified (2 Chron. 30:17-18a). When **Hezekiah** realized this, he **prayed** on their behalf that **God** might be more impressed with the sincerity of their hearts and motives than with matters of mere ceremonialism (vv. 18b-19). The essence of God's grace is seen in His favorable response to the king's prayer (v. 20).

30:21-27. During the seven-day **Feast of Unleavened Bread,** which followed the Passover, the people praised **the LORD** with joy. **The Levites** also faithfully discharged their office (singing **praise,** eating the **assigned portion** of the sacrifices, and offering **fellowship offerings;** cf. Lev. 3; 7:11-21), which **Hezekiah** encouraged them to do. In fact all the people were so caught up in their devotion to and **joy** in the Lord that they decided to extend the festivities for another week.

This impressed the **king** and his officials, so he **provided** at his own expense **1,000 bulls and 7,000 sheep and goats for** sacrifice by the people, and the officials **provided . . . 1,000 bulls and 10,000 sheep and goats. Since the days of Solomon,** the chronicler related, **there had** never **been** anything **like this. God** heard from **heaven, His . . . dwelling place** (cf. 2 Chron. 6:21, 30, 33, 39; Ps. 11:4; Hab. 2:20), and blessed their outpouring of praise and consecration.

31:1. The most reasonable follow-up of the great 15-day festival ensued. **The Israelites** (and probably the Judeans) **went** through **Judah and Benjamin** destroying **all** remaining remnants of Baal's sacred **places** (cf. comments on 14:3). They then did the same **in Ephraim and Manasseh,** and **returned to their** homes.

3. REESTABLISHMENT OF PROPER WORSHIP (31:2-21)

31:2-4. Based on the requirements and guidelines of the Law, **Hezekiah** next proceeded to reestablish proper temple worship. He gave instruction concerning the service of **the priests and Levites** (v. 2), assigning them their 24 **divisions** (1 Chron. 24); he **contributed** animals for **the burnt offerings** for daily, weekly, monthly, and annual sacrifices (2 Chron. 31:3; cf. Num. 28–29; 1 Chron. 23:30-31); and he directed **the people** to support **the priests and Levites** (2 Chron. 31:4).

31:5-13. The citizens of Jerusalem and the surrounding towns and cities complied by presenting **the firstfruits** (cf. Ex. 23:19a; Num. 18:12) and tithes (cf. Lev. 27:30-33; Num. 18:21-24) of their produce of field crops and livestock and all other goods (2 Chron. 31:5-6). For four months they continued bringing their gifts to the temple (v. 7). **The third month** was May-June, the beginning of grain harvesting, and **the seventh month**

was September-October, the time of vine and fruit harvesting (see the chart "Calendar in Israel" near Ex. 12).

The people's gifts were **piled** in great **heaps** (2 Chron. 31:8). In fact **Azariah the chief priest** said that the quantities **Hezekiah** saw represented a surplus beyond what **the priests and Levites** needed. So the king ordered that **storerooms** be prepared **in the temple** to accommodate the excess (vv. 9-11). **Conaniah** with **his brother Shimei** were placed over 10 **supervisors** whose ministry was to oversee the collection and distribution of all these **gifts** (vv. 12-13).

31:14-21. As for the **gifts** made **to the LORD** Himself—a way of describing **freewill** (voluntary) **offerings** (cf. Lev. 7:11-21), these were the responsibility of **Kore** and his six associates. It was their duty to distribute them to **the priests** who lived in 13 towns outside Jerusalem (2 Chron. 31:14-15; cf. Josh. 21:13-19). Even the priests' young boys **three years old** and above received freewill offerings for they would someday serve as priests (2 Chron. 31:16). **The Levites,** on the other hand, received their portions only if they were at least **20 years old** (cf. 1 Chron. 23:24). Obviously there were many more **Levites** than **priests.** The **families** of both the priests and the Levites were, of course, supported similarly (2 Chron. 31:17-18) since the Law of Moses forbade the clergy from engaging in secular work to provide for themselves (cf. Num. 18:21-24). Finally, any **priests** or **Levites** who did not live in either Jerusalem or a designated priestly town were not to be overlooked (2 Chron. 31:19). All these things, the chronicler wrote, **Hezekiah** did **wholeheartedly** (a word used by the chronicler six times: 1 Chron. 29:9; 2 Chron.6:14; 15:15; 19:9; 25:2; 31:21) and in strict compliance with the Lord's **commands** (31:20-21).

4. SENNACHERIB'S INVASION (32:1-23)

32:1-8. Shortly **after . . . Hezekiah** began his independent reign he broke the treaty which had existed between his father Ahaz and the Assyrians (2 Kings 16:7) and rebelled against Assyria (2 Kings 18:7). This probably occurred at the time Sargon II (722–705 B.C.) of **Assyria** was preoccupied with rebellions in his Babylonian provinces and so could not punish Hezekiah. Sargon's successor

Sennacherib (705–681) did decide to bring **Judah** into line, however, so he led a campaign against **Hezekiah** in that king's 14th year (2 Kings 18:13), 701 B.C. At first the Assyrians **laid siege** to the various military towns, but then moved **on Jerusalem** (2 Chron. 32:1-2).

Hoping to prevent Jerusalem's capture, Hezekiah took measures to conceal the city's **outside** water supplies (vv. 3-4). **The stream** was probably the Gihon spring (v. 30). **Then he** repaired breaches in **the wall** and built **towers on it.** He even constructed an outer **wall,** greatly strengthened the **terraces** (the meaning of the Heb. word *millô*) below the walls of the city (v. 5; cf. 1 Kings 9:24), and added to the nation's weaponry. Next he mobilized **the people** under army **officers** and **encouraged them. . . . not** to fear but to trust **the LORD,** a Power far superior to Assyria. Hezekiah's reassurance that **God** was **with** them **to help** them (cf. 2 Chron. 14:11; 20:4; 25:8) helped build the people's **confidence** in the Lord in the face of the awesome Assyrians (cf. comments about the Assyrians in the Book of Nahum). Not mentioned in 2 Chronicles is the fact that Hezekiah tried to stave off Sennacherib by giving him huge amounts of gold and silver (2 Kings 18:14-16).

32:9-15. Before **Sennacherib** arrived in person he sent an embassy from **Lachish** (a key city 30 miles southwest of **Jerusalem**), bearing terms of surrender **for Hezekiah** to accept (vv. 10-15). In his message he boasted that **no** other **god** had **been able** to protect **his people from** the Assyrians. (Some of those nations and cities are listed in 2 Kings 19:12-13.) How then could Israel expect the Lord to do so since He was just another **god**? In fact Israel, Sennacherib said, had no god since **Hezekiah** had removed His **high places and altars.** (Assyria of course worshiped many **gods.**)

32:16-23. Sennacherib's taunt was followed by still other addresses and **letters** bearing the same theme—**the LORD** is just another impotent **god** unable to save **His people.** The Assyrian delegation even spoke **in Hebrew** to the Judeans **on the wall,** to make sure that even the common people would hear and understand every word and so become demoralized (vv. 16-19).

Desperate, **Hezekiah** turned to **the**

LORD with **the Prophet Isaiah** and together they sought divine deliverance. God gave the **king** a reassuring answer through the prophet (2 Kings 19:20-34) and then **sent an angel** who destroyed the Assyrian host, forcing Sennacherib to retreat in humility (2 Chron. 32:20-21a). The author of 2 Kings elaborated by stating that 185,000 Assyrians were slaughtered (2 Kings 19:35). Sometime after Sennacherib's return (though the chronicler did not seem to suggest a passing of time), the Assyrian king was murdered by two **of his sons** (identified in 2 Kings 19:37) in **the temple of his god** Nisroch (cf. Isa. 37:38) in Nineveh. According to Assyrian historical annals this assassination occurred in 681 B.C., 20 years after the aborted campaign against Jerusalem in 701. As a result of this miraculous deliverance of **Jerusalem** and similar experiences, Judah's God and king were given **gifts** and recognition from **all the** surrounding **nations** (2 Chron. 32:22-23).

5. HEZEKIAH'S SICKNESS AND PROSPERITY (32:24-33)

32:24-30. The story of **Hezekiah's** illness and miraculous healing (on the **sign** see 2 Kings 20:11) and extension of life is greatly abbreviated by the chronicler (2 Chron. 32:24; cf. 2 Kings 20:1-11; Isa. 38:1-8) perhaps because his intent here was to emphasize **the pride** of the king and not his piety (2 Chron. 32:25-26). The reasons for such pride could well be the accomplishments which the historian cataloged in verses 27-31. He had wealth **and honor**; he **built** storage facilities, agricultural settlements, and **villages**; he rerouted the city's **water** supply from **the Gihon spring** (in the Kidron Valley on the east) **to the west side,** and **succeeded** in these and many other undertakings. The tunnel of Hezekiah was dug through solid rock from the Gihon spring to the Pool of Siloam, a distance of 1,777 feet with workmen digging from each end and meeting in the middle.

32:31-33. However, Hezekiah foolishly and proudly displayed all the wealth of the temple and his palace to the Babylonian envoys of Merodach-Baladan (2 Kings 20:12-19; Isa. 39). The chronicler without details simply recorded that **God** allowed all this **to test him and to know everything that was in his heart.** That is, God wanted to show Hezekiah himself the consequences of pride. After Hezekiah died he **was buried** with honor among **his fathers** (royal ancestors). His **other** deeds, the historian said, were found in the records of **Isaiah** (cf. Isa. 36–39) and **of the kings of Israel and Judah.**

N. *Manesseh (33:1-20)*

33:1-9. In complete contrast with his godly father was **Manasseh,** an **evil** king of Judah who **reigned** for **55 years** (697–642). Though he reigned with Hezekiah for some 11 years, the young king either learned nothing from his father or quickly repudiated it, for he set about to rebuild **the high places . . . altars,** and sacred **poles** dedicated **to the Baals and Asherah,** the female fertility goddess of the Canaanites (cf. comments on 14:3). Manasseh also **worshiped** the gods of the heavens, represented in the pagan mind by **the starry hosts** (i.e., the sun, moon, stars, and planets) in violation of Deuteronomy 4:19. In fact he even placed pagan shrines (**altars**) of the stellar gods within **the temple of the LORD** itself. Like his grandfather Ahaz, he also offered **his** own **sons** as human sacrifices **in the Valley of Ben Hinnom** (cf. 2 Chron. 28:3 and comments there). Manasseh also **practiced sorcery** (seeking to gain power from evil spirits), **divination** (seeking to interpret the future by omens), **and witchcraft** (seeking to control others through communication with evil spirits), all of which were commonly employed in other nations of the ancient Near East to discern the planned activities of the gods.

Manasseh **consulted mediums and spiritists,** diviners whose specialty was to seek to consult the dead. Perhaps most serious of all, he set up the **image** (of Asherah; cf. 2 Kings 21:7) within the **temple,** which was to be reserved exclusively for the Lord (2 Chron. 33:7-8; cf. 7:16). The king also caused innocent people to die (2 Kings 21:16). So **Manasseh led** his nation away from God (2 Chron. 33:9).

33:10-13. Because **Manasseh and his people** ignored the LORD, His punishment was swift and sure. **Assyria,** the instrument of the Lord, came down **against** Judah. With great ruthlessness they bound **Manasseh . . . put a hook in his nose** as though he were a wild bull, and **took him** off **to Babylon,** Assyria's southern province. After a time Manasseh repented before **the LORD** and soon was allowed to return to his own land and people. The chronicler included this fact about Manasseh's restoration (not given in 2 Kings) to emphasize, no doubt, the fact that even the most wicked scions in David's dynasty could and did receive forgiveness if they met the Lord's conditions. This would give hope to the exilic and postexilic community of Jews.

33:14-17. When Manasseh returned **he rebuilt the outer wall** on the east side of Jerusalem from **the Gihon spring** (cf. 32:30) northwesterly to **the Fish Gate** (see the map "Jerusalem in the Time of Nehemiah," near Neh. 2) and from Gihon south to encircle **Ophel,** the original old city. He also regarrisoned the fortress **cities** throughout **Judah,** probably in anticipation of another Assyrian onslaught (2 Chron. 33:14). He then removed all the pagan idols and other accoutrements for which he had been responsible (v. 15; cf. vv. 3-5) and **restored** the proper worship of **the Lord** (v. 16). But **the people** had become used to worshiping **at the high places,** and so continued there though they only worshiped **the Lord** (v. 17).

33:18-20. Manasseh's **other** activities and achievements were recorded **in the annals of the kings of Israel** (v. 18) and the documents **of the seers** (v. 19). "Israel" here, as in 20:34, probably stands for Judah, since only the Southern Kingdom was in the land (cf. comments on "the annals" in 1 Kings 14:19 and under "Authorship" in the *Introduction* to 1 Chron.). Because of his general wickedness he was not **buried** in the tombs of the kings but **in his** own **palace** (2 Chron. 33:20).

O. Amon (33:21-25)

33:21-25. Amon, in his brief **two**-year reign (642–640 B.C.), imitated the wickedness of **Manasseh. But unlike his father, he did not** repent. So **Amon's** top leaders **assassinated him.** As it turned out this was an unpopular move for the assassins themselves were disposed of and **Josiah,** Amon's **son,** was put in power by the masses.

P. Josiah (chaps. 34–35)

1. JOSIAH'S REFORMATION (CHAP. 34)

a. Preparations for temple repairs (34:1-13)

34:1-7. Josiah, son of Amon, who was only **eight years old when** his father

died, ruled over Judah for **31 years** (640–609 B.C.) Much like his great-grandfather Hezekiah, Josiah loved **the Lord** and **began to** demonstrate this actively by the time he was 16 years old. **In his 12th year** as king (age 20) he initiated a campaign to rid the land of all vestiges of Canaanite religion. Apparently Manasseh's purge (33:15) related only to the **idols** and pagan **altars** in the temple, not to those throughout the land (33:3).

Josiah went so far as to scatter the **smashed . . . idols** and other paraphernalia **over the graves** of their worshipers and to burn **the bones of the** pagan **priests on their** very **altars.** And this purge was not limited to Judah. In Israel all the way up to **Naphtali** in the north the work of extirpation of idolatry went on.

34:8-13. Then, in Josiah's **18th year** (age 26) he commissioned **Shaphan . . . Maaseiah,** and **Joah** to **repair** and refurbish **the temple.** (This was one of several times that kings of Judah restored the temple.) These men took **money** which had been collected for that purpose from all over Israel and Judah and gave it **to Hilkiah the high priest** to enable him to hire workmen and **to purchase** materials for the task ordered by the king. The supervisors were **Levites,** two of the **Merari** branch and two of the Kohath branch. Those four were skillful musicians, a statement that probably attests to their artistry and sensitivity in all things pertaining to the temple and worship. It was their task to oversee the workmen at every point. **Levites** with other skills and assignments served as foremen.

b. Discovery of the Book of the Law (34:14-33)

34:14-21. In the course of paying **out** some of the temple **money** one day, **Hilkiah the** high **priest** (cf. v. 9) **found a** copy of **the Book of the Law of the Lord.** Because of certain higher critical assumptions, many scholars limit this document to Deuteronomy. There is no reason to do so, however, even though Deuteronomy may be in mind in certain places in the present narrative. The "book" may well have included the entire Pentateuch (Gen.–Deut.).

When **Shaphan** (cf. v. 8) **the secretary** took the scroll to Josiah and **reported** on the progress of the work, **Shaphan** began to **read** a few passages **from it** to **the king.** Realizing the significance of the message, **the king . . . tore his robes** (as an expression of grief; cf. comments on 23:13) and issued a command **to Hilkiah** and the others that the entire text be studied and that the mind of **the Lord** in relation to it be ascertained. He was concerned that his ancestors had incurred God's **anger** by not obeying God's **Word.** Josiah's personal display of grief may have been in reaction to statements in Deuteronomy concerning the role and responsibility of the king as covenant leader, a role he probably felt he had not fulfilled (cf. Deut. 17:18-20).

34:22-28. Strange as it may seem, the Books of Moses had apparently been destroyed except for this one copy preserved in the temple. How or when this happened is a mystery but the most likely occasion was the almost complete eradication of the worship of the Lord in the days of Manasseh and Amon (chap. 33). To find out what needed to be done **Hilkiah** and his colleagues **went to . . . the Prophetess Huldah,** who resided in a suburb (**the Second District**) of **Jerusalem.** Her husband **Shallum** was the overseer **of the wardrobe** for either the king or the priests. **She** related to them that **God** was **going to bring** His judgment on the land—all according to **the curses written in the** newly found scroll (cf. Deut. 28:15-68; Lev. 26:14-39). Though the wrath of God was sure because of the nation's apostasy and idolatry, Josiah himself would be spared because of his wholehearted devotion to **the Lord.** The impending doom would be postponed until after Josiah's death.

34:29-33. When Josiah heard Huldah's message, he gathered **all the elders** and **all the people** to **the temple** and **read** to them **the Book of the Covenant which had been found.** This may be the section known by that phrase in Exodus 20:1–23:33, or it may be all of Deuteronomy. Then, as **king** and representative of the **people,** Josiah **stood** and affirmed his intent to renew his **covenant** vows and keep all the statutes prescribed by **the covenant.** He **then** had all **the people** of the kingdom do the same. In summation, he **removed** idolatry from the land and in its place established faithful worship of **the Lord** and adherence to His covenant demands.

2. JOSIAH'S GREAT PASSOVER (35:1-19)

a. *Preparation for the Passover (35:1-9)*

35:1-4. In Josiah's 18th year (v. 19, age 26), the same year in which the temple was repaired (34:8), he **celebrated the Passover** (cf. Hezekiah's Passover celebration, chap. 30). Having charged **the priests** and **the Levites** to fulfill their designated responsibilities for the occasion, he instructed that the **ark** be left **in the temple** and **not . . . carried** in procession as had been done in the wilderness before there was a permanent place for it. They were free now to do other things. First, they were to divide up by their stated **divisions** as **David** had instructed (cf. 1 Chron. 24), and **Solomon** reaffirmed (2 Chron. 8:14). In the court of the temple they were to perform their ministry on behalf of the people according to clans.

35:5-9. Next the priests and **Levites** were to **slaughter the Passover lambs** and **prepare** them for consumption by the people (cf. 30:16-17). Out of the royal flocks and herds the king **provided** for the **people . . . 30,000 sheep and goats** and **3,000 cattle.** (Hezekiah, for the Passover celebration in his day, had given 7,000 sheep and 1,000 bulls, 30:24.) Josiah's leading **officials also** gave generously. Finally, the chief priests **gave** their fellow **priests 2,600 Passover offerings** (i.e., sheep and goats) **and 300 cattle** while the heads of **the Levites** gave their Levitical colleagues **5,000 Passover offerings** (sheep and goats) **and 500 cattle.**

b. *Celebration of the Passover (35:10-19)*

35:10-14. When all was ready the festival began with the slaughter of the **lambs** by **the Levites** who then handed over **the blood** to **the priests** for sprinkling on the great altar. The **burnt offerings,** those sheep and goats not intended for use in the Passover, were distributed along with the **cattle** to **the people. The Passover** sacrifices were then **roasted** and **boiled** as the Law required (cf. Ex. 12:7-9; Deut. 16:7). **After** that the Levites prepared **the burnt offerings** for their own and the priests' consumption since the priests were so busy with the Passover service. Since only lambs and goats were sacrificed as Passover victims and for evening and morning offerings (cf. Ex. 29:38-45) the cattle were used for thank or fellowship offerings (cf. Lev. 3:1-5).

35:15-19. In addition to the **Levites** involved in sacrifice were **the** Levite **musicians** and **gatekeepers,** all of whom could remain at **their posts because their** comrades attended to their sacrificial meals. The festivities of **the Passover** continued on through the whole **seven**-day period of **the Feast of Unleavened Bread.** Not since . . . **Samuel,** the chronicler reported, had **such a Passover** been **celebrated.**

3. JOSIAH'S FATAL ENCOUNTER WITH NECO (35:20-27)

35:20. By the year 609 B.C. Assyria had become so weak that she had lost practically all her empire, especially to the Babylonians (or Chaldeans). Nineveh had fallen in 612 so the Assyrians had concentrated their forces around Haran and Carchemish on the upper Euphrates River. The Babylonians decided to advance against them there to destroy them once for all, but **Egypt,** more fearful of Babylonia than Assyria, launched an attack through Palestine with the idea of coming to Assyria's assistance at Carchemish. **Josiah** in the meantime favored the Babylonians and therefore set out to intercept the Egyptians under Pharaoh **Neco** (609–595 B.C.) and prevent them from getting to **Carchemish.**

35:21-27. Neco tried his best to dissuade **Josiah** from this course of action, arguing that **God** was **with** him (Neco) in his mission and would **destroy** Josiah if he did not back off. Neco had indeed received such instructions from the Lord God, but **Josiah** intervened anyway and despite disguising **himself** (like Ahab; cf. 18:29) was fatally **wounded** on the battlefield at **Megiddo.** For centuries the flat plains of Megiddo have been the scene of many battles. Armageddon (lit., the mountain of Megiddo) will be the scene of Christ's battle at His second coming (Rev. 16:16; cf. Rev. 19).

Though Josiah survived till he reached **Jerusalem . . . he died** there and **was buried** with **his fathers.** So shocking was the good king's death that **Jeremiah** the prophet **composed laments** for the occasion which, the chronicler wrote, were sung to his very **day. The Laments** are probably not the Book of Lamentations. **Other** incidents **of Josiah's** life were recorded **in the book of the kings of Israel and Judah.**

Q. Jehoahaz (36:1-4)

36:1-4. Josiah had at least four sons (cf. 1 Chron. 3:15), three of whom became kings of Judah (see the chart "The Last Five Kings of Judah," near 2 Kings 23:31-35). The first of these (though not the oldest; cf. 2 Chron. 36:5) was **Jehoahaz,** an appointee by **the people** after Josiah's tragic death. He remained in power for only **three months** because for reasons not given, Neco **dethroned him,** levied on **Judah** a tax of **100 talents of silver** (3¾ tons) **and a talent of gold** (75 pounds).

Then Neco replaced Jehoahaz with his brother **Eliakim** whom Neco renamed **Jehoiakim.** The act of renaming showed Neco's superiority and control over the new king. **Jehoahaz** was then taken prisoner **to Egypt.** All this presupposes Egyptian control of Judah, a situation which prevailed from 609 to 605 B.C.

R. Jehoiakim (36:5-8)

36:5-8. Jehoiakim, a wicked king, reigned **in Jerusalem 11 years** (609–598 B.C.), part of the time under Neco and the Egyptians and part of the time under **Nebuchadnezzar** and the Babylonians. Because of his wickedness (cf. Jer. 26:21-24) **the** LORD allowed him to fall to **Nebuchadnezzar** who had driven the Egyptians out of Palestine by 605 B.C. In that year Daniel and his friends were taken captive to Babylon (cf. comments on Dan. 1:1). Jehoiakim had at first been loyal to Nebuchadnezzar but after three years (in 602) he rebelled (cf. 2 Kings 24:1). The chronicler (but not the author of 2 Kings) reported that Jehoiakim was then **bound . . . with bronze shackles** and taken **to Babylon** along with sacred objects **from the temple.** This was Nebuchadnezzar's first of three attacks on Jerusalem—in 605, 597, and 586 B.C. Apparently Jehoiakim was released or escaped from Babylon because he was given a dishonorable burial outside the gates of Jerusalem (Jer. 22:18-19). His wicked reign was also recorded **in the book of the kings of Israel and Judah.**

S. Jehoiachin (36:9-10)

36:9-10. Jehoiachin, son of Jehoiakim, **was 18 when he** succeeded his father (most Heb. mss. have 8; cf. NIV marg., which seems unlikely since he had wives; cf. 2 Kings 24:15). **He reigned**

only **three months and 10 days** (598–597
B.C.). He too was **evil** so when **Nebuchadnezzar** undertook his next western
campaign in the spring (NIV marg.) he
took the young king and his family into
captivity (along with 10,000 Jews, 2 Kings
24:13-14) and set **Zedekiah** on Judah's
throne. In 2 Kings 25:27-30 is the additional information that Jehoiachin was released from Babylonian imprisonment in
the 37th year of his captivity (560 B.C.)
and was placed on a royal pension in
Babylon for the rest of his life. This is
now confirmed in the Neo-Babylonian
texts (James B. Pritchard, ed., *Ancient
Near Eastern Texts Relating to the Old Testament*, 3rd ed. Princeton, N.J.: Princeton
University Press, 1969, p. 308). This was
two years after Nebuchadnezzar died
and may have been because of Daniel's
influence.

T. Zedekiah (36:11-16)

36:11-16. Having removed Jehoiachin, Nebuchadnezzar replaced him with
his uncle (cf. v. 10) **Zedekiah**, Judah's
last king in Old Testament times. His **11-
year reign** (597–586 B.C.) was **evil**, a situation well documented by the Prophet **Jeremiah** (cf. Jer. 21:3-7; 32:1-5). Zedekiah
rebelled against King Nebuchadnezzar
in his ninth year (588 B.C.; cf. 2 Kings
25:1), and despite the increasing peril of
his predicament he **would not turn to the
Lord** nor would any of the other **leaders**
or the general population. Yet **the Lord**
in His mercy (**pity**) continued to send
warnings through the prophets (**His
messengers**) but the people **despised** the
word of the Lord and **mocked** His prophets. Thus **there was no remedy** (cf. Jer.
5:10-13; 7:12-15).

U. The Babylonian Conquest and Exile (36:17-21)

36:17-20. At last Nebuchadnezzar's
army came (under God's leading) and
delivered a smashing blow that brought
Judah's independence to an end. **Young**
and **old** alike were **killed** and many of
the others taken as prisoners. The valuable treasures of **the temple** were looted
and the building itself burned and reduced to rubble, along with **the palaces.**
Also the city's **wall** was broken down.
Those who **escaped** death were taken **to
Babylon** where they existed as slaves till
Babylon's fall to **Persia** in 539 B.C.

36:21. The historian then observed
that **the land** of Judah at last **enjoyed its
Sabbath rests,** a period of **70 years**
prophesied **by Jeremiah** (cf. Jer. 29:10).
This probably refers to the approximately
70-year period from the first deportation
under Nebuchadnezzar (605 B.C.) to the
rebuilding of the temple foundation by
the returning exiles in 536 (cf. Dan. 9:2;
Ezra 1:1). Since Israel and Judah had
failed to keep the sabbatical years (every
seventh year the land was supposed to
lie fallow, Lev. 25:1-7) throughout her
history, the Lord would enforce on the
land a 70-year "sabbath" (cf. Lev. 26:34-
35).

V. The Decree of Cyrus (36:22-23)

36:22-23. The chronicler closed his
historical narrative on an optimistic note.
God had brought His people into the
judgment of exile but He also eventually
delivered them, a chastened and repentant people who would form the nucleus
of a continuing Davidic dynasty. To accomplish this the Lord raised up the
mighty **Cyrus king of Persia** (559–530
B.C.). In his **first year** over Babylon (538)
he issued a decree which allowed the
people of **Judah** to return to their land
and rebuild their **temple.** This proclamation—identical to Ezra 1:2-3a (see comments there) and confirmed by the discovery of a Babylonian inscription—was
prompted by **the Lord . . . God** as fulfillment of Jeremiah's prophetic word
(Jer. 25:12; 29:10; cf. Daniel's prayer in
Dan. 9:4-19). Most of the kings of Israel
and Judah had failed to obey the Lord
and to lead the people in godliness. Ironically God stirred up the spirit of a pagan
king to make possible the historical
events which will eventually lead to the
second coming of Jesus Christ, the incarnate God and King of Israel.

BIBLIOGRAPHY

Ackroyd, Peter R. *I and II Chronicles, Ezra,
Nehemiah.* Torch Bible Commentaries. London:
SCM Press, 1973.

Coggins, R.J. *The First and Second Books of
the Chronicles.* New York: Cambridge University Press, 1976.

Curtis, Edward Lewis, and Madsen, Albert Alonzo. *A Critical and Exegetical Commen-*

tary on the Books of Chronicles. The International Critical Commentary. Edinburgh: T. & T. Clark, 1910.

Keil, C.F. "The Books of the Chronicles." In Commentary on the Old Testament in Ten Volumes. Vol. 3. Reprint (25 vols. in 10). Grand Rapids: Wm. B. Eerdmans Publishing Co., 1982.

Myers, Jacob M. II Chronicles. The Anchor Bible. Garden City, N.Y.: Doubleday & Co., 1965.

Sailhamer, John. First and Second Chronicles. Chicago: Moody Press, 1983.

Slotki, I.W. Chronicles: Hebrew Text and English Translation with an Introduction and Commentary. London: Soncino Press, 1952.

Williamson, H.G.M. 1 and 2 Chronicles. The New Century Bible Commentary. Grand Rapids: Wm. B. Eerdmans Publishing Co., 1982.

Zöckler, Otto. "The Books of the Chronicles." In Commentary on the Holy Scriptures, Critical, Doctrinal, and Homiletical. Vol. 4. Reprint (24 vols. in 12). Grand Rapids: Zondervan Publishing House, 1960.

EZRA

John A. Martin

INTRODUCTION

Name. Josephus (*Against Apion* 1. 8), Jerome (*Preface to the Commentary on Galatians*), and the Talmud (*Baba Bathra* 15a) considered the Books of Ezra and Nehemiah as one. Also the Hebrew Bible has the books together as a single work. However, there is evidence that the two books were originally separate. The lists in Ezra 2 and Nehemiah 7 are basically the same. This would militate against the idea that the two books were originally one, for it would seem strange to repeat the same list in one volume. The name Ezra for the title of the first work comes from the major person in the second half of the book, who also appears in chapters 8 and 12 of the Book of Nehemiah.

The name of the Book of Ezra is complicated by the way the Septuagint named some of its books. In the Septuagint the name Esdras (Ezra) refers to a number of books. First Esdras (also called Esdras A) is an apocryphal book. Second Esdras (Esdras B) contains the canonical Books of Ezra and Nehemiah. However, sometimes Nehemiah is called Esdras C (or G if one accurately reflects the third Heb. letter, which is *gimel*). The Apocrypha has still another Esdras, alternately called II Esdras or IV Esdras.

Canonicity. The Book of Ezra has been accepted as canonical since before the time of the Septuagint (ca. 200 B.C.), which may have been only about 250 years after the book was written. Few scholars in modern times have therefore questioned the canonicity of the Book of Ezra.

Author. Though Ezra is not referred to in the book as having written it, he has long been supposed to be the book's author. Internal evidence points to this fact for in 7:27–9:15 the author refers to himself in the first person. Hebrew tradition also

has considered Ezra the author. He was a priest and a scribe of the Law (7:21). Undoubtedly Ezra had documents at his disposal for the historical sections in chapters 1–6. Many Bible students have noted similarities between the style of Ezra and the style of 1 and 2 Chronicles. Therefore some suppose that Ezra was the author of all three. (See comments in *Introduction to 1 Chron.*)

Date. The Book of Ezra covers two distinct time periods. Chapters 1–6 cover the 23 years from the edict of Cyrus to the rebuilding of the temple in Jerusalem (538–515 B.C.). Chapters 7–10 deal with the events after Ezra returned from Babylon (458 B.C.). The two exceptions are 4:6, which refers to an event in the reign of Xerxes (485–465) and verses 7-23, which parenthetically include a letter written later during the reign of Artaxerxes (464–424). The time of writing of the completed book could not have been earlier than about 450 B.C. (when the events recorded in 10:17-44 took place). Ezra was a contemporary of Nehemiah (Neh. 8:1-9; 12:36).

Historical Setting. The setting of the book is the postexilic era when the faithful Israelites were returning from Babylon to Judah so that they could reestablish their temple worship. In all the books written during the postexilic period the temple and temple worship are vital subjects. (These include 1 and 2 Chron.; Ezra; Neh.; Hag.; Zech.; and Mal.—all except Es. in which the people were unfaithful to the command of the Lord given through Isaiah and Jeremiah to return to the land after the Captivity.) The people who returned to the land of promise were publicly acknowledging that they believed God would reestablish the nation and usher in a time of kingdom blessing.

There were three returns from Bab-

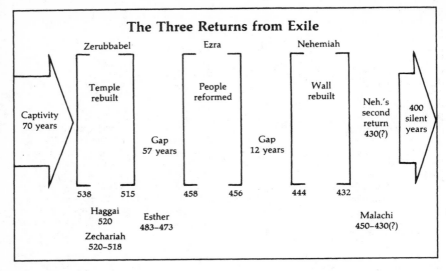

The Three Returns from Exile

| Captivity 70 years | Zerubbabel — Temple rebuilt | Gap 57 years | Ezra — People reformed | Gap 12 years | Nehemiah — Wall rebuilt | Neh.'s second return 430(?) | 400 silent years |

538   515   458   456   444   432

Haggai 520
Zechariah 520–518

Esther 483–473

Malachi 450–430(?)

ylon to the land of Israel (in 538, 458, and 444 B.C.), just as there had been three deportations from the land to Babylon (605, 597, and 586 B.C.). The first return was led by Zerubbabel (Ezra 1–6; Hag.; Zech.) in 538 B.C. The rebuilding of the temple was of vital importance for this group. The second return was under Ezra (Ezra 7–10) in 458 B.C. The people needed reforming; they needed to return to their covenant obligations. The third return was led by Nehemiah in 444 B.C. Nehemiah's concerns were to rebuild the walls of Jerusalem and, as in Ezra's time, to lead the people back to obedience to the Lord. The Book of Malachi was probably written in Nehemiah's time. The events in the Book of Esther occurred between the events recorded in Ezra 6 and Ezra 7. (See the chart "The Three Returns from Exile." Also see the chart "Chronology of the Postexilic Period" near Ezra 1:1.)

The Text. Nearly a fourth of the Book of Ezra was written in Aramaic; the rest was written in Hebrew. The Aramaic sections (67 of 280 verses) are 4:8–6:18 and 7:12-26. The material in these verses was mainly copied from official correspondence for which Aramaic was the standard language (*lingua franca*) of the day.

Purpose. The Book of Ezra was written not simply to record miscellaneous his-

torical facts in the history of Israel during the Jews' return to the land. This book, like all books in the Bible, had a theological purpose. The purpose of Ezra's book can be seen by reflecting on the audience for which it was written. As stated earlier, the book may have been written around 450 B.C. Thus the original readers were exiles who had returned under Zerubbabel and Ezra, but who were then wavering in their relationship to God. Ezra wrote to encourage the remnant to be involved in true temple worship and to remind them to fulfill their covenantal obligations because of God's mercy. The highlight of the book is in chapters 9–10, which tells of the people's proper response after sin was found in their midst. Ezra wanted his readers to emulate that same attitude of dependence on God, which believers of all times should have.

OUTLINE

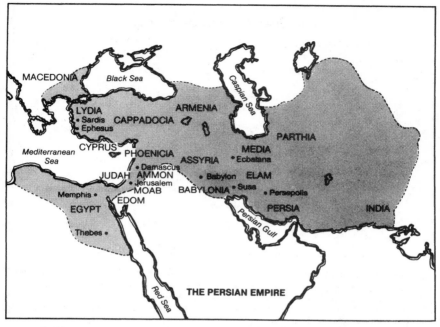

THE PERSIAN EMPIRE

COMMENTARY

I. The First Return and Rebuilding under Zerubbabel (chaps. 1–6)

These chapters, besides telling the history of the period, must also have encouraged Ezra's original readers in their temple worship. As they read about the rebuilding process they would have been made aware of the great personal sacrifices the Jews had made in constructing the temple. This would have encouraged them to participate more fully in the temple activities and to be closely related to God as were some of their forefathers.

A. The proclamation of Cyrus (1:1-4)

1:1. Cyrus, the **king of** the extensive Persian **realm** (see the map "The Persian Empire"), drafted **a proclamation** that allowed the Israelites to return to their land and rebuild their temple. **Cyrus** made the proclamation in his **first year** (538 B.C.). This was the first year of his reign over

Chronology of the Postexilic Period

Persian Kings	Dates of Their Reigns	Biblical Events	Scripture References	Dates
Cyrus	559–530 B.C.	Edict of Cyrus for the return	Ezra 1:1-4	538 B.C.
		First return of 49,897 exiles, under Zerubbabel (to build the temple)	Ezra 2	538
		The altar and temple foundation built	Ezra 3:1–4:5	536
Cambyses	530–522			
Smerdis	522			
Darius I	521–486	Haggai prophesied	Book of Haggai	520
		Zechariah prophesied	Book of Zechariah	520–518
		The temple completed	Ezra 5–6	515
Xerxes (Ahasuerus)	485–465	Accusation against Judah	Ezra 4:6	486
		Esther became queen	Esther 2:17	479
Artaxerxes I (Artashasta)	464–424	Artaxerxes stopped the rebuilding of Jerusalem	Ezra 4:7-23	ca. 464–458
		Second return of 4,000-5,000 exiles, under Ezra (to beautify the temple and reform the people)	Ezra 7–10	458
		Third return of exiles, under Nehemiah (to build the walls of Jerusalem)	Book of Nehemiah	444
		Nehemiah's second return	Nehemiah 13:6	ca. 430
		Malachi prophesied	Book of Malachi	450–430 (?)

Babylon, but he had been king over other territories for more than 20 years. He had been in power since 559 when he became the king of Anshan. Then he became **king of** Medo-**Persia** about 550 B.C. He conquered Babylon in October 539, and became the king of Babylon, a title of honor denoting the highest position in the civilized world. (See the chart "Chronology of the Postexilic Period.")

As is evidenced from Cyrus' attitude concerning the God of Israel (whom he did not worship) he was not a true believer in Yahweh. Cyrus' concern was to establish strong buffer states around his empire which would be loyal to him. Also by having his subject peoples resettled in their own countries he hoped to have the gods in various parts of his empire praying for him to his gods Bel and Nebo. The famous Cyrus Cylinder (538

B.C.), which records his capture of Babylon and his program of repatriating his subject peoples in their homelands, includes this statement: "May all the gods whom I have resettled in their sacred cities daily ask Bel and Nebo for a long life for me."

The fulfilling of Jeremiah's words (Jer. 29:10; cf. Jer. 25:11-12) was totally God's doing. Seventy years of Jewish captivity in Babylon were about to end. The first deportation of Jews to Babylon was in 605 B.C. Cyrus' decree in 538 was 67 years later. By the time the people returned and built the altar in 536, 70 years were almost up.

The edict came about because **the LORD moved the heart of Cyrus.** The Hebrew words translated "moved the heart" (also trans. "stirred [up] the spirit") were a favorite expression of biblical writers in the postexilic period (Ezra 1:5; 1 Chron. 5:26; 2 Chron. 21:16, "aroused"; 36:22; Jer. 51:11; Hag. 1:14). This shows the sovereign hand of God behind the events of history.

1:2-3. Cyrus said that Yahweh, **the God of heaven,** had **appointed** him **to build a temple . . . at Jerusalem.** Part of this decree is recorded in 2 Chronicles 36:23. Also the decree was filed in Ecbatana, where Darius I found it about 520–518 B.C. (Ezra 6:1-5). God had promised the Jewish remnant that He would raise up Cyrus as His servant to restore the fortunes of His people (Isa. 44:28; 45:1, 13). Under the Holy Spirit's guidance, the Prophet Isaiah referred to Cyrus by name about 150 years before the king made his decree. Josephus wrote that Cyrus was shown the prophecy in Isaiah 44:28 and wanted to fulfill it (*The Antiquities of the Jews* 11. 1. 1).

"The God of heaven" is a title of God used 9 times in Ezra (1:2; 5:11-12; 6:9-10; 7:12, 21, 23 [twice]—more than in any other Bible book—and 10 times in other exilic and postexilic books (2 Chron. 36:23; Neh. 1:4-5; 2:4, 20; Dan. 2:18-19, 28, 37, 44). Elsewhere in the Old Testament that phrase occurs only four times (Gen. 24:3, 7; Ps. 136:26; Jonah 1:9). It points to God's sovereignty. He is the One who made heaven (Gen. 14:19, 22; 2 Chron. 2:12; Ps. 115:15), who is in heaven (Deut. 4:39; 1 Kings 8:30, 39, 43, 49; Ecc. 5:2), and who reigns from His throne in heaven (Isa. 66:1). Though Cyrus was a monarch over an extensive empire, Yahweh is far greater for He rules from heaven.

The emphasis in Ezra 1:2-3 on **the temple** sets the tone for this and other postexilic books. The temple was of utmost importance in the life of the people of Israel. Without the temple there could be no sacrificial system, which was the nation's lifeblood in its relationship to **God.** "The God of heaven" (v. 2) is also **the God of Israel** who Cyrus said was **in Jerusalem.**

1:4. Cyrus' edict also instructed the returnees' neighbors in Persia to give them the equivalent of money (**silver and gold**), material **goods . . . livestock,** and **freewill offerings** (cf. v. 6). The freewill offerings were **for the temple** and the other gifts were for the people themselves. This is reminiscent of the Exodus

from Egypt when God miraculously took the nation out of bondage and had the Egyptians aid them with gifts of silver, gold, and clothing (Ex. 3:22; 11:2; 12:35). Now God was effecting a new "Exodus," again bringing His people who had been in bondage back into the land of promise, much as He had done under Moses and Joshua. The people had been in bondage to Babylon because of their failure to keep their covenantal obligations, which Moses had given them during the first Exodus. Once more God was miraculously working in the life of the nation.

B. The reaction of the Israelites (1:5-11)

1:5-11. The religious leaders (**priests and Levites**) along with the **heads** of the two tribes (**Judah and Benjamin**) that had been taken into exile by the Babylonians spearheaded the return to Israel to rebuild the temple, **the house of the LORD.** The Jews who returned totaled 49,897 (2:64-65). The **neighbors** of the returnees obeyed the king's decree by contributing to the effort (1:6). Even **Cyrus** contributed to the return by giving back **the articles belonging to the temple of the LORD.** These were the **dishes . . . pans . . . bowls,** and **other articles** (vv. 9-10) **Nebuchadnezzar had** taken **from** the **Jerusalem** temple in 605 B.C. (Dan. 1:2), in 597 B.C. (2 Kings 24:13), and in 586 B.C. (2 Kings 25:14-15; Jer. 27:16; 52:18-19; cf. Ezra 5:14; 6:5; Dan. 5:2-3) and placed in a **temple** in Babylon, perhaps the Esagila temple built in honor of the god Marduk. **Mithredath** is a Persian name, and the word for **treasurer** (*gizbār*) is also Persian.

In Ezra 1:9-10 the **articles** total 2,499 but in verse 11 the total number of **gold** and **silver** items was **5,400.** Why the difference? Surely Ezra would not be so foolish as to make a major mistake such as that when he so carefully wrote the rest of the book under the Holy Spirit's inspiration. Even if one were to assume (as do many critics) that a redactor brought together in verses 9-11 two variant traditions, it would seem likely that Ezra would try to reconcile them in some way. It seems better to suppose Ezra first listed some of the items, perhaps the bigger and more valuable ones (vv. 9-10), then referred to the total number of items both the larger and more valuable and the smaller and less significant (v. 11).

Another problem pertains to **Sheshbazzar** (v. 11), who was called **the prince of Judah** (v. 8). Three views about his identity are suggested: (1) Some feel that **Sheshbazzar** was a Persian name for Zerubbabel. Both are said to have laid the foundation of the temple (3:8-10; 5:16). Zerubbabel, which means "begotten in Babel," was a grandson of Jehoiachin (1 Chron. 3:17-19), who had been deported to Babylon but had been released from confinement (2 Kings 25:27-30). Zerubbabel's relationship to Jehoiachin would explain the title "the prince of Judah." However, it would seem strange that Zerubbabel would have a second pagan name rather than having one name that reflected Yahweh worship (Sheshbazzar being a pagan deity). If Zerubbabel and Sheshbazzar were two names of the same person, it is strange that he was never again referred to by the name Sheshbazzar except in Ezra 5:15-16.

(2) A second view is that this man was a Jew who was appointed governor by Cyrus but who died shortly after arriving in Palestine and was replaced by Zerubbabel. Though plausible, no solid evidence exists for this view.

(3) A third view is that Sheshbazzar was the Shenazzar in 1 Chronicles 3:17, and therefore was Zerubbabel's uncle.

(4) A fourth view is that Sheshbazzar was a Persian official who was sent to oversee the use of the king's money and to make sure the king's wishes were carried out. It has been suggested that because Sheshbazzar was a Persian official the returnees later referred to him (Ezra 5:15-16) to support their claim of legitimacy for their building project. (See comments on 5:13-16.)

C. The list of people who returned (chap. 2)

1. THE LIST RECORDED (2:1-63)

2:1-63. The list is divided into several parts. All of **the people of the province** (i.e., of **Judah**) returned to their hometowns (v. 1). Ezra first recorded the 11 civil and religious leaders who were prominent (v. 2). **Jeshua** was the high priest (3:2); his name is spelled Joshua in the Books of Haggai and Zechariah. He was a grandson of Seraiah (cf. 1 Chron. 6:14 with Hag. 1:1), a priest whom **Nebuchadnezzar** killed at Riblah (2 Kings 25:18-21). The **Nehemiah** in Ezra 2:2 was

not the Nehemiah who returned to Jerusalem more than 90 years later, 444 B.C. Nor was the **Mordecai** here Esther's cousin (Es. 2:5-7), who lived in Susa about 60 years after the Jews' first return.

Nehemiah 7:7 records 12 names rather than 11 (cf. Ezra 2:2). (Three names have different spellings. In verse 2 **Seraiah, Reelaiah,** and **Rehum** are probably the same persons as Azariah, Raamiah, and Nehum, respectively, in Neh. 7:7.) Nahamani's name, not in Ezra's list, may have been dropped out by an early scribal error in the copying of the original manuscripts. It is likely that 12 men would have originally been listed as symbolic heads of the 12-tribe nation (cf. 12 male goats offered for the 12 tribes of Israel, Ezra 6:17).

Then Ezra listed people by their 18 families and clans, totaling 15,604 (2:3-20). Next came a listing of inhabitants (totaling 8,540) from 21 towns and villages (vv. 21-35; see the map "Postexilic Samaria and Judah"). Then **the priests** (4,289 of them) were listed (vv. 36-39), followed by 341 **Levites** which included **singers** and **gatekeepers** (vv. 40-42). **The temple servants** (vv. 43-54) and **descendants of the** royal **servants** (vv. 55-58) totaled **392. The 652** returnees who **could not** clearly trace their ancestry (vv. 59-63) were listed last. **The priests** who could not delineate their genealogies were not allowed by **the governor** (*tiršāṯā*', a Persian term, possibly a reference to Sheshbazzar [cf. comments on 1:8] or to Zerubbabel) **to eat . . . the most sacred food** till **a priest** was **ministering with the Urim and Thummim.** The Urim and Thummim were parts of the high priest's breastplate, probably two stones used in some way in determining God's will (cf. Ex. 28:30; Lev. 8:8; Num. 27:21; Deut. 33:8; 1 Sam. 28:6; Neh. 7:65).

Though such a list of names and locations seems unnecessary to some modern readers, it would have been of great encouragement to the original readers as they saw their own families and towns represented.

2. THE TOTAL NUMBERS GIVEN (2:64-67)

2:64-67. When added together the numbers in verses 2-42, 58, and 60 which list the returnees come to 29,829 (including the 11 prominent men listed in v. 2). However, the total in verses 64-65—**the**

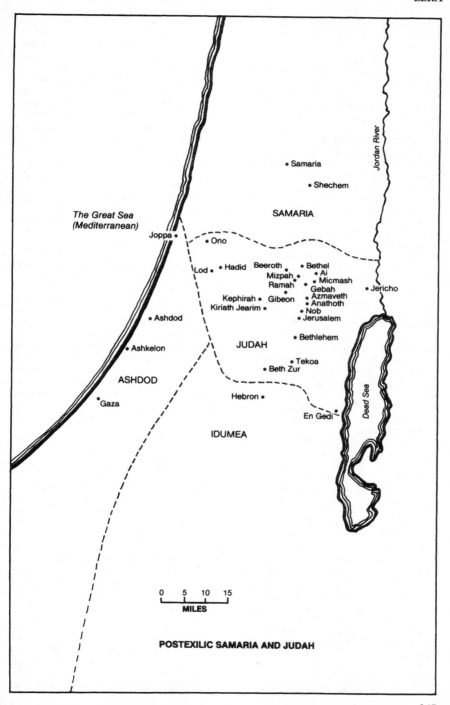

POSTEXILIC SAMARIA AND JUDAH

whole company—is 49,897. The larger number may include women and children. It may also include Jews from the 10 Northern tribes who might have joined the remnant of the two Southern tribes of Judah and Benjamin (cf. 1:5). It may also have included the priests who could not delineate their genealogies (2:61-62).

Ezra's grand total of 49,897 is very close to Nehemiah's total of 49,942 (Neh. 7:66-67). Nehemiah's extra 45 people are in the singers (Ezra had 200 but Nehemiah referred to 245). This may have been a scribal error, an error not in the original manuscripts but in the numerous copyings of the text in its transmission. A scribe, in copying Nehemiah 7:67, may have inadvertently picked up the 245 in verse 68, in reference to mules, and inserted that number for the 200 singers. This kind of error may also account for several variations in the other numbers in these lists. (For further discussion see the comments on Neh. 7. Also see the chart "The Lists of Exile Returnees in Ezra 2 and Nehemiah 7," near Neh. 7:8-62.)

Even the animals were counted—a total of 8,136, most of them **donkeys,** commonly used for riding (Ezra 2:66-67).

The journey from Babylon to Israel was about 900 miles and took about four months (cf. 7:8-9), but Ezra did not state how long the return trip took. His focus was not on the people's hardships but on their task of rebuilding the temple.

3. THE RESTORATION BEGUN (2:68-70)

2:68-69. When the returnees **arrived** back in Palestine **at the house of the Lord** (i.e., at its location site) they **gave** of their possessions **according to their ability.** They gave large amounts of money and material to begin the temple-building project. The list of precious metals and materials differs from the corresponding list in Nehemiah 7:70-72. Ezra's **61,000 drachmas of gold** are 41,000 in Nehemiah. Ezra recorded **5,000 minas of silver** while Nehemiah referred to 4,200. Ezra mentioned **100 priestly garments** whereas Nehemiah recorded 597. These differences were probably early scribal errors.

2:70. The people then **settled in** their ancestors' **towns** and villages (see the map "Postexilic Samaria and Judah").

D. The rebuilding of the temple (3:1–6:15)

1. THE ALTAR AND THE FOUNDATION REBUILT (CHAP. 3)

3:1-2. The first task facing the people was the rebuilding of **the altar** of **burnt** offering, directly east of where the temple building itself would be located. This was essential for reestablishing the sacrificial system which set these people apart as a nation and which was used by God as a means for atoning for their sins. **The seventh month** may refer to the seventh month after the people left Babylon or to the seventh month after they arrived in **Jerusalem.** This was in September-October (see the chart "Calendar in Israel" near Ex. 12). In years past, the seventh month had been a great month religiously for Israel. Three religious festivals were held in the seventh month: the Feast of Trumpets on the 1st day (Lev. 23:23-25), the Day of Atonement on the 10th day (Lev. 23:26-32), and the Feast of Tabernacles on days 15-21 (Lev. 23:33-36, 39-43; Num. 29:12-39; cf. Ezra 3:4).

The words, **The people assembled as one man,** suggest they all agreed that the building project must begin. The men who headed up the constructing of the altar were **Jeshua,** the religious leader (a descendant of Aaron), **and Zerubbabel,** the civil leader (a descendant of David), along with **fellow priests** (other descendants of Aaron) and **associates** (other descendants of David). They built the altar so that they could offer sacrifices **in accordance with what** was **written in the Law of Moses.** It was imperative that the returnees would come back to the Mosaic Covenant. Because their forefathers had left the covenant, the nation had been driven into Captivity. The former exiles did not want to make that same mistake.

3:3-6. Even though the returnees had **fear of the peoples around them,** foreigners who had been deported by the Assyrian Empire into Palestine, **they built the altar,** and offered **burnt offerings on it** (cf. Lev. 1; 6:8-13), starting **on the first day of the . . . month** (Ezra 3:6). These were the first sacrifices made there in 50 years—since 586 B.C. when the temple was torn down. Other **sacrifices** were offered in connection with **all the appointed feasts,** including, for example, **the Feast of Tabernacles** on days 15-21 of that seventh month (cf. Lev. 23:33-36, 39-43; Num. 29:12-39). The **sacrifices** showed that the people wanted to be responsive to the Law of God.

3:7-9. There was a period of preparation for building the temple foundation for **the work** did not begin till **the second month of the second year after their arrival** (May-June 536, exactly 70 years after the first deportation in 605). Why this delay of seven months after the altar was built? Because they had to get organized and secure the building materials. The wood (**cedar logs**) came **from Lebanon,** shipped along the coast **to Joppa** and then carried overland to **Jerusalem** (see the map "The Persian Empire" near 1:1). Lebanon was well known for its cedar forests and its fine woodworkers. For the first temple, 430 years earlier (in 966 B.C.), Solomon had received much of his building materials (cedar, pine, and algum logs) and craftsmen from Lebanon (1 Kings 5:1-10, 18; 2 Chron. 2:1-16). Solomon began his project in the second month (May-June; 1 Kings 6:1), the same month this rebuilding began under Zerubbabel. Since **Tyre** and **Sidon** in Lebanon were under the Persian Empire, **Cyrus** had to authorize this transaction (cf. Ezra 6:3-4), in which the logs, as in Solomon's time, were paid for by **money . . . food . . . drink, and oil.**

Zerubbabel appointed **the Levites** as supervisors of the construction project. Centuries earlier Levites were involved in the tabernacle construction (Ex. 38:21) and in caring for and transporting it (Num. 1:50-51; 3:21-37). Now they were involved in the temple construction. Three Levite groups of supervisors were mentioned (Ezra 3:9)—**Jeshua** and his family, **Kadmiel** (cf. 2:40) and his family, and the family **of Henadad.**

3:10-11. Nothing is mentioned about the actual process of laying the temple **foundation** or the length of time involved. This is because the focus was on the results of this project on that community of people who had braved the rugged conditions. They were following the command of Cyrus but, more importantly, they were following the command of their God with whom they were in covenant. As **the foundation . . . was laid** the **people** were careful to follow in the traditions of their forefathers who had been rightly related to God under the

Mosaic Covenant. As **the priests . . . and the Levites** led the dedication service for the temple's foundations, they did the things that were **prescribed by David.** The order followed was the same as when David brought the ark to Jerusalem. At that time priests blew trumpets and Asaph sounded cymbals (1 Chron. 16:5-6). Here the priests blew **trumpets** and **sons** (descendants) of Asaph played the **cymbals.** The order was also similar to the time when the ark was brought to the temple in Solomon's day (2 Chron. 5:12-13), when Asaph and others played cymbals, harps, and lyres; and the priests blew trumpets. In this rebuilding service the priests and Levites sang, **He is good; His love to Israel endures forever,** words almost identical to the song of praise in 2 Chronicles 5:13 (cf. Ps. 136:1). This song of praise is highly significant for by it the religious leaders were acknowledging that Yahweh had again established His loving protection over the nation. The word "love" (*ḥeseḏ*) is God's covenantal loyal love which exists forever with His people Israel. Now that the temple worship was being reestablished, the people again recognized the commitment of God's unending covenantal love.

3:12-13. In contrast with the joy many people experienced on that occasion, a few of **the older priests and Levites and family heads, who had seen the former temple** (destroyed 50 years earlier in 586 B.C.) were discouraged. Perhaps they contrasted the roughness of the current project with the grandeur of the Solomonic temple. Sixteen years later (in 520 B.C.) the same emotion of discouragement again hit the builders of the **temple** (Hag. 2:1-9). The two sounds, the **joy** and the **weeping** (from sadness), mingled together and were so loud that they were **heard far away.**

2. THE REBUILDING OPPOSED (4:1–6:12)

Ezra did not record all the events in those 21 years (from 536) till the temple was finished (in 515). That is because he was making a theological point that the temple of the Lord was completed despite opposition that might have stopped any other project. The temple was the basis for the postexilic community's fellowship with God. Not till the temple was built could the people really live in accord with the covenant. Ezra's account of this interim period differs in tone from Haggai's account of opposition (from 520 to 518). Ezra did not dwell on the sinful condition of the people as they lived in the land as did Haggai (Hag. 1). Ezra's account focused on external pressures from the surrounding peoples, whereas Haggai focused on the internal attitudes of the people who valued material possessions above spiritual things (Hag. 1:4-6).

a. *Attempts of enemies to stop the building (4:1-5)*

4:1-2. The enemies used two methods of opposition to try to keep the **temple** from being built. First they offered to **help** in the construction process, thereby hoping to infiltrate the ranks and sidetrack the building project. When that did not work, they frightened the builders (perhaps with threats on their lives) and even hired counselors to frustrate them (vv. 4-5). **The enemies of Judah and Benjamin** refer to the people living in Palestine since the time of the fall of the Northern Kingdom in 722 B.C. The Assyrian Empire, which conquered the 10 Northern tribes, deported some of the people away to Assyria and brought in other peoples to intermarry (2 Kings 17:23-24). This tactic prevented strong nationalistic uprisings in the conquered lands.

The "enemies" (called "the peoples around them," Ezra 4:4) were the descendants of these mixed peoples and the forefathers of the New Testament Samaritans. These people in Ezra's day claimed that they worshiped the same God, that is, Yahweh, the God of Israel. But they had a syncretistic form of worship; they worshiped both Yahweh and others (2 Kings 17:29, 32-34, 41). Therefore their statement (Ezra 4:2) was not fully accurate and was apparently made to mislead the leadership of the returned band. **Esarhaddon, king of Assyria, who brought us here,** was the Assyrian monarch who aggressively pursued the policy of partial deportation and to whose reign these enemies could trace their ancestry in Palestine. Esarhaddon, a son of Sennacherib, ruled from 681 to 669 B.C. Some people, however, had been displaced into Samaria earlier by the Assyrian kings Sargon II (722–705) and Sennacherib (705–681). Judah and Benjamin's enemies

were also appealing on the basis of the fact that they, like the Jews, were a "displaced people," having been brought in from the outside. In a sense they were downplaying the nation of Israel's "roots" in the land.

4:3-5. The response by the governmental side (**Zerubbabel**) and the religious side (**Jeshua**) was decisive and immediate. They had two reasons for not wanting to be sidetracked by this offer of help. First, the temple was for **the LORD the God of Israel,** who was not the god these people worshiped. Second, they had been commissioned by **King Cyrus** himself to undertake the **building** project and therefore had every right to carry it out on their own. This rebuff brought on the second form of opposition. As already stated, the enemies tried **to discourage** the workers **and make them afraid.** This policy of harassment continued on till **the reign of Darius, king of Persia,** who ruled from 521 to 486. It was during his reign, in 515, that the temple was completed. The account of the building program under Darius is resumed in Ezra 4:24 after a parenthesis in verses 6-23.

b. *Parenthetical letters (4:6-23)*

These letters to and from Artaxerxes are out of place chronologically, but they follow here logically to show that the opposition Ezra had begun to describe (vv. 1-5) continued on for many years—to 485 B.C., the year Xerxes began to reign (v. 6) and on into the days of Artaxerxes (464-424). Artaxerxes was the king who was reigning during the events recorded in chapters 7–10. For the names and dates of the Persian kings in the postexilic period, see the chart "Chronology of the Postexilic Period" near 1:1. Thus the letters may have been written at the time of Ezra's return (458 B.C.). Therefore the letters were written nearly 80 years later than the account into which they were placed. Ezra was not being deceptive by placing the letters here in his book since he clearly dated them by the ruler under which they were written. Anyone familiar with the history of that part of the world at that time (as were the inhabitants of Israel when the Book of Ezra was written) would have clearly seen what Ezra was logically doing.

4:6. Opposition continued during

the time of **Xerxes**. Xerxes, also known as Ahasuerus in the Book of Esther, ruled from 485 to 465. Ezra recorded nothing of the nature or results of the **accusation** except that it apparently kept the Israelites from working on building projects. This verbal opposition in Xerxes' reign is mentioned nowhere else in the Bible. This verse sets the stage for the following letter which was written in the reign of Persia's next king.

4:7. Opposition against the Jews was strong during the time of **Artaxerxes**. The focus of the narrative is on two letters written during his reign (464–424). Because the enemies' **letter** and the king's reply brought the work on the city walls and foundations to a halt, it seems logical that **the letter was written** before the return of Nehemiah, for under Nehemiah the building projects resumed and were completed. Though the letter was composed by people who spoke a northwest Semitic dialect (like Hebrew) it was written **in the Aramaic language** (the trade language of the day). It was in square **Aramaic script** rather than in the slanted Hebrew type of script or in cuneiform signs. Ezra 4:8–6:18 and 7:12-26 are in Aramaic. Perhaps **Bishlam, Mithredath,** and **Tabeel** were men from Samaria.

4:8-10. Rehum the commanding officer and Shimshai the secretary were probably Persians who were persuaded to write the letter. In their introduction Rehum and Shimshai tried to point out to King **Artaxerxes** that the participants in this opposition were from various parts of the world. Their complaint was not merely from a single isolated group. **Judges and officials** from various parts of the Persian Empire (see the map "The Persian Empire" near 1:1) and people who had been deported to **Samaria** under the reign of the Assyrian King **Ashurbanipal** 200 years earlier were opposed to the work. Ashurbanipal (669–626) continued the deporting done by his father Esarhaddon (4:2).

4:11-16. The writers **of the letter** (cf. **This is a copy** of the letter, v. 23; 5:6; 7:11) identified with the Persian king by noting that they were his **servants**. The letter itself is recorded in 4:12-16. The opponents noted that **the Jews were restoring the walls and repairing the foundations**. Their opposition was obviously not against the rebuilding of the temple, for it had been completed in 515 B.C. The opposition was against an attempt to begin rebuilding the **walls** of **Jerusalem** which the opponents called that **rebellious and wicked city** (cf. vv. 15, 19). The apparent reason for the complaint was that if the city was allowed to be fortified, then Jerusalem and the territory which Jerusalem would control would no longer pay **taxes** or **tribute** money to the crown. This would dishonor **the king**. Therefore the complainers felt it was their patriotic duty to tell **the king** what was happening so that he could **search** the **records** and see that Jerusalem was **a rebellious city**, which is **why** it **was destroyed**. The letter added that if the city of Jerusalem was fortified then the Jews would take back all the territory they had previously occupied and the Persian **king** would have no territory left **in Trans-Euphrates**. They claimed he would lose a huge portion of his empire.

4:17-23. In his **reply** the king actually strengthened the position of the Israelites by leaving open the possibility that their work might resume later by his permission. This, of course, did happen under the leadership of Nehemiah. The king did **search** the archives and **found** that **Jerusalem** had been **powerful** at one time. What an encouragement this must have been to Ezra's original readers to recall the years of David and Solomon and to know that even a pagan king acknowledged the sovereignty of their empire centered at Jerusalem. The **king** commanded that the building projects **stop . . . until I so order.** This was the same king who later (444 B.C.) changed this edict and allowed Nehemiah to return and rebuild the walls of Jerusalem (Neh. 2:1-9). However, the immediate result was a forced cessation of the building activity because the enemies used **force** to back up a legal document from the Persian king.

c. The result of the opposition (4:24)

4:24. The narrative now picks up where it left off after verse 5 (vv. 6-23 are a lengthy parenthesis). The result of the opposition during Cyrus' reign was that **work** on the temple was suspended **until the second year of . . . Darius** (520 B.C.), some 18 years after the people had returned to the land for the purpose of rebuilding **the house of God.**

d. The continuation of the work (5:1–6:12)

This section informs the readers of certain historical events under the reign of Darius, and also helps its readers understand that the temple rebuilding was sovereignly ordained by God and carried out through pagan rulers, this time Darius I (521–486).

5:1-2. The work on the temple had been stopped (4:1-5, 24), from 535 to 520 B.C. Now under the influence of two important prophets, **Haggai** and **Zechariah,** it was resumed. The preaching of these two men is recorded in the biblical books bearing their respective names. Haggai prophesied from August to December 520 B.C., and Zechariah prophesied for two years beginning in October-November 520. They were **helping** by exhorting and encouraging (cf. 6:14; Hag. 1:8; 2:4; Zech. 4:7-9). They were vitally concerned with the building of the temple because they realized that their nation could never fulfill the obligations of the Mosaic Covenant till the temple worship was reinstated. Both of these **prophets** placed the blame for the hard times the nation experienced during this period on the people's lack of obedience in not rebuilding the temple. However, Ezra did not deal with that question in his book. He stressed the outside opposition which was also a factor in slowing the work. The building process itself was spearheaded by **Zerubbabel** and **Jeshua,** the civil and religious leaders, respectively.

5:3-5. But as soon as the work was resumed, another effort (cf. 4:1-5) was made to stop it. Israel's leaders came into direct conflict with the duly established local authorities who were responsible to the Persian crown. In a Babylonian record dated 502 B.C. the name **Tattenai** and his office as **governor of Trans-Euphrates** are mentioned. Syria-Palestine was under him, an area including but much larger than Israel. **Shethar-Bozenai** was probably an assistant to Tattenai. It would have been Tattenai's responsibility, on hearing of this building activity in his territory, to investigate it. Major political unrest was seething at the beginning of Darius' reign. Possibly Tattenai thought the temple-**building** project in Jerusalem would grow into a full-scale rebellion against the empire.

The group of officials **asked** Zerubbabel and Jeshua **who authorized** the project (the word **structure** is lit., "wooden structure"), and asked for **the names of** the people responsible for it (cf. 5:9-10). But despite this challenge, the work did not stop because **the eye of their God was watching over** them (cf. "God . . . was over them," v. 1). Occurring frequently in Ezra and Nehemiah are the words "the *hand* of the LORD was on him" and similar expressions (Ezra 7:6, 9, 28; 8:18, 22, 31; Neh. 2:8, 18). God was providentially caring for them (by His "eye") and blessing them (by His "hand"). Clearly God was at work in spite of this opposition because through it the project was eventually given help.

5:6-10. Ezra recorded **the letter** (cf. **This is a copy** of the letter; 4:11, 23; 7:11) **Tattenai . . . sent to King Darius** about the building activity going on in Jerusalem (5:7-16). Tattenai began his letter by noting that **work** was being done on **the temple of the great God** in Jerusalem. This does not mean that Tattenai believed Yahweh of Israel was the supreme God. Most likely he meant that the God to whom the Jews were building the **temple** was the major God of the area. In the ancient Near East there was a highly developed belief in local deities. Tattenai noted that **large stones** and **timbers** (cf. 6:4; 1 Kings 6:36) were being used in the work and that the Jews were working **with diligence** and were **making rapid progress.** He added that he had asked **who authorized** the work (cf. Ezra 5:3) and that he had asked for **the names** of those who were leading the building program (cf. v. 4).

5:11-12. Tattenai's letter then included the Jews' answers to his questions (vv. 11-16). Zerubbabel and Jeshua called themselves **servants of the God of heaven and earth,** not servants of Persia! For comments on the title "the God of heaven" see 1:2. The true God, Yahweh, was superior to Darius' god, Ahura Mazda, whom Darius called "the god of heaven." **Years** earlier **Israel** had **a great king,** Solomon, and had had a beautiful **temple.** It was a prominent structure in the ancient world. **But because** of sin (**our fathers angered the God of heaven**), God **handed them over to Nebuchadnezzar.** The Jews knew why the **temple** was **destroyed** and the people **deported.** In

God's promise/threat (Deut. 28) He said that the people would be taken into captivity if they did not live according to the covenant He instituted with them as they were ready to enter the land of promise. Not only was Nebuchadnezzar involved in the fall of Jerusalem; God Himself was responsible! Nebuchadnezzar was merely an agent of God's anger on His people (cf. "My servant Nebuchadnezzar" in Jer. 25:9; 27:6; 43:10)—an anger which was designed to purify the nation so that some would return to the land as a believing remnant. The Exile did not mean that Yahweh was defeated by Nebuchadnezzar's gods.

5:13-17. In response to Tattenai Zerubbabel and Jeshua stated that Cyrus had allowed a remnant to return to **Jerusalem** to **rebuild** the temple and even gave them **articles** which had been taken from Solomon's **temple** (cf. 1:2-4, 7-11). The letter-writers also recounted the fact that **Cyrus** gave **Sheshbazzar** the task of carrying out the king's command—to return the **articles** and to build another **temple** in the city. Sheshbazzar was mentioned to show Tattenai that the building program was legal. Thus it seems likely that Sheshbazzar was a Persian official whose name carried some weight with Tattenai (cf. comments on 1:8 on several views of Sheshbazzar's identity). Are **Sheshbazzar** and Zerubbabel the same person? Many think so because Sheshbazzar **laid the** temple **foundations,** and so did Zerubbabel (3:8-10). However, this is not absolute proof that the two men were identical. Sheshbazzar could have been responsible, as the king's representative, to see that the work was begun, and Zerubbabel the Jewish leader who completed the task. Tattenai and the officials asked that the king research the records in Babylon (cf. 6:1-2) to find out if what the Jews had said about **a decree** from Cyrus was true. That such records were carefully kept is attested by archeology.

6:1-5. Tattenai had requested that Babylon's archives be **searched** for the document (5:17) but it was not found there. Instead the **scroll** (of papyrus or leather) **was found in . . . Ecbatana** (modern Hamadan), 300 miles northeast of Babylon and capital **of Media** (6:1-2). The scroll was in Ecbatana, because that is where **Cyrus** had spent the summer of

538, when he issued the **decree.** This Ecbatana record was an official "minute" with three details that the verbal and written proclamation (1:1-4) apparently did not contain: (1) **The temple** was **to be 90 feet high and 90 feet wide, with three courses of large stones and one of timbers** (cf. 5:8; 1 Kings 6:36). (2) The project was to be financed by funds from **the royal treasury.** This shows the earnestness of Cyrus' repatriation program. (3) The returned **gold and silver articles** were to be put in **their places in the temple.**

6:6-12. King **Darius** then gave three instructions to **Tattenai** and his associates: (1) He told them to leave the Jews alone and **not interfere** with the building of the **temple** (vv. 6-7). The words **stay away from there** were a common Aramaic legal statement. This was to be in accord with the edict of the great King Cyrus. (2) Tax money was to be used to help finance the project and animals were to be supplied **daily** so that **sacrifices** could be made at the altar of the new temple along with food items for the **offerings** (vv. 8-10). Flour (from **wheat**), **salt,** and **oil** were to be used in the grain offerings (Lev. 2:1-2, 7, 13), and **wine** for drink offerings (Lev. 23:13) on feast days. (3) **Anyone** who disobeyed the edict was to suffer a horrible fate (Ezra 6:11-12). He was to be **impaled on** a **beam** taken from his own **house,** and **his house** was to be demolished. Execution by impaling was practiced in the Assyrian and Persian Empires. Darius wanted no disturbance in this part of his vast kingdom. The pagan king acknowledged that **God** had **caused His name to dwell** at **Jerusalem.** Darius probably thought of Yahweh as a local deity (cf. comments on 5:6-10), whereas Ezra, in recording that statement, knew of the covenantal significance in Yahweh's name dwelling in Jerusalem.

So Tattenai's inquiry backfired. Instead of stopping the temple work, he had to let it proceed and even had to help pay for it out of his **revenues!** Darius' curse on anyone who would **destroy** the **temple** was fulfilled in: (a) Antiochus Epiphanes, who desecrated it in 167 B.C., and died insane three years later; (b) Herod the Great (37–4 B.C.), who added extensively to the temple to glorify himself, and who had domestic trouble and died

EZRA

of disease; and (c) the Romans, who destroyed the temple in A.D. 70, and later had their empire destroyed.

3. THE TEMPLE COMPLETED (6:13-15)

6:13-15. Tattenai, to his credit, **carried . . . out** the instructions of **Darius,** and did so **with diligence** (cf. "with diligence" in 5:8; 6:12; 7:21, 23). The work was done by **the** Jewish **elders** who were encouraged by **the preaching of** the Prophets **Haggai** and **Zechariah** (cf. 5:1). Ezra noted that the ultimate decree for the building of **the temple** was from **God** Himself. God worked through the commands of the pagan Persian kings, **Cyrus, Darius,** and **Artaxerxes.** Workers, **prophets,** and God were all involved. Artaxerxes had nothing to do with building the temple; apparently his name was added to round out the account, for he had decreed the building of Jerusalem's walls (Neh. 2:1, 8). He also helped provide for sacrifices at the temple (Ezra 7:12-17). Some have suggested that Artaxerxes' name may have been added by an early scribe but there is no textual evidence of that. Actually in the Hebrew the words "the temple" are not in 6:14. It reads literally, **They finished their building,** thus speaking in general terms of the total reconstruction of Jerusalem under the decrees of the three kings. But verse 15 specifically mentions **the temple.**

The temple was completed in Adar (February-March) of 515—21 years after the work started in 536, and 4½ years after Haggai began his prophesying. This was 70½ years after the temple had been destroyed on August 12, 586.

E. The dedication of the temple and the celebration of the Passover (6:16-22)

1. THE TEMPLE DEDICATED (6:16-18)

6:16-18. After the temple was finished, it was then dedicated. The comparatively small number of animals sacrificed (**100 bulls, 200 rams, 400 male lambs,** and **12 male goats**) contrasted sharply with the tremendous amount sacrificed by Solomon at the dedication of the first temple (22,000 cattle and 120,000 sheep and goats; 1 Kings 8:63). This points up the comparative poverty of the postexilic community. The 12 goats for the **sin offering** show that the postexilic community still envisioned a unified Israel consisting of all 12 **tribes** even though only 2 had survived with any strength.

The leaders of the sacrificial system—**the priests** and **the Levites**—were **installed . . . according to . . . the Book of Moses,** that is, according to that portion of the Law in which the legal system is described—in parts of Leviticus and Numbers (Lev. 8; Num. 3:5-10; 8:5-14). One of the motifs of Ezra, Nehemiah, and 1 and 2 Chronicles is that the postexilic community was under the leadership of godly men who were steeped in the Scriptures and attempted to do everything according to the Law. This shows that they had learned from the Exile that God's people suffer if they do not live up to their covenantal obligations.

2. THE PASSOVER CELEBRATED (6:19-22)

6:19-21. Beginning with verse 19 the text is again in Hebrew (4:8–6:18 are in Aramaic). **On the 14th day of the first month** (April 515 B.C.) **the Passover** was **celebrated.** The temple had been completed in the 12th month (Adar; v. 15) and fittingly, in the very next month, **the Passover** was reinaugurated. This was the first time in 70 years that the people partook of this feast which commemorated their forefathers' release from Egyptian bondage (cf. Ex. 12:1-14; Lev. 23:5).

The Israelite returnees ate the Passover **with all who had separated themselves from the unclean practices of their Gentile neighbors.** This second group might have been: (a) Gentiles living in Judah (cf. Num. 9:14), or more likely (b) Jews who had remained in the land and had defiled themselves by practices that went against the Law, and then repented of those sins, thereby "separating" themselves.

6:22. The **seven**-day **Feast of Unleavened Bread** was on days 15-21 of the first month, immediately after the Passover (cf. Lev. 23:6-8). The reference to Darius as **the king of Assyria** is not an anachronism (though the Assyrian Empire had ended in 609 B.C.) for the Persian Empire included what was once Assyria. Perhaps this title was a grim reminder that Assyria's harsh tactics were now ended. She was the first to deport Israelites from their land; but now a contingent of Jews was settled back in their land.

This eight-day celebration (the Pass-

354

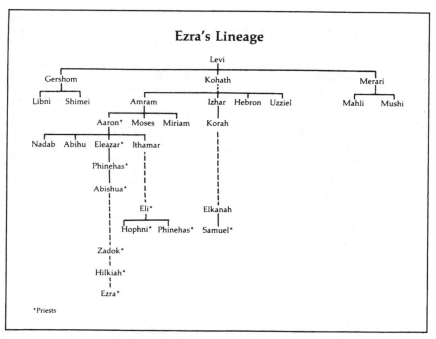

Ezra's Lineage

Levi
- Gershom
  - Libni
  - Shimei
- Kohath
  - Amram
    - Aaron*
      - Nadab
      - Abihu
      - Eleazar*
        - Phinehas*
          - Abishua*
            - Zadok*
              - Hilkiah*
                - Ezra*
      - Ithamar
        - Eli*
          - Hophni*
          - Phinehas*
    - Moses
    - Miriam
  - Izhar
    - Korah
  - Hebron
  - Uzziel
  - Elkanah
    - Samuel*
- Merari
  - Mahli
  - Mushi

*Priests

over, Ezra 6:19, and the seven-day Feast of Unleavened Bread, v. 22), 900 years after the first Passover, signaled the end of the Exile for a remnant of the nation was once again back in fellowship with Yahweh. Since the temple worship was restored, it was important for people who wanted to be in fellowship with God and live according to the covenantal obligations to be in the place where the sacrificial system was being practiced. The people had seen firsthand that God works through history, for He had caused pagan kings to issue decrees which let them return to the land of promise (much as He had caused Egypt's Pharaoh to release Israel). The original readers of Ezra's book would rejoice in that fact and would be encouraged to participate fully in the temple worship, which had been reestablished at such great cost.

II. The Second Return and Reform under Ezra (chaps. 7–10)

These chapters describe a second return of exiles from Babylon, this time under Ezra in 458 B.C. (7:7). Here Ezra often wrote in the first person ("I" and "we"). Ezra, a priest who knew the

Scriptures, knew the importance of having the people back where the sacrificial system was being practiced.

A. The return to the land (chaps. 7–8)

The emphasis in these chapters is on the character of Ezra, which sets the scene for chapters 9 and 10 where sin is uncovered in the postexilic community. Ezra is presented as a man who was strongly motivated by the Law of God.

1. THE INTRODUCTION OF EZRA (7:1-10)

The events which transpire in this section of the narrative occurred during the reign of Artaxerxes who was introduced earlier in the book (4:8-23; 6:14). The return occurred in the king's seventh year, which was 458 B.C.

7:1-5. After these things points to a gap of 57 years since the events at the end of chapter 6. The temple was completed in 515 B.C. in the reign of Darius I. After Darius' death in 486 his son Xerxes ruled for 20 years (485–465). Since Xerxes was the Ahasuerus mentioned in the Book of Esther, the events of that book occurred between Ezra 6 and 7. Then Xerxes' son Artaxerxes ruled from 464 to 424. From 515 to 458 (Artaxerxes' seventh year, 7:7) was 57 years.

Ezra's lineage is traced back to **Aaron,** the first **priest** (see the chart "Ezra's Lineage"). This list is abbreviated, for it does not name every generation. Between **Azariah** and **Meraioth** (v. 3) six names appear in the genealogy in 1 Chronicles 6:7-10 (cf. comments there). Since **Seraiah** was the high priest when Jerusalem fell in 586 (2 Kings 25:18), Ezra may have been his great-grandson. Because of his priestly ancestry, Ezra, like the priests, had authority to teach (cf. Lev. 10:11; Ezra 7:10).

7:6. Ezra . . . was a teacher well-versed in the Law of Moses. The word "teacher" translates *sōpēr,* a broad word that means, a "recorder, scribe, secretary, or writer" (e.g., 2 Sam. 8:17; Es. 3:12; 8:9; Ps. 45:1). The word also referred to a learned man who could read and write (e.g., Jehudi in Jer. 36:23) and a learned man who could teach what he read in God's Law. Ezra was called a "teacher" (*sōpēr*) four times (Ezra 7:6, 11-12, 21; cf. v. 25). And he was called "Ezra the scribe" six times in Nehemiah (8:1, 4, 9, 13; 12:26, 36). "Well versed" translates *māhîr,* which is rendered "skillful" in Psalm 45:1.

Ezra had the blessing of the pagan King Artaxerxes as well as the blessing of the covenant **God of Israel.** A few years later Nehemiah had an official position before **the king** (Neh. 1:11), but Ezra held no such position. It is enough for the author to note that he was a teacher who was well versed in the Law. That was to be his major function in life. Because of the king's favor Ezra was promised that he could have whatever he wanted. Rather than ask for something personal, Ezra used the monarch's favor to advance the cause of **God** and His people.

For the first of eight times in the Books of Ezra and Nehemiah, mention is made of God's **hand** being on Ezra and Nehemiah (Ezra 7:6, 9, 28; 8:18, 22, 31; Neh. 2:8, 18).

7:7-10. Not much is said here about the trip **from Babylon** to **Jerusalem** or the preparations for it. These few verses are a summary of the journey that is detailed in the rest of chapter 7 and in chapter 8. Returning with **Ezra** were groups of people corresponding to the groups in Zerubbabel's return (chap. 2). The trip back to the land took exactly four months, from **the first** to **the fifth** months, from Nisan 1 (March-April) to Ab 1 (July-August). **The good hand of . . . God was on** Ezra because he **devoted himself to the study and observance of the Law of the LORD, and to teaching** it. "Devoted himself" is literally, "set his heart firmly" (cf. 2 Chron. 19:3; 30:19), which gives the idea that Ezra was inwardly determined. His determination was directed toward doing three things: studying God's Law, obeying it, and teaching it to others—an inviolable order for a successful ministry!

2. THE CIRCUMSTANCES PROMPTING THE RETURN (7:11-28)

7:11-12. **Artaxerxes** wrote a letter (cf. **This is a copy of the letter;** 4:11, 23; 5:6) **to Ezra** that allowed Ezra and others to return to Israel. (On Ezra as **a teacher** see comments on 7:6.) No reason for the decree was given. It can be surmised that Ezra had asked for permission to take a group back and that this decree was the official granting of his request. The decree was sent **to Ezra** personally.

7:13-26. **Artaxerxes** listed certain freedoms the people were to have as they journeyed to and lived in **Israel.** He gave them permission **to go to Jerusalem** (v. 13). He gave them **silver and gold** to take with them and he allowed them to get more in **Babylon** (vv. 15-16, 20). He said that they could offer sacrifices **on the altar** at **the temple** (v. 17). They were also given freedom to make their own decisions (v. 18). They could take back the utensils of **worship** for **the temple** (vv. 19-20). (Apparently not all of them had been carried back with Zerubbabel; cf. 1:7-11.) They could have **whatever** else they needed for the temple **up to** a certain limit (7:21-22). The wheat, oil, and salt were for use in the **grain offerings** (cf. 6:9; Lev. 2:1-2, 7, 13), and the wine was for **drink offerings** (cf. Ezra 6:9; Lev. 12:13). As noted in the NIV margin, the amounts were enormous: **100 talents** (3¾ tons) **of silver, 100 cors** (600 bushels) **of wheat, 100 baths** (600 gallons) **of wine, 100 baths** of olive oil, **and salt without limit. The priests** and **Levites** were not to be taxed (Ezra 7:24).

In return for granting these privileges the king was to receive some benefits from the expedition. He wanted to avoid uprisings or feelings of anger against him (v. 23) and to have order in that part of his empire (vv. 25-26). **Ezra was responsible to administer justice to all the people** of the area, that is, to **all who knew the laws of** his God—the Jewish people. Ezra also was to administer the judicial system by handing out punishment to any who would **not obey** (v. 26).

7:27-28. Ezra's response to the king's decree shows what kind of man he was. He praised the LORD for what was being done under him. By calling Yahweh **the God of our fathers** he linked himself with the godly line that had been concerned with proper sacrificial worship. He also noted that God had given this idea to the king (**put it into the king's heart**). Ezra added that the purpose of all this was **to bring honor to the house of the LORD.** The privileges granted by Artaxerxes were for God's glory, not Ezra's.

Ezra also said that God's **good favor** was shown to him in front of all the king's pagan **advisers** and **officials.** "Good favor" translates ḥesed, God's covenantal love for His people. (That Heb. word is rendered "love" in 3:11, in each verse in Ps. 136, and elsewhere.) It refers to more than love; it means covenantal love, love borne out of loyalty to a commitment. Because Ezra saw that God was working through him (**the hand of the LORD my God was on me;** cf. Ezra 7:6, 9; 8:18, 22, 31), he began the task of selecting people to make the difficult trip. This probably was difficult and must have involved much personal contact and persuasion. But he was successful in enlisting **leading men . . . to go** with him.

3. THE LIST OF THE RETURNEES (8:1-14)

8:1-14. This list consists of the major men (**family heads**) who returned as well as the numbers of those who accompanied them. Most of the people listed were related to the families who had returned previously under Zerubbabel (537 B.C.) 79 years earlier (chap. 2). Many of the family names in 8:3c-14 are mentioned in 2:3-15. **Gershom was a descendant of Phinehas,** son of Aaron's third son Eleazar (Ex. 6:25), and **Daniel** was descended from **Ithamar,** Aaron's fourth son (Ex. 6:23). The total number of men who returned was 1,514 including 18 heads of families and 1,496 other men.

With the 258 Levites assembled later (Ezra 8:15-20) the number came to 1,772. With women and children, the group may have totaled between 4,000 and 5,000. Even so, this group was much smaller than the near-50,000 on the first return (2:64-65).

4. THE DETAILS OF THE JOURNEY AND ARRIVAL (8:15-36)

a. Levites recruited for the journey (8:15-20)

8:15. Levites were to function as teachers of the Law (cf. Lev. 10:11; Deut. 33:10). Therefore they were to have an extremely important role in the reestablished community. **The people** desperately needed to understand the importance of the Law as they faced their situation as returnees from exile. The **Levites** would have a difficult time in the new land for they were to be involved in the disciplined ministry of temple service. Perhaps that is why none were present when Ezra and his group were ready to depart from **the canal** of **Ahava** (cf. Ezra 8:21, 31), whose location is unknown. This canal may have been a tributary of the Euphrates River. Even Zerubbabel had comparatively few Levites on his return (733 [2:40-58], less than 1.5% of the 49,897 [2:64-65]).

8:16-17. Therefore Ezra **sent 9 leaders** and 2 **men of learning** to secure some Levites and **temple servants** from the man **Iddo.** Ezra **told** the messengers **what to say,** which seems to indicate that this was a delicate task which needed to have some weight behind the message. The 11 messengers were sent to **Casiphia,** whose location is no longer known.

8:18-20. The men were able to secure 38 Levites from two families—18 from **Sherebiah's** family and 20 from Jeshaiah's relatives—as well as **220 . . . temple servants.** Only then was Ezra ready to start on the important journey. Without the Levite teachers of the Law and people to serve at the temple all would be lost and the trip futile.

b. Preparations made for the journey (8:21-30)

8:21-23. First, spiritual preparation was made for the journey. Ezra was concerned with matters pertaining to God's people. So Ezra **proclaimed a fast** in preparation for the journey. He wanted the assembled group thereby to **humble themselves before . . . God** in order to **ask Him for a safe journey** for themselves, their **children,** and their **possessions.** Being humble before God shows one's spiritual dependence, his acknowledgment that God is in total control. Ezra did not want **to ask** for military protection **(soldiers and horsemen)** because he had already publicly announced that God would take care of the people as they returned. In contrast, Nehemiah readily accepted a military escort on his way back to the land (Neh. 2:9).

8:24-27. Next, physical preparation was made for the journey. Ezra divided the **silver . . . gold,** and **articles** among 24 of the key men in the group. These items were gifts for the temple, given by Persian officials and by nonreturning Israelites. They included 25 tons **of silver, silver articles** weighing 3¾ tons, 3¾ tons **of gold, 20 bowls of gold** that weighed about 19 pounds, and **two** expensive **bronze** objects. All this would be valued at many millions of dollars today. No wonder Ezra was concerned about the people's safety (v. 21).

8:28-30. Ezra charged these key men with the responsibility of getting the precious metals and valuables back to **Jerusalem** safely. In his charge he said that these material possessions were **consecrated to the LORD** and that **the silver and gold** were freely given by God's people. He emphasized the need for guarding the money and articles **carefully** by noting that they would all be **weighed** on arrival to be sure none had disappeared. **The priests and Levites** accepted the responsibility of taking the metals and utensils to **Jerusalem.**

c. The people journeyed and arrived (8:31-36)

8:31-34. Only a few statements were made about the journey and the arrival. The group left Babylon on the 1st day of the first month (7:9) and they left **the Ahava Canal** on **the 12th** of the same month. Since they were at the canal three days (8:15), the site of their canal encampment was about nine days' travel from Babylon, perhaps 100-130 miles away.

The total journey was about 900 miles and must have been difficult for a group without a military escort. However, Ezra was content merely to relate that

the hand of our God was on us (cf. 7:6, 9, 28; 8:18, 22) and that the Lord granted the returnees protection. On arriving in **Jerusalem,** after a **three-**day rest, **everything** was turned over to the priests and **Levites** and **weighed** (vv. 33-34). Several of these temple officials are also mentioned in the Book of Nehemiah: **Meremoth** (Neh. 3:4, 21), **Jozabad** (Neh. 11:16), and **Binnui** (Neh. 3:24).

8:35-36. Then the exiles offered sacrifices to God. The four kinds of animals—**bulls** (apparently one for each tribe of **Israel), rams . . . lambs,** and **goats**—were the same as those offered at the temple dedication (6:17), but now the number was smaller. A copy of **the king's** edict was given to the surrounding officials **(royal satraps** and **governors),** who were to carry out his wishes under Ezra's leadership. This caused the surrounding peoples to assist the Jewish postexilic community. The section ends in an interesting climax—God's good hand was so evident on His people that even surrounding peoples helped them in the sacrificial system, the means of fellowship with God.

B. The reform in the land (chaps. 9–10)

In contrast with the highpoint of God's blessing on the people at the end of the previous section (8:36), this section opens with a statement about the severe sin into which the people of the postexilic community had fallen. The reason the people were back in the land was so that they would be able to worship God according to the ways of their forefathers under the Law. However, when the people returned to the land they still had a tendency to wander away from the words of God that had been written by Moses.

1. THE PEOPLE'S SIN OF INTERMARRIAGE REPORTED (9:1-4)

9:1-2. Ezra's return had a profound effect on the people of Israel. The man who was devoted to the accurate teaching of the Law became the focal point of a major reform. This occurred less than five months after his arrival (cf. 7:9 with 10:9). **The leaders came to me** suggests that these were men who had previously returned to the land under Zerubbabel and had established themselves as leaders and had looked into the problem.

Ezra's return may have pricked their consciences as they reflected on the Law of God. They realized that something had to be done about the situation if the nation was to enjoy fellowship with the Lord. Outward sacrifice was fine, but only if it was accompanied by an inward conformity to the Word of God (Hosea 6:6; Micah 6:6-8).

The Jewish leaders reported to Ezra that some Israelites had been involved with their pagan neighbors' **detestable practices** (cf. Ezra 9:11, 14) which meant they had married Gentiles. One of God's major prohibitions was that His people were not to marry outside the community of believers (Ex. 34:11-16; Deut. 7:1-4). This was not because of racial difference, for the peoples of the surrounding areas were of the same Semitic race. The reason was strictly religious. If God's people married outside Israel they would be tempted (as was Solomon; 1 Kings 11:3-5) to get caught up in pagan idolatrous worship. Intermarrying with people who did not worship Yahweh was symptomatic of the way the people forsook other aspects of God's Law. If they would break this aspect of the Law in the most intimate of human relationships then they would probably also break the Law in other less intimate human relationships. The peoples listed in Ezra 9:1 were many of those God had warned about centuries before (Deut. 7:1), as well as the surrounding nations of Ammon, Moab, and Egypt. Unfortunately some religious and civil **leaders** had been in the forefront of this evil practice.

9:3-4. Ezra's response was typical of the response of godly people in the Old Testament when they found out about sin. Tearing his **tunic and cloak** was a sign of mourning (cf. Num. 14:6; Josh. 7:6; Es. 4:1; Job 1:20), and pulling **hair from** his **head and beard** was a sign of unusual grief or of intense anger (Isa. 22:12). He was **appalled** because of the people's sin (Ezra 9:3; cf. v. 4). Ezra knew that it was for just this sort of sin that his nation had gone into captivity (cf. v. 7). Perhaps he was afraid they would go into captivity again (cf. v. 8).

2. EZRA'S PRAYER TO GOD (9:5-15)

Ezra's prayer reveals much about him. He identified with the nation in their sin even though he himself was in-

nocent of the offense (cf. Dan. 9:5-6, 8-11, 13, 15-16). Ezra understood that the nation stood together under the covenant and that this breach of responsibility, especially since it had been led by leaders of the nation, could jeopardize the entire nation before God.

9:5. The evening sacrifice was around 3 P.M. Ezra's physical position (**on his knees with his hands spread out to the Lord**) showed that he was throwing himself on the mercy of God. Ezra knew that the nation was guilty (vv. 6-7; cf. vv. 13, 15) so he assumed a position of begging before the Lord. There was no excuse for the people's actions. Ezra's prayer was made at the temple with weeping (10:1).

9:6-7. Ezra confessed the continuing problem of sin among the people of the nation. He reacted to the sin with embarrassment, using terms such as **ashamed and disgraced.** He felt embarrassed because it was for **guilt** like this that the nation had gone into **captivity** in the first place **at the hand of foreign kings** (viz., Sargon II and Nebuchadnezzar). The Captivity was to be a method of purifying the people and reestablishing a close relationship between them and God. Apparently the Exile had not accomplished its purpose because of the people's tendency to stray from their covenantal obligations. Like a flood their **sins,** Ezra said, had engulfed them for their sins were **higher than** their **heads.**

9:8-9. Ezra acknowledged the grace of **God** in allowing the people to return to the land. He reminded God and himself that it was the Lord's graciousness that allowed **the kings of Persia** to grant the Jews freedom to return to the land of promise **to rebuild** the temple. But now they were back in **bondage**—bondage to sin.

9:10-12. Ezra then confessed the men's present sin of intermarriage. Ezra asked, **What can we say after this?** By this question he was acknowledging that the nation had no excuse before God (cf. v. 6). No explanation was given for the leaders' disobedience. They had broken God's **commands** to remain pure before Him, and to separate from the **corruption** and **detestable practices** (cf. vv. 1, 14) in **the land.** They had directly disobeyed the clear Word of God. Foreign marriages contaminated Israel, fostered the foreigners' **prosperity,** weakened Israel spiritually, and decreased her opportunity to enjoy the land's crops.

9:13-14. The conclusion Ezra reached was that **God** would be totally just in destroying them in His anger so that **no remnant** would be left (cf. "remnant" in vv. 8, 13, 15). They deserved even greater punishment than God was giving them (cf. v. 6). In a nutshell, Ezra was describing the position of all mankind before God. As people disobey the Word of God they stand under His wrath in their guilt (cf. "guilt" in vv. 6-7, 13, 15; cf. John 16:8; James 2:10).

9:15. Ezra's prayer included no specific request; he simply threw himself on God's mercy. By this he concluded his prayer in the same way he began. He acknowledged that no one in the entire community was worthy to **stand** before the **righteous** God. In his prayer Ezra affirmed several attributes of **God:** grace (v. 8), kindness (v. 9), anger (v. 14), and righteousness (v. 15). Ezra was asking God to be merciful on the basis of His loyal love for the nation.

3. THE PEOPLE'S CONFESSION OF SIN (CHAP. 10)

As already noted, the leaders were sensitive to the fact that there was a problem (9:1-2). Now other concerned Israelites joined Ezra in his grief.

a. The people acknowledged their sin (10:1-4)

10:1-4. Many people acknowledged that something had to be done about the situation. Apparently this sin had gone on and had been tolerated for some time. Children were born to some of those who had intermarried (vv. 3, 44). No doubt some devout Jews were grieved because of this sin in the community. Perhaps they were afraid to speak up or had tried and were rebuffed. In any case, now that some of the leaders were joining Ezra in bemoaning the sin, these righteous people joined in the mourning and began to demand that something be done. **A large crowd of Israelites** gathered with **Ezra** and **wept bitterly.**

One man, **Shecaniah,** spoke for all the people who were weeping. He acknowledged the unfaithfulness of the nation but he felt that **there** was **still hope for Israel.** He suggested that the people **covenant before . . . God** to divorce the

foreign **women** and **send** them **away** along with the **children** they had borne. This was to be done **according to the Law.** Shecaniah promised Ezra that the people would stand behind him in such a decision. Shecaniah was calling on the nation to do something distasteful and difficult, something that could cause bitter division between family members and friends. However, he appealed on the basis of the Law of God which was supposed to be the people's rule of life. The Law also was a safeguard for this situation, for an Israelite could marry a woman from outside the nation if she had become Jewish in faith. Perhaps that is why each marriage was investigated thoroughly (vv. 16-19)—to see if any women had become Jewish proselytes.

Though divorce was not the norm, it may have been preferable in this situation because the mixed marriages, if continued, would lead the nation away from true worship of Yahweh. Eventually they would destroy the nation. On the other hand some Bible students believe this plan was not in accord with God's desires (cf. Mal. 2:16). Do two "wrongs" make one "right"? Perhaps Ezra wrongly followed Shecaniah's advice in requiring these divorces. However, no specific support for this view is indicated in Ezra 10.

b. The people took an oath (10:5-8)

10:5-8. The people's sincerity in their confession and repentance was shown by the fact that they **took** an **oath** before **God.** Taking an oath was not a light matter; it bound the oath-taker to do what he had promised. If he did not, he would be punished.

Ezra withdrew to fast and mourn by himself. **Jehohanan** was the same as Johanan (Neh. 12:23). He was the grandson of Eliashab (Neh. 12:10-11), who was the high priest (Neh. 13:28). Hence, **son of Eliashab** (Ezra 10:6) means "grandson of Eliashab" ("son" in Heb. often means a grandson or even a later descendant). **A proclamation** was sent out to **all the exiles to assemble in Jerusalem. Anyone who** did not come would lose **his property** and would **be expelled from the assembly of the exiles.** In effect such a person would no longer have any legal rights. Ezra had this authority to send out a proclamation with threat of punishment, because of the edict of the king (cf. 7:26).

c. The people gathered at the temple (10:9-15)

10:9-11. The **square** to the east of the temple could accommodate thousands of people. The temple area was always the center of action in the Book of Ezra. On the appointed day (**three days** after the proclamation, in November-December 457) as the people were gathering, a rainstorm was in progress. This was the rainy season (v. 13). However, because of the oath (v. 5) and because of the threat of punishment the meeting went on as scheduled. The people were **distressed** out of fear of God's wrath and over concern about their families being separated. As **Ezra** addressed the group, he cited their sin of unfaithfulness, pronounced their **guilt**, and challenged them to acknowledge their sin and do something about it by becoming **separate** from their **foreign wives.**

10:12-15. The people **responded** that they agreed, but that the matter would take some time because of the large number of people involved and because of the rain. (In fact, it took three months, vv. 16-17.) Someone suggested that each man who had **married a foreign woman** should make an appointment **with the elders and judges** of his hometown so that the matter could be settled locally. This was a good suggestion because the elders and judges of each town would know the individuals involved. They would know whether the women involved were worshipers of the Lord or were still involved in pagan worship. Four leaders **opposed** the plan, though it is not clear why. Perhaps they wanted to take care of the matter right away; or perhaps they did not want to take care of it at all. At least one of them, **Meshullam,** was guilty (v. 29).

d. The marriages examined (10:16-17)

10:16-17. In just 11 days the examining began (cf. vv. 9, 16). It took three months for all the marriages to be examined, from **the first day of the 10th month** (December-January 457) to the **first day of the 1st month** of the next year (March-April 456). Obviously the problem was widespread and could not be settled in a day (v. 13). Each case was judged individually so that justice would

be done. By this action the community was not saying that divorce was good. It was a matter of following God's Law about the need for religious purity in the nation (Ex. 34:11-16; Deut. 7:1-4). **Ezra** wrote nothing about what happened to these **foreign women** or their children. Presumably they returned to their pagan countries.

e. The offenders listed (10:18-44)

10:18-44. Ezra concluded his account by listing the offenders in the **foreign** marriages. Involved in this serious sin were 17 **priests** (vv. 18-22) and 10 **Levites** including a singer and 3 **gatekeepers** (vv. 23-24), and 84 others from around the nation (vv. 25-43). As the leaders had said (9:1), some priests and Levites were guilty. The guilty priests each offered **a ram . . . as a guilt offering** in accord with Leviticus 5:14-15. The family names in Ezra 10:25-43 correspond closely to those in 2:3-20. **Some of** these **had children by these** marriages (10:44). This was a grievous separation from God's covenant. Unfortunately the people would again slip into the same kind of sin only one generation later (Neh. 13:23-28).

The narrative ends abruptly at this point. The message of the book is complete. In order for the people to be back in fellowship with the Lord it was absolutely necessary for them to have proper temple worship (Ezra 1–6) and to live according to God's Word (chaps. 7–10).

BIBLIOGRAPHY

Ackroyd, Peter R. *I and II Chronicles, Ezra and Nehemiah.* London: SCM Press, 1973.

Batten, Loring. *The Books of Ezra and Nehemiah.* The International Critical Commentary. Edinburgh: T. & T. Clark, 1913.

Coggins, R.J. *The Books of Ezra and Nehemiah.* The Cambridge Bible Commentary on the New English Bible. Cambridge: University Press, 1976.

Fensham, F. Charles. *The Books of Ezra and Nehemiah.* The New International Commentary on the Old Testament. Grand Rapids: Wm. B. Eerdmans Publishing Co., 1982.

Ironside, H.A. *Notes on Ezra, Nehemiah, and Esther.* Neptune, N.J.: Loizeaux Brothers, 1972.

Keil, C.F. "Ezra." In *Commentary on the Old Testament in Ten Volumes*. Vol. 3. Reprint (25 vols. in 10). Grand Rapids: Wm. B. Eerdmans Publishing Co., 1982.

Kidner, Derek. *Ezra and Nehemiah*. The Tyndale Old Testament Commentaries. Downers Grove, Ill.: InterVarsity Press, 1979.

Laney, J. Carl. *Ezra and Nehemiah*. Every-man's Bible Commentary. Chicago: Moody Press, 1982.

Myers, Jacob M. *Ezra, Nehemiah*. The Anchor Bible. Garden City, N.Y.: Doubleday & Co., 1965.

Ryle, H.E. *The Books of Ezra and Nehemiah*. Cambridge: University Press, 1917.

Slotki, Judah J. *Daniel, Ezra, Nehemiah*. London: Soncino Press, 1951.

NEHEMIAH

Gene A. Getz

INTRODUCTION

Historical Background. God had promised Israel that if they obeyed Him, He would bless them as a nation. If they did not, then He would judge them and cause them to be taken into captivity (Deut. 28). That promise was repeated to Solomon with a specific application to his own life. If he, as king of Israel, obeyed the Lord he would experience God's continual blessing. If Solomon did not obey Him, God would take away his power and position as king of Israel (1 Kings 9:1-9).

As happened so frequently among many of Israel's leaders, a good beginning had an unfortunate ending. Solomon sinned against God, particularly by marrying many foreign wives and worshiping their false gods (1 Kings 11:1-5). So the kingdom was split in 931 B.C. The 10 Northern tribes were initially ruled by Jeroboam, and the Southern tribes (Judah and Benjamin) were ruled at first by Rehoboam.

Both kingdoms, however, continued to be characterized by idolatry and immorality. And as God had forewarned, His hand of judgment fell on all Israel because of their sin. The Northern Kingdom fell first and the people were taken into captivity by the Assyrians in 722 B.C. The Babylonians brought about the fall of the Southern Kingdom in 586 B.C.

The Israelites of the Northern Kingdom were absorbed into Assyria and eventually into other cultures. However, the people of the Southern Kingdom remained intact in Babylon, and after the power of Babylon was broken by the Medes and Persians in 539 B.C., many Jews returned to their homeland.

In 538 B.C. the first group returned to Judah under the leadership of Zerubbabel (Ezra 1:1–2:2). Over a period of years and tremendous opposition from the Samaritans, the returnees eventually succeeded in rebuilding the temple in 515 B.C. (See the chart "The Three Returns from Exile," in the *Introduction* to Ezra.)

A number of years later—in 458 B.C.—a second group of Jews returned, led by Ezra (Ezra 7:1-10). Arriving on the scene, they found the Jews in Israel in a state of spiritual and moral degradation. They had intermarried with the unbelieving peoples of the surrounding nations and were participating in their pagan practices. However, through Ezra's faithful teaching ministry, the majority of these people turned from their sins and once again followed God's will for their lives.

In 444 B.C., 14 years after Ezra's return to Jerusalem, Nehemiah also returned and God used him to guide Judah in rebuilding the city's walls and in reordering the people's social and economic lives. What he accomplished in a brief period of time was an incredible feat. How he accomplished this goal is one of the major emphases in the book that bears his name.

Name. On the name of the Book of Nehemiah in relation to the Book of Ezra see "Name" in the *Introduction* to Ezra.

Author. Most Bible expositors agree that Nehemiah authored the book that bears his name. Much of the book is a first-person account of the circumstances surrounding his return to Jerusalem (chaps. 1–7; 12:31–13:31).

Nothing is known about Nehemiah's childhood, youth, or family background, except that his father's name was Hacaliah (1:1) and he had a brother named Hanani (1:2). Possibly Nehemiah's great-grandparents were taken into captivity when Jerusalem fell to the Babylonians. Nehemiah was probably born in Persia sometime during or soon after Zerubbabel's ministry in Jerusalem.

Nehemiah had risen to a position of prominence in his pagan environment. He was serving King Artaxerxes as his personal cupbearer (1:11; cf. 2:1).

This important position in the king's court gives insight into Nehemiah's life and character. A mighty monarch such as the king of Persia would select for that position a man who was wise and discreet, and consistently honest and trustworthy. Nehemiah's position alone reveals much about his intellectual capabilities, his emotional maturity, and his spiritual status.

Nehemiah probably wrote the book that bears his name soon after all its events were completed. This means the book was written about 430 B.C. or shortly thereafter.

OUTLINE

COMMENTARY

I. The Rebuilding of the Walls (chaps. 1–6)

A. Nehemiah's prayer voiced (chap. 1)

1. THE REPORT FROM JERUSALEM (1:1-3)

1:1-3. While serving at the Persian winter palace in **Susa** (cf. Es. 1:2; Dan. 8:1; also see the map "The Persian Empire," in the *Introduction* to Ezra), **Nehemiah** one day received a report from several **men** who had come **from Judah.** One of them was his own brother, **Hanani;** later Nehemiah appointed him to a high position in Jerusalem (7:2). This report came **in the month of Kislev,** that is, November-December (see the chart "Calendar in Israel," near Ex. 12:1) **in the 20th year** of Artaxerxes the king (cf. Neh. 2:1). Artaxerxes, Persia's sixth king, began reigning in 464 B.C., so this year was 444.

The report instantly depressed Nehemiah. It pertained to his people and their land. The Jews in Judah (a **province** of Persia) were greatly troubled and disgraced, and Jerusalem's **wall** was **broken down and its gates** had **been burned.** (Six gates were later repaired, 3:1, 3, 6, 13-15.) This left the city defenseless against enemy attacks. The people had been rebuilding the walls (Ezra 4:12) but were stopped by Artaxerxes who was pressured by some Samaritans and Rehum, the commanding officer, who may have been a Persian responsible to Artaxerxes (Ezra 4:17-23).

Because of Nehemiah's position in the king's court, he must have been aware of Rehum's initial letter and Artaxerxes' subsequent response. However, he had probably not received word as to the results of the letter, though no doubt he feared for his brothers in **Jerusalem.** It is with this prior knowledge that he received the disappointing report from Jerusalem with a sense of deep regret and despair.

2. THE RESPONSE OF NEHEMIAH (1:4)

1:4. On receiving this dismal report, Nehemiah **sat down and wept** (cf. Ezra 10:1). For a number of **days** he **mourned . . . fasted, and prayed** to **the God of heaven** (cf. Neh. 1:5; 2:4, 20; see comments on Ezra 1:2). His praying was continual ("day and night," Neh. 1:6). Fasting, though not a requirement of the Law except on the annual Day of Atonement, often evidenced one's distraught condition (cf. 2 Sam. 12:16; 1 Kings 21:27; Ezra 8:23).

3. THE CONTENTS OF THE CUPBEARER'S PRAYER (1:5-11)

a. Nehemiah's acknowledgment of God's greatness (1:5)

1:5. Nehemiah faced a situation he knew he could not solve by himself. But he also knew that with God all things are possible (cf. Jer. 32:17). Nehemiah began his prayer by acknowledging that fact: **O LORD, God of heaven** (cf. Neh. 1:4), **the great and awesome God** (cf. 4:14; 9:32). "LORD" (Yahweh) speaks of His covenant relationship to Israel, "God of heaven" refers to His sovereignty, and the words "great and awesome" are mindful of His power and majesty. Surely such a God could answer Nehemiah's prayer. As the "LORD" He **keeps His covenant of love** (ḥesed, "loyal love") **with those who love . . . and obey** Him.

b. Nehemiah's confession of Israel's sins (1:6-7)

1:6-7. In this **prayer** of confession of **the sins** of **the people of Israel,** Nehemiah included himself. As the Prophet Daniel had prayed almost 100 years before (Dan. 9:4-6) and as Ezra had prayed (Ezra 9:6-15), Nehemiah acknowledged that he shared the responsibility for Israel's disobedience to God's laws. He said **I confess** and three times he said **we.**

He placed himself and Israel in a submissive attitude under the Lord by calling himself God's **servant** (cf. Neh. 1:10-11) and by calling them His **servants** (cf. vv. 10-11; also note **Your servant Moses,** vv. 7-8).

c. Nehemiah's request for God's help (1:8-11)

1:8-11. Nehemiah reminded God—to lead Him to act, not to recall for Him something forgotten—that He had told **Moses** that if the nation Israel was **unfaithful** He would disperse them from their homeland (Lev. 26:27-28, 33; Deut. 28:64), **but** that if they obeyed Him then those who were exiled would be regathered to Jerusalem (Deut. 30:1-5). On Jerusalem as a place where God would cause His **name** to dwell, see comments on

Deuteronomy 12:5; 2 Chronicles 6:6. Since the Jews belonged to God (**Your servants and Your people;** cf. Deut. 9:29) and He had **redeemed** them, it was reasonable that God should respond to Nehemiah's **prayer** on their behalf, keeping His "covenant of love" (Neh. 1:5). Speaking for fellow Jews who revered God's **name** (i.e., honored His revealed character), Nehemiah asked that He hear their **prayer** (v. 11; cf. v. 6).

Humanly speaking only one person could make it possible for Nehemiah to help the Jews in Jerusalem—the king he served. Years earlier, Artaxerxes had issued a decree to stop the construction work in Jerusalem (Ezra 4:21; see comments on Neh. 1:1-3), and he was the only one who could reverse that order. That is why Nehemiah prayed specifically, **Give Your servant** (cf. v. 6) **success today by granting him favor** (lit., "compassion") **in the presence of this man.** Nehemiah was referring of course to King Artaxerxes (cf. 2:1). A favorable relationship with the king could open the door for his petition.

As the king's **cupbearer,** Nehemiah was responsible for tasting the wine before serving it to the king to be sure it was not poisoned. Nehemiah therefore had frequent access **to the king.**

B. Nehemiah's prayer answered (2:1-8)

1. NEHEMIAH'S OPPORTUNITY AND RESPONSE (2:1-4A)

2:1-4a. Four months went by before Nehemiah's opportunity came—from Kislev (1:1, November-December) to **Nisan** (March-April). Nisan was still in Artaxerxes' **20th year** (cf. 1:1) because the regnal year started in Tishri (September-October). As Nehemiah was going about his usual duties **the king** noticed something different about Nehemiah's countenance. He was **sad. The king** was immediately curious about Nehemiah's state of depression, since this was the first time he had seen his cupbearer dejected. **The king asked** a pointed question, **Why does your face look so sad when you are not ill?**

Nehemiah was careful in replying. In fact he was even **afraid.** A servant was never to let his negative emotions show before the king, for it might suggest dissatisfaction with the king. To do so might jeopardize his position or even his life.

Also Nehemiah knew that his request was a bold one. As already stated, a few years earlier this king had stopped the rebuilding of Jerusalem and now Nehemiah was going to ask that the order be reversed. The cupbearer was risking his life! But his response was wise, no doubt reflecting the fact that he had been thinking about this opportunity, should it come, for a number of months.

In Nehemiah's response he avoided naming Jerusalem, perhaps so that he would not touch a sensitive "political nerve" in **the king.** He appealed to the king's sense of respect—his sense of "rightness" regarding proper respect for the dead. Nehemiah said **the city where** his ancestors were **buried** was **in ruins** and the **gates** had been burned (cf. 1:3). This was a sad state of affairs for the Jewish city. Seventy-one years before (in 515 B.C.), the temple had been rebuilt. The year was now 444; yet the city itself still needed much rebuilding.

Artaxerxes' heart responded to Nehemiah's statements. So he asked Nehemiah what **the king** might do about the situation. With Judea being a Persian province, the cupbearer may have reasoned that perhaps the king would now be sensitive to Jerusalem's condition.

2. NEHEMIAH'S REQUEST TO THE KING (2:4B-8A)

2:4b-6. Obviously Nehemiah had prepared for this moment he had **prayed** for. Besides seeking God's help in prayer, he utilized all the human resources available, including his intellectual capabilities, his past experiences, his accumulated wisdom, his role and position in life, and people with whom he came in contact (in this instance, the king of Persia).

Between the king's question (v. 4a) and Nehemiah's answer (v. 5), the cupbearer "breathed" a brief prayer **to the God of heaven** (cf. 1:4-5). This short prayer—whatever its unvoiced words— was built on his praying for four months. No doubt he asked for wisdom in stating his request properly and for a favorable reply from **the king.**

Speaking with courtesy (**If it pleases the king;** cf. 2:7; this appears elsewhere only in Es. 1:19; 3:9; 5:4, 8; 7:3; 8:5; 9:13) and humility (**your servant**), Nehemiah asked the king to **send** him **to the city in Judah where** his ancestors were **buried so that** he might **rebuild** the city. Again the cupbearer avoided mentioning Jerusalem specifically (see comments on "the city" in Neh. 2:3). The fact that **the queen** was seated there suggests this was a private gathering, since it was not customary for queens to appear at formal banquets.

The king then **asked** Nehemiah when he would return. This question indicated that the king would give him permission. Nehemiah responded immediately with a specific **time** frame, again indicating forethought on his part.

2:7-8a. Nehemiah then asked for the biggest favor yet. Knowing he would face opposition from his enemies, he requested **letters** of permission from **the king** to allow him to pass through the various provinces in the **Trans-Euphrates,** the large area west of the Euphrates River. Nehemiah also asked that the king write **a letter to Asaph,** the man in charge **of the king's forest.** Nehemiah knew he would need access to **timber** for rebuilding **the gates** and the **wall** and other parts of **the city. The citadel** (cf. 7:2) was a fortification to protect **the temple.** The fact that Nehemiah knew the name of the man in charge of the king's forest near Jerusalem may indicate that he had done some careful research.

Artaxerxes' permission to rebuild the city of Jerusalem is the decree Daniel had prophesied 95 years earlier in 539 B.C. This decree was issued on March 5, 444 B.C. (see comments on Dan. 9:25).

3. NEHEMIAH'S TRIBUTE TO GOD (2:8B)

2:8b. Though Nehemiah had worked diligently to prepare himself for the time when he would have opportunity to share his burden with the king, and though he demonstrated unusual wisdom in responding to the king's questions, he knew that ultimately his success depended on God's help. So he wrote that the king's granting of his **requests** was **because** God's **gracious hand . . . was upon** him (cf. v. 18; Ezra 7:6, 9, 28; 8:18, 22, 31).

C. Nehemiah's preparation for the work (2:9-20)

1. HIS ARRIVAL IN JERUSALEM (2:9-10)

2:9-10. The journey to Jerusalem, even though Nehemiah probably took the shortest route possible, would have taken at least two months (see comments on 6:15). Ezra's trip, 14 years earlier, took four to five months (Ezra 7:8-9). On the way Nehemiah showed the governors of the provinces the king's letters of authorization. Also the king even provided a military escort for him! But as soon as Nehemiah arrived, he began to face opposition. When Sanballat the Horonite (perhaps meaning he was from Beth-Horon about 15 miles northeast of Jerusalem) and his associate Tobiah, from Ammon, heard that Nehemiah had arrived on the scene to help Israel, they were very displeased. Immediately they began to plan how to stop Nehemiah from achieving his goal. Perhaps they were hoping to gain control of Judah. In fact in the Elephantine papyri written in 407 B.C., 37 years after this event, Sanballat was called "governor of Samaria." But Nehemiah's motivation remained undaunted. He knew that God had brought him to this moment in Israel's history and he was about to tackle a project that others, for almost 100 years before him, had been unable to complete.

2. HIS SURVEY OF THE WALLS (2:11-16)

2:11-16. Nehemiah knew there was no way he could share with the people in Jerusalem what God led him to accomplish without first doing some research and planning. After taking time (three days), presumably to think, pray, and get acquainted with some people there, he took a few men into his confidence, men he could trust.

Then he made a careful survey of the walls to analyze the problem he faced. He did so at night, apparently to avoid letting others know his plans before they were firmly fixed in his mind. During these night hours he gained perspective and, as outlined in chapter 3, developed an effective plan to accomplish the task he had come to Jerusalem to perform. In his nighttime inspection he rode his horse or mule (mount, 2:14) from the Valley Gate in the southwest wall east to the Jackal Well, the site of which is unknown, and to the Dung Gate in the southeast part of the city. Possibly this is the same as the Potsherd Gate (Jer. 19:2). The Fountain Gate was north of the Dung Gate on the eastern wall. The King's Pool may be the same as the Pool of Siloam which was near the King's Garden (Neh. 3:15), or the King's Pool may have been south of the Pool of Siloam. Apparently the rubble there kept him from proceeding on his mount so he went up the valley (probably the Kidron Valley east of the city). Either he went all round the entire wall or, more likely, he retraced his steps from the eastern wall. He went back into the city at his starting place, the Valley Gate. (See the map "Jerusalem in the Time of Nehemiah," near 3:1.)

3. HIS CHALLENGE TO THE PEOPLE (2:17-20)

2:17-18. After Nehemiah had completed his secret survey and was satisfied that he had developed a workable plan, the time had come to reveal to the Jews why he was in Jerusalem. Them refers to the people mentioned in verse 16: "Jews [i.e., common people], priests . . . nobles . . . officials." First he challenged them to notice their deplorable circumstances, which had brought them trouble and disgrace (cf. 1:3). Then he challenged them to rebuild the wall of Jerusalem, and followed his challenge with a personal testimony as to how God's gracious hand (cf. 2:8) had granted him favor before King Artaxerxes.

When Nehemiah gave his challenge, the people's negative feelings became positive. Despair turned to hope. They responded and began the rebuilding process.

2:19-20. Apparently word spread quickly regarding the Jews' response to Nehemiah's challenge. As soon as their enemies heard the news they stepped up their efforts to hinder the process. They used every demoralizing technique they knew, beginning with ridicule (bûz means "to despise or regard with contempt") and the suggestion that they were rebels. Joining Sanballat and Tobiah (cf. v. 10) was Geshem (cf. 6:1-2, 6) the Arab.

But Nehemiah was ready for their insidious attack. He affirmed that the God of heaven (cf. 1:4-5; 2:4) would enable them to succeed. The Jews, God's servants, would rebuild, but the three opponents had no share or claim (present) or historic right (past) to the city. Once again Nehemiah brought the task—both in the eyes of Judah and his enemies—into clear focus. Their dependence was not to be on their abilities, human resources, or personal genius. Their hope was in the God of heaven!

Nehemiah exhibited many characteristics necessary for effective leadership. Donald K. Campbell lists 21 such factors (*Nehemiah: Man in Charge*, p. 23):

1. He established a reasonable and attainable goal.
2. He had a sense of mission.
3. He was willing to get involved.
4. He rearranged his priorities in order to accomplish his goal.
5. He patiently waited for God's timing.
6. He showed respect to his superior.
7. He prayed at crucial times.
8. He made his request with tact and graciousness.
9. He was well prepared and thought of his needs in advance.
10. He went through proper channels.
11. He took time (three days) to rest, pray, and plan.
12. He investigated the situation firsthand.
13. He informed others only after he knew the size of the problem.
14. He identified himself as one with the people.
15. He set before them a reasonable and attainable goal.
16. He assured them God was in the project.
17. He displayed self-confidence in facing obstacles.
18. He displayed God's confidence in facing obstacles.
19. He did not argue with opponents.
20. He was not discouraged by opposition.
21. He courageously used the authority of his position.

D. Nehemiah's delegation of the work (chap. 3)

A task so enormous as rebuilding the walls of Jerusalem, especially under adverse conditions, called for unusual organizational effort. The uniqueness of Nehemiah's plan is evident in this chapter. Several aspects of his delegation of the work are evident.

He assigned everyone a specific place to work. This coordination stands out in the phrases "next to him," "next to them," "next to that," "the next section," "beside him," and "beyond

them," which occur 28 times in this chapter.

Assignments were made near people's houses (vv. 21, 23-24, 26, 28-30). Reasons for this plan are obvious. First, people who were assigned to sections of the wall near their homes would be more personally involved and consequently more highly motivated. Second, they would not have to travel to another part of the city to do the job, wasting valuable time. Third, in case of attack they would not be tempted to leave their posts, but would stay and protect their families. Fourth, the whole task would be a family effort, utilizing all available talent.

Commuters also had a part. Men whose homes were outside of Jerusalem—in Jericho (v. 2), Tekoa (vv. 5, 27), Gibeon (v. 7), and Mizpah (v. 7)—were assigned to sections of the wall where there were few homes. Those workers were asked to complete tasks that would not be as conveniently handled by the permanent residents in Jerusalem.

Assignments were also made by vocation. For example, the high priest and his fellow priests were assigned to rebuild the Sheep Gate (v. 1). This was of particular interest to them, because animals were brought through that gate to the temple for sacrifice. Other priests are mentioned in verses 22, 28. Other workers whose vocations are listed include goldsmiths (vv. 8, 31-32), perfume-makers (v. 8), district and half-district rulers (vv. 9-12, 14-19), Levites (v. 17), and merchants (vv. 31-32). Even one man's daughters were involved (v. 12).

1. WORKERS ON THE NORTH WALL (3:1-5)

The map "Jerusalem in the Time of Nehemiah" shows the 10 gates and four towers mentioned in this chapter. Of the 10 gates, 6 were repaired (vv. 1, 3, 6, 13-15).

3:1-2. Nehemiah's account of the repairs begins with **the Sheep Gate** at the northeast of the wall, and proceeds counterclockwise. The Sheep Gate is known to have been in that location because it was near the Pool of Bethesda (John 5:2), which archeologists have located in that area.

Eliashib the high priest (cf. Neh. 13:4) was a grandson of Jeshua (12:10), the high priest in Zerubbabel's day (Ezra 3:2). Eliashib and other **priests** (cf. Neh.

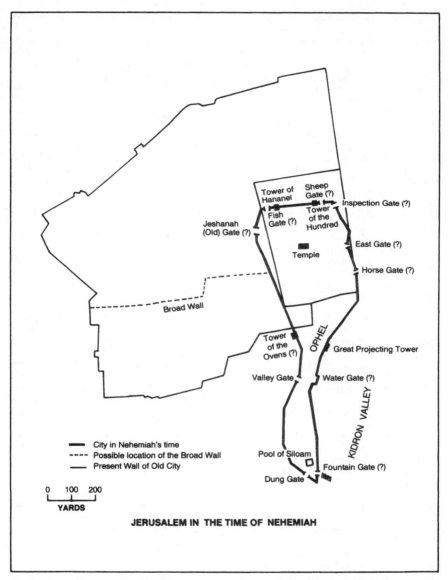

JERUSALEM IN THE TIME OF NEHEMIAH

3:22) repaired and **dedicated** the Sheep Gate and then repaired the walls to **the Tower of the Hundred** and **the Tower of Hananel** (also mentioned in 12:39; Jer. 31:38; Zech. 14:10). The exact locations of these two towers are not known, but they were between the Sheep Gate and the Fish Gate.

3:3-5. The Fish Gate may have been the gate through which the people of Tyre brought fish they sold (13:16). **Meremoth,** a priest's **son** (cf. Ezra 8:33), also worked on a second **section** (Neh. 3:21), as did **Meshullam** (v. 30), whose daughter was married to Tobiah's son (6:18). **The men of Tekoa,** Amos' hometown (Amos 1:1) about 12 miles south of Jerusalem, **repaired** a section. Though the

369

nobles of Tekoa did **not** help in the project, others from Tekoa took on another section, on the east wall (Neh. 3:27).

2. WORKERS ON THE WEST WALL (3:6-12)

3:6-12. Between the **Jeshanah** (or "Old"; cf. NIV marg.) **Gate** (v. 6) and **the Broad Wall** (v. 8) was the Gate of Ephraim (cf. 12:39). **Gibeon and Mizpah** were a few miles northwest of Jerusalem. (Meronoth's site is unknown.) Somewhat surprisingly, those towns were **under . . . the governor of Trans-Euphrates** (cf. 2:9). The exact sites of those gates and of **the Tower of the Ovens** (3:11) is not known, but the tower may have been near the ovens in the street of the bakers (Jer. 37:21). A goldsmith and a perfume-maker (Neh. 3:8) took on a different line of work when they went into construction labor. Even rulers of Jerusalem's districts and half-districts (vv. 9, 12; cf. vv. 14-15) took up tools for the building project.

3. WORKERS ON THE SOUTH WALL (3:13-14)

3:13-14. The Valley Gate was where Nehemiah's nighttime inspection tour began and ended (2:13, 15). **The Dung Gate** was so named because it led to the Hinnom Valley south of the city where refuse was dumped.

4. WORKERS ON THE SOUTHEAST WALL (3:15-27)

3:15-16. The Fountain Gate was on the east wall, north of the Dung Gate. **The Pool of Siloam** was near **the King's Garden,** near which Zedekiah, Judah's last king, had gone in his attempt to escape from Jerusalem while the Babylonians were conquering the city (Jer. 39:4). **The tombs of David** refer to those of David and his descendants, the kings of Judah. David was buried in this area, "the city of David" (1 Kings 2:10). **The artificial pool** may be the King's Pool (Neh. 2:14) or perhaps the "lower pool" (Isa. 22:9). **The House of the Heroes** may have been the barracks of David's select soldiers, or "mighty men" (2 Sam. 23:8).

3:17-27. Binnui (v. 18) also **repaired another section** (v. 24). **The armory** (v. 19) is another point near the eastern wall. **The angle** was apparently some turn in the wall. Another **angle** is mentioned in verses 24-25.

Private houses were some of the points of reference: **the house of Eliashib the high priest** (vv. 20-21; cf. v. 1), **Benjamin** and Hasshub's **house** (v. 23), and **Azariah's house** (vv. 23-24). Other houses were mentioned later including the priests' houses (v. 28), Zadok's house (v. 29), Meshullam's house (v. 30), and "the house of the temple servants and the merchants" (v. 31).

Meremoth (v. 21) **repaired** two sections (cf. v. 4), as did the Tekoites (vv. 5, 27). **Priests** (v. 22; cf. v. 1) and **Levites** (v. 17) were involved in the repair work, closer to the temple than to other parts of the wall. The **tower** (v. 25) was near the **palace,** presumably the palace built by Solomon (1 Kings 7:1-8). **The court of the guard** may have been part of Solomon's great courtyard near his palace (1 Kings 7:9-12). **The hill of Ophel** (Neh. 3:26) was the area between the city of David and the temple mount. Understandably **the temple servants** lived near the temple area.

5. WORKERS ON THE NORTHEAST WALL (3:28-32)

3:28-32. The Horse Gate (v. 28) on the east wall may have been where horses entered the palace area. **The East Gate** (v. 29) was directly east of the temple area. **Malkijah** (v. 31) is the third man by this name in this chapter (see vv. 11, 14). His wall **repairs** extended south to **the house of the temple servants,** who are mentioned in verse 26 as living on the hill of Ophel. **Merchants** also lived in that area near the temple servants. **The Inspection Gate** was at the northeast corner of the wall (cf. **the corner** in v. 24). **The room above the corner** was a room on the wall whose purpose is not known. **The Sheep Gate** brings the reader back to the starting point (cf. v. 1).

E. Nehemiah's reactions to opposition (chap. 4)

Chapter 3 might give the impression that once Nehemiah had carefully assigned everyone to a particular section of the wall, from that time on everything progressed smoothly. Not so! God's work seldom goes forward without opposition. In fact, as seen in the chart "Nehemiah's Problems and His Responses," this new leader in Judah faced many problems.

Nehemiah's Problems and His Responses

Problems	Responses
1. Walls broken and gates burned (1:2-3)	1. Grief and *prayer* (1:4), and motivation of the people to rebuild (2:17-18)
2. False accusation of the workers (2:19)	2. Confidence that God would give them success (2:20)
3. Ridicule of the workers (4:1-3)	3. *Prayer* (4:4-5) and action (greater diligence in the work, 4:6)
4. Plot to attack the workers (4:7-8)	4. *Prayer* and action (posting of a guard, 4:9)
5. Physical exhaustion and threat of murder (4:10-12)	5. Positioning of people by families with weapons (4:13, 16-18) and encouragement of the people (4:14, 20)
6. Economic crisis and greed (5:1-5)	6. Anger (5:6), reflection, rebuke (5:7), and action (having the people return the debtors' interest, 5:7b-11)
7. Plot to assassinate (or at least harm) Nehemiah (6:1-2)	7. Refusal to cooperate (6:3)
8. Slander against Nehemiah (6:5-7)	8. Denial (6:8) and *prayer* (6:9)
9. Plot to discredit Nehemiah (6:13)	9. Refusal to cooperate (6:11-13) and *prayer* (6:14)
10. Tobiah moved into a temple storeroom (13:4-7)	10. Tossing out Tobiah's furniture (13:8)
11. Neglect of temple tithes and offerings (13:10)	11. Rebuke (13:11a), stationing the Levites at their posts (13:11b), and *prayer* (13:14)
12. Violation of the Sabbath by business activities (13:15-16)	12. Rebuke (13:17-18), posting of guards (13:19), and *prayer* (13:22)
13. Mixed marriages (13:23-24)	13. Rebuke (13:25-27), removal of a guilty priest (13:28), and *prayer* (13:29)

1. SANBALLAT'S PSYCHOLOGICAL WARFARE (4:1-3)

4:1-3. As noted earlier (2:10) **Sanballat** was displeased when he **heard** that Nehemiah had returned to Jerusalem to help the Jews. Sanballat, however, did not know of God's interest in His people. Sanballat's displeasure turned to intense anger (4:1; cf. v. 7). So with **his associates,** including Tobiah (2:19; 4:3; also cf. v. 7; 6:1, 12, 14) and Geshem (2:19), and **in the presence of** Samaritan soldiers, Sanballat **ridiculed the Jews.** He accused them of rebelling against King Artaxerxes (2:19) and by a series of questions he suggested they were incapable of completing the project (4:2). Calling them **feeble** he asked if they would **offer sacrifices.** That is, could they possibly complete the walls so that they could then give sacrifices of thanksgiving? The question about finishing **in a day** suggests that the Jews did not know what they were undertaking. And how, Sanballat asked, could they use **burned,** weakened bricks from the **heaps of** debris? **Tobiah the Ammonite** (cf. 2:19), standing nearby, also tried to discourage the Jews. Ridiculing them, he said they were so inept in their work that **a fox,** weighing only a few pounds, **would break** it down by merely climbing **up on it.**

2. NEHEMIAH'S SPIRITUAL RESPONSE (4:4-6)

4:4-5. Prayer was a distinct and consistent part of Nehemiah's approach to problem-solving. When faced with Sanballat's demoralizing attack, he immediately asked God for help: **Hear us, O our God, for we are despised.**

Like some of the imprecatory prayers in which the psalmists invoked God's condemnation on His enemies, Nehemiah's prayer in this instance was severe and condemning. He prayed that Sanballat and his cohorts would be taken captive and that they would be judged for **their sins.**

How should a Christian interpret this kind of praying, especially in view of what Jesus Christ said about praying for one's enemies? (Matt. 5:44; cf. Rom. 12:14, 20) Several facts need to be noted. First, in opposing the Jews, Sanballat "and company" were actually opposing God. Second, God had already pronounced judgment on Israel's enemies. Nehemiah was praying according to God's will—that God would deliver Jerusalem from her enemies (Josh. 1:5). Third, Nehemiah was praying that God would bring about what He had promised Abraham regarding those who curse His people (Gen. 12:3). Fourth, vengeance belongs to God, not to Nehemiah or other believers (cf. Deut. 32:35; Rom. 12:19). Also see comments on the imprecatory psalms in the *Introduction* to the Book of Psalms.

4:6. After praying, Nehemiah and the Jews continued with the work. Some Christians pray and then wait for things to happen, but not Nehemiah! As in all his efforts, he blended the divine perspective with the human. He faced Sanballat's opposition with *both* prayer and hard work. Once he committed the problem to the Lord, he trusted God to help them achieve their goal. And while praying and trusting, they **rebuilt the wall** to **half its height.** At this juncture their task was half completed. Sanballat and Tobiah's efforts at demoralizing the Jews failed. The Jews rose above their enemies' attempts at discouragement. Because **the people worked** so diligently and enthusiastically (**with all their heart**), they were able to complete half the job in a surprisingly short period of time. Nehemiah wrote later (6:15) that the entire task was completed in 52 days (about eight weeks of 6 days each), so possibly this halfway point took about four weeks.

3. SANBALLAT'S CONSPIRACY (4:7-12)

4:7-9. The Jewish workers' rapid progress naturally increased the threat to their enemies, who became **very angry** (cf. v. 1). So they decided to take more overt and corporate action. Joining **Sanballat** and the Samaritans from the north, **Tobiah** and **the Ammonites** from the east, Geshem (cf. 2:19) and **the Arabs** from the south, were **men** from **Ashdod,** a Philistine city, from the west. **They all plotted together to** attack **Jerusalem,** apparently from all sides.

The corporate strategy of Judah's enemies was met by a corporate response. Again the people (**we**) **prayed** for help, and then added action to their prayers by posting **a guard** round the clock **to meet this threat.**

4:10-12. However, the problem was not automatically solved. In fact the builders faced some new problems. They were physically and psychologically exhausted and the work seemed endless (v. 10). Furthermore they faced the threat of a secret attack (v. 11) which Nehemiah knew was not idle talk (v. 12).

4. NEHEMIAH'S STRATEGY (4:13-15)

4:13-15. Nehemiah established a new strategy to meet the threat of enemy infiltration. He positioned **some of the people behind the lowest points of the wall** with **swords, spears, and bows.**

This must have been a difficult decision for Nehemiah. To place *whole* **families** together—including women and children—put tremendous pressure on fathers particularly. In case of outright attack, they would have no choice but to stay and fight for and with their family members. But Nehemiah knew it was the only decision he could make if they were to survive and succeed in rebuilding the walls.

Obviously fear gripped these people. So Nehemiah gathered them together and charged them to face the situation courageously (**don't be afraid**) and to **remember** the **great and awesome** Lord (cf. 1:5) who was on their side, and to **fight** to save their families. **When** their **enemies heard** that **their plot** had been discovered, they did not attack and the people resumed their construction **work.**

5. THE COMPLETION OF THE WALLS (4:16-23)

4:16-18a. As the Jews continued their work they were more cautious. Nehemiah had **half** the **men . . . work while the other half** guarded them **with spears,**

shields, bows, and armor. Perhaps they were divided around the wall: a few workers, next to them a few guards, a few more workers, more guards next to them, and so on. The officers in Jerusalem, who apparently had not yet been given responsibilities in the project, were enlisted to stand guard behind the workers. As some workers carried materials, presumably bricks and mortar, they each did so with one hand, while holding a weapon (probably a spear or sword) in the other. Each of the wall-workers (masons) worked with both hands but had his sword at his side. Though this arrangement meant fewer bricklayers were on the job, the work was well defended!

4:18b-20. In addition Nehemiah stationed a trumpeter next to him—a man who would follow Nehemiah everywhere he went as he supervised the work. In case of an attack, the trumpet blast would rally the people to the place of attack. Again Nehemiah encouraged the people (cf. 2:20; 4:14), this time stating that their God would fight for them.

4:21-23. The people worked diligently, from early morning till nighttime. Those living outside the city did not even return to their homes. Venturing outside Jerusalem at night would have been a dangerous risk. Through each night some workers stood guard, knowing the city was vulnerable to attack even then. They did not even take off their clothes to clean up after work; they kept a diligent watch at all times.

F. Nehemiah's handling of internal problems (5:1-13)

Some say the events in this chapter happened after the wall was completed. It is argued (a) that calling a large assembly (v. 7) would have endangered the city, leaving it almost defenseless, and (b) that Nehemiah would not have been appointed governor till after the wall was completed. However, verse 16 suggests that the "wall work" was continuing.

1. THE PROBLEMS AND NEHEMIAH'S INITIAL RESPONSE (5:1-7A)

5:1-5. Up to this point Nehemiah's challenges as a spiritual leader focused primarily on those outside of Judah. But before the walls were finally rebuilt, he encountered the most difficult and intense kind of problem almost every spiritual leader has to face sometime—problems within. For Nehemiah, those problems centered not on Sanballat, Tobiah, or Geshem but on his own people, the Jews. There were four such difficulties. First, the people face a food shortage. They said they needed to get grain for food to keep themselves and their families alive (v. 2). The work on the wall hindered their tending their crops. And this crop failure was called a famine. Second, others had grain (buying it from others), but to get it they had to mortgage their fields . . . vineyards, and homes (v. 3). Third, others, not wanting to mortgage their property, had to borrow money from their Jewish brothers to pay property taxes to King Artaxerxes (v. 4). This problem was compounded by the fact that they were charged exorbitant interest rates by their own Jewish brothers.

This led to a fourth problem. To repay their creditors they had to sell their children into slavery (v. 5; cf. Ex. 21:2-11; Deut. 15:12-18). This of course left them in a hopeless state.

All these difficulties created an internal crisis in Judah. And they meant "double trouble" for Nehemiah. Not only were their enemies a constant threat to their security and state of well-being, but now many Jews were actually taking advantage of other Jews. Morale, which was already low (Neh. 4:10-12) because of external pressures, physical exhaustion, and fear, now took another plunge because of these internal problems.

5:6-7a. Nehemiah's initial response to all this was deep anger. His intense emotion was directed at certain people's selfishness, greed, and insensitivity. Some people were hurting and suffering, and those who should have been the most compassionate (the nobles and officials) were most guilty of exploitation.

Though Nehemiah's anger was certainly righteous indignation, he did not take immediate action. Spending time reflecting on the problem enabled him to cool down, to see the facts in proper perspective, and to decide on a course of action (v. 7a).

2. NEHEMIAH'S ACTION (5:7B-11)

5:7b-9. After regaining his emotional equilibrium, Nehemiah confronted the situation head on. First, he rebuked those who were violating God's command not to charge their own people interest (cf. Ex. 22:25; Lev. 25:35-38; Deut. 23:19-20). Money could be loaned (Deut. 15:7-8) but not to gain interest from another person's distresses. Second, calling **a large meeting,** Nehemiah pointed out the inconsistencies of their behavior compared with what he and others in exile had done personally to help their **brothers.** He and others had already purchased (redeemed) some indentured Jews who were sold to foreigners (cf. Lev. 25:47-55). But now the opposite was happening; Jews were **selling** their fellow Jews *into* slavery.

Also God's reputation was at stake. This immoral and unethical behavior was bringing reproach on the One who had delivered their country from both Egyptian bondage and Babylonian Captivity. So he exhorted them to live **in the fear of . . . God** (i.e., to trust, obey, and serve Him) and thus avoid **the reproach** of their **Gentile enemies.**

5:10-11. Nehemiah's final action was intensely personal. He referred to his own example and that of others who were already helping those in need by **lending** them **money and grain.** He was already doing something about the problem. So he was not asking the people to do something he was not exemplifying in his own life.

Some Bible translations and commentaries suggest that Nehemiah was admitting his own guilt of charging interest on his loans. This, however, seems inconsistent with his high leadership qualities and his charge to the nobles and officials about their guilt (v. 7).

Nehemiah then asked those guilty of exploitation to return what they had taken from others. Mortgaged **fields, vineyards, olive groves** (the groves are mentioned here for the first time; they were not referred to in vv. 3-5), **and houses** were to be returned (perhaps with the income made from the **grain, new wine, and oil** from those fields), charging interest (**usury**) was to stop, and the interest received from the loans was to be returned. The interest was a **100th part,** that is, one percent a month. He emphasized the urgency of this exhortation by asking them to act **immediately.**

3. THE PEOPLE'S RESPONSE (5:12-13)

5:12-13. No doubt Nehemiah was pleased when the people responded to his exhortations. But knowing that words are cheap and easy to say on the spur of the moment under public pressure, he **made the** guilty leaders (**nobles and officials;** cf. v. 7) take another step—to **take an oath** affirming that they would **do what they had** said. **The priests** witnessed the oath-taking. Nehemiah visualized for them the grave consequences that would come if they lied to God. Shaking **out the folds of** his **robe** (cf. Paul's action in Acts 18:6), which served as pockets, he asked that **God** similarly **shake out of His house . . . every** person who failed to keep his oath. This gesture indicated rejection, something like shaking the dust off one's feet (Matt. 10:14; Acts 13:51).

G. Nehemiah's service as governor (5:14-19)

Presumably sometime while the city wall was being rebuilt, Nehemiah was appointed governor of Judah. This was the highest position of leadership in the nation at that time.

Later, as Nehemiah wrote this historical account of his years in Jerusalem, he evidently inserted these observations (vv. 14-19) about his perspective on that leadership position. Apparently he included these verses here in the narrative because of their relationship to the events described in verses 1-13.

1. HIS REFUSAL TO USE HIS PRIVILEGES (5:14-15, 17-18)

5:14-15. Nehemiah served as Judah's **governor** for **12 years,** from Artaxerxes' **20th year** (444 B.C.) to **his 32nd year** (432 B.C.) This Hebrew word for governor is *peḥâh* derived from the Akkadian word *pāḥatu.* (The word for governor in 7:65, 70; 8:9; 10:1 is a Persian word.) One of the "fringe benefits" of being **governor** was a **food** allowance, granted him by the Persian officials, perhaps for official entertaining of guests. However, Nehemiah did not take advantage of what was rightfully his. In providing food for many Jews and in entertaining dignitaries from other nations (v. 17), he served food and wine out of his personal resources. This practice contrasted with the former **governors,** who charged **the** Jewish **peo-**

ple . . . **40 shekels** (about one pound; cf.
NIV marg.) **of silver** besides the food allowance of **food and wine.** Even those
governors' **assistants** took advantage of
their position and oppressed **the people,**
demanding their payments. Nehemiah's
reverence for God kept him from placing
a heartless burden on his fellow Jews.
This is still another evidence of his ster-
ling leadership qualities: compassion for
those under him and refusal to use his
privileges at the expense of others.

5:17-18. Exactly who all the **150 Jews**
were for whom Nehemiah provided food
is not known, though some of them were
officials. The cost to supply **one ox,
six . . . sheep, and some poultry** daily
was no doubt great. Even so, Nehemiah
willingly bore the cost "out of his own
pocket" rather than place **heavy** demands **on** the **people.**

2. HIS INNOCENCE OF CONFLICT OF INTEREST
(5:16, 19)

5:16. As governor, Nehemiah could
have loaned people money to pay their
taxes, having them use their land as col-
lateral. And then, when they could not
pay back what they had borrowed, he
could have applied the world's standard
and taken their land. He, along with
other leaders in Judah, could have ex-
ploited the poor. But he did **not acquire
any land** in this way, or by outright pur-
chases. He was careful not to abuse his
position as governor in any way, thereby
jeopardizing the people's respect for
him. In fact he continued working right
along with the people in the construction
project. He did not hesitate to "get his
hands dirty" in this important building
program, and was never sidetracked by
other interests. His motives were pure,
and he never lost sight of God's calling in
his life. He was in Jerusalem to help the
people, not exploit them. He was there to
exemplify God's Law, not violate it. He
was there to rebuild the **wall,** not a personal empire.

5:19. As a man of prayer, Nehemiah
was in touch with God. He prayed that
God would **remember** him (i.e., not fail
to act on his behalf) because of his concern **for** the **people.** Seven times in his
prayers recorded in this book Nehemiah
asked God to remember (v. 19; 6:14
[twice]; 13:14, 22, 29, 31). Remember **me
with favor** is the same prayer he voiced

at the end of the book (13:31).

H. *Nehemiah's response to opposition against him personally (6:1-14)*

1. THE FIRST SCHEME: ASSASSINATION PLOT
(6:1-4)

**6:1-3. When . . . Sanballat, Tobiah,
Geshem** (cf. 2:19), and other **enemies**
heard that **the wall** was completed and
that the only thing remaining was to **set
the doors in the gates,** those "wall opponents" again attempted to halt the work.
This time they were more subtle; their
sole object of attack was Nehemiah himself. By removing him from the scene or
by at least destroying his credibility with
the Jews, they reasoned that they might
be able to defeat the work. Each of their
three attacks on him was different, but
each was designed to take his life or dis-
credit his effectiveness as a leader.

This first attack was more subtle
than the others. **Sanballat and Geshem**
invited Nehemiah to **meet** with them **in
one of the villages on the plain of Ono.**
The plain of Ono was named after the
town of that name (cf. 1 Chron. 8:12; Ezra
2:33; Neh. 7:37; 11:35). It was near Lod
about 25 miles northwest of Jerusalem,
about 6 miles southeast of Joppa. As seen
on the map "Postexilic Samaria and Judah," near Ezra 2, Ono was near the
border of Samaria, Sanballat's home
province. On the surface it appeared that
Sanballat and his cohorts wanted to have
a peace conference, but their hidden motive was to harm Nehemiah.

Nehemiah suspected foul play. Why
would they want him a day's journey
away from Jerusalem? Then he could not
oversee the **work,** and by outnumbering
him they might do him **harm.** Though he
could not prove his enemies' motives at
the moment, he chose a method that
would eventually demonstrate whether
they were sincere. He simply **sent messengers to** tell **them** he was involved in **a
great** (important) **project** and could not
leave it unsupervised. By responding in
this way Nehemiah was not openly ques-
tioning their motives. In fact he was giving them an opportunity to prove their
motives were sincere, if they had really
wanted to make peace.

6:4. Sanballat and Geshem's response tipped their hand. Rather than
countering with an offer to meet with
Nehemiah in Jerusalem, **four times they**

sent . . . **the same message** and Nehemiah responded four times with his **same** refusal.

Nehemiah could have impatiently attacked their motives on their third or fourth request. But he patiently waited it out till *they* revealed their motives. And this they did with their fifth response, which involved their second scheme.

2. THE SECOND SCHEME: SLANDER (6:5-9)

6:5-7. When Nehemiah's enemies realized he would not leave Jerusalem and meet with them, they tried another tactic. They put pressure on him, trying to force him to meet with them in the plain of Ono. **Sanballat sent his** servant to Nehemiah **with an unsealed letter.** The letter reported an alleged rumor that Nehemiah was trying to set himself up as the **king** of **the Jews,** which in turn would be a threat to Artaxerxes **(the king).**

This letter was insidious in several ways. First, the letter made it seem as if they had Nehemiah's welfare at heart. The letter implied that their reason for conferring with him was to protect him.

Second, and more basic to their motive, they were attempting to get Nehemiah to respond out of fear, Third, the letter may have contained an element of truth. Possibly some well-meaning religious leader in Judah had interpreted Nehemiah's presence as a fulfillment of Old Testament prophecies regarding the coming Messiah-**King.**

6:8-9. Nehemiah's bold response demonstrated his trust in God. He outrightly denied the accusation. He told his fellow workers that the letter was designed **to frighten** them into **thinking** their wall-building would bring Artaxerxes' wrath down on them. Then, as Nehemiah regularly did, he **prayed,** this time asking God for strength.

3. THE THIRD SCHEME: TREACHERY (6:10-14)

6:10. Persisting in their evil planning, Nehemiah's enemies then tried to destroy his credibility by luring him into **the temple.** They hired **Shemaiah,** a man "on the inside," to propose a solution to Nehemiah. Claiming to be a prophet, he purposely locked himself in his house, supposedly from some debility or ritual defilement, and sent word for Nehemiah to visit him. Perhaps Shemaiah devised

an urgent situation that would arouse Nehemiah's curiosity.

Shemaiah must have been a man Nehemiah trusted, for it would have been illogical for him to meet secretly with someone he did not trust. When Nehemiah arrived, Shemaiah suggested they **meet in the temple** behind closed **doors.** He pretended to be protecting Nehemiah from would-be nighttime assassins.

6:11-14. Nehemiah discerned two flaws in Shemaiah's so-called prophecy. First, God would hardly ask Nehemiah to **run** when the project on the walls was nearing completion. Second, no true prophet would ask someone to violate God's Law. Only priests were allowed in the sanctuary (Num. 3:10; 18:7). If Nehemiah, not being a priest, entered the temple, he would have desecrated it and brought himself under God's judgment. He would **not** disobey God to try to gain safety from his enemies. Nehemiah was convinced that Shemaiah was a false prophet, employed by **Tobiah and Sanballat** to trick him. If the governor had entered the temple and lived, his people would know he disregarded God's commands. Once again Nehemiah prayed, this time that God would **remember** (see comments on Neh. 5:19) his enemies and judge them for their evil scheming. In this imprecation he also included **the Prophetess Noadiah,** mentioned only here, who with other false **prophets** was seeking **to intimidate** him.

I. Nehemiah's completion of the project (6:15-19)

6:15-19. The walls were **completed . . . in 52 days,** on **the 25th day of Elul,** which was about September 20. The project began in the last few days of July and continued through August and into September. The previous November-December (Kislev) was when Nehemiah first heard about the problem (1:1), and in March-April (Nisan) he presented his plan to the king (2:1). As stated earlier, the trip to Jerusalem took two or three months (April or May to June or July), as long as or longer than the building program itself.

The enemies' **self-confidence** dissipated as they saw that the **work** was **done** with God's **help.** Opposing Him, they were fighting a losing battle! One reason **Tobiah** the Ammonite (cf. 2:10,

19) was able to make some inroads into Judah was that he was related to the Jews in two ways (also cf. 13:4). His father-in-law was **Shecaniah son of Arah** (cf. Ezra 2:5), and his daughter-in-law was **the daughter of Meshullam son of Berekiah**, who worked on two sections of the wall (Neh. 3:4, 30). **Many** Jews were therefore loyalists to **Tobiah,** perhaps having trading contracts with him, and they **kept** telling Nehemiah **good** things about Tobiah. Yet **Tobiah** tried **to intimidate** the governor-builder with threatening **letters.**

II. The Restoration of the People (chaps. 7–13)

A. The security of the city (7:1-3)

7:1-3. Besides repairing the walls, the builders repaired the gates. The last part of the project was setting **the doors in** the gates (cf. 6:1). **Hanani** was Nehemiah's **brother** who had reported the Jerusalem problems to the cupbearer (1:2). **Hananiah . . . a man of integrity,** had deep spiritual convictions. Nehemiah, knowing that his enemies were still around, ordered that security measures be maintained: **the** city **gates** were **to be opened** only a few hours each day; and citizens, probably many of whom had been wall-repairers, were to serve **as guards.**

B. The census of the returnees (7:4-73a)

7:4-7a. Comparatively **few people** were residing in **Jerusalem** (v. 4) so Nehemiah wanted to populate it with people of pure Jewish descent (cf. 11:1-24). To register the present population Nehemiah began with the **record of those who had. . . . returned** with **Zerubbabel** and others (7:5-7). The list of names in verse 7 is almost identical with the list in Ezra 2:2, except that Nehemiah included **Azariah** and **Nahamani.**

7:7b-65. Some scholars suggest that the list in Ezra 2 is that of the returnees before they departed from Babylon and that Nehemiah 7 gives **the list of** those who actually arrived in Jerusalem or the list of the community sometime after their arrival. The two chapters, however, give no indication of those differences. The variations in the lists are seen in the chart "The Lists of Exile Returnees in Ezra 2 and Nehemiah 7." The list included people by 18 families and clans (vv. 8-

25) and a listing of inhabitants from 20 towns and villages (vv. 26-38; see the map "Postexilic Samaria and Judah," near Ezra 2). Then **the priests** (4,289 of them) were listed (Neh. 7:39-42), followed by mention of 360 **Levites** which included **singers** and **gatekeepers** (vv. 43-45). **The temple servants** (vv. 46-56) **and descendants of** Solomon's **servants** (vv. 57-59) totaled **392** (v. 60). These were followed by reference to **642** returnees who could **not** trace their ancestries (vv. 61-62). Some of **the priests** could **not** clearly trace their genealogies so they were not allowed by **the governor** (*tiršātā'*, a Persian term, possibly a reference to Sheshbazzar—see comments on Ezra 1:8—or to Zerubbabel) **to eat** the **sacred food** till **a priest** was **ministering with the Urim and Thummim** (see comments on Ezra 2:63).

The groups enumerated in Nehemiah 7:8-62 total 31,089, whereas the groups enumerated in Ezra 2:3-60 total 29,818. The difference of 1,281 is seen in 19 of the 41 items. These variations may be copyists' errors or Ezra and Nehemiah may have had reasons for the different figures which were unstated and therefore unknown today.

7:66-69. Nehemiah's grand total of 49,942 people is very close to Ezra's total of 49,897 (Ezra 2:64-65). The extra 45 in Nehemiah's total are the **singers** (Nehemiah **had 245** whereas Ezra referred to 200). A scribe, in copying Nehemiah 7:67, might have inadvertently picked up the 245 in verse 68, in reference to mules, and inserted that number for the 200 singers. He then might have mistakenly omitted verse 68 (cf. NIV marg.). The total then was probably as Ezra recorded it—49,897.

But how does one account for the difference between the enumerated 31,089 and the 49,897—a difference of 18,808? The larger number may include women and children. Or it may include Jews from the Northern tribes who might have joined the remnant in Judah and Benjamin. It may also include the priests who could not delineate their genealogies (vv. 63-64).

Nehemiah's enumeration even included the animals—a total of 8,136, most of them **donkeys,** used for riding. There was about one donkey available for every seven people.

The Lists of Exile Returnees in Ezra 2 and Nehemiah 7

Family Clans	Ezra 2:3-60	Nehemiah 7:8-62	Difference
Parosh	2,172	2,172	
Shephatiah	372	372	
Arah	775	652	− 123
Pahath-Moab	2,812	2,818	+ 6
Elam	1,254	1,254	
Zattu	945	845	− 100
Zaccai	760	760	
Bani (Binnui)*	642	648	+ 6
Bebai	623	628	+ 5
Azgad	1,222	2,322	+1,100
Adonikam	666	667	+ 1
Bigvai	2,056	2,067	+ 11
Adin	454	655	+201
Ater	98	98	
Bezai	323	324	+ 1
Jorah (Hariph)*	112	112	
Hashum	223	328	+105
Gibbar (Gibeon)*	95	95	
Inhabitants from Towns			
Bethlehem and Netophah	179	188	+ 9
Anathoth	128	128	
Azmaveth (Beth Azmaveth)*	42	42	
Kiriath Jearim, Kephirah, and Beeroth	743	743	
Ramah and Geba	621	621	
Micmash	122	122	
Bethel and Ai	223	123	− 100
Nebo	52	52	
Magbish†	156	—	− 156
The other Elam	1,254	1,254	
Harim	320	320	
Lod, Hadid, and Ono	725	721	− 4
Jericho	345	345	
Senaah	3,630	3,930	+300
Priests			
Jedaiah	973	973	
Immer	1,052	1,052	
Pashhur	1,247	1,247	
Harim	1,017	1,017	
Levites	74	74	
Asaph singers	128	148	+ 20
Gatekeepers	139	138	− 1
Temple servants	392	392	
Descendants of Delaiah, Tobiah, and Nekoda	652	642	− 10
Totals	29,818	31,089	+1,271

*The names in parentheses are the variant spellings in the Book of Nehemiah.
† This name and number may have been omitted from Nehemiah's list by a copyist's oversight.

7:70-72. Heads of the families and even **the governor** (see comments on v. 65) and **the people** gave large amounts of money and materials to begin the work of the temple. Nehemiah's 41,000 **drachmas of gold** are 61,000 in Ezra 2:69. Nehemiah referred to 4,200 **minas of silver** (totaling more than 2½ tons; cf. NIV marg.) whereas Ezra refers to 5,000 silver minas. The 597 priests' **garments** mentioned by Nehemiah are 100 in Ezra. Again these differences are probably caused by scribal errors in copying the manuscripts.

7:73a. The people **settled in their** ancestors' **towns** and villages.

C. The ministry of Ezra (7:73b–10:39)

1. THE ISRAELITES' OBEDIENCE TO THE LAW (7:73B–8:18)

The pattern in 7:73b–10:39 reflects the suzerainty-vassal treaties of the ancient Near East (see comments on 9:5b-31). The covenant was to be read at regular intervals (chap. 8), sin was confessed (chap. 9), and obedience was promised (chap. 10).

7:73b–8:9. When the seventh month arrived the **Israelites** were **settled in their towns** (cf. 7:73a). The seventh month was September-October (see the chart "Calendar in Israel," near Ex. 12:1). Then the **people** met near **the Water Gate** or the east wall (cf. Neh. 3:26, and see the map "Jerusalem in the Time of Nehemiah," near 3:1) to hear **Ezra, a scribe** (cf. 8:4, 9, 13; 12:26, 36) and also a **priest** (8:2, 9; 12:26), **read** and teach **the Law of Moses** (the five books of Moses).

Ezra had returned to Jerusalem in 458 B.C., 14 years before Nehemiah, also with the blessing of King Artaxerxes (Ezra 7). His primary purpose in going to his homeland was to teach the Jews God's Law.

In Ezra 7:6, 11-12, 21 he was called a teacher. Of course Ezra and Nehemiah were contemporaries (cf. Neh. 12:33, 36). Ezra's descent from Eleazar, Aaron's third son, is seen in the chart "Ezra's Lineage," near Ezra 7:1-5.

When Ezra first arrived in Jerusalem, the moral and spiritual condition of the people was deplorable (Ezra 9:1-4; 10:2, 10). But as he prayerfully taught them God's Word, they began to respond to and to obey the laws of God. A few years later Nehemiah arrived in Jerusalem and challenged them to trust God to help them rebuild the walls.

The effectiveness of Ezra's ministry is also reflected in the people's behavior after the walls were completed. The two-month building program was an interlude in Ezra's teaching, but apparently it helped motivate the people to want to know more of God's Law. They themselves asked Ezra to continue his teaching ministry among them (Neh. 8:1). This was **the first day of the seventh month,** the day which was to be the Feast of Trumpets (Lev. 23:24; Num. 29:1). Adults and children **who were** old enough **to understand** (Neh. 8:2-3) listened attentively all morning as Ezra **faced** west by **the Water Gate** (cf. v. 1).

Standing **on a . . . platform** (not a podium as in the NASB or a pulpit as in the KJV) above the people **Ezra** read from the Law, while 13 men, perhaps priests (cf. v. 7), **stood** on the platform **beside him.** As he read, **the people . . . stood** (v. 5). He then **praised the LORD, the great God** (cf. 1:5; 4:14).

The people's response to the reading of the Scriptures and to Ezra's praises must have been an emotional experience for this scribe and priest. Lifting **their hands** toward heaven they shouted **Amen! Amen!** in an expression of agreement with God's Word. **Then they** fell on their knees and **bowed** low as they **worshiped the LORD** (8:6).

Nehemiah did not explain exactly how Ezra and the Levites read and explained God's **Law** to this large crowd that may have numbered between 30,000 and 50,000 people (7:66-67). Possibly Ezra read sections of the Law in the presence of **all the people** (8:3), and then at certain times **the Levites** circulated among them and made it clear (*pāraš*, "to make distinct or interpret," possibly means here "to translate" from Heb. to Aram.) and explained (gave **the meaning** of) what Ezra had read as the people stood in groups (vv. 7-8).

The most gratifying thing that happened, of course, is that the people obeyed God's Word. What they heard touched their emotions, for they wept as they heard **the Law** (v. 9). Apparently they were remorseful over their past disobedience to the Law and contrite over their sins.

8:10-18. Nehemiah then encouraged

the people to consider the **day . . . sacred** and **to eat,** give to others in need, and rejoice in **the LORD,** their source of **strength.** Holiness and **joy** were to go together!

The next **day** the spiritual leaders— **heads of . . . families** (i.e., heads of clans), **priests and . . . Levites—gathered** to hear more of God's Word from **Ezra.** Another response of the people was their celebrating the Feast of Tabernacles. The sequence in chapter 8 is striking: intellectual response to the Word (vv. 1-8), emotional response to the Word (vv. 9-12), and volitional response to the Word (vv. 13-18).

The spiritual leaders discovered this instruction about **the feast** in Leviticus 23:37-43. This was celebrated from the 15th to the 22nd of **the seventh month** (Tishri). Since they discovered these instructions on the second day of the seventh month (Neh. 8:2, 13), the timing was perfect. They had exactly two weeks to prepare for it. So they had **the people** get **branches from** various kinds of **trees** (v. 15) and build **booths** (temporary shelters) in various places, including **the square . . . by the Gate of Ephraim** (see the map "Jerusalem in the Time of Nehemiah," near 3:1). This recalled their days of wandering in the wilderness (Lev. 23:43). Their celebration of the Feast of Tabernacles was unmatched since **the days of Joshua.** When the altar was completed in 536 B.C. the people then celebrated the Feast of Tabernacles (Ezra 3:4), but here the **joy** and involvement was much greater. **Ezra read** the **Law** during the Feast of Tabernacles, because Moses had indicated that this was to be done every seven years (Deut. 31:10-13).

2. THE ISRAELITES' CONFESSION OF SIN (9:1-37)

"The Word of God had a tremendous impact on the Restoration community. It pointed the people to their sin (8:9), led them to worship (8:12, 14), and gave them great joy (8:17)" (J. Carl Laney, *Ezra/Nehemiah,* p. 104). Now the Word led to their confession of sin.

9:1-5a. The Feast of Tabernacles concluded on the 22nd day of the month (see comments on 8:14). After one day's interval, the 23rd, the people assembled **on the 24th.** They **separated** from **foreigners** (cf. 10:28). Then they confessed their sins, evidenced by **fasting** (cf. comments on 1:4), **wearing sackcloth** (cf. Gen. 37:24; Es. 4:1-4; Pss. 30:11; 35:13; 69:11; Isa. 22:12; 32:11; 37:1-2; Lam. 2:10; Dan. 9:3), a dark coarse cloth made from goats' hair, **and having dust on their heads** (cf. Josh. 7:6; 1 Sam. 4:12; 2 Sam. 1:2; 15:32; Job 2:12; Lam 2:10; Ezek. 27:30). These were signs of mourning and grief.

For about three hours the people again **stood** (cf. Neh. 8:7) while **the Law** was **read.** Then for another three hours they **confessed their sins** and worshiped **the LORD.** Several **Levites,** some of whom were mentioned in 8:7, were involved in leading the people in their **praise** of the eternal **God.** Five of the eight Levites in 9:4 are listed in the group of eight in verse 5 (**Pethahiah** is also mentioned in 11:24). These five may have been the same or different men. One group was involved in petition (v. 4) and the other in praise (v. 5). **The stairs** (lit., "ascent") may have led to some part of the temple complex or they may refer to the platform mentioned in 8:4.

9:5b-31. The material in 9:5b-10:39 follows the normal covenant form used in the ancient Near East: preamble (9:5b-6), historical prologue (9:7-37), acceptance of the covenant (9:38-10:29), and the stipulations (10:30-39). The prayer in 9:5b-31 was voiced by the Levites on the people's behalf. It rehearses major events in Israel's history, first stating God's glory (v. 5b), uniqueness (v. 6a), and Creation of the universe (v. 6b). The Levites then spoke of God's work with **Abram—** calling him from **Ur** (Gen. 12:1) and making **a covenant with him** (Gen. 15:4-21). Then they recounted God's deliverance of Israel from **Egypt** (Neh. 9:9-12; cf. Ex. 1–15), and the giving of the Law (Neh. 9:13-14) and of manna (**bread from heaven**) and **water** (v. 15; cf. Ex. 16–17). On God's swearing an oath by His **uplifted hand,** see comments on Exodus 6:8.

But the Israelites' ancestors became disobedient and rebellious against God even to the point of worshiping a **calf-** idol (Neh. 9:16-18; cf. Ex. 32). However, God was still **gracious and compassionate, slow to anger and abounding in love** (cf. Ex. 34:6; Num. 14:18; Pss. 86:15; 103:8; 145:8; Joel 2:13; Jonah 4:2). God continued to **guide them . . . instruct them,** and provide for them (Neh. 9:19-21). He helped them conquer their enemies **Sihon** and **Og** (v. 22; cf. Num.

21:21-35), and brought them into **the Promised Land** under Joshua (Neh. 9:23-25). In all this they enjoyed God's **great goodness** (cf. v. 35).

Again the people **rebelled** (v. 26; cf. v. 17) so God gave them over to oppressors. But because of His **great compassion** He raised up **deliverers,** the Judges, who freed them (vv. 27-28). Through the centuries of Israel's sin (v. 29) God continued to be **patient** and to admonish them **by** the Holy **Spirit . . . through** the **prophets** (v. 30). But as a result of their ongoing sinning they were taken into exile (vv. 30-31).

9:32-37. In this concluding part of the Levites' prayer, they asked for relief, again acknowledging God's power, majesty (cf. 1:5; 4:14), and loyalty. Throughout Israel's history she experienced **hardship** because of her disobedience. **Assyria** was the first great power after Egypt that menaced Israel and Judah, beginning in the ninth century, over 400 years before Nehemiah's time. Even while the Israelites were **enjoying** God's blessings (from His **great goodness**; cf. 9:25) in the **land,** they were still sinful.

Now they were **slaves** in their own land! (v. 36) Being slaves meant that they had to pay taxes to Persia, and Judah's governmental leaders had to give the Persian **kings** tribute from the produce of the land. Nehemiah's prayer ended with a plaintive admission of their **great distress.**

3. THE ISRAELITES' PROMISE TO OBEY (9:38–10:39)

a. *The signatories (9:38–10:27)*

9:38–10:27. The civil **leaders,** religious leaders (**Levites and . . . priests**), and all the people agreed to put **their seals** to a written **agreement** that they would obey the stipulations of the Mosaic Law (cf. v. 29). The list begins with **Nehemiah,** who again set an excellent example for the people. Many of the 24 names in 10:1-8 are listed in 12:12-21, names of heads of families. **These were . . . priests** (10:8). Ezra is not listed, but he was a descendant of **Seraiah** (v. 1). After the priests, 17 **Levites** were listed, 6 of whom were involved in reading the Law (8:7). The other group of signers of the agreement were 44 **leaders,** that is, heads of families. Some of them are listed in 7:8-25.

b. *The stipulations (10:28-39)*

10:28-29. The rest of the people did not place their seals to the written agreement, but they did **join** in binding **themselves . . . to follow** God's Law. Gatekeepers, singers, and **temple servants** were listed in 7:44-60. All others are included under the rubric **all who separated themselves from** foreign **peoples** (cf. 9:2). Their commitment, though not indicated by seals, was evidenced by **a curse** (that called down calamity if they failed to carry through on their agreement) **and an oath.** The curse may refer to the cursings God stated in the Deuteronomic Covenant (Deut. 28:15-68).

10:30-39. The stipulations they spelled out in the agreement include (a) avoidance of intermarriages (v. 30; cf. Ex. 34:16; Deut. 7:3-4), (b) keeping **the Sabbath** and the sabbatical **year** (Neh. 10:31; cf. Ex. 20:8-11; 23:11-12; 31:15-17; Lev. 25:2-7; Deut. 15:1-3), and (c) supporting the temple **service** by giving a **third of a shekel** (about one-eighth of an ounce) annually (Neh. 10:32-33). According to Exodus 30:11-16 the temple gift was to be one-half a shekel annually, but here it was valued lightly. These temple **offerings** gave the **priests** and **Levites** money for maintaining the bread on the table of the Presence (Ex. 35:13; 39:36; Num. 4:7), for making various **offerings,** for celebrating monthly and annual **festivals,** and carrying out other **duties.** (See comments on Neh. 13:10-11 regarding the people's failure to keep this commitment.)

Other responsibilities to which the leaders and people pledged themselves were (d) contributing **wood** for the fire on **the altar** of burnt offering, which was to burn continually (Lev. 6:12-13), (e) giving **the firstfruits of** their **crops** (Ex. 23:19; Deut. 26:1-3) and their **firstborn . . . sons** and animals (Num. 18:15-17; Deut. 12:6) to the Lord, and (f) paying annual **tithes** (Lev. 27:30; Num. 18:21-24). **The Levites** were to tithe **the tithes** they received (Neh. 10:38-39; cf. Num. 18:26) to help provide for the priests' needs.

The final statement of the agreement, **We will not neglect the house of our God** (Neh. 10:39), summarizes obligations (c) through (f). Under Ezra's and Nehemiah's leadership the people had been led to place a higher priority on spiritual things, including the care of the restored temple. This was even more important than restoring the city's walls.

D. The list of Judean residents (11:1–12:26)

Comparatively few people lived in Jerusalem because of the rubble in the city (7:4). Now that the walls and gates were repaired, the city was ready to be occupied by more people.

1. OCCUPANTS IN JERUSALEM (11:1-24)

11:1-4a. Along with **the leaders,** one-tenth of the Israelites were to reside **in Jerusalem,** here called **the Holy City** (cf. v. 18; Isa. 52:1; Dan. 9:24; Rev. 11:2). They were chosen by **lots** (cf. Prov. 16:33). Those **who volunteered** (Neh. 11:2) were either the ones chosen by lots who gladly moved to the city, or were additional **men.** Some **priests** and **Levites** including **temple servants . . . lived in** surrounding **towns** and villages and "commuted" to **Jerusalem** when they served in the temple. Others who were not civil or religious leaders took up residence **in Jerusalem.** They were of the tribes of **Judah and Benjamin.**

11:4b-19. The descendants of various family heads who moved into Jerusalem included **468** laymen of the tribe **of Judah** (vv. 4b-6), **928** laymen of the tribe **of Benjamin** (vv. 7-9), 1,192 **priests** (vv. 10-14), **284 Levites** (vv. 15-18), and 172 **gatekeepers** (v. 19)—3,044 men in all. According to 1 Chronicles 9:3 descendants of Ephraim and Manasseh also lived in Jerusalem. The total of "provincial leaders" (Neh. 11:3) from Judah included **Athaiah . . . a descendant of Perez, and Maaseiah . . . a descendant of Shelah** (vv. 4-5). Perez and Shelah were sons of Judah (cf. Gen. 38:2-5, 26-29). Another son of Judah, Zerah, mentioned in Genesis 38:30 and 1 Chronicles 9:6, is not referred to in Nehemiah 11:4-6. This explains why 1 Chronicles 9:6 has 690 and Nehemiah 11:6 has 468 in the census. In the Benjamite list Nehemiah named one line of descendants (v. 7) but the chronicler included four lines of descent. This may or may not account for Nehemiah's figure of 928 Benjamites (v. 8) being slightly lower than the Chronicles figure of 956 (1 Chron. 9:9).

The priests were from six family heads (Neh. 11:10-14): **Jedaiah; the son of Joiarib; Jakin; Seraiah . . . Adaiah;** and **Amashsai.** In 1 Chronicles 9:10-13, the names refer to the same individuals, with a few spelling variations. The son of Joiarib is Jehoiarib, Seraiah is Azariah, and Amashsai is Maasai. It is difficult to know why the 1,192 priests differ from the total of 1,760 in 1 Chronicles 9:13.

The list of Levite family heads in Nehemiah 11:15-18 and the list in 1 Chronicles 9:14-16 have several variations in spelling and additions or omissions (e.g., **Bakbukiah** may be the same as Bakkakkar, and **Abda** may be Obadiah; cf. Neh. 12:25). The chronicler listed Heresh, Galal, and Berekiah whereas Nehemiah does not, and Nehemiah lists **Shabbethai** and **Jozabad,** who did **outside work** on the temple (11:16) whereas 1 Chronicles does not.

The gatekeepers' family heads were two, whereas 1 Chronicles 9:17 names four. This may account for the difference in the total gatekeepers: **172** in Nehemiah 11:19 and 212 in 1 Chronicles 9:22.

11:20-24. The rest of the Israelites . . . were in Judean **towns** (v. 20) except for **temple** servants in Ophel (cf. 3:26), the hill in the city that led north to the temple. **Uzzi was** over **the Levites** (11:22). **The singers were under the . . . orders** of the king (v. 23), presumably Artaxerxes. **Pethahiah** (v. 24; cf. 9:5) was the **agent** who represented the Jews' affairs to Artaxerxes and informed them of **the king's** wishes and directives.

2. OCCUPANTS IN VILLAGES OF JUDAH AND BENJAMIN (11:25-36)

11:25-30. In the postexilic period under Nehemiah **some of the people of Judah** settled in 17 towns and their surrounding villages as far south as **Beersheba** (vv. 27, 30), about 32 miles south of Jerusalem, **to the Valley of Hinnom,** immediately south of Jerusalem (cf. Josh. 15:8). **Kiriath Arba** was an older name for Hebron (Josh. 14:15).

11:31-35. The 15 places where **the descendants of** Benjamin lived were north of Judah. **The Valley of the Craftsmen** may have been near **Lod and Ono.** (See the locations of many of the cities in vv. 25-35 on the map "Postexilic Samaria and Judah," near Ezra 2.)

11:36. Some of the . . . Levites who were living in **Judah** moved north to **Benjamin.**

3. LIST OF PRIESTS AND LEVITES (12:1-26)

12:1-7. David had appointed 24 priestly divisions to serve in the temple (1 Chron. 24:7-19) when it would be built. Now Nehemiah listed the 22 **leaders of the priests** who had **returned** from Babylon **with Zerubbabel** and **Jeshua,** almost 100 years earlier, in 538 B.C. Perhaps two names were dropped from the list in copying or perhaps it was not possible to fill the roster of 24.

12:8-9. The names of 8 of the Levites who returned with Zerubbabel are listed here. **Their associates** brought the number to 74 (Ezra 2:40), or to 202 if the Levite singers (Ezra 2:41) are included. Of the 8 names, Ezra listed only 2, **Jeshua** and **Kadmiel** (Ezra 2:40). **Mattaniah** and **Bakbukiah** (Neh. 12:8-9) in Zerubbabel's day (v. 1) should not be confused with men by the same names in Nehemiah's day (11:17) though their work of leading **songs of thanksgiving** (cf. 12:24) was similar.

12:10-11. The many generations of high priests extended from Aaron to Jehozadak, who was taken into exile to Babylon (1 Chron. 6:3-15). Then **Jeshua** the high priest returned from Babylon with Zerubbabel (Ezra 2:1-2; Neh. 11:1). Jeshua's descendant **Eliashib** (12:10) was the high priest in Nehemiah's day (3:1; 13:4, 7, 28). Some scholars suggest that the reference to Eliashib's line to **Jaddua,** three generations later, was added by someone after Nehemiah's time. However, it was certainly possible that Eliashib's great-grandson was born while Nehemiah was still living. **Jonathan** is probably the same as Johanan in 12:22.

12:12-21. These verses list **the heads of the priestly families** in **the days of Joiakim,** the son of Jeshua the high priest (cf. v. 10). Twenty names are listed here, corresponding roughly to the 22 names in verses 1-7. Hattush in verse 2 and Maadiah in verse 5 are not in the list in verses 12-21. Harim (v. 15; cf. 10:5) is spelled Rehum in 12:3. Minjamin in verse 17 is spelled Mijamin in verse 5.

12:22-26. Darius is probably Darius II who ruled Persia from 423 to 404 B.C. According to the Elephantine papyri **Johanan** was high priest in 408 B.C. Possibly Nehemiah lived to see Johanan's son **Jaddua** become high priest sometime between 408 and 404.

The book of the annals was an official record book of the Levite **family heads. . . . up to the days of Johanan.** The Levites mentioned in verses 24-25 **served in the days of** the high priest **Joiakim** (cf. vv. 10, 12), **and in the days of Nehemiah** and Ezra. Hashabiah may be the man mentioned in 3:17; **Sherebiah** and **Jeshua** are mentioned in 12:8 as being involved in leading songs of thanksgiving, sung antiphonally. Possibly Jeshua **son of Kadmiel** should read "Jeshua, Binnui, Kadmiel," as in verse 8.

Mattaniah and **Bakbukiah** (cf. 11:17) were associated with music in 12:8 but here (v. 25) they were gatekeepers. **Obadiah** was probably the same as Abda (11:17). Possibly they served in both capacities. **Meshullam** (also mentioned in 3:4, 30) may be a variant spelling for Shallum, who along with **Talmon and Akkub were gatekeepers** (cf. 1 Chron. 9:17).

E. The dedication of the wall (12:27-47)

1. THE PREPARATION FOR THE DEDICATION (12:27-30)

12:27-30. Nehemiah had **the Levites,** who had settled in various towns around **Jerusalem** (cf. 11:3, 20) join the others in the holy city for the ceremonies to dedicate the rebuilt **wall.** It was to be a time of singing **songs of thanksgiving** (cf. 12:8) to God with musical instruments (cf. 1 Chron. 25:1). **Singers,** who were Levites, assembled from south of **Jerusalem (the villages of** Netophah), the east (assuming **Beth Gilgal** is the same as Gilgal), and the north (the Benjamite towns of **Geba and Azmaveth**). The preparations also included ceremonial cleansing of all **the people** and of **the gates and the wall.** This was done no doubt by sprinkling the blood of sacrificed animals.

2. THE PROCESSION OF THE TWO CHOIRS (12:31-42A)

12:31-42a. Nehemiah assembled **two** great **choirs to** sing thanks (cf. vv. 8, 27); the number in each choir is not indicated. The choirs probably began near the Valley Gate, which interestingly is the place where Nehemiah began and ended his nighttime inspection of the ruined walls months earlier (2:13-15). The first procession moved counterclockwise on the southern and eastern wall **toward the Dung Gate** (12:31) and past **the Fountain Gate up to the Water Gate.** Because both **choirs** entered the temple (v. 40), the first one may have proceeded on the wall up to the East Gate (see the map "Jerusalem in the Time of Nehemiah," near 3:1). The procession included the following: **Ezra,** who **led the** group (12:36), the choir, **Hoshaiah . . . half the leaders of Judah** (v. 32), **priests** (seven of them named and **some** with **trumpets**), and **Zechariah** and his eight **associates . . . with musical instruments.**

The second choir moved clockwise, presumably starting at the Valley Gate and going past various gates and towers (see comments on chap. 3) till they arrived at **the Gate of the Guard.** This group included the choir, Nehemiah, **half the officials** (12:40), **priests** (seven of them named and with **trumpets**), and eight others who apparently were singers. The parallel arrangement of the two processions is striking.

Their walking **on top of the wall** (vv. 31, 38) visually demonstrated that the walls were strong, a rejoinder to Tobiah's earlier mocking claim that the wall would be so weak that even a fox on top of it would break it down (4:3). Perhaps Nehemiah wanted Tobiah to see that with God's help the project was completed in spite of his and others' opposition. Since the people now carried no spears, swords, or bows (cf. 4:16, 18), the enemies had no doubt withdrawn. Seeing the two large processions marching on the walls must have been an impressive sight.

3. THE PARTICIPATION IN WORSHIP (12:42B-43)

12:42b-43. In the temple ("the house of God," v. 40) the choir leader **Jezrahiah** led the two large **choirs. Sacrifices** were made and the people **rejoiced** so loudly that they **could be heard far away.**

4. THE PROVISION OF CONTRIBUTIONS (12:44-47)

12:44-47. Nehemiah took advantage of this celebration to provide for ongoing worship. **The storerooms** to which the people were to bring their **contributions, firstfruits, and tithes** that were **required by the Law** were side rooms on the temple (cf. 1 Kings 6:5; 1 Chron. 28:11; 2 Chron. 31:11; Neh. 10:37-39; 12:25; 13:4, 12-13). Nehemiah had **the ministering priests and Levites** follow the order of responsibilities outlined more than 500 years earlier by **David** (1 Chron. 22–26)

and presumably established by **Solomon.** Music had been an important part of David's preparations for the temple, under the leadership of the musician **Asaph** (1 Chron. 15:19; 16:4-5,,37). Besides being an effective administrator Nehemiah was also a man of worship. He was concerned with praise by music and praise by gifts.

The people had made a binding agreement to provide for the priests and Levites (see comments on Neh. 10:37-39).

F. The reforms under Nehemiah (chap. 13)

For 12 years Nehemiah served as governor of Judah, from Artaxerxes' 20th year to his 32nd year (5:14; cf. 13:6), that is, from 444 B.C. to 432 B.C. Other than his rebuilding and dedicating the wall, getting the people to agree to keep the Law, and organizing the work of the priests and Levites in the temple, little is known about Nehemiah's 12-year rule. Undoubtedly that was a successful period of time in his life.

When the 12 years were up Nehemiah returned to Persia (perhaps to the city of Susa; cf. 1:1; or to the capital, Persepolis), evidently once again to serve King Artaxerxes (cf. 2:6). How long he remained in this position is not known. Perhaps it was two years or so. While he was gone some rather startling changes took place in Judah, changes involving serious violations of the Mosaic Law. When Nehemiah once again returned to Judah (perhaps around 430 or later), he faced a task that in some respects must have been even more difficult than rebuilding the wall.

1. ISRAEL'S EXCLUSION OF FOREIGNERS (13:1-3)

13:1-3. On that day refers not to 12:44 but to the time after Nehemiah returned to Jerusalem to be governor again, as indicated in 13:4-7. The portion of the Law (**the Book of Moses**) that **was read** is Deuteronomy 23:3-5. The Ammonites and Moabites had resisted Israel's march to Canaan, and the Moabites **had hired Balaam** to **curse** Israel but God . . . turned that attempted **curse into a blessing** (Num. 22–25). Therefore Ammonites and Moabites were to have no part in Israel's temple worship. Being reminded of this **the people** in Nehemiah's day eliminated those foreigners (as stated in

Neh. 13:4-9, 23-28). Interestingly once again the reading of God's Word had an effect on **the people** (cf. 8:1-6, 13-17; 9:3).

2. NEHEMIAH'S ENCOUNTER WITH TOBIAH (13:4-9)

13:4-5. When Nehemiah returned to Jerusalem he was shocked to find that **Eliashib, the** high **priest** in Judah (cf. 3:1, 20; 13:28), had prepared **a large** room in the temple for **Tobiah.** Eliashib and Tobiah were **closely associated,** which may mean family ties (cf. Tobiah's relationships by marriage with several Jews, 6:17-18). Tobiah had been an enemy of Nehemiah, opposing the wall-building (2:10-19; 4:3, 7; 6:1, 12, 17, 19); but now that Nehemiah was gone (13:6) Tobiah the Ammonite (cf. comments on vv. 1-3) moved into the **temple!** The room he occupied had been one of the temple storerooms (v. 4; see comments on 12:44), a side room for storing **grain offerings** (13:4-5). There Tobiah could oppose God's work while posing to assist it!

13:6-9. Artaxerxes is called the **king of Babylon** because his rule over the Persian Empire included Babylon. Nehemiah's return to Artaxerxes (at either Persepolis, the capital, or Susa) was in 432. **Some time later** (perhaps two years or more) Nehemiah asked to return **to Jerusalem.** How long he stayed this second time is not stated. Malachi may have ministered about that same time (see the chart "Chronology of the Postexilic Period," near Ezra 1:1).

Hearing what the high priest **had done** for **Tobiah** (Nehemiah called it an **evil thing;** cf. Neh. 13:17), Nehemiah was deeply distressed. **Eliashib** had been involved in restoring the walls (3:1), but now inconsistently he had allowed an opponent to reside inside the temple complex! Understandably Nehemiah was so angry that he went into the temple room and tossed out **all Tobiah's household goods.** He then had the **rooms** (apparently Tobiah had also occupied some rooms adjacent to the large chamber) purified, either ceremonially or by fumigation or both, and restored the temple articles and **offerings** that belonged there.

3. NEHEMIAH'S ENCOUNTER WITH THE OFFICIALS IN JUDAH (13:10-14)

13:10. Nehemiah's next task pertains to why Tobiah was able to occupy one of the temple storerooms. They were empty because the people had failed in their commitment to bring their tithes and offerings **to the Levites.** As a result **the Levites** and others who were to live off these offerings as they performed spiritual services for the people had to work in the **fields** caring for **their** livestock (cf. Num. 35:1-5). This meant they had less time to work in the temple.

13:11-14. Nehemiah reprimanded **the** Jewish **officials** for neglecting this aspect of the work of the temple (**the house of God;** cf. vv. 4, 7, 9, 14). Malachi addressed this problem too (Mal. 3:8-10). The officials had failed to make sure the people of Judah obeyed the Lord in these matters. What made this problem even more distressing for Nehemiah, and difficult to believe, is that these leaders had previously signed a document promising before the Lord and the people that they would never again let this happen (Neh. 9:38; 10:14-29, 35, 37, 39). They had even said specifically, "We will not neglect the house of our God" (10:39b).

Besides rebuking the leaders for their neglect, Nehemiah took action to correct the problem (cf. 13:17-19). He **stationed** the Levites **at their posts** in the temple and appointed four men—a **priest,** a **scribe,** a **Levite,** and an **assistant,** all **trustworthy** (v. 13)—to oversee the distribution of the peoples' **tithes** (**grain, new wine, and oil,** v. 12; cf. v. 5; 10:39). Also Nehemiah, as he so often did, prayed for God's help in the matter (13:14). **Remember** was a plea for help, not merely a request that **God . . . not** forget something (cf. "remember" in vv. 22, 29, 31; 5:19; 6:14 [twice]). Judah's leader did not want his efforts of reform to be undone by the people's neglect.

4. NEHEMIAH'S ENCOUNTER WITH THOSE WHO WERE PROFANING THE SABBATH (13:15-22)

13:15-16. Another commitment Israel had made in writing was to keep God's laws regarding **the Sabbath** (10:31). But when Nehemiah returned to Jerusalem he found that the people had also violated this promise. They were working on **the Sabbath** as they did on the other days of the week. They were **treading** grapes in the **winepresses,** and transporting the **wine,** along with grain . . . **grapes, figs,** and **other** merchandise, **into**

Jerusalem to sell it. They also were buying fish and other items from people of Tyre who resided in Jerusalem.

13:17-22. Again Nehemiah met the problem with a rebuke and action (cf. vv. 11-13). In rebuking their **Sabbath** desecration (calling it a **wicked thing**; cf. v. 7), he referred to a similar sin in Jeremiah's day (cf. Jer. 17:19-27) which God punished by the Exile (**calamity**). Nehemiah had the city **doors . . . shut** on **the Sabbath,** beginning on Friday evening, with guards posted to see that merchandise was not **brought in.** Even so, some **merchants** stayed all **night outside** the walls, perhaps hoping people would slip outside in the darkness to purchase their goods. When Nehemiah heard of this, he threatened to use force against them. Then he told **the Levites** (cf. Neh. 13:30) to help **guard the gates** (cf. 7:1; 11:19). Again (cf. 13:14) he asked **God** to help in this problem, showing **mercy** to him out of His **great love** (*ḥeseḏ*, "loyal love").

5. NEHEMIAH'S ENCOUNTER WITH THOSE WHO VIOLATED THEIR MARRIAGE COMMITMENTS (13:23-31)

13:23-24. The people **of Judah** had also promised in writing that they would not intermarry with pagan people (10:30). Yet when Nehemiah arrived back in Jerusalem, he found that many of the **men** had violated this commitment also (cf. Ezra 9:1-4; 10:44; Mal. 2:10-11) by marrying **women from** the Philistine city of **Ashdod,** and Ammonite and Moabite (cf. comments on Ezra 10:1-3) women. This too had been forbidden in the Mosaic Law (Ex. 34:12-16; Deut. 7:1-5). These mixed marriages even meant that **their children** were speaking their mothers' **language,** not Hebrew (**the language of Judah**).

13:25-27. Again Nehemiah responded with a rebuke (cf. vv. 11, 17). Also he asked God to judge them (**called curses down on them**) and even struck some of them physically, pulling **out their hair,** probably from their beards. To lose one's beard was a disgrace (2 Sam. 10:4; also see Isa. 50:6). He **made them** swear before **God** that they would not continue to commit this violation of God's Law. He reminded them of Solomon's **sin** in marrying **foreign women** (cf. 1 Kings 11:1-8). This was **wickedness,** an act of unfaithfulness.

Nehemiah's pulling out the men's hair may seem to be violent and inappropriate for a man of God. However, Nehemiah was concerned that God's judgment not fall again on Judah. He knew **God** would not tolerate this sin.

13:28-29. Even the priesthood was contaminated by this sin! A grandson of **the high priest** Eliashib (cf. 3:1, 20; 13:4) had married Sanballat's daughter. **Sanballat,** perhaps governor of Samaria, had vigorously opposed Nehemiah's work (cf. 2:10, 19; 4:1, 7; 6:1-2, 5, 12, 14), and now he, like Tobiah (cf. 6:17-18; 13:4), had apparently planned through this family relationship to destroy God's work. Nehemiah had thrown Tobiah's furniture out of the storeroom (v. 8); now he chased the guilty husband **away.**

Nehemiah prayed that **God** would judge the high priest's grandson. Who else is included in his word **them** is not specified, but probably Sanballat was in mind. Mixed marriages **defiled** the priesthood for a priest was to marry "only a virgin from his own people" (Lev. 21:14).

13:30-31. This problem, like the others reported in this chapter (cf. vv. 9, 22), called for ceremonial purifying. Again **the priests and the Levites** were **assigned** their **duties.** (Nehemiah was great at getting people to work!) He **also made** sure the people brought their **contributions** and **firstfruits** to the temple (cf. comments on vv. 10-13).

For the fourth time in this chapter this great leader prayed that **God** would **remember** him (see comments on v. 14), that is, that God would bestow His blessings on him in return for his diligence.

This book underscores the importance of physical protection for God's people in Jerusalem but, more importantly, it stresses the need for His people to obey His Word, not giving in to sin through neglect, compromise, or outright disobedience.

BIBLIOGRAPHY

Ackroyd, Peter R. *I and II Chronicles, Ezra, Nehemiah.* Torch Bible Commentaries. New York: Harper & Row, 1973.

Barber, Cyril J. *Nehemiah and the Dynamics of Effective Leadership.* Neptune, N.J.: Loizeaux Brothers, 1976.

Brockington, L.H. *Ezra, Nehemiah, and Esther*. New Century Bible. Greenwood, S.C.: Attic Press, 1969.

Campbell, Donald K. *Nehemiah: Man in Charge*. Wheaton, Ill.: SP Publications, Victor Books, 1979.

Fensham, F. Charles. *The Books of Ezra and Nehemiah*. The New International Commentary on the Old Testament. Grand Rapids: Wm. B. Eerdmans Publishing Co., 1982.

Getz, Gene A. *Nehemiah: A Man of Prayer and Persistence*. Ventura, Calif.: G/L Publications, Regal Books, 1981.

Ironside, H.A. *Notes on Ezra, Nehemiah, Esther*. Neptune, N.J.: Loizeaux Brothers, 1972.

Jamieson, Robert. "The Book of Nehemiah." In *A Commentary Critical, Experimental and Practical on the Old and New Testaments*. Vol. 2.

Grand Rapids: Wm. B. Eerdmans Publishing Co., 1945.

Keil, C.F. "Nehemiah." In *Commentary on the Old Testament in Ten Volumes*. Vol. 3. Reprint (25 vols. in 10). Grand Rapids: Wm. B. Eerdmans Publishing Co., 1982.

Kidner, Derek. *Ezra and Nehemiah: An Introduction and Commentary*. The Tyndale Old Testament Commentaries. Downers Grove, Ill.: InterVarsity Press, 1979.

Laney, J. Carl. *Ezra/Nehemiah*. Everyman's Bible Commentary. Chicago: Moody Press, 1982.

Myers, Jacob M. *Ezra, Nehemiah*. The Anchor Bible. Garden City, N.Y.: Doubleday & Co., 1965.

Swindoll, Charles R. *Hand Me Another Brick*. Nashville: Thomas Nelson Publishers, 1978.

ESTHER

John A. Martin

INTRODUCTION

Historical Setting. The Book of Esther is unique in several ways. For one thing it is a book with several historical problems. The book contains interesting and informative eyewitness accounts about the Persian Empire which were true to life in that period of history but which are difficult to verify from outside sources (see comments under "Historicity").

The book takes place in the Persian period (539–331 B.C.) after many Israelites had returned from the Exile to the land of Palestine to rebuild the temple and set up the sacrificial system. Most Israelite captives, however, chose not to return to their homeland. They should have done so for Isaiah and Jeremiah had urged the yet-to-be-exiled nation to come out of Babylon (Isa. 48:20; Jer. 50:8; 51:6) after 70 years (Jer. 29:10) and return to the place where the Lord could bless them under the covenantal promises (Deut. 28). Esther and Mordecai had not returned to the land and did not seem interested in complying with the prophetic command to return. The Persian monarch mentioned in the Book of Esther is Xerxes (485–465), known from other sources as Ahasuerus (see NIV marg.), a strong, effective ruler. The events in this book occurred between those recorded in Ezra 6 and Ezra 7 (see the chart "Chronology of the Postexilic Period" near Ezra 1:1). The events in the Book of Esther extend over a decade—from 483 B.C. (Xerxes' 3rd year, Es. 1:3) to 473 (the end of Xerxes' 12th year, 3:7).

Characteristics. Esther is the only book of the Bible in which the name of God is not mentioned. The New Testament does not quote from the Book of Esther, nor have copies of it been found among the Dead Sea Scrolls. The Law is never mentioned in the book nor are sacrifices or offerings referred to. This fits the view that the Jewish people residing in the Persian Empire were not following God's will. They were shunning their responsibility to return to Palestine and to become involved in temple worship.

Prayer is never mentioned in the book, though fasting is. In other postexilic books prayer is important to the main characters (both the books of Ezra and Neh. are good examples), but in the Book of Esther nothing is said about Mordecai or Esther praying. Both Esther and Mordecai seem to have lacked spiritual awareness except in their assurance that God would protect His people.

Recipients. Knowing who the original recipients of a Bible book were helps in interpreting that book. The Book of Esther includes a number of dates which tie the account to a particular time in the Persian Empire, but no hint is given when the book was written nor is there any explicit evidence about its original readers.

Some scholars suggest that the book was composed in the Persian Empire and then transported back to Palestine and added to the collection of biblical books (OT mss. considered canonical). More likely, however, is the view that the author lived in Palestine and wrote this account of events transpiring in the Persian Empire for the benefit of his fellow returnees to the land. It is unlikely that the book was written for Persian readers. No doubt it was composed to encourage Israelites that God was working on their behalf, even through some people who had refused to come back to the land.

At the time of the writing of the book (see comments under "Author and Date") the Jews in Palestine were going through difficult times in their struggle to rebuild their nation and to reestablish temple worship. It had taken the nation 21 years to complete the building of the temple (536–515) and, as is evident from the last half of the Book of Ezra, the people were not in good spiritual condition during the reign of Artaxerxes (464–424). Of course both Ezra and Nehemiah noted the reason for the nation's lowly condition: the people had not been following the Deuteronomic Covenant and therefore were under God's curse rather than under His promise of blessing. The Book of Esther, then, would have been a great encouragement to these struggling Jews. It would have helped them realize that the surrounding peoples which seemed so awesome could never conquer the unique people of God. Israel was protected by God even though a large number of them were outside the land. The Book of Esther would also encourage them to worship the God of Israel, though He is not mentioned by name in it.

Author and Date. The book gives no hint of who wrote it. But whoever it was knew the Persian culture well. The account has all the marks of a person who was there for he described the events as an eyewitness. And he was probably a Jew. Some have suggested that Ezra or Nehemiah wrote the account but no specific evidence supports that view. Many critics of the Book of Esther claim that it was written at a much later date because of its language and style, but recent investigations have shown this idea to be unfounded. The document as it stands could have been written sometime between 470 and 465, during the latter years of Xerxes' reign (cf. 10:2-3), or in the reign of his son Artaxerxes (464–424). There is no need to suppose that a well-known person was the author.

Historicity. Objections to the historicity of the events in the Book of Esther are usually along three lines:

1. One of the purposes of the Book of Esther (see under "Purpose") is to describe the origin of the religious Feast of Purim. Though scholars debate what the word "Purim" means and what it signifies, the Book of Esther explains that the feast is a celebration of God's miraculous deliverance of His people from Haman. What appeared to be an event of "chance" was, of course, the sovereign intervention of God. Many critics, however, argue that this is too simple an

explanation and that the story of the Feast of Purim arose as a folktale. However, no evidence whatever contradicts the Esther account as a reliable explanation of how the Feast of Purim began. It cannot be shown to have derived from another source.

2. Many doubt that the account is historical because they say no outside records mention any of the characters in the book. But outside records do refer to Xerxes; however, they make no reference to a queen named Esther or to Mordecai or Haman. In response, it must be admitted that there is no mention of Esther outside this book. (Mordecai, though, is referred to; cf. comments on 2:5-7.) But the fact that Esther is not mentioned in other sources does not prove that she did not exist. Herodotus and Ctesias recorded that a woman named Amestris was Xerxes' queen. She was the mother of the next ruler, Artaxerxes. However, Herodotus discussed Amestris not in connection with the reign of Xerxes, but with the reign of her son many years later. If Amestris is identified with the biblical woman named Vashti who was deposed in 482 (Artaxerxes was born in 483) and then is not mentioned again until her son assumed the throne in 464, there would be time for Esther to have assumed the throne as queen all the way up to the death of Xerxes or at least till the time when the Book of Esther ends. Even if Vashti were deposed before the book was written, the author might have included that fact because it would have fit the book's purpose. The idea that Esther could not have existed because no extant historical record mentions her by name is an argument from silence. Her existence actually fits nicely into the chronology of the Persian period.

3. Some critics presume that the account of King Xerxes seems improbable. Why would the king pick a new queen in such an irrational manner? In response, it must be repeated that no evidence whatever exists which shows that the biblical account is unreliable. In fact the irrationality of Xerxes and the large harem he acquired in Susa have been referred to in other sources.

Much evidence does support the historicity of the facts in this book. Xerxes was a real king in Persia. His drinking parties were well known. Xerxes did have an irrational temper, occasionally exhibiting fits of rage (1:12; 7:10). He did have a palace in Susa and a large harem there. Various features of the court can also be substantiated from other sources.

Purpose. As noted earlier, the Book of Esther was written to encourage the returned Jewish exiles by reminding them of the faithfulness of God who would keep His promises to the nation. The author was describing God's unfailing preservation of His people (even "disobedient people" such as Esther and Mordecai—those not back in the land). The author was also explaining how the Feast of Purim began. That feast, each time it was celebrated, would encourage the remnant.

OUTLINE

COMMENTARY

I. Esther Placed in a Position of Prominence (1:1–2:20)

This first major section of the book describes the need for God's deliverance of His people, and the background of that deliverance. Undoubtedly many of the original readers, like readers today, would be helped by knowing the background of the story. The author described in some detail the setting of the Persian banquet and the reasons Esther came into a prominent position. Besides carefully conveying historical facts, the author was also a good narrator.

A. Vashti deposed by Xerxes (chap. 1)

1. THE KING'S 187-DAY CELEBRATION (1:1-9)

1:1. The account opens with the mention of **Xerxes who ruled over 127 provinces . . . from India to Cush** (cf. 8:9). Xerxes, called Ahasuerus throughout the Hebrew text of Esther (cf. NIV marg.), ruled the Persian Empire for 21 years from 485 to 465 B.C. He is mentioned elsewhere in the Bible only in Ezra 4:6 and Daniel 9:1. The vast extent of his empire has been confirmed by several outside sources which state the size of that empire in similar words (see the map "The Persian Empire" near Ezra 1:1). Judah was one of the provinces over which the king ruled (cf. Neh. 1:2). "India" corresponds to present-day West Pakistan; "Cush" was a term for the upper Nile region which included present-day southern Egypt, all of Sudan, and northern Ethiopia.

1:2. King Xerxes had an elaborate palace in Persepolis as well as a winter **citadel** (palace) in **Susa** (cf. Neh. 1:1). Persepolis and Ecbatana (Ezra 6:2) were other major cities in the Persian Empire (see the map "The Persian Empire," near Ezra 1:1). An inscription from the time of Xerxes' son Artaxerxes noted that the palace was destroyed by fire sometime in Artaxerxes' reign. Reference in Esther 1:2 to this citadel has been confirmed by archeological work at Susa. An author from a later period probably would not have known about the palace so it can be inferred that the author of this book was someone who was close to the events chronologically.

1:3-4. In the third year of his reign (483 B.C.) Xerxes **gave a banquet** to which he invited **his nobles and officials** as well as **military leaders . . . princes,** and **nobles of the provinces.** Mention of these leaders fits the known fact that the Persian Empire had a large administrative system. Though not stated, this banquet probably corresponds to the great feast Xerxes gave when he was planning to invade Greece. According to Herodotus it took Xerxes four years to get ready for the invasion he launched in 481. (Herodotus' four years would extend from the beginning of Xerxes' reign in 485.) No doubt the **180 days** involved planning sessions in which all the provinces' leaders were being prepared for the war effort, as well as being impressed with Xerxes' **wealth** and **splendor**. The campaign was to be a costly affair.

The Book of Esther says nothing about Xerxes' invasion of Greece, but other sources state that he wanted to avenge his father's defeat at Marathon near Athens. Xerxes' immense fleet defeated the Greeks at Thermopylae but was defeated at the famous Battle of Salamis in 480 B.C. and the Battle of Plataea in 479. He had to retreat home. Esther gained the favor of the king in 479 B.C., the seventh year of his reign (2:16). This would have been after his defeat by Greece. Thus these events recorded in Esther fit the facts known from secular sources.

1:5-9. At the end of the 180 days Xerxes gave another **banquet;** this one lasted **seven days** for **people** in **Susa**. Both great and small were invited. The descriptions of the decor of the king's palace **garden** (vv. 6-7) add to the feeling that the writer had firsthand knowledge of the setting and the occasion. Perhaps Mordecai was among the guests at the seven-day banquet. **Linen . . . silver,** and **marble,** and **other costly stones** are known to have been used in Persia, and Persian **couches** (cf. 7:8) **of gold and silver** were referred to by Herodotus. **Blue** and **white** were the royal colors (cf. 8:15). Drinking vessels (**goblets**) of expensive material were a Persian luxury. The feast was livened by the fact that any **guest** could **drink in his own way,** that is, he could drink as much or as little as he desired. In other words the king was liberal with the **wine.** Meanwhile **Queen Vashti** was giving a separate **banquet for the women.** Separate banquets were not unusual in that culture.

2. VASHTI DEPOSED (1:10-22)

1:10-12. Xerxes told his **seven eunuchs** (cf. 6:14) **to bring . . . Vashti** into his banquet hall so that **her beauty** could be admired by the male guests. **But she refused to come.** One of the eunuchs named here is referred to later (**Harbona** in 7:9). This order was given **on the seventh day,** that is, the last day of the feast which had turned into a drunken party. The mention of "seven eunuchs" serving the king fits the era in which the account took place. It was a well-known practice then for young men who served the **king** to be castrated so they would have no illusions of starting their own dynasties.

Vashti's refusal is not explained by the author. There is no implication that the king wanted her to do anything immoral or to expose herself. Perhaps she simply did not wish to be in mixed company at that time. It has been suggested that if this queen was Amestris, perhaps she refused to go to the banquet because she was pregnant with Artaxerxes, who was born in 483. Regardless of the reason for her refusal, her action was a breach of etiquette. **The king** was used to getting whatever he desired whenever he desired it. Therefore her response made him **furious** (cf. 7:7).

1:13-15. The king consulted **wise**

men about what he should do. These seven men had special access to the king and were the ones who knew the law well. Herodotus has confirmed the fact that this use of wise men was a feature of ancient Near Eastern courts. Throughout the ancient Near East wise men played important roles in governments (e.g., Daniel's position in the Babylonian and Persian Empires). The crime the queen had committed was that she disobeyed a command of the king. Obviously the king and queen did not share an emotionally intimate relationship. This was true of Xerxes and the women in his harem. This is again apparent later when Esther noted to Mordecai that she had not even seen the king for a month and was afraid to ask to see him (4:11).

1:16-22. Memucan, one of Xerxes' wise men, suggested that he have the queen deposed (v. 19) so that other noble women (v. 18) of the empire (and in fact all the women, v. 20) would not follow Vashti's example and despise their husbands (v. 17) and the empire be filled with female disrespect and marital discord (v. 18). It is difficult to see how this punishment would cause the women of the empire to respect their husbands but that was the idea behind the decree. This is partially explained by the fact that the men had been drinking heavily (v. 10). (The words "if it pleases the king" occur nine times in the OT, seven of them in the Book of Es.: Neh. 2:5, 7; Es. 1:19; 3:9; 5:4, 8; 7:3 ["your majesty" is lit., "the king"] 8:5; 9:13.)

The idea pleased the king and his nobles so an edict was sent throughout the empire in various languages (cf. 3:12), stating that every man should be ruler over his own household. A vast relay communications system, something like an ancient pony express, made it possible to spread news throughout the empire quickly (cf. 3:13; 8:10). This bit of information helps set the stage for the rise of Esther.

B. Esther elevated to queen (2:1-20)

Esther, a Jewess, was placed in a position in which she could help the nation Israel. Her being elevated to queen happened even before Israel needed help. The original readers would realize that this was another instance of God protecting His covenant people.

1. SOLUTION PROPOSED FOR A NEW QUEEN (2:1-4)

2:1-4. After the anger of the king subsided, apparently sometime later, he realized that he had been foolish in his actions. Throughout the book it is evident that the king was led along by his officials. It appears that he was somewhat provincial in his outlook. Like all men of power he had to rely on others to be his eyes and ears on the outside, and did not always receive the best information.

In this case it was suggested to the king that beautiful young virgins (unmarried women) be brought to Susa, placed under Hegai (the eunuch . . . in charge of the harem) and given beauty treatments (cf. v. 9), and that the king be allowed to pick from them a woman to replace Vashti. His personal attendants (probably "the wise men who understood the laws . . . seven nobles," 1:13-14) had suggested that Vashti be deposed. So now they certainly did not want Xerxes to reinstate her for fear that she would turn against them. The suggestion appealed to the king and he followed it. The fact that he had a harem in Susa is known from other sources. New women were constantly being brought into the Persian harem to replace the older women.

2. ESTHER TAKEN INTO THE HAREM (2:5-11)

2:5-7. Mordecai is a Babylonian name taken from the god Marduk. The name mrdk is attested in fifth-century Aramaic documents. Mordecai was a Jew of the tribe of Benjamin. He had tried to hide the fact that he and his cousin were Jews (vv. 10, 20). Verse 6 may mean that Mordecai was deported by Nebuchadnezzar along with Jehoiachin (597 B.C.). But this would mean that Mordecai would have been about 115 years old by the time of Xerxes' third year and Esther would have been 80. It is better to understand that Kish, Mordecai's great-grandfather, was the one who was carried away in the 597 deportation.

Mordecai's cousin, Esther, also a Benjamite, had been raised by him, apparently because her parents died when she was young. Her father was Abihail (v. 15; 9:29). The name Esther ("star") is Persian. Her Hebrew name, Hadassah, means myrtle. She was beautiful, lovely in form and features.

2:8-11. Esther was taken into Xerxes' harem to await **the king's** choice, along with **many** other young women of the kingdom who were summoned to **Susa.** Esther immediately pleased **Hegai,** the eunuch (cf. v. 3) and as a result was given a favorable position **in the harem.** He saw that she had **beauty treatments** (cf. v. 3) **and special food,** apparently food of a better-than-ordinary quality. Esther was even given **seven maids** to serve her. The wait in the harem was at least 12 months (v. 12) so Esther must have appreciated her favored position.

Esther kept her Jewish nationality a secret (cf. v. 20), not telling Hegai, her maids, or anyone else **because Mordecai had** told **her** not to. From this and other statements in the book it is clear the author was making the point that God protected and used Esther and Mordecai *in spite of* the fact that they were not living according to the Law commanded by God to the people of Israel. By Law Esther was not to marry a pagan (Deut. 7:1-4) or have sexual relations with a man who was not her husband (Ex. 20:14), and yet this was the purpose of her being included in the harem. **Esther** could be contrasted with Daniel who refused to eat the things from the king's table (Dan. 1:5) because the food would include items considered unclean by the Jewish Law. Apparently Esther had no qualms about the food she ate (Es. 2:9). She certainly did not set herself apart as Daniel had done.

3. ESTHER CHOSEN TO BE QUEEN (2:12-20)

2:12-15. Esther became extremely popular during her year of preparation for her night with the king. Each girl's **beauty treatments** were designed to enhance her attractiveness. **Myrrh,** a gum from a small tree, gives a fragrant smell. Esther was not in a beauty contest simply to win the king's affections; the women were being prepared to have sexual relations with **the king.** This is suggested by the words **in the evening she would go there and in the morning return.** After that they would be transferred to another harem, under **Shaash- gaz,** which consisted of **the concubines.** Most of the women were relegated to living the rest of their lives in the harem of the concubines, many probably never

again seeing **the king.** When Esther went to **the king** she followed the instructions of **Hegai** the eunuch.

2:16-20. Esther **was taken to King Xerxes** in 479 B.C., his **seventh year,** the 10th month (Tebeth was the Babylonian name for December-January). **The king was attracted to Esther** and therefore **made her queen** in place **of Vashti.** Then a big **banquet** was prepared and **he proclaimed a holiday** and gave away many **gifts.** Throughout all this, Esther had still not revealed that she belonged to the Jewish nation (cf. v. 10). Apparently there was a gathering of another harem of **virgins** during the time Mordecai **was . . . at the king's gate** (cf. v. 21; 3:2). His being at the king's gate probably meant that Mordecai held an official position in the empire's judicial system. His position thus helped set the stage for the following events. This fact about Mordecai shows how he could have uncovered an assassination plot and how a feud started that threatened the entire Jewish nation.

II. The Jews Marked for Extermination (2:21–4:3)

Many have noted that the ,Book of Esther is a great short story. Like Ruth, another little book in the Bible about a woman, Esther has all the earmarks of great literature, including a conflict, an antagonist, tension, and irony. The antagonist, Haman, is introduced here and his conflict with Mordecai began.

A. A feud and Haman's hatred of the Jews (2:21–3:6)

1. KING SAVED BY MORDECAI (2:21-23)

2:21-23. Again a reference to Mordecai's position **at the king's gate** (cf. v. 19) as a judiciary official points to God's sovereign control over these events. Learning about a plot by **Bigthana and Teresh,** royal guards, **to assassinate** the **king,** Mordecai **told Queen Esther,** who reported this **to the king.** She gave **credit to Mordecai** for uncovering the scheme. **The two** men involved in the plot **were hanged on a gallows** (or "post," NIV marg.; cf. 5:14). Rather than being hanged by the neck on a modern-type gallows, the men were probably impaled on a stake or post (cf. Ezra 6:11). This was not an unusual method of execution in the Persian Empire. Darius, Xerxes' father, was known to have once impaled 3,000 men. A record of this assassination attempt was written in **the annals,** the official royal record (cf. Es. 6:1-2).

2. HAMAN PROMOTED (3:1-6)

3:1. Haman was promoted to the highest position by **Xerxes.** This occurred **after these events** (i.e., after Mordecai saved the king from the assassination and the two men were executed). It is reasonable to suppose that Mordecai expected a reward for his work on behalf of the king. But no reward was given then, possibly because of some bureaucratic bungle. Later this neglect appalled and surprised the king (cf. 6:1-3).

Because Haman was an **Agagite,** some have supposed that he was descended from Agag, king of the Amalekites (1 Sam. 15:8). However, it seems unlikely that a high-ranking Persian official would be related to a west Semite who lived 600 years earlier. Archeologists have uncovered an inscription which indicates that Agag was also the name of a province in the Persian Empire. This probably explains why Haman was called an Agagite.

3:2-4. Haman's promotion meant that the other nobles had to kneel **down** to him, that is, they had to pay him special respect. This was not an act of worship, such as that commanded of the three Hebrew young men in Daniel 3:8-15. Since the **officials at the king's gate** had to kneel before **Haman,** the people probably also had to bow before the king himself. **Mordecai** said he would not bow to **Haman** (cf. Es. 5:9) because **he** (Mordecai) **was a Jew.** Probably this persistent (**day after day**) refusal stemmed more from pride than from religious scruples. For several years **Mordecai** had not let Esther tell the king she was a Jewess (2:10, 20), but now Mordecai was using their national heritage as an excuse for not giving honor to a high Persian official.

3:5-6. Haman . . . enraged by Mordecai's refusal (cf. 5:9), set out to find **a way to kill all . . . the Jews,** not just **Mordecai.** This was an early case of anti-Semitism. In this literary plot, a climax is now reached in the tension. (Later a second climax was reached when Haman was revealed to be the plotter against the Jews; 7:6.) If the Jews were killed

throughout the whole kingdom of Xerxes, this would include those in the land of Palestine. These latter Jews were faithful to the Lord, worshiping in the rebuilt temple and living according to the stipulations of the Law (cf. comments on Ezra 1–6). A massive execution of thousands of Jews would thwart God's program. However, God cannot be thwarted (Job 42:2). He can overturn man's diabolical efforts, sometimes by miraculous acts, and sometimes through seeming acts of happenstance as in the following sequence. God is always working on behalf of His people.

B. King persuaded by Haman to destroy the Jews (3:7-15)

1. LOT CAST BY HAMAN (3:7-9)

3:7. The author included a seemingly obscure part of the account by recording that Haman used a *pur,* a Babylonian word for **the lot,** to decide when the Jews should be killed. The original readers of this book would have understood that God was working to protect His people even in the timing of events. As things worked out, the Jews had almost a year in which to prepare themselves for the conflict with their enemies.

A little more than four years had gone by since Esther had become queen, in 478 B.C. (2:16). On the first day of the year, in **Nisan** (April-May) 474 B.C., at the beginning of Xerxes' **12th year,** the *pur* was cast **to select a day and month.** *Pur* is the basis of the name of the Feast of Purim (9:26). Presumably the day selected was when the execution of the Jews was to begin. **Haman,** along with many people in the Persian Empire, was extremely superstitious (cf. 6:13). The Persian religious system stressed fate and chance. Haman was allowing fate, by the casting of the lot, to dictate his move against the Jewish nation. Little did he then realize that the God who created all things and controls all events was in control of that situation, the lot-casting (Prov. 16:33; cf. comments on Acts 1:26). God had already prepared a means of delivering His people from Haman's plot. The month chosen by the lot was **the 12th month** (February-March)—almost a year later. The day, stated later (Es. 3:13), was the 13th of the month (cf. 8:12; 9:1).

3:8-9. Haman went in to the **king** to

present his plan. Falsely accusing all Jews of refusing to obey the king's laws, he suggested that the king would be better off if the Jews, scattered throughout the empire, were exterminated. Haman said he himself was willing to bear the costs involved in carrying out this decree. Haman must have been a man of immense wealth. As the highest official he undoubtedly had many opportunities to add to his personal fortune. Ten thousand talents of silver weighed about 750,000 pounds, an enormous amount worth millions of dollars in present-day currency. That was the staggering sum which Haman was willing to pay. Possibly this huge sum made the king suspicious of Haman. Surely he could not have acquired so much money without being crooked. (Interestingly, however, the king did not make him pay the money; v. 11.) At that time Persia used silver as its monetary standard.

2. KING'S PERMISSION GIVEN (3:10-11)

3:10-11. Xerxes, as before, was easily influenced by his officials (cf. 1:16-22; 2:2-4). He accepted Haman's advice and acquiesced. By giving his signet ring to Haman, Xerxes was allowing the enemy of the Jews, as Haman was now called, to send out a proclamation to the empire in the king's name. Five times in the Book of Esther, Haman is called the Jews' enemy (cf. 7:6; 8:1; 9:10, 24). The signet ring, when impressed on clay, made a special imprint, which, like a signature, represented the king's authority (cf. 3:12; 8:2, 8; Gen. 41:42; Dan 6:17; Hag. 2:23). The king noted that Haman could do with the people as he pleased. Little did the king realize that his queen, Esther, was a Jewess and would be included in this hideous plan.

3. PROCLAMATIONS SENT OUT (3:12-15)

3:12-15. Haman's proclamation, sent out under the king's name to all the provinces and in various languages (cf. 1:22), called for the death of all Jewish people including women and little children. Haman intended to rid the world of God's covenant people. Also the executioners were ordered to confiscate property owned by Jews. The day the decree was dispatched was in March 474 B.C. (On the quick dispatching of this edict see comments on 1:22.)

The edict . . . bewildered the people in the city of Susa (cf. 8:15). Apparently such a decree had never before come from the royal court. Haman's bloodthirstiness, along with Xerxes' seeming indifference to such atrocities, was incredible even to a sophisticated society which was used to cruel behavior. Perhaps other minority populations wondered if they would be the next to be annihilated.

C. Mordecai mourned (4:1-3)

4:1-3. Whatever had been Mordecai's reasons for not bowing to Haman, he was now in great mourning. His feud with Haman, whether legitimate or not, had caused a great crisis for his whole nation. He feared that God's Chosen People would be destroyed and God's program thwarted. He knew the amount of money Haman had agreed to spend on this vast project as he had a copy of the edict (vv. 7-8). Wearing sackcloth and ashes and crying publicly signified mourning (cf. Gen. 37:34; Jer. 49:3; Dan. 9:3; Joel 1:13; Jonah 3:6). Mordecai was identifying himself to the public as one in great distress. Perhaps he was remorseful for having revealed his nationality (Es. 3:4) and thus having endangered the lives of thousands of his people. Everywhere Jews heard of the edict, and they had the same response. Certainly many Jewish people must have prayed fervently, though the Book of Esther does not mention it. Meanwhile God was working behind the scenes to deliver His people.

III. Calamity Averted by Esther (4:4—9:19)

Nothing has been said so far in the Book of Esther to suggest Esther and Mordecai were people of great faith in Yahweh. But here it is revealed that they at least believed that God was concerned for the welfare of His Chosen People. In this climactic section the interworkings of various events reveal God's sovereignty in working on behalf of His own. Though God's name is not mentioned, the abundance of "happenstances" surely point to God's control.

A. Communications between Esther and Mordecai (4:4-17)

4:4-8. The action in this section centers around Hathach, one of the king's eunuchs assigned to Esther. Though Esther had not been in the presence of the king for a month (v. 11), this did not mean that she had fallen from his favor. As his queen she had many luxuries and was waited on by maids and eunuchs, who told her about Mordecai's mourning. She assigned Hathach . . . to find out why Mordecai was carrying on that way in public places. Esther may have been embarrassed about him. Or perhaps she was concerned for his welfare since she sent out new clothes for him to wear so he would not be seen in sackcloth and ashes. Esther's unique position in the harem apparently shut her off from normal lines of communication. She did not seem to be aware of the edict about the execution of the Jews.

In response to Hathach's inquiry to Mordecai in the open square, Mordecai gave him a copy of the edict to show to Esther. He also told Hathach to tell her all the details of how the edict came about and to urge her to go to the king on behalf of her people to beg for their lives. The words "her people" revealed to the eunuch Hathach, if he did not know it before, that Esther was a Jewess. Without some reprieve from the king, Esther and Mordecai and all their people would die.

4:9-11. Esther's response to Mordecai was not encouraging. Persian monarchs (like those in most ancient nations) were protected against unwanted visitors. Esther reminded Mordecai that she could not simply enter the king's inner chambers unannounced or she might be put to death. The king had the power to execute anyone who disturbed him without an appointment. For the king to extend the golden scepter to someone showed that he approved of the visit and that the person was welcome and not in danger of death (cf. 5:2). Since Esther had not been summoned by him for a month she did not know whether his attitude toward her would be favorable.

4:12-14. Mordecai's response to Esther has often been taken as a great confession of faith. Actually, though, Mordecai apparently was expecting help from the Persian monarch. However, Mordecai did believe God in some way would protect His people: deliverance would arise from another place if Esther would not approach Xerxes about the Jews' plight. Though Mordecai is not pictured as a pious man who was righteous in his dealings before God, he at least had a sense of the covenantal relationship between God and Israel. He was aware that the promises to Abraham, Moses, and David would not be fulfilled if the entire nation was wiped out. Therefore he was confident that God would act on their behalf. He hoped that God would work through Esther because of her unique position.

Mordecai reminded Esther that if she did not attempt to avert this terrible calamity she would surely die, even though she was a member of the royal household. Whether Haman's power was great enough to reach to the palace and execute the queen is not stated. Mordecai simply planted the idea in Esther's mind that she would die if she did not act. Therefore death by order of the king for entering into his presence would be no worse than waiting and meeting death at the hands of Haman.

4:15-17. Esther understood the situation well. In concluding her reply to Mordecai she noted, If I perish, I perish. She resolved to carry out the wishes of Mordecai and go to the king even if it meant her death. In this section, as elsewhere in the book, Esther and Mordecai are seen as great patriots on behalf of the Jewish nation, but are not presented as righteous people, like others in the Old Testament who fully trusted the Lord. Nothing is said about Esther praying (though many commentators say that her fasting meant she also prayed). She simply instructed Mordecai to fast. . . . for three days (with the Jews . . . in Susa) as she and her maids would also do.

B. Plot exposed by Esther (chaps. 5–7)

These chapters mark the climax of the book. Here the tables are turned and evil is overcome by good. God's people are preserved through an unlikely set of circumstances. It is obvious to readers who trust the Lord that He was sovereignly at work, accomplishing His purposes. The original readers in postexilic Palestine would also be reminded that God would protect them against anything that might come their way. Even the forgetfulness of a pagan king could be used by God to preserve and protect His people.

1. BANQUET PREPARED (5:1-4)

5:1-4. After the three days of fasting in which **Esther** participated (cf. 4:16) she was ready to go to **the king** with her request. Actually she went **on the third day** because part of a day was counted as a whole day (cf. comments on Matt. 12:40). Even though she had not been with the king in over a month (Es. 4:11), **he was pleased** that she came (though she had passed apprehensive) and **he held out . . . the gold scepter** toward **her** (cf. 4:11; 8:4). He sensed that she had come to request something so he asked her for her **request.** And he even offered to give her whatever she wanted **even up to half the kingdom** (cf. 5:6; 7:2; Mark 6:23). This apparently was an idiom to express the point that **Esther** could request whatever she desired and that her wish would be fulfilled. Esther's request was simple: she asked that Xerxes and **Haman come . . . to a banquet** she had **prepared.**

2. SECOND BANQUET PREPARED (5:5-8)

5:5-8. The banquet was readied and **Haman** was told to come as **Esther** had requested. It was an unusual honor to be invited to a banquet with the queen, for Persian officials were protective of their wives. When **the king** asked what she wanted and again promised to fulfill her wish (cf. v. 3; 7:2), **Esther replied** that she would tell him the next day at a second **banquet.** Why **Esther** did not relate Haman's plot at the first banquet is not stated. Perhaps **Esther** was afraid to voice her complaint to **the king.** Perhaps she had second thoughts about telling him at all. Or perhaps she sensed that he was not in the right frame of mind for her to tell him on that day. From a literary standpoint, this delay raises the tension level as the story moves to its climax. A person reading Esther for the first time would be in a high state of agitation as the tension increased. Xerxes' response to Esther's suggestion is not given here, but Haman's later boasting (5:12) shows that **the king** was in obvious agreement with the idea.

3. HAMAN GLOATED, AND BUILT GALLOWS (5:9-14)

5:9-14. Haman was euphoric (**happy and in high spirits**) about his sudden good fortune with **the king** and the queen (v. 12) but, in contrast, he was enraged about **Mordecai,** the **Jew,** who still refused to bow down to him (cf. 3:2, 5). Haman was so overwrought about Mordecai that he could not enjoy his good position. On this occasion, to relieve himself of his rage and anxiety about **Mordecai,** he gathered his family and **friends** and spent time boasting about the **wealth** he had amassed and the family he had raised (he had 10 **sons;** 9:7-10, 12). As a social braggart (cf. 6:6) he also reminded them of his promotions in rank in the government, capping it off by telling them that on two successive days he was to be the guest of honor at a private **banquet** with only **the king** and **queen** present. However, he admitted that all his money and fame did not satisfy him because of **Mordecai.**

Haman's **wife, Zeresh, and all his friends** were no better than he was. They suggested that Haman **have a gallows built** that would be **75 feet high** and that he **have Mordecai hanged on it** before the banquet so he would have nothing bothering him when he went to the feast. **The gallows** probably was an impaling stake, a common method of execution in the ancient world (cf. comments on 2:23). The purpose in suggesting such a tall stake was so it would be a lesson to all who saw it. The person on the stake would be visible from all directions, since he would be higher than all the trees. This spectacle would solemnly emphasize that Haman was in control (cf. 3:1) and that no one should try to stand in his way.

Haman undoubtedly felt that with Mordecai gone there would be no organized opposition from the Jewish camp. He would be freed from his enemy forever. Here the tension in the Haman-Mordecai conflict reached its peak. From this point on it was relieved little by little through circumstances that had already been set in motion. As the events unfold, the reader is reminded of seemingly insignificant or forgotten events that the skillful narrator had previously mentioned but had not highlighted. God was sovereignly at work behind even such a hateful act as building a gallows (cf. Acts 2:23; 4:27-28).

4. MORDECAI HONORED BY XERXES (CHAP. 6)

The tension which had been building throughout the account now began to dissipate. Previously understated facts take on new meanings. Almost incredible circumstances point to God's hand guiding the course of events. The entire course of history for the Jewish nation was changed because a pagan king, hundreds of miles from the center of God's activities in Jerusalem, could not sleep. Jewish people all over the Persian Empire, and especially in Palestine itself, were unaware of God's dealings till long after the fact. But read in the light of God's covenants to Abraham, Moses, and David, the readers could well appreciate the sovereign action of God.

6:1-3. During the **night** before Esther's second banquet, **Xerxes** was unable to **sleep** (cf. Dan. 6:18). The author had not written why Esther asked for a delay before telling the king her request (Es. 5:7), but the reason was now made clear. God was going to elevate **Mordecai,** to prepare **the king** to react unfavorably to Haman. Because of the king's sleeplessness he asked for some **of the chronicles** (court annals; cf. 2:23) to be **read to him.** Sometimes, as is known by many people with insomnia, reading can help put a person to sleep! Through Xerxes' insomnia God caused him to learn about Mordecai's deed. Of all the texts that could have been selected by the librarian (from the records of Xerxes' 12 years of rule up to that time), the one that contained the account of Mordecai's uncovering the assassination plot (2:21-23) was read to **the king.** Extrabiblical sources confirm that the Persian kings maintained an elaborate recording system (cf. Ezra 6:1-2). Herodotus noted that the king kept especially clear records of those who served him well. Once again God's sovereignty is evident. When Xerxes asked **what honor** Mordecai had been given for saving the king's life (about five years before; cf. Es. 2:16 with 3:7), the king found that he had not been rewarded. Undoubtedly a bureaucratic oversight had occurred. However, if Mordecai had been immediately rewarded for his saving the king there would have been no need for the elaborate plan which would soon be carried out by the king through the mouth of Haman (6:6-10). Once again unusual circumstances worked to preserve God's people.

6:4-6. In the morning (cf. 5:14) **Haman . . . entered the** palace **outer court**

to ask that **Mordecai** be hanged. **The king** asked **who** was **in the court** and **Haman** "just happened" to be there. Obviously the tables were being turned. Everything that was meant for evil against the Jews was turning out for good for them. What a comfort this must have been to the original Jewish readers in postexilic Palestine as they observed their tenuous position among the nations. They could rejoice in the fact that God cared about them and that He would continue to preserve them as He had under Xerxes.

When **Haman** was ushered into the king's presence, he must have felt honored. And when **the king asked . . . What should be done for the man the king delights to honor?** the egotistical **Haman** was beside **himself** with joy and enthusiasm. He thought that **the king** was speaking about him.

6:7-9. Haman responded to **the king** by mentioning several things that should be done for the person **the king** wished **to honor:** (1) Haman recommended that such a man should have the appearance of royalty, by wearing a kingly **robe** and riding **a royal** steed, one **the king** had already **ridden.** Some have suggested that the Bible is in error when it speaks of a horse wearing **a royal crest . . . on its head.** They think that the man, not the horse, should have worn the crown. However, a relief actually shows a horse with a crown on its head, signifying that it was a royal horse. (2) Haman said that the honored man should be served by one of the **most noble princes.** (3) The princes were to take the man **through the city** on this **horse,** clearing the way before him and pointing out to all who watched that this **man** was honored by **the king** (cf. Gen. 41:42-43). Haman did not need money (cf. Es. 3:9). He craved respect from his peers and from the population at large (cf. 5:11). Even though he was fabulously wealthy and had more power than anyone outside the royal family (3:1), he wanted even more respect from the people of the city. Haman's lust for respect (from Mordecai) is what got him into trouble in the first place (cf. 3:2, 5; 5:9, 13).

6:10-13. Haman's ideas apparently appealed to **the king;** he **commanded Haman** to carry them out **for Mordecai the Jew.** This is the first of five times Mordecai is called "the Jew" (cf. 8:7; 9:29, 31; 10:3), apparently to highlight the fact that a Jew, though opposed by **Haman,** was given a prominent position in Susa in the Persian Empire. What a turn of events; what irony for Haman! **Mordecai,** whom he hated, had to be honored by **Haman.** He who wanted respect *from* Mordecai had to give respect *to* Mordecai. Haman had to carry out the king's order even though it embarrassed and angered him greatly. **Afterward** he **rushed home,** had **his head covered in grief,** and **told Zeresh his wife** and **friends** the reversal of his fortunes.

Earlier Mordecai had publicly grieved over his people (4:1); now Haman privately grieved over his own humiliation. When Haman had left his wife in the morning he had been elated. Now the bottom had fallen out from under him. To make matters worse, **his advisers and his wife** all saw nothing but trouble for him in the future. They noted that Mordecai's **Jewish origin** meant that Haman was doomed. Exactly what they meant by that statement is difficult to determine. It is known that in the Persian religions much was made of omens and signs. Fate, chance, and luck were considered important in everyday life. The Book of Esther stands as a polemic against such a fatalistic view of the world. To many who are not of the covenant community, Israel, the world's events appear to be fatalistic and to happen by chance. But those who are the people of God's covenant know that God overrules fate. He moves events and circumstances for His good pleasure. Pagan advisers and the pagan wife of an evil man unknowingly stated the central thrust of this book: neither Haman nor any other human can possibly **stand against** God's Chosen People, the Jewish nation (many of whom were then back in the Promised Land with a rebuilt temple, offering sacrifices to God at Jerusalem).

6:14. Now, with his world crashing down around his head, **Haman** was hustled off to Esther's second **banquet,** which once he desired but now dreaded. He may have well wondered what the king would say to him at the banquet.

Haman stands as a prototype of all anti-God activists who oppose God's people. Like authors of many short stories, God led the author of the Book of

Esther to make his historical figures into symbols of much larger proportions. As the regathered nation read this account, they could have looked back over their history and noted other times when men had tried to set aside God's promises to their nation and had failed. They could therefore rest assured that in the future God would do the same. Even though God's people often disobeyed Him, even though they were often not spiritually or even physically where God wanted them to be, deliverance would come. God would so work in history that He would be vindicated and His people delivered.

5. XERXES TOLD OF PLOT, HAMAN HANGED (CHAP. 7)

7:1-4. What **Haman** knew about **Esther** is not stated. If he knew of the connection between Mordecai and Esther he may have been even more terrified at the prospect of attending this second banquet given by Esther. This was the fifth banquet mentioned in the Book of Esther: two were given by **the king** (1:3, 5), one by Queen Vashti (1:9), and two by **Queen Esther** (5:4, 8). During the banquet **the king** again asked Esther her **request,** and again he promised that he would grant it to her (cf. 5:3, 6). This time Esther got right to the point and gave her **petition** and **request . . . life** for her and her **people.** It was now clear to Xerxes what her nationality was (cf. 2:10, 20). She explained that all her **people** had been **sold** (i.e., the king was offered a bribe by Haman; cf. 3:9; 4:7) into extinction (cf. 3:13). Showing her subservient position to the king, she added that if they had merely been **sold** into slavery she certainly would not have bothered **the king.** Esther's statement not only shows the unbelievable power of the king, but also the condition to which she was reduced. **Esther** may have been apprehensive, not knowing if the king would grant her request. It was quite possible that he would fly into a rage, as he had done with Vashti (1:12).

7:5-6. However, this time **the king** did not become furious. He requested more information about who was doing **such a thing** to **Esther** and her people. Undoubtedly a look of terror was on Haman's face as he realized that he was about to be exposed before the most powerful man on the face of the earth.

Haman must have known that his execution was assured now that "fate" was working against him. Esther revealed that vile Haman was the enemy (cf. 3:10; 8:1; 9:10, 24).

7:7-8. *Now* the king was filled with rage (cf. 1:12 and cf. Haman's anger on two occasions, 3:5; 5:9). The reason why the king left the palace to go outside to his **palace garden** is not given. It has been suggested that he went out to control his anger, but that is unlikely in view of his other behavior. Others have suggested that he was thinking up a way to execute Haman legally, but that is unlikely because any word of the king was law. Others have said that Xerxes was trying to figure out a way to spare Esther and her nation. Whatever the reason, Esther and Haman were left together in the banquet hall.

While begging Esther to spare his life—though he realized that the king had already decided his fate—Haman fell on the couch (cf. 1:6) on which Esther was reclining. Persians (and later Greeks, Romans, and Jews) reclined on couches when they ate. At just that moment (another so-called "happenstance" in the sovereignty of God) the king returned and accused Haman of assaulting the queen. However, Haman was not assaulting her but was merely falling on her couch. It is highly unlikely that Haman and Esther were alone in that banquet hall. No doubt people who were serving the meal and the guards were also present. The word they (7:8) suggests that several people were there. What is meant by their covering Haman's face is uncertain. Probably they did this because Haman was now a doomed man, condemned to death.

7:9-10. Harbona, one of the king's seven eunuchs (cf. 1:10), told the king about the gallows which Haman had built during the previous night to kill Mordecai (5:14). Possibly Haman was hated by many people in the city of Susa, especially in government circles. Many might have been glad to see Haman killed. Harbona obviously knew of Haman's plot to kill Mordecai. At the king's orders, Haman was taken and hanged . . . on his own gallows (i.e., impaled; cf. comments on 2:23). The tables had now been turned, but the Jews were still left with a major problem. The king's edict to eradicate them was still in effect. Per a Persian decree there would still be a great slaughter of many innocent people because of the wicked actions of a now-dead man.

C. Jews delivered, and took revenge (8:1–9:19)

God had sovereignly worked in various circumstances so that the Jews could be delivered. Now it was the Jews' turn. They would have to fight to retain what was theirs. They had to take part actively in their own deliverance. The Jewish people back in the land would also be encouraged to work hard and carry out their responsibilities before God in His sovereign plan.

1. MORDECAI RECEIVED ROYAL POSITION (8:1-2)

8:1-2. Apparently Haman was considered a criminal, for his property was confiscated. The king's signet ring, which had been given Haman to authorize the edict against the Jews (3:10), was now given to Mordecai. Again the tables turned against Haman, even after his death. For one thing Mordecai now had the power that Haman previously had. For another, Haman, who had hoped to confiscate the Jews' property (3:13), now had his own property removed and given to, of all people, Esther, who in turn appointed Mordecai to oversee it.

2. SECOND PROCLAMATION SENT OUT (8:3-14)

8:3-6. Since the edict to exterminate the Jews (3:13) was still in effect, something had to be done. So Esther appeared before the king a second time without an invitation (cf. 5:1-2). This time she begged him to put an end to the evil plan which was in effect because of Haman. The king was favorable toward her and once again held out the gold scepter to her (cf. 4:11; 5:2).

Esther's request was simple. She wanted a second decree written and sent out which would override the first decree. Again she was willing to be known as a Jewess for she spoke of my people and my family (cf. 7:3).

8:7-8. The king noted that Esther and Mordecai now had the power and resources that previously belonged to Haman and therefore they should use that power to their advantage. Though

Haman's decree could not be revoked, a second one could supersede it. Xerxes even gave Mordecai authority to **write** the **decree** any way he wished and to stamp it with **the king's** authority by using his **signet ring** (cf. 3:10, 12; 8:2).

8:9-14. The decree Mordecai wrote was **sent** out in **the third month . . . Sivan** (June-July) 474. Since this was a little over two months after Haman's decree (3:12) the Jews had about nine months to prepare themselves for the conflict (up to the 13th day of the 12th month, the date Haman had chosen by lot; cf. 3:7, 13; 9:1). As was the case with the previous decree (cf. 3:12), this one too was dispatched (cf. 1:22; 3:15) by horsemen throughout the whole empire **from India to Cush** (cf. 1:1) and was **written in the** appropriate languages for **each province.** The edict gave the Jews . . . **the right** to **protect themselves** and the right to **annihilate** (cf. 3:13; 7:4) and **plunder** any group that fought against them. **The Jews** could take away the property of **their enemies** as Mordecai had "taken away" the property of Haman.

3. JEWS REJOICED (8:15-17)

8:15-17. Mordecai wore clothes which told of his royal position—**royal garments . . . a large crown,** and a **purple** linen **robe. Blue and white** were the Persian royal colors (cf. 1:6). He now held the position and status Haman had held (3:1). Previously under Haman's edict the city of Susa had been "bewildered" (3:15). Now under the edict of Mordecai **the city of Susa held a joyous celebration.** And obviously **the Jews** were elated. Their rise to power caused **many** Gentiles to become Jewish proselytes. God's good hand was then becoming obvious to the world at large. No longer were these events being viewed simply as happenstance; now people were beginning to realize that the God of **the Jews** was protecting them.

4. JEWS TOOK REVENGE (9:1-19)

9:1-4. When the appointed **day** of the battle came, **the tables were turned** on **the enemies of the Jews.** As **the Jews assembled** in various **cities** to face their attackers, the Gentiles became **afraid of them.** In fact even the government authorities **helped the Jews.** The people who attacked the Jews may have seen this as an opportunity to get rich at someone else's expense. However, since they had no backing from others they were in a cause which they could not win.

Only by God's sovereign intervention was **Mordecai** now in a position of authority. **He became more . . . powerful** and enjoyed a good **reputation.**

9:5-15. On the day of the battle (13th day of the 12th month, i.e., in March 473) **in the citadel of Susa the Jews killed . . . 500 men** plus Haman's **10 sons.** When **the king** asked **Esther** what she wanted, she requested that **the Jews in Susa** be given one more day to carry out the task of rooting out the ones who were trying to destroy them and that **Haman's 10** slain **sons be hanged on gallows** (i.e., impaled; cf. 2:23; 7:10). On the second day the Jews killed an additional **300 men.** The Jews were not doing this for money, as Haman had hoped to do (cf. 3:13), for three times it is stated that the Jews **did not lay their hands on the plunder** (9:10, 15-16). Many have questioned why the Jews wanted to impale the already dead bodies of Haman's 10 sons. This was not an unusual practice in the ancient Near East. It was a visual warning that others better not commit the same crime as the punished ones.

9:16-19. In the outlying **provinces . . . 75,000** individuals were **killed by the Jews** in one day, but there, as well as in Susa, **they did not** take any **plunder** from the victims. Only in Susa did the fighting last for two days. For that reason **Jews in Susa** celebrated **on the 15th** day of the 12th month (after the slaughters on **the 13th and 14th**), whereas Jews in the villages celebrated **on the 14th** (after the slaughter on **the 13th**).

IV. Feast of Purim Established (9:20-32)

9:20-22. The Feast of Purim was not established by the Mosaic Law. It was commanded by **Mordecai** (vv. 20-28) and by Esther (vv. 29-32). The two-day feast was for remembering the goodness of God working through a number of circumstances to protect His people from extinction. Mordecai wrote a proclamation that **the Jews** were to **celebrate** the event **annually** with eating, rejoicing (cf. 8:17), **giving . . . food,** and sharing with **the poor.**

9:23-32. The feast was **called Purim**

4

(v. 26) **because of** Haman's use of **the** *pur* . . . **the lot** to determine the time of the execution (3:7). **The** *pur* became a symbol of God's using circumstances to deliver His own.

Esther . . . **along with Mordecai,** wrote a **second letter** confirming that **the Jews** were to celebrate the feast (9:29-32). Unlike Haman's decree her **words,** sent to the Jews (her "people") throughout the vast empire, were for **good will and assurance.** A copy of her letter was also included in the royal archives (cf. 2:23; 6:1; 10:2).

V. Greatness of Mordecai Described (chap. 10)

10:1-3. The book closes by speaking of **King** Xerxes' power; but more importantly the closing verses extol **Mordecai,** once a hated Jew in the Persian **Empire.** He was promoted by **Xerxes** and revered by **the Jews.** He was their great patriot **because he worked** hard for them **and spoke up** on their behalf to Xerxes. However, it is noteworthy that the Book of Esther nowhere states that Mordecai was a righteous individual or that he was careful to follow the Law. Many have doubted that a Jew could have such a high rank in the Persian Empire. However, it is known that many foreign people were fully assimilated into the mainstream of life in the empire (e.g., Daniel; Dan. 5:29; 6:1-2, 28).

As the original Jewish readers read this account they would have been struck by the way God was sovereignly protecting them, often when they did not even know it. Many things in the Book of Esther happened that were beyond anyone's control except that of God, who oversees history. And the Book of Esther is filled with irony, with ways in which events turned out unexpectedly and in favor of God's people. Queen Vashti, a Persian, was deposed so that Esther, a Jewess, could become queen and save her people. Haman, once exalted, was brought low, and **Mordecai** and **the Jews,** once hated, were exalted and hon-

ored. A decree that would have wiped out the Jews was overruled by one which led to the destruction of nearly 76,000 enemies of the Jews. No wonder Purim was celebrated yearly with such rejoicing: to help the Jews remember that God is in control and that people should faithfully worship and serve their great God.

BIBLIOGRAPHY

Baldwin, Joyce G. *Esther.* The Tyndale Old Testament Commentaries. Downers Grove Ill.: InterVarsity Press, 1984.

Berg, Sandra Beth. *The Book of Esther: Motifs, Themes and Structure.* Missoula, Mont.: Scholars Press, 1979.

Cohen, A. "Esther." In *The Five Megilloth.* London: Soncino Press, 1946.

Hess, Margaret. *Esther: Courage in Crisis.* Wheaton, Ill.: Scripture Press Publications, Victor Books, 1980.

Ironside, H.A. *Notes on Ezra, Nehemiah, Esther.* Neptune, N.J.: Loizeaux Brothers, 1972.

Keil, C.F. "Esther." In *Commentary on the Old Testament in Ten Volumes.* Vol. 3. Reprint (25 vols. in 10). Grand Rapids: Wm. B. Eerdmans Publishing Co., 1982.

Knight, G.A.F. *Esther, Song of Songs, Lamentations.* London: SCM Press, 1955.

McGee, J. Vernon. *Esther: The Romance of Providence.* Pasadena, Calif.: Thru the Bible Books, n.d.

Moore, Carey A. *Esther.* The Anchor Bible. Garden City, N.Y.: Doubleday & Co., 1971.

_____. *Studies in the Book of Esther.* New York: KTAV Publishing House, 1982.

Strean, A.W. *The Book of Esther.* The Cambridge Bible for Schools and Colleges. Cambridge: University Press, 1907.

Whitcomb, John C. *Esther: Triumph of God's Sovereignty.* Everyman's Bible Commentary. Chicago: Moody Press, 1979.

At David C Cook, we equip the local church around
the corner and around the globe to make disciples.
Come see how we are working together—go to
www.davidccook.com. Thank you!

transforming lives together